# Saab 9-5
# Service and Repair Manual

## A K Legg LAE MIMI and Peter T Gill

*(4156 - 288 - 1AN2)*

**Models covered**

Saloon & Estate models, including special/limited editions
2.0 litre (1985cc) & 2.3 litre (2290cc) 4-cyl petrol
Does NOT cover 3.0 litre V6 petrol models or Diesel variants

ISBN **978 1 78521 289 5**

**British Library Cataloguing in Publication Data**
A catalogue record for this book is available from the British Library.

**Haynes Group Limited**
**Haynes North America, Inc**

**www.haynes.com**

Authorised representative in the EU

HaynesPro BV
Stationsstraat 79 F, 3811MH Amersfoort, The Netherlands
gpsr@haynes.co.uk

## Disclaimer

There are risks associated with automotive repairs. The ability to make repairs depends on the individual's skill, experience and proper tools. Individuals should act with due care and acknowledge and assume the risk of performing automotive repairs.

The purpose of this manual is to provide comprehensive, useful and accessible automotive repair information, to help you get the best value from your vehicle. However, this manual is not a substitute for a professional certified technician or mechanic.

This repair manual is produced by a third party and is not associated with an individual vehicle manufacturer. If there is any doubt or discrepancy between this manual and the owner's manual or the factory service manual, please refer to the factory service manual or seek assistance from a professional certified technician or mechanic.

Even though we have prepared this manual with extreme care and every attempt is made to ensure that the information in this manual is correct, neither the publisher nor the author can accept responsibility for loss, damage or injury caused by any errors in, or omissions from, the information given.

# Contents

# Contents

## REPAIRS AND OVERHAUL

### Engine and Associated Systems

### Transmission

### Brakes and suspension

### Body equipment

### Wiring diagrams

## REFERENCE

### Index

Working on your car can be dangerous. This page shows just some of the potential risks and hazards, with the aim of creating a safety-conscious attitude.

# General hazards

## Scalding

• Don't remove the radiator or expansion tank cap while the engine is hot.
• Engine oil, automatic transmission fluid or power steering fluid may also be dangerously hot if the engine has recently been running.

## Burning

• Beware of burns from the exhaust system and from any part of the engine. Brake discs and drums can also be extremely hot immediately after use.

## Crushing

• When working under or near a raised vehicle, always supplement the jack with axle stands, or use drive-on ramps. *Never venture under a car which is only supported by a jack.*
• Take care if loosening or tightening high-torque nuts when the vehicle is on stands. Initial loosening and final tightening should be done with the wheels on the ground.

## Fire

• Fuel is highly flammable; fuel vapour is explosive.
• Don't let fuel spill onto a hot engine.
• Do not smoke or allow naked lights (including pilot lights) anywhere near a vehicle being worked on. Also beware of creating sparks (electrically or by use of tools).
• Fuel vapour is heavier than air, so don't work on the fuel system with the vehicle over an inspection pit.
• Another cause of fire is an electrical overload or short-circuit. Take care when repairing or modifying the vehicle wiring.
• Keep a fire extinguisher handy, of a type suitable for use on fuel and electrical fires.

## Electric shock

• Ignition HT voltage can be dangerous, especially to people with heart problems or a pacemaker. Don't work on or near the ignition system with the engine running or the ignition switched on.

• Mains voltage is also dangerous. Make sure that any mains-operated equipment is correctly earthed. Mains power points should be protected by a residual current device (RCD) circuit breaker.

## Fume or gas intoxication

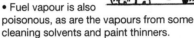

• Exhaust fumes are poisonous; they often contain carbon monoxide, which is rapidly fatal if inhaled. Never run the engine in a confined space such as a garage with the doors shut.
• Fuel vapour is also poisonous, as are the vapours from some cleaning solvents and paint thinners.

## Poisonous or irritant substances

• Avoid skin contact with battery acid and with any fuel, fluid or lubricant, especially antifreeze, brake hydraulic fluid and Diesel fuel. Don't syphon them by mouth. If such a substance is swallowed or gets into the eyes, seek medical advice.
• Prolonged contact with used engine oil can cause skin cancer. Wear gloves or use a barrier cream if necessary. Change out of oil-soaked clothes and do not keep oily rags in your pocket.
• Air conditioning refrigerant forms a poisonous gas if exposed to a naked flame (including a cigarette). It can also cause skin burns on contact.

## Asbestos

• Asbestos dust can cause cancer if inhaled or swallowed. Asbestos may be found in gaskets and in brake and clutch linings. When dealing with such components it is safest to assume that they contain asbestos.

# Special hazards

## Hydrofluoric acid

• This extremely corrosive acid is formed when certain types of synthetic rubber, found in some O-rings, oil seals, fuel hoses etc, are exposed to temperatures above 400°C. The rubber changes into a charred or sticky substance containing the acid. *Once formed, the acid remains dangerous for years. If it gets onto the skin, it may be necessary to amputate the limb concerned.*
• When dealing with a vehicle which has suffered a fire, or with components salvaged from such a vehicle, wear protective gloves and discard them after use.

## The battery

• Batteries contain sulphuric acid, which attacks clothing, eyes and skin. Take care when topping-up or carrying the battery.
• The hydrogen gas given off by the battery is highly explosive. Never cause a spark or allow a naked light nearby. Be careful when connecting and disconnecting battery chargers or jump leads.

## Air bags

• Air bags can cause injury if they go off accidentally. Take care when removing the steering wheel and/or facia. Special storage instructions may apply.

## Diesel injection equipment

• Diesel injection pumps supply fuel at very high pressure. Take care when working on the fuel injectors and fuel pipes.

⚠️ *Warning: Never expose the hands, face or any other part of the body to injector spray; the fuel can penetrate the skin with potentially fatal results.*

---

# Remember...

## DO

• Do use eye protection when using power tools, and when working under the vehicle.

• Do wear gloves or use barrier cream to protect your hands when necessary.

• Do get someone to check periodically that all is well when working alone on the vehicle.

• Do keep loose clothing and long hair well out of the way of moving mechanical parts.

• Do remove rings, wristwatch etc, before working on the vehicle – especially the electrical system.

• Do ensure that any lifting or jacking equipment has a safe working load rating adequate for the job.

## DON'T

• Don't attempt to lift a heavy component which may be beyond your capability – get assistance.

• Don't rush to finish a job, or take unverified short cuts.

• Don't use ill-fitting tools which may slip and cause injury.

• Don't leave tools or parts lying around where someone can trip over them. Mop up oil and fuel spills at once.

• Don't allow children or pets to play in or near a vehicle being worked on.

# Introduction 0•5

The Saab 9-5 was introduced in the UK in August 1997 as an executive class model. Like the 9-3 which is essentially a re-badged 900, the 9-5 is based on a Vauxhall Vectra chassis, and competes with other models such as the BMW 5-Series, Mercedes E-Class and the Audi A6. It was originally available as a 4-door Saloon with turbocharged 2.0 and 2.3 litre, balancer-shaft, 16-valve engines. The 3.0 litre V6 engine (not covered by this Manual) was introduced in February 1998, and was available with automatic transmission and traction control. The Estate version was launched in November 1998.

Standard equipment includes power-assisted steering, ABS brakes, remote deadlock central locking, twin front and side airbags, electric windows and mirrors, and air conditioning. Optional extras include electric sunroof, electric front seats, leather upholstery and CD autochanger.

Models may be fitted with a five-speed manual transmission or four-speed automatic transmission mounted on the left-hand side of the engine. The automatic transmission was changed to five-speed as from September 2001.

All models have front-wheel-drive with fully-independent front and rear suspension, incorporating struts, gas-filled shock absorbers, and coil springs.

For the home mechanic, the Saab 9-5 is a relatively straightforward vehicle to maintain and repair, since design features have been incorporated to reduce the actual cost of ownership to a minimum, and most of the items requiring frequent attention are easily accessible.

## Your Saab 9-5 manual

The aim of this manual is to help you get the best value from your vehicle. It can do so in several ways. It can help you decide what work must be done (even should you choose to get it done by a garage), provide information on routine maintenance and servicing, and give a logical course of action and diagnosis when random faults occur. However, it is hoped that you will use the manual by tackling the work yourself. On simpler jobs, it may even be quicker than booking the car into a garage and going there twice, to leave and collect it. Perhaps most important, a lot of money can be saved by avoiding the costs a garage must charge to cover its labour and overheads.

The manual has drawings and descriptions to show the function of the various components, so that their layout can be understood. Then the tasks are described and photographed in a clear step-by-step sequence.

References to the 'left' or 'right' are in the sense of a person in the driver's seat, facing forward.

## Acknowledgements

Thanks are also due to Draper Tools Limited, who provided some of the workshop tools, and to all those people at Sparkford who helped in the production of this manual.

**We take great pride in the accuracy of information given in this manual, but vehicle manufacturers make alterations and design changes during the production run of a particular vehicle of which they do not inform us. No liability can be accepted by the authors or publishers for loss, damage or injury caused by any errors in, or omissions from, the information given.**

## Project vehicle

The main vehicle used in the preparation of this manual, and which appears in many of the photographic sequences, was a 2001 Saab 9-5 Estate Aero fitted with the 2.3 litre turbocharged petrol engine and automatic transmission.

The following pages are intended to help in dealing with common roadside emergencies and breakdowns. You will find more detailed fault finding information at the back of the manual, and repair information in the main chapters.

## If your car won't start and the starter motor doesn't turn

☐ If it's a model with automatic transmission, make sure the selector is in the P or N position.
☐ Open the bonnet and make sure that the battery terminals are clean and tight.
☐ Switch on the headlights and try to start the engine. If the headlights go very dim when you're trying to start, the battery is probably flat. Get out of trouble by jump starting (see next page) using another car.

## If your car won't start even though the starter motor turns as normal

☐ Is there fuel in the tank?
☐ Is there moisture on electrical components under the bonnet? Switch off the ignition, then wipe off any obvious dampness with a dry cloth. Spray a water-repellent aerosol product (WD-40 or equivalent) on ignition and fuel system electrical connectors like those shown in the photos. Pay special attention to the ignition coils wiring connector.

A Check that the battery cables are securely connected.

B Check that the ignition discharge module wiring is securely connected.

C Check that the mass airflow meter wiring is securely connected.

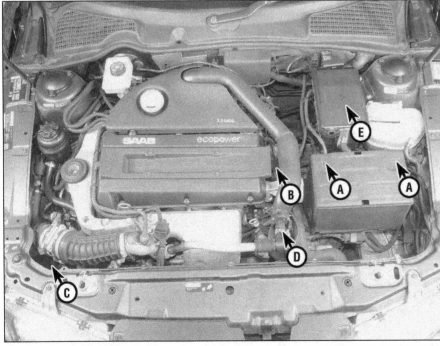

Check that electrical connections are secure (with the ignition switched off) and spray them with a water dispersant spray like WD-40 if you suspect a problem due to damp

D Check the engine wiring loom multi-plugs for security.

E Check that none of the engine compartment fuses have blown.

# Jump starting

When jump-starting a car using a booster battery, observe the following precautions:

✔ Before connecting the booster battery, make sure that the ignition is switched off.

✔ Ensure that all electrical equipment (lights, heater, wipers, etc) is switched off.

✔ Take note of any special precautions printed on the battery case.

✔ Make sure that the booster battery is the same voltage as the discharged one in the vehicle.

✔ If the battery is being jump-started from the battery in another vehicle, the two vehicles MUST NOT TOUCH each other.

✔ Make sure that the transmission is in neutral (or PARK, in the case of automatic transmission).

**HAYNES HINT** *Jump starting will get you out of trouble, but you must correct whatever made the battery go flat in the first place. There are three possibilities:*

**1** *The battery has been drained by repeated attempts to start, or by leaving the lights on.*

**2** *The charging system is not working properly (alternator drivebelt slack or broken, alternator wiring fault or alternator itself faulty).*

**3** *The battery itself is at fault (electrolyte low, or battery worn out).*

**1** Connect one end of the red jump lead to the positive (+) terminal of the flat battery

**2** Connect the other end of the red lead to the positive (+) terminal of the booster battery.

**3** Connect one end of the black jump lead to the negative (-) terminal of the booster battery

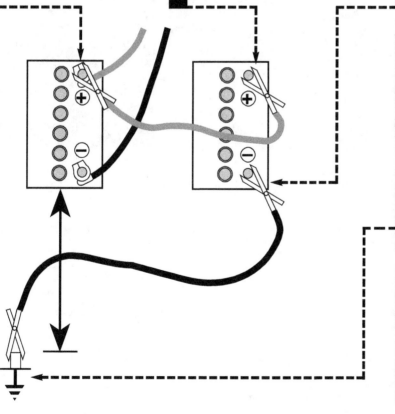

**4** Connect the other end of the black jump lead to a bolt or bracket on the engine block, well away from the battery, on the vehicle to be started.

**5** Make sure that the jump leads will not come into contact with the fan, drive-belts or other moving parts of the engine.

**6** Start the engine using the booster battery and run it at idle speed. Switch on the lights, rear window demister and heater blower motor, then disconnect the jump leads in the reverse order of connection. Turn off the lights etc.

# Identifying leaks

Puddles on the garage floor or drive, or obvious wetness under the bonnet or underneath the car, suggest a leak that needs investigating. It can sometimes be difficult to decide where the leak is coming from, especially if the engine bay is very dirty already. Leaking oil or fluid can also be blown rearwards by the passage of air under the car, giving a false impression of where the problem lies.

 **Warning: Most automotive oils and fluids are poisonous. Wash them off skin, and change out of contaminated clothing, without delay.**

 *The smell of a fluid leaking from the car may provide a clue to what's leaking. Some fluids are distinctively coloured. It may help to clean the car carefully and to park it over some clean paper overnight as an aid to locating the source of the leak. Remember that some leaks may only occur while the engine is running.*

### Sump oil

Engine oil may leak from the drain plug...

### Oil from filter

...or from the base of the oil filter.

### Gearbox oil

Gearbox oil can leak from the seals at the inboard ends of the driveshafts.

### Antifreeze

Leaking antifreeze often leaves a crystalline deposit like this.

### Brake fluid

A leak occurring at a wheel is almost certainly brake fluid.

### Power steering fluid

Power steering fluid may leak from the pipe connectors on the steering rack.

# Towing

When all else fails, you may find yourself having to get a tow home – or of course you may be helping somebody else. Long-distance recovery should only be done by a garage or breakdown service. For shorter distances, DIY towing using another car is easy enough, but observe the following points:

☐ Use a proper tow-rope – they are not expensive. The vehicle being towed must display an ON TOW sign in its rear window.

☐ Always turn the ignition key to the 'on' position when the vehicle is being towed, so that the steering lock is released, and that the direction indicator and brake lights will work.

☐ Only attach the tow-rope to the towing eyes provided. The front towing eye is in the vehicle

tool kit, and screws into the hole in the centre of the subframe; use the wheelbrace to tighten it. The rear towing eye is located beneath the centre of the rear bumper and is permanent.

☐ Before being towed, release the handbrake and select neutral on the transmission.

☐ On models with automatic transmission, special precautions apply as follows (if in doubt, do not tow, or transmission damage may result):

a) Only tow the car in a forward direction.

b) The gear selector lever must be in the N position.

c) The vehicle must not be towed at a speed exceeding 31 mph (50 km/h), nor for a distance of more than 31 miles (50 km).

☐ Note that greater-than-usual pedal pressure will be required to operate the brakes, since the vacuum servo unit is only operational with the engine running. Similarly, greater-than-usual steering effort will also be required.

☐ The driver of the car being towed must keep the tow-rope taut to avoid snatching.

☐ Make sure that both drivers know the route before setting off.

☐ Only drive at moderate speeds and keep the distance towed to a minimum. Drive smoothly and allow plenty of time for slowing down at junctions.

# Wheel changing

 *Warning: Do not change a wheel in a situation where you risk being hit by another vehicle. On busy roads, try to stop in a lay-by or a gateway. Be wary of passing traffic while changing the wheel - it is easy to become distracted by the job in hand.*

## Preparation

☐ When a puncture occurs, stop as soon as it is safe to do so.
☐ Park on firm level ground, if possible, and well out of the way of other traffic.
☐ Use hazard warning lights if necessary.

☐ If you have one, use a warning triangle to alert other drivers of your presence.
☐ Apply the handbrake and engage first or reverse gear (or Park on models with automatic transmission).

☐ Chock the wheel diagonally opposite the one being removed – a couple of large stones will do for this.
☐ If the ground is soft, use a flat piece of wood to spread the load under the jack.

## Changing the wheel

1 The spare wheel, jack and wheel removal tools are stored beneath a cover in the luggage compartment.

2 Unscrew the retaining nut and lift out the spare wheel. Place it beneath the sill as a precaution against the jack failing. Note that the spare wheel is a the 'space saver' type.

3 Where fitted, pull the wheel trim off the wheel. On models with alloy wheels, use the plastic tool provided to prise the cap from the locking wheel bolt, then fit the adapter.

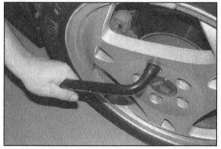

4 Before you raise the car, loosen each wheel bolt by half a turn only.

5 Locate the jack head below the jacking points (indicated by the cut-outs in the sill), nearest the wheel to be changed. Turn the handle until the base of the jack touches the ground directly below the sill. Raise the vehicle until the wheel is clear of the ground.

6 Remove the bolts and lift the wheel from the vehicle. Place it beneath the sill in place of the spare as a precaution against jack failing.

7 Fit the spare wheel, then insert each of the wheel bolts and tighten them moderately using the wheel brace.

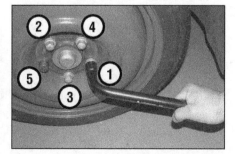

8 Lower the vehicle to the ground, then tighten the wheel bolts in a diagonal sequence. Remove the wheel chocks. Note that the wheel bolts should be tightened to the specified torque at the earliest opportunity.

## Finally...

☐ Stow the jack and tools in the correct locations in the car.
☐ Check the tyre pressure on the wheel just fitted. If it is low, or if you don't have a pressure gauge with you, drive slowly to the next garage and inflate the tyre to the correct pressure.
☐ Have the damaged tyre or wheel repaired as soon as possible, or another puncture will leave you stranded.

*Warning: You should not exceed 50 mph when driving the vehicle with a 'Space Saver' spare wheel fitted – consult your vehicle handbook for further information.*

# Introduction

There are some very simple checks which need only take a few minutes to carry out, but which could save you a lot of inconvenience and expense.

These *Weekly checks* require no great skill or special tools, and the small amount of time they take to perform could prove to be very well spent, for example;

☐ Keeping an eye on tyre condition and pressures, will not only help to stop them wearing out prematurely, but could also save your life.

☐ Many breakdowns are caused by electrical problems. Battery-related faults are particularly common, and a quick check on a regular basis will often prevent the majority of these.

☐ If your car develops a brake fluid leak, the first time you might know about it is when your brakes don't work properly. Checking the level regularly will give advance warning of this kind of problem.

☐ If the oil or coolant levels run low, the cost of repairing any engine damage will be far greater than fixing the leak, for example.

# Underbonnet check points

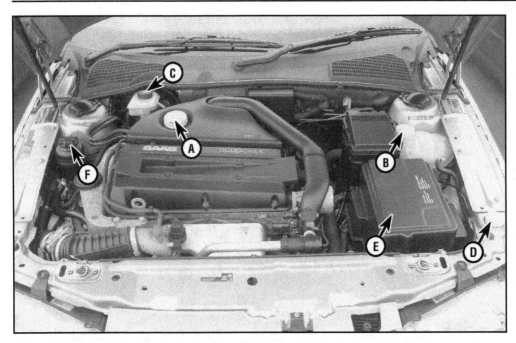

## ◄ 2.0 litre engine

**A** *Engine oil level filler cap and dipstick*

**B** *Coolant reservoir (expansion tank)*

**C** *Brake fluid reservoir*

**D** *Washer fluid reservoir*

**E** *Battery*

**F** *Power steering fluid reservoir*

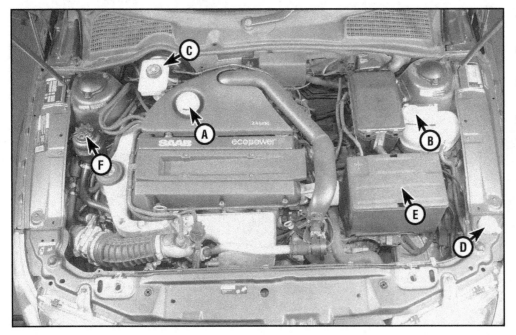

## ◄ 2.3 litre engine

**A** *Engine oil level filler cap and dipstick*

**B** *Coolant reservoir (expansion tank)*

**C** *Brake fluid reservoir*

**D** *Washer fluid reservoir*

**E** *Battery*

**F** *Power steering fluid reservoir*

# Engine oil level

### Before you start
✔ Make sure that your car is on level ground.
✔ Check the oil level before the car is driven, or at least 5 minutes after the engine has been switched off.

### The correct oil
Modern engines place great demands on their oil. It is very important that the correct oil for your car is used (See *Lubricants and fluids*).

### Car Care
● If you have to add oil frequently, you should check whether you have any oil leaks. Place some clean paper under the car overnight, and check for stains in the morning. If there are no leaks, the engine may be burning oil.

● Always maintain the level between the upper and lower dipstick marks (see photo 3). If the level is too low severe engine damage may occur. Oil seal failure may result if the engine is overfilled by adding too much oil.

> **HAYNES HINT** *If the oil is checked immediately after driving the vehicle, some of the oil will remain in the upper engine components, resulting in an inaccurate reading on the dipstick.*

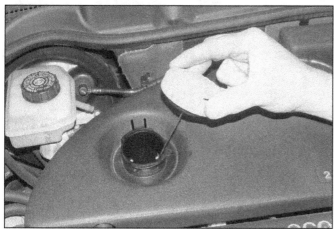

1 The dipstick is integral with the oil filler cap, located on the right-hand rear of the engine (see *Underbonnet Check Points* on page 0•11 for exact location). Unscrew the cap and withdraw the integral dipstick

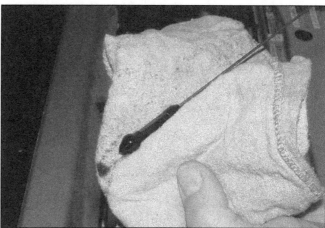

2 Using a clean rag or paper towel remove all oil from the dipstick. Insert the clean dipstick into the tube and tighten the filler cap, then withdraw it again.

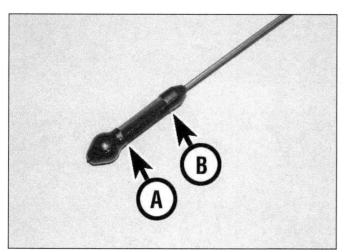

3 Note the oil level on the end of the dipstick, which should be between the upper mark (B) and lower mark (A). Approximately 1.0 litre of oil will raise the level from the lower mark to the upper mark.

4 Oil is added through the filler cap hole. Unscrew the cap and withdraw it. Top-up the level. A funnel may help to reduce spillage. Add the oil slowly, checking the level on the dipstick often. Do not overfill. Refit the cap on completion.

# Coolant level

**Warning: DO NOT attempt to remove the expansion tank pressure cap when the engine is hot, as there is a very great risk of scalding. Do not leave open containers of coolant about, as it is poisonous.**

## Car Care

● With a sealed-type cooling system, adding coolant should not be necessary on a regular basis. If frequent topping-up is required, it is likely there is a leak. Check the radiator, all hoses and joint faces for signs of staining or wetness, and rectify as necessary.

● It is important that antifreeze is used in the cooling system all year round, not just during the winter months. Don't top-up with water alone, as the antifreeze will become too diluted.

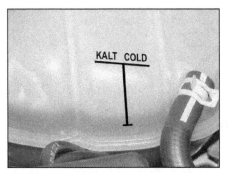

**1** The coolant level varies with the temperature of the engine. When the engine is cold, the coolant level should be on or slightly above the KALT/COLD mark on the side of the tank. When the engine is hot, the level will rise.

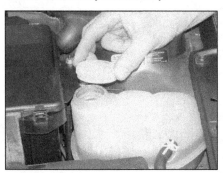

**2** If topping up is necessary, **wait until the engine is cold**. Slowly unscrew the expansion tank cap, to release any pressure present in the cooling system, and remove it.

**3** Top up the level by adding a mixture of water and antifreeze to the expansion tank. A funnel may help to reduce spillage. Refit the cap and tighten it securely.

# Brake (and clutch) fluid level

**Warning:**
● **Brake fluid can harm your eyes and damage painted surfaces, so use extreme caution when handling and pouring it.**
● **Do not use fluid that has been standing open for some time, as it absorbs moisture from the air, which can cause a dangerous loss of braking effectiveness.**

● *Make sure that your car is on level ground.*
● *The fluid level in the reservoir will drop slightly as the brake pads wear down, but the fluid level must never be allowed to drop below the MIN mark.*

## Safety First!

● If the reservoir requires repeated topping-up this is an indication of a fluid leak somewhere in the system, which should be investigated immediately.
● If a leak is suspected, the car should not be driven until the braking system has been checked. Never take any risks where brakes are concerned.

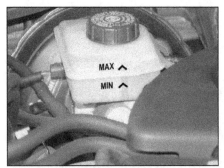

**1** The MAX and MIN marks are indicated on the front of the reservoir located in the right-hand rear corner of the engine compartment. The fluid level must always be kept between the marks.

**2** If topping-up is necessary, first wipe clean the area around the filler cap to prevent dirt entering the hydraulic system. Unscrew the cap and place it on an absorbent rag.

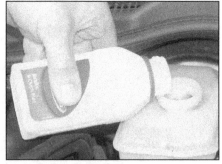

**3** Carefully add fluid, taking care not to spill it onto the surrounding components. Use only the specified fluid; mixing different types can cause damage to the system. After topping-up to the correct level, securely refit the cap and wipe off any spilt fluid.

# Tyre condition and pressure

It is very important that tyres are in good condition, and at the correct pressure - having a tyre failure at any speed is highly dangerous. Tyre wear is influenced by driving style - harsh braking and acceleration, or fast cornering, will all produce more rapid tyre wear. As a general rule, the front tyres wear out faster than the rears. Interchanging the tyres from front to rear ("rotating" the tyres) may result in more even wear. However, if this is completely effective, you may have the expense of replacing all four tyres at once!

Remove any nails or stones embedded in the tread before they penetrate the tyre to cause deflation. If removal of a nail does reveal that the tyre has been punctured, refit the nail so that its point of penetration is marked. Then immediately change the wheel, and have the tyre repaired by a tyre dealer.

Regularly check the tyres for damage in the form of cuts or bulges, especially in the sidewalls. Periodically remove the wheels, and clean any dirt or mud from the inside and outside surfaces. Examine the wheel rims for signs of rusting, corrosion or other damage. Light alloy wheels are easily damaged by "kerbing" whilst parking; steel wheels may also become dented or buckled. A new wheel is very often the only way to overcome severe damage.

New tyres should be balanced when they are fitted, but it may become necessary to re-balance them as they wear, or if the balance weights fitted to the wheel rim should fall off. Unbalanced tyres will wear more quickly, as will the steering and suspension components. Wheel imbalance is normally signified by vibration, particularly at a certain speed (typically around 50 mph). If this vibration is felt only through the steering, then it is likely that just the front wheels need balancing. If, however, the vibration is felt through the whole car, the rear wheels could be out of balance. Wheel balancing should be carried out by a tyre dealer or garage.

**1  Tread Depth - visual check**
The original tyres have tread wear safety bands (B), which will appear when the tread depth reaches approximately 1.6 mm. The band positions are indicated by a triangular mark on the tyre sidewall (A).

**2  Tread Depth - manual check**
Alternatively, tread wear can be monitored with a simple, inexpensive device known as a tread depth indicator gauge.

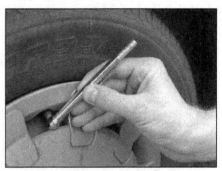

**3  Tyre Pressure Check**
Check the tyre pressures regularly with the tyres cold. Do not adjust the tyre pressures immediately after the vehicle has been used, or an inaccurate setting will result.

# Tyre tread wear patterns

### Shoulder Wear

**Underinflation (wear on both sides)**
Under-inflation will cause overheating of the tyre, because the tyre will flex too much, and the tread will not sit correctly on the road surface. This will cause a loss of grip and excessive wear, not to mention the danger of sudden tyre failure due to heat build-up.
*Check and adjust pressures*
**Incorrect wheel camber (wear on one side)**
*Repair or renew suspension parts*
**Hard cornering**
*Reduce speed!*

### Centre Wear

**Overinflation**
Over-inflation will cause rapid wear of the centre part of the tyre tread, coupled with reduced grip, harsher ride, and the danger of shock damage occurring in the tyre casing.
*Check and adjust pressures*

*If you sometimes have to inflate your car's tyres to the higher pressures specified for maximum load or sustained high speed, don't forget to reduce the pressures to normal afterwards.*

### Uneven Wear

Front tyres may wear unevenly as a result of wheel misalignment. Most tyre dealers and garages can check and adjust the wheel alignment (or "tracking") for a modest charge.
**Incorrect camber or castor**
*Repair or renew suspension parts*
**Malfunctioning suspension**
*Repair or renew suspension parts*
**Unbalanced wheel**
*Balance tyres*
**Incorrect toe setting**
*Adjust front wheel alignment*
**Note:** *The feathered edge of the tread which typifies toe wear is best checked by feel.*

# Wiper blades

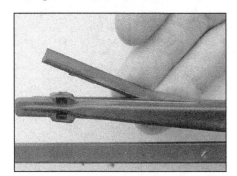

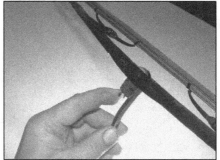

**1** Check the condition of the wiper blades; if they are cracked or show any signs of deterioration, or if the glass swept area is smeared, renew them. For maximum clarity of vision, wiper blades should be renewed annually.

**2** To remove a windscreen wiper blade, pull the arm fully away from the glass until it locks. Swivel the blade through 90°, then squeeze the locking clip, and detach the blade from the arm. When fitting the new blade, make sure that the blade locks securely into the arm, and that the blade is orientated correctly.

**3** Don't forget to check the tailgate wiper blade as well on Estate models. The blade is clipped onto the arm.

# Screen washer fluid level

● Screenwash additives not only keep the windscreen clean during bad weather, they also prevent the washer system freezing in cold weather – which is when you are likely to need it most. Don't top up using plain water, as the screenwash will become diluted and will freeze in cold weather.

● Check the operation of the windscreen and rear window washers. Adjust the nozzles using a pin if necessary, aiming the spray to a point slightly above the centre of the swept area. *On no account use coolant antifreeze in the washer system - this could discolour or damage paintwork.*

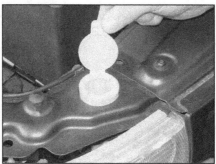

**1** The reservoir for the windscreen, headlight and rear window (where applicable) washer systems is located on the front left-hand side of the engine compartment. If topping-up is necessary, open the cap.

**2** When topping-up the reservoir a screen-wash additive should be added in the quantities recommended on the bottle.

# Battery

*Caution: Before carrying out any work on the vehicle battery, read the precautions given in 'Safety first!' at the start of this manual.*

✔ Make sure that the battery tray is in good condition, and that the clamp is tight. Corrosion on the tray, retaining clamp and the battery itself can be removed with a solution of water and baking soda. Thoroughly rinse all cleaned areas with water. Any metal parts damaged by corrosion should be covered with a zinc-based primer, then painted.

✔ Periodically (approximately every three months), check the charge condition of the battery, as described in Chapter 5A.

✔ If the battery is flat, and you need to jump start your vehicle, see *Jump starting*.

**1** The battery is located at the front, left-hand side of the engine compartment, and is covered with a protective casing. As from 2002 models, the battery is located with its terminals in line with the left-hand front wing, however, on earlier models they are in line with the engine compartment front crossmember. The exterior of the battery should be inspected periodically for damage such as a cracked case or cover.

**2** Check the tightness of battery clamps to ensure good electrical connections. You should not be able to move them. Also check each cable for cracks and frayed conductors.

**HAYNES HiNT**

*Battery corrosion can be kept to a minimum by applying a layer of petroleum jelly to the clamps and terminals after they are reconnected.*

**3** If corrosion (white, fluffy deposits) is evident, remove the cables from the battery terminals, clean them with a small wire brush, then refit them. Automotive stores sell a tool for cleaning the battery post . . .

**4** . . . as well as the battery cable clamps.

# Electrical systems

✔ Check all external lights and the horn. Refer to the appropriate Sections of Chapter 12 for details if any of the circuits are found to be inoperative, and replace the fuse if necessary.

✔ Visually check all accessible wiring connectors, harnesses and retaining clips for security, and for signs of chafing or damage.

 *If you need to check your brake lights and indicators unaided, back up to a wall or garage door and operate the lights. The reflected light should show if they are working properly.*

1 If a single indicator light, stop-light or headlight has failed, it is likely that a bulb has blown and will need to be renewed. Refer to Chapter 12 for details. If both stop-lights have failed, it is possible that the switch has failed (see Chapter 9).

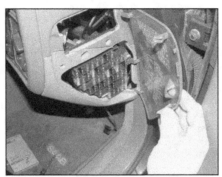

2 If more than one indicator light or headlight has failed, it is likely that either a fuse has blown or that there is a fault in the circuit (see Chapter 12). The main fuses are accessed by removing a cover on the driver's end of the facia. Additional fuses and relays are located in the left-hand side of the engine compartment.

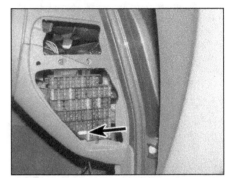

3 To renew a blown fuse, remove it using the plastic tool provided. Fit a new fuse of the same rating, available from car accessory shops. If the fuse blows repeatedly, refer to Chapter 12 to locate the fault.

## Lubricants and fluids

| | |
|---|---|
| Engine . . . . . . . . . . . . . . . . . . . . . . . . . . . . . . . . . . . . . | Saab Turbo Engine Oil or fully synthetic, Long Life Mobil 1 to specification GM-LL-A-025, viscosity 0W30 |
| Cooling system . . . . . . . . . . . . . . . . . . . . . . . . . . . . . . . | Saab original coolant/antifreeze only |
| Manual gearbox . . . . . . . . . . . . . . . . . . . . . . . . . . . . . . | Saab manual gearbox oil MTF 0063 |
| Automatic transmission . . . . . . . . . . . . . . . . . . . . . . . | Saab automatic transmission fluid 3309 (mineral oil based) or Dexron III ATF |
| Power steering reservoir . . . . . . . . . . . . . . . . . . . . . . . | Saab Power Steering Fluid CHF 11S |
| Brake fluid reservoir . . . . . . . . . . . . . . . . . . . . . . . . . . | Hydraulic fluid to DOT 4 |

## Choosing your engine oil

Engines need oil, not only to lubricate moving parts and minimise wear, but also to maximise power output and to improve fuel economy.

### HOW ENGINE OIL WORKS

#### • Beating friction

Without oil, the moving surfaces inside your engine will rub together, heat up and melt, quickly causing the engine to seize. Engine oil creates a film which separates these moving parts, preventing wear and heat build-up.

#### • Cooling hot-spots

Temperatures inside the engine can exceed 1000° C. The engine oil circulates and acts as a coolant, transferring heat from the hot-spots to the sump.

#### • Cleaning the engine internally

Good quality engine oils clean the inside of your engine, collecting and dispersing combustion deposits and controlling them until they are trapped by the oil filter or flushed out at oil change.

### OIL CARE - FOLLOW THE CODE

To handle and dispose of used engine oil safely, always:

OIL BANK LINE
**0800 66 33 66**
www.oilbankline.org.uk

• *Avoid skin contact with used engine oil. Repeated or prolonged contact can be harmful.*
• *Dispose of used oil and empty packs in a responsible manner in an authorised disposal site. Call 0800 663366 to find the one nearest to you. Never tip oil down drains or onto the ground.*

## Tyre pressures (cold)

**Note:** *Pressures apply to original-equipment tyres, and may vary if any other make or type of tyre is fitted; check with the tyre manufacturer or supplier for correct pressures if necessary.*

| Tyre size | Front | Rear |
|---|---|---|
| 195/65 R15 91Q: | | |
|   1 to 3 persons, up to 100 mph . . . . . . . . . . . . . . . . | 35 psi (2.4 bar) | 35 psi (2.4 bar) |
|   4 to 5 persons, up to 100 mph . . . . . . . . . . . . . . . . | 38 psi (2.6 bar) | 38 psi (2.6 bar) |
| 205/55 R16 91Q and 215/55 R16 93Q: | | |
|   1 to 3 persons, up to 100 mph . . . . . . . . . . . . . . . . | 35 psi (2.4 bar) | 35 psi (2.4 bar) |
|   4 to 5 persons, up to 100 mph . . . . . . . . . . . . . . . . | 38 psi (2.6 bar) | 38 psi (2.6 bar) |
| 205/65 R15 94V: | | |
|   1 to 5 persons, up to 100 mph . . . . . . . . . . . . . . . . | 33 psi (2.3 bar) | 30 psi (2.1 bar) |
|   1 to 5 persons, 100 mph plus . . . . . . . . . . . . . . . . | 41 psi (2.8 bar) | 38 psi (2.6 bar) |
| 215/55 R16 93V: | | |
|   1 to 5 persons, up to 100 mph . . . . . . . . . . . . . . . . | 35 psi (2.4 bar) | 32 psi (2.2 bar) |
|   1 to 5 persons, 100 mph plus . . . . . . . . . . . . . . . . | 42 psi (2.9 bar) | 39 psi (2.7 bar) |
| 225/45 R17 94 WXL: | | |
|   1 to 5 persons, up to 120 mph . . . . . . . . . . . . . . . . | 36 psi (2.5 bar) | 35 psi (2.4 bar) |
|   1 to 5 persons, 120 mph plus . . . . . . . . . . . . . . . . | 43 psi (3.0 bar) | 42 psi (2.9 bar) |
| T115/70 R16 (space saver spare) . . . . . . . . . . . . . . . . | 60 psi (4.1 bar) | 60 psi (4.1 bar) |

# Chapter 1
# Routine maintenance and servicing

## Contents

## Degrees of difficulty

| | | | | |
|---|---|---|---|---|
| **Easy,** suitable for novice with little experience  | **Fairly easy,** suitable for beginner with some experience  | **Fairly difficult,** suitable for competent DIY mechanic | **Difficult,** suitable for experienced DIY mechanic  | **Very difficult,** suitable for expert DIY or professional  |

## Lubricants and fluids

See end of *Weekly checks* on page 0•17

## Capacities

**Engine oil**

| | |
|---|---|
| All engines (drain and refill, with filter change) . . . . . . . . . . . . . . . . . . . . | 4.0 litres |
| Total from dry, including engine oil cooler . . . . . . . . . . . . . . . . . . . . . . . | 5.4 litres |
| Between dipstick MAX and MIN markings . . . . . . . . . . . . . . . . . . . . . . | 1.0 litres |

| | |
|---|---|
| **Cooling system** . . . . . . . . . . . . . . . . . . . . . . . . . . . . . . . . . . . . . . . . . | 7.4 litres |

**Transmission**

Manual:

| | |
|---|---|
| Drain and refill . . . . . . . . . . . . . . . . . . . . . . . . . . . . . . . . . . . . . . . | 1.5 litres |
| Total from dry . . . . . . . . . . . . . . . . . . . . . . . . . . . . . . . . . . . . . . . | 1.8 litres |

Automatic:

| | |
|---|---|
| Drain and refill . . . . . . . . . . . . . . . . . . . . . . . . . . . . . . . . . . . . . . . | 3.5 litres |
| Total from dry (including torque converter and cooler) . . . . . . . . . . | 7.0 litres |

**Braking system**

| | |
|---|---|
| System capacity . . . . . . . . . . . . . . . . . . . . . . . . . . . . . . . . . . . . . . . . | 0.9 litres |

**Fuel tank**

| | |
|---|---|
| | 68.0 litres |
| 2.0 and 2.3 litre Ecopower models . . . . . . . . . . . . . . . . . . . . . . . . . . . . | 75.0 litres (16.5 gallons) |
| 2.3 litre Aero HOT models . . . . . . . . . . . . . . . . . . . . . . . . . . . . . . . . . | 70.0 litres (15.4 gallons) |

**Power-assisted steering**

| | |
|---|---|
| System capacity . . . . . . . . . . . . . . . . . . . . . . . . . . . . . . . . . . . . . . . . | 1.3 litres |

## Cooling system

Antifreeze mixture:*

| | |
|---|---|
| 50% antifreeze . . . . . . . . . . . . . . . . . . . . . . . . . . . . . . . . . . . . . . . | Protection down to -37°C |
| 55% antifreeze . . . . . . . . . . . . . . . . . . . . . . . . . . . . . . . . . . . . . . . | Protection down to -45°C |

***Note:** Refer to antifreeze manufacturer for latest recommendations.*

## Ignition system

| | | |
|---|---|---|
| Firing order . . . . . . . . . . . . . . . . . . . . . . . . . . . . . . . . . . . . . . . . . . | 1 – 3 – 4 – 2 | |
| Spark plugs: | **Type** | **Electrode gap** |
| All engines . . . . . . . . . . . . . . . . . . . . . . . . . . . . . . . . . . . . . . . . . | Bosch FR 5 DP 222 | 1.0 mm |

## Brakes

| | |
|---|---|
| Front brake pad friction material minimum thickness . . . . . . . . . . . . . . | 5.0 mm at time of service (acoustic warning at 3.0 mm) |
| Rear brake pad friction material minimum thickness . . . . . . . . . . . . . . | 5.0 mm |

## Tyre pressures

Refer to the end of *Weekly checks* on page 0•17

## Torque wrench settings

| | Nm | lbf ft |
|---|---|---|
| Automatic transmission drain plug . . . . . . . . . . . . . . . . . . . . . . . . . . . . | 40 | 30 |
| Engine oil sump drain plug . . . . . . . . . . . . . . . . . . . . . . . . . . . . . . . . . | 25 | 18 |
| Manual transmission drain, level and filler plugs . . . . . . . . . . . . . . . . . | 50 | 37 |
| Spark plugs . . . . . . . . . . . . . . . . . . . . . . . . . . . . . . . . . . . . . . . . . . . | 28 | 21 |
| Wheel bolts . . . . . . . . . . . . . . . . . . . . . . . . . . . . . . . . . . . . . . . . . . . | 110 | 81 |

The maintenance intervals in this manual are provided with the assumption that you will be carrying out the work yourself. These are the minimum maintenance intervals recommended by the manufacturer for vehicles driven daily. If you wish to keep your vehicle in peak condition at all times, you may wish to perform some of these procedures more often. We encourage frequent maintenance, because it enhances the efficiency, performance and resale value of your vehicle.

If the vehicle is driven in dusty areas, used to tow a trailer, or driven frequently at slow speeds (idling in traffic) or on short journeys, more frequent maintenance intervals are recommended.

When the vehicle is new, it should be serviced by a factory-authorised dealer service department, in order to preserve the factory warranty.

## Every 250 miles (400 km) or weekly
☐ Refer to *Weekly checks*

## Every 6000 miles (10 000 km)
☐ Engine oil and filter – renewal (Section 3)

**Note**: *Frequent oil and filter changes are good for the engine. We recommend changing the oil at the mileage specified here, or at least twice a year if the mileage covered is a less.*

## At first 6000 miles (10 000 km) and thereafter every 12 000 miles (20 000 km)
☐ Service indicator – resetting (Section 4)
☐ Hoses and fluids – leak check (Section 5)
☐ Steering and suspension components – check (Section 6)
☐ Handbrake – check and adjustment (Section 7)
☐ Seat belt condition – check (Section 8)
☐ Airbag system – check (Section 9)
☐ Headlight beam alignment – check (Section 10)
☐ Power steering fluid level – check (Section 11)
☐ Road test (Section 12)

## Every 12 000 miles (20 000 km)
**Note:** *The 12 000 mile intervals start at 18 000 miles (30 000 km), ie, at 18 000 miles, 30 000 miles, 42 000 miles, 54 000 miles, etc.*
☐ Coolant antifreeze concentration – check (Section 13)
☐ Automatic transmission fluid level – check (Section 14)
☐ Driveshaft joints and gaiters – check (Section 15)
☐ Exhaust system – check (Section 16)
☐ Brake pad wear – check (Section 17)
☐ Hinges and locks – lubrication (Section 18)
☐ Air conditioning drain hoses – check (Section 19)
☐ Pollen air filter – renew (Section 20)
☐ Auxiliary drivebelt condition – check (Section 21)
☐ Spark plugs (B205E engine only) – renewal (Section 22)

## Every 24 000 miles (40 000 km)
**Note:** *The 24 000 mile intervals start at 30 000 miles (50 000 km), ie, at 30 000 miles, 54 000 miles, 78 000 miles, 102 000 miles, etc.*
☐ Manual transmission oil level – check (Section 23)
☐ Air filter element – renewal (Section 24)
☐ Spark plugs (except B205E engine) – renewal (Section 25)

## Every 3 years
☐ Coolant – renewal (Section 26)

**Note:** *The interval for this service item is based on time **and** mileage. It must be carried out every 3 years **or** every 48 000 miles (80 000 km), whichever comes sooner.*

## Every 60 000 miles (100 000 km)
**Note:** *The 60 000 mile intervals start at 66 000 miles (110 000 km), ie, at 66 000 miles, 126 000 miles, etc.*
☐ Fuel filter – renewal (Section 27)
☐ Auxiliary drivebelt – renewal (Section 28)
☐ Automatic transmission fluid – renewal (Section 29)

## Every 4 years
☐ Brake fluid – renewal (Section 30)

## Underbonnet view of a 2.3 litre turbocharged petrol engine

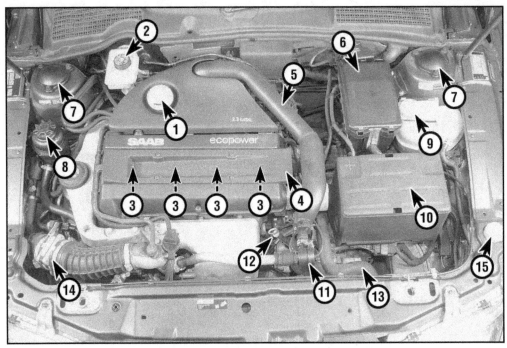

1  Engine oil filler cap and dipstick
2  Hydraulic brake fluid reservoir
3  Spark plugs (hidden)
4  Ignition coil module
5  Turbocharger-to-engine air inlet pipe
6  Engine compartment fusebox
7  Front suspension strut top mountings
8  Power steering fluid reservoir
9  Coolant expansion tank
10  Battery
11  Turbocharger control by-pass valve
12  Automatic transmission fluid level dipstick
13  Radiator top hose
14  Fuel injection system air-mass meter
15  Windscreen washer fluid reservoir filler cap

## Front underbody view

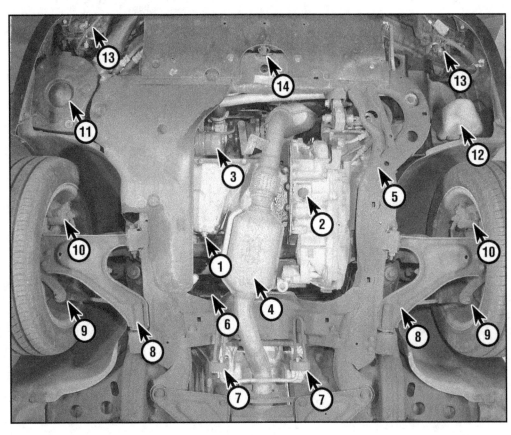

1  Engine oil drain plug
2  Automatic transmission fluid drain plug
3  Engine oil filter
4  Exhaust front pipe
5  Front suspension/engine subframe
6  Steering gear
7  Exhaust mounting rubbers
8  Front suspension lower arms
9  Steering track rod ends
10  Front brake calipers
11  Air filter housing
12  Windscreen washer fluid reservoir
13  Front foglights
14  Front towing eye position

## Rear underbody view

1   Rear suspension
    crossmember
2   Rear anti-roll bar
3   Rear suspension lower
    transverse link
4   Brake hydraulic flexible
    hoses
5   Handbrake cables
6   Fuel tank
7   Rear suspension trailing
    arms
8   Rear suspension
    strut/shock absorbers
9   Exhaust rear silencer and
    tailpipe

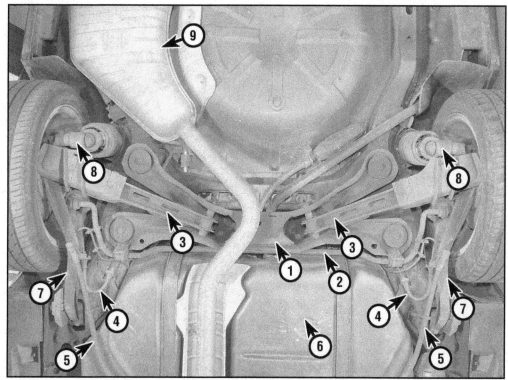

## 1   General information

1 This Chapter is designed to help the home mechanic maintain his/her vehicle for safety, economy, long life and peak performance.
2 The Chapter contains a master maintenance schedule, followed by Sections dealing specifically with each task in the schedule. Visual checks, adjustments, component renewal and other helpful items are included. Refer to the accompanying illustrations of the engine compartment and the underside of the vehicle for the locations of the various components.
3 Servicing your vehicle in accordance with the mileage/time maintenance schedule and the following Sections will provide a planned maintenance programme which should result in a long and reliable service life. This is a comprehensive plan, so maintaining some items but not others at the specified service intervals will not produce the same results.
4 As you service your vehicle, you will discover that many of the procedures can – and should – be grouped together, because of the particular procedure being performed, or because of the close proximity of two otherwise-unrelated components to one another. For example, if the vehicle is raised for any reason, the exhaust system could be inspected at the same time as the suspension and steering components.

5 The first step in this maintenance programme is to prepare yourself before the actual work begins. Read through all the Sections relevant to the work to be carried out, then make a list and gather together all the parts and tools required. If a problem is encountered, seek advice from a parts specialist, or a dealer service department.

## 2   Regular maintenance

1 If, from the time the vehicle is new, the routine maintenance schedule is followed closely, and frequent checks are made of fluid levels and high-wear items, as suggested throughout this manual, the engine will be kept in relatively good running condition, and the need for additional work will be minimised.
2 It is possible that there will be times when the engine is running poorly due to the lack of regular maintenance. This is even more likely if a used vehicle, which has not received regular and frequent maintenance checks, is purchased. In such cases, additional work may need to be carried out, outside of the regular maintenance intervals.
3 If engine wear is suspected, a compression test (refer to Chapter 2A) will provide valuable information regarding the overall performance of the main internal components. Such a test can be used as a basis to decide on the

extent of the work to be carried out. If, for example, a compression test indicates serious internal engine wear, conventional maintenance as described in this Chapter will not greatly improve the performance of the engine, and may prove a waste of time and money, unless extensive overhaul work (Chapter 2B) is carried out first.
4 The following series of operations are those most often required to improve the performance of a generally poor-running engine:

### Primary operations

a)  Clean, inspect and test the battery ('Weekly checks' and Chapter 5A)
b)  Check all the engine-related fluids ('Weekly checks').
c)  Check the condition and tension of the auxiliary drivebelt (Section 21).
d)  Renew the spark plugs (Section 22 and 25).
e)  Check the condition of the air filter element, and renew if necessary (Section 24).
f)  Renew the fuel filter (Section 27).
g)  Check the condition of all hoses, and check for fluid leaks (Section 5).

5 If the above operations do not prove fully effective, carry out the following secondary operations:

### Secondary operations

a)  Check the charging system (Chapter 5A).
b)  Check the ignition system (Chapter 5B).
c)  Check the fuel system (Chapter 4).

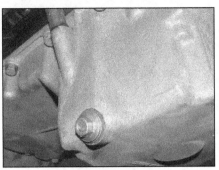

3.4 Engine oil drain plug

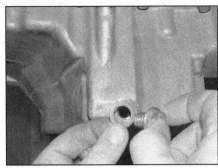

3.6 Renew the sump oil drain plug washer if necessary

3.8 Removing the oil filter

# Every 6000 miles

## 4 Engine oil and filter – renewal

1 Frequent oil changes are the most important preventative maintenance the DIY home mechanic can give the engine, because ageing oil becomes diluted and contaminated, which leads to premature engine wear.
2 Before starting this procedure, gather together all the necessary tools and materials. Also make sure that you have plenty of clean rags and newspapers handy, to mop up any spills. Ideally, the engine oil should be warm, as it will drain better, and more built-up sludge will be removed with it. Take care, however, not to touch the exhaust or any other hot parts of the engine when working under the vehicle. To avoid any possibility of scalding, and to protect yourself from possible skin irritants and other harmful contaminants in used engine oils, it is advisable to wear gloves when carrying out this work.
3 Apply the handbrake, then jack up the front of the vehicle and support it on axle stands (see *Jacking and vehicle support*).
4 The engine oil drain plug is located on the front of the sump; slacken the plug about half a turn. Position the draining container under the drain plug, then remove the plug completely – recover the sealing washer **(see illustration)**.

**HAYNES HINT** *Keep the plug pressed into the sump while unscrewing it by hand the last couple of turns. As the plug releases from the threads, move it away sharply so the stream of oil issuing from the sump runs into the container, not up your sleeve.*

5 Allow some time for the old oil to drain, noting that it may be necessary to reposition the container as the oil flow slows to a trickle.
6 After all the oil has drained, wipe off the drain plug with a clean rag. Check the sealing washer for condition, and renew it if necessary **(see illustration)**. Clean the area around the drain plug opening, and refit the plug. Tighten the plug to the specified torque.
7 Move the container into position under the oil filter which is located on the rear of the cylinder block and accessed from under the vehicle.
8 Using an oil filter removal tool or strap, slacken the filter initially, then unscrew it by hand the rest of the way **(see illustration)**. Empty the oil from the old filter into the container, and discard the filter.
9 Use a clean rag to remove all oil, dirt and sludge from the filter sealing area on the mounting bracket.
10 Apply a light coating of clean engine oil to the sealing ring on the new filter, then screw it

into position on the engine. Tighten the filter firmly by hand only – **do not** use any tools. Wipe clean the filter and sump drain plug.
11 Remove the old oil and all tools, then lower the vehicle to the ground.
12 Remove the oil filler cap and withdraw the dipstick from the top of the filler tube. Fill the engine, using the correct grade and type of oil (see *Lubricants and fluids*). An oil can spout or funnel may help to reduce spillage. Pour in half the specified quantity of oil first, then wait a few minutes for the oil to run to the sump. Continue adding oil a small quantity at a time until the level is up to the lower mark on the dipstick. Adding a further 1.0 litre will bring the level up to the upper mark on the dipstick. Insert the dipstick, and refit the filler cap.
13 Start the engine and run it for a few minutes; check for leaks around the oil filter seal and the sump drain plug. Note that there may be a delay of a few seconds before the oil pressure warning light goes out when the engine is first started, as the oil circulates through the engine oil galleries and the new oil filter, before the pressure builds-up.
14 Switch off the engine, and wait a few minutes for the oil to settle in the sump once more. With the new oil circulated and the filter completely full, recheck the level on the dipstick, and add more oil as necessary.
15 Dispose of the used engine oil safely, in accordance with the guidance given in the Reference Section.

# At first 6000 miles and thereafter every 12 000 miles

## 4 Service indicator – resetting

1 The facia-mounted SID (Saab Information Display) system incorporates a service interval indicator. When the distance covered between services approaches the next service, a visual message is displayed. The service indicator is then manually reset to zero after the vehicle has been serviced. **Note:** *The*

*indicator is automatically reset after the message has been displayed for 20 times.* The indicator can be reset at any time using the Saab diagnostic tool.
2 On the SID panel, press and hold the CLEAR button (furthermost left) for 8 seconds, then release it. During this period, the display should read CLEARED for the first four seconds, followed by SERVICE for the remaining 4 seconds. An audible signal will also be sounded during this time. The service indicator will then be reset.

## 5 Hoses and fluids – leak check

### Cooling system

⚠ *Warning: Refer to the safety information given in 'Safety First!' and Chapter 3 before disturbing any of the cooling system components.*

**1** Carefully check the radiator and heater coolant hoses along their entire length. Renew any hose which is cracked, swollen or which shows signs of deterioration. Cracks will show up better if the hose is squeezed. Pay close attention to the clips that secure the hoses to the cooling system components. Hose clips that have been overtightened can pinch and puncture hoses, resulting in cooling system leaks.

**2** Inspect all the cooling system components (hoses, joint faces, etc) for leaks. Where any problems of this nature are found on system components, renew the component or gasket with reference to Chapter 3 (see Haynes Hint).

### Fuel system

 **Warning: Refer to the safety information given in 'Safety First!' and Chapter 4A before disturbing any of the fuel system components.**

**3** Petrol leaks can be difficult to pinpoint, unless the leakage is significant and hence easily visible. Fuel tends to evaporate quickly once it comes into contact with air, especially in a hot engine bay. Small drips can disappear before you get a chance to identify the point of leakage. If you suspect that there is a fuel leak from the area of the engine bay, leave the vehicle overnight then start the engine from cold, with the bonnet open. Metal components tend to shrink when they are cold, and rubber seals and hoses tend to harden, so any leaks will be more apparent whilst the engine is warming-up from a cold start.

**4** Check all fuel lines at their connections to the fuel rail, fuel pressure regulator and fuel filter. Examine each rubber fuel hose along its length for splits or cracks. Check for leakage from the crimped joints between rubber and metal fuel lines. Examine the unions between the metal fuel lines and the fuel filter housing. Also check the area around the fuel injectors for signs of O-ring leakage.

**5** To identify fuel leaks between the fuel tank and the engine bay, the vehicle should be raised and securely supported on axle stands (see Jacking and vehicle support). Inspect the petrol tank and filler neck for punctures, cracks and other damage. The connection between the filler neck and tank is especially critical. Sometimes a rubber filler neck or connecting hose will leak due to loose retaining clamps or deteriorated rubber.

**6** Carefully check all rubber hoses and metal fuel lines leading away from the petrol tank. Check for loose connections, deteriorated hoses, kinked lines, and other damage. Pay particular attention to the vent pipes and hoses, which often loop up around the filler neck and can become blocked or kinked, making tank filling difficult. Follow the fuel supply and return lines to the front of the vehicle, carefully inspecting them all the way for signs of damage or corrosion. Renew damaged sections as necessary.

### Engine oil

**7** Inspect the area around the camshaft cover, cylinder head, oil filter and sump joint faces. Bear in mind that, over a period of time, some very slight seepage from these areas is to be expected – what you are really looking for is any indication of a serious leak caused by gasket failure. Engine oil seeping from the base of the timing belt cover or the transmission bellhousing may be an indication of crankshaft or transmission input shaft oil seal failure. Should a leak be found, renew the failed gasket or oil seal by referring to the appropriate Chapters in this manual.

### Automatic transmission fluid

**8** Where applicable, check the hoses leading to the transmission fluid cooler which is integral with the radiator. Look for deterioration caused by corrosion and damage from grounding, or debris thrown up from the road surface. Automatic transmission fluid is a thin oil and is usually red in colour.

### Power-assisted steering fluid

**9** Examine the hose running between the fluid reservoir and the power steering pump, and the return hose running from the steering rack to the fluid reservoir. Also examine the high pressure supply hose between the pump and the steering rack.

**10** Check the condition of each hose carefully. Look for deterioration caused by corrosion and damage from grounding, or debris thrown up from the road surface.

**11** Pay particular attention to crimped unions, and the area surrounding the hoses that are secured with adjustable worm drive clips. Like automatic transmission fluid, PAS fluid is a thin oil, and is usually red in colour.

### Air conditioning refrigerant

 **Warning: Refer to the safety information given in 'Safety First!' and Chapter 3, regarding the dangers of disturbing any of the air conditioning system components.**

**12** The air conditioning system is filled with a liquid refrigerant, which is retained under high pressure. If the air conditioning system is opened and depressurised without the aid of specialised equipment, the refrigerant will immediately turn into gas and escape into the atmosphere. If the liquid comes into contact with your skin, it can cause severe frostbite. In addition, the refrigerant contains substances which are environmentally damaging; for this reason, it should not be allowed to escape into the atmosphere in an uncontrolled fashion.

**13** Any suspected air conditioning system leaks should be immediately referred to a Saab dealer or air conditioning specialist. Leakage will be shown up as a steady drop in the level of refrigerant in the system.

**14** Note that water may drip from the condenser drain pipe, underneath the car, immediately after the air conditioning system

*A leak in the cooling system will usually show up as white- or rust-coloured, crusty deposits around the area of the leak.*

has been in use. This is normal, and should not be cause for concern.

### Brake (and clutch) fluid

**Warning: Refer to the safety information given in 'Safety First!' and Chapter 9, regarding the dangers of handling brake fluid.**

**15** With reference to Chapter 9, examine the area surrounding the brake pipe unions at the master cylinder for signs of leakage. Check the area around the base of fluid reservoir, for signs of leakage caused by seal failure. Also examine the brake pipe unions at the ABS hydraulic unit.

**16** If fluid loss is evident, but the leak cannot be pinpointed in the engine bay, the brake calipers and underbody brake lines should be carefully checked with the vehicle raised and supported on axle stands (see Jacking and vehicle support). Leakage of fluid from the braking system is a serious fault that must be rectified immediately.

**17** Brake/clutch hydraulic fluid is a toxic substance with a watery consistency. New fluid is almost colourless, but it becomes darker with age and use.

### Unidentified fluid leaks

**18** If there are signs that a fluid of some description is leaking from the vehicle, but you cannot identify the type of fluid or its exact origin, park the vehicle overnight and slide a large piece of card underneath it. Providing that the card is positioned in roughly the right location, even the smallest leak will show up on the card. Not only will this help you to pinpoint the exact location of the leak, it should be easier to identify the fluid from its colour. Bear in mind, though, that the leak may only be occurring when the engine is running!

### Vacuum hoses

**19** Although the braking system is hydraulically-operated, the brake servo unit amplifies the effort applied at the brake pedal by making use of the vacuum in the inlet manifold, generated by the engine. Vacuum is ported to the servo by means of a large-bore hose. Any leaks that develop in this hose will reduce the effectiveness of the braking system, and may affect the running of the engine.

**20** In addition, a number of the underbonnet components, particularly the emission control components, are driven by vacuum supplied from the inlet manifold via narrow-bore hoses. A leak in a vacuum hose means that air is being drawn into the hose (rather than escaping from it) and this makes leakage very difficult to detect. One method is to use an old length of vacuum hose as a kind of stethoscope – hold one end close to your ear and use the other end to probe the area around the suspected leak. When the end of the hose is directly over a vacuum leak, a hissing sound will be heard clearly through the hose. Care must be taken to avoid contacting hot or moving components, as the engine must be running, when testing in this manner. Renew any vacuum hoses that are found to be defective.

### 6 Steering and suspension components – check

#### *Front suspension and steering*

**1** Raise the front of the vehicle, and securely support it on axle stands (see *Jacking and vehicle support*).

**2** Visually inspect the balljoint dust covers and the steering rack-and-pinion gaiters for splits, chafing or deterioration. Any wear of these components will cause loss of lubricant, together with dirt and water entry, resulting in rapid deterioration of the balljoints or steering gear.

**3** Check the power steering fluid hoses for chafing or deterioration, and the pipe and hose unions for fluid leaks. Also check for signs of fluid leakage under pressure from the steering gear rubber gaiters, which would indicate failed fluid seals within the steering gear.

**4** Grasp the roadwheel at the 12 o'clock and 6 o'clock positions, and try to rock it **(see illustration)**. Very slight free play may be felt,

**6.4 Check for wear in the hub bearings by grasping the wheel and trying to rock it**

but if the movement is appreciable, further investigation is necessary to determine the source. Continue rocking the wheel while an assistant depresses the footbrake. If the movement is now eliminated or significantly reduced, it is likely that the hub bearings are at fault. If the free play is still evident with the footbrake depressed, then there is wear in the suspension joints or mountings.

**5** Now grasp the wheel at the 9 o'clock and 3 o'clock positions, and try to rock it as before. Any movement felt now may again be caused by wear in the hub bearings or the steering track rod balljoints. If the outer balljoint is worn, the visual movement will be obvious. If the inner joint is suspect, it can be felt by placing a hand over the rack-and-pinion rubber gaiter and gripping the track rod. If the wheel is now rocked, movement will be felt at the inner joint if wear has taken place.

**6** Using a large screwdriver or flat bar, check for wear in the suspension mounting bushes by levering between the relevant suspension component and its attachment point. Some movement is to be expected, as the mountings are made of rubber, but excessive wear should be obvious. Also check the condition of any visible rubber bushes, looking for splits, cracks or contamination of the rubber.

**7** With the car standing on its wheels, have an assistant turn the steering wheel back-and-forth, about an eighth of a turn each way. There should be very little, if any, lost movement between the steering wheel and roadwheels. If this is not the case, closely observe the joints and mountings previously described. In addition, check the steering column universal joints for wear, and also check the rack-and-pinion steering gear itself.

**8** The front suspension mountings should be checked for tightness.

#### *Rear suspension*

**9** Chock the front wheels, then jack up the rear of the vehicle and support securely on axle stands (see *Jacking and vehicle support*).

**10** Working as described previously for the front suspension, check the rear hub bearings, the suspension bushes and the strut or shock absorber mountings (as applicable) for wear.

**11** The rear suspension mountings should be checked for tightness.

#### *Shock absorber*

**12** Check for any signs of fluid leakage around the shock absorber bodies, or from the rubber gaiters around the piston rods. Should any fluid be noticed, the shock absorber is defective internally, and should be renewed. **Note:** *Shock absorbers should always be renewed in pairs on the same axle.*

**13** The efficiency of the shock absorber may be checked by bouncing the vehicle at each corner. Generally speaking, the body will return to its normal position and stop after being depressed. If it rises and returns on a rebound, the shock absorber is probably suspect. Also

examine the shock absorber upper and lower mountings for any signs of wear.

#### *Removable towbar attachment*

**14** Where applicable, clean the coupling pin then apply a little grease to the socket. Make sure that the removable towbar attachment fits easily to its mounting and locks correctly in position.

### 7 Handbrake – check and adjustment

**1** Chock the front wheels, then jack up the rear of the vehicle and support on axle stands (see *Jacking and vehicle support*).

**2** Fully release the handbrake lever.

**3** Apply the lever to the 4th notch position, and check that both rear wheels are locked when attempting to turn them by hand.

**4** If adjustment is necessary, refer to Chapter 9.

**5** Lower the vehicle to the ground.

### 8 Seat belt condition – check

**1** Working on each seat belt in turn, carefully examine the seat belt webbing for cuts, or for any signs of serious fraying or deterioration. Pull the belt all the way out, and examine the full extent of the webbing.

**2** Fasten and unfasten the belt, ensuring that the locking mechanism holds securely, and releases properly when intended. Check also that the retracting mechanism operates correctly when the belt is released.

**3** Check the security of all seat belt mountings and attachments which are accessible, without removing any trim or other components, from inside the vehicle.

**4** Check the function of the seat belt reminder lamp.

### 9 Airbag system – check

**1** The following work can be carried out by the home mechanic, however if an electronic fault is apparent, it will be necessary to take the car to a Saab dealer, who will have the necessary diagnostic equipment to extract fault codes from the system.

**2** Turn the ignition switch to the drive position (ignition warning lights on), and check that the SRS (Supplementary Restraint System) warning light is illuminated for 3 to 4 seconds. After this period the light should go out, indicating that the system has been checked and is functioning correctly.

**3** If the warning light remains on or refuses to light, have the system checked by a Saab dealer.

11.1 Power steering fluid reservoir

11.3 Fluid level marks on the dipstick

11.4 Topping-up the power steering fluid level

**4** Visually examine the steering wheel centre pad and the passenger airbag module for external damage. Also check the exterior of the front seats around the side airbag locations. If damage is evident, consult a Saab dealer.

**5** In the interests of safety, make sure that there are no loose items inside the car which could be thrown onto the airbag modules in the event of an accident.

## 10 Headlight beam alignment – check

Refer to Chapter 12 for details

## 11 Power steering fluid level – check

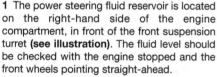

**1** The power steering fluid reservoir is located on the right-hand side of the engine compartment, in front of the front suspension turret **(see illustration)**. The fluid level should be checked with the engine stopped and the front wheels pointing straight-ahead.

**2** First wipe the filler cap and surrounding area of the reservoir. Unscrew the cap from the top of the reservoir, and wipe all fluid from the cap dipstick with a clean rag.

**3** Screw on the cap completely again, then remove it and check the fluid level on the dipstick. When the engine is cold at an ambient temperature of 20°C, the fluid level should be between the upper (MAX) and lower (MIN) marks on the dipstick, preferably near the MAX mark **(see illustration)**. If the engine is warm, the level can be slightly higher, but the level must never be allowed to be lower than the MIN mark.

**4** Top-up the fluid level using the specified type of fluid (do not overfill the reservoir) **(see illustration)**, then refit and tighten the filler cap.

## 12 Road test

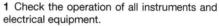

### Instruments and electrical equipment

**1** Check the operation of all instruments and electrical equipment.

**2** Make sure that all instruments read correctly, and switch on all electrical equipment in turn to check that it functions properly. Check the function of the heating, air conditioning and automatic climate control systems.

### Steering and suspension

**3** Check for any abnormalities in the steering, suspension, handling or road 'feel'.

**4** Drive the vehicle, and check that there are no unusual vibrations or noises.

**5** Check that the steering feels positive, with no excessive 'sloppiness', or roughness, and check for any suspension noises when cornering, or when driving over bumps. Check that the power steering system operates correctly.

### Drivetrain

**6** Check the performance of the engine, clutch (manual transmission), transmission and driveshafts. Check that the turbo boost pressure needle moves up to the upper limit during sharp acceleration. The needle may occasionally enter the red zone for an instant, but if this happens frequently, or for extended periods, a problem may exist within the turbo boost control mechanism.

**7** Listen for any unusual noises from the engine, clutch (manual transmission) and transmission.

**8** Make sure that the engine runs smoothly when idling, and that there is no hesitation when accelerating.

**9** On manual transmission models, check that the clutch action is smooth and progressive, that the drive is taken up smoothly, and that the pedal travel is correct. Also listen for any noises when the clutch pedal is depressed. Check that all gears can be engaged smoothly, without noise, and that the gear lever action is smooth and not abnormally vague or 'notchy'.

**10** On automatic transmission models, make sure that all gearchanges occur smoothly without snatching, and without an increase in engine speed between changes. Check that all the gear positions can be selected with the vehicle at rest. If any problems are found, they should be referred to a Saab dealer.

**11** Listen for a metallic clicking sound from the front of the vehicle, as the vehicle is driven slowly in a circle with the steering on full lock. Carry out this check in both directions. If a clicking noise is heard, this indicates wear in a driveshaft joint, in which case, refer to Chapter 8.

### Braking system

**12** Make sure that the vehicle does not pull to one side when braking, and that the wheels do not lock when braking hard.

**13** Check that there is no vibration through the steering when braking.

**14** Check that the handbrake operates correctly, without excessive movement of the lever, and that it holds the vehicle stationary on a slope.

**15** Test the operation of the brake servo unit as follows. With the engine off, depress the footbrake four or five times to exhaust the vacuum, then start the engine while holding the brake pedal depressed. As the engine starts, there should be a noticeable 'give' in the brake pedal as vacuum builds-up. Allow the engine to run for at least two minutes, and then switch it off. If the brake pedal is now depressed again, it should be possible to detect a 'hiss' from the servo as the pedal is depressed. After about four or five applications, no further sound should be heard, and the pedal should feel considerably harder.

**14.3a** Withdrawing the automatic transmission fluid level dipstick

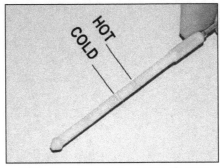

**14.3b** Fluid level marks on the dipstick

**15.2** Checking the condition of the driveshaft gaiters

# Every 12 000 miles

### 13 Coolant antifreeze concentration – check

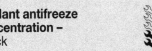

1 The cooling system should be filled with the recommended antifreeze and corrosion protection fluid. Over a period of time, the concentration of fluid may be reduced due to topping-up (this can be avoided by topping-up with the correct antifreeze mixture) or fluid loss. If loss of coolant has been evident, it is important to make the necessary repair before adding fresh fluid. The exact mixture of antifreeze-to-water which you should use depends on the weather conditions. The mixture should contain at least 40% antifreeze, but not more than 70%. Consult the mixture ratio chart on the antifreeze container before adding coolant. Hydrometers are available at most automotive accessory shops to test the coolant. Use antifreeze which meets the vehicle manufacturer's specifications.
2 With the engine **cold**, carefully remove the cap from the expansion tank. If the engine is not completely cold, place a cloth rag over the cap before removing it, and remove it slowly to allow any pressure to escape.
3 Antifreeze checkers are available from car accessory shops. Draw some coolant from the expansion tank and observe how many plastic balls are floating in the checker. Usually, 2 or 3 balls must be floating for the correct concentration of antifreeze, but follow the manufacturer's instructions.
4 If the concentration is incorrect, it will be necessary to either withdraw some coolant and add antifreeze, or alternatively drain the old coolant and add fresh coolant of the correct concentration.

### 14 Automatic transmission fluid level – check

1 The fluid level is checked using the dipstick located on the front of the transmission, on the left-hand side of the engine compartment, beneath the battery location.
2 With the engine idling, select D for approximately 15 seconds, then engage R and wait a further 15 seconds. Do this again in position P, and leave the engine idling.
3 Withdraw the dipstick from the tube, and wipe all the fluid from its end with a clean rag or paper towel. Insert the clean dipstick back into the tube as far as it will go, then withdraw it once more. Note the fluid level on the end of the dipstick – there are level marks for cold and hot fluid conditions **(see illustrations)**. Use the hot marks if the engine has reached normal operating temperature.
4 If topping-up is necessary, add fluid as necessary through the dipstick tube. **Note:** *Never overfill the transmission so that the fluid level is above the upper mark. Use a funnel with a fine mesh gauze, to avoid spillage and to ensure that no foreign matter enters the transmission.* Note that the quantity of oil between the MIN and MAX marks is 0.4 litres.
5 After topping-up, take the car on a short run to distribute the fresh fluid, then recheck the level again, topping-up if necessary.
6 Always maintain the fluid at the correct level. If the level is allowed to fall below the lower mark, fluid starvation may result, which could lead to severe transmission damage.

### 15 Driveshaft joints and gaiters – check

1 The driveshaft rubber gaiters are very important, because they prevent dirt, water and foreign material from entering and damaging the constant velocity (CV) joints. External contamination can cause the gaiter material to deteriorate prematurely, so it's a good idea to wash the gaiters with soap and water occasionally.
2 With the vehicle raised and securely supported on axle stands, turn the steering onto full-lock, then slowly rotate each front wheel in turn. Inspect the condition of the outer constant velocity (CV) joint rubber gaiters, squeezing the gaiters to open out the folds **(see illustration)**. Check for signs of cracking, splits, or deterioration of the rubber, which may allow the escape of grease, and lead to the ingress of water and grit into the joint. Also check the security and condition of the retaining clips. Repeat these checks on the inner CV joints. If any damage or deterioration is found, the gaiters should be renewed as described in Chapter 8.
3 At the same time, check the general condition of the outer CV joints themselves, by first holding the driveshaft and attempting to rotate the wheels. Repeat this check on the inner joints, by holding the inner joint yoke and attempting to rotate the driveshaft.
4 Any appreciable movement in the CV joint indicates wear in the joint, wear in the driveshaft splines, or a loose driveshaft retaining nut.

### 16 Exhaust system – check

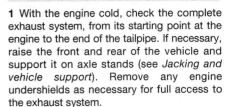

1 With the engine cold, check the complete exhaust system, from its starting point at the engine to the end of the tailpipe. If necessary, raise the front and rear of the vehicle and support it on axle stands (see *Jacking and vehicle support*). Remove any engine undershields as necessary for full access to the exhaust system.
2 Check the exhaust pipes and connections for evidence of leaks, severe corrosion, and damage. Make sure that all brackets and mountings are in good condition and that all relevant nuts and bolts are tight. Leakage at any of the joints or in other parts of the system will usually show up as a black sooty stain in the vicinity of the leak.
3 Rattles and other noises can often be traced to the exhaust system, especially the brackets and rubber mountings. Try to move the pipes and silencers. If the components are able to come into contact with the body or suspension parts, secure the system with new mountings. Otherwise separate the joints (if possible) and twist the pipes as necessary to provide additional clearance.

### 17 Brake pad wear – check

#### Front brake pads

**Note:** *An acoustic wear warning device is fitted to the outer pad, consisting of a metal strip which contacts the brake disc when the thickness of the friction material is less than 3.0 mm. This device causes a scraping noise which warns the driver that the pads are worn excessively (see illustration).*

**1** To check the front brake pads, firmly apply the handbrake, then jack up the front of the vehicle and support it securely on axle stands (see *Jacking and vehicle support*). Remove the front roadwheels.

**2** For a quick check, the pad thickness can be checked via the inspection hole on the front of the caliper (**see illustration**). Using a steel rule, measure the thickness of the pad lining excluding the backing plate. This must not be less than that indicated in the Specifications.

**3** The view through the caliper inspection hole gives an indication of the **inner** brake pad wear only. For a comprehensive check, the brake pads should be removed and cleaned. The operation of the caliper can then also be checked, and the condition of the brake disc itself can be fully examined on both sides.

**4** If any pad's friction material is worn to the specified thickness or less, *all four pads must be renewed as a set*. Refer to Chapter 9 for details.

**5** On completion, refit the roadwheels and lower the vehicle to the ground.

#### Rear brake pads

**6** To check the rear brake pads, chock the front wheels then jack up the rear of the vehicle and support it securely on axle stands (see *Jacking and vehicle support*). Remove the rear roadwheels.

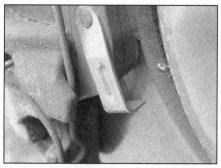

**17.0 Acoustic wear warning device fitted to the outer front brake pad**

**7** For a quick check, the pad thickness can be carried out via the inspection hole on the rear of the caliper. Using a steel rule, measure the thickness of the pad lining including the backing plate. This must not be less than that indicated in the Specifications.

**8** The view through the caliper inspection hole gives a rough indication of the state of the brake pads. For a comprehensive check, the brake pads should be removed and cleaned. The operation of the caliper can then also be checked, and the condition of the brake disc itself can be fully examined on both sides.

**9** If any pad's friction material is worn to the specified thickness or less, *all four pads must be renewed as a set*. Refer to Chapter 9 for details.

**10** On completion, refit the roadwheels and lower the vehicle to the ground.

### 18 Hinges and locks – lubrication

**1** Work around the vehicle and lubricate the hinges of the bonnet, doors and tailgate with a light machine oil.

**2** Lightly lubricate the two bonnet release locks with a smear of grease.

**3** Check carefully the security and operation of all hinges, latches and locks. Check that the central locking system operates correctly.

**4** Check the condition and operation of the bonnet and tailgate struts, renewing them if either is leaking or no longer able to support the bonnet/tailgate.

### 19 Air conditioning drain hoses – check

**1** Working beneath the glovebox, remove the side trim from the filter housing.

**2** Remove the sound insulation from both sides of the heater unit.

**3** Fold down the carpet from both sides of the centre console, and remove the insulation from the passenger's side.

**4** Loosen the clips and remove both drain hoses from the side of the heater unit.

**5** Ideally, blow compressed air through the drain hoses to clear them, alternatively use a cloth rag. Also clear the spigots on the heater unit.

**6** Refit the hoses using a reversal of the removal procedure.

### 20 Pollen air filter – renew

**1** Remove the glovebox as described in Chapter 11.

**2** Remove the side trim/carpet from the centre console with reference to Chapter 11. At the same time, cut the plastic ties holding the wiring harness to the cover, and the cooler hose to the glovebox.

**3** Undo the screws and remove the cover from over the pollen air filter (**see illustrations**).

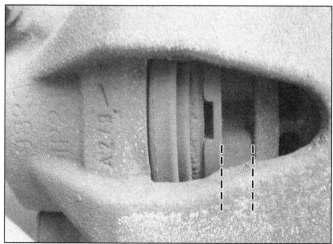

**17.2 The inner brake pad wear can be measured through the aperture in the front brake caliper**

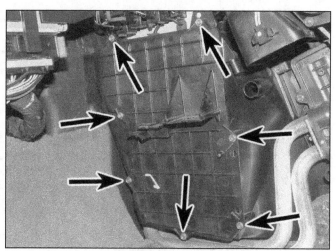

**20.3a Undo the screws . . .**

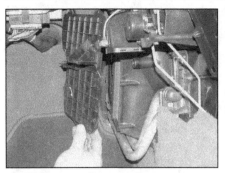

**20.3b . . . and remove the cover . . .**

**20.4 . . . then slide the pollen filter from the housing**

**4** Slide the pollen filter from the housing **(see illustration)**. Note the arrows indicating the direction of airflow through the filter.
**5** Check that a seal is fitted to the top of the filter; if not, obtain and fit one. On models which have had air conditioning fitted after original manufacture, break off the plastic lugs from the top of the filter.
**6** Loosen the clips and disconnect the two drain hoses from each side of the heater unit. Ideally, blow compressed air through the hoses to clear any accumulated debris, alternatively, clear the hoses with a suitable internal brush. Also, clear the spigots on the heater unit.
**7** Refit the drain hoses and tighten the clips, then fit the new pollen filter using a reversal of the removal procedure.

## 21 Auxiliary drivebelt condition – check

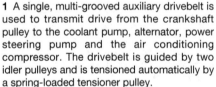

**1** A single, multi-grooved auxiliary drivebelt is used to transmit drive from the crankshaft pulley to the coolant pump, alternator, power steering pump and the air conditioning compressor. The drivebelt is guided by two idler pulleys and is tensioned automatically by a spring-loaded tensioner pulley.
**2** For better access to the drivebelt, apply the

*It is very often difficult to insert spark plugs into their holes without cross-threading them. To avoid this possibility, fit a short length of hose over the end of the spark plug.*

handbrake then jack up the front of the car and support it on axle stands (see *Jacking and vehicle support*). Remove the right-hand front roadwheel, then remove the lower section of the plastic liner from under the right-hand wheel arch to expose the crankshaft pulley and drivebelt.
**3** Check that the mark on top of the tensioner arm (right-hand rear of engine) is positioned within the two marks on the fixed tensioner mounting bracket. If it is outside the rearmost mark, the belt has stretched excessively and should be renewed.
**4** Depress the front section of drivebelt between the power steering pump and compressor pulleys, then release the belt and check that it returns to its tensioned position again, proving that the tensioner is operating correctly. If the tensioner does not operate freely, it should be removed for examination and renewed if necessary.
**5** Using a suitable socket and extension bar fitted to the crankshaft pulley bolt, rotate the crankshaft so that the entire length of the drivebelt can be examined. Examine the drivebelt for cracks, splitting, fraying, or other damage. Check also for signs of glazing (shiny patches) and for separation of the belt plies. Renew the belt if worn or damaged.

## 22 Spark plugs (B205E engine only) – renewal

**Note:** *The spark plugs should be renewed at 12 000 mile (20 000 km) intervals on models with the B205E engine only. On all other models they should be renewed at 24 000 mile (40 000 km) intervals.*
**1** The correct functioning of the spark plugs is vital for the correct running and efficiency of the engine. It is essential that the plugs fitted are appropriate for the engine. If this type is used and the engine is in good condition, the spark plugs should not need attention between scheduled renewal intervals.
**2** Remove the ignition discharge module as described in Chapter 5A.

 **Warning: When the ignition discharge module is removed, it must be kept in the upright**

position. If the ignition discharge module has been turned upside down for a length of time, leave it in the fitted position for a couple of hours before starting.
**3** It is advisable to remove the dirt from the spark plug recesses using a clean brush, vacuum cleaner or compressed air before removing the plugs, to prevent dirt dropping into the cylinders.
**4** Unscrew the plugs using a spark plug spanner or a deep socket and extension bar. Keep the socket aligned with the spark plug – if it is forcibly moved to one side, the ceramic insulator may be broken off. As each plug is removed, examine it as follows.
**5** Examination of the spark plugs will give a good indication of the condition of the engine. If the insulator nose of the spark plug is clean and white, with no deposits, this is indicative of a weak mixture or too hot a plug (a hot plug transfers heat away from the electrode slowly, a cold plug transfers heat away quickly).
**6** If the tip and insulator nose are covered with hard black-looking deposits, then this is indicative that the mixture is too rich. Should the plug be black and oily, then it is likely that the engine is fairly worn, as well as the mixture being too rich.
**7** If the insulator nose is covered with light tan to greyish-brown deposits, then the mixture is correct, and it is likely that the engine is in good condition.
**8** The electrode gap is of considerable importance as, if it is too large or too small, the size of the spark and its efficiency will be seriously impaired. The gap should be set to the value given in the Specifications.
**9** To set the gap, measure it with a feeler blade or wire gauge and then bend open, or closed, the outer plug electrode until the correct gap is achieved. The centre electrode should never be bent, as this will crack the insulator and cause plug failure, if nothing worse. If using feeler blades, the gap is correct when the appropriate-size blade is a firm sliding fit. Note that some models may be fitted with multi-electrode spark plugs – no attempt to adjust the electrode gap should be made on this type of spark plug.
**10** Special spark plug electrode gap adjusting tools are available from most motor accessory shops, or from some spark plug manufacturers.
**11** Before fitting the spark plugs, check that the threaded connector sleeves are tight, and that the plug exterior surfaces and threads are clean. It is very often difficult to insert spark plugs into their holes without cross-threading them. To avoid this possibility, fit a short length of hose over the end of the spark plug **(see Haynes Hint)**.
**12** Remove the rubber hose (if used), and tighten the plug to the specified torque (see Specifications) using the spark plug socket and a torque wrench. Refit the remaining plugs in the same way.
**13** Refit the ignition discharge module with reference to Chapter 5A.

23.2 Unscrew the transmission oil level plug, using an Allen key

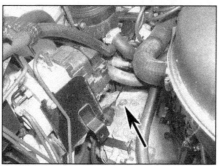

23.3a The transmission oil filler plug is located at the top of the transmission casing

23.3b Unscrew the plug using an Allen key

# Every 24 000 miles (40 000 km)

## 23 Manual transmission oil level – check

**Note:** *A suitable Allen key will be required to unscrew the manual transmission filler and level plugs. This can be obtained from most motor factors, or from your Saab dealer.*

1 Make sure that the car is parked on a level surface. Wipe clean the area around the level plug, which is located on the left hand side of the differential casing at the rear of the transmission, behind the left-hand driveshaft. Access to the plug can be gained from the engine compartment, or alternatively, apply the handbrake, then jack up the vehicle and support it on axle stands (see *Jacking and vehicle support*), but note that the vehicle must be level.

2 Unscrew the plug, using a suitable Allen key and wipe it clean **(see illustration)**. The oil level should reach the lower edge of the level hole. A certain amount of oil will have gathered behind the level plug, and will trickle out when it is removed; this does **not** necessarily indicate that the level is correct. To ensure that a true level is established, wait until the initial trickle has stopped, then use a length of clean wire, bent into a right angle, as a dipstick.

3 If the oil level requires topping-up, wipe clean the area around the filler plug, which is located on top of the transmission. Unscrew the plug, and wipe it clean **(see illustrations)**.

4 Add oil as necessary until a steady trickle of oil can be seen emerging from the level hole **(see illustration)**. Use **only** specified grade of oil. A funnel will be helpful when adding oil to the transmission through the filler plug aperture.

5 When the level is correct, refit and tighten the filler plug (and where necessary, the level plug) to the specified torque wrench setting. Wipe off any spilt oil.

23.4 Topping-up the transmission

## 24 Air filter element – renewal

1 The air cleaner is located beneath the front right-hand wing, behind the front bumper, and the air inlet is taken from the front of the car behind the radiator grille area. For improved access to the filter, apply the handbrake, then jack up the front of the vehicle and support it on axle stands (see *Jacking and vehicle support*), then undo the single screw and pull aside the front bumper/spoiler **(see illustration)**.

2 Undo the screws and remove the cover together with filter element from the bottom of the air filter housing **(see illustrations)**. Recover the O-ring seal.

3 Note how the element is fitted, then remove it from the cover.

4 Wipe clean the inner surfaces of the cover and main housing.

5 Locate the new element on the cover, then fit the cover complete with O-ring seal to the bottom of the housing. Insert and tighten the screws.

6 Lower the vehicle to the ground.

## 25 Spark plugs (except B205E engine) – renewal

Refer to Section 22.

24.1 For improved access, remove the screw from the front bumper/spoiler

24.2a Undo the screws . . .

24.2b . . . then remove the cover and air filter element

# Every 3 years

### 26 Coolant – renewal

**Note:** *The interval for this service item is based on time and mileage. It must be carried out every 3 years or every 48 000 miles (80 000 km), whichever comes sooner.*

⚠️ **Warning: Wait until the engine is cold before starting this procedure. Do not allow anti-freeze to come into contact with your skin, or with the painted surfaces of the vehicle. Rinse off spills immediately with plenty of water.**

### Cooling system draining

1 With the engine completely cold, remove the expansion tank filler cap. Turn the cap anti-clockwise, wait until any pressure remaining in the system is released, then unscrew it and lift it off.

2 Where applicable, remove the engine undershield, then position a suitable container beneath the left-hand side of the radiator.

3 Loosen the drain plug located on the left-hand lower mounting stub, and allow the coolant to drain into the container. If necessary, attach a hose to the drain plug to direct the coolant into the container.

4 When the flow of coolant stops, tighten the drain plug and where necessary refit the undershield.

5 If the coolant has been drained for a reason other than renewal, then provided it is clean and less than two years old, it can be re-used, though this is not recommended.

### Cooling system flushing

6 If coolant renewal has been neglected, or if the antifreeze mixture has become diluted, then in time the cooling system may gradually lose efficiency, as the coolant passages become restricted due to rust, scale deposits and other sediment. The cooling system efficiency can be restored by flushing the system clean.

7 The radiator should be flushed independently of the engine, to avoid unnecessary contamination.

### Radiator flushing

8 Disconnect the top and bottom hoses and any other relevant hoses from the radiator, with reference to Chapter 3.

9 Insert a garden hose into the radiator top inlet. Direct a flow of clean water through the radiator, and continue flushing until clean water emerges from the radiator bottom outlet.

10 If after a reasonable period, the water still does not run clear, the radiator can be flushed with a good proprietary cleaning agent. It is important that the manufacturer's instructions are followed carefully. If the contamination is particularly bad, remove the radiator and insert the hose in the bottom outlet, and reverse-flush the radiator, then refit it.

### Engine flushing

11 Remove the thermostat as described in Chapter 3, then temporarily refit the thermostat cover. If the radiator top hose has been disconnected, temporarily reconnect the hose.

12 With the top and bottom hoses disconnected from the radiator, insert a garden hose into the radiator top hose. Direct a clean flow of water through the engine, and continue flushing until clean water emerges from the radiator bottom hose.

13 On completion of flushing, refit the thermostat and reconnect the hoses with reference to Chapter 3.

### Cooling system filling

14 Before attempting to fill the cooling system, make sure that all hoses and clips are in good condition, and that the clips are tight. Note that an antifreeze mixture must be used all year round, to prevent corrosion of the engine components.

15 Make sure that the air conditioning (A/C) or automatic climate control (ACC) is switched off. This is to prevent the air conditioning system starting the radiator cooling fan before the engine is at normal temperature when refilling the system.

16 Remove the expansion tank filler cap and slowly fill the system until the coolant level reaches the MAX mark on the side of the expansion tank.

17 Refit and tighten the expansion tank filler cap.

18 Start the engine and set the heater to hot, then run the engine until it reaches normal operating temperature (until the cooling fan cuts in and out). Running the engine at varying speeds will allow the engine to warm-up quickly.

19 Stop the engine, and allow it to cool, then recheck the coolant level with reference to *Weekly checks*. Top-up the level if necessary and refit the expansion tank filler cap. Refit the splash cover beneath the radiator.

### Antifreeze mixture

20 The antifreeze should always be renewed at the specified intervals. This is necessary not only to maintain the antifreeze properties, but also to prevent corrosion which would otherwise occur as the corrosion inhibitors become progressively less effective.

21 Always use an ethylene-glycol based antifreeze which is suitable for use in mixed-metal cooling systems. The quantity of antifreeze and levels of protection are given in the Specifications.

22 Before adding antifreeze, the cooling system should be completely drained, preferably flushed, and all hoses checked for condition and security.

23 After filling with antifreeze, a label should be attached to the expansion tank, stating the type and concentration of antifreeze used, and the date installed. Any subsequent topping-up should be made with the same type and concentration of antifreeze.

24 Do not use engine antifreeze in the windscreen/tailgate washer system, as it will cause damage to the vehicle paintwork. A screenwash additive should be added to the washer system in the quantities stated on the bottle.

# Every 60 000 miles (100 000 km)

### 27 Fuel filter – renewal

⚠️ **Warning: Before carrying out the following operation, refer to the precautions given in 'Safety first!' at the beginning of this manual, and follow them implicitly. Petrol is a highly-dangerous and volatile liquid, and the** precautions necessary when handling it cannot be overstressed.p

1 On all models, the fuel filter is mounted adjacent to the fuel tank underneath the rear of the car.

2 Depressurise the fuel system with reference to Chapter 4A.

3 Chock the front wheels, then jack up the rear of the car and support on axle stands (see *Jacking and vehicle support*).

4 Pull off the plastic guard where fitted, then clean the areas around the fuel filter inlet and outlet unions **(see illustration)**.

5 Position a small container or cloth rags beneath the filter to catch spilt fuel.

6 Unscrew the banjo coupling bolts from each end of the filter, while holding the coupling with a further spanner. Recover the sealing washers **(see illustrations)**.

7 Undo the mounting clamp securing screw **(see illustration)**.

8 Remove the filter from its mounting bracket,

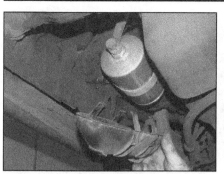

27.4 Removing the fuel filter plastic guard

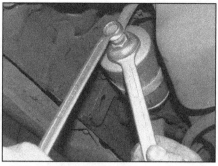

27.6a Use two spanners to unscrew the banjo coupling bolts from each end of the fuel filter . . .

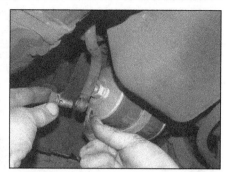

27.6b . . . and recover the sealing washers

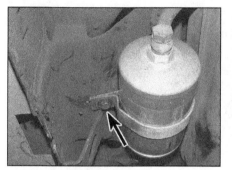

27.7 Undo the screw . . .

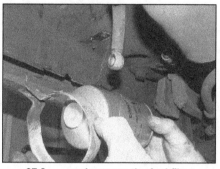

27.8 . . . and remove the fuel filter

27.9 Make sure that the direction of flow arrow on the filter body is pointing towards the outlet which leads to the engine compartment

noting the direction of the arrow marked on the filter body, loosen the retaining clip and withdraw the filter from under the car **(see illustration)**.

**9** Locate the new filter in the retaining clip, then fit and tighten the securing screw. Make sure that the direction of flow arrow on the filter body is pointing towards the outlet which leads to the engine compartment **(see illustration)**.

**10** Check the condition of the sealing washers, and renew them if necessary.

**11** Refit the banjo couplings and hoses to each end of the filter, together with the sealing washers. Tighten the bolts securely, while holding the couplings with a second spanner.

**12** Wipe away any excess fuel, refit the plastic cover where fitted, then lower the car to the ground.

**13** Start the engine, and check the filter hose connections for leaks.

**14** The old filter should be disposed of safely, bearing in mind that it will be highly inflammable.

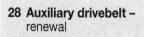

## 28 Auxiliary drivebelt –
renewal

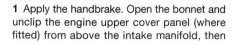

**1** Apply the handbrake. Open the bonnet and unclip the engine upper cover panel (where fitted) from above the intake manifold, then

slacken its two retaining clips and withdraw the mass airflow sensor's rubber intake hose; cover the sensor's intake to prevent the entry of dirt or other foreign matter into the inlet tract **(see illustration)**. Jack up the front of the car and support it on axle stands (see *Jacking and vehicle support*). Remove the right-hand front roadwheel, then undo the retaining screws and withdraw the lower section of the plastic liner from under the right-hand wheel arch and the wheel arch liner itself as necessary to expose the crankshaft pulley and drivebelt. Unbolt the clip securing the power steering pipe to the subframe, immediately beneath the crankshaft pulley.

**2** Position a trolley jack underneath the engine and raise the jack head until it is just taking the

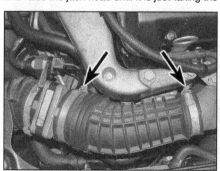

28.1 Undo the retaining screws (arrows) and withdraw the mass airflow sensor's rubber intake hose . . .

weight of the engine. Ensure that the jack head does not bear on the underside of the sump; place a block of wood between the sump and the jack head. Alternatively, position a lifting beam across the engine bay and support the engine by the lifting eyelet located at the rear right-hand side of the cylinder head. Unbolt the engine right-hand mounting bracket from the engine and remove the retaining nut on top of the engine mounting **(see illustration)**. Withdraw the engine mounting bracket, releasing the power steering hose from its retaining clip underneath.

**3** The tensioner pulley spring must now be compressed and locked in position. Insert a 1/2 in drive straight extension bar or similar into the square hole in the lug at the top of the

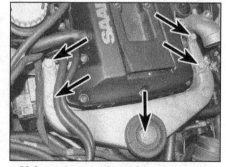

28.2 . . . then unclip engine cover panel and remove engine mounting bracket (nut and bolts arrowed) to reach auxiliary drivebelt and tensioner

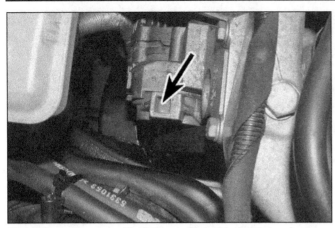

28.3a  To compress and lock the auxiliary drivebelt's tensioner . . .

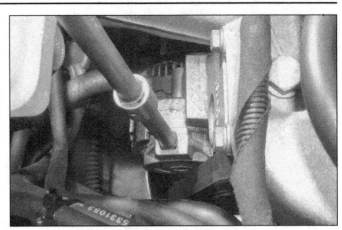

28.3b  . . . insert a 1/2 in drive straight extension bar into lug at top of outboard (moving) part of tensioner . . .

28.3c  . . . and rotate tensioner against spring tension until hole in stop lug aligns with hole in inboard (fixed) part of tensioner; insert 3 mm dia. tool to lock tensioner assembly in position

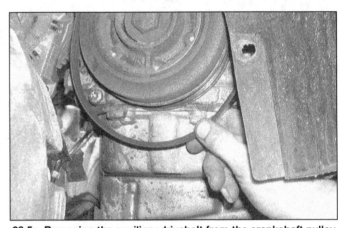

28.5a  Removing the auxiliary drivebelt from the crankshaft pulley

outboard (moving) part of the tensioner assembly. Rotate the tensioner clockwise, against the spring tension, until the hole in the stop lug lines up with the corresponding hole in the inboard (fixed) part of the tensioner assembly. Note that the tensioner spring is very strong, and considerable pressure is required to compress it, but do not try to force

it beyond the limit of its travel, or allow it to snap back against spring pressure; it will break **(see illustrations)**.
**4** Hold the tensioner in that position and slide a 3 mm Allen key (or drill bit) through the holes in the stop lug and in the inboard (fixed) part of the tensioner assembly **(see illustration)**. Release slowly the effort on the straight

extension bar, checking that the tensioner remains locked in position.
**5** Slip the drivebelt from the pulleys and remove it **(see illustration)**. Carefully check the pulleys (particularly the tensioner and idlers) and renew any that are damaged or that show signs of roughness or jerkiness when rotated **(see illustration)**.

28.5b  Check carefully tensioner and idler pulleys . . .

28.5c  . . . and renew any that are damaged or that rotate roughly or jerkily

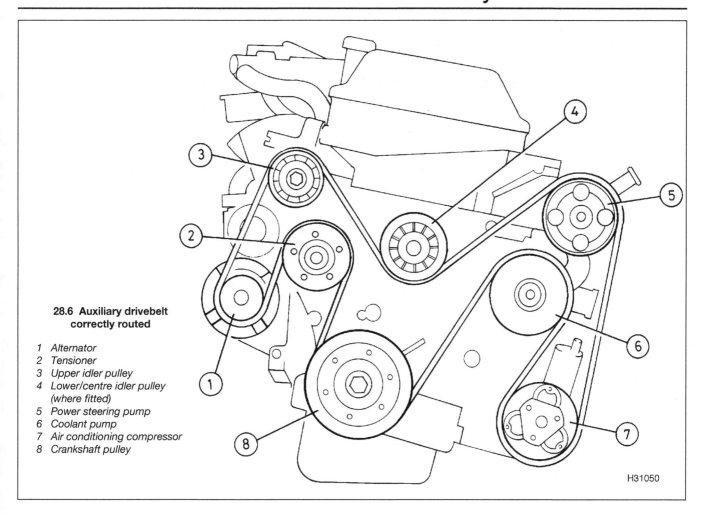

**28.6 Auxiliary drivebelt
correctly routed**

1 Alternator
2 Tensioner
3 Upper idler pulley
4 Lower/centre idler pulley
   (where fitted)
5 Power steering pump
6 Coolant pump
7 Air conditioning compressor
8 Crankshaft pulley

H31050

**6** On refitting, route the drivebelt over all the pulleys as shown, making sure that, where applicable, the multi-grooved side is correctly engaged with the pulley grooves **(see illustration). Note:** *A shorter drivebelt may be found on some vehicles, running straight from the upper idler (item 3) to the power steering pump pulley (item 5) the lower, or centre, idler pulley (item 4) having been deleted.*
**7** Compress the tensioner spring as described for the removal procedure. Remove the locking tool and then slowly release the tensioner, allowing it to apply pressure to the drivebelt.
**8** Ensure that the belt is correctly seated on all the pulleys, then refit the engine right-hand mounting bracket, clipping the power steering hose on its underside and tightening its nut and bolts to the torque wrench settings specified (see Chapter 2A). Tighten securely the bolt securing the power steering hose clip to the subframe, then refit the plastic wheel arch liner and its lower section. Refit the roadwheel and lower the car to the ground. Uncover the mass airflow sensor and refit its rubber intake hose, then refit the engine upper cover panel to the intake manifold.
**9** On completion, start the engine and allow it

to idle for a few minutes. This will allow the tensioner to settle in position and distribute the tension evenly throughout the belt. Stop the engine and check once again that the belt is correctly seated on all the pulleys.

## 29 Automatic transmission fluid – renewal

**1** Take the car on a short journey to warm the transmission up to normal operating temperature. Position the car over an inspection pit, or alternatively jack up the front and rear of the car and support on axle stands (see *Jacking and vehicle support*). Whichever method is used, make sure that the car is level for checking the fluid level later.
**2** Position a suitable container beneath the transmission, then unscrew the drain plug and allow the fluid to drain **(see illustration)**. Note that a special adapter key will be required to unscrew the plug.

⚠️ *Warning: The fluid will be very hot, so take necessary precautions to prevent scalding. The use of thick waterproof gloves is recommended.*

**3** With all the fluid drained, wipe clean the plug and refit it to the automatic transmission housing. Where applicable fit a new sealing washer. Tighten the plug to the specified torque.
**4** Fill the automatic transmission with the specified grade and quantity of fluid. Referring to Section 14, top it up to the correct level. Use the low temperature set of dipstick markings first, then take the car for a run. With the fluid at operating temperature, recheck the fluid level using the high temperature set of dipstick markings.

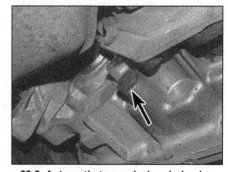

**29.2 Automatic transmission drain plug**

# Every 4 years

### 30 Brake fluid – renewal

⚠ *Warning: Brake hydraulic fluid can harm your eyes and damage painted surfaces, so use extreme caution when handling and pouring it. Do not use fluid that has been standing open for some time, as it absorbs moisture from the air. Excess moisture can cause a dangerous loss of braking effectiveness.*

**1** The procedure is similar to that for the bleeding of the hydraulic system as described in Chapter 9.

**2** Working as described in Chapter 9, open the first bleed screw in the sequence, and pump the brake pedal gently until nearly all the old fluid has been emptied from the master cylinder reservoir. Top-up to the MAX level with new fluid, and continue pumping until only the new fluid remains in the reservoir, and new fluid can be seen emerging from the bleed screw. Tighten the screw, and top the reservoir level up to the MAX level line.

**HAYNES HiNT** *Old hydraulic fluid is invariably much darker in colour than the new, making it easy to distinguish the two.*

**3** Work through all the remaining bleed screws in the sequence until new fluid can be seen at all of them. Be careful to keep the master cylinder reservoir topped-up to above the MIN level at all times, or air may enter the system and greatly increase the length of the task.

**4** When the operation is complete, check that all bleed screws are securely tightened, and that their dust caps are refitted. Wash off all traces of spilt fluid, and recheck the master cylinder reservoir fluid level.

**5** Check the operation of the brakes before taking the car on the road.

# Chapter 2 Part A:
## Engine in-car repair procedures

# Contents

# Degrees of difficulty

| **Easy,** suitable for novice with little experience |  | **Fairly easy,** suitable for beginner with some experience |  | **Fairly difficult,** suitable for competent DIY mechanic | | **Difficult,** suitable for experienced DIY mechanic | | **Very difficult,** suitable for expert DIY or professional | |
|---|---|---|---|---|---|---|---|---|---|

# Specifications

### Engine (general)

Designation:
| | |
|---|---|
| 1985 cc engine ...................................... | B205 |
| 2290 cc engine ...................................... | B235 |

Bore ................................................. 90.00 mm

Stroke:
| | |
|---|---|
| 1985 cc engine ...................................... | 78.00 mm |
| 2290 cc engine ...................................... | 90.00 mm |

Direction of crankshaft rotation ........................... Clockwise (viewed from right-hand side of vehicle)

No 1 cylinder location .................................. At timing chain end of engine

Compression ratio:
| | |
|---|---|
| B205 ............................................... | 8.8 : 1 |
| B235 ............................................... | 9.3 : 1 |

Maximum power/torque:
| | |
|---|---|
| B205 ............................................... | 110 kW @ 5500 rpm/240 Nm @ 1800 rpm |
| B205 (with accessory kit fitted) ...................... | 136 kW @ 5500 rpm/300 Nm @ 3500 rpm |

B235E:
| | |
|---|---|
| 1998-2000 ......................................... | 125 kW @ 5500 rpm/280 Nm @ 1800 rpm |
| 2000-on ........................................... | 136 kW @ 5500 rpm/280 Nm @ 1800 rpm |

B235L ............................................... 162 kW @ 5500 rpm/310 Nm @ 2500 rpm

B235R:
| | |
|---|---|
| 2000 models ....................................... | 169 kW @ 5500 rpm/350 Nm @ 1900 rpm |
| 2001-on models .................................... | 184 kW @ 5500 rpm/370 Nm @ 1900 rpm |

## Engine codes

**Note:** *The engine code is situated on the front of the engine at the transmission end, stamped directly onto the cylinder block.*

Character 1:

| | |
|---|---|
| B | Petrol engine |

Characters 2 & 3:

| | |
|---|---|
| 20 | 1985 cc |
| 23 | 2290 cc |

Character 4:

| | |
|---|---|
| 5 | 4 cylinders, in-line block with 2 balancer shafts, double overhead camshafts with 4 valves per cylinder |

Character 5:

| | |
|---|---|
| E | Low-pressure turbocharged engine with intercooler |
| L | Turbocharged engine with intercooler – Stage 1 |
| R | Turbocharged engine with intercooler – Stage 2 |

Character 6:

| | |
|---|---|
| D | Saab 9-3 |
| E | Saab 9-5 |

Character 7:

| | |
|---|---|
| A | Automatic transmission |
| M | Manual transmission |

Characters 8 & 9:

| | |
|---|---|
| 00 | Basic engine |
| 18 | Engine adapted for automatic |
| 19 | Engine with oil cooler |
| 20 | Engine with OBD II |

Character 10:

| | |
|---|---|
| W | 1998 |
| X | 1999 |
| Y | 2000 |
| 1 | 2001 |
| 2 | 2002 |
| 3 | 2003 |
| 4 | 2004 |
| 5 | 2005 |

Characters 11 to 16 .............................. Serial numbers

## Camshafts

| | |
|---|---|
| Drive | Chain from crankshaft |
| Number of bearings | 5 per camshaft |
| Camshaft bearing journal diameter (outside diameter) | 28.922 to 28.935 mm |
| Cam lift | 8.31 mm |
| Endfloat | 0.08 to 0.35 mm |

## Lubrication system

| | |
|---|---|
| Oil pump type | Bi-rotor type, driven off the crankshaft |
| Minimum oil pressure at 80°C | 2.5 bars at 2000 rpm, using 10W30 engine oil. |
| Oil pressure warning switch operating pressure | 0.3 to 0.5 bar |
| Clearance between pump outer rotor and timing cover housing | 0.03 to 0.08 mm |
| Pressure release valve opens at | 3.8 bar |
| Oil cooler thermostat opens at | 105°C approx. |

## Torque wrench settings

| | Nm | lbf ft |
|---|---|---|
| Balance shaft chain idler sprocket | 25 | 18 |
| Balance shaft sprockets | 22 | 16 |
| Big-end bearing cap nuts: | | |
| Stage 1 | 20 | 15 |
| Stage 2 | Angle-tighten a further 70° | |
| Camshaft bearing cap | 15 | 11 |
| Camshaft sprockets | 63 | 46 |
| Crankshaft pulley bolt | 175 | 129 |
| Cylinder head bolts: | | |
| Stage 1 | 40 | 30 |
| Stage 2 | 60 | 44 |
| Stage 3 | Angle-tighten a further 90° | |
| Cylinder head cover | 15 | 11 |
| Driveplate | 95 | 70 |
| Engine oil drain plug | 25 | 18 |
| Engine-to-transmission bolts | 70 | 52 |

## Torque wrench settings (continued)

| | Nm | lbf ft |
|---|---|---|
| Flywheel | 80 | 59 |
| Front engine mounting: | | |
|     Bracket to engine | 47 | 35 |
|     Torque arm to body | 121 | 89 |
|     Torque arm to bracket | 47 | 35 |
| Left-hand transmission mounting: | | |
|     Mounting nut | 85 | 63 |
|     Mounting to body | 60 | 44 |
|     Bracket to transmission: | | |
|         Manual | 40 | 30 |
|         Automatic | 84 | 62 |
| Main bearing cap bolts: | | |
|     Stage 1 | 20 | 15 |
|     Stage 2 | Angle-tighten a further 70° | |
| Oil cooler hose unions | 8 | 6 |
| Piston cooling jet | 18 | 13 |
| Plug for camshaft chain tensioner | 22 | 16 |
| Plug for oil cooler thermostat | 60 | 44 |
| Plug for oil pressure reducing valve | 30 | 22 |
| Rear engine mounting: | | |
|     Bracket to transmission | 84 | 62 |
|     Mounting to subframe | 26 | 19 |
|     Mounting nut | 26 | 19 |
| Right-hand engine mounting: | | |
|     Mounting-to-inner wing bolts | 47 | 35 |
|     Mounting-to-bracket to engine bolts | 47 | 35 |
|     Mounting-to-bracket nut | 105 | 77 |
| Sump bolts | 22 | 16 |
| Timing chain tensioner body | 63 | 47 |
| Timing chain tensioner spring plug | 22 | 16 |
| Timing cover bolts | 22 | 16 |

## 1 General information

### How to use this Chapter

This Part of Chapter 2 describes those repair procedures that can reasonably be carried out on the engine while it remains in the car. If the engine has been removed from the car, and is being dismantled as described in Part B, any preliminary dismantling procedures can be ignored.

Note that, while it may be possible physically to overhaul items such as the piston/connecting rod assemblies while the engine is in the car, such tasks are not normally carried out as separate operations. Usually, several additional procedures (not to mention the cleaning of components and oilways) have to be carried out. For this reason, all such tasks are classed as major overhaul procedures, and are described in Part B of this Chapter.

Part B describes the removal of the engine/transmission from the vehicle, and the full overhaul procedures that can then be carried out.

### Engine description

The engine is of in-line four-cylinder, double-overhead camshaft (DOHC), 16-valve type, mounted transversely at the front of the car with the transmission attached to its left-hand end. The Saab 9-5 is fitted with 1985 cc or 2290 cc engine versions, which have balance shafts that are situated in the cylinder block, to smooth out vibrations. All engines are fuel-injected using a Saab-manufactured 'Trionic' engine management system.

The crankshaft runs in five main bearings. Thrustwashers are fitted to the centre main bearing (upper half only) to control crankshaft endfloat.

The connecting rods rotate on horizontally-split bearing shells at their big-ends. The pistons are attached to the connecting rods by fully-floating gudgeon pins, which are retained in the pistons by circlips. The aluminium-alloy pistons are fitted with three piston rings – two compression rings and an oil control ring.

The cylinder block is of cast-iron, and the cylinder bores are an integral part of the cylinder block. The inlet and exhaust valves are closed by coil springs, and operate in guides pressed into the cylinder head; the valve seat inserts are also pressed into the cylinder head, and can be renewed separately if worn. There are four valves per cylinder.

The camshafts are driven by a single-row timing chain, and they operate the 16 valves via hydraulic cam followers. The hydraulic cam followers maintain a predetermined clearance between the cam lobe and the end of the valve stem, using hydraulic chambers and a tension spring. The followers are fed with oil from the main engine lubrication circuit.

The balance shafts are driven in counter-rotation by a small single-row chain from a sprocket on the front of the crankshaft. The balance shaft chain run is controlled by two fixed guide rails and an idler sprocket. The chain is located on the outside of the main camshaft timing chain, with its tension being controlled by a dedicated oil pressure-driven tensioner.

Lubrication is by means of a bi-rotor oil pump, driven from the front of the crankshaft and located in the timing cover. A relief valve in the timing cover limits the oil pressure at high engine speeds by returning excess oil to the sump. Oil is drawn from the sump through a strainer and, after passing through the oil pump, is forced through an externally-mounted filter and oil cooler into galleries in the cylinder block/crankcase. From there, the oil is distributed to the crankshaft (main bearings), balance shafts, camshaft bearings and hydraulic cam followers. It also lubricates the water-cooled turbocharger and the crankcase-mounted piston cooling jets. The big-end bearings are supplied with oil via internal drillings in the crankshaft, while the camshaft lobes and valves are lubricated by splash, as are all other engine components.

### Repairs with engine in car

The following work can be carried out with the engine in the car:

a) Compression pressure – testing.
b) Cylinder head cover – removal and refitting.

c) Camshaft oil seals – renewal.
d) Camshafts – removal, inspection and refitting.
e) Cylinder head – removal and refitting.
f) Cylinder head and pistons – decarbonising (refer to Part B of this Chapter).
g) Sump – removal and refitting.
h) Oil pump – removal, overhaul and refitting.
i) Crankshaft oil seals – renewal.
j) Flywheel/driveplate – removal, inspection and refitting.
k) Engine/transmission mountings – inspection and renewal.

## 2 Compression test – description and interpretation

1 When engine performance is down, or if misfiring occurs which cannot be attributed to the ignition or fuel systems, a compression test can provide diagnostic clues as to the engine's condition. If the test is performed regularly, it can give warning of trouble before any other symptoms become apparent.
2 The engine must be fully warmed-up to normal operating temperature, the battery must be fully charged, and all the spark plugs must be removed (Chapter 1). The aid of an assistant will also be required.
3 Disable the ignition system by disconnecting the wiring plug from the Direct Ignition cartridge.
4 To prevent unburnt fuel from being supplied to the catalytic converter, the fuel pump must also be disabled by removing the relevant fuse and/or relay; see Chapter 4A as applicable for further details.
5 Fit a compression tester to the No 1 cylinder spark plug hole – the type of tester which screws into the plug thread must be used to obtain accurate readings.
6 Have the assistant depress the accelerator pedal fully, and crank the engine on the starter motor; after one or two revolutions, the compression pressure should build-up to a

maximum figure, and then stabilise. Record the highest reading obtained.
7 Repeat the test on the remaining cylinders, recording the pressure in each.
8 All cylinders should produce very similar pressures; a difference of more than 2 bars between any two cylinders indicates a fault. Note that the compression should build-up quickly in a healthy engine; low compression on the first stroke, followed by gradually-increasing pressure on successive strokes, indicates worn piston rings. A low compression reading on the first stroke, which does not build-up during successive strokes, indicates leaking valves or a blown head gasket (a cracked cylinder head could also be the cause). Deposits on the undersides of the valve heads can also cause low compression.
9 Saab specify that the expected compression pressures required are 12 bars for the B205 (1985 cc) engine and 14 bars for the B235 (2290 cc) engine. Any cylinder pressure of below 10 bars for the B205 engine or 12 bars for the B235 engine can be considered as less than healthy. Refer to a Saab dealer or other specialist if in doubt as to whether a particular pressure reading is acceptable.
10 If the pressure in any cylinder is low, carry out the following test to isolate the cause. Introduce a teaspoonful of clean oil into that cylinder through its spark plug hole, and repeat the test.
11 If the addition of oil temporarily improves the compression pressure, this indicates that bore or piston wear is responsible for the pressure loss. No improvement suggests that leaking or burnt valves, or a blown head gasket, may be to blame.
12 A low reading only from two adjacent cylinders is almost certainly due to the head gasket having blown between them; the presence of coolant in the engine oil will confirm this.
13 If one cylinder is about 20 percent lower than the others and the engine has a slightly rough idle, a worn camshaft lobe could be the cause.

14 On completion of the test, refit the spark plugs and reconnect the ignition system and fuel pump as necessary.

## 3 Top dead centre (TDC) for No 1 piston – locating

1 TDC timing marks are provided in the form of a slot machined into the crankshaft pulley and a corresponding bar cast into the timing chain cover. In addition, TDC marks are provided on the flywheel and oil seal housing – these are useful if the engine is being dismantled on the bench (see illustration).
Note: With the timing marks correctly aligned, piston Nos 1 (at the timing chain end of the engine) and 4 (at the flywheel end of the engine) will be at top dead centre (TDC), with piston No 1 on its compression stroke.
2 For access to the crankshaft pulley bolt, jack up the front of the car and support on axle stands (see Jacking and vehicle support). Remove the right-hand front wheel, then remove the screws and detach the inspection cover from the right-hand wheel arch liner.
3 Using a socket on the crankshaft pulley, turn the engine until the TDC slot in the crankshaft pulley is aligned with the slot on the timing cover (see illustration). No 1 piston (at the timing chain end of the engine) will be at the top of its compression stroke. The compression stroke can be confirmed by removing the No 1 spark plug, and checking for compression with a finger over the plug hole as the piston approaches the top of its stroke. No compression indicates that the cylinder is on its exhaust stroke and is therefore one crankshaft revolution out of alignment.
4 Remove the cylinder head cover with reference to Section 4.
5 Check that the TDC marks at the sprocket ends of the camshafts are aligned with the corresponding TDC marks on the camshaft bearing caps (see illustration). If necessary, turn the crankshaft to bring the marks into alignment.

3.1 TDC timing marks (arrowed) on the flywheel and engine backplate

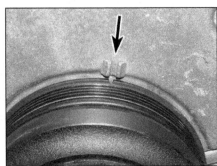
3.3 TDC timing marks (arrowed) on the timing chain cover and crankshaft pulley

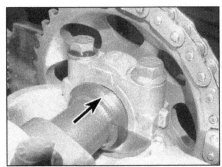
3.5 TDC timing marks (arrowed) on the camshaft and bearing cap

**4.1 Where applicable, undo the retaining bolt (arrowed) to disconnect breather pipe**

**4.2 Disconnect the breather hose (arrowed) from the cover**

**4.3a Disconnecting the wiring connector from the ignition cartridge . . .**

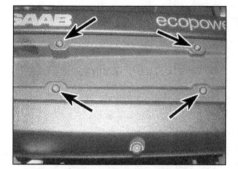

**4.3b . . . then remove the cylinder head cover retaining screws (arrowed)**

**4.5a Refitting the cylinder head cover inner gasket . . .**

**4.5b . . . and outer gasket, securely in the groove**

## 4 Cylinder head cover – removal and refitting

### Removal

**1** Open the bonnet and unclip the intake manifold cover away from the inlet manifold. Undo the retaining screw (where applicable) and disconnect the wiring and crankcase breather pipe bracket from the right-hand end of the cylinder head cover **(see illustration)**.
**2** Disconnect the crankcase breather hose (and where applicable, the vacuum hose), and position them to one side **(see illustration)**. **Note:** *On later models, release the securing clip to disconnect the hose.*
**3** Disconnect the wiring connector, then undo the screws and remove the ignition cartridge from the centre of the cylinder head cover; refer to Chapter 5B, Section 3, if necessary **(see illustrations)**.
**4** Unbolt and remove the cylinder head cover, and remove the gasket. If the cover is stuck, tap it gently with the palm of your hand to free it.

### Refitting

**5** Clean the contact surfaces of the cylinder head cover and cylinder head. Locate the gasket securely in the groove in the cylinder head cover. **Note:** *The gasket is in two parts, inner and outer gaskets* **(see illustrations)**.
**6** Refit the cylinder head cover, and insert the securing bolts. Tighten the bolts progressively and in sequence **(see illustration)** until all the

bolts are tightened to the specified torque.
**7** Reconnect the crankcase breather hose (and where applicable, the vacuum hose) to the cylinder head cover.
**8** Refit the direct ignition cartridge to the centre of the cylinder head cover, and tighten the screws, refer to Chapter 5B if necessary.
**9** Refit the engine upper cover.

## 5 Camshafts and hydraulic cam followers – removal, inspection and refitting

**Note:** *The following procedure describes removal and refitting of the camshafts and hydraulic cam followers with the cylinder head in position in the car. If necessary, the work can be carried out on the bench, with the cylinder head removed from the engine. In this*

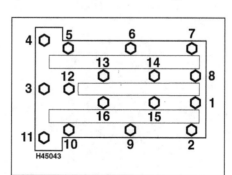

**4.6 Tightening sequence for the cylinder head cover bolts**

*case, start the procedure at paragraph 8, after removing the cylinder head.*

### Removal

**1** Open the bonnet, and clean the engine around the cylinder head.
**2** Apply the handbrake, then jack up the front of the car and support on axle stands (see *Jacking and vehicle support*). Remove the right-hand front wheel.
**3** Remove the screws, and withdraw the front wing moulding and wheel arch liner from under the right-hand front wing.
**4** Remove the battery cover then disconnect the battery negative lead, and position the lead away from the battery terminal.
**5** Unbolt and remove the cylinder head cover as described in Section 4.
**6** Using a socket on the crankshaft pulley, turn the engine until the TDC slot in the crankshaft pulley is aligned with the timing bar on the timing cover. If necessary, refer to Section 3 for more information. Check also that the TDC marks on the sprocket ends of the camshafts are aligned with the corresponding TDC marks on the camshaft bearing caps.
**7** Unscrew the bolt on the idler sprocket and remove the timing chain tensioner, use a 27 mm socket after removing the plug with spring and pushrod.
**8** While holding each camshaft stationary with a spanner on the special flats at the transmission end of the camshaft, unscrew the bolts, then withdraw the sprockets and allow them to rest on the timing chain guides.

**5.9 The camshaft bearing caps are marked for position (arrowed – No 10 bearing cap)**

Note that the sprockets have projections which engage with cut-outs in the ends of the camshafts. The timing chain cannot come off the crankshaft sprocket, since there is a guide located below the sprocket.

**9** Check that the camshaft bearing caps and the camshafts are identified for position. They have stamped markings on the caps – do not mix up these when refitting, 1 to 5 for the inlet

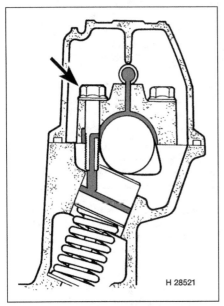

**5.10a The camshaft bearing cap inner bolts (arrowed) are hollow for the oil supply to the hydraulic cam followers**

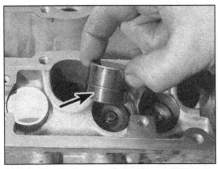

**5.11a Removing a hydraulic cam follower**

side and 6 to 10 for the exhaust side **(see illustration)**.

**10** Progressively unscrew the bearing cap bolts, so that the caps are not stressed unduly by the valve springs. Ensure that the bearing caps closest to the open valves are removed last, to avoid stressing the camshaft unduly. Fully remove the bolts and lift off the caps, then lift the camshafts from the cylinder head. Note that the bearing cap inner bolts (except at the timing chain end) have black heads, and incorporate drillings for the oil supply to the hydraulic cam followers; always make sure that the correct bolts are fitted **(see illustrations)**. Keep the camshafts carefully identified for location.

**11** Obtain sixteen small, clean plastic containers, and number them 1i to 8i (inlet) and 1e to 8e (exhaust). Alternatively, divide a larger container into sixteen compartments, similarly marked for the inlet and exhaust camshafts. Using a rubber sucker or a magnet, withdraw each hydraulic cam follower in turn, and place it in its respective container **(see illustrations)**. **Do not** interchange the cam followers. To prevent the oil draining from the hydraulic cam followers, pour fresh oil into the containers until it covers them.

*Caution: Take great care to avoid scratching the cylinder head bores as the followers are withdrawn.*

### Inspection

**12** Examine the camshaft bearing surfaces and cam lobes for signs of wear ridges and scoring. Renew the camshaft if any of these

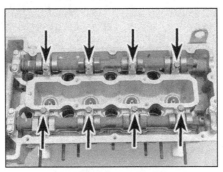

**5.10b Locations (arrowed) of the black-headed inner bearing cap bolts incorporating oil drillings**

**5.11b Hydraulic cam follower removed from the cylinder head. Store cam followers in an oil bath while removed**

conditions are apparent. Examine the condition of the bearing surfaces on the camshaft journals, in the camshaft bearing caps, and in the cylinder head. If the head or cap bearing surfaces are worn excessively, the cylinder head will need to be renewed. If the necessary measuring equipment is available, camshaft bearing journal wear can be checked by direct measurement and comparison with the specifications given.

**13** Camshaft endfloat can be measured by locating each camshaft in the cylinder head, refitting the sprockets, and using feeler blades between the shoulder on the front of the camshaft and the front bearing surface on the cylinder head.

**14** Check the hydraulic cam followers where they contact the bores in the cylinder head for wear, scoring and pitting. Occasionally, a hydraulic cam follower may be noisy and require renewal, and this will have been noticed when the engine was running. It is not easy to check a cam follower for internal damage or wear once it has been removed; if there is any doubt, the complete set of cam followers should be renewed.

**15** Clean the internal drillings of the hollow camshaft bearing cap bolts, to ensure oil supply to the hydraulic cam followers.

### Refitting

**16** Lubricate the bores for the hydraulic cam followers in the cylinder head, and the followers themselves, then insert them in their original positions **(see illustration)**.

**17** Lubricate the bearing surfaces of the camshafts in the cylinder head.

**18** Locate the camshafts in their correct positions in the cylinder head, so that the valves of No 1 cylinder (timing chain end) are closed, and the valves of No 4 cylinder are 'rocking'.

**19** The timing marks on the sprocket ends of the camshafts should be aligned **(see illustration 3.5)**.

**20** Lubricate the bearing surfaces in the bearing caps, then locate them in their correct positions and insert the retaining bolts. Progressively tighten the bolts to the specified torque. **Note:** *Ensure that the black-coloured oil supply bolts are in their correct positions (see illustration 5.10b).*

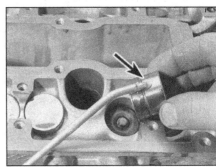

**5.16 Oiling a hydraulic cam follower prior to fitting**

**5.26 Tighten the camshaft sprocket retaining bolts, using a spanner on the camshaft flats (arrowed) to hold it stationary**

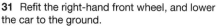

**6.8 Disconnect the wiring plug from the charge air control valve**

**6.9 Slackening the banjo bolt for the crankcase breather pipe**

**21** Check that each camshaft is at its TDC position – the timing marks are located on the front of the camshafts, and must be aligned with the mark on the bearing caps – see Section 3.

**22** Check that the TDC slot in the crankshaft pulley is aligned with the timing bar on the timing cover **(see illustration 3.3)**.

**23** Locate the sprockets on the camshafts, fitting the exhaust one first, followed by the inlet one. Do not fully tighten the bolts at this stage. Check that the timing chain is correctly located on the guides and sprockets.

**24** Refit the timing chain tensioner, with reference to Chapter 2B .

**25** Using a socket on the crankshaft pulley, rotate the engine two complete turns clockwise, then check that the TDC timing marks are still correctly aligned.

**26** Fully tighten the camshaft sprocket retaining bolts to the specified torque, while holding them stationary with a spanner on the special flats provided **(see illustration)**.

**27** Clean the contact surfaces of the cylinder head cover and cylinder head. Refit the cylinder head cover with reference to Section 4.

**28** Refit the inspection cover or DI ignition cartridge to the centre of the cylinder head cover, and tighten the securing screws.

**29** Reconnect the crankcase breather hose.

**30** Refit the front wing moulding and wheel arch liner under the right-hand front wing, and tighten the screws.

**31** Refit the right-hand front wheel, and lower the car to the ground.

**32** Reconnect the battery negative lead and refit the covers to the battery and the engine.

## 6 Cylinder head – removal and refitting

### Removal

**1** Open the bonnet, and clean the engine around the cylinder head. Run the engine at idling speed and remove the fuel pump fuse (up to 2001 – fuse number 19, from 2001 – fuse number 15. Check in Chapter 12, for exact location for your model). Turn the ignition off after the engine has stopped, there will be no fuel pressure in the fuel lines. Refit the fuse.

**2** Apply the handbrake, then jack up the front of the car and support on axle stands (see *Jacking and vehicle support*). Remove the right-hand front wheel and remove the lower engine cover.

**3** Remove the battery cover and disconnect the battery negative lead, and position the lead away from the battery terminal.

**4** Remove the retaining screws, and withdraw the wheel arch liner from under the right-hand front wing.

**5** Drain the cooling system, with reference to Chapter 1.

**6** Remove the oil filler cap/dipstick and unclip

the intake manifold cover away from the inlet manifold.

**7** Support the engine under the right-hand side, then undo the retaining bolts and remove the right-hand upper engine mounting assembly from the vehicle. For further information see Section 13.

**8** With reference to Chapter 4A, Section 14, remove the mass airflow sensor and rubber gaiter from the engine compartment. Pull back the rubber cover and disconnect the wiring plug from the charge air control valve **(see illustration)**. Release the hose clips and remove the turbocharger-to-intercooler and intercooler-to-throttle body intake air ducts. Cover the turbocharger port with a cloth to prevent the ingress of debris.

**9** Undo the banjo bolt (or quick-release securing clip on later models) and disconnect the crankcase breather pipe from the air intake hose **(see illustration)**.

**10** Unbolt and remove the engine lifting eye from the front right-hand side of the cylinder head **(see illustration)**.

**11** Remove the charge air pipe, bypass valve and pressure/temperature sensor connector. Disconnect the bypass valve vacuum hose. Plug the throttle body and the hose by the charge air cooler **(see illustrations)**.

**12** Refer to Chapter 1 and remove the auxiliary drivebelt.

**13** Remove the alternator to one side (referring to Chapter 5A), then unbolt the alternator bracket from the cylinder head **(see illustration)**.

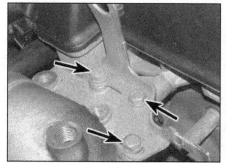

**6.10 Undo the retaining bolts (arrowed) to remove the engine lifting eye**

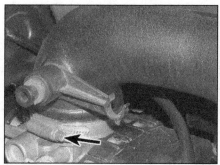

**6.11a Slacken the retaining clip (arrowed) . . .**

**6.11b . . . then disconnect the sensor wiring connector (arrowed) and vacuum pipe (arrowed)**

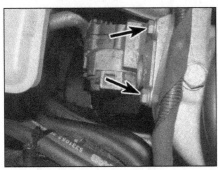

6.13 Undo the alternator bracket upper mounting bolts (arrowed)

6.16 Remove the cover to access the throttle linkage/cable

6.19 Undo the two intake manifold bracing bracket retaining bolts (arrowed)

14 Disconnect the wiring connector from the temperature sensor in the left-hand end of the cylinder head.

15 Slacken the hose clips and disconnect the coolant hoses from the cylinder head.

16 Unbolt the cover from the throttle body lever, and disconnect the throttle cable from the throttle body (see illustration).

17 Unbolt the support bracket and release the engine oil dipstick tube and dipstick from the cylinder head.

18 Slacken the hose clips and disconnect the hoses from the throttle body.

19 From under the vehicle, unbolt and remove the intake manifold bracing bracket from the rear of the engine (see illustration).

20 Refer to Chapter 4A and remove the exhaust heat shield, then unbolt the exhaust system front pipe from the turbocharger.

21 Unbolt the power steering pump from its mountings, with reference to Chapter 10, and

secure to one side using nylon cable ties or similar. Note that there is no need to disconnect the hydraulic fluid hoses from the pump. Slacken and remove the lower retaining bolt in the power steering pump bracket (see illustration).

22 Unbolt and remove the rear engine lifting eye from the intake manifold and move the wiring harness bracket to one side. Refer to Chapter 4A and remove the intake manifold from the cylinder head.

23 Unbolt and remove the cylinder head cover, and remove the gasket with reference to Section 4. If the cover is stuck, tap it gently with the palm of your hand to free it. If necessary, remove all four spark plugs, as described in Chapter 1.

24 Using a socket on the crankshaft pulley, turn the engine until the TDC mark on the crankshaft pulley is aligned with the timing mark on the timing cover, and No 1 piston (at

the timing chain end of the engine) is at the top of its compression stroke. If necessary, refer to Section 3 for more information. Check also that the TDC marks on the sprocket ends of the camshafts are aligned with the corresponding TDC marks on the camshaft bearing caps.

25 While holding each camshaft stationary with a spanner on the special flats at the flywheel/driveplate end of the camshaft, slacken the bolts (see illustration 5.26). Do not remove at this stage.

26 Unscrew the bolt on the idler roller and remove the timing chain tensioner (see illustration), use a 27 mm socket after removing the plug with spring and pushrod.

27 Unscrew the camshaft sprocket retaining bolts, then disengage the sprockets from the chain and remove from the engine. Fit a rubber band/cable tie around the chain guides, to prevent the chain from dropping down.

28 Unscrew and remove the two bolts securing the timing cover to the cylinder head (see illustration).

29 Working in the reverse sequence (see illustration 6.44), progressively slacken the ten cylinder head bolts by half a turn at a time, until all bolts can be unscrewed by hand. The bolts require the use of a Torx socket to unscrew them, as they have six external splines.

30 With all the cylinder head bolts removed, check that the timing chain is positioned so that the pivoting chain guide will not obstruct removal of the head. Lift the cylinder head directly from the top of the cylinder block and place it on a clean workbench, without damaging the mating surface. If necessary, enlist the help of an assistant, since the cylinder head is quite heavy. If the cylinder head is stuck, try rocking it slightly to free it from the gasket – do not insert a screwdriver or similar tool between the gasket joint, otherwise the gasket mating faces will be damaged. The head is located on dowels, so do not try to free it by tapping it sideways.

31 Remove the gasket from the top of the block, noting the two locating dowels. If the locating dowels are a loose fit, remove them and store them with the head for safe-keeping (see illustration). Do not discard the gasket – it may be needed for identification purposes.

6.21 Remove the lower retaining bolt (arrowed) from the power steering pump bracket

6.26 Remove the idler roller, then slacken and remove the timing chain tensioner (arrowed)

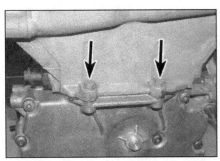

6.28 Slacken and remove the two bolts (arrowed) securing the timing cover to the cylinder head

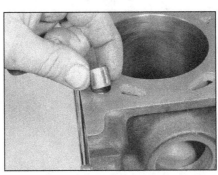

6.31 Removing a cylinder head locating dowel

**32** If the cylinder head is to be dismantled for overhaul, remove the camshafts as described in Section 5.

### Preparation for refitting

**33** The mating faces of the cylinder head and cylinder block must be perfectly clean before refitting the head. Use a hard plastic or wood scraper to remove all traces of gasket and carbon; also clean the piston crowns. Take particular care during the cleaning operations, as the soft aluminium alloy is damaged easily. Also, make sure that the carbon is not allowed to enter the oil and water passages – this is particularly important for the lubrication system, as carbon could block the oil supply to the engine's components. Using adhesive tape and paper, seal the water, oil and bolt holes in the cylinder block. After cleaning each piston, use a small brush to remove all traces of grease and carbon from the gap, then wipe away the remainder with a clean rag. Clean all the pistons in the same way.

 **To prevent carbon entering the gap between the pistons and bores, smear a little grease in the gap.**

**34** Check the mating surfaces of the cylinder block and the cylinder head for nicks, deep scratches and other damage. If slight, they may be removed carefully with a file, but if excessive, machining may be the only alternative to renewal.

**35** If warpage of the cylinder head gasket surface is suspected, use a straight-edge to check it for distortion. Refer to Part B of this Chapter if necessary.

**36** Check the condition of the cylinder head bolts, and particularly their threads, whenever they are removed. Wash the bolts in suitable solvent, and wipe them dry. Check each for any sign of visible wear or damage, renewing any bolt if necessary. Measure the length of each bolt, and compare with the length of a new bolt. Although Saab do not specify that the bolts must be renewed, it is strongly recommended that the bolts are renewed as a complete set if the engine has completed a high mileage.

### Refitting

**37** Where removed, refit the camshafts with reference to Section 5.

**38** Wipe clean the mating surfaces of the cylinder head and cylinder block/crankcase. Check that the two locating dowels are in position on the cylinder block.

**39** Position a new gasket on the cylinder block surface, making sure that it is fitted the correct way round.

**40** Check that each camshaft is at its TDC position – the timing marks are located on the front of the camshaft, and must be aligned with the marks on the bearing caps – see Section 3.

**41** Rotate the crankshaft one quarter of a turn away from TDC; this will position all four pistons part-way along their bores, keeping them out of way during cylinder head refitting.

**42** Check that the timing chain is located correctly on the chain guides, then carefully lower the cylinder head onto the block, aligning it with the locating dowels.

**43** Apply a smear of grease to the threads, and to the underside of the heads, of the cylinder head bolts. Insert the bolts, and screw them in finger-tight.

**44** Working progressively and in sequence, tighten the cylinder head bolts to their Stage 1 torque setting, using a torque wrench **(see illustration)**.

**45** Using the same sequence, tighten the cylinder head bolts to their Stage 2 torque setting.

**46** With all the cylinder head bolts tightened to their Stage 2 setting, working again in the given sequence, angle-tighten the bolts further through the specified Stage 3 angle, using a socket and extension bar. It is recommended that an angle-measuring gauge is used during this stage of the tightening, to ensure accuracy **(see illustration)**.

 **If a gauge is not available, use white paint to make alignment marks between the bolt head and cylinder head prior to tightening; the marks can then be used to check that the bolt has been rotated through the correct angle during tightening.**

**47** Rotate the crankshaft through one quarter of a turn back to its TDC position (see Section 3).

**48** Insert and tighten the two bolts securing the timing cover to the cylinder head.

**49** With reference to Section 3, check that the camshafts are both aligned at their respective TDC positions. Engage the camshaft sprockets with the timing chain (with reference to Chapter 2B, Section 10 if necessary) and then locate the sprockets on the camshafts, fitting the inlet one first, followed by the exhaust one. Do not fully tighten the bolts at this stage. Check that the timing chain is correctly located on the guides and sprockets.

**50** Refit the timing chain tensioner with reference to Chapter 2B, Section 10, if necessary.

**51** Using a socket on the crankshaft pulley, rotate the engine two complete turns clockwise, then check that the TDC timing marks are still correctly aligned.

**52** Fully tighten the camshaft sprocket retaining bolts to the specified torque, while holding each camshaft stationary, using a spanner on the special flats machined into the transmission end of each shaft.

**53** Refit the cylinder head cover as described

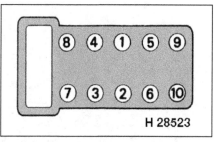

**6.44 Cylinder head bolt tightening sequence**

in Section 4, then refit the spark plugs with reference to Chapter 1.

**54** Refit the inlet manifold with reference to Chapter 4A. Bolt the engine lifting eyelets and the wiring harness support bracket in position.

**55** Reconnect the coolant hoses for the throttle body, thermostat housing and cabin heater to their respective ports on the cylinder head, tightening the hose clips securely.

**56** Position the engine oil dipstick tube against the cylinder head and secure it with the retaining bolt.

**57** Reconnect the vacuum and crankcase breather hoses to the cylinder head cover.

**58** With reference to Chapter 4A refit the exhaust system front pipe to the turbocharger and tighten the bolts to the specified torque.

**59** Refit the power steering pump with reference to Chapter 10.

**60** Refit the alternator with reference to Chapter 5A, then refit the auxiliary drivebelt with reference to Chapter 1.

**61** Refit the intake air ducting and mass air flow meter with reference to Chapter 4A.

**62** Refit the turbocharger crankcase breather pipe, then refit the intercooler-to-throttle body intake air ducts.

**63** Refit the cover panel to the top of the inlet manifold and insert the oil filler cap/dipstick.

**64** Reconnect the battery negative lead and refit the battery cover.

**65** Refit the central panel under the radiator, followed by the right-hand front wing wheel arch liner and moulding.

**66** Refit the right-hand front wheel, and lower the car to the ground.

**67** Refill the cooling system (see Chapter 1).

**68** Start the engine, observing the precautions given in Chapter 2B, Section 23.

**6.46 Using an angle-measuring gauge to tighten the cylinder head bolts through their Stage 3 angle**

**7.4 Oxygen sensor wiring connectors (arrowed) – model with two oxygen sensors fitted**

## 7 Sump – removal and refitting

### Removal

**1** Firmly apply the handbrake, then jack up the front of the car and support it on axle stands (see *Jacking and vehicle support*). Remove the battery cover and disconnect the negative lead.

**2** Remove both front roadwheels, and undo the securing screws and lower the undertray from under the vehicle

**3** Remove the engine upper cover then drain the engine oil, clean and refit the engine oil drain plug, tightening it to the specified torque. Remove the dipstick from its tube and place clean rag over the engine oil filler neck to prevent the ingress of debris. If the engine is nearing its service interval when the oil and filter are due for renewal, it is recommended that the filter is also removed, and a new one fitted. After reassembly, the engine can then be refilled with fresh oil. Refer to Chapter 1 for further information.

**4** Unplug the oxygen sensor wiring connectors, located on a bracket at the left-hand end of the cylinder head **(see illustration)**.

**5** With reference to Chapter 4A, unbolt the exhaust system front pipe from the turbocharger. Unbolt the front pipe from its support bracket and withdraw it from the underside of the engine compartment. **Note:** *the flexible section of the exhaust pipe MUST*

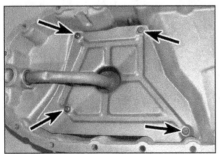

**7.11 Remove the retaining bolts (arrowed) to remove the oil pump pick-up and strainer**

**7.6 Remove the retaining bolts (arrowed) and remove the cover plate**

*NOT be put under excessive strain, as it may cause it to leak and eventually break.*

**6** Undo the retaining bolts and remove the flywheel cover plate from the transmission end of the sump **(see illustration)**.

**7** Where applicable, disconnect the crankcase breather hose from the rear of the sump.

**8** Progressively unscrew and remove the bolts securing the sump to the cylinder block, leaving one or two bolts in position to prevent the sump falling.

**9** Remove the remaining bolts, and lower the sump to the ground. Break the joint between the sump and crankcase by striking the sump with the palm of your hand.

**10** It may be necessary to use a lever between the inner wing panel and the crankshaft pulley to move the engine to the left for the sump to be removed.

**11** While the sump is removed, take the opportunity to check the oil pump pick-up/strainer for signs of clogging or damage **(see illustration)**.

### Refitting

**12** Clean all traces of sealant from the mating surfaces of the cylinder block/crankcase and sump, then use a clean rag to wipe out the sump and the engine's interior.

**13** Ensure that the sump and cylinder block/crankcase mating surfaces are clean and dry, then apply a bead of suitable sealant approximately 1mm thick to the sump flange **(see illustration)**.

**14** Offer up the sump and refit its retaining bolts, tightening them progressively to the specified torque.

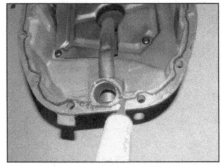

**7.13 Apply a bead of sealant to the sump flange**

**15** Refer to Chapter 4A and refit the exhaust system front pipe. Apply a suitable anti-seize agent to the front pipe-to-turbocharger securing nut studs, and tighten the nuts to the specified torque. Fit the front pipe-to-support bracket securing bolt and tighten it securely.

**16** Refit the flywheel cover plate to the transmission end of the sump.

**17** Refit the undertray(s) to the front of the vehicle and tighten the securing screws.

**18** Refit both front roadwheels and lower the vehicle to the ground.

**19** Reconnect the oxygen sensor wiring block connectors.

**20** Refill the engine with the correct quantity and grade of oil as described in Chapter 1, then clean and refit the dipstick/filler cap.

**21** Start the engine and allow it to warm-up. Check around the sump mating surface for signs of leakage.

## 8 Oil pump – removal, inspection and refitting

### Removal

**1** Apply the handbrake, then jack up the front of the car and support on axle stands (see *Jacking and vehicle support*). Remove the right-hand front wheel.

**2** Undo the securing screws and withdraw the wheel arch liner from under the wing, then unclip the power steering pipe from the subframe.

**3** Support the engine under the right-hand side, then undo the retaining bolts and remove the right-hand upper engine mounting assembly from the vehicle.

**4** Remove the auxiliary drivebelt with reference to Chapter 1.

**5** Slacken the centre bolt from the crankshaft pulley. To do this, the crankshaft must be held stationary using one of the following methods. On manual transmission models, have an assistant depress the brake pedal and engage 4th gear. Alternatively, remove the flywheel cover or starter motor as described in Chapter 5A, then insert a stout flat-bladed screwdriver through the transmission bellhousing and engage it with the starter ring gear to prevent the crankshaft turning. On automatic transmission models, use the latter method only.

**6** Remove the crankshaft pulley bolt, then withdraw the crankshaft pulley and hub from the end of the crankshaft. If it is tight, careful use of two levers may be required **(see illustration)**.

**7** Extract the large circlip, then withdraw the oil pump cover from the timing cover. Note that the circlip has a high tension, and a large pair of circlip pliers will be required to compress it. Also note the alignment arrows on the cover and timing cover **(see illustrations)**.

**8.6 Remove the crankshaft pulley bolt and withdraw the crankshaft pulley**

**8** Remove the O-ring seal from the groove in the cover **(see illustration)**.

**9** Note the position of the crankshaft oil seal in the oil pump cover, then prise it out with a screwdriver **(see illustrations)**.

## Inspection

**10** Wipe clean the inner faces of the pump rotors, and identify them for position with a marker pen. It is important that the rotors remain in their correct original positions on reassembly. Note that the outer rotor position is identified by the punch hole facing outwards.

**11** Remove the rotors from the timing cover (oil pump body), keeping them identified for position **(see illustrations)**.

**12** Unscrew the plug, and remove the relief valve spring and plunger, noting which way round they are fitted **(see illustration)**. Recover the plug washer.

**8.7a Using circlip pliers to remove the oil pump cover circlip**

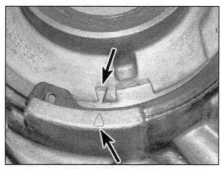

**8.7c Alignment arrows on the oil pump cover**

**13** Clean all components, and examine them for wear and damage. Examine the pump rotors and body for signs of wear ridges and scoring. Using a feeler blade check the clearance between the outer rotor and the timing cover,

**8.7b Withdrawing the oil pump cover from the timing cover**

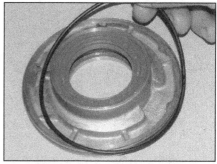

**8.8 Removing the O-ring seal from the groove in the oil pump cover**

with reference to the Specifications **(see illustration)**. If worn excessively, the complete pump assembly must be renewed.

**14** Examine the relief valve plunger for signs of wear or damage, and renew if necessary.

**8.9a Using a vernier gauge to check the depth of the oil seal in the cover . . .**

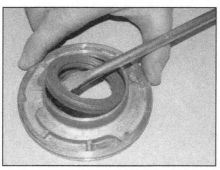

**8.9b . . . then prise out the crankshaft oil seal from the oil pump cover**

**8.11a Removing the inner rotor . . .**

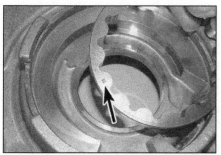

**8.11b . . . and outer rotor from the timing cover. Note that the position mark (arrowed) is facing outwards**

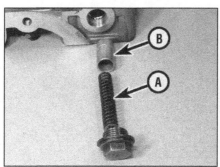

**8.12 Unscrew the plug and remove the relief valve spring (A) and plunger (B)**

**8.13 Checking the clearance between the oil pump outer rotor and the timing cover**

The condition of the relief valve spring can only be measured by comparing it with a new one; if there is any doubt about its condition, it should also be renewed.

**15** If there are any signs of dirt or sediment in the oil pump, it will be necessary to remove the sump (see Section 7), and clean the pick-up/strainer.

**16** Insert the relief valve plunger and spring, then refit the plug together with a new washer, and tighten the plug.

**17** Lubricate the rotors with fresh engine oil, then insert them in the oil pump body in their original positions. The rotors must be positioned with the identification mark facing outwards, see paragraph 11.

### Refitting

**18** Wipe clean the oil seal seating in the oil pump casing, then drive a new oil seal into the casing **(see illustration)**, making sure that it enters squarely and is fitted in the previously-noted position.

**19** Fit a new O-ring seal, then insert the oil pump in the timing cover, making sure that the alignment arrows point to each other. Refit the large circlip in the groove with its chamfer facing outwards, and the opening facing downwards.

**20** Locate the crankshaft pulley and hub on the end of the crankshaft. Insert the centre bolt and tighten it to the specified torque, holding the crankshaft stationary using one of the methods described in paragraph 5.

**21** Refit the auxiliary drivebelt with reference to Chapter 1.

**22** Refit the wing liner and moulding, and tighten the screws.

**9.4a Undo the oil pipe retaining bolt (arrowed) . . .**

**9.5 Slacken and remove the mounting bolts (arrowed) to remove the oil cooler**

**8.18 Fitting a new oil seal to the oil pump cover**

**23** Refit the right-hand front wheel, and lower the car to the ground.

**24** Before running the engine, disconnect the ignition wiring harness to the DI ignition cartridge to disable the ignition system (see Chapter 5B), then remove the fuel pump fuse (see Chapter 12). Crank the engine on the starter motor until oil pressure is restored and the oil pressure warning light is extinguished. Restore the ignition and fuel systems, and run the engine to check for oil leaks.

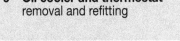

**9  Oil cooler and thermostat –**
removal and refitting

### Oil cooler/adapter

#### Removal

**1** An oil cooler/adapter is fitted between the

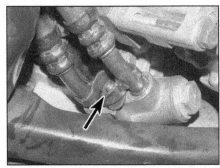

**9.4b . . . and the oil pipe retaining bracket and nut (arrowed) from the oil cooler**

**9.9 Slacken and remove plug to access thermostat**

oil filter and cylinder block. If the engine is nearing its service interval when the oil and filter are due for renewal, it is recommended that the filter is removed, and a new one fitted. After reassembly, the engine can then be refilled with fresh oil. Refer to Chapter 1 for further information.

**2** Drain the engine oil as described in Chapter 1, then refit and tighten the drain plug.

**3** Jack up the front of the car and support it securely on axle stands (see *Jacking and vehicle support*). Slacken and withdraw the securing screws, and remove the front lower cover/spoiler.

**4** Position a suitable container beneath the oil cooler on the right-hand side front of the engine compartment. Unscrew the unions from the top and bottom of the oil cooler **(see illustrations)**. Allow any oil to drain into the container.

**5** Unscrew the mounting bolts and remove the oil cooler from the engine compartment **(see illustration)**.

#### Refitting

**6** Refitting is a reversal of removal, but tighten the unions to the specified torque. Fill the engine with oil with reference to Chapter 1. On completion, start the engine and run it at a fast idle speed for several minutes, to allow the oil to fill the oil cooler. Check and if necessary top-up the engine oil level with reference to *Weekly checks*.

### Thermostat

#### Removal

**7** The oil temperature thermostat is mounted on the right-hand side front of the oil filter cooler/adapter.

**8** Drain the engine oil as described in Chapter 1, then refit and tighten the drain plug.

**9** Position a suitable container beneath the thermostat, then unscrew the plug, recover the seal/washer and allow the surplus oil to run into the container **(see illustration)**.

**10** Withdraw the thermostat and spring from the filter adapter **(see illustration)**.

#### Refitting

**11** Fit the new thermostat into the filter adapter, ensuring that the flange rests on the machined recess in the housing.

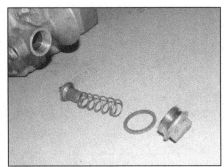

**9.10 Thermostat, spring, sealing washer and securing bolt/plug**

**12** Slide the spring into position, then fit the seal/washer to the plug and screw the plug into the filter housing, tightening it to the correct torque.

**13** Fill the engine with oil with reference to Chapter 1. On completion, start the engine and run it at a fast idle speed for several minutes, then check around the thermostat plug for signs of leakage. Check the engine oil level and top-up if necessary (see *Weekly checks*).

## 10 Oil pressure warning light switch – removal and refitting

### *Removal*

**1** The oil pressure switch is screwed into the rear of the cylinder block, beneath the inlet manifold and behind the starter motor **(see illustration)**. First jack up the front of the car, and support on axle stands (see *Jacking and vehicle support*).

**2** Trace the wiring back from the switch and disconnect the wiring block connector **(see illustration)**.

**3** Unscrew the switch from the cylinder block; be prepared for slight loss of oil **(see illustration)**. If the switch is to be left removed for any length of time, plug the hole, to prevent the entry of debris.

### *Refitting*

**4** Wipe clean the threads of the switch and the location aperture. Do not insert tools or wire into the hole at the tip of the switch, in an attempt to clean it out; as this may damage the internal components.

**5** Insert the switch into the cylinder block and tighten it securely.

**6** Reconnect the switch wiring block connector.

**7** Start the engine and check for leakage, then lower the car to the ground. Check the engine oil level and top-up if necessary (see *Weekly checks*).

## 11 Crankshaft oil seals – renewal

### *Right-hand oil seal*

**Note:** *This procedure explains the fitting of the seal in situ. See Section 8, for the removal of the oil pump cover and renewing the seal off the engine.*

**1** Apply the handbrake, then jack up the front of the car and support on axle stands (see *Jacking and vehicle support*). Remove the right-hand front wheel, undo the securing screws and withdraw the wheel arch liner. Where applicable, unclip the power steering pipe from the subframe.

**2** Support the engine under the right-hand

**10.1 The oil pressure switch (arrowed) is screwed into the rear of the cylinder block**

side, then undo the retaining bolts and remove the right-hand upper engine mounting assembly from the vehicle (with reference to Section 13).

**3** Remove the auxiliary drivebelt with reference to Chapter 1.

**4** Unscrew and remove the centre bolt from the crankshaft pulley. To do this, the crankshaft must be held stationary using one of the following methods. On manual transmission models, have an assistant depress the brake pedal and engage 4th gear. Alternatively, remove the flywheel cover plate or starter motor as described in Chapter 5A, then insert a flat-bladed screwdriver through the bellhousing and jam the starter ring gear to prevent the crankshaft turning. On automatic transmission models, use the latter method only.

**5** Pull the crankshaft pulley and hub from the end of the crankshaft. If it is tight, careful use of two levers may be required.

**6** Note the fitted depth of the oil seal in its housing, then using a screwdriver, carefully prise the oil seal from the oil pump casing. Alternatively, punch or drill two small holes opposite each other in the seal. Thread a self-tapping screw into each hole, and pull on the screw heads with pliers to extract the seal. Another method is to remove the oil pump cover as described in Section 8, and remove the oil seal on the bench **(see illustrations in Section 8)**.

**7** Clean the seating in the oil pump casing, then lubricate the lips of the new oil seal with clean engine oil, and locate it squarely on the oil pump casing. Make sure that the closed

**10.3 Using a ring spanner to remove the oil pressure switch**

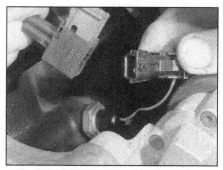

**10.2 Disconnecting the wiring from the oil pressure switch**

side is facing outwards. Using a suitable tubular drift (such as a socket) which bears only on the hard outer edge of the seal, tap the seal into position, to the same depth in the casing as the original was prior to removal.

**8** Locate the crankshaft pulley and hub on the end of the crankshaft. Insert the centre bolt and tighten it to the specified torque, holding the crankshaft stationary using one of the methods described in paragraph 4.

**9** Refit the auxiliary drivebelt with reference to Chapter 1, then refit the engine mounting assembly.

**10** Refit the wheel arch liner front section and moulding, and tighten the screws.

**11** Refit the right-hand front wheel, and lower the car to the ground.

### *Left-hand oil seal*

**12** Remove the flywheel/driveplate as described in Section 12.

**13** Make a note of the fitted depth of the seal in its housing. Punch or drill two small holes opposite each other in the seal. Thread a self-tapping screw into each hole, and pull on the screw heads with pliers to extract the seal. Alternatively, use a screwdriver to prise out the oil seal.

**14** Clean the seal housing, then lubricate the lips of the new seal with clean engine oil, and carefully locate the seal on the end of the crankshaft.

**15** Using a suitable tubular drift, which bears only on the hard outer edge of the seal, drive the seal into position, to the same depth in the housing as the original was prior to removal.

**16** Wipe clean the oil seal, then refit the fly-wheel/driveplate as described in Section 12.

## 12 Flywheel/driveplate – removal, inspection and refitting

### *Removal*

**1** Remove the transmission as described in Chapter 7A or 7B.

**2** On manual transmission models, remove the clutch assembly as described in Chapter 6.

**3** Prevent the flywheel/driveplate from turning by jamming the ring gear teeth with a wide-bladed screwdriver or similar tool.

**12.10 Apply locking fluid to the bolt threads, and tighten to the specified torque**

Alternatively, bolt a metal link between the flywheel/driveplate (using the clutch or torque converter bolt holes) and the cylinder block/crankcase.

**4** Unscrew and remove the retaining bolts, remove the locking tool, then remove the flywheel/driveplate from the crankshaft flange. Note that the unit is located by a dowel pin, and must be fitted correctly.

### Inspection

**5** On manual transmission models, if the flywheel's clutch mating surface is deeply scored, cracked or otherwise damaged, the flywheel must be renewed. However, it may be possible to have it surface-ground; seek the advice of a Saab dealer or engine reconditioning specialist.
**6** Similarly check the condition of the driveplate on automatic transmission models.
**7** If the ring gear is badly worn or has missing teeth, it may be possible to renew it. This job is best left to a Saab dealer or engine reconditioning specialist. The temperature to which the new ring gear must be heated for installation is critical and, if not done accurately, the hardness of the teeth will be destroyed.

### Refitting

**8** Clean the mating surfaces of the flywheel/driveplate and crankshaft. Clean the threads of the retaining bolts and the crankshaft holes.

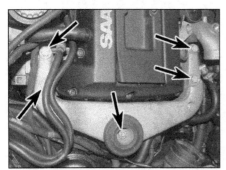

**13.10 Slacken and remove the bolts and nut (arrowed) to remove the engine mounting bracket**

**HAYNES HiNT** *If a suitable tap is not available, cut two slots into the threads of an old flywheel bolt, and use the bolt to clean the threads.*

**9** Ensure that the locating dowel is in position, then offer up the flywheel and locate it on the dowel.
**10** Apply locking fluid to the threads of the retaining bolts. Insert and tighten them to the specified torque, holding the flywheel/driveplate stationary using one of the methods described in paragraph 3 **(see illustration)**.
**11** On manual transmission models, refit the clutch assembly as described in Chapter 6.
**12** Refit the transmission with reference to Chapter 7A or 7B.

---

### 13 Engine/transmission mountings – inspection and renewal

### Inspection

**1** For improved access, raise the front of the car and support it securely on axle stands (see *Jacking and vehicle support*).
**2** The engine mountings are located at the front right-hand side, the left-hand side of the transmission under the battery tray, at the rear of the engine and, on some models, a torque arm mounting at the front.
**3** Check the mounting rubbers to see if they are cracked, hardened or separated from the metal at any point; renew the mounting if any such damage or deterioration is evident.
**4** Check that all the mounting's fasteners are securely tightened.
**5** Using a large screwdriver or a crowbar, check for wear in the mounting by carefully levering against it to check for freeplay. Where this is not possible, enlist the aid of an assistant to move the engine/transmission back-and-forth, or from side-to-side, while you watch the mounting. While some freeplay is to be expected even from new components, excessive wear should be obvious. If excessive freeplay is found, check

**13.11 Unclipping the power steering hose from the retaining clip under the engine mounting**

first that the fasteners are securely tightened, then if necessary renew any worn components as described below.

### Renewal

#### Right-hand mounting

**6** Apply the handbrake, then jack up the front of the car and support on axle stands (see *Jacking and vehicle support*). Remove the right-hand front wheel.
**7** Remove the screws, and withdraw the right-hand front wing plastic moulding and front wheel arch liner.
**8** Remove the securing screws and detach the plastic undertray from under the engine.
**9** Position a trolley jack underneath the engine and raise the jack head until it is just taking the weight of the engine. Ensure that the jack head does not bear on the underside of the sump, use a block of wood between the sump and the jack head. Alternatively, position a lifting beam across the engine bay and support the engine by the lifting eyelet located at the rear right-hand side of the cylinder head.
**10** Undo the bolts securing the engine mounting bracket to the engine and the retaining nut on the top of the engine mounting **(see illustration)**. Take care to avoid straining the other engine mountings as you do this.
**11** Withdraw the engine mounting bracket from the vehicle, unclipping the power steering hose from its retaining clip **(see illustration)**. Undo the three retaining bolts and remove the engine mounting from the inner wing panel.
**12** Fit the new mountings using a reversal of the removal procedure, making sure that the bolts/nuts are tightened to the correct torque.

#### Left-hand mounting

**13** Apply the handbrake, then jack up the front of the car and support on axle stands (see *Jacking and vehicle support*).
**14** Remove the battery cover and disconnect the battery leads (negative first), and position the leads away from the battery terminals.
**15** Remove the securing screws and detach the plastic undertray from under the engine.
**16** Position a trolley jack underneath the transmission and raise the jack head until it is just taking the combined weight of the engine and transmission. On models with automatic transmission, ensure that the jack head does not bear on the underside of the transmission sump; use a block of wood between the sump and the jack head. Alternatively, position a lifting beam across the engine bay and support the engine by the lifting eyelet located at the rear left-hand side of the cylinder head.
**17** Undo the securing nut and remove the battery from the vehicle (disconnect the vent hose, where applicable), slacken and remove the four retaining bolts and withdraw the battery tray from the vehicle **(see illustration)**.
**18** Unscrew the bolts securing the engine/transmission mounting bracket to the

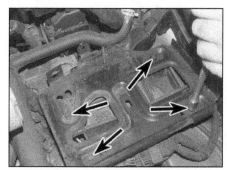

**13.17 Removing the mounting bolts (arrowed) to withdraw the battery tray**

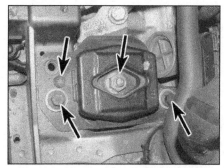

**13.18 Slacken and remove the bolts, nut and retaining screw (arrowed) to remove the engine mounting bracket**

bodywork and the centre nut from the mounting **(see illustration)**. Make sure the transmission is supported, taking care to avoid straining the other engine mountings as you do this.

**19** Withdraw the mounting from the inner wing panel and transmission. Where applicable, disconnect the clutch hydraulic hose from the mounting bracket.

**20** If required the transmission mounting bracket can then be withdrawn from the transmission by removing the retaining bolts from the transmission casing.

**21** Fit the new mounting using a reversal of the removal procedure, making sure that the nuts are tightened to the correct torque.

### Rear mounting

**22** Mount a lifting beam across the engine compartment, in-line with the front suspension turrets. Attach the jib to the engine lifting eyelet at the left hand end of the cylinder head. Raise the jib until the beam just starts to take the weight of the engine.

**23** Remove the battery cover and disconnect the battery leads (negative first), and position the leads away from the battery terminals. Remove the engine upper cover.

**24** On manual models, release the stay for the gearchange linkage from the rear engine mounting bracket.

**25** Undo the upper nut and bolts securing the rear engine mounting to the subframe.

**26** Disengage the bypass pipe and valve from the turbo intake pipe, then undo the retaining bolts and remove the exhaust manifold heat shield.

**27** Unplug the oxygen sensor wiring at the connector, located on a bracket at the left hand end of the cylinder head and release it from any cable ties.

**28** Ensure that the lifting beam is supporting the engine and transmission adequately, then slacken and withdraw the rear engine mounting centre bolts.

**29** Raise the front of the vehicle and support it securely on axle stands (see *Jacking and vehicle support*). Remove both front roadwheels.

**30** With reference to Chapter 4A, unbolt the exhaust system front pipe from the turbocharger. Unbolt the front pipe from its support bracket and withdraw it from the underside of the engine compartment. **Note:** *the flexible section of the exhaust pipe MUST*

*NOT be put under excessive strain, as it may cause it to leak and eventually break.*

**31** Unbolt the engine mounting bracket from the rear of the transmission casing and remove it from the engine compartment complete with engine mounting **(see illustration)**.

**32** Fit the new mounting using a reversal of the removal procedure, making sure that the nuts are tightened to the correct torque.

### Front mounting

**33** Raise the front of the vehicle and support it securely on axle stands (see *Jacking and vehicle support*).

**34** Remove the securing screws and detach the plastic undertray from under the engine.

**35** Slacken and remove the two nut and bolts securing the torque arm mounting to the transmission and subframe **(see illustration)**. It can then be withdrawn from the vehicle.

**36** If required the transmission mounting bracket can then be withdrawn from the transmission by removing the retaining bolts from the transmission casing.

**37** Fit the new mounting using a reversal of the removal procedure, making sure that the nuts are tightened to the correct torque.

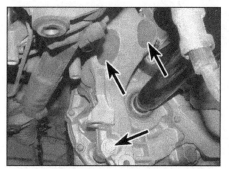

**13.31 Undo the bolts (arrowed – two upper bolts inside housing) to remove the rear engine mounting bracket**

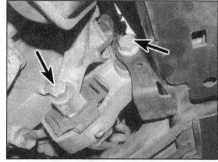

**13.35 Slacken and remove the bolts (arrowed) on the front engine mounting/torque arm**

# Notes

# Chapter 2 Part B:
# Engine removal and general overhaul procedures

## Contents

## Degrees of difficulty

| **Easy,** suitable for novice with little experience  | **Fairly easy,** suitable for beginner with some experience  | **Fairly difficult,** suitable for competent DIY mechanic  | **Difficult,** suitable for experienced DIY mechanic  | **Very difficult,** suitable for expert DIY or professional |
|---|---|---|---|---|

## Specifications

### Cylinder head

| | |
|---|---|
| Height (new) . . . . . . . . . . . . . . . . . . . . . . . . . . . . . . . . . . . . . . . . . . . . . . . . . . . . . . . | 139.4 to 139.6 mm |
| Height (minimum) . . . . . . . . . . . . . . . . . . . . . . . . . . . . . . . . . . . . . . . . . . . . . . . . . . . | 139.0 mm |
| Valve guide-to-valve stem clearance (max): | |
|    Inlet . . . . . . . . . . . . . . . . . . . . . . . . . . . . . . . . . . . . . . . . . . . . . . . . . . . . . . . . . . . | 0.17 mm |
|    Exhaust . . . . . . . . . . . . . . . . . . . . . . . . . . . . . . . . . . . . . . . . . . . . . . . . . . . . . . . . | 0.22 mm |

### Valves

| | |
|---|---|
| Valve head diameter: | |
|    Inlet . . . . . . . . . . . . . . . . . . . . . . . . . . . . . . . . . . . . . . . . . . . . . . . . . . . . . . . . . . . | 33.0 mm |
|    Exhaust . . . . . . . . . . . . . . . . . . . . . . . . . . . . . . . . . . . . . . . . . . . . . . . . . . . . . . . . | 29.0 mm |
| Valve stem diameter: | |
|    Inlet . . . . . . . . . . . . . . . . . . . . . . . . . . . . . . . . . . . . . . . . . . . . . . . . . . . . . . . . . . . | 4.970 to 4.985 mm |
|    Exhaust . . . . . . . . . . . . . . . . . . . . . . . . . . . . . . . . . . . . . . . . . . . . . . . . . . . . . . . . | 4.950 to 4.965 mm |
| Valve spring: | |
|    Free length . . . . . . . . . . . . . . . . . . . . . . . . . . . . . . . . . . . . . . . . . . . . . . . . . . . . . . | 57.1 to 60.1 mm |
|    Fitted length . . . . . . . . . . . . . . . . . . . . . . . . . . . . . . . . . . . . . . . . . . . . . . . . . . . . . | 37.5 mm |
| Valve length: | |
|    Inlet . . . . . . . . . . . . . . . . . . . . . . . . . . . . . . . . . . . . . . . . . . . . . . . . . . . . . . . . . . . | 107.30 mm |
|    Exhaust . . . . . . . . . . . . . . . . . . . . . . . . . . . . . . . . . . . . . . . . . . . . . . . . . . . . . . . . | 107.84 mm |

### Cylinder block

| | |
|---|---|
| Cylinder bore diameter: | |
|    Standard (A) . . . . . . . . . . . . . . . . . . . . . . . . . . . . . . . . . . . . . . . . . . . . . . . . . . . . . | 90.000 to 90.020 mm |
|    Standard (B) . . . . . . . . . . . . . . . . . . . . . . . . . . . . . . . . . . . . . . . . . . . . . . . . . . . . . | 90.020 to 90.040 mm |
|    First oversize . . . . . . . . . . . . . . . . . . . . . . . . . . . . . . . . . . . . . . . . . . . . . . . . . . . . | 90.500 to 90.520 mm |
|    Second oversize . . . . . . . . . . . . . . . . . . . . . . . . . . . . . . . . . . . . . . . . . . . . . . . . . | 91.000 to 91.020 mm |

## Balance shafts

Endfloat . . . . . . . . . . . . . . . . . . . . . . . . . . . . . . . . . . . . . . . . . . . . . . . 0.060 to 0.460 mm
Diameter of journal:
    Larger, inner . . . . . . . . . . . . . . . . . . . . . . . . . . . . . . . . . . . . . . . . . 39.892 to 39.908 mm
    Smaller, outer . . . . . . . . . . . . . . . . . . . . . . . . . . . . . . . . . . . . . . . . 19.947 to 19.960 mm
Diameter of bearing:
    Larger, inner . . . . . . . . . . . . . . . . . . . . . . . . . . . . . . . . . . . . . . . . . 39.988 to 40.043 mm
    Smaller, outer . . . . . . . . . . . . . . . . . . . . . . . . . . . . . . . . . . . . . . . . 20.000 to 20.021 mm
Bearing running clearance . . . . . . . . . . . . . . . . . . . . . . . . . . . . . . . . . . 0.080 to 0.151 mm

## Pistons

**Note:** *Piston diameter is measured at right-angles to the gudgeon pin holes, 11mm from the bottom of the piston skirt. The piston classification is stamped on the crown.*
Piston diameter:
    AB . . . . . . . . . . . . . . . . . . . . . . . . . . . . . . . . . . . . . . . . . . . . . . . . . . 89.964 to 89.975 mm
    B . . . . . . . . . . . . . . . . . . . . . . . . . . . . . . . . . . . . . . . . . . . . . . . . . . . 89.975 to 89.982 mm
    First oversize (+0.5 mm) . . . . . . . . . . . . . . . . . . . . . . . . . . . . . . . . 90.457 to 90.475 mm
    Second oversize (+1.0 mm) . . . . . . . . . . . . . . . . . . . . . . . . . . . . . 90.957 to 90.975 mm
Nominal piston clearance (new) . . . . . . . . . . . . . . . . . . . . . . . . . . . . . 0.025 to 0.056 mm

## Connecting rods

Length (centre to centre):
    B205 . . . . . . . . . . . . . . . . . . . . . . . . . . . . . . . . . . . . . . . . . . . . . . . 159 mm
    B235 . . . . . . . . . . . . . . . . . . . . . . . . . . . . . . . . . . . . . . . . . . . . . . . 153 mm

## Crankshaft

Endfloat . . . . . . . . . . . . . . . . . . . . . . . . . . . . . . . . . . . . . . . . . . . . . . . . 0.08 to 0.34 mm
Maximum bearing journal out-of-round . . . . . . . . . . . . . . . . . . . . . . . 0.005 mm
Main bearing journal diameter:
    Standard . . . . . . . . . . . . . . . . . . . . . . . . . . . . . . . . . . . . . . . . . . . . 57.981 to 58.000 mm
    First undersize . . . . . . . . . . . . . . . . . . . . . . . . . . . . . . . . . . . . . . . 57.731 to 57.750 mm
    Second undersize . . . . . . . . . . . . . . . . . . . . . . . . . . . . . . . . . . . . . 57.481 to 57.500 mm
Main bearing running clearance . . . . . . . . . . . . . . . . . . . . . . . . . . . . . 0.014 to 0.062 mm
Big-end bearing journal diameter:
    Standard . . . . . . . . . . . . . . . . . . . . . . . . . . . . . . . . . . . . . . . . . . . . 51.981 to 52.000 mm
    First undersize . . . . . . . . . . . . . . . . . . . . . . . . . . . . . . . . . . . . . . . 51.731 to 51.750 mm
    Second undersize . . . . . . . . . . . . . . . . . . . . . . . . . . . . . . . . . . . . . 51.481 to 51.500 mm
Big-end bearing running clearance . . . . . . . . . . . . . . . . . . . . . . . . . . . 0.020 to 0.068 mm

## Piston rings

End gaps in cylinder:
    Upper compression ring . . . . . . . . . . . . . . . . . . . . . . . . . . . . . . . . . 0.30 to 0.50 mm
    Lower compression ring . . . . . . . . . . . . . . . . . . . . . . . . . . . . . . . . . 0.30 to 0.50 mm
    Scraper ring . . . . . . . . . . . . . . . . . . . . . . . . . . . . . . . . . . . . . . . . . 0.75 to 1.00 mm
Side clearance in groove:
    Top compression ring . . . . . . . . . . . . . . . . . . . . . . . . . . . . . . . . . . 0.035 to 0.080 mm
    Second compression ring . . . . . . . . . . . . . . . . . . . . . . . . . . . . . . . 0.040 to 0.075 mm
    Oil control ring . . . . . . . . . . . . . . . . . . . . . . . . . . . . . . . . . . . . . . . Not applicable

## Torque wrench settings

*Refer to Chapter 2A Specifications.*

## 1  General information

Included in this Part of Chapter 2 are details of removing the engine from the vehicle, and general overhaul procedures for the cylinder head, cylinder block/crankcase, and all engine internal components.

The information given ranges from advice concerning preparation for an overhaul and the purchase of new parts, to detailed step-by-step procedures covering removal, inspection, renovation and refitting of engine internal components.

After Section 8, all instructions are based on the assumption that the engine has been removed from the vehicle. For information concerning in-car engine repair, as well as the removal and refitting of those external components necessary for full overhaul, refer to Part A of this Chapter. Ignore any preliminary dismantling operations described in Part A that are no longer relevant once the engine has been removed from the vehicle.

## 2  Engine overhaul – general information

It is not always easy to determine when, or if, an engine should be completely overhauled, as a number of factors must be considered.

High mileage is not necessarily an indication that an overhaul is needed, while low mileage does not preclude the need for an overhaul. Frequency of servicing is probably the most important consideration. An engine which has had regular and frequent oil and filter changes, as well as other required maintenance, should give many thousands of miles of reliable service. Conversely, a neglected engine may require an overhaul very early in its life.

Excessive oil consumption is an indication that piston rings, valve seals and/or valve guides are in need of attention. Make sure that oil leaks are not responsible before deciding that the rings and/or guides are worn. Perform a compression test, as described in Part A of this Chapter, to determine the likely cause of the problem.

Check the oil pressure with a gauge fitted in place of the oil pressure switch, and compare it with that specified. If it is extremely low, the main and big-end bearings, and/or the oil pump, are probably worn out.

Loss of power, rough running, knocking or metallic engine noises, excessive valve gear noise, and high fuel consumption may also point to the need for an overhaul, especially if they are all present at the same time. If a complete service does not remedy the situation, major mechanical work is the only solution.

An engine overhaul involves restoring all internal parts to the specification of a new engine. During an overhaul, the cylinders are rebored (where necessary) and the pistons and the piston rings are renewed. New main and big-end bearings are generally fitted; if necessary, the crankshaft may be renewed or reground, to restore the journals. The valves are also serviced as well, since they are usually in less-than-perfect condition at this point. While the engine is being overhauled, other components, such as the distributor (where applicable), starter and alternator, can be overhauled as well. The end result should be an as-new engine that will give many trouble-free miles.

**Note:** *Critical cooling system components such as the hoses, thermostat and water pump should be renewed when an engine is overhauled. The radiator should be checked carefully, to ensure that it is not clogged or leaking. Also, it is a good idea to renew the oil pump whenever the engine is overhauled.*

Before beginning the engine overhaul, read through the entire procedure, to familiarise yourself with the scope and requirements of the job. Overhauling an engine is not difficult if you follow carefully all of the instructions, have the necessary tools and equipment, and pay close attention to all specifications. It can, however, be time-consuming. Plan on the car being off the road for a minimum of two weeks, especially if parts must be taken to an engineering works for repair or reconditioning. Check on the availability of parts, and make sure that any necessary special tools and equipment are obtained in advance. Most work can be done with typical hand tools, although a number of precision measuring tools are required for inspecting parts to determine if they must be renewed. Often the

engineering works will handle the inspection of parts, and will offer advice concerning reconditioning and renewal.

**Note:** *Always wait until the engine has been completely dismantled, and until all components (especially the cylinder block/crankcase and the crankshaft) have been inspected, before deciding what service and repair operations must be performed by an engineering works. The condition of these components will be the major factor to consider when determining whether to overhaul the original engine, or to buy a reconditioned unit. Do not, therefore, purchase parts or have overhaul work done on other components until they have been thoroughly inspected.* As a general rule, time is the primary cost of an overhaul, so it does not pay to fit worn or sub-standard parts.

As a final note, to ensure maximum life and minimum trouble from a reconditioned engine, everything must be assembled with care, in a spotlessly-clean environment.

## 3   Engine removal –
### methods and precautions

If you have decided that the engine must be removed for overhaul or major repair work, several preliminary steps should be taken.

Locating a suitable place to work is extremely important. Adequate workspace, along with storage space for the vehicle, will be needed. If a workshop or garage is not available, at the very least, a flat, level, clean work surface is required.

Cleaning the engine compartment and engine/transmission before beginning the removal procedure will help keep tools clean and organised.

An engine hoist or A-frame will also be necessary. Make sure the equipment is rated in excess of the combined weight of the engine and transmission. Safety is of primary importance, considering the potential hazards involved in lifting the engine/transmission out of the vehicle.

If this is the first time you have removed an engine, an assistant should ideally be available. Advice and aid from someone more experienced would also be helpful. There are many instances when one person cannot simultaneously perform all of the operations required when lifting the engine out of the vehicle.

Plan the operation ahead of time. Before starting work, arrange for the hire of, or obtain, all of the tools and equipment you will need. Some of the equipment necessary to perform engine/transmission removal and installation safely and with relative ease (in addition to an engine hoist) is as follows: a heavy-duty trolley jack, complete sets of spanners and sockets as described in the back of this manual, wooden blocks, and plenty of rags and cleaning solvent for

mopping-up spilled oil, coolant and fuel. If the hoist must be hired, make sure that you arrange for it in advance, and perform all of the operations possible without it beforehand. This will save you money and time.

Plan for the vehicle to be out of use for quite a while. An engineering works will be required to perform some of the work which the do-it-yourselfer cannot accomplish without special equipment. These places often have a busy schedule, so it would be a good idea to consult them before removing the engine, in order to accurately estimate the amount of time required to rebuild or repair components that may need work.

Always be extremely careful when removing and refitting the engine/transmission. Serious injury can result from careless actions. Plan ahead and take your time, and a job of this nature, although major, can be accomplished successfully.

The engine and transmission is removed by lowering it from the underside of the engine compartment.

## 4   Engine and transmission –
### removal, separation and refitting

**Note:** *The engine is removed from the car as a unit complete with the transmission, the engine and transmission can then be separated for overhaul. The engine/transmission is lowered and removed from the underside of the engine compartment. Note that it is possible to remove the transmission, leaving the engine in situ – refer to Chapter 7A or 7B (as applicable) for details.*

### Removal

**1** Park the vehicle on firm, level ground. Chock the rear wheels, then firmly apply the handbrake. It may be useful at this point, to slacken the front wheel bolts. Jack up the front of the vehicle, and securely support it on axle stands (see *Jacking and vehicle support*).
**2** Remove both front wheels, then unbolt both wing mouldings and front wheel arch liners, for access to either side of the engine bay.
**3** Unbolt and remove the lower covers from under the engine and radiator.
**4** Drain the coolant with reference to Chapter 1. Save the coolant in a clean container if it is fit for re-use.

 *Warning: The engine should be cold before draining the coolant.*

**5** With the coolant drained, tighten the drain plug on the left-hand bottom of the radiator.
**6** If required, remove the bonnet as described in Chapter 11. Alternatively, disconnect the support struts from the bonnet, and support it in the fully-open position.
**7** Remove the covers from the top of the engine, intake manifold and battery, then remove the battery with reference to Chapter 5A.

4.9 Disconnecting the breather hose from the top of the automatic transmission

4.12 Disconnect the vacuum hose (arrowed) from the rear of the intake manifold

4.13a Where applicable, press the red sleeve in and pull the vacuum hose (arrowed) from the pump . . .

4.13b . . . then press the red sleeve down and pull the vacuum hose from the intake manifold

4.16 Unplug the automatic transmission control system wiring harness

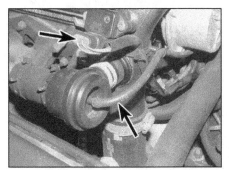

4.18 Disconnect the vacuum hose and the wiring connector (arrowed)

**8** Unbolt the battery tray from the side of the engine bay, and disconnect the earth cable(s) between the transmission and the vehicle body.

**9** On models with automatic transmission, disconnect the breather hose from the top of the transmission **(see illustration)**; plug the open port to prevent the ingress of foreign material.

**10** On manual models, unplug the wiring from the reversing lamp switch at the connector on the top of the transmission casing.

**11** Detach the throttle cable from the throttle body, with reference to Chapter 4A.

**12** Release the retaining clip and disconnect the EVAP canister purge valve's vacuum hose from the intake manifold **(see illustration)**.

**13** Where applicable, press the red sleeve inwards and pull the braking system vacuum hose to disconnect it from the vacuum pump

and intake manifold **(see illustrations)**; see Chapter 9 for further details.

**14** Disconnect the fuel supply and return hoses at the quick-release unions as described in Chapter 4A. Plug both sides of the open fuel lines to minimise leakage and to prevent the ingress of foreign material.

**15** On manual models, release the securing clip and disconnect the connection for the clutch fluid delivery at the top of the transmission. Refit the securing clip to the connector after it has been disconnected for safe-keeping. Plug both sides of the open clutch fluid lines to minimise leakage and to prevent the ingress of foreign material.

**16** Disconnect the gear selector cable (automatic models) or shaft (manual models) at the rear of the transmission casing; refer to Chapter 7A or 7B for details. On automatic models, also unplug the transmission control system wiring harness, at the two multiway

connectors located to the front of the battery tray **(see illustration)**.

**17** Slacken the hose clip and disconnect the cooling system top hose from the thermostat housing and the expansion tank hose on the end of the cylinder head. Also disconnect the heater hoses from the rear of the engine; refer to Chapter 3 for further information.

**18** Disconnect the vacuum hose from the bypass valve at the front of the engine bay, then disconnect the wiring connector from the pressure/temperature sensor **(see illustration)**.

**19** Undo the retaining clips and securing bolt, then remove the air intake pipe to the throttle body. Undo the securing bolt from the air bypass pipe and withdraw from the vehicle **(see illustrations)**.

**20** Remove the mass airflow sensor and air intake hose from the vehicle as described in Chapter 4A, Section 14.

**21** Slacken the hose clip and disconnect the radiator bottom hose from the coolant pump; refer to Chapter 3 for further information.

**22** Remove the wiper arms and windscreen lower trim panel which covers the wiper motor, as described in Chapter 12.

**23** Undo the four retaining nuts and withdraw the rubber cover, then disconnect the wiring connector from the electronic control module. Pull the rubber grommet from the bulkhead and rest the wiring harness on the top of the engine. Remove the wiring connection cover on the rear of the bulkhead and release any retaining clips/cable ties as required **(see illustrations)**.

4.19a Slacken and remove the air intake pipe retaining bolt (arrowed) . . .

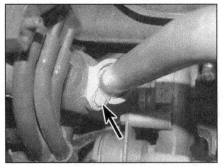

4.19b . . . and the air bypass pipe retaining bolt (arrowed)

**24** Release the tension on the auxiliary belt and remove it from the pulleys. Refer to Chapter 1 for further information.
**25** Disconnect the power steering pump from the engine mounting bracket, then using suitable straps/cable ties suspend it from the radiator upper crossmember.
**26** Slacken and remove the air conditioning compressor retaining bolts, then using suitable straps/cable ties suspend the compressor, condenser cooler, and charge air cooler from the radiator upper crossmember. Note that the engine oil cooler will be removed with the engine.
**27** Disconnect the wiring connector to the air conditioning compressor and release the coupling on the vacuum hose connected to the wastegate.
**28** Undo the retaining nut and disconnect the oil cooler pipes from the oil filter housing, then undo the retaining bolts and remove the engine oil cooler, complete with cooler pipes from the vehicle **(see illustrations)**.
**29** On models with automatic transmission, disconnect the quick-release connectors to the transmission oil cooler. Plug ends of the open fluid lines to minimise leakage and to prevent the ingress of foreign material.
**30** Position an engine lifting hoist over the engine compartment. Attach the lifting jib to the eyelets at either end of the cylinder head. It may be necessary to attach an extra lifting eye to the transmission to allow the engine/transmission to be kept level for removal. Raise the hoist until it is just taking the weight of the engine/transmission.
**31** Referring to Chapter 8, unbolt and remove the both driveshafts.
**32** Referring to Chapter 10, unbolt and remove the front subframe.
**33** Unbolt and remove the right- and left-hand engine/transmission mountings, with reference to Chapter 2A, Section 13.
**34** Make a final check that any components which would prevent the removal of the engine/transmission from the car have been removed or disconnected. Ensure that components such as the gearchange selector rod, clutch cable and accelerator cable are secured so that they cannot be damaged on removal.
**35** Slowly lower the engine/transmission assembly from the engine compartment,

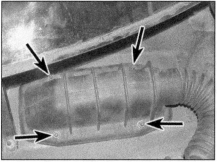
**4.23a  Remove the four retaining nuts (arrowed) . . .**

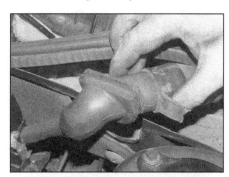
**4.23c  Withdraw the rubber wiring grommet from the bulkhead panel**

making sure that it clears the components on the surrounding panels. In particular, make sure that it clears the ABS unit and the radiator. Enlist the help of an assistant during this procedure, as it may be necessary to tilt and twist the assembly slightly to clear the body panels. Lower the assembly to the ground and remove it from the underside of the engine compartment.

### Separation from transmission

**36** If the engine is to be dismantled, working as described in Chapter 1, drain the oil and if required remove the oil filter. Clean and refit the drain plug, tightening it securely.
**37** Support the engine/transmission assembly on suitable blocks of wood, on a workbench (or failing that, on a clean area of the workshop floor).
**38** Remove the starter motor with reference to Chapter 5A.

**4.23b  . . . and release the multiplug wiring connector from the control module**

**4.23d  Unclip the cover from the wiring block connector on the bulkhead**

### Manual transmission models

**39** Unscrew the bolt securing the turbo oil pipe bracket to the transmission.
**40** Unbolt and remove the flywheel protection plate from the underside of the transmission bellhousing.
**41** Ensure that both engine and transmission are adequately supported, then with reference to Chapter 7A, unscrew the bolts securing the transmission housing to the engine. Note the correct fitted positions of each bolt as they are removed, to use as a reference on refitting. Withdraw the transmission directly from the engine. Take care not to allow the weight of the transmission to bear on the input shaft and clutch friction plate.

### Automatic transmission models

**42** Working through the aperture exposed by the removal of the starter motor, unscrew the bolts securing the flywheel to the torque

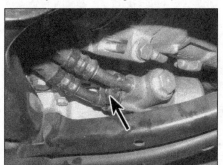
**4.28a  Undo the retaining nut (arrowed) . . .**

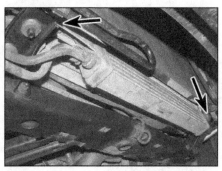
**4.28b  . . . and the retaining bolts (arrowed)**

**4.42  Undo the bolts (one shown) securing the torque converter to the flywheel**

converter **(see illustration)**. To bring each bolt into view, turn the engine using a socket on the crankshaft pulley bolt.

**43** Saab technicians use a special tool to hold the torque converter inside the transmission while the transmission is separated from the engine. The tool is quite basic, and consists of a plate which engages the torque converter through the timing hole in the top of the transmission.

**44** Support the weight of the transmission, preferably using a hoist.

**45** Ensure that both engine and transmission are adequately supported, then unscrew the bolts securing the transmission housing to the engine. Note the correct fitted positions of each bolt as they are removed, to use as a reference on refitting. Withdraw the transmission directly from the engine (see Chapter 7B for details). Make sure that the torque converter stays inside the transmission bellhousing, otherwise it may fall out and be damaged.

### Reconnection to transmission

#### Automatic transmission models

**46** Carefully offer the transmission to the engine. Make sure that the torque converter is held fully engaged with the transmission, using the special tool described earlier in this procedure (refer to Chapter 7B for settings and further details).

**47** Insert and tighten to the specified torque the bolts securing the transmission to the engine.

**48** Remove the special tool, then insert and tighten to the specified torque the bolts securing the driveplate to the torque converter. Turn the engine by means of a socket on the crankshaft pulley.

#### Manual transmission models

**Caution: If a new clutch slave cylinder has been fitted, or if any hydraulic fluid has been allowed to drain from the existing slave cylinder, the cylinder must be primed and bled BEFORE the transmission is refitted; see Chapter 6 for details.**

**49** Apply a smear of high-melting-point grease to the splines of the transmission input shaft. Do not apply too much, otherwise there is a possibility of the grease contaminating the clutch friction plate.

**50** Carefully offer the transmission to the engine. Ensure that the weight of the transmission is not allowed to hang on the input shaft as it is engaged with the clutch friction plate. Insert and tighten the bolts securing the transmission to the engine to the specified torque.

**51** Where applicable, insert and tighten the bolts securing the turbo oil pipe bracket to the transmission.

#### All models

**52** Refit the lower cover plate to the transmission bellhousing, and tighten the bolts.

**53** Refit the starter motor with reference to Chapter 5A.

### Refitting

**54** Refit the engine and transmission by following the removal procedure in reverse, noting the following points:
a) *Hoist the engine and transmission into position in the engine compartment, then refit the right- and left-hand engine mountings as described in Chapter 2A.*
b) *Refit the front subframe with reference to Chapter 10, refit the driveshafts with reference to Chapter 8.*
c) *Tighten all nuts and bolts to the specified torque.*
d) *Renew all copper sealing washers on unions, as applicable.*
e) *Reconnect the accelerator cable with reference to Chapter 4A.*
f) *With reference to Chapter 6, reconnect the fluid supply pipe to the slave cylinder, then bleed the clutch hydraulic system.*
g) *Ensure that all wiring has been securely reconnected, and all nuts and bolts have been tightened.*
h) *Refill the engine and transmission with the correct quantity and grade of oil/fluid, with reference to Chapter 1.*
i) *Refill the cooling system with reference to Chapter 1.*
j) *Check and if necessary top-up the power steering fluid, with reference to Chapter 1.*

## 5  Engine overhaul –
dismantling sequence

**1** It is much easier to dismantle and work on the engine if it is mounted on a portable engine stand. These stands can often be hired from a tool hire shop. Before the engine is mounted on a stand, the flywheel/driveplate should be removed, so that the stand bolts can be tightened into the end of the cylinder block/crankcase.

**2** If a stand is not available, it is possible to dismantle the engine with it blocked up on a sturdy workbench, or on the floor. Be extra-careful not to tip or drop the engine when working without a stand.

**3** If you are going to obtain a reconditioned engine, all the external components must be removed first, to be transferred to the new engine (just as they will if you are doing a complete engine overhaul yourself). These components normally include the following, but check with your engine supplier first:
a) *Alternator mounting bracket (Chapter 5A).*
b) *The Direct Ignition cartridge and spark plugs (Chapter 1 and Chapter 5B).*
c) *Thermostat and housing (Chapter 3).*
d) *The dipstick tube.*
e) *Air conditioning compressor mounting bracket (Chapter 3).*
f) *The fuel injection system and emission control components (Chapter 4A and 4B).*
g) *All electrical switches and sensors, and the engine wiring harness.*
h) *Inlet and exhaust manifolds (Chapter 4A).*
i) *Oil cooler (Chapter 2A).*
j) *Engine mounting brackets (Chapter 2A).*
k) *Flywheel/driveplate (Chapter 2A).*

**HAYNES HINT** *When removing the external components from the engine, pay close attention to details that may be helpful or important during refitting. Note the fitted position of gaskets, seals, spacers, pins, washers, bolts and other small items.*

**4** If you are obtaining a 'short' engine (which consists of the engine cylinder block/crankcase, crankshaft, pistons and connecting rods all assembled), then the cylinder head and sump will have to be removed also.

**5** If you are planning a complete overhaul, the engine can be dismantled, and the internal components removed, in the order given below:
a) *Inlet and exhaust manifolds (Chapter 4A).*
b) *Cylinder head (Chapter 2A).*
c) *Timing chain and balance shaft chain, sprockets and tensioner (Sections 10 and 11).*
d) *Flywheel/driveplate (Chapter 2A).*
e) *Balance shafts (Section 12).*
f) *Sump (Chapter 2A).*
g) *Piston/connecting rod assemblies (Section 13).*
h) *Crankshaft (Section 14).*

**6** Before beginning the dismantling and overhaul procedures, make sure that you have all of the correct tools necessary. Refer to *Tools and working facilities* for further information.

## 6  Cylinder head –
dismantling

**Note:** *New/reconditioned cylinder heads are obtainable from Saab, or from engine overhaul specialists. Be aware that some specialist tools are required for the dismantling and inspection procedures, and new components may not be readily available. It may therefore be more practical and economical for the home mechanic to purchase a reconditioned head, rather than dismantle, inspect and recondition the original head.*

**1** Remove the cylinder head as described in Part A, then unbolt the external components – these include the right-hand engine mounting bracket and the engine lifting eyes, etc, depending on model.

**2** Remove the camshafts and hydraulic cam followers, with reference to Chapter 2A, Section 5.

**3** Before removing the valves, consider

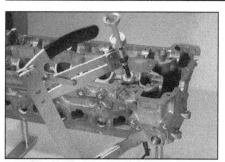

6.4a Using a compressor to compress the valve springs in order to remove the split collets

6.4b Removing the spring retainer . . .

6.4c . . . valve spring . . .

6.4d . . . and seat

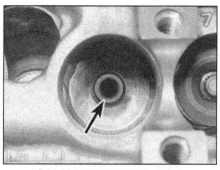

6.4e Valve stem seal location

6.4f Removing a valve stem seal

obtaining plastic protectors for the hydraulic cam follower bores. When using certain valve spring compressors, the bores can easily be damaged should the compressor slip off the end of the valve.

**HAYNES HiNT** *The cam follower bore protectors can be obtained from a Saab dealer; alternatively, a protector may be made out of plastic cut from a washing-up liquid container or similar.*

**4** Position the protector in the cam follower bore then, using a valve spring compressor, compress the valve spring until the split collets can be removed. Release the compressor, and lift off the spring retainer, spring and seat. Using a pair of pliers, carefully extract the valve stem seal from the top of the guide **(see illustrations)**.
**5** If, when the valve spring compressor is screwed down, the spring retainer refuses to free and expose the split collets, gently tap the top of the tool, directly over the retainer, with a light hammer. This will free the retainer.
**6** Withdraw the valve through the combustion chamber.
**7** It is essential that each valve is stored together with its collets, retainer, spring, and spring seat. The valves should also be kept in their correct sequence, unless they are so badly worn that they are to be renewed. If they are going to be kept and used again, place each valve assembly in a labelled polythene bag or similar small container **(see**

**illustrations)**. Note that No 1 cylinder is nearest to the timing chain end of the engine.

### 7 Cylinder head and valves – cleaning and inspection

**1** Thorough cleaning of the cylinder head and valve components, followed by a detailed inspection, will enable you to decide how much valve service work must be carried out during the engine overhaul. **Note:** *If the engine has been severely overheated, it is best to assume that the cylinder head is warped – check carefully for signs of this.*

### Cleaning

**2** Scrape away all traces of old gasket material from the cylinder head.

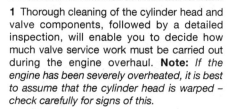

6.7a The valve spring components

**3** Scrape away the carbon from the combustion chambers and ports, then wash the cylinder head thoroughly with paraffin or a suitable solvent.
**4** Scrape off any heavy carbon deposits that may have formed on the valves, then use a power-operated wire brush to remove deposits from the valve heads and stems.

### Inspection

**Note:** *Be sure to perform all the following inspection procedures before concluding that the services of a machine shop or engine overhaul specialist are required. Make a list of all items that require attention.*

**Cylinder head**

**5** Inspect the head very carefully for cracks, evidence of coolant leakage, and other damage. If cracks are found, a new cylinder head should be obtained.

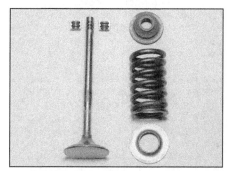

6.7b Place each valve and its associated components in a labelled polythene bag

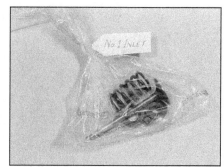

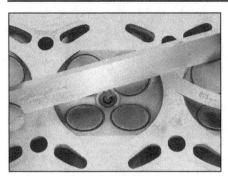

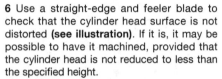

**7.6  Checking the cylinder head gasket face for distortion**

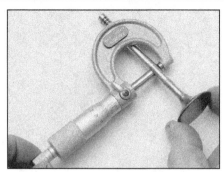

**7.10  Measuring a valve stem diameter**

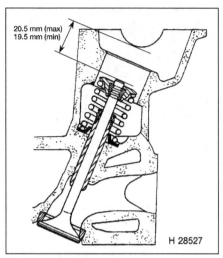

**7.16  Check the depth of the valve stems below the camshaft bearing surface**

**6** Use a straight-edge and feeler blade to check that the cylinder head surface is not distorted **(see illustration)**. If it is, it may be possible to have it machined, provided that the cylinder head is not reduced to less than the specified height.

**7** Examine the valve seats in each of the combustion chambers. If they are severely pitted, cracked, or burned, they will need to be renewed or recut by an engine overhaul specialist. If they are only slightly pitted, this can be removed by grinding-in the valve heads and seats with fine valve-grinding compound, as described below. Note that the exhaust valves have a hardened coating and, although they may be ground-in with paste, they must not be machined.

**8** Check the valve guides for wear by inserting the relevant valve, and checking for side-to-side motion of the valve. A very small amount of movement is acceptable. If the movement seems excessive, remove the valve. Measure the valve stem diameter (see below), and renew the valve if it is worn. If the valve stem is not worn, the wear must be in the valve guide, and the guide must be renewed. The renewal of valve guides is best carried out by a Saab dealer or engine overhaul specialist, who will have the necessary tools available.

### Valves

**9** Examine the head of each valve for pitting, burning, cracks, and general wear. Check the valve stem for scoring and wear ridges. Rotate the valve, and check for any obvious indication that it is bent. Look for pits and excessive wear on the tip of each valve stem. Renew any valve that shows any such signs of wear or damage.

**10** If the valve appears satisfactory at this stage, measure the valve stem diameter at several points using a micrometer **(see illustration)**. Any significant difference in the readings obtained indicates wear of the valve stem. Should any of these conditions be apparent, the valve(s) must be renewed.

**11** If the valves are in satisfactory condition, they should be ground (lapped) into their respective seats, to ensure a smooth, gas-tight seal. If the seat is only lightly pitted, or if it has been recut, fine grinding compound should be used to produce the required finish. Coarse valve-grinding compound should *not* be used, unless a seat is badly burned or deeply pitted. If this is the case, the cylinder head and valves should be inspected by an expert, to decide whether seat recutting, or even the renewal of the valve or seat insert (where possible) is required.

**12** Valve grinding is carried out as follows. Place the cylinder head upside-down on a bench.

**13** Smear a trace of (the appropriate grade of) valve-grinding compound on the seat face, and press a suction grinding tool onto the valve head. With a semi-rotary action, grind the valve head to its seat, lifting the valve occasionally to redistribute the grinding compound. A light spring placed under the valve head will greatly ease this operation.

**14** If coarse grinding compound is being used, work only until a dull, matt even surface is produced on both the valve seat and the valve, then wipe off the used compound, and repeat the process with fine compound. When a smooth unbroken ring of light grey matt finish is produced on both the valve and seat, the grinding operation is complete. *Do not* grind-in the valves any further than absolutely necessary, or the seat will be prematurely sunk into the cylinder head.

**15** When all the valves have been ground-in, carefully wash off *all* traces of grinding compound using paraffin or a suitable solvent, before reassembling the cylinder head.

**16** To ensure that the hydraulic cam followers operate correctly, the depth of the valve stems below the camshaft bearing surface must be within certain limits. It may be possible to obtain a Saab checking tool from a dealer, but if not, the check may be made using a steel rule and straight-edge. Check that the dimension is within the limits given in the illustration by inserting each valve it its guide in turn, and measuring the dimension between the end of the valve stem and the camshaft bearing surface **(see illustration)**.

**17** If the dimension is not within the specified limits, adjustment must be made either to the end of the valve stem or to the valve seat height. If lower than the minimum amount, the length of the valve stem must be reduced, and if more than the maximum amount, the valve seat must be milled. Seek the advice of a Saab dealer or engine reconditioning specialist.

### Valve components

**18** Examine the valve springs for signs of damage and discoloration, and measure their free length **(see illustration)**.

**19** Stand each spring on a flat surface, and check it for squareness **(see illustration)**. If any of the springs are less than the minimum free length, or are damaged, distorted or have lost their tension, obtain a complete new set of springs.

**20** Obtain new valve stem oil seals, regardless of their apparent condition.

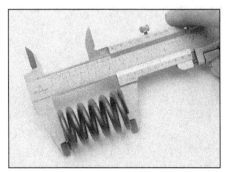

**7.18  Checking the valve spring free length**

**7.19  Checking the valve springs for squareness**

## 8 Cylinder head – reassembly

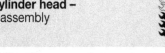

**1** Lubricate the stems of the valves, and insert the valves into their original locations **(see illustration)**. If new valves are being fitted, insert them into the locations to which they have been ground.
**2** Working on the first valve, dip the new valve stem seal in fresh engine oil. Carefully locate it over the valve and onto the guide. Take care not to damage the seal as it is passed over the valve stem. Use a suitable socket or metal tube to press the seal firmly onto the guide **(see illustration)**.
**3** Refit the valve spring followed by the spring retainer, then locate the plastic protector in the hydraulic cam follower bore.
**4** Compress the valve spring, and locate the split collets in the recess in the valve stem. Release the compressor and remove the protector, then repeat the procedure on the remaining valves.

**HAYNES HINT** *Use a little dab of grease to locate the collets on the valve stems, and to hold them in place while the spring compressor is released.*

**5** With all the valves installed, place the cylinder head flat on the bench and, using a hammer and interposed block of wood, tap

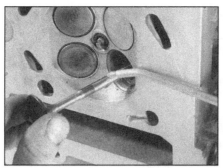

**8.1 Inserting a valve in the cylinder head**

the end of each valve stem to settle the components.
**6** Refit the hydraulic cam followers and camshafts with reference to Chapter 2A, Section 5.
**7** Refit the external components removed in Section 6.
**8** The cylinder head may now be refitted as described in Chapter 2A.

## 9 Timing cover – removal and refitting

**Note:** *This procedure describes removal of the timing cover, leaving the cylinder head in position. The alternative method (which is less likely to damage the cylinder head gasket) is to remove the cylinder head first, as described in Chapter 2A.*

**8.2 Using a socket to fit the valve stem seals**

### Removal

**1** Unbolt and remove the auxiliary drivebelt tensioner unit and idler pulley **(see illustrations)**.
**2** Remove the alternator as described in Chapter 5A, then undo the retaining bolts and remove the mounting bracket from the rear of the cylinder block **(see illustration)**.
**3** Undo the retaining bolts and remove the power steering pump mounting bracket including lifting eye from the front of the cylinder head.
**4** Remove the water pump as described in Chapter 3.
**5** Have an assistant hold the crankshaft/flywheel by inserting a flat-bladed screwdriver through the bellhousing and locking the starter ring gear to prevent the crankshaft turning. Loosen the crankshaft pulley bolt using a long socket bar. Note that the bolt is tightened to a very high torque.
**6** Fully unscrew the crankshaft pulley bolt, and slide the pulley off the end of the crankshaft **(see illustrations)**.
**7** Remove the sump as described in Chapter 2A, Section 7.
**8** Remove the two locating dowels (one in the left-hand bottom corner and one in the top right-hand corner) in the timing cover by cutting an internal thread in them using a 3/8 in UNC thread tap and withdraw them with sliding hammer. A bolt can be threaded into the locating dowels, then attached to the end of the slide hammer **(see illustrations)**.
**9** Unscrew and remove the bolts securing the timing cover to the cylinder block and cylinder

**9.1a Unscrewing the tensioner retaining bolt . . .**

**9.1b . . . and idler pulley retaining bolt**

**9.2 Unscrew the mounting bracket retaining bolts (arrowed) . . .**

**9.6a Remove the crankshaft pulley bolt . . .**

**9.6b . . . and slide the pulley off the crankshaft**

9.8a Cutting an internal thread in the dowel using a thread tap

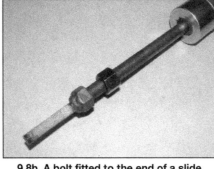

9.8b A bolt fitted to the end of a slide hammer

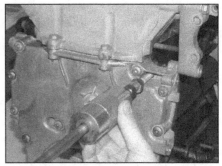

9.8c Using the slide hammer to withdraw the dowels from the timing cover

9.9a Note two upper bolts securing the timing cover to the cylinder head

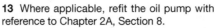
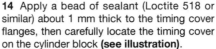

9.9b Removing the timing cover from the engine

head. Note the fitted position of the bolts, the two upper bolts on the cylinder head and the two lower bolts in the sump are different **(see illustrations)**.

10 Taking care not to damage the cylinder head gasket, withdraw the timing cover complete with the oil pump from the end of the crankshaft. Carefully move the timing cover down and outwards, away from the cylinder block.

11 Thoroughly clean all traces of sealant from the contact faces of the timing cover, sump, cylinder head and block. **Note:** *Check the condition of the cylinder head gasket, if there is any damage to the gasket, then the cylinder head will need to be removed to renew the gasket.*

12 If required, remove the oil pump from the timing cover, with reference to Chapter 2A, Section 8.

### Refitting

13 Where applicable, refit the oil pump with reference to Chapter 2A, Section 8.

14 Apply a bead of sealant (Loctite 518 or similar) about 1 mm thick to the timing cover flanges, then carefully locate the timing cover on the cylinder block **(see illustration)**.

15 Insert the timing cover retaining bolts including the two upper cylinder head bolts but do not tighten them at this stage. Tap the locating dowels back into place **(see illustration)**, then tighten the cover retaining bolts to the specified torque, including the two upper cylinder head bolts.

16 Refit the sump as described in Chapter 2A, Section 7.

17 Slide the crankshaft pulley onto the crankshaft, then insert the pulley bolt. Tighten the bolt to the specified torque, while an assistant holds the crankshaft stationary

using a wide-bladed screwdriver inserted in the starter ring gear.

18 Refit the water pump, with reference to Chapter 3.

19 Refit the alternator and power steering pump mounting brackets, and tighten the retaining bolts.

20 Refit the alternator with reference to Chapter 5A.

21 Refit the drivebelt tensioner assembly and idler pulley, and tighten the bolts.

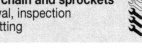

## 10 Timing chain and sprockets
– removal, inspection and refitting

### Removal

1 Position the crankshaft at TDC compression for No 1 piston (timing chain end of the engine) as described in Chapter 2A, Section 3.

2 Remove the timing cover as described in Section 9. Also remove the oil pump drive dog from the crankshaft **(see illustration)**.

3 The balance shafts are 'timed' at TDC, but since they rotate at twice the speed of the crankshaft, they may also be correctly 'timed' at BDC. Check that the timing marks on the shafts are correctly aligned with the marks on the front of the cylinder block/bearing housing. Note that the balance shaft sprockets are marked 'inlet' and 'exhaust' for their positions, but both front bearings are marked identically. However, as the bearings

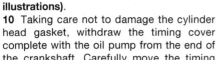

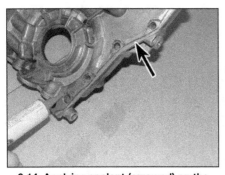

9.14 Applying sealant (arrowed) on the timing cover flanges

9.15 Using the slide hammer to tap the dowels back into the timing cover

10.2 Removing the oil pump drive dog from the crankshaft

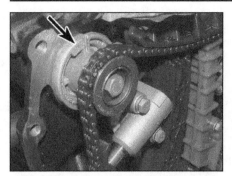

10.3a INL mark on the inlet balance shaft front bearing

10.3b EXH mark on the exhaust balance shaft front bearing

10.4a Unscrew the bolts (arrowed) and remove the balance shaft chain upper guide

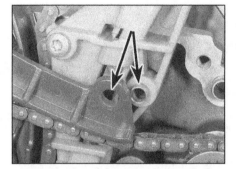

10.4b Note how the upper guide locates on the dowel

10.4c Removing the balance shaft chain tensioner . . .

10.4d . . . and side guide

are located with single bolts, the 'inlet' and 'exhaust' marks will always be correctly located at the top of the bearings (see illustrations).

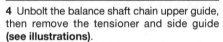

HAYNES HINT  Apply alignment markings (small dabs of paint are ideal) to the chain and sprockets, to ensure correct refitting.

4 Unbolt the balance shaft chain upper guide, then remove the tensioner and side guide (see illustrations).
5 Unbolt the idler from the block, then release the chain from the balance shaft sprockets and crankshaft sprocket. Note that the idler is in two parts (see illustrations).
6 Slide the balance shaft chain sprocket from the front of the crankshaft (see illustration). Note that the word 'Saab' is facing outwards.
7 Unscrew the retaining bolts, and remove

the sprockets from the ends of the balance shafts. To do this, hold the sprockets stationary with a chain-type oil filter removal tool or similar. Keep the sprockets identified for position.

10.5a Loosen . . .

8 Remove the cylinder head cover as described in Section 4.
9 Unscrew and remove the timing chain tensioner from the rear of the cylinder head. To do this, first unscrew the centre bolt and

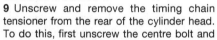

10.5b . . . and remove the idler retaining bolt (note alignment marks between idler and chain) . . .

10.5c . . . then withdraw the idler and remove the balance shaft chain

10.5d The idler is in two parts

10.6 Removing the balance shaft chain sprocket from the front of the crankshaft

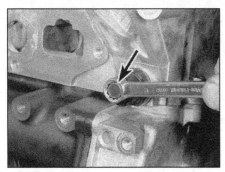

**10.9a** Unscrew the centre bolt . . .

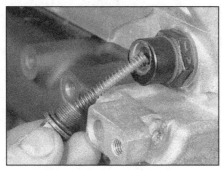

**10.9b** . . . and remove the spring . . .

**10.9c** . . . then unscrew the tensioner . . .

**10.9d** . . . and remove it from the cylinder head

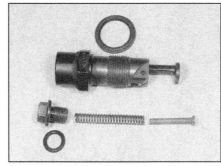

**10.9e** The timing chain tensioner components

**10.11** Removing the sprocket from the end of the inlet camshaft

remove the spring, then unscrew and remove the tensioner from the cylinder head **(see illustrations)**.

**10** While holding each camshaft stationary with a spanner on the flats at the

flywheel/driveplate end of the camshaft, loosen (but do not remove) the camshaft sprocket securing bolts.

**11** Unscrew and remove the bolt, and withdraw the sprocket from the end of the

inlet camshaft **(see illustration)**. Hold the timing chain with one hand, and release the sprocket from it with the other hand.

**12** Identify each sprocket for position. Note that each sprocket has a projection which engages with a cut-out in the end of the camshaft.

**13** Unscrew the bolt and withdraw the sprocket from the end of the exhaust camshaft, then disengage it from the chain **(see illustrations)**.

**14** Unscrew the bolts, and remove the timing chain fixed guide from the cylinder block **(see illustrations)**.

**15** Unbolt the chain retainer from the cylinder block, then disengage the timing chain and remove the sprocket from the end of the crankshaft **(see illustrations)**. If necessary, remove the Woodruff key from the groove in the crankshaft using a screwdriver.

**10.13a** Remove the retaining bolt . . .

**10.13b** . . . then disengage the sprocket from the chain

**10.14a** Unscrew the bolts . . .

**10.14b** . . . and remove the timing chain fixed guide

**10.15a** Removing the timing chain retainer (arrowed) from the cylinder block

## Inspection

**16** The timing chain **(see illustration)** (and where applicable, the balance shaft chain) should be renewed if the sprockets are worn, or if the chain is loose and noisy in operation. It's a good idea to renew the chain as a matter of course if the engine is stripped down for overhaul. The rollers on a very badly worn chain may be slightly grooved. To avoid future problems, if there's any doubt at all about the chain's condition, renew it. The chain tensioner and guides should be examined and if necessary renewed at the same time (refer to Section 11).

**17** Examine the teeth on the crankshaft sprocket, camshaft sprockets (and where applicable, the balance shaft sprockets) for wear. Each tooth forms an inverted V. If worn, the side of each tooth under tension will be slightly concave (hooked) in shape, when compared with the other side of the tooth (ie, one side of the inverted V will be concave when compared with the other). If the teeth appear to be worn, the sprockets must be renewed.

## Refitting

**18** Locate the Woodruff key in the groove in the crankshaft. Tap it fully into the groove, making sure that its plane surface is parallel to the crankshaft.

**19** Engage the timing chain with the crankshaft sprocket, then locate the crankshaft sprocket on the end of the crankshaft, making sure that it locates correctly on the Woodruff key. Where the timing chain has bright links, locate the single bright link at the bottom of the sprocket, aligned with the slot in the sprocket. Refit the chain retainer and tighten the bolts **(see illustrations)**.

**20** Locate the timing chain in the fixed guide, then refit the guide and tighten the bolts.

**21** Refit the sprocket to the end of the exhaust camshaft, insert the bolt and finger-tighten it at this stage. **Do not** apply thread-locking fluid to the threads of the bolt.

**22** Check that the crankshaft and camshafts are still aligned at their TDC positions.

**23** Feed the timing chain up through the cylinder head aperture, and locate it on the exhaust camshaft sprocket, making sure that it is taut between the two sprockets. Check that it is correctly located on the guides. Where the chain has a bright link, make sure that it is aligned with the timing mark.

**24** Engage the inlet sprocket with the timing chain so that the engagement cut-out and projection are in alignment, then locate the sprocket on the inlet camshaft, and insert the bolt. Finger-tighten the bolt at this stage. **Do not** apply thread-locking fluid to the threads of the bolt. Where the chain has a bright link, make sure that it is aligned with the timing mark.

**25** Set the timing chain tensioner by pressing down on the ratchet with a screwdriver, then push the plunger fully into the tensioner, and

**10.15b Removing the crankshaft sprocket from the end of the crankshaft**

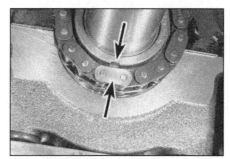

**10.19a Where timing chain has bright links, these must be aligned with the slot in the sprocket (arrowed)**

release the ratchet **(see illustration)**. Check the tensioner washer for condition and renew it if necessary.

**26** Insert the tensioner body in the cylinder head, and tighten to the specified torque.

**27** Insert the spring and plastic guide pin in the tensioner, then fit the plug together with a new O-ring, and tighten it to the specified torque. **Note:** *New tensioners are supplied with the tensioner spring held pretensioned with a pin. Do not remove this pin until after the tensioner has been tightened into the cylinder head.* When the engine is started, hydraulic pressure will take up any remaining slack.

**28** Temporarily refit the crankshaft pulley bolt, and rotate the engine two complete turns clockwise. Check that the timing marks still align correctly. Remove the pulley bolt. Where the chain has bright links, note that these will not now be aligned with the timing marks.

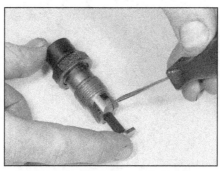

**10.25 Setting the timing chain tensioner**

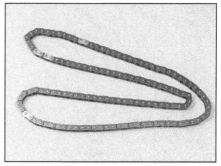

**10.16 Timing chain removed from the engine**

**10.19b Tightening the timing chain retainer bolts**

**29** Fully tighten the camshaft sprocket bolts to the specified torque, while holding the camshafts with a spanner on the flats.

**30** Refit the cylinder head cover with reference to Section 4.

**31** Refit the sprockets to the ends of the balance shafts, and tighten the retaining bolts.

**32** Locate the balance shaft chain sprocket on the front of the crankshaft, with the word 'Saab' facing outwards.

**33** Fit the chain to the sprockets, making sure that the timing marks are aligned correctly **(see illustration)**.

**34** Refit the idler to the front of the block, and tighten the retaining bolt.

**35** Refit the side guide, tensioner and upper guide to the balance shaft chain **(see illustration and Tool Tip overleaf)**.

**36** Rotate the crankshaft one turn, and check that the balance shaft timing marks are still correctly aligned.

**10.33 The balance shaft timing marks must be correctly aligned before refitting the chain**

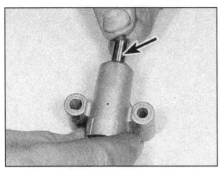

**10.35 Depress the balance shaft chain tensioner plunger (arrowed) and retain with a plastic cable-tie**

**37** Refit the timing cover with reference to Section 5.

*Before refitting the tensioner, hold its plunger depressed by fitting a plastic cable-tie around it. Cut the tie after refitting.*

## 11 Timing chain guides and tensioner – removal, inspection and refitting

### Removal

**1** Remove the timing chain as described in Section 10; note that this procedure includes removal of the fixed guide and balance shaft chain guides. The timing chain need not be removed from the crankshaft sprocket.
**2** Unbolt and remove the fixed timing chain guide and release the pivoting guide from the pin on the cylinder block **(see illustration)**.

### Inspection

**3** Inspect the chain guides for damage and excessive wear, and renew them if necessary.
**4** Clean the tensioner plunger and body, and examine them for damage and wear **(see illustration)**. The plunger may be removed by depressing the ratchet against the spring. If the plunger or body is excessively scored, the complete tensioner should be renewed.

### Refitting

**5** Locate the pivoting guide on the pin on the cylinder block, then refit the fixed guide and tighten the retaining bolts.
**6** Refit the timing chain with reference to Section 10.

## 12 Balance shafts – removal, inspection and refitting

### Removal

**1** Position the crankshaft at TDC compression for No 1 piston (timing chain end of the engine) as described in Chapter 2A, Section 3.
**2** Remove the timing cover as described in Section 9.
**3** The balance shafts are 'timed' at TDC, but since they rotate at twice the speed of the crankshaft, they may also be correctly 'timed'

at BDC. Check that the timing marks on the shafts are correctly aligned with the marks on the bearing brackets. As an extra precaution, apply dabs of paint to the chain and sprockets, to ensure correct refitting. Note that the balance shaft sprockets are marked 'inlet' and 'exhaust' for position, but the front bearings are marked identically. However, as the bearings are located with single bolts, the 'inlet' and 'exhaust' marks will always be correctly located at the top of the bearings – refer to Section 10 for further information.
**4** Unbolt the balance shaft chain upper guide, then remove the tensioner and side guide (see illustrations in Section 10 of this Chapter).
**5** Unscrew the retaining bolt and remove the idler from the block.
**6** Release the chain from the balance shaft sprockets and crankshaft sprocket.
**7** Unscrew the bearing retaining bolts, and

**12.7a Unscrew the bearing retaining bolts . . .**

**12.7c Removing the inlet balance shaft from the cylinder block**

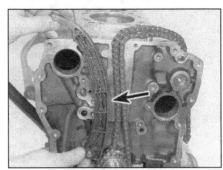

**11.2 Removing the pivoting guide from the pin on the cylinder block**

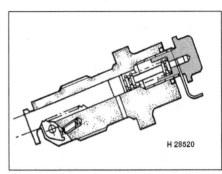

**11.4 Cross-section of the timing chain tensioner**

withdraw the balance shafts from the cylinder block **(see illustrations)**. Keep the shafts identified for position.
**8** Unscrew the retaining bolts, and remove

**12.7b . . . and withdraw the exhaust balance shaft from the cylinder block**

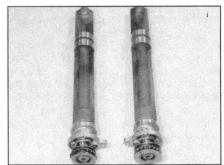

**12.7d The two balance shafts removed from the engine**

the sprockets from the ends of the balance shafts, while holding each shaft in a soft-jawed vice.

### Inspection

**9** Clean the balance shafts and examine the bearing journals for wear and damage. The bearings inside the cylinder block should also be examined. If these are excessively worn or damaged, get advice from a Saab dealer or engine reconditioner.

### Refitting

**10** Fit the sprockets to the ends of the balance shafts, and tighten the retaining bolts.
**11** Lubricate the bearing journals with clean engine oil, then insert the balance shafts in the cylinder block in their correct positions.
**12** Locate the balance shaft chain sprocket on the front of the crankshaft, with the word 'Saab' facing outwards.
**13** Fit the chain to the sprockets, and refit the idler to the front of the block, making sure that the timing marks remain aligned correctly.
**14** Refit the side guide, tensioner and upper guide to the balance shaft chain.
**15** Rotate the crankshaft one turn, and check that the balance shaft sprockets are still correctly aligned.
**16** Refit the timing cover with reference to Section 9.

### 13 Piston/connecting rod assembly – removal

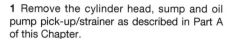

**1** Remove the cylinder head, sump and oil pump pick-up/strainer as described in Part A of this Chapter.
**2** If there is a pronounced wear ridge at the top of any bore, it may be necessary to remove it with a scraper or ridge reamer, to avoid piston damage during removal. Such a ridge indicates excessive wear of the cylinder bore.
**3** Using a hammer and centre-punch, paint or similar, mark each connecting rod big-end bearing cap with its respective cylinder number on the flat machined surface provided; if the engine has been dismantled before, note carefully any identifying marks

**13.5a Removing a big-end bearing cap**

made previously. Note that No 1 cylinder is at the transmission (flywheel/driveplate) end of the engine.
**4** Turn the crankshaft to bring pistons 1 and 4 to BDC (bottom dead centre).
**5** Unscrew the nuts from No 1 piston big-end bearing cap. Take off the cap, and recover the bottom half bearing shell. If the bearing shells are to be re-used, tape the cap and the shell together **(see illustrations)**.
**6** To prevent the possibility of damage to the crankshaft bearing journals, tape over the connecting rod stud threads.
**7** Using a hammer handle, push the piston up through the bore, and remove it from the top of the cylinder block. Recover the bearing shell, and tape it to the connecting rod for safe-keeping.
**8** Loosely refit the big-end cap to the connecting rod, and secure with the nuts – this will help to keep the components in their correct order.
**9** Remove No 4 piston assembly in the same way.
**10** Turn the crankshaft through 180° to bring pistons 2 and 3 to BDC (bottom dead centre), and remove them in the same way.

### 14 Crankshaft – removal

**1** Remove the timing chain and sprocket, the sump and oil pump pick-up/strainer/transfer tube, and the flywheel/driveplate, as described in Chapter 2A.

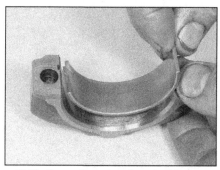

**13.5b Removing a bearing shell from a big-end bearing cap**

**2** Remove the pistons and connecting rods, as described in Section 13. **Note:** *If no work is to be done on the pistons and connecting rods, there is no need to remove the cylinder head, or to push the pistons out of the cylinder bores. The pistons should just be pushed far enough up the bores that they are positioned clear of the crankshaft journals.*
**3** Check the crankshaft endfloat with reference to Section 17, then proceed as follows.
**4** Unbolt and remove the crankshaft oil seal housing from the end of the cylinder block, noting the correct fitted locations of the locating dowels. If the locating dowels are a loose fit, remove them and store them with the housing for safe-keeping. Remove the gasket.
**5** Identification numbers should already be cast onto the base of each main bearing cap **(see illustration)**. If not, number the cap and crankcase using a centre-punch, as was done for the connecting rods and caps.
**6** Unscrew and remove the main bearing cap retaining bolts, and withdraw the caps, complete with bearing shells **(see illustrations)**. Tap the caps with a wooden or copper mallet if they are stuck.
**7** Remove the bearing shells from the caps, but keep them with their relevant caps and identified for position to ensure correct refitting **(see illustration)**.
**8** Carefully lift the crankshaft from the crankcase **(see illustration)**.
**9** Remove the upper bearing shells from the crankcase, keeping them identified for position. Also remove the thrustwashers at

**14.5 The main bearing caps are numbered from the timing chain end of the engine**

**14.6a Unscrew and remove the main bearing cap bolts . . .**

**14.6b . . . and remove the main bearing caps**

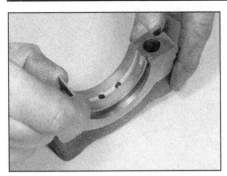

14.7 Removing a main bearing shell from its cap

14.8 Lifting the crankshaft from the crankcase

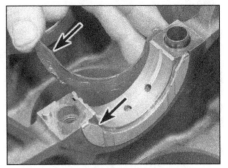

14.9a Removing the thrustwashers (arrowed) . . .

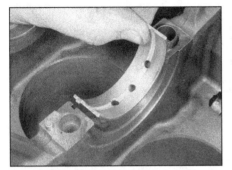

14.9b . . . and main bearing shells

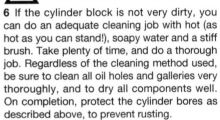

14.10 Location of the screws securing the crankshaft position sensor reluctor

each side of the centre main bearing, and store them with the bearing cap (see illustrations).

**10** With the crankshaft removed, the crankshaft position sensor reluctor may be removed if necessary, by unscrewing the screws and withdrawing the reluctor over the end of the crankshaft (see illustration). Note that the screws are arranged so that it is only possible to refit the reluctor in one position.

## 15 Cylinder block/crankcase – cleaning and inspection

### Cleaning

**1** Remove all external components and electrical switches/sensors from the block. For complete cleaning, the core plugs should

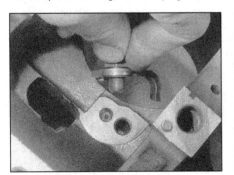

15.1 Removing an oil jet from the crankcase

ideally be removed, as follows. Drill a small hole in the plugs, then insert a self-tapping screw into the hole. Pull out the plugs by pulling on the screw with a pair of grips, or by using a slide hammer. Also unbolt the four oil jets (where fitted) from the lower part of the crankcase (see illustration).

**2** Scrape all traces of sealant from the cylinder block/crankcase, taking care not to damage the gasket/sealing surfaces.

**3** Remove all oil gallery plugs (where fitted). The plugs are usually very tight – they may have to be drilled out, and the holes retapped. Use new plugs when the engine is reassembled.

**4** If the cylinder block/crankcase is extremely dirty, it should be steam-cleaned.

**5** Clean all oil holes and oil galleries, and flush all internal passages with warm water until the water runs clear. Dry thoroughly, and apply a light film of oil to all mating surfaces, to

15.7 Cleaning a cylinder head bolt hole in the cylinder block using a tap

prevent rusting. Also oil the cylinder bores. If you have access to compressed air, use it to speed up the drying process, and to blow out all the oil holes and galleries.

> **Warning: Wear eye protection when using compressed air.**

**6** If the cylinder block is not very dirty, you can do an adequate cleaning job with hot (as hot as you can stand!), soapy water and a stiff brush. Take plenty of time, and do a thorough job. Regardless of the cleaning method used, be sure to clean all oil holes and galleries very thoroughly, and to dry all components well. On completion, protect the cylinder bores as described above, to prevent rusting.

**7** All threaded holes must be clean, to ensure accurate torque readings during reassembly. To clean the threads, run the correct-size tap into each of the holes to remove rust, corrosion, thread sealant or sludge, and to restore damaged threads (see illustration). If possible, use compressed air to clear the holes of debris produced by this operation.

> **HAYNES HINT** *A good alternative to compressed air is to inject aerosol-applied water-dispersant lubricant into each hole, using the long tube usually supplied.*
>
> **Warning: Wear eye protection when cleaning out these holes in this way.**

**8** Apply suitable sealant to the new oil gallery plugs, and insert them into the holes in the block. Tighten them securely. Apply suitable sealant to new core plugs and tap them into place with a socket or tube. Refit and tighten the oil jets to the bottom of the crankcase where applicable.

**9** If the engine is not going to be reassembled right away, cover it with a large plastic bag to keep it clean; protect all mating surfaces and the cylinder bores as described above, to prevent rusting.

### Inspection

**10** Visually check the cylinder block for cracks and corrosion. Look for stripped

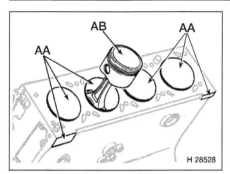

**15.12a Piston and cylinder bore classification code locations**

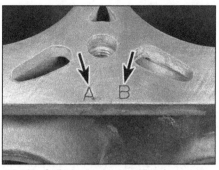

**15.12b Cylinder bore classification on the front of the block**

**15.12c Piston classification on the piston crown**

threads in the threaded holes. If there has been any history of internal water leakage, it may be worthwhile having an engine overhaul specialist check the cylinder block/crankcase with special equipment. If defects are found, have them repaired if possible; otherwise, a new block will be needed.

**11** Check each cylinder bore for scuffing and scoring. Check for signs of a wear ridge at the top of the cylinder, indicating that the bore is excessively worn.

**12** The cylinder bores and pistons are matched and classified according to five codes – AB, B, C, 1 (0.5 mm oversize), and 2 (1.0 mm oversize). The code is stamped on the piston crowns, and on the front of the cylinder block **(see illustrations)**. Note that all classifications may occur in the same cylinder block.

**13** Wear of the cylinder bores and pistons can be measured by inserting the relevant piston (without piston rings) in its bore and using a feeler blade. Make the check with the piston near the top of its bore. If the clearance is more than the nominal (new) amount given in the Specifications, a rebore should be considered, and the opinion of an engine reconditioner sought.

## 16 Piston/connecting rod assembly – inspection

**1** Before the inspection process can begin, the piston/connecting rod assemblies must be cleaned, and the original piston rings

removed from the pistons **(see illustration)**.

**2** Carefully expand the old rings over the top of the pistons. The use of two or three old feeler blades will be helpful in preventing the rings dropping into empty grooves **(see illustrations)**. Be careful not to scratch the piston with the ends of the ring. The rings are brittle, and will snap if they are spread too far. They're also very sharp – protect your hands and fingers. Note that the third ring incorporates an expander. Always remove the rings from the top of the piston. Keep each set of rings with its piston, if the old rings are to be re-used.

**3** Scrape away all traces of carbon from the top of the piston. A hand-held wire brush (or a piece of fine emery cloth) can be used, once the majority of the deposits have been scraped away.

**4** Remove the carbon from the ring grooves in the piston, using an old ring. Break the ring in half to do this (be careful not to cut your fingers – piston rings are sharp). Be careful to remove only the carbon deposits – do not remove any metal, and do not nick or scratch the sides of the ring grooves.

**5** Once the deposits have been removed, clean the piston/connecting rod assembly with paraffin or a suitable solvent, and dry thoroughly. Make sure that the oil return holes in the ring grooves are clear.

**6** If the pistons and cylinder bores are not damaged or worn excessively, and if the cylinder block does not need to be rebored, the original pistons can be refitted. Normal piston wear shows up as even vertical wear on the piston thrust surfaces, and slight looseness of the top ring in its groove.

**7** Carefully inspect each piston for cracks around the skirt, around the gudgeon pin holes, and at the piston ring 'lands' (between the ring grooves).

**8** Look for scoring and scuffing on the piston skirt, holes in the piston crown, and burned areas at the edge of the crown. If the skirt is scored or scuffed, the engine may have been suffering from overheating, and/or abnormal combustion which caused excessively high operating temperatures. The cooling and lubrication systems should be checked thoroughly. Scorch marks on the sides of the pistons show that blow-by has occurred. A hole in the piston crown, or burned areas at the edge of the piston crown, indicates that abnormal combustion (pre-ignition, knocking, or detonation) has been occurring. If any of the above problems exist, the causes must be investigated and corrected, or the damage will occur again. The causes may include incorrect ignition timing and/or fuel/air mixture.

**9** Corrosion of the piston, in the form of pitting, indicates that coolant has been leaking into the combustion chamber and/or the crankcase. Again, the cause must be corrected, or the problem may persist in the rebuilt engine.

**10** Where needed, pistons can be purchased from a Saab dealer.

**11** Examine each connecting rod carefully for signs of damage, such as cracks around the big-end and small-end bearings. Check that the rod is not bent or distorted. Damage is highly unlikely, unless the engine has been seized or badly overheated. Detailed checking

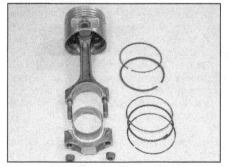

**16.1 Piston/connecting rod assembly components**

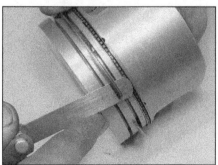

**16.2a Removing a piston compression ring with the aid of a feeler blade**

**16.2b Removing the oil control ring**

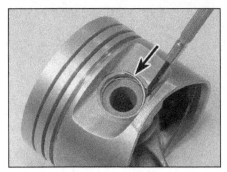

**16.13a Prise out the gudgeon pin circlip . . .**

**16.13b . . . then withdraw the gudgeon pin, and separate the piston from the connecting rod**

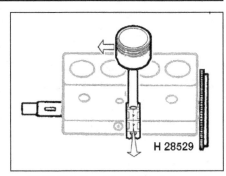

**16.17 Relationship of the piston and connecting rod**

of the connecting rod assembly can only be carried out by a Saab dealer or engine repair specialist with the necessary equipment.

**12** The gudgeon pins are of the floating type, secured in position by two circlips, and the pistons and connecting rods can be separated and reassembled as follows.

**13** Using a small flat-bladed screwdriver, prise out the circlips, and push out the gudgeon pin **(see illustrations)**. Hand pressure should be sufficient to remove the pin. Identify the piston, gudgeon pin and rod to ensure correct reassembly.

**14** Examine the gudgeon pin and connecting rod small-end bearing for signs of wear or damage. Wear can be cured by renewing both the pin and bush. Bush renewal, however, is a specialist job – press facilities are required, and the new bush must be reamed accurately.

**15** The connecting rods themselves should not be in need of renewal, unless seizure or some other major mechanical failure has occurred. Check the alignment of the connecting rods visually, and if the rods are not straight, take them to an engine overhaul specialist for a more detailed check.

**16** Examine all components, and obtain any new parts from your Saab dealer. If new pistons are purchased, they will be supplied complete with gudgeon pins and circlips. Circlips can also be purchased individually.

**17** Position the piston so that the notch on the edge of the crown faces the timing end of the engine, and the numbers on the connecting rod and big-end cap face the exhaust side of the cylinder block. With the piston held in your hand and the notch facing

the left, the connecting rod numbering should face towards you **(see illustration)**. Apply a smear of clean engine oil to the gudgeon pin. Slide it into the piston and through the connecting rod small-end. Check that the piston pivots freely on the rod, then secure the gudgeon pin in position with the circlips. Ensure that each circlip is correctly located in its groove in the piston.

**18** Measure the piston diameters, and check that they are within limits for the corresponding bore diameters. If the piston-to-bore clearance is excessive, the block will have to be rebored, and new pistons and rings fitted.

**19** Examine the mating surfaces of the big-end caps and connecting rods, to see if they have ever been filed in a mistaken attempt to take up bearing wear. This is extremely unlikely, but if evident, the offending connecting rods and caps must be renewed.

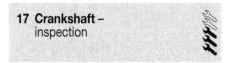

**17 Crankshaft –**
inspection

### Checking endfloat

**1** If the crankshaft endfloat is to be checked, this must be done when the crankshaft is still installed in the cylinder block/crankcase, but is free to move (see Section 14).

**2** Check the endfloat using a dial gauge in contact with the end of the crankshaft. Push the crankshaft fully one way, and then zero the gauge. Push the crankshaft fully the other

way, and check the endfloat **(see illustration)**. The result can be compared with the specified amount, and will give an indication as to whether new thrustwashers are required.

**3** If a dial gauge is not available, feeler blades can be used. First push the crankshaft fully towards the flywheel end of the engine, then use feeler blades to measure the gap between the No 3 crankpin web and the centre main bearing thrustwasher **(see illustration)**.

### Inspection

**4** Clean the crankshaft using paraffin or a suitable solvent, and dry it, preferably with compressed air if available. Be sure to clean the oil holes with a pipe cleaner or similar probe, to ensure that they are not obstructed.

⚠ *Warning: Wear eye protection when using compressed air.*

**5** Check the main and big-end bearing journals for uneven wear, scoring, pitting and cracking.

**6** Big-end bearing wear is accompanied by distinct metallic knocking when the engine is running (particularly noticeable when the engine is pulling from low speed), and some loss of oil pressure.

**7** Main bearing wear is accompanied by severe engine vibration and rumble – getting progressively worse as engine speed increases – and again by loss of oil pressure.

**8** If there are any signs of wear, take the crankshaft to your local engine reconditioning specialist, where they will check the bearing journals. Any roughness (which will be accompanied by obvious bearing wear) indicates that the crankshaft requires regrinding (where possible) or renewal.

**9** If the crankshaft has been reground, check for burrs around the crankshaft oil holes (the holes are usually chamfered, so burrs should not be a problem, unless regrinding has been carried out carelessly). Remove any burrs with a fine file or scraper, and thoroughly clean the oil holes as described previously.

**10** Using a micrometer, measure the diameter of the main and big-end bearing journals, and compare the results with the Specifications **(see illustration)**. By measuring the diameter at a number of points

**17.2 Using a dial gauge to check the crankshaft endfloat**

**17.3 Using feeler blades to check the crankshaft endfloat**

**17.10 Measuring a crankshaft big-end bearing journal diameter**

around each journal's circumference, you will be able to determine whether or not the journal is out-of-round. Take the measurement at each end of the journal, near the webs, to determine if the journal is tapered. Compare the results obtained with those given in the Specifications.

11 Check the oil seal contact surfaces at each end of the crankshaft for wear and damage. If the seal has worn a deep groove in the surface of the crankshaft, consult an engine overhaul specialist; repair may be possible, but otherwise a new crankshaft will be required.

## 18 Main and big-end bearings – inspection

1 Even though the main and big-end bearings are renewed during the engine overhaul, the old bearings should be retained for close examination, as they may reveal valuable information about the condition of the engine. The bearing shells are graded by thickness, the grade of each shell being indicated by the colour code marked on it – they may also have markings on their backing faces **(see illustration)**.
*The thinnest shells are red –*
   *0.005mm thinner than yellow.*
*The standard shells are yellow (only size stocked as spare part).*
*The first undersize shells are blue –*
   *0.005mm thicker than yellow.*
2 Bearing failure can occur due to lack of

**18.1 STD marking on the backing of a big-end bearing shell**

lubrication, the presence of dirt or other foreign particles, overloading the engine, or corrosion **(see illustration)**. Regardless of the cause of bearing failure, the cause must be corrected (where applicable) before the engine is reassembled, to prevent it from happening again.
3 When examining the bearing shells, remove them from the cylinder block/crankcase, the main bearing caps, the connecting rods and the connecting rod big-end bearing caps. Lay them out on a clean surface in the same general position as their location in the engine. This will enable you to match any bearing problems with the corresponding crankshaft journal. *Do not* touch any shell's bearing surface with your fingers while checking it, or the delicate surface may be scratched.
4 Dirt and other foreign matter gets into the engine in a variety of ways. It may be left in the engine during assembly, or it may pass through filters or the crankcase ventilation system. It may get into the oil, and from there into the bearings. Metal chips from machining operations and normal engine wear are often present. Abrasives are sometimes left in engine components after reconditioning, especially when parts are not thoroughly cleaned using the proper cleaning methods. Whatever the source, these foreign objects often end up embedded in the soft bearing material, and are easily recognised. Large particles will not embed in the bearing, and will score or gouge the bearing and journal. The best prevention for this cause of bearing failure is to clean all parts thoroughly, and keep everything spotlessly-clean during engine assembly. Frequent and regular engine oil and filter changes are also recommended.
5 Lack of lubrication (or lubrication breakdown) has a number of interrelated causes. Excessive heat (which thins the oil), overloading (which squeezes the oil from the bearing face) and oil leakage (from excessive bearing clearances, worn oil pump or high engine speeds) all contribute to lubrication breakdown. Blocked oil passages, which usually are the result of misaligned oil holes in a bearing shell, will also oil-starve a bearing, and destroy it. When lack of lubrication is the cause of bearing failure, the bearing material is wiped or extruded from the steel backing of the bearing. Temperatures may increase to the point where the steel backing turns blue from overheating.
6 Driving habits can have a definite effect on bearing life. Full-throttle, low-speed operation (labouring the engine) puts very high loads on bearings, tending to squeeze out the oil film. These loads cause the bearings to flex, which produces fine cracks in the bearing face (fatigue failure). Eventually, the bearing material will loosen in pieces, and tear away from the steel backing.
7 Short-distance driving leads to corrosion of bearings, because insufficient engine heat is produced to drive off the condensed water

and corrosive gases. These products collect in the engine oil, forming acid and sludge. As the oil is carried to the engine bearings, the acid attacks and corrodes the bearing material.
8 Incorrect bearing installation during engine assembly will lead to bearing failure as well. Tight-fitting bearings leave insufficient bearing running clearance, and will result in oil starvation. Dirt or foreign particles trapped behind a bearing shell result in high spots on the bearing, which lead to failure.
9 *Do not* touch any shell's bearing surface with your fingers during reassembly; there is a risk of scratching the delicate surface, or of depositing particles of dirt on it.

> **HAYNES HiNT** *Bearing shells should be renewed as a matter of course during engine overhaul; to do otherwise is false economy.*

## 19 Engine overhaul – reassembly sequence

1 Before reassembly begins, ensure that all new parts have been obtained, and that all necessary tools are available. Read through the entire procedure, to familiarise yourself with the work involved, and to ensure that all items necessary for reassembly of the engine are at hand. In addition to all normal tools and materials, thread-locking compound will be needed. A suitable tube of sealant will also be required for the joint faces that are fitted without gaskets.

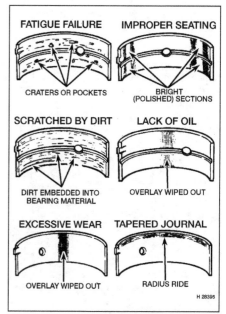

**18.2 Typical bearing failures**

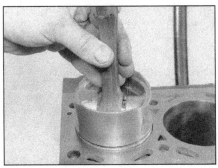

**20.3 Using the top of a piston to push a piston ring into the bore**

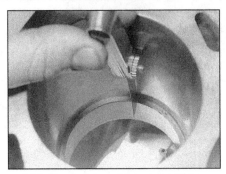

**20.4 Measuring a piston ring end gap**

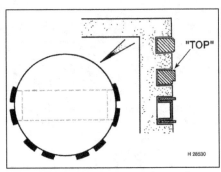

**20.9 Piston ring cross-section and gap positioning**

**2** In order to save time and avoid problems, engine reassembly can be carried out in the following order:

a) Crankshaft (Section 21).
b) Piston/connecting rod assemblies (Section 22).
c) Sump (Chapter 2A).
d) Balance shafts (Section 12).
e) Flywheel/driveplate (Chapter 2A).
f) Timing chain and balance shaft chain, sprockets and tensioner (Section 10 and 11).
g) Cylinder head (Chapter 2A).
h) Inlet and exhaust manifolds (Chapter 4A).
i) Engine external components.

**3** At this stage, all engine components should be absolutely clean and dry, with all faults repaired. The components should be laid out (or in individual containers) on a completely clean work surface.

## 20 Piston rings – refitting

**1** Before fitting new piston rings, the ring end gaps must be checked as follows.
**2** Lay out the piston/connecting rod assemblies and the new piston ring sets, so that the ring sets will be matched with the same piston and cylinder during the end gap measurement and subsequent engine reassembly.
**3** Insert the top ring into the first cylinder, and push it down the bore using the top of the

piston **(see illustration)**. This will ensure that the ring remains square with the cylinder walls. Position the ring near the bottom of the cylinder bore, at the lower limit of ring travel. Note that the top and second compression rings are different.
**4** Measure the end gap using feeler blades, and compare the measurements with the figures given in the Specifications **(see illustration)**.
**5** If the gap is too small (unlikely if genuine Saab parts are used), it must be enlarged, or the ring ends may contact each other during engine operation, causing serious damage. Ideally, new piston rings providing the correct end gap should be fitted. As a last resort, the end gap can be increased by filing the ring ends very carefully with a fine file. Mount the file in a vice with soft jaws, slip the ring over the file with the ends contacting the file face, and slowly move the ring to remove material from the ends. Take care, as piston rings are sharp, and are easily broken.
**6** With new piston rings, it is unlikely that the end gap will be too large. If the gaps are too large, check that you have the correct rings for your particular engine.
**7** Repeat the checking procedure for each ring in the first cylinder, and then for the rings in the remaining cylinders. Remember to keep rings, pistons and cylinders matched up.
**8** Once the ring end gaps have been checked and if necessary corrected, the rings can be fitted to the pistons.
**9** Fit the piston rings using the same technique as for removal. Fit the bottom (oil control) ring first, and work up. When fitting the oil control ring, first insert the expander, then fit the lower and upper rings with the ring gaps both on the non-thrust side of the piston, with approximately 60° between them. Ensure that the second compression ring is fitted the correct way up, with the word TOP uppermost. Arrange the gaps of the top and second compression rings on opposite sides of the piston, above the ends of the gudgeon pin **(see illustration)**. **Note:** *Always follow any instructions supplied with the new piston ring sets – different manufacturers may specify different procedures. Do not mix up the top and second compression rings, as they have different cross-sections.*

## 21 Crankshaft – refitting

**1** Refit the crankshaft position sensor reluctor if removed and tighten the screws, with reference to Section 14.
**2** Using a little grease, stick the upper thrustwashers to each side of the centre main bearing upper location; ensure that the oil way grooves on each thrustwasher face outwards (away from the cylinder block).
**3** Place the bearing shells in their locations in the caps, ensuring that the tab on each shell engages in the notch in the cylinder block or main bearing cap location. Take care not to touch any shell's bearing surface with your fingers. If new shells are being fitted, ensure that all traces of protective grease are cleaned off, using paraffin. Wipe dry the shells and connecting rods with a lint-free cloth. Liberally lubricate each bearing shell in the cylinder block/crankcase with clean engine oil **(see illustration)**.
**4** Lower the crankshaft into position so that Nos 2 and 3 cylinder crankpins are at TDC. In this position, Nos 1 and 4 cylinder crankpins will be at BDC, ready for fitting No 1 piston. Check the crankshaft endfloat as described in Section 17.
**5** Lubricate the lower bearing shells in the main bearing caps with clean engine oil. Make sure that the locating lugs on the shells engage with the corresponding recesses in the caps.
**6** Fit the main bearing caps to their correct locations, ensuring that they are fitted the correct way round (the bearing shell lug recesses in the block and caps must be on the same side). Insert the bolts loosely.
**7** Progressively tighten the main bearing cap bolts to the specified torque wrench setting.
**8** Check that the crankshaft rotates freely.
**9** Refit the piston/connecting rod assemblies to the crankshaft, as described in Section 22.
**10** Before refitting the crankshaft oil seal housing, fit a new oil seal in the housing, with reference to Chapter 2A. Use a mallet and block of wood to drive it into the housing, or alternatively, use the block of wood in a vice **(see illustrations)**.

**21.3 Lubricating the main bearing shells**

21.10a  Driving the crankshaft oil seal into the housing

21.10b  Fitting the crankshaft oil seal using a block of wood in a vice

21.11a  Adhesive tape over the end of the crankshaft will prevent damage to the oil seal when refitting

**11** Apply suitable sealant to the contact faces of the oil seal housing, then smear a little oil on the oil seal lips, and refit the locating dowels where necessary. Locate the housing on the cylinder block. To prevent damage to the oil seal as it locates over the crankshaft, make up a guide out of a plastic container, or alternatively use adhesive tape. Once the housing is in position, remove the guide or tape, then insert the bolts and tighten them securely **(see illustrations)**.

**12** Refit the flywheel/driveplate, oil pick-up/strainer/transfer tube and sump, with reference to Chapter 2A.

**13** Where removed, refit the cylinder head as described in Chapter 2A.

**14** Refit the timing chain and sprocket as described in Chapter 2A.

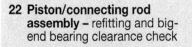

**22 Piston/connecting rod assembly** – refitting and big-end bearing clearance check

### Running clearance check

**1** One method of checking the clearance is to refit the big-end bearing cap to the connecting rod before refitting the pistons to the cylinder block, ensuring that they are fitted the correct way round, with the bearing shells in place. With the cap retaining nuts correctly tightened, use an internal micrometer or vernier caliper to measure the internal diameter of each assembled pair of bearing shells. If the diameter of each corresponding crankshaft journal is measured and then

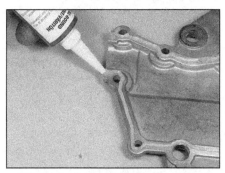

21.11b  Applying sealant to the oil seal housing

subtracted from the bearing internal diameter, the result will be the big-end bearing running clearance.

**2** The second, and more accurate, method is to take the components to your local engine reconditioning specialist, where they will be able to do a more comprehensive check.

### Refitting

**3** Lubricate the cylinder bores, pistons, piston rings and bearing shells with clean engine oil, then lay out each piston/connecting rod assembly in its respective position on a clean dust free surface.

**4** Press the bearing shells into their locations, ensuring that the tab on each shell engages in the notch in the connecting rod and cap. Take care not to touch any shell's bearing surface with your fingers. If the original bearing shells are being used for the check, ensure that they are refitted in their original locations.

21.11c  Refitting the oil seal housing (engine backplate)

**5** Start with assembly No 1. Position No 1 crankpin at the bottom of its stroke. Make sure that the piston rings are still spaced as described in Section 20, then clamp them in position with a piston ring compressor **(see illustration)**.

**6** Insert the piston/connecting rod assembly into the top of cylinder No 1, taking care not to mark the cylinder bores. Ensure that the notch or arrow on the piston crown is pointing towards the timing chain end of the engine. Using a block of wood or hammer handle against the piston crown, tap the assembly into the cylinder bore until the piston crown is flush with the top of the cylinder **(see illustrations)**.

**7** With the No 1 crankpin at the bottom of its stroke, guide the connecting rod onto it while tapping the top of the piston with the hammer handle.

**8** Refit the big-end bearing cap, using the

22.5  Piston ring compressor fitted over the piston rings

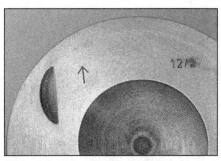

22.6a  The arrow on the piston crown must point towards the timing chain end of the engine

22.6b  Using a hammer handle to tap the piston down the cylinder bore

**22.8 Tightening the big-end bearing cap nuts**

marks made or noted on removal to ensure that they are fitted the correct way round. Tighten the bearing cap nuts to the specified torque **(see illustration)**.

**9** Rotate the crankshaft. Check that it turns freely; some stiffness is to be expected if new components have been fitted, but there should be no signs of binding or tight spots.

**10** Refit the remaining three piston/connecting rod assemblies to their crankpins in the same way.

**11** Refit the oil pump pick-up/strainer, sump and cylinder head with reference to chapter 2A.

## 23 Engine –
initial start-up after overhaul

**1** With the engine refitted in the vehicle, double-check the engine oil and coolant levels. Make a final check that everything has been reconnected, and that there are no tools or rags left in the engine compartment.

**2** Disconnect the wiring plug from the ignition discharge module (refer to Chapter 5B if necessary) and remove the spark plugs.

**3** Turn the engine on the starter until the oil pressure warning light goes out. Refit the spark plugs, and reconnect the ignition discharge module wiring connector.

**4** Start the engine, noting that this may take a little longer than usual, due to the fuel system components having been disturbed.

**5** While the engine is idling, check for fuel, water and oil leaks. Don't be alarmed if there are some odd smells and smoke from parts getting hot and burning off oil deposits.

**6** Assuming all is well, keep the engine idling until hot water is felt circulating through the top hose then switch off the engine.

**7** After a few minutes, recheck the oil and coolant levels as described in *Weekly checks*, and top-up as necessary.

**8** There is no requirement to retighten the cylinder head bolts once the engine has first run after reassembly.

**9** If new pistons, rings or crankshaft bearings have been fitted, the engine must be treated as new, and run-in for the first 500 miles (800 km). *Do not* operate the engine at full-throttle, or allow it to labour at low engine speeds in any gear. It is recommended that the oil and filter be changed at the end of this period.

# Chapter 3
# Cooling, heating and ventilation systems

## Contents

## Degrees of difficulty

| Easy, suitable for novice with little experience  | Fairly easy, suitable for beginner with some experience  | Fairly difficult, suitable for competent DIY mechanic | Difficult, suitable for experienced DIY mechanic | Very difficult, suitable for expert DIY or professional |
|---|---|---|---|---|

## Specifications

### General
Expansion tank cap opening pressure ......................... 1.4 to 1.5 bars

### Thermostat
Opening temperature ...................................... 89°C ± 2°C

### Electric cooling fan
Cut-in temperature:
    Stage 1 ............................................. 100° ± 2°C
    Stage 2 ............................................. 113° ± 2°C
Cut-out temperature:
    Stage 1 ............................................. 96° ± 1°C
    Stage 2 ............................................. 109° ± 1°C

### Coolant temperature sensor

| | Resistance (kOhm) | Voltage |
|---|---|---|
| At -30°C | 20 to 30 | approx. 4.8 |
| At -10°C | 7.0 to 11.4 | approx. 4.5 |
| At 20°C | 2.1 to 2.9 | approx. 3.6 |
| At 40°C | 1.0 to 1.3 | approx. 2.7 |
| At 60°C | 0.565 to 0.670 | approx. 1.9 |
| At 80°C | 0.295 to 0.365 | approx. 1.2 |
| At 90°C | 0.24 to 0.26 | approx. 1.0 |
| At 110°C | 0.14 to 0.16 | approx. 0.65 |

### Torque wrench settings

| | Nm | lbf ft |
|---|---|---|
| Air conditioning compressor mounting: | | |
|     M8 bolts | 24 | 18 |
|     M10 bolts | 40 | 30 |
| Coolant temperature sensor | 13 | 10 |
| Electric cooling fan unit | 8 | 6 |
| Hose to air conditioning compressor | 20 | 15 |
| Rigid heater pipe: | | |
|     To turbocharger | 25 | 18 |
|     To water pump | 20 | 15 |
|     To cylinder block | 10 | 7 |
| Thermostat housing | 22 | 16 |
| Water pump | 22 | 16 |

## 1 General information and precautions

### General information

The cooling system is of pressurised type, comprising a water pump driven by the auxiliary drivebelt, a crossflow radiator, electric cooling fan, a thermostat, heater matrix and all associated hoses. The expansion tank is located on the left-hand side of the engine compartment.

The system functions as follows. Cold coolant in the bottom of the radiator passes through the bottom hose to the water pump, where it is pumped around the cylinder block and head passages. After cooling the cylinder bores, combustion surfaces and valve seats, the coolant reaches the underside of the thermostat, which is initially closed. The coolant passes through the heater, and is returned to the water pump. A small proportion of coolant is channelled direct from the cylinder head through the throttle body, and a further amount is channelled through the turbocharger.

When the engine is cold, the coolant circulates only through the cylinder block, cylinder head, throttle body, heater and turbocharger. When the coolant reaches a predetermined temperature, the thermostat opens, and the coolant passes through the top hose to the radiator. As the coolant circulates through the radiator, it is cooled by the inrush of air when the car is in forward motion, and also by the action of the electric cooling fan when necessary. Upon reaching the bottom of the radiator, the coolant has now cooled, and the cycle is repeated.

When the engine is at normal operating temperature, the coolant expands, and some of it is displaced into the expansion tank. Coolant collects in the tank, and is returned to the radiator when the system cools.

A double-speed electric cooling fan is mounted on the rear of the radiator, and is controlled by a thermostatic switch. At a predetermined coolant temperature, the switch/sensor actuates the fan. On models with air conditioning, two double-speed fans are fitted.

### Precautions

 **Warning: Do not attempt to remove the expansion tank filler cap, or to disturb any part of the cooling system, while the engine is hot, as there is a high risk of scalding. If the expansion tank filler cap must be removed before the engine and radiator have fully cooled (even though this is not recommended), the pressure in the cooling system must first be relieved. Cover the cap with a thick layer of cloth, to avoid scalding, and slowly unscrew the filler cap until a hissing sound is heard. When the** hissing has stopped, indicating that the pressure has reduced, slowly unscrew the filler cap until it can be removed; if more hissing sounds are heard, wait until they have stopped before unscrewing the cap completely. At all times, keep well away from the filler cap opening, and protect your hands.

 **Warning: Do not allow antifreeze to come into contact with your skin, or with the painted surfaces of the vehicle. Rinse off spills immediately, with plenty of water. Never leave antifreeze lying around in an open container, or in a puddle in the driveway or on the garage floor. Children and pets are attracted by its sweet smell, but antifreeze can be fatal if ingested.**

 **Warning: If the engine is hot, the electric cooling fan may start rotating even if the engine is not running. Be careful to keep your hands, hair and any loose clothing well clear when working in the engine compartment.**

 **Warning: Refer to Section 10 for precautions to be observed when working on models with air conditioning.**

## 2 Cooling system hoses – disconnection and renewal

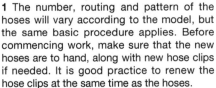

1 The number, routing and pattern of the hoses will vary according to the model, but the same basic procedure applies. Before commencing work, make sure that the new hoses are to hand, along with new hose clips if needed. It is good practice to renew the hose clips at the same time as the hoses.

2 Drain the cooling system, as described in Chapter 1, saving the coolant if it is fit for re-use. Squirt a little penetrating oil onto the hose clips if they are corroded.

3 Loosen and release the hose clips from the hose concerned.

4 Unclip any wires, cables or other hoses which may be attached to the hose being removed. Make notes for reference when reassembling if necessary. The hoses can be removed with relative ease when new, however on an older vehicle they may be stuck to the outlet.

5 If a hose proves stubborn, try to release it by rotating it before attempting to work it off. Take care not to damage the pipe stubs or hoses. Note in particular that the radiator hose stubs are fragile; do not use excessive force when attempting to remove the hoses.

6 Before fitting the new hose, smear the stubs with washing-up liquid or a suitable rubber lubricant to aid fitting. Do not use oil or grease, which may attack the rubber.

7 Fit the hose clips over the ends of the hose, then fit the hose to the stub. Work the hose into position. When satisfied, locate and tighten the hose clips.

8 Refill the cooling system as described in Chapter 1. Run the engine, and check that there are no leaks.

9 Top-up the coolant level if necessary (see *Weekly checks*).

## 3 Radiator – removal, inspection and refitting

**Note:** *If the reason for removing the radiator is to cure a leak, bear in mind that minor leaks can often be cured using a radiator sealant added to the coolant.*

### Removal

1 Drain the cooling system as described in Chapter 1. This procedure includes removing the splash cover from under the radiator. If the coolant is relatively new or in good condition, drain it into a clean container and re-use it.

2 Loosen the clip and disconnect the top hose from the upper left-hand side of the radiator.

3 Remove the electric cooling fan as described in Section 5.

4 On automatic transmission models the fluid oil cooler is incorporated in the radiator. Position suitable containers beneath the radiator and transmission, then disconnect the oil cooler-to-transmission hoses or pipes (as applicable) and allow the hydraulic fluid to drain. Tape over or plug the ends of the hoses/pipes, and discard the O-rings/seals as applicable.

5 Loosen the clip and disconnect the air purge hose from the radiator.

6 Disconnect the wiring from the air conditioning compressor.

7 Loosen the clip and disconnect the bottom hose from the lower right-hand side of the radiator. Alternatively, if the radiator clip is not accessible, disconnect the hose from the coolant pump on the right-hand end of the engine.

8 Release the top mountings and lift the radiator from the lower mounting rubbers. Take care not to damage the radiator cooling fins. On models with an engine oil cooler, unbolt the cooler from the bottom of the radiator.

### Inspection

9 If the radiator has been removed due to suspected blockage, reverse-flush it as described in Chapter 1. Clean dirt and debris from the radiator fins, using an air line or a soft brush.

10 If necessary, a radiator specialist can perform a 'flow test' on the radiator, to establish whether an internal blockage exists. A leaking radiator must be referred to a specialist for permanent repair. Do not attempt to weld or solder a leaking radiator. If the radiator is to be sent for repair, or is to be renewed, remove the cooling fan thermostatic switch.

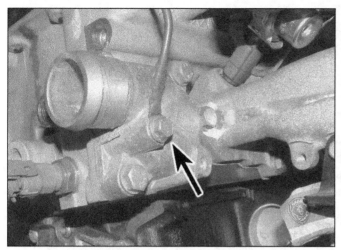

**4.3 Earth cable bolted to the thermostat housing**

**4.5 Thermostat housing bolts**

11 Inspect the condition of the upper and lower radiator mounting rubbers, and renew them if necessary.

### Refitting

12 Before refitting the radiator, fit the bottom hose making sure that the retaining clip will be accessible when in the car. Also, on models with an engine oil cooler, refit the oil cooler to the radiator and tighten the bolts securely.
13 Lower the radiator into the mounting rubbers and reconnect the top mountings.
14 Reconnect the wiring to the air conditioning compressor.
15 Reconnect the air purge hose and tighten the clip.
16 On automatic transmission models, reconnect the oil cooler hoses/pipes together with new O-rings/seals and tighten the mounting nuts.
17 Refit the electric cooling fan with reference to Section 5.
18 Reconnect the top hose and tighten the clip.
19 Refill and bleed the cooling system as described in Chapter 1. Check and if necessary top up the fluid level in the automatic transmission with reference to Chapter 1.
20 Finally, check the cooling system for leaks.

## 4  Thermostat –
removal, testing and refitting

### Removal

1 Drain the cooling system as described in Chapter 1. This procedure includes removing the splash cover from under the radiator. If the coolant is relatively new or in good condition, drain it into a clean container and re-use it.
2 At the left-hand end of the cylinder head, loosen the clip and disconnect the top hose

from the thermostat housing. Move the hose to one side.
3 Unscrew the bolt securing the earth cable to the thermostat housing and move the cable to one side (see illustration).
4 Unbolt the hose support bracket from the thermostat housing.
5 Unscrew and remove the upper and lower mounting bolts, and withdraw the thermostat housing and thermostat from the cylinder head (see illustration). On early models, it is only necessary to loosen the upper bolt as the housing bolt hole is open-ended. Recover the sealing ring.

### Testing

6 A rough test of the thermostat may be made by suspending it with a piece of string in a container full of water. Heat the water to boiling point and check that the thermostat opens. If not, renew it.
7 If a thermometer is available, the precise opening temperature of the thermostat may be determined and compared with the figures given in the Specifications. The opening temperature is normally marked on the thermostat.
8 A thermostat which fails to close as the water cools must also be renewed.

### Refitting

9 Clean the surfaces of the thermostat housing and cylinder head.
10 Locate the thermostat and sealing ring in the cylinder head, making sure that the vent hole is located at the top. The hole is to allow air to purge from the system.
11 Refit the thermostat housing and tighten the bolts to the specified torque.
12 Refit the hose support bracket and tighten the bolts.
13 Refit the earth cable and tighten the bolt.
14 Reconnect the top hose and tighten the clip.
15 Refill and bleed the cooling system with reference to Chapter 1.

## 5  Electric cooling fan –
testing, removal and refitting

### Testing

1 Current supply to the cooling fan is controlled by the DICE Control Module (see Chapter 12). The module is supplied with information from the coolant temperature sensor, air conditioning pressure, vehicle speed and outside temperature. Models with air conditioning are fitted with two cooling fans controlled by the DICE Control Module.
2 If the fan does not appear to work, first check that the wiring plug located near the cooling fan is intact. Note that Saab technicians use an electronic tester to check the DICE Control Module for fault codes, and if necessary a Saab dealer should carry out a diagnostic check to locate the fault.
3 If the wiring is in good condition, use a voltmeter to check that 12 volts is reaching the motor when the engine temperature dictates. The motor itself can be checked by disconnecting it from the wiring loom, and connecting a 12 volt supply directly to it.

### Removal

4 Remove the bypass pipe and valve from the left-hand end of the cylinder head, noting that an O-ring is fitted on the turbo inlet pipe.
5 Disconnect the wiring for the cooling fan(s) from the top of the radiator.
6 Release the clip holding the expansion tank vent hose to the engine compartment crossmember. On automatic transmission models, also release the wiring or pipes from the top of the fan cowling.
7 Unscrew the bolts securing the electric cooling fan unit to the radiator side tanks; a single bolt is located on each side of the unit.
8 Lift the electric cooling fan unit slightly and release it from the lower mounting hooks, then move the unit to one side and withdraw it from the engine compartment.

**9** To remove a motor and fan blade unit, unclip the cowl and wiring, then undo the retaining screws. Where fitted, also remove the resistor.

## Refitting

**10** Refitting is a reversal of removal but tighten the mounting bolts to the specified torque.

## 6 Coolant temperature sensor – testing, removal and refitting

### Testing

**1** The engine coolant temperature sensor is located on the thermostat housing, on the left-hand end of the cylinder head. The resistance of the sensor varies according to the temperature of the coolant.

**2** To test the sensor, disconnect the wiring at the plug then connect an ohmmeter to the sensor **(see illustration)**.

**3** Determine the temperature of the coolant, then compare the resistance with the information given in the Specifications. If the reading is incorrect, the sender must be renewed.

### Removal

**4** Drain the cooling system as described in Chapter 1. Alternatively, the new sensor may be fitted immediately after removing the old one, or a suitable plug may be fitted in the aperture while the sensor is removed. If the

**6.2 Disconnecting the wiring from the engine coolant temperature sensor**

latter option is used, carefully loosen the expansion tank filler cap to release any pressure in the cooling system, then retighten the cap.

**5** With the wiring disconnected, unscrew the sensor and remove it from the cylinder head. If the new sensor is at hand, place a finger over the aperture to prevent loss of coolant from the cylinder head. Where applicable, remove the sealing washer.

### Refitting

**6** Apply some copper grease to its threads, then insert the sensor, together with a new sealing washer where applicable, and tighten it to the specified torque.

**7** Reconnect the wiring.

**8** Refill the cooling system as described in Chapter 1. If the system was not completely drained, top it up (*Weekly checks*).

**7.15 Water pump removed from the engine**

**7.16b The adaptor locates in cut-outs in the water pump body**

**7.16a 'Wide' location tab on the adaptor which locates in the 'wide' cut-out on the water pump**

**7.16c Removing the O-ring seals from the adaptor**

## 7 Water pump – removal and refitting

### Removal

**1** Drain the cooling system as described in Chapter 1. This procedure includes removing the splash cover from under the radiator. If the coolant is relatively new or in good condition, drain it into a clean container and re-use it.

**2** Disconnect the wiring from the mass airflow sensor in the front right-hand corner of the engine compartment, then loosen the clips and remove the air hose complete with airflow sensor.

**3** Remove the auxiliary drivebelt as described in Chapter 1.

**4** Disconnect the crankcase ventilation hose and release it from the turbocharger inlet pipe and camshaft cover.

**5** Disconnect the wiring from the turbocharger boost pressure control valve.

**6** Unbolt the engine lifting eye from the cylinder head.

**7** Disconnect the hoses from the turbocharger wastegate valve.

**8** Disconnect the turbocharger bypass pipe and valve, noting that there is an O-ring at the connection to the turbo inlet pipe.

**9** Unscrew the nut and unclip the heat shield from the exhaust manifold.

**10** Disconnect the crankcase ventilation hose at the quick-release coupling.

**11** Remove the turbocharger inlet pipe, and cover the inlet aperture with tape or a plastic bag to prevent entry of dust and dirt.

**12** Refer to Chapter 10 and remove the power steering pump, however, do not disconnect the fluid hoses.

**13** Loosen the clip and disconnect the inlet hose from the water pump.

**14** Unscrew the two bolts from the left-hand end of the cylinder block, and remove the rigid heater return pipe from the water pump. Recover the O-ring from the water pump. Also, unscrew the bolt and remove the rigid heater supply pipe support from the turbocharger.

**15** Unscrew the three coolant pump mounting bolts and carefully ease the pump from the bracket and connecting adaptor on the cylinder block **(see illustration)**.

**16** Remove the adaptor from the cylinder block, and examine the O-ring seals for deterioration. It is recommended that new seals are fitted. Note that on later models, the adaptor has two location tabs of different widths which locate in the water pump; the adaptor can only be fitted one way round; this ensures the correct direction of the internal channel **(see illustrations)**.

**17** The water pump may be obtained as a complete unit, or alternatively just the impeller/pulley section may be obtained. To separate the two sections, first mark them in relation to each other. Unscrew the bolts and separate the halves (see illustrations).

### Refitting

**18** If separated, clean the mating faces and assemble the halves together with a new gasket. Insert the bolts and tighten securely.
**19** Refit the adaptor to the cylinder block together with new O-rings. Apply a little petroleum jelly to the O-rings to help them enter the cylinder block. On later models, make sure the adaptor is positioned correctly.
**20** Locate the water pump on the adaptor then insert the bolts and tighten to the specified torque.
**21** Refit the rigid heater pipes together with a new O-ring on the return pipe, and also refit the pipe support. Tighten the retaining bolts to the specified torque.
**22** Reconnect the inlet hose to the water pump and tighten the clip.
**23** Refit the power steering pump with reference to Chapter 10.
**24** Refit the turbocharger inlet pipe.
**25** Reconnect the crankcase ventilation hose at the quick-release coupling.
**26** Refit the heat shield to the exhaust manifold.
**27** Reconnect the turbocharger bypass pipe and valve together with a new O-ring at the connection to the turbo inlet pipe.
**28** Reconnect the hoses to the turbocharger wastegate valve.
**29** Refit the engine lifting eye to the cylinder head and tighten the bolt.
**30** Reconnect the wiring to the turbocharger boost pressure control valve.
**31** Reconnect the crankcase ventilation hose to the turbocharger inlet pipe and camshaft cover.
**32** Refit the auxiliary drivebelt as described in Chapter 1.
**33** Refit the air hose and airflow sensor, and reconnect the wiring.
**34** Refit the splash cover beneath the radiator.
**35** Refill and bleed the cooling system with reference to Chapter 1.

## 8  Heating and ventilation system – general information

**1** Three types of heating/ventilation system are fitted – the Standard Manual Climate Control (MCC) system, the Standard Air Conditioning (A/C) system, and the Automatic Climate Control (ACC) system which maintains the temperature inside the car at a selected temperature, regardless of the temperature outside the car (see illustration). The basic heating/ventilation unit is common to all versions, and consists of air ducting from the centrally-located heater assembly to a central vent and two side vents, with an extension leading from the bottom of the

**7.17a  Unscrew the bolts . . .**

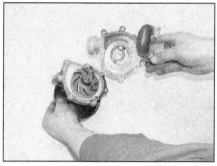

**7.17b  . . . and separate the halves of the water pump**

heater through the centre console to the rear passenger footwell areas. A four-speed heater blower motor is fitted.
**2** The heating and ventilation controls are mounted in the centre of the facia. Cable-controlled flap valves are contained in the air distribution housing, to divert the air to the various ducts and vents.
**3** Cold air enters the system through the grille at the bottom of the windscreen. If required,

the airflow is boosted by the blower, and then flows through the various ducts, according to the settings of the controls. Stale air is expelled through ducts at the rear of the vehicle. If warm air is required, the cold air is passed over the heater matrix, which is heated by the engine coolant.
**4** On models fitted with air conditioning, a recirculation switch enables the outside air supply to be closed off, while the air inside the

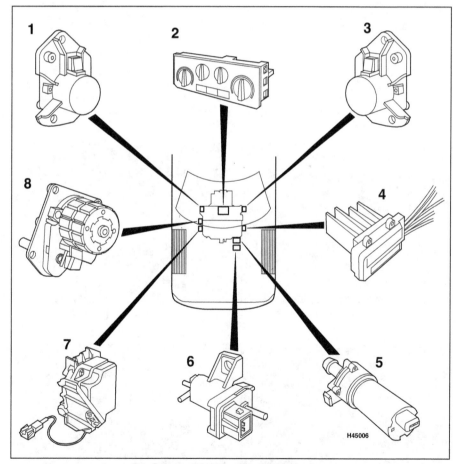

**8.1  Standard heating/ventilation system**

| | |
|---|---|
| 1  *Right-hand mixed air stepping motor* | 5  *Circulation pump (certain versions only)* |
| 2  *Control module* | 6  *Heat exchanger shut-off valve* |
| 3  *Left-hand mixed air stepping motor* | 7  *Air recirculation motor* |
| 4  *Ventilation fan control* | 8  *Air distribution stepping motor* |

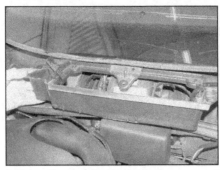

9.3a Unscrew the nuts . . .

9.3b . . . then unclip the frame from around the blower motor

9.3c Removing the weatherstrip from the groove

9.4 Remove the wiper arm bracket . . .

9.5 . . . release the wiring harness from the blower motor cover . . .

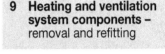

### 9 Heating and ventilation system components – removal and refitting

## Heater blower motor

1 Set the air recirculation control to OFF.
2 Remove the wiper motor and linkage as described in Chapter 12.
3 Unscrew the nuts then unclip the frame from around the blower motor. If necessary, remove the weatherstrip from the groove (see illustrations).
4 Unbolt and remove the wiper arm bracket (see illustration).
5 Release the wiring harness from the blower motor cover (see illustration).
6 Undo the screws and remove the blower motor cover by lifting it to one side, at the same time releasing the wiring (see illustrations).
7 Lift out the blower motor sufficiently to disconnect the wiring. Also cut the plastic cable tie and release the wiring.
8 Withdraw the blower motor from the bulkhead. On right-hand drive models, there may be insufficient clearance between the windscreen and engine compartment rear panel, in which case the panel must be temporarily pulled back using a ratchet strap between the panel and front crossmember (see illustration).
9 Refitting is a reversal of removal, but make sure that the wiring is clear of the fan before refitting the cover.

vehicle is recirculated. This can be useful to prevent unpleasant odours entering from outside the vehicle, but should only be used briefly, as the recirculated air inside the vehicle will soon become stale.

5 A solar sensor located on top of the facia panel detects increased solar radiation, and increases the speed of the blower motor. This is necessary in order to increase the throughput of air in the vehicle.

9.6a . . . undo the upper screws . . .

9.6b . . . and lower screws . . .

9.6c . . . and remove the blower motor cover . . .

9.6d . . . at the same time releasing the wiring

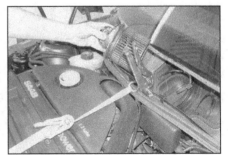

9.8 Using a ratchet strap to pull back the panel when removing the heater blower motor

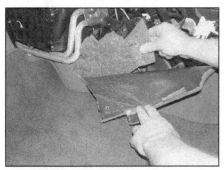

**9.12 Removing the console side trim and packing**

**9.13a Undo the screws . . .**

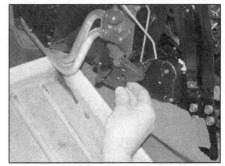

**9.13b . . . and remove the plastic bracket from the side of the heater**

**9.14a Undo the centre screw . . .**

**9.14b . . . remove the clamp plate . . .**

**9.14c . . . and remove the O-ring seals**

## Heater matrix

**10** Drain the cooling system as described in Chapter 1. This procedure includes removing the splash cover from under the radiator. If the coolant is relatively new or in good condition, drain it into a clean container and re-use it.

**11** At the rear of the engine compartment, identify the two heater hoses for position, then disconnect them from the heater pipes. Place a container beneath the pipes to catch spilt coolant. To remove most of the coolant from the matrix, blow through one of the pipes, and the coolant will escape from the other.

**12** Remove the glovebox and centre console side trim and packing with reference to Chapter 11 **(see illustration)**.

**13** On right-hand drive models, undo the screws and remove the plastic bracket from the side of the heater **(see illustrations)**. On left-hand drive models, remove the air vent

**9.15 Removing the matrix from the heater housing**

from the air duct on the right-hand side of the heater unit, however, do not remove the seal.

**14** Undo the centre screw and remove the clamp plate, then withdraw the two pipes from the matrix. Recover the O-ring seals and check them for deterioration, renewing them as necessary **(see illustrations)**.

**15** Undo the four screws and carefully slide the heater matrix from the housing **(see illustration)**.

**16** Refitting is a reversal of removal, but renew the O-rings and finally refill the cooling system with reference to Chapter 1.

## Heater unit

**17** On models with air conditioning, the refrigerant must be evacuated by a qualified engineer.

⚠ *Warning: Do not attempt to carry out this work yourself, as it is potentially dangerous.*

**18** Drain the cooling system as described in Chapter 1. This procedure includes removing the splash cover from under the radiator. If the coolant is relatively new or in good condition, drain it into a clean container and re-use it.

**19** At the rear of the engine compartment, identify the two heater hoses for position, then disconnect them from the heater pipes. Place a container beneath the pipes to catch spilt coolant. To remove most of the coolant from the matrix, blow through one of the pipes, and the coolant will escape from the other.

**20** Remove the centre console and front seats as described in Chapter 11.

**21** Fold up the carpet and remove the air ducts located under the front seat positions.

**22** Remove the facia panel as described in Chapter 11.

**23** Unscrew the nuts and remove the heater earth cables from the facia mounting crossmember. Also unscrew the nuts and detach the wiring loom support from the crossmember **(see illustration)**. Cut the plastic cable ties securing the wiring harness as required.

**24** Unscrew the nuts and remove the central wiring conduit.

**25** Unscrew the nuts and remove the driver's knee shield.

**26** Unbolt the relay holder and place to one side.

**27** Remove the steering column as described in Chapter 10.

**28** Unbolt and remove the pedal bracket, the two braces supporting the facia mounting crossmember, and the centre mounting from the crossmember.

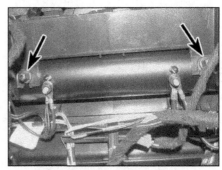

**9.23 Nuts securing the wiring loom support to the crossmember**

9.29 Facia mounting crossmember side retaining bolts

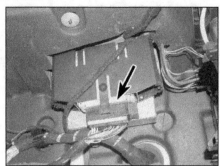

9.30a Disconnect the wiring from the automatic transmission control module, located next to the Trionic engine management ECU mounting box

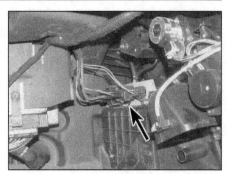

9.30b Disconnect the wiring from the side of the heater unit

29 Unbolt the facia mounting crossmember and withdraw it through one of the front door apertures (see illustration).

30 On automatic transmission models remove the automatic transmission control module from its mounting box, and disconnect the upper wiring, then disconnect the wiring from the side of the heater unit and place the module to one side (see illustrations).

31 In the engine compartment, remove the air pipe leading from the intercooler to the throttle body.

32 Remove the turbocharger bypass valve solenoid valve holder from the bulkhead as follows. Remove the cover, disconnect the wiring and unbolt the holder.

33 Either remove the heater matrix as described earlier, or disconnect the two pipes from the matrix leaving it fitted to the heater unit.

34 Unbolt and remove the expansion valve.

35 Disconnect the drain hoses from the heater unit.

36 Working in the engine compartment, undo the three heater unit mounting bolts from the bulkhead.

37 Inside the vehicle, place cloth rags on the floor to soak up spilled coolant, then raise the rear of the heater unit and withdraw it past the gear selector housing. Remove it through one of the front door apertures.

38 Refitting is a reversal of removal, but refill the cooling system as described in Chapter 1. Have the air conditioning system recharged by a qualified engineer.

### Manual Climate Control Module

39 Remove the radio/cassette unit as described in Chapter 12.

40 Reach in through the radio aperture and push out the manual climate control unit. It is retained by plastic tabs on each side of the unit.

41 Disconnect the wiring and withdraw the unit from the facia.

42 If necessary, remove the control knobs by carefully pulling them from their spindles. The bulbholders may also be twisted from the rear of the unit.

43 Refitting is a reversal of removal.

### Automatic Climate Control Module

44 Remove the radio/cassette unit as described in Chapter 12.

45 Reach in through the radio aperture and push out the automatic climate control unit. It is retained by plastic tabs on each side of the unit (see illustration).

46 Disconnect the wiring and withdraw the unit from the facia (see illustration).

47 Refitting is a reversal of removal, but on completion calibrate the ACC system by pressing the AUTO and OFF buttons simultaneously.

### Solar sensor

48 At the centre top of the facia panel, slide the solar sensor cover forwards to release it from the facia (see illustration).

49 Disconnect the wiring and remove the anti-theft LED (see illustration).

50 With the cover on the bench, depress and twist the solar sensor anti-clockwise to remove it from the cover (see illustration).

9.45 Remove the automatic climate control (ACC) module . . .

9.46 . . . and disconnect the wiring

9.48 Slide the solar sensor cover forwards and lift from the facia

9.49 Disconnect the LED and sensor wiring

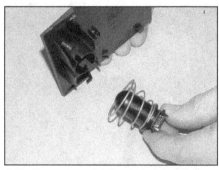

9.50 Depress and twist the solar sensor to remove it from the cover

**51** Refitting is a reversal of removal, but on completion calibrate the ACC system by pressing the AUTO and OFF buttons simultaneously.

### Interior temperature sensor

**52** Carefully prise out the roof console lens with a screwdriver.
**53** Undo the screw and remove the sensor from the clips.
**54** Disconnect the wiring.
**55** Refitting is a reversal of removal, but on completion calibrate the ACC system by pressing the AUTO and OFF buttons simultaneously.

### Mixed air sensor

#### Driver's side

**56** Remove the facia lower trim panel, then undo the screws and remove the datalink connector and disconnect the floor lighting wiring.
**57** Pull out the sensor from the air duct leading to the lower panel.
**58** Remove the radio/cassette unit and control panel as described in Chapter 12 and this Section.
**59** Disconnect the black upper wiring plug, then note the locations of the sensor pins and remove them from the connector. **Note:** *It may be necessary to cut the wires and fit new ones on refitting.*
**60** Refitting is a reversal of removal, but on completion calibrate the ACC system by pressing the AUTO and OFF buttons simultaneously.

#### Passenger's side

**61** Remove the glovebox and the centre console side trim as described in Chapter 11.
**62** Pull out the sensor from the air duct leading to the lower panel.
**63** Remove the radio/cassette unit and control panel as described in Chapter 12 and this Section.
**64** Disconnect the grey lower wiring plug, then note the locations of the sensor pins and remove them from the connector. **Note:** *It may be necessary to cut the wires and fit new ones on refitting.*
**65** Refitting is a reversal of removal, but on completion calibrate the ACC system by pressing the AUTO and OFF buttons simultaneously.

### Air distribution stepping motor

**66** Remove the glovebox and the centre console side trim as described in Chapter 11.
**67** Undo the screws and remove the stepping motor.
**68** Disconnect the wiring.
**69** Refitting is a reversal of removal, but on completion calibrate the ACC system by pressing the AUTO and OFF buttons simultaneously.

### Air blending stepping motor

#### Driver's side

**70** Set the air blending control to MAX HEAT or MAX COLD before commencing work.
**71** Remove the facia lower trim panel, then undo the screws and remove the datalink connector and disconnect the floor lighting wiring.
**72** Disconnect the wiring.
**73** Undo the screws and withdraw the air blending stepping motor.
**74** Refitting is a reversal of removal, but when fitting the stepping motor, hold the flap by the floor air duct to prevent the flap coming out of its mounting. On completion calibrate the ACC system by pressing the AUTO and OFF buttons simultaneously.

#### Passenger's side

**75** Set the air blending control to MAX HEAT or MAX COLD before commencing work.
**76** Remove the glovebox and the centre console side trim as described in Chapter 11.
**77** Disconnect the wiring.
**78** Undo the screws and withdraw the air blending stepping motor.
**79** Refitting is a reversal of removal, but on completion calibrate the ACC system by pressing the AUTO and OFF buttons simultaneously.

### Heater blower motor control unit

**Note:** *The following sub-section describes removal of the control unit on a left-hand drive model. The procedure is similar for a right-hand drive model.*
**80** The control unit is located on the right-hand side of the heater assembly. First, remove the facia lower trim panel from the driver's side, then undo the screws and remove the diagnostic/datalink connector and disconnect the floor lighting wiring.
**81** Unhook the inner cable end fitting from the top of the accelerator pedal, then unscrew the nuts and remove the pedal assembly complete.
**82** Remove the glovebox as described in Chapter 11.
**83** Disconnect the two front wiring plugs located above the pollen filter. Detach the plugs from the plate and cut the plastic cable tie.
**84** Temporarily switch on the ignition and set the air recirculation flap to OFF, then switch off the ignition.
**85** Remove the windscreen wiper arms (see Chapter 12), and remove the rubber seals from the spindles.
**86** Pull off the weatherstrip located at the rear of the engine compartment, then undo the screws and remove the scuttle cover by lifting its front edge and pulling it from the rear retaining clips.
**87** Remove the wiper motor and linkage as described in Chapter 12.

**88** Unscrew the nuts then unclip the frame from around the blower motor.
**89** Unbolt and remove the wiper arm bracket.
**90** Release the wiring harness from the blower motor cover.
**91** Unbolt and remove the blower motor cover by lifting it to one side.
**92** Lift out the blower motor sufficient to disconnect the wiring. Also cut the plastic cable tie and release the wiring.
**93** Note the location of the wiring harness on the blower motor control unit, then pull it up together with the rubber seal and cut the plastic cable tie.
**94** Unbolt and remove the control unit.
**95** Refitting is a reversal of removal.

## 10 Air conditioning system – general information and precautions

### General information

**1** Air conditioning is available as an option on all models. It enables the temperature of air inside the car to be lowered, and also dehumidifies the air, which makes for rapid demisting and increased comfort.
**2** The cooling side of the system works in the same way as a domestic refrigerator. Refrigerant gas is drawn into a belt-driven compressor, and passes into a condenser mounted in front of the radiator, where it loses heat and becomes liquid. The liquid passes through a receiver and expansion valve to an evaporator, where it changes from liquid under high pressure to gas under low pressure. This change is accompanied by a drop in temperature, which cools the

*Many car accessory shops sell one-shot air conditioning recharge aerosols. These generally contain refrigerant, compressor oil, leak sealer and system conditioner. Some also have a dye to help pinpoint leaks.*

⚠️ *Warning: These products must only be used as directed by the manufacturer, and do not remove the need for regular maintenance.*

evaporator. The refrigerant returns to the compressor, and the cycle begins again.

3 Air drawn through the evaporator passes to the air distribution unit. The air conditioning system is switched on with the switch located on the heater panel.

4 The heating side of the system works in the same way as on models without air conditioning.

5 The compressor operation is controlled by an electromagnetic clutch on the drive pulley. Any problems with the system should be referred to a Saab dealer.

## Precautions

6 When working on the air conditioning system, it is necessary to observe special precautions. If for any reason the system must be disconnected, entrust this task to your Saab dealer or a refrigeration engineer.

 *Warning: The refrigeration circuit contains a liquid refrigerant under pressure, and it is therefore dangerous to disconnect any part of the system without specialised knowledge and equipment. The refrigerant is potentially dangerous, and should only be handled by qualified persons. If it is splashed onto the skin, it can cause frostbite. It is not itself poisonous, but in the presence of a naked flame (including a cigarette) it forms a poisonous gas. Uncontrolled discharging of the refrigerant is dangerous, and potentially damaging to the environment. Do not operate the air conditioning system if it is known to be short of refrigerant, as this may damage the compressor.*

## 11 Air conditioning system components – removal and refitting

 *Warning: Do not attempt to open the refrigerant circuit. Refer to the precautions given in Section 10.*

1 The only operation which can be carried out easily without discharging the refrigerant is renewal of the compressor drivebelt. This is described in Chapter 1. All other operations must be referred to a Saab dealer or an air conditioning specialist.

2 If necessary for access to other components, the compressor can be unbolted and moved aside, **without** disconnecting its flexible hoses, after removing the drivebelt.

3 Access to the condenser is gained by removing the grille and both headlight units.

# Chapter 4 Part A:
# Fuel and exhaust systems

## Contents

## Degrees of difficulty

| Easy, suitable for novice with little experience  | Fairly easy, suitable for beginner with some experience  | Fairly difficult, suitable for competent DIY mechanic | Difficult, suitable for experienced DIY mechanic | Very difficult, suitable for expert DIY or professional |
|---|---|---|---|---|

## Specifications

### System type
All models ........................................ Saab Trionic SFi engine management system

### Manifold absolute pressure (MAP) sensor
| Pressure: | Voltage (approx) |
|---|---|
| -0.75 bar | 0.9 |
| -0.50 bar | 1.3 |
| 0 bar | 2.1 |
| 0.25 bar | 2.5 |
| 0.50 bar | 2.9 |
| 0.75 bar | 3.3 |
| Manifold absolute pressure (MAP) sensor – supply voltage | 5 volts |

### Intake air temperature (IAC) sensor
| Temperature (°C): | Voltage (approx) |
|---|---|
| -30 | 4.5 |
| -10 | 3.9 |
| 20 | 2.4 |
| 40 | 1.5 |
| 60 | 0.9 |
| 80 | 0.54 |
| 90 | 0.41 |
| Intake air temperature (IAC) sensor – supply voltage | 5 volts |

### Throttle body
Throttle motor – pins 10 and 5 at 20°C ...................... 1.13 ± 0.5 ohms
Throttle position sensor 1:
  Closed – pins 6 and 9 ................................... 0.065 to 1.090 volts
  Fully open – pins 6 and 9 ............................... 3.930 to 4.775 volts
Throttle position sensor 2:
  Closed – pins 8 and 9 ................................... 3.910 to 4.935 volts
  Fully open – pins 8 and 9 ............................... 0.025 to 1.070 volts

### Pedal switch
Pedal position sensor 1:
  Released – pins 1 and 9 ................................. 3.990 to 4.645 volts
  Fully depressed – pins 1 and 9 .......................... 0.400 to 1.055 volts
Pedal position sensor 2:
  Released – pins 3 and 9 ................................. 0.355 to 1.010 volts
  Fully depressed – pins 3 and 9 .......................... 3.945 to 4.600 volts

## Crankshaft position sensor
Resistance (pins 1 and 2) at 20°C ........................... 860 ± 90 ohms

## Fuel pressure regulator
Pressure ................................................. 3.0 ± 0.1 bars

## Injectors
Type ..................................................... Bosch EV6 E
Version .................................................. 4 hole nozzle
Nozzle colour code:
  1998/1999
    B205 ............................................. green
    B205 (with tuning kit) ........................... red
    B235 ............................................. red
  2000:
    B205 ............................................. green
    B205 (with tuning kit) ........................... red
    B235 ............................................. brown
  2001-on:
    All engines ...................................... brown
Resistance at 20°C ....................................... 15.95 ± 0.8 ohms
Flow rating (at 3 bar fuel pressure):
  B205 (up to 2000) ................................... 126 ± 5 ml/30 seconds
  B205 (2001-on) ...................................... 176 ± 7 ml/30 seconds
  B235 ................................................ 176 ± 7 ml/30 seconds
Maximum flow difference between injectors:
  B205 (up to 2000) ................................... 10 ml
  B235 (up to 2000) ................................... 14 ml
  B205/B235 (2001 on) ................................. 20 ml

## Idle air control valve
Resistance at 20°C ....................................... 8.0 ± 1 ohms
Fuel filter capacity ..................................... 0.6 litres

## Fuel pump
Type ..................................................... Electric immersed in fuel tank
Capacity at 3.0 bars ..................................... 700 ml/30 seconds (minimum)
Resistance (ohms):
  Fuel level sensor in full position .................. 425 ± 6.5
  Fuel level sensor in empty position ................. 50 ± 1.5

## Turbocharger
Type:
  B205E ............................................... Garrett GT17
    Pressure ......................................... 0.40 ± 0.03 bars
  B235E ............................................... Garrett GT17
    Pressure ......................................... 0.40 ± 0.03 bars
  B235R ............................................... Mitsubushi TD04HL-15T-5
    Pressure ......................................... 0.45 ± 0.03 bars
  B235R (305 bhp) ..................................... Garrett TB28
    Pressure ......................................... 0.45 ± 0.03 bars
Wastegate preload (all types) ............................ 2.0 mm
Turbo shaft play (axial) ................................. 0.036 to 0.091 mm

## Fuel system
System pressure .......................................... 3.0 bars
Residual pressure (after 20 mins) ........................ 2.3 bars (min)

## Recommended fuel
2.0t and 2.3t ............................................ 95 RON unleaded
2.3 Turbo HOT (Aero) and 2.3T ............................ 98 RON unleaded

## Idle speed
All models ............................................... Controlled by ECM (not adjustable)

## Exhaust gas CO content
All models ............................................... Controlled by ECM (not adjustable)

## Torque wrench settings

| | Nm | lbf ft |
|---|---|---|
| Coolant temperature sensor | 13 | 10 |
| Exhaust heat shield | 20 | 15 |
| Exhaust manifold to cylinder head | 25 | 18 |
| Exhaust manifold-to-turbocharger nuts | 24 | 18 |
| Exhaust pipe to turbocharger | 24 | 18 |
| Exhaust system joint nuts and bolts | 22 | 16 |
| Fuel filter banjo fittings | 21 | 15 |
| Fuel pump screw ring | 75 | 55 |
| Intake manifold | 24 | 18 |
| Oxygen sensor | 55 | 41 |
| Throttle body to intake manifold | 8 | 6 |
| Turbocharger to exhaust manifold | 24 | 18 |

## 1 General information and precautions

The fuel supply system consists of a fuel tank mounted under the rear of the car (with an electric fuel pump immersed in it), a fuel filter, and the fuel feed and return lines. The fuel pump supplies fuel to the fuel rail, which acts as a reservoir for the four fuel injectors which inject fuel into the intake tracts. A fuel filter is incorporated in the feed line from the pump to the fuel rail to ensure that the fuel supplied to the injectors is clean. The filter is mounted adjacent to the fuel tank.

The engine management system is of Saab Trionic type, refer to the relevant Sections for further information on the operation of the system.

A cruise control system is fitted as standard equipment on most of the later Saab models, and is available as an option on earlier models.

The turbocharger fitted is of a water-cooled type. Boost pressure is controlled by the Saab Trionic engine management.

### Precautions

• Many of the procedures in this Chapter require the disconnection of fuel lines, which may result in some fuel spillage. Before carrying out any operation on the fuel system, refer to Section 8. See the precautions given in 'Safety first!' at the front of this manual and follow them implicitly. Petrol is a highly-dangerous and volatile liquid, and the precautions necessary when handling it cannot be overstressed.

## 2 Air cleaner assembly – removal and refitting

### Removal

1 Remove the front grille as described in Chapter 11.
2 Remove the right-hand headlight and indicator units as described in Chapter 12.
3 Slacken the retaining clip, and disconnect the intake pipe from the top of the air cleaner assembly (see illustration 2.5).
4 Apply the handbrake, then jack up the front of the car and support on axle stands (see Jacking and vehicle support). Remove the right-hand front wheel, undo the retaining screws and remove the wheel arch liner.
5 From under the vehicle, slacken the retaining clip, and disconnect the intake pipe from the bottom of the air cleaner assembly (see illustration).
6 Unscrew the lower mounting nuts (see illustration), and lower the air cleaner assembly from under the inner wing. Note: It may be necessary to remove a couple of retaining screws from the right-hand side of the front bumper to allow removal of the air cleaner assembly.
7 If required, undo the retaining bolt(s) and remove the bracket for the air intake pipe (see illustration), then withdraw the air intake pipe from across the front of the radiator.

 Warning: Do not run the engine with the air cleaner housing and/or ducting removed – the depression at the turbocharger intake may increase very suddenly if the engine speed is raised above idle.

### Refitting

8 Refitting is a reversal of the removal procedure. Note: Make sure the peg at the top of the air cleaner assembly, locates in the hole in the inner wing panel.

## 3 Accelerator cable – removal and refitting

### Removal

1 From inside the vehicle, undo the retaining screws and withdraw the facia lower panel from the driver's footwell as described in Chapter 11.
2 While holding the accelerator pedal, slide the bush backwards and disconnect the cable from the top of the accelerator pedal (see illustration).
3 Working under the bonnet, remove the engine oil filler cap/dipstick then unclip and remove the cover from the top of the engine. Undo the retaining bolts and remove the cover from the throttle linkage (see illustrations).
4 Attach a piece of string (or wire) to the end of the accelerator cable inside the vehicle, then pull the cable (with string or wire connected) into the engine compartment.

2.5 Slacken the retaining clips (arrowed) and disconnect the intake pipes

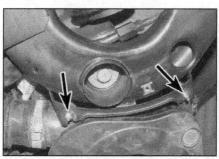

2.6 Remove the lower mounting nuts (arrowed) and withdraw the air cleaner housing

2.7 Undo the retaining bolt (arrowed) from the air intake pipe

**3.2 Disconnect the inner cable (arrowed) from the top of the accelerator pedal**

**3.3b . . . and remove the throttle linkage cover**

Disconnect the string (or wire) and leave it through the bulkhead for refitting.

**5** Rotate the throttle housing sector and disconnect the inner cable.

**6** Pull out the locking clip (noting its position in the grooves on the sleeve), and disconnect the accelerator outer cable from the bracket on the throttle housing **(see illustration)**.

### Refitting

**7** Apply a little petroleum jelly to the rubber bush (grommet) in the bulkhead, connect the string (or wire) to the accelerator cable, and draw it back through the bulkhead.

**8** Untie the string, and reconnect the cable and bushing to the accelerator pedal inside the car.

**9** Refit the accelerator outer cable to the bracket on the throttle housing, and secure with the locking clip in the position noted on removal.

**4.3a Undo the two retaining bolts (arrowed) . . .**

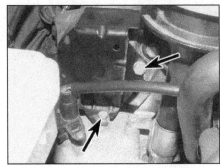

**3.3a Undo the two bolts (arrowed) . . .**

**3.6 Remove the outer cable clip (arrowed) securing the accelerator cable to the bracket**

**10** Reconnect the inner cable to the throttle housing sector. If there is too much slack in the inner cable, move the locking clip further along the grooves in the outer cable sleeve.

**11** Refit the inner facia lower trim panel, this is a reversal of the removal procedure; see Chapter 11.

**12** Refit the engine upper cover and throttle valve cover, this is a reversal of the removal procedure.

### 4 Accelerator pedal – removal and refitting

### Removal

**1** From inside the vehicle, undo the retaining screws and withdraw the facia lower panel from the driver's footwell as described in Chapter 11.

**4.3b . . . then remove the three pedal securing nuts (arrowed)**

**2** While holding the accelerator pedal, slide the bush backwards and disconnect the cable from the top of the accelerator pedal.

**3** Unscrew the bolts on the pedal bracket, and remove the pedal **(see illustrations)**.

### Refitting

**4** Refitting is a reversal of removal, but make sure that the mounting bolts are tightened securely. If necessary, adjust the accelerator cable as described in Section 3, paragraph 10.

### 5 Cruise control system – description and component renewal

### Description

**1** The cruise control system allows the driver to preselect the speed of the car and then release the accelerator pedal. The cruise control system then adjusts the throttle automatically to maintain a constant road speed. The system is deactivated when either the clutch or brake pedals are depressed, when neutral gear is selected (models with automatic transmission) or when the main cruise control switch is switched off. The system has a memory function which allows a preselected cruising speed to be resumed if the operation of the cruise control has been interrupted by depressing the brake or clutch pedals.

**2** When the cruise control system is active, the preselected road speed may be increased or decreased in small increments, by means of the multi-function cruise control system switch.

**3** In the event of a fault in the cruise control system, first check all relevant wiring for security. Further testing is best left to a Saab dealer, who will have the necessary diagnostic equipment to find the fault quickly.

**4** The main components of the system are as follows:

a) **Electronic Control Module (ECM):** *The module is supplied with the speed of the car by signals sent from the speedometer in the instrument panel. The system is not operative at speeds below 25 mph. When the cruise control system is active, the engine management system ECM is informed of this fact by a signal, to ensure smoother control of the car's speed. The ECM determines the vehicle's road speed from a signal supplied by the Anti-lock Braking System (ABS) ECM.*

b) **Switches:** *the main multi-function control switch for the cruise control system is integral with the steering column left-hand stalk switch. Switches mounted behind the facia and operated by the brake and clutch pedals deactivate the system when either pedal is depressed. As a fail-safe, the brake pedal cruise control switch is earthed through the brake stop-light bulbs, via the main stop-light switch – if* this circuit develops a fault, the cruise control system will not operate.

c) *Indicator light*: the CRUISE indicator light on the instrument panel is illuminated whenever the cruise control system is operating.

## Component renewal

### Electronic Control Module

**5** The cruise control uses the same electronic control module as the engine management system. Refer to the information given in Section 14 of this Chapter, for the removal and refitting procedure.

### Multi-function control switch

**6** Refer to the information given in Chapter 12, Section 4, for the removal of the steering column switch.

### Stop-light switch

**7** Refer to the information given in Chapter 9.

### Pedal switches

**8** From inside the vehicle, undo the retaining screws and withdraw the facia lower panel from the drivers footwell as described in Chapter 11.

**9** Reach behind the facia and unplug the wiring from the relevant switch.

**10** Carefully prise the switch from its mounting bracket.

**11** To refit the switch, carefully pull the switch plunger out, then depress the brake/clutch pedal (as applicable). Insert the switch into its mounting bracket, and slowly release the pedal until it contacts the switch plunger. Reconnect the wiring securely.

## 6  Unleaded petrol – general information and usage

**Note:** *The information given in this Chapter is correct at the time of writing, and applies only to fuels currently available in the UK. If updated information is thought to be required, check with a Saab dealer. If travelling abroad, consult one of the motoring organisations (or a similar authority) for advice on the petrols available, and their suitability for your vehicle.*

**1** The fuel recommended by Saab is given in the Specifications at the start of this Chapter.

**2** RON and MON are different testing standards; RON stands for Research Octane Number (also written as RM), while MON stands for Motor Octane Number (also written as MM).

**3** All Saab 9-5 models covered in this manual are designed to run on unleaded fuel with a minimum octane rating of 91 RON; 95 RON and 98 RON unleaded fuel is recommended. All models are equipped with a catalytic converter, and must be run on unleaded fuel **only**. Under no circumstances should leaded fuel/LRP be used, as this will damage the catalytic converter.

## 7  Engine management system – general information

The Saab Trionic engine management system controls three functions of the engine from a single electronic control unit (ECM). The three functions comprise the fuel injection system, ignition system, and the turbocharger boost control system. Details of the components related to the ignition function are given in Chapter 5B.

The system is microprocessor-controlled, and the fuel system provides the correct amount of fuel necessary for complete combustion under all engine conditions. Data from various sensors is processed in the ECM, in order to determine the opening period of the fuel injectors for the exact amount of fuel to be injected into the intake manifold.

The system is of sequential type, where fuel is injected in sequence with the engine's firing order. Conventional sequential fuel injection systems requires a camshaft sensor, which works in conjunction with the crankshaft position sensor to indicate which cylinder at TDC is on its compression stroke and which is on its exhaust stroke. The Trionic system has no camshaft sensor, it determines each cylinder's stroke by applying a small, direct current voltage across each spark plug. When a cylinder on its combustion stroke approaches TDC, this voltage causes an ionisation current to flow across the terminals of the spark plug, thus indicating which cylinder requires fuel injection and ignition next. Sequential control of the ignition timing to control combustion knock is achieved in the same manner (see Chapter 5B).

When the ignition is initially switched on and after the fuel pump is operating, all the injectors operate simultaneously for a short period; this helps to minimise cold start cranking times.

The main components of the system are as follows:

a) *ECM*: the electronic control module controls the entire operation of the fuel injection system, ignition system, cruise control and turbocharger boost control system.

b) *Crankshaft position sensor*: the crankshaft position sensor provides a datum for the ECM to calculate the position of the crankshaft in relation to TDC. The sensor is triggered by a reluctor disc that rotates inside the crankcase.

c) *Manifold absolute pressure (MAP) sensor*: the MAP sensor provides a voltage to the ECM, proportional to the pressure in the intake manifold.

d) *Charge air (boost) pressure/temperature sensor*: the air pressure/temperature sensor is integrated into one component and informs the ECM of the pressure and temperature of the air in the hose between the intercooler and the throttle body.

e) *Engine coolant temperature sensor*: the engine coolant temperature sensor informs the ECM of the engine temperature.

f) *Mass airflow sensor*: is located behind the right-hand headlamp. The engine load is measured by means of a hot-film type air mass flow meter, rather than by measuring intake manifold depression. The meter houses a heated metal filament which is mounted in the flow of the air intake. The temperature reduction in the wire caused by the flow of air over it causes a change in electrical resistance, which is converted to a variable voltage output signal. Measuring air mass flow, rather than volume flow compensates for the changes in air density encountered when driving on roads at different altitudes above sea level. Note that this method of measurement also precludes the need for a measurement of intake air temperature.

g) *Throttle position sensor*: the throttle position sensor informs the ECM of the throttle valve position.

h) *Charge air (boost) control valve*: the boost pressure control valve (also referred to as the solenoid valve) is located on a bracket at the front of the cylinder head. It controls the operation of the turbo-charger. Under certain conditions (ie, in 1st gear), boost pressure is reduced.

i) *Charge air (boost) bypass valve*: the bypass valve is located on the engine wiring harness connector bracket at the rear of the engine compartment on the bulkhead. It is a safety device to prevent any damage to the turbocharger. Under certain conditions, when there is a build-up of pressure the valve is opened by the vacuum from the intake manifold.

j) *Fuel pressure regulator*: is connected to the end of the fuel rail on the intake manifold and regulates the fuel pressure to approximately 3.0 bars.

k) *Fuel pump*: the fuel pump is housed in the fuel tank. The pump housing incorporates a separate feed pump which supplies the main fuel pump with pressurised fuel, free of air bubbles.

l) *Injectors*: each fuel injector consists of a solenoid-operated needle valve, which opens under the commands from the ECM. Fuel from the fuel rail is then delivered through the injector nozzle into the intake manifold.

m) *Oxygen sensor*: the oxygen sensor provides the ECM with constant feedback on the oxygen content of the exhaust gases (see Chapter 4B).

n) *EVAP canister-purge valve*: the EVAP canister-purge valve is operated when the engine is started, to purge fuel accumulated in the canister. In order to allow the oxygen sensor to compensate for the additional fuel, the system is operated in short phases (see Chapter 4B).

9.2a Lift up the carpet under the rear seat . . .

o) **Ignition discharge module and spark plugs**: *the ignition discharge module (or cartridge) contains four HT coils connected directly to the spark plugs (see Chapter 5B).*

p) **Limp-home solenoid** : *the limp-home solenoid is located on the rear of the throttle body. If a safety related fault occurs in the throttle control, it will go into the limp-home mode. The* **Check Engine** *lamp will go on immediately and the diagnostic trouble code will have to be cleared with the diagnostic tool.*

### Check Engine indicator lamp

If the Check Engine warning light comes on, the car should be taken to a Saab dealer at the earliest opportunity. A complete test of the engine management system can then be carried out, using dedicated Saab electronic diagnostic test equipment.

### 8 Fuel supply system – precautions and depressurisation

**Note:** *Refer to the Precautions at the end of Section 1 before proceeding.*

⚠️ *Warning: The following procedure will merely relieve the pressure in the fuel system – remember that fuel will still be present in the system components, and to take precautions accordingly before disconnecting any of them.*
1 The fuel system referred to in this Section is defined as the tank-mounted fuel pump, the

9.2b . . . and prise out the fuel pump cover

fuel filter, the fuel injectors, the fuel rail and the pressure regulator, and the metal pipes and flexible hoses connected between these components. All these contain fuel, which will be under pressure while the engine is running and/or while the ignition is switched on.

⚠️ *Warning: Residual fuel pressure may remain for some time after the ignition has been switched off, and must be relieved before any of these components are disturbed for servicing work.*
2 Open the fusebox, beneath a cover panel on the right-hand side of the facia panel (see *Weekly checks*) and remove the fuel pump fuse (up to 2001 – fuse number 19, from 2001 – fuse number 15. Check in Chapter 12 for exact location for your model).
3 Turn the ignition key and crank the engine. If it starts and runs, allow it to idle until it stops through fuel starvation; this should not take more than a few seconds. Try to start it two more times, to ensure that all pressure has been relieved.
4 Disconnect the battery negative terminal, then refit the fuel pump fuse.
5 Place a suitable container beneath the relevant connection/union to be discon-nected, and have a large rag ready to soak up any escaping fuel not being caught by the container.
6 Slowly loosen the connection or union nut (as applicable) to avoid a sudden release of pressure, and position the rag around the connection to catch any fuel spray which may be expelled. Once the pressure is released, disconnect the fuel line.

 **Cut the fingers from an old pair of rubber gloves and secure them over the open fuel lines or ports with elastic bands, to minimise fuel loss and to prevent the entry of dirt into the fuel system.**

### 9 Fuel pump – removal and refitting

⚠️ *Warning: Refer to the precautions given in Section 8 and the infor-mation detailed in the 'Safety First!' Section of this manual, before disturbing any component in the fuel supply system.*
**Note:** *On all models, the fuel pump also incorporates the fuel gauge sender unit.*

### Removal

1 Release the pressure in the fuel system as described in Section 8, then disconnect the battery negative cable and position it away from the terminal.
2 Lift up the rear seat cushion as described in Chapter 11. Fold the carpet out of the way and unclip the fuel pump cover from the floor panel **(see illustrations)**.
3 Disconnect the upper wiring plug connector. DO NOT disconnect the connector directly on the top of the fuel pump sender **(see illustration)**.
4 Remove the two fuel lines/check valves from the fuel pump/sender unit. Use a screwdriver to carefully release the yellow retaining hooks **(see illustration)**, position a rag around the connection to catch any fuel spray which may be expelled. Note the fitted position of the fuel lines, the white one is the pressure feed line and the black one is the return (which is also marked on the top of the fuel pump/sender unit).
5 The unit is secured by a screwed ring. Saab technicians use a special tool to unscrew the ring, but a large pair of grips (water pump pliers) inserted between the serrations on the inside edge of the ring will achieve the same result. Unscrew and remove the ring **(see illustration)**. Note the location arrows on the top of the pump and tank.

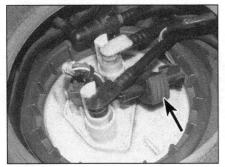

9.3 Disconnect the wiring plug at the position (arrowed)

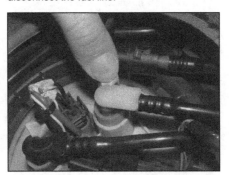

9.4 Disconnecting the fuel pipes from the pump

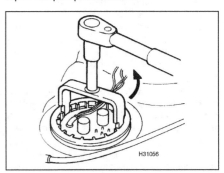

9.5 Unscrew and remove the locking ring from the top of the fuel pump

**6** Carefully lift the pump flange away from the surface of the fuel tank. Allow the excess fuel to drain back into the tank, then rotate the pump clockwise through about one quarter of a turn and withdraw it from the fuel tank **(see illustration)**, have a large rag ready to soak up any escaping fuel not drained out of the unit. Recover the O-ring seal from the tank aperture.

### Refitting

**7** Fit a new O-ring seal to the fuel tank aperture, pressing it firmly into its recess.
**8** Lower the fuel pump into the fuel tank, rotating it to ensure that the alignment markings on the fuel pump and tank line up **(see illustration)**.
**9** Screw the large plastic locking ring into position and tighten it using the method described for its removal. Apply acid-free petroleum jelly to the screw threads.
**10** Refit the fuel lines and wiring connectors to the fuel pump/sender unit, noting the correct fitted position (see paragraph 4). The refitting is a reversal of removal procedure.
**11** Refit the rear seat cushion, then reconnect the battery negative cable.

## 10 Fuel pump relay – removal and refitting

### Removal

**1** The fuel pump relay is located on the main relay board, behind the facia (see Chapter 12 for further information).
**2** Remove the battery cover, then disconnect the battery negative cable and position it away from the terminal.
**3** Release the fasteners and detach the lower cover panel from the driver's side of the facia.
**4** Remove the securing screw and lower the fuseboard away from the facia.
**5** The fuel pump relay is the one labelled G; 1st column from the left, 3rd row from the top **(see illustration)**.
**6** Grasp the relay and pull it squarely from the relay board.

### Refitting

**7** Refitting is a reversal of removal. Ensure that the relay is pushed firmly into its base.

**10.5 Fuel pump relay (arrowed)**

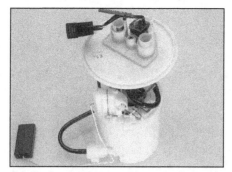
**9.6 Fuel pump removed from the fuel tank**

## 11 Fuel gauge sender unit – removal and refitting

On all models, the fuel gauge sender unit is integral with the fuel pump and can only be purchased as a complete assembly; refer to Section 9 for fuel pump removal and refitting.

## 12 Fuel tank – removal, repair and refitting

⚠ **Warning: Refer to the precautions given in Section 8, and the information detailed in the 'Safety First!' Section of this manual, before disturbing any component in the fuel supply system.**
**1** Before removing the fuel tank, it is preferable that all the fuel is first removed from the tank. Since a fuel tank drain plug is not provided, carry out the removal operation when the tank is almost empty.

### Removal

**2** Release the pressure in the fuel system as described in Section 8, then disconnect the battery negative cable and position it away from the terminal.
**3** Select first gear (manual transmission) or Park (automatic transmission) and chock the front wheels securely. Raise the rear of the car and support it securely on axle stands (see *Jacking and vehicle support*).

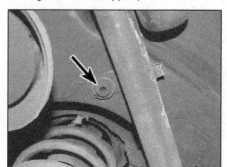
**12.7 Undo the fuel filler pipe retaining bolt (arrowed)**

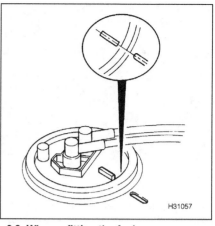
**9.8 When refitting the fuel pump, ensure that the markings on the fuel pump and tank are aligned**

**4** With reference to Section 9 (fuel pump removal), carry out the procedures from paragraphs 2 to 4, disconnecting the fuel pipes and wiring connectors from the fuel pump.
**5** Remove the rear section of the exhaust system as described in Section 20.
**6** Release the locking clip and disconnect the purge pipe.
**7** Undo the retaining bolt and detach the filler neck hose from the tank **(see illustration)**.
**8** With reference to Chapter 9, disconnect the both handbrake cables from the rear brakes.
**9** Position a trolley jack centrally underneath the fuel tank, with a plank of wood placed on the jack head. Raise the jack until it just starts to take the weight of the fuel tank.
**10** Progressively undo the bolts securing the fuel tank support straps to their respective mounting brackets **(see illustrations)**. Unhook the ends of each support strap from their brackets, as they become slack.
**11** Disconnect any remaining breather hoses or cables that may prevent the removal of the tank.
**12** With the help of an assistant, lower the fuel tank to the ground and remove it from under the car.

### Repair

**13** If the tank is contaminated with sediment or water, remove the fuel pump and wash the tank

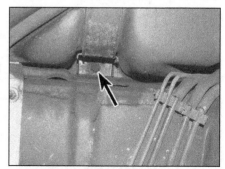
**12.10a Progressively undo one fuel tank support strap bolt (arrowed) . . .**

**12.10b ... and then the other strap bolt (arrowed) to release the fuel tank**

out with clean fuel. In certain cases, it may be possible to have small leaks or minor damage repaired. Seek the advice of a suitable specialist before attempting to repair the fuel tank.

### Refitting

**14** Refitting is a reversal of removal, noting the following points:
a) *Inspect the O-rings at the fuel supply and return quick-release unions, on the top of the fuel pump.*
b) *Ensure that all fuel lines and breather hoses are correctly routed and are not kinked or twisted.*
c) *Tighten the fuel tank support straps securely.*

## 13 Engine management system – general information

**1** The engine idle speed and air-to-fuel mixture (and hence the exhaust gas CO content) are automatically controlled by the ECM. The *checking* of idle speed and mixture is possible on all models by using a tachometer and exhaust gas analyser, note some difficulty may be experienced connecting a conventional tachometer to the engine because of the Direct Ignition system. In addition, as all models are fitted with catalytic converters, the levels of CO, HC and NOx produced may be difficult to measure accurately with anything other than professional test equipment if the system is operating normally. However, it may be

**13.3 Diagnostic connector (arrowed) under driver's side facia panel**

possible to at least confirm the existence of a fuelling or ignition fault, by detecting high levels of one or more of these exhaust gas pollutants, using a commercially-available exhaust gas analyser.
**2** If a fault appears to be present in the engine management system, first ensure that all the system wiring connectors are securely connected and free of corrosion. Then ensure that the fault is not due to poor maintenance – ie, check that the air cleaner filter element is clean, that the fuel filter has been renewed at the specified interval, and that the spark plugs and associated HT components are in good condition. Also check that the engine breather hoses are clear and undamaged. Finally, check that the cylinder compression pressures are correct, referring to Chapters 1, 2A and 5B for further information.
**3** If these checks fail to reveal the cause of the problem, the car should be taken to a Saab dealer for testing. A diagnostic connector is incorporated in the engine management system wiring harness, into which a special Saab electronic diagnostic tester can be plugged. The tester will identify any faults detected by the engine management system ECM by interpreting fault codes stored in the ECM's memory. It also allows system sensors and actuators to be tested remotely without disconnecting them or removing them from the vehicle. This alleviates the need to test all the system components individually, using conventional test equipment. The diagnostic connector is located on the underside of the facia, on the driver's side of the vehicle **(see illustration)**.

**4** If the Check Engine warning light comes on, the car should be taken to a Saab dealer at the earliest opportunity. A complete test of the engine management system can then be carried out, using dedicated Saab electronic diagnostic test equipment.

## 14 Engine management system components – removal and refitting

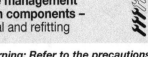

⚠️ *Warning: Refer to the precautions given in Section 8, and the information detailed in the 'Safety First!' Section of this manual, before disturbing any component in the fuel supply system.*

### Electronic Control Module (ECM)

#### Removal

**1** Ensure that the ignition is switched off. Disconnect the battery negative cable and position it away from the terminal.
**2** Remove the windscreen wipers and windscreen lower scuttle panel as described in Chapter 12.
**3** Undo the retaining nuts from the control module cover inside the scuttle panel **(see illustration)**.
**4** Carefully lift the cover, release the locking lever and disconnect the multiconnector from the control module **(see illustration)**.
**5** Undo the two retaining nuts (a magnetic socket will be useful for this) and withdraw the ECM straight up from the vehicle **(see illustration)**.

#### Refitting

**6** Refitting is a reversal of removal. Ensure that the wiring harness multiway connector is secured with the locking lever. Note that if a new ECM has been fitted, it will gradually 'learn' the engine's characteristics as the vehicle is driven. Driveability, performance and fuel economy may be slightly reduced during this period.

### Charge air (boost) pressure/temperature sensor

#### Removal

**7** The pressure/temperature sensor is located

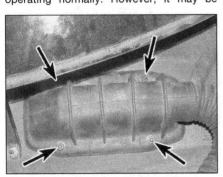

**14.3 Undo the four retaining nuts (arrowed)**

**14.4 Unclip the multi-plug wiring connector from the control module**

**14.5 Undo the two retaining nuts (arrowed) to withdraw the ECM**

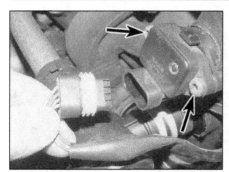

**14.8 Disconnect the wiring plug, then undo the two retaining screws (arrowed)**

**14.10 Removing the engine upper cover panel**

**14.11a Disconnect the wiring plug . . .**

in the main air intake duct to the throttle housing.

**8** Disconnect the wiring connector from the sensor, unscrew the sensor from the air intake duct, and recover the sealing washer **(see illustration)**.

### Refitting

**9** Refitting is a reversal of removal, but check and if necessary renew any sealing washers.

## Manifold absolute pressure sensor

### Removal

**10** Unclip the engine upper cover panel from above the intake manifold **(see illustration)**.
**11** Disconnect the wiring plug, then remove the securing screws and withdraw the sensor from the intake manifold **(see illustrations)**.

### Refitting

**12** Refitting is a reversal of removal, but check and if necessary renew any sealing washers.

## Mass airflow sensor

### Removal

**13** The mass airflow sensor is located in the right-hand front corner of the engine bay behind the right-hand headlamp unit. Slacken the two retaining clips and withdraw the rubber intake hose from the vehicle **(see illustration)**.
**14** Slacken the hose clip on the intake hose and withdraw the air flow sensor. Note the direction of the arrow on the sensor, this is for the correct direction of the airflow **(see illustrations)**.
**15** Disconnect the wiring connector from the bottom of the sensor as it is removed **(see illustration)**.

### Refitting

**16** Refitting is a reversal of removal, but check that the arrows on the sensor are pointing in the direction of flow and the wiring connector is secure.

## Coolant temperature sensor

### Removal

**17** The sensor is threaded into the left-hand side of the cylinder head. Ensure that the

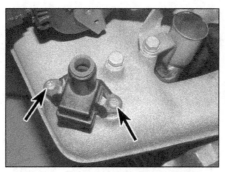

**14.11b . . . then undo the two retaining screws (arrowed)**

engine is completely cold, then release the pressure in the cooling system by removing and then refitting the expansion tank filler cap (see *Weekly checks*).
**18** To make access easier, it may be

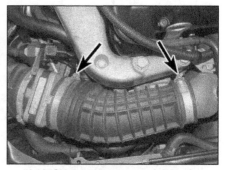

**14.13 Slacken the two retaining clips (arrowed)**

necessary to slacken the hose clips and remove the air intake assembly from the top of the throttle body.
**19** Unplug the wiring connector from the sensor **(see illustration)**.

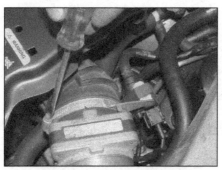

**14.14a Slacken the hose clip, and withdraw the airflow sensor . . .**

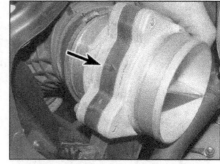

**14.14b . . . note the direction of the arrow**

**14.15 Disconnecting the wiring connector as the sensor is withdrawn**

**14.19 Disconnect the wiring connector (arrowed) . . .**

**14.20 . . . then remove the sensor (arrowed) from the coolant housing**

**14.24 Crankshaft sensor is located behind a shield on the front of the cylinder block**

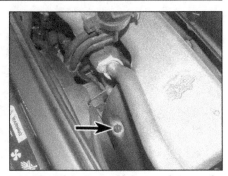

**14.25a Undo the retaining nut (arrowed) and remove the heat shield**

**20** Unscrew the sensor from the coolant housing on the left-hand end of the cylinder head. Be prepared for some coolant loss **(see illustration)**.

### Refitting

**21** Clean the threads, then insert the sensor into the intake manifold, and tighten securely. Fit new sealing washer if necessary.
**22** Ensure that the wiring connector is securely refitted.
**23** Top-up the cooling system with reference to *Weekly checks*.

## Crankshaft position sensor

### Removal

**24** The crankshaft position sensor is located on the front surface of the cylinder block, at the transmission end **(see illustration)**.
**25** Undo the retaining nut and unclip the heat

shield from the exhaust manifold, then undo the securing bolt and remove the shield/cover from the sensor **(see illustrations)**.

 *Warning: The exhaust system and turbocharger may be hot.*

**26** Withdraw the sensor from its location on the front left-hand side of the cylinder block **(see illustration)**. Recover the O-ring, noting how it is fitted. Clean the seating in the cylinder block.
**27** Note the routing of the wiring around the left-hand end of the cylinder head, then disconnect the wiring at the connector **(see illustrations)**. Release the wiring from any retaining clips along its length.

### Refitting

**28** Refitting is a reversal of removal, ensuring that the O-ring is properly seated. Tighten the sensor retaining screw securely. Ensure that

the wiring is retained with the clips/cable ties, following its original routing, and that the multiway connector is securely reconnected.

## Throttle body

### Removal

**29** Ensure that the ignition switch is turned to the OFF position. Making sure the engine is completely cold, release the pressure in the cooling system by removing and then refitting the expansion tank filler cap (see *Weekly checks*).
**30** Unclip the engine upper cover panel from the top of the throttle body, then undo the retaining bolts and remove the cover from the throttle linkage **(see illustration)**.
**31** Remove the lower vacuum hose from the throttle body **(see illustration)**.
**32** Clamp the two coolant hoses that are connected to the throttle body, then release

**14.25b Undo the retaining screw and remove the sensor shield**

**14.26 Withdraw the sensor and recover the O-ring**

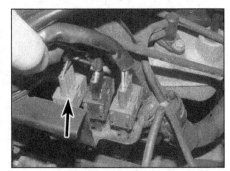

**14.27a Wiring plug connector location (arrowed)**

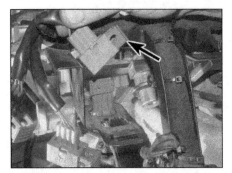

**14.27b Pull out locking clip (arrowed) to disconnect the wiring plug connector**

**14.30 Undo the retaining bolts (arrowed) and remove the cover**

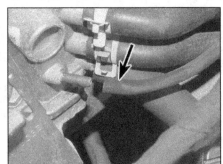

**14.31 Disconnect the vacuum pipe (arrowed)**

the retaining clips and disconnect the hoses **(see illustrations)**.

**33** Remove the air bypass hose from the front lower part of the throttle body. Slacken the securing clip and disconnect the hose at the rear of the throttle body, below the limp-home solenoid **(see illustration)**.

**34** Undo the retaining bolt on the front of the cylinder head for the turbocharger delivery pipe. Slacken the retaining clip and carefully lift the delivery pipe from the top of the throttle body **(see illustrations)**.

**35** Unclip the accelerator inner cable from the throttle linkage, then remove the rubber cover and disconnect the wiring connector from the limp-home solenoid on the back of the throttle body **(see illustration)**.

**36** Disconnect the 10-pin multiplug connector from the side of the throttle body **(see illustration)**.

**37** Undo the three retaining bolts and remove the throttle body from the intake manifold **(see illustration)**.

### Refitting

**38** Refitting is a reversal of removal. Renew the seal if necessary and ensure that all connections are secure.

### *Fuel supply rail, injectors and pressure regulator*

### Removal

**39** Depressurise the fuel system as described in Section 8. Ensure that the ignition switch is then turned to the OFF position.

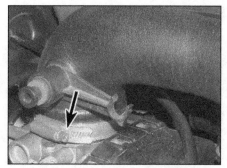
14.34b ... then slacken the retaining clip on the air intake pipe

14.37 Undo the three throttle body retaining bolts (arrowed)

14.32a Clamp the coolant hoses ...

14.33 Disconnect the hose (arrowed) from the rear of the throttle body

**40** Unclip the engine upper cover panel from the top of the throttle body.

**41** Disconnect the crankcase breather hose from the cylinder head cover **(see illustration). Note:** *On later models, release*

14.35 Disconnecting the wiring plug from the limp-home solenoid

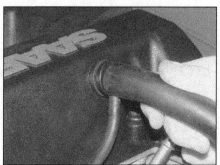
14.41 Disconnect the breather hose from the cylinder head cover

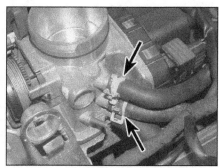
14.32b ... then release the securing clips (arrowed) and disconnect the coolant hoses

14.34a Undo the retaining bolt (arrowed) ...

*the securing clip to disconnect the hose.*
**42** Unbolt the dipstick/filler tube from the rear of the cylinder head and remove **(see illustrations)**. Plug up the pipe to prevent dirt entering the engine.

14.36 Pull out locking clip (arrowed) to disconnect the wiring plug connector from the throttle body

14.42a Undo the retaining bolt (arrowed) ...

14.42b . . . and withdraw the oil filler tube

14.43 Using a plastic sleeve to release the securing clips on the fuel lines

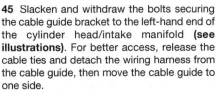

**45** Slacken and withdraw the bolts securing the cable guide bracket to the left-hand end of the cylinder head/intake manifold (see illustrations). For better access, release the cable ties and detach the wiring harness from the cable guide, then move the cable guide to one side.

**46** Release the locking clips and then unplug the wiring from all four injectors (see illustrations), release any cable ties and move wiring loom to one side.

**47** Remove the two bolts securing the fuel rail to the cylinder head (see illustration). Place a cloth beneath the fuel rail, to soak up fuel which will escape as the fuel rail is removed.

**48** Disconnect the vacuum hose from the fuel pressure regulator, then lift the fuel rail from the intake manifold complete with the fuel injectors (see illustrations). Recover the O-ring seals and discard, new ones should be used on refitting. Plug up the holes in the cylinder head to prevent dirt entering the engine.

**49** If required, release the metal clamp and remove the fuel pressure regulator from the end of the fuel rail (see illustration).

**50** To remove the injectors from the fuel rail, release the retaining clips and pull the injectors from the fuel rail. Recover the rubber O-ring seals and discard, new ones should be used on refitting (see illustrations).

### Refitting

**51** Refitting is a reversal of the removal procedure. Fit the injectors to the fuel rail (using new O-rings), then press the fuel rail

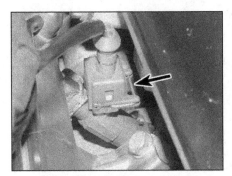

14.45a Undo the two lower retaining bolts (arrowed) . . .

14.45b . . . and the upper retaining bolt (arrowed) from the wiring harness guide

**43** Refer to Section 3 and disconnect the accelerator cable from the throttle body. Disconnect the quick-release fuel lines from the fuel rail, fit caps to the open fuel lines to prevent ingress of dirt (see illustration).

**44** Undo the retaining bolt on the front of the cylinder head for the turbocharger delivery pipe. Slacken the retaining clip and carefully lift the delivery pipe from the top of the throttle body (see illustrations 14.34a and 14.34b).

14.46a Press in the securing clip (arrowed) . . .

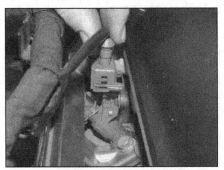

14.46b . . . and disconnect the wiring connector from the injector

14.47 Fuel rail securing bolts (arrowed)

14.48a Disconnect the vacuum hose from the regulator . . .

14.48b . . . then withdraw the fuel rail from the intake manifold

14.49 Undo the retaining screw (arrowed) to release the regulator from the fuel rail

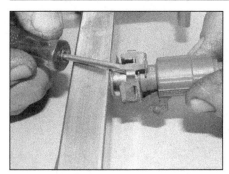

14.50a Prise out the retaining clips . . .

14.50b . . . and pull the injectors from the fuel rail

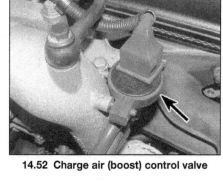

14.52 Charge air (boost) control valve

and injectors into the intake manifold as an assembly. Before locating the new rubber O-rings in the intake manifold, apply a little petroleum jelly to them, to facilitate entry of the injectors. Make sure that all the wiring plugs are connected securely. When refitting the turbocharger air intake to the throttle body, ensure that the O-ring seals are properly seated.

## Charge air (boost) control valve

### Removal

52 The valve is located at the front right-hand corner of the engine, mounted on a bracket on the air intake pipe (see illustration).
53 Ensure that the ignition is switched off, then unplug the wiring connector from the valve (see illustration).
54 Mark each of the hoses leading to the valve to identify their fitted positions, then

release the clips and detach the hoses from the valve ports (see illustration).
55 Slide the control valve off the two locating pegs and remove from the engine compartment.

### Refitting

56 Refitting is a reversal of removal. It is vitally important that the hoses are refitted to the correct ports on the boost control valve.

## Charge air (boost) bypass valve

### Removal

57 Unclip the engine upper cover panel from the top of the throttle body, then unclip the cover from the engine harness bracket on the bulkhead (see illustration).
58 Undo the two retaining nuts from the mounting bracket (see illustration), then lift the control valve mounting plate and unhook it from the bulkhead.

59 As the unit is withdrawn, disconnect the lower multiplug connector from the bypass valve (see illustration).
60 Mark each of the vacuum hoses leading to the valve to identify their fitted positions, then detach the hoses from the valve body.
61 Drill out the two rivets and remove the control valve (see illustration).

### Refitting

62 Refitting is a reversal of removal. Using new pop rivets, fasten the control valve to the mounting plate.

## Limp-home solenoid

### Removal

63 Unclip the engine upper cover panel from above the intake manifold (see illustration 14.10).

14.53 Pull back rubber cover and disconnect the wiring connector

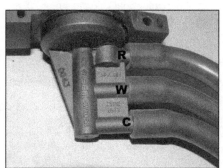

14.54 Note the markings on the valve for the hoses

14.57 Unclip the cover from the engine harness on the bulkhead

14.58 Undo the two retaining nuts (arrowed)

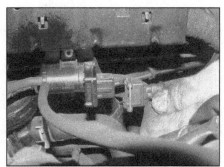

14.59 Disconnect the wiring connector from the valve

14.61 Drill out the two rivets (arrowed)

**14.64a Disconnect the wiring plug from the limp-home solenoid (arrowed) . . .**

64 Pull back the rubber cover then disconnect the wiring plug from the limp-home solenoid. Remove the securing screws and withdraw the sensor from the throttle body **(see illustrations)**.

### Refitting

65 Refitting is a reversal of removal, but check and if necessary renew any sealing washers.

### *Oxygen sensor*

66 Refer to the information given in Chapter 4B.

## 15 Turbocharger –
description and precautions

### *Description*

1 The turbocharger increases engine efficiency and performance by raising the pressure in the intake manifold above atmospheric pressure. Instead of the intake air being sucked into the combustion chambers, it is forced in under pressure. This leads to a greater charge pressure increase during combustion and improved fuel burning, which raises the thermal efficiency of the engine. Under these conditions, additional fuel is supplied by the fuel injection system, in proportion to the increased air flow.
2 Energy for the operation of the turbocharger comes from the exhaust gas. The gas flows through a specially-shaped housing (the turbine housing) and in so doing spins the turbine wheel. The turbine wheel is attached to a shaft, at the end of which is another vaned wheel known as the compressor wheel. The compressor wheel spins in its own housing, and compresses the intake air on the way to the intake manifold.
3 Between the turbocharger and the intake manifold, the compressed air passes through an intercooler. This is an air-to-air heat exchanger, mounted in front of the radiator and supplied with cooling air from the front grille and electric cooling fans. The temperature of the intake air rises due to the compression action of the turbocharger – the purpose of the intercooler is to cool the intake air again, before it enters the engine. Because

**14.64b . . . then undo the two retaining screws (arrowed)**

cool air is denser than hot air, this allows a greater mass of air (occupying the same volume) to be forced into the combustion chambers, resulting in a further increase in the engine's thermal efficiency.
4 Boost pressure (the pressure in the intake manifold) is limited by a wastegate, which diverts the exhaust gas away from the turbine wheel in response to a pressure-sensitive actuator. The wastegate valve is controlled by the engine management system ECM, via an electronic boost control valve. The ECM opens and closes (modulates) the boost valve several times a second, which results in manifold vacuum being applied to the wastegate valve in a series of rapid pulses – the duty ratio of the pulses depends primarily on engine speed and load. The ECM monitors boost pressure via the manifold pressure sensor, and uses the boost control valve to maintain pressure at an optimum level throughout the engine speed range. If the ECM detects that combustion pre-ignition ('pinking' or 'knocking') is taking place, the boost pressure is reduced accordingly to prevent engine damage; see Chapter 5B for greater detail.
5 A boost bypass valve fitted in the airflow between the low pressure supply and high pressure delivery sides of the turbocharger compressor allows excess boost to be dumped into the intake air ducting when the throttle is closed at high engine speed (ie, during overrun or deceleration). This improves driveability by preventing compressor stall (and therefore reducing turbo 'lag'), and also by eliminating the surging that would

**16.3 Undo the two retaining bolts (arrowed) from the exhaust stay bracket**

otherwise occur when the throttle is reopened.
6 The turbo shaft is pressure-lubricated by an oil feed pipe from the main oil gallery. The shaft 'floats' on a cushion of oil and has no moving bearings. A drain pipe returns the oil to the sump. The turbine housing is water-cooled and has a dedicated system of coolant supply and return pipes.

### *Precautions*

• The turbocharger operates at extremely high speeds and temperatures. Certain precautions must be observed during servicing activities, to avoid injury to the operator, or premature failure of the turbo.
• Do not operate the turbo with any of its parts exposed, or with any of its hoses removed. Foreign objects falling onto the rotating vanes could cause excessive damage, and (if ejected) personal injury.
• Do not race the engine immediately after start-up, especially if it is cold. Give the oil a few seconds to circulate.
• Always allow the engine to return to idle speed before switching it off – do not blip the throttle and switch off, as this will leave the turbo spinning without lubrication.
• Allow the engine to idle for a few minutes before switching off after a high-speed run. This will allow the turbine housing to cool before the coolant stops circulating under pressure.
• Observe the recommended intervals for oil and filter changing, and use a reputable oil of the specified quality. Infrequent oil changes, or use of inferior oil, can cause carbon formation on the turbo shaft, leading to subsequent failure.

## 16 Turbocharger –
removal and refitting

*Note 1: The exhaust system and turbocharger may still be hot, make sure the vehicle has cooled down before working on the engine.*
*Note 2 : Saab recommend that the oil and filter should be changed (as described in Chapter 1), when removing the turbocharger.*

### *Removal*

1 Apply the handbrake, then jack up the front of the car and support on axle stands (see *Jacking and vehicle support*).
2 Remove the shield from beneath the radiator, then drain the cooling system as described in Chapter 1.
3 Undo the retaining bolts and remove the turbocharger stay bracket **(see illustration)**.
4 Slacken the unions and disconnect the oil supply and return pipes from the turbocharger **(see illustrations)**. Plug the open ports to prevent contamination.
5 Working at the top of the engine, undo the retaining nut and unclip the heat shield from the exhaust manifold.

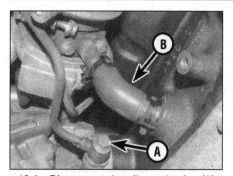

16.4a Disconnect the oil supply pipe (A) and oil return pipe (B)

16.4b On some models the return pipe (arrowed) is a metal corrugated pipe

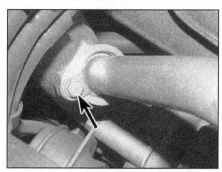

16.6a Undo the retaining bolt (arrowed) . . .

**6** Undo the retaining bolt/clips and remove the air bypass hose (see illustrations). Note that there is an O-ring seal at the connection to the intake pipe.
**7** Disconnect the wiring connectors from the charge air control valve (see illustration).
**8** Slacken retaining clip on the hose to the intake pipe/turbo unit and disconnect the breather pipe (banjo bolt or quick-release coupling) from the intake pipe (see illustrations).
**9** Undo the retaining bolt (or unclip) the breather pipe and wiring loom from the right-hand end of the camshaft cover and move them to one side.
**10** Undo the retaining bolt(s) and remove the lifting eye from the front of the cylinder head (see illustration).
**11** Disconnect the quick-release coupling on the EVAP hose (see illustration).

16.6b . . . and release the securing clip (arrowed)

**12** Undo the retaining bolt and withdraw the intake pipe V-clamp from the turbo, then withdraw the intake pipe (see illustrations). Disconnect the vacuum hose as the intake pipe is removed.

16.7 Remove the rubber cover (arrowed) and disconnect the wiring connector

**13** From under the vehicle, slacken the securing clip on the hose from the charge air cooler to the turbo and disconnect (see illustration). Plug the open ports to prevent contamination or damage to the turbo.

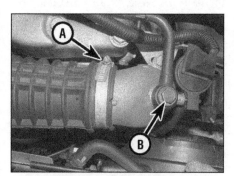

16.8a Slacken the retaining clip (A) and breather pipe banjo bolt (B)

16.8b On some models the breather pipe has a quick-release coupling (arrowed)

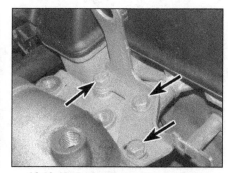

16.10 Undo the three retaining bolts (arrowed)

16.11 Disconnect the coupling on the EVAP hose

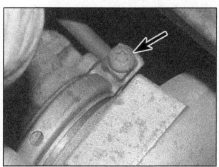

16.12a Slacken the clamp securing bolt (arrowed)

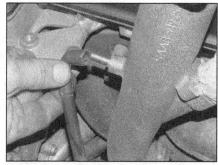

16.12b Disconnect the vacuum pipe as the intake pipe is removed

**14** Unbolt and remove the exhaust system front pipe from the turbo, carefully lower the front pipe on to an axle stand (or similar) taking care not to damage it (see Section 20 of this Chapter).

⚠️ **Warning: The flexible section of the exhaust should not be bent out of alignment by anymore than 5° as this can cause damage to the exhaust causing leakage and noise.**

**15** Undo the unions and detach the coolant supply pipe from the coolant pump and the turbo housing **(see illustrations)**, retrieve the copper sealing washers. Plug the open ports to prevent contamination.

**16** Undo the unions and detach the coolant return pipe from the turbo housing **(see illustration)**. Retrieve the copper sealing washers, then plug the open ports to prevent contamination.

**17** Apply some easing oil to the exhaust manifold studs, then slacken the turbocharger securing nuts and remove the turbocharger from the vehicle **(see illustration)**. Check around the turbocharger for any pipes that may still be connected.

### Refitting

**18** Refitting is a reversal of removal, noting the following points:

a) Fill the turbocharger interchamber with clean engine oil, through the oil supply union on the turbocharger. This is important, as the turbocharger must have oil in it when the engine is started.

b) Thoroughly clean the exhaust manifold mating surface, before refitting the turbocharger.

c) Renew all copper union sealing washers, O-ring seals and gaskets, where applicable.

d) Tighten all nuts, bolts and oil and coolant unions to the correct torque settings, where specified.

e) Apply a suitable high-temperature, anti-seize compound to the threads of the exhaust system-to-turbocharger and exhaust manifold-to-turbocharger studs and nuts.

f) Ensure that the charge air (boost) control valve hoses are refitted correctly to the turbocharger, wastegate actuator and air hose **(see illustration 14.54)**.

**19** On completion, check that the radiator drain plug is tight, then refit the shield panel.

**20** Lower the car to the ground, then check and if necessary top-up the engine oil level (see *Weekly checks*). If not already done, it is strongly recommended that the engine oil is changed before starting the engine if a new turbocharger has been fitted, as this will protect the turbo bearings during the 'running-in' period.

**21** Refill the cooling system (see Chapter 1).

**22** It is recommended that the boost pressure is checked by a Saab dealer at the earliest opportunity.

## 17 Intercooler – removal and refitting

### Removal

**1** Remove the radiator as described in Chapter 3.

**2** Raise the front of the vehicle and support it securely on axle stands (see *Jacking and vehicle support*).

**3** Undo the retaining bolts and remove the intercooler bracket from the oil cooler. Suspend the oil cooler from the subframe by using cable-ties or similar.

**4** Release the hose clips and disconnect the air hoses from the left-hand end and the right-hand end of the intercooler. Slacken and withdraw the intercooler securing screws, together with any washers and grommets.

**5** Remove the front grille as described in Chapter 11.

**6** Refer to Chapter 12 and remove the both headlights and direction indicators and put safely to one side.

**7** Move the capacitor to one side and suspend it from the subframe using a cable-tie or similar.

**8** Remove the intercooler bracket from the condensor.

**9** Move the intercooler away from the front panel, lift it from its mountings, and withdraw it from the engine compartment.

### Refitting

**10** Refitting is a reversal of removal, using the relevant Chapters for reference. Ensure that the air hose clips are securely tightened.

## 18 Intake manifold – removal and refitting

⚠️ **Warning: Refer to the precautions given in Section 1, and the information detailed in the 'Safety First!' Section of this manual, before disturbing any component in the fuel supply system.**

**16.13 Slacken the retaining clip (arrowed) from the hose**

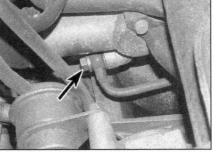

**16.15a Undo the coolant pipe (arrowed) from the coolant pump . . .**

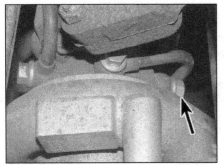

**16.15b . . . and the coolant pipe (arrowed) from the front of the turbocharger**

**16.16 Undo the coolant pipe (arrowed) from the rear of the turbocharger**

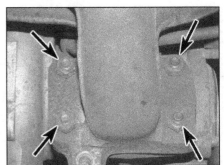

**16.17 Slacken the four turbocharger securing bolts (arrowed)**

## Removal

**1** Disconnect the battery negative lead.
**2** Refer to Section 14, and remove the throttle body from the intake manifold.
**3** Remove the fuel rail and fuel injectors from the intake manifold as described in Section 14.
**4** Disconnect the brake servo vacuum hose from the intake manifold **(see illustration)**.
**5** Unplug the wiring from the coolant temperature sensor **(see illustration)**.
**6** Unscrew the mounting bolts securing the intake manifold to the cylinder head. Also unscrew the lower bolt from the steady bar **(see illustration)**.
**7** Withdraw the intake manifold from the cylinder head **(see illustration)**. Where applicable, carefully withdraw the intake air heating plate, unplugging the wiring at the multiway connector. Recover the gasket from the cylinder head.

## Refitting

**8** Refitting is a reversal of removal. Fit a new gasket and where applicable, reconnect the intake air heating plate wiring. Ensure that the manifold retaining bolts are tightened to the specified torque.

---

### 19 Exhaust manifold – removal and refitting

## Removal

**1** Apply the handbrake, then jack up the front of the car and support on axle stands (see *Jacking and vehicle support*).
**2** Disconnect the oxygen sensor wiring with reference to Chapter 4B, Section 2.
**3** Remove the exhaust system front pipe and catalytic converter with reference to Section 20.
**4** Remove the auxiliary drivebelt as described in Chapter 1. To gain access to the right-hand exhaust manifold nuts, the power steering fluid pump must be unbolted and moved aside; see Chapter 10 for details. Note that there is no need to disconnect the hydraulic fluid pipes.
**5** Unscrew and remove the exhaust manifold mounting nuts, then lift the manifold from the cylinder head. Note the position of the sleeves fitted beneath some of the stud nuts **(see illustration)**.
**6** Remove the gasket from the studs on the cylinder head **(see illustration)**.

## Refitting

**7** Clean the contact surfaces of the cylinder head and exhaust manifold.
**8** Refit the exhaust manifold to the studs on the cylinder head together with a new gasket, then tighten the mounting nuts to the specified torque. Make sure that the sleeves are correctly located, as previously noted.
**9** Refit the power steering pump with reference to Chapter 10.

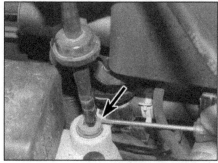
**18.4 Press the collar down and release the vacuum pipe**

**18.6 Remove the upper and lower retaining bolts (arrowed)**

**10** Refit the auxiliary drivebelt as described in Chapter 1.
**11** Refit the exhaust front pipe with reference to Section 20.
**12** Reconnect the oxygen sensor wiring with reference to Chapter 4B, Section 2.
**13** Lower the car to the ground.

### 20 Exhaust system – general information and component removal

## General information

**1** The exhaust system consists of two sections:
*1) The front section (incorporating one catalytic converter on B205E models, and two catalytic converters on B235E/R models).*

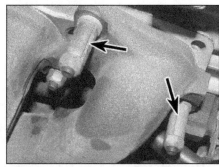
**19.5 Note the position of the sleeves fitted beneath some of the stud nuts (two shown)**

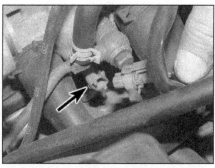
**18.5 Disconnecting the wiring connector from the temperature sensor (arrowed)**

**18.7 Removing the intake manifold and gasket**

*2) The rear section (incorporating two silencers, which are a combination of resonance and absorption types).*

**2** If one of the silencers in the rear section of exhaust is leaking or damaged, it can be renewed by cutting the exhaust pipe approximately 95mm ahead of the rear silencer. A new silencer can then be fitted (making the system into three sections). Check with your local exhaust dealer for availability of parts.
**3** The exhaust system sections are joined by flanges with no gaskets, this is for the ease of removing the exhaust and ensuring a good fit. The outer exhaust casing is aluminized to protect against corrosion and the silencers are made of stainless 12% chrome steel.
**4** On B205E models, there is one oxygen sensor located in the front pipe. On B235E/R models, there are two oxygen sensor located in the front pipe.

**19.6 Renew the manifold gasket**

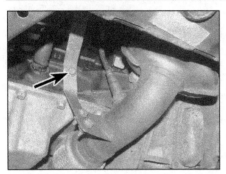

**20.12 Undo the exhaust bracket bolt (arrowed)**

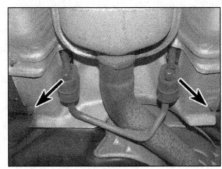

**20.19 Heat shield retaining nuts (arrowed) – two shown**

**5** The front pipe incorporates a support bracket which is also connected to the turbocharger.

**6** On all models, the system is suspended throughout its entire length by rubber mountings.

### Removal

**7** Each exhaust section can be removed individually as described in the following paragraphs. Alternatively, it is possible to remove the complete exhaust system in one piece, but without disconnecting the flange between the front and rear sections.

**8** To remove a section of the system, first jack up the front or rear of the car and support it on axle stands (see *Jacking and vehicle support*). Alternatively, position the car over an inspection pit, or on car ramps.

#### Front section

**Note:** *Do not drop the catalytic converter, as it contains a fragile ceramic element.*

**9** Remove the front oxygen sensor as described in Chapter 4B, Section 2.

**10** Undo the retaining nut and unclip the heat shield from the exhaust manifold. Slacken the three nuts securing the front pipe to the turbocharger, do not fully remove at this point.

**11** Where applicable, remove the lower engine cover from under the vehicle.

**12** Remove the bolts securing the front pipe to its support bracket under the front of the engine **(see illustration)**.

**13** Unscrew the nuts and separate the flange joint between the front pipe and the rear exhaust section.

**14** Support the exhaust front section and remove the three retaining nuts which where slackened in paragraph 10.

**15** Remove the clips from the rubber mountings, then unhook the mounting rubbers from the underbody and lower the pipe between the engine and the subframe crossmember.

> ⚠ **Warning: The flexible section of the exhaust should not be bent out of alignment by anymore than 5° as this can cause damage to the exhaust causing leakage and noise.**

#### Rear section

**16** Unscrew the nuts and separate the flange joint between the front pipe and the rear exhaust section.

**17** Remove the clips from the rubber mountings, then support the exhaust and unhook the mounting rubbers from the underbody of the vehicle. Lower the exhaust rear section to the ground.

**18** If either one of the silencers in the rear section of exhaust is leaking or damaged, then it can be renewed individually by cutting the exhaust pipe as described above.

#### Heat shields

**19** The heat shields are secured to the underbody by securing nuts **(see illustration)**. Each shield can be removed once the relevant exhaust section has been removed.

### Refitting

**20** Each section is refitted by a reversal of the removal sequence, noting the following points:

  a) *Ensure that all traces of corrosion have been removed from the flared tube ends in the flanges, and where applicable, renew the front pipe-to-exhaust manifold/turbocharger gasket(s).*

  b) *When tightening the nuts on the front section of exhaust to the turbo, tighten them alternately to avoid distortion of the flange.*

  c) *Inspect the rubber mountings for signs of damage or deterioration, and renew as necessary.*

  d) *Refit the oxygen sensor with reference to Chapter 4B, Section 2.*

  e) *Make sure that all rubber mountings are correctly located with their retaining clips, and that there is adequate clearance between the exhaust system and underbody.*

  f) *Make sure the rear of the exhaust is aligned centrally with the cut-out in the rear bumper and matches the bumper profile.*

# Chapter 4 Part B:
# Emissions control systems

## Contents

## Degrees of difficulty

| | | | | |
|---|---|---|---|---|
| **Easy,** suitable for novice with little experience  | **Fairly easy,** suitable for beginner with some experience  | **Fairly difficult,** suitable for competent DIY mechanic  | **Difficult,** suitable for experienced DIY mechanic  | **Very difficult,** suitable for expert DIY or professional |

## Specifications

**EVAP canister-purge valve**

Resistance at 20°C . . . . . . . . . . . . . . . . . . . . . . . . . . . . . . . . . . . . . . 45 ± 5 ohms

**EVAP pressure sensor**

| | |
|---|---|
| Pressure . . . . . . . . . . . . . . . . . . . . . . . . . . . . . . . . . . . . . . . . . . . . . . | Voltage (approx) |
| -0.038 bar . . . . . . . . . . . . . . . . . . . . . . . . . . . . . . . . . . . . . . . . . . . . | 0.1 |
| 0 bar . . . . . . . . . . . . . . . . . . . . . . . . . . . . . . . . . . . . . . . . . . . . . . . . | 2.5 |
| 0.012 bar . . . . . . . . . . . . . . . . . . . . . . . . . . . . . . . . . . . . . . . . . . . . | 2.0 |

**EVAP shut-off control valve**

Resistance at 20°C . . . . . . . . . . . . . . . . . . . . . . . . . . . . . . . . . . . . . . 24.5 ±1.5 ohms

**Heated oxygen sensors**

| | |
|---|---|
| Type . . . . . . . . . . . . . . . . . . . . . . . . . . . . . . . . . . . . . . . . . . . . . . . . | Bosch LSF 4.7 (with preheating) |
| Resistance at 20°C (pins 1 and 2) . . . . . . . . . . . . . . . . . . . . . . . . . | 9.0 ohms (approx) |

| Torque wrench setting | Nm | lbf ft |
|---|---|---|
| Oxygen sensor . . . . . . . . . . . . . . . . . . . . . . . . . . . . . . . . . . . . . . . | 55 | 41 |

## 1 General information

All models use unleaded petrol and various features are built into the fuel system to help minimise harmful emissions. All models have a crankcase emissions control system, and are equipped with a three-way catalytic converter. Some models are also fitted with exhaust gas recirculation and evaporative emissions control systems.

In certain non-UK territories, having strict emissions laws, a secondary air injection system is fitted.

### Evaporative emissions control

To minimise the escape into the atmosphere of unburned hydrocarbons, an evaporative emissions control system is fitted. The system is sometimes referred to as the 'evaporative-loss control device' (ELCD). The fuel tank filler cap is sealed, and a charcoal canister is mounted on the front right-hand side of the car beneath the right-hand wing on B205E (and B235E models up to 09/01). On B235R (and B235E models after 09/01) the charcoal canister is located on top of the fuel tank. The charcoal canister collects the petrol vapours generated in the tank when the car is parked. The vapours are stored until they can be cleared from the canister (under the control of the fuel system ECU via the purge valve, into the inlet tract, to be burned by the engine during normal combustion.

To ensure that the engine runs correctly when it is cold and/or idling, and to protect the catalytic converter from the effects of an over-rich mixture, the purge control valve is not opened by the ECU until the engine has warmed-up, and the engine is under load; the valve solenoid is then modulated on and off, to allow the stored vapour to pass into the inlet tract.

### Crankcase emissions control

To reduce emissions of unburned hydrocarbons from the crankcase into the atmosphere, the engine is sealed. The blow-by gases and oil vapour are drawn from inside the crankcase, through an external oil trap which is connected to the crankcase via the camshaft cover and breather hose. The gases are then evacuated to the throttle housing and also via the turbocharger to the inlet manifold.

Under conditions of high manifold depression (idling, deceleration) the gases will be sucked positively out of the crankcase to the throttle housing. Under conditions of low manifold depression (acceleration, full-throttle running) the gases are forced out of the crankcase by the (relatively) higher crankcase pressure; if the engine is worn, the raised crankcase pressure (due to increased blow-by) will cause some of the flow to return under all manifold conditions.

### Exhaust emissions control

To minimise the amount of pollutants which escape into the atmosphere all models are fitted with a catalytic converter in the exhaust system. The catalytic converter system is of the 'closed-loop' type, in which an oxygen sensor (two on some models) in the exhaust system provides the fuel-injection/ignition system ECU with constant feedback on the oxygen content of the exhaust gases. This enables the ECU to adjust the mixture to provide the best possible conditions for the converter to operate.

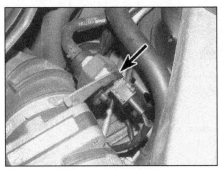

**2.16 Purge valve (arrowed) mounted on the airflow sensor retaining clip**

**2.18 Pull the valve rubber mounting from the mounting bracket**

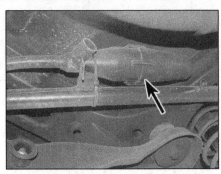

**2.21 Shut-off valve (arrowed) mounted on the fuel filler pipe**

The oxygen sensors have a built-in heating element, controlled by the ECU through the sensor relay, to quickly bring the sensor's tip to an efficient operating temperature. The sensor's tip is sensitive to oxygen, and sends the ECU a varying voltage depending on the amount of oxygen in the exhaust gases; if the inlet air/fuel mixture is too rich, the sensor sends a high-voltage signal. The voltage falls as the mixture weakens. Peak conversion efficiency of all major pollutants occurs if the inlet air/fuel mixture is maintained at the chemically-correct ratio for the complete combustion of petrol – 14.7 parts (by weight) of air to 1 part of fuel (the 'stoichiometric' ratio). The sensor output voltage alters in a large step at this point, the ECU using the signal change as a reference point, and correcting the inlet air/fuel mixture accordingly by altering the fuel injector pulse width (injector opening time).

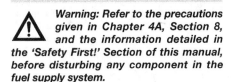

## 2 Emissions control systems – component renewal

⚠️ **Warning: Refer to the precautions given in Chapter 4A, Section 8, and the information detailed in the 'Safety First!' Section of this manual, before disturbing any component in the fuel supply system.**

### Evaporative emission control

#### Pressure sensor

1 The pressure sensor is located on top of the fuel tank, remove the fuel tank as described in Chapter 4A, Section 12.
2 Clean around the pressure sensor, to make sure no dirt enters the fuel tank when the sensor is removed.
3 Undo the retaining screw and withdraw the sensor and O-ring seal from the fuel tank.
4 Refitting is a reversal of removal procedure. **Note:** *Renew the sensor O-ring seal and lubricate with acid-free petroleum jelly or similar.*

#### Charcoal canister (B205E and B235E up to 09/01)

5 The charcoal canister is mounted on the

front right-hand side of the car beneath the right-hand wing with the purge valve.
6 Apply the handbrake, then jack up the front of the car and support on axle stands (see *Jacking and vehicle support*). Remove the right-hand front wheel.
7 Remove the right-hand front wing plastic moulding, followed by the front section of the wheel arch liner.
8 Note the positions of the hoses on the canister (A is connected to the tank and B is connected to the purge valve) then disconnect them from the canister.
9 Unhook the canister from its mounting bracket and remove it from under the wing.
10 Refitting is a reversal of the removal procedure. **Note:** *Make sure the retaining clips for the hoses are not damaged and the hoses are securely fitted, in the position noted on removal.*

#### Charcoal canister (B235R and B235E after 09/01)

11 The charcoal canister is located on top of the fuel tank, remove the fuel tank as described in Chapter 4A, Section 12.
12 Clean around the charcoal canister, to make sure no dirt enters the fuel tank when the canister is removed.
13 Release the retaining clips on the hoses to the canister and disconnect them, noting their fitted position.
14 Undo the retaining screw and withdraw the canister, unhooking it from its holder in the top of the fuel tank.
15 Refitting is a reversal of removal procedure. **Note:** *Make sure the retaining clips for the hoses are not damaged and the hoses are securely fitted, in the position noted on removal.*

#### Purge valve

16 The purge valve is mounted on the front right-hand side inner wing panel **(see illustration)**. Check that the hoses from the purge control valve are clear by removing them and blowing through them. If the purge control valve is thought to be faulty, it must be renewed.
17 Release the retaining clip(s) on the hose(s) to the valve and disconnect them, noting their fitted position.
18 Remove purge valve from the mounting

bracket, noting its fitted position **(see illustration)**.
19 Twist the valve and unplug the connector, then withdraw the purge valve from the vehicle.
20 Refitting is a reversal of the removal procedure, but make sure that the purge valve is fitted in the correct position as noted on removal.

#### Shut-off control valve

21 The shut-off valve (where fitted), is clipped to the side of the fuel filler pipe at the rear of the vehicle **(see illustration)**. Park the vehicle on a firm level surface, then select first gear (manual transmission) or Park (automatic transmission) and chock the front wheels securely. Raise the rear of the car and support it securely on axle stands (see *Jacking and vehicle support*).
22 Cut the cable tie and disconnect the wiring connector to the shut-off valve.
23 Using a screwdriver carefully prise the control valve, to unclip it from the fuel filler pipe.
24 Clean off any dirt from around the control valve, then unclip the cover from the top of the valve. Disconnect the wiring connector from the top of the valve and withdraw the washer.
25 Unclip the cover from the bottom of the valve, then release the securing clip and disconnect the hose from the bottom of the valve. If required, the filter can now be renewed.
26 Refitting is a reversal of the removal procedure, but make sure that the wiring at the top of the valve locates correctly in the recess in the washer.

### Crankcase emissions control

27 The components of this system require no attention other than to check at regular intervals that the hose(s) and the external oil trap on the cylinder block are clear and undamaged **(see illustrations)**.

### Oxygen sensors

⚠️ *Warning: On some early models Bosch LSH25P oxygen sensors where used, later models have the Bosch LSF 4.7 oxygen sensor fitted. These are not interchangeable, when*

*renewing the sensors, check the type fitted and refit with the same type.*
**Note:** *On B235E and B235R models there are two oxygen sensors fitted, one before the catalytic converter and one after. On B205E models there is one oxygen sensor fitted to the front of the catalytic converter. The oxygen sensor is DELICATE. It will not work if it is dropped or knocked, if its power supply is disrupted, or if any cleaning materials are used on it.*

### Front oxygen sensor

**28** Open the bonnet and remove the upper cover from the intake manifold **(see illustration)**.
**29** Release the securing clip and disconnect the wiring plug connectors, then press lugs together to release from the mounting bracket at the left-hand side rear of the cylinder head **(see illustration)**.
**30** Remove the heat shield from above the exhaust manifold, disconnect the by-pass pipe from across the top of the heat shield if required.
**31** Release the cable-tie from the wiring to the oxygen sensor, and withdraw the wiring harness.
**32** Unscrew the sensor from the exhaust system downpipe **(see illustration)**, and remove it. The sensor may be tight, in which case it will help if it is turned back-and-forth on its threads as it is being removed. Note that it is possible to obtain a special slotted socket, which locates on the sensor without causing any damage to the wiring.

**33** Refitting is a reverse of the removal procedure. Prior to installing the sensor, apply a smear of high-temperature grease to the sensor threads. Tighten the sensor to the specified torque. The wiring must be correctly routed, and in no danger of contacting the exhaust system.

### Rear oxygen sensor

**34** Open the bonnet and remove the upper cover from the intake manifold **(see illustration 2.28)**.
**35** Release the securing clip and disconnect the wiring plug connectors then press the lugs together and release the wiring plug from the mounting bracket at the rear left-hand side of the cylinder head **(see illustration 2.29)**.
**36** Release the cable-tie from the wiring to the oxygen sensor, and withdraw the wiring harness.
**37** Apply the handbrake, then jack up the front of the car and support on axle stands (see *Jacking and vehicle support*).
**38** Pull the wiring harness down, then unscrew the sensor from the exhaust system front pipe **(see illustration)**, and remove it. The sensor may be tight, in which case it will help if it is turned back-and-forth on its threads as it is being removed. Note that it is possible to obtain a special slotted socket, which locates on the sensor without causing any damage to the wiring.
**39** Refitting is a reverse of the removal procedure. Prior to installing the sensor, apply a smear of high-temperature grease to the sensor threads. Tighten the sensor to the

specified torque. The wiring must be correctly routed, and in no danger of contacting the exhaust system.

### Testing

**40** The oxygen sensors may be tested with a multi-meter by disconnecting the wiring at the connector, trace the wiring back from the sensor and disconnect the wiring plug.
**41** Connect an ohmmeter between terminals 1 and 2 on the sensor wiring plug. **Do not** connect the ohmmeter to the ECU wiring. The resistance should be approximately 9 ohms, when the temperature of the sensor is 20°C.
**42** Reconnect the wiring after making the test.

### *Catalytic converter*

**43** Removal and refitting of the catalytic converter is described in Chapter 4A, Section 20, as part of the exhaust system procedures.

### Testing

**44** The performance of the catalytic converter can be checked only by measuring the exhaust gases using a good-quality, carefully-calibrated exhaust gas analyser.
**45** If the CO level at the tailpipe is too high, the vehicle should be taken to a Saab dealer so that the fuel injection and ignition systems, including the oxygen sensor, can be thoroughly checked using special diagnostic equipment. Once these have been checked and are known to be free from faults, the fault must be in the catalytic converter, which must be renewed as described in Chapter 4A.

**2.27a Oil trap (arrowed) mounted on the rear of the cylinder block**

**2.27b On later models the hoses (arrowed) have quick-release connections on the oil trap**

**2.28 Removing the upper cover from the intake manifold**

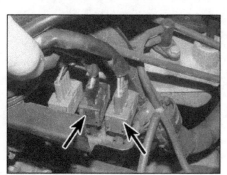

**2.29 Disconnect the two wiring connectors (arrowed) for the oxygen sensors**

**2.32 Slacken and remove the oxygen sensor (arrowed)**

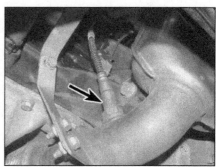

**2.38 Slacken and remove the oxygen sensor (arrowed)**

### 3  Catalytic converter –
general information
and precautions

**1** The catalytic converter is a reliable and simple device which needs no maintenance in itself, but there are some facts of which an owner should be aware if the converter is to function properly for its full service life.

a) *DO NOT use leaded petrol/LRP in a car with a catalytic converter – the lead will coat the precious metals, reducing their converting efficiency, and may eventually destroy the converter.*

b) *Always keep the ignition and fuel systems well-maintained in accordance with the manufacturer's schedule (see Chapter 1).*

c) *If the engine develops a misfire, do not drive the car at all (or at least as little as possible) until the fault is cured.*

d) *DO NOT push- or tow-start the car – this will soak the catalytic converter in unburned fuel, causing it to overheat when the engine does start.*

e) *DO NOT switch the engine off at high engine speeds – ie, do not 'blip' the throttle before switching off. Allow it to return to idle first.*

f) *DO NOT use fuel or engine oil additives – these may contain substances harmful to the catalytic converter.*

g) *DO NOT continue to use the car if the engine burns oil to the extent of leaving a visible trail of blue smoke.*

h) *Remember that the catalytic converter operates at very high temperatures. DO NOT, therefore, park the car in dry undergrowth, over long grass, or over piles of dead leaves, after a long run.*

i) *Remember that the catalytic converter is FRAGILE – do not strike it with tools during servicing work.*

# Chapter 5 Part A:
## Starting and charging systems

## Contents

## Degrees of difficulty

| **Easy,** suitable for novice with little experience |  | **Fairly easy,** suitable for beginner with some experience | 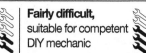 | **Fairly difficult,** suitable for competent DIY mechanic | | **Difficult,** suitable for experienced DIY mechanic |  | **Very difficult,** suitable for expert DIY or professional | |
|---|---|---|---|---|---|---|---|---|---|

## Specifications

**System type** ........................................ 12 volt, negative earth

### Battery
Type ................................................. Lead-acid, low-maintenance or 'maintenance-free' (sealed for life)
Battery capacity ...................................... 70 amp-hour
Charge condition ..................................... More than 12 volts

### Alternator
Type ................................................. Bosch NC–14V 65-130A or Bosch E8–14V 75-140A
Rated voltage ........................................ 14V
Slip-ring diameter:
  Min. ............................................. 15.4 mm
  New ............................................. 14.4 mm
Minimum brush protrusion from holder ..................... 7.5 mm
Output current:
  Bosch NC:
    At 1800 rpm .................................. 65 amps
    At 6000 rpm .................................. 130 amps
  Bosch E8:
    At 1800 rpm .................................. 75 amps
    At 6000 rpm .................................. 140 amps

### Starter motor
Type ................................................. Bosch DW
Output .............................................. 1.4 kW
No of teeth on pinion .................................. 9
No of teeth on ring gear ............................... 9
Ratio – engine/starter motor ............................ 15:1

| Torque wrench settings | Nm | lbf ft |
|---|---|---|
| Alternator belt tensioner | 45 | 33 |
| Engine mounting nut – right-hand side | 50 | 37 |
| Engine mounting nut – rear | 25 | 18 |

## 1 General information and precautions

### General information

Because of their engine-related functions, the components of the starting and charging systems are covered separately from the body electrical devices such as the lights, instruments, etc (which are covered in Chapter 12). Refer to Part B of this Chapter for information on the ignition system.

The electrical system is of the 12 volt negative earth type. The battery fitted as original equipment is of low-maintenance or 'maintenance-free' (sealed for life) type. The battery is charged by the alternator, which is belt-driven from the crankshaft pulley. During the life of the car, the original battery may have been renewed with a standard type battery.

The starter motor is of the pre-engaged type, incorporating an integral solenoid. On starting, the solenoid moves the drive pinion into engagement with the flywheel/driveplate ring gear before the starter motor is energised. Once the engine has started, a one-way clutch prevents the motor armature being driven by the engine until the pinion disengages from the ring gear. Unlike some modern starter motors, it incorporates epicyclic reduction gears between the armature and the pinion.

### Precautions

• Further details of the various systems are given in the relevant Sections of this Chapter. While some repair procedures are given, the usual course of action is to renew the component concerned. The owner whose interest extends beyond mere component renewal should obtain a copy of the *Automotive Electrical & Electronic Systems Manual*, available from the publishers of this manual.

• It is necessary to take extra care when working on the electrical system, to avoid damage to semi-conductor devices (diodes and transistors), and to avoid the risk of personal injury. In addition to the precautions given in *Safety first!* observe the following when working on the system:

• *Always remove rings, watches, etc, before working on the electrical system.* Even with the battery disconnected, capacitive discharge could occur if a component's live terminal is earthed through a metal object. This could cause a shock or nasty burn.

• *Do not reverse the battery connections.* Components such as the alternator, electronic control units, or any other components having semi-conductor circuitry, could be irreparably damaged.

• If the engine is being started using jump leads and a slave battery, refer to *Jump starting* on page 0•8.

**Caution: Never disconnect the battery terminals, the alternator, any electrical wiring, or any test instruments, when the engine is running.**

• Do not allow the engine to turn the alternator when the alternator is not connected.
• Never 'test' for alternator output by 'flashing' the output lead to earth.
• Never use an ohmmeter of the type incorporating a hand-cranked generator for circuit or continuity testing.
• Always ensure that the battery negative lead is disconnected when working on the electrical system.
• Before using electric-arc welding equipment on the car, disconnect the battery, alternator, and components such as the fuel injection/ignition electronic control unit, to protect them from the risk of damage.

## 2 Electrical fault finding – general information

Refer to Chapter 12.

## 3 Battery – testing and charging

### Testing

#### Standard and low-maintenance battery

**1** If the vehicle covers a small annual mileage, it is worthwhile checking the specific gravity of the electrolyte every three months, to determine the state of charge of the battery. Use a hydrometer to make the check, and compare the results with the following table. Note that the specific gravity readings assume an electrolyte temperature of 15°C (60°F); for every 10°C (18°F) below 15°C (60°F), subtract 0.007. For every 10°C (18°F) above 15°C (60°F), add 0.007. However, for convenience, the temperatures quoted in the following table are **ambient** (outdoor air) temperatures, above or below 25°C (77°F):

|  | Above 25°C (77°F) | Below 25°C (77°F) |
|---|---|---|
| Fully-charged | 1.210 to 1.230 | 1.270 to 1.290 |
| 70% charged | 1.170 to 1.190 | 1.230 to 1.250 |
| Discharged | 1.050 to 1.070 | 1.110 to 1.130 |

**2** If the battery condition is suspect, first check the specific gravity of electrolyte in each cell. A variation of 0.040 or more between any cells indicates loss of electrolyte or deterioration of the internal plates.
**3** If the specific gravity variation is 0.040 or more, the battery should be renewed. If the cell variation is satisfactory but the battery is discharged, it should be charged as described later in this Section.

### Maintenance-free battery

**4** In cases where a 'sealed for life' maintenance-free battery is fitted, topping-up and testing of the electrolyte in each cell is not possible. The condition of the battery can therefore only be tested using a battery condition indicator or a voltmeter.
**5** A battery with a built-in charge condition indicator may be fitted. The indicator is located in the top of the battery casing, and indicates the condition of the battery from its colour. If the indicator shows green, then the battery is in a good state of charge. If the indicator turns darker, eventually to black, then the battery requires charging, as described later in this Section. If the indicator shows clear/yellow, then the electrolyte level in the battery is too low to allow further use, and the battery should be renewed. **Do not** attempt to charge, load or jump start a battery when the indicator shows clear/yellow.
**6** If testing the battery using a voltmeter, connect the voltmeter across the battery, and compare the result with those given in the Specifications under 'charge condition'. The test is only accurate if the battery has not been subjected to any kind of charge for the previous six hours, including charging by the alternator. If this is not the case, switch on the headlights for 30 seconds, then wait four to five minutes after switching off the headlights before testing the battery. All other electrical circuits must be switched off, so check (for instance) that the doors and tailgate or boot lid are fully shut when making the test.
**7** If the voltage reading is less than 12.2 volts, then the battery is discharged. A reading of 12.2 to 12.4 volts indicates a partially-discharged condition.
**8** If the battery is to be charged, remove it from the vehicle (Section 4) and charge it as described in the following paragraphs.

### Charging

**Note:** *The following is intended as a guide only. Always refer to the manufacturer's recommendations (often printed on a label attached to the battery) before charging a battery.*

#### Standard and low-maintenance battery

**9** Charge the battery at a rate of 3.5 to 4 amps, and continue to charge the battery at this rate until no further rise in specific gravity is noted over a four hour period.
**10** Alternatively, a trickle charger charging at the rate of 1.5 amps can safely be used overnight.
**11** Specially rapid 'boost' charges which are claimed to restore the power of the battery in 1 to 2 hours are not recommended, as they can cause serious damage to the battery plates through overheating.
**12** While charging the battery, note that the temperature of the electrolyte should never exceed 37.8°C (100°F).

## Maintenance-free battery

**13** This battery type requires a longer period to fully recharge than the standard type, the time taken being dependent on the extent of discharge, but it can take anything up to three days.

**14** A constant-voltage type charger is required, to be set, where possible, to 13.9 to 14.9 volts with a charger current below 25 amps. Using this method, the battery should be usable within three hours, giving a voltage reading of 12.5 volts, but this is for a partially-discharged battery and, as mentioned, full charging can take considerably longer.

**15** Use of a normal trickle charger should not be detrimental to the battery, provided excessive gasing is not allowed to occur, and the battery is not allowed to become hot.

## 4 Battery – removal and refitting

### Removal

**1** The battery is located at the front left-hand side of the engine compartment. Unclip the cover from the battery **(see illustration)**.

**2** Loosen the clamp nut and disconnect the lead at the negative (earth) terminal **(see illustration)**. Disconnect the lead at the positive terminal in the same way.

**3** Unscrew the retaining nut and remove the battery retaining clamp which secures the battery to the mounting bracket.

**4** Lift the battery out of the engine compartment (take care not to tilt it excessively).

### Refitting

**5** Refitting is a reversal of removal. Smear petroleum jelly on the terminals after reconnecting the leads, and always reconnect the positive lead first, and the negative lead last.

## 5 Charging system – testing

**Note:** *Refer to the warnings given in 'Safety first!' and in Section 1 of this Chapter before starting work.*

**1** If the ignition/no-charge warning light does not come on when the ignition is switched on, first check the alternator wiring connections for security. If satisfactory, check that the warning light bulb has not blown, and that the bulbholder is secure in its location in the instrument panel. If the light still fails to illuminate, check the continuity of the warning light feed wire from the alternator to the bulbholder. If all is satisfactory, the alternator is at fault, and should be taken to an auto-

**4.1 Removing the battery cover from the battery**

electrician for testing and repair, or else renewed.

**2** If the ignition warning light comes on when the engine is running, stop the engine. Check that the drivebelt is intact and correctly tensioned (see Chapter 1), and that the alternator connections are secure. If all is satisfactory, check the alternator brushes and slip-rings as described in Section 8. If the fault persists, the alternator should be taken to an auto-electrician for testing and repair, or else renewed.

**3** If the alternator output is suspect even though the warning light functions correctly, the regulated voltage may be checked as follows.

**4** Connect a voltmeter across the battery terminals, and start the engine.

**5** Increase the engine speed until the voltmeter reading remains steady; the reading should be approximately 12 to 13 volts, and no more than 14 volts.

**6** Switch on as many electrical accessories (eg, the headlights, heated rear window and heater blower) as possible, and check that the alternator maintains the regulated voltage at around 13 to 14 volts.

**7** If the regulated voltage is not as stated, the fault may be due to worn brushes, weak brush springs, a faulty voltage regulator, a faulty diode, a severed phase winding, or worn or damaged slip-rings. The brushes and slip-rings may be checked (see Section 8), but if the fault persists, the alternator should be taken to an auto-electrician for testing and repair, or else renewed.

**7.7 Removing the auxiliary belt tensioner . . .**

**4.2 Loosen the clamp nut and disconnect at the negative (earth) terminal first**

## 6 Alternator drivebelt – removal, refitting and tensioning

Refer to the procedure given for the auxiliary drivebelt in Chapter 1.

## 7 Alternator – removal and refitting

### Removal

**1** Open the bonnet and unclip the covers from top of the intake manifold and battery, then disconnect the battery negative lead.

**2** Apply the handbrake, then jack up the front of the car and support on axle stands (see *Jacking and vehicle support*). Remove the right-hand front wheel.

**3** Remove the right-hand front wing inner plastic moulding/wheel arch liner for access to the rear of the engine.

**4** Remove the auxiliary drivebelt as described in Chapter 1, Section 28.

**5** Remove the intake manifold as described in Chapter 4A, Section 18.

**6** Remove the front exhaust pipe section (including catalytic converter) as described in Chapter 4A, Section 20.

**7** Undo the retaining bolt and remove the auxiliary belt tensioner **(see illustration)**.

**8** Unscrew and remove the alternator upper mounting bolt **(see illustration)**.

**7.8 . . . then remove the upper alternator mounting bolt (arrowed)**

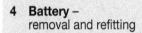

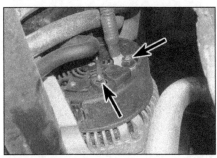

**7.9  Unscrew the terminal nuts (arrowed) and disconnect the wiring from the rear of the alternator**

**7.10 Removing the alternator lower mounting bolt**

**12** Lift the alternator upwards from its position to remove from the engine compartment.

### Refitting

**13** Refitting is a reversal of removal. Ensure that the alternator mountings are securely tightened, and refit the components referring to the relevant Chapters.

---

## 8  Alternator brushes and regulator – inspection and renewal

**1** Remove the alternator as described in Section 7.

**2** Unscrew the large terminal nut and the screws securing the cover to the rear of the alternator **(see illustrations)**.

**3** Using a screwdriver, lever off the cover, and remove it from the rear of the alternator **(see illustrations)**.

**4** Unscrew and remove the two retaining screws, and remove the regulator/brush holder from the rear of the alternator **(see illustrations)**.

**5** Measure the protrusion of each brush from its holder, using a steel rule or vernier calipers **(see illustration)**. If less than 7.5 mm, a new regulator/brush assembly should be obtained.

**6** If the brushes are in good condition, clean them and check that they move freely in their holders.

**7** Clean the alternator slip-rings with a fuel-moistened cloth. Check for signs of scoring or

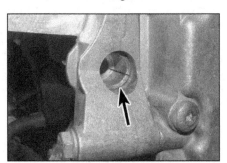

**7.11a  Metal sleeve (arrowed) in the mounting bracket . . .**

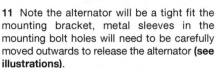

**7.11b  . . . this sleeve (arrowed) will need to be tapped outwards to release the alternator**

**9** Note the position of the wires on the rear of the alternator, then unscrew the terminal nuts and disconnect the wires **(see illustration)**.

**10** Unscrew the alternator lower mounting bolt **(see illustration)**.

**11** Note the alternator will be a tight fit the mounting bracket, metal sleeves in the mounting bolt holes will need to be carefully moved outwards to release the alternator **(see illustrations)**.

**8.2a Unscrew the large terminal nut . . .**

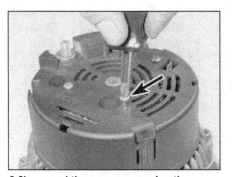

**8.2b . . . and the screws securing the cover to the rear of the alternator**

**8.3a Lever off the cover . . .**

**8.3b . . . and remove it from the alternator**

**8.4a Remove the screws (arrowed) . . .**

**8.4b . . . and withdraw the regulator/brush holder from the rear of the alternator**

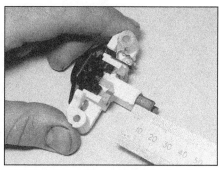

**8.5 Measuring the brush protrusion from the holder**

burning on the surface of the slip-rings. It may be possible to have the slip-rings renovated by an electrical specialist.

**8** Refit the regulator/brush holder assembly, and securely tighten the retaining screws.

**9** Refit the cover, then insert and tighten the retaining screws and refit the large terminal nut.

**10** Refit the alternator with reference to Section 7.

## 9 Starting system – testing

**Note:** *Refer to the precautions given in 'Safety first!' and in Section 1 of this Chapter before starting work.*

**1** If the starter motor fails to operate when the ignition key is turned to the appropriate position, the following possible causes may apply:

a) *The battery is faulty.*
b) *The electrical connections between the switch, solenoid, battery and starter motor are somewhere failing to pass the necessary current from the battery through the starter to earth.*
c) *The solenoid is faulty.*
d) *The starter motor is mechanically or electrically defective.*

**2** To check the battery, switch on the headlights. If they dim after a few seconds, this indicates that the battery is discharged – recharge (see Section 3) or renew the battery. If the headlights glow brightly, operate the starter

on the ignition switch, and observe the lights. If they dim, this indicates that current is reaching the starter motor – therefore, the fault must lie in the starter motor. If the lights continue to glow brightly (and no clicking sound can be heard from the starter motor solenoid), this indicates that there is a fault in the circuit or solenoid – see the following paragraphs. If the starter motor turns slowly when operated, but the battery is in good condition, then this indicates that either the starter motor is faulty, or that there is considerable resistance somewhere in the circuit.

**3** If a fault in the circuit is suspected, disconnect the battery leads, the starter/solenoid wiring and the engine/transmission earth strap. Thoroughly clean the connections, and reconnect the leads and wiring, then use a voltmeter or test light to check that full battery voltage is available at the battery positive lead connection on the solenoid, and that the earth is sound.

**4** If the battery and all connections are in good condition, check the circuit by disconnecting the wire from the solenoid terminal. Connect a voltmeter or test light between the wire end and a good earth (such as the battery negative terminal), and check that the wire is live when the ignition switch is turned to the 'start' position. If it is, then the circuit is sound – if not, the circuit wiring can be checked as described in Chapter 12.

**5** The solenoid contacts can be checked by connecting a voltmeter or test light between the terminal on the starter side of the solenoid, and earth. When the ignition switch is turned to the 'start' position, there should be a reading or lighted bulb, as applicable. If there is no reading or lighted bulb, the solenoid or contacts are faulty and the solenoid should be renewed.

**6** If the circuit and solenoid are proved sound, the fault must lie in the starter motor. Begin checking the starter motor by removing it (see Section 10), and checking the brushes (see Section 11). If the fault does not lie in the brushes, the motor windings must be faulty. In this event, it may be possible to have the starter motor overhauled by a specialist, but check on the availability and cost of spares before proceeding, as it may prove more economical to obtain a new or exchange motor.

## 10 Starter motor – removal and refitting

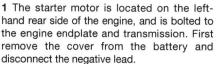

### Removal

**1** The starter motor is located on the left-hand rear side of the engine, and is bolted to the engine endplate and transmission. First remove the cover from the battery and disconnect the negative lead.

**2** Apply the handbrake, then jack up the front of the car and support on axle stands (see *Jacking and vehicle support*).

**3** From inside the engine compartment, remove the starter motor upper mounting bolt **(see illustration)**.

**4** Unscrew the nut(s) and disconnect the wiring terminal(s) from the starter/solenoid.

**5** Cut and release the cable-tie/strap from around the solenoid to release the wiring loom **(see illustration)**.

**6** From under the vehicle, unscrew the lower starter motor mounting nut, then lower the starter motor from the engine compartment **(see illustration)**.

### Refitting

**7** Refitting is a reversal of removal. Tighten all wire connections securely.

## 11 Starter motor – testing and overhaul

**Note:** *At the time of writing, no individual starter motor components were available from Saab. An auto-electrical specialist should be able to supply and fit parts such as brushes.*

If the starter motor is thought to be defective, it should be removed from the vehicle (as described in Section 10) and taken to an auto-electrician for assessment. In the majority of cases, new starter motor brushes can be fitted at a reasonable cost. However, check the cost of repairs first as it may prove more economical to purchase a new or exchange motor.

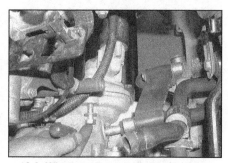

**10.3 Withdraw the upper starter motor mounting bolt, from the top of the transmission bellhousing**

**10.5 Remove the cable-tie (arrowed) to release the wiring loom**

**10.6 Unscrew the starter motor lower mounting nut (arrowed)**

Notes

Notes

# Chapter 5 Part B:
# Ignition system

## Contents

## Degrees of difficulty

| | | | | | | | | | |
|---|---|---|---|---|---|---|---|---|---|
| **Easy,** suitable for novice with little experience |  | **Fairly easy,** suitable for beginner with some experience |  | **Fairly difficult,** suitable for competent DIY mechanic |  | **Difficult,** suitable for experienced DIY mechanic |  | **Very difficult,** suitable for expert DIY or professional |  |

## Specifications

### System type
System type . . . . . . . . . . . . . . . . . . . . . . . . . . . . . . . . . . . . . . . . . . . Direct Ignition (DI) system incorporated in Trionic engine management system

### Direct Ignition (DI) system
Ignition discharge module:
   Capacitor voltage . . . . . . . . . . . . . . . . . . . . . . . . . . . . . . . . . . . . . 400 volts
   Ignition voltage (maximum) . . . . . . . . . . . . . . . . . . . . . . . . . . . . . . 40 000 volts
Ignition timing . . . . . . . . . . . . . . . . . . . . . . . . . . . . . . . . . . . . . . . . . Pre-programmed in ECU

### Firing order . . . . . . . . . . . . . . . . . . . . . . . . . . . . . . . . . . . . . . . . . 1-3-4-2 (No 1 cylinder at timing chain end)

### Torque wrench settings

| | Nm | lbf ft |
|---|---|---|
| Crankshaft pulley bolt . . . . . . . . . . . . . . . . . . . . . . . . . . . . . . . . . . . | 175 | 130 |
| Ignition discharge module . . . . . . . . . . . . . . . . . . . . . . . . . . . . . . . | 12 | 9 |
| Spark plugs . . . . . . . . . . . . . . . . . . . . . . . . . . . . . . . . . . . . . . . . . . | 28 | 21 |

## 1 General information

1 All models have a Direct Ignition system which is incorporated into the Saab Trionic engine management system. With this system, a single electronic control unit (ECU) controls both the fuel injection and ignition functions. More information on the system components are given in Chapter 4A.

2 The Direct Ignition system uses a separate HT coil for each spark plug **(see illustration)**. The system electronic control unit (ECU) monitors the engine by means of various sensors, in order to determine the most efficient ignition timing.

3 The components of the system are a crankshaft position/speed sensor, ignition discharge module with one coil per plug, diagnostic socket, ECU, pressure sensor in the inlet manifold (to determine engine load), and a solenoid valve (to regulate the turbocharger operation).

4 During starting at a crankshaft speed in excess of 150 rpm, HT sparks are triggered in the cylinder pair with the pistons at TDC. Under difficult conditions, multi-sparking occurs during this period, to aid starting. The ECU determines in which cylinder combustion is taking place by monitoring the flow of current across the spark plug electrodes, and then uses this information to determine the firing.

5 When the engine starts, the ignition timing is always set to 10° BTDC, and will remain at this setting until the engine speed exceeds 825 rpm. The ECU will regulate the ignition timing at engine speeds above 825 rpm.

6 When the ignition is switched off and the engine stops, the main relay remains operational for a further 6 seconds. During this period, the Trionic control module earths all the trigger leads 210 times a second for 5 seconds, in order to burn off impurities from the spark plug electrodes.

7 Because the system does not use any HT leads, radio suppression must be incorporated in the spark plugs, so resistor-type plugs must always be used.

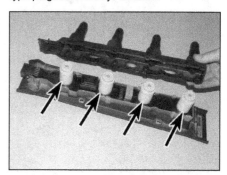

1.2 Separate coils (arrowed) – one for each cylinder

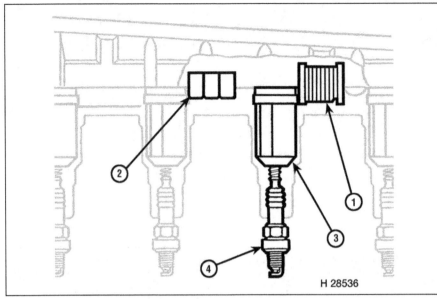

1.8a Direct Ignition cartridge

1  Transformer (12 volts/400 volts)    3  Ignition coil
2  Capacitor    4  Spark plug

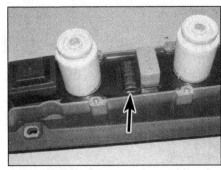

1.8b Direct Ignition capacitor (arrowed)
located in the cartridge

8 The Direct Ignition system uses the capacitive discharge method of producing an HT spark. Approximately 400 volts is stored in a capacitor (see illustrations), and at the time of ignition, this voltage is discharged through the primary circuit of the relevant coil. Approximately 40 000 volts is induced in the HT secondary coil, and this is discharged across the spark plug electrodes.

9 Should a fault occur in the system, a fault code is stored in the ECU. This code can only be accessed by a Saab dealer, using dedicated equipment.

10 Note that the starter motor must never be operated with the ignition cartridge disconnected from the spark plugs but still connected to the wiring loom. This can cause irreversible damage to the cartridge.

11 The engine management system controls engine precombustion via a knock sensor incorporated into the ignition system. Mounted onto the cylinder block, the sensor detects the high frequency vibrations caused when the engine starts to pre-ignite, or 'pink'. Under

these conditions, the knock sensor sends an electrical signal to the ECU, which in turn retards the ignition advance setting in small steps until the 'pinking' ceases. With the Saab Trionic system, the spark plugs themselves are used as knock sensors, instead of employing a separate knock detector in the cylinder block. It achieves this by applying a small, direct current voltage across each spark plug. When two cylinders approach TDC, this voltage causes an ionisation current to flow across the terminals of the spark plug in the cylinder under combustion; a high current indicates that knock is occurring thus indicating which cylinder requires ignition retardation. Sequential control of the fuel injection is achieved in the same manner (see Chapter 4A).

## 2  Ignition system – testing

⚠️ *Warning: Voltages produced by an electronic ignition system are considerably higher than those produced by conventional ignition systems. Extreme care must be taken when working on the system with the ignition switched on. Persons with surgically-implanted cardiac pacemaker devices should keep well clear of the ignition circuits, components and test equipment. Refer to the precautions in Chapter 5A, Section 1, before starting work. Always switch off the ignition before disconnecting or connecting any component, and when using a multi-meter to check resistances.*

1 If a fault appears in the engine management system, first check that all wiring is secure and in good condition. If necessary, individual components of the Direct Ignition system may be removed for visual investigation as described later in this Chapter. Coils are best checked by substituting a suspect one with a known good coil, and checking if the misfire is cured.

2 Due to the location of the spark plugs beneath the ignition discharge module, it is not possible to easily check the HT circuit for faults. Further testing should be carried out by a Saab dealer, who will have equipment to access fault codes stored in the system ECU.

## 3  Ignition discharge module – removal and refitting

### Removal

1 Open the bonnet, unclip the cover from the top of the battery and disconnect the battery negative lead.

2 Unscrew the four screws securing the ignition cartridge to the top of the cylinder head (see illustration).

3 Disconnect the wiring plug, located on the left-hand end of the ignition discharge module (see illustration).

4 Where applicable, disconnect any wiring support clips or earth lead.

5 Lift the ignition cartridge, at the same time releasing it from the tops of the spark plugs (see illustration).

3.2 Slacken and remove the four screws (arrowed) securing the ignition cartridge

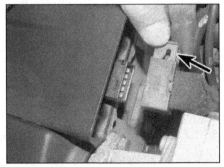

3.3 Release the retaining clip (arrowed) and disconnect the wiring connector

3.5 Lift the cartridge straight up to release it from the spark plugs

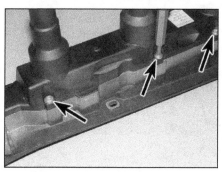

3.6a Unscrew the screws (three shown) . . .

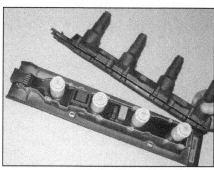

3.6b . . . and separate the black lower shroud from the cartridge

**Warning: When the ignition discharge module is removed, it must be kept in the upright position. If the ignition discharge module has been turned upside down for a length of time, leave it in the fitted position for a couple of hours before starting.**

6 If necessary, the shroud may be removed from the bottom of the cartridge, by inverting it and removing the retaining screws. Separate the black (lower) shroud from the cartridge **(see illustrations)**.

7 The HT springs may be removed from the shroud by careful use of a screwdriver **(see illustration)**.

## Refitting

8 Refitting is a reversal of removal, but tighten the retaining screws to the specified torque.

### 4 Ignition HT coils – general information

The four ignition coils are an integral part of the ignition discharge module upper assembly and can only be purchased from Saab as a complete unit.

If required, the ignition discharge module can be removed from the vehicle as described

in Section 3, then taken to your local Saab dealer or motor vehicle electrical specialist, where they can check the ignition module.

**Warning: When the ignition discharge module is removed, it must be kept in the upright position. If the ignition discharge module has been turned upside down for a length of time, leave it in the fitted position for a couple of hours before starting.**

### 5 Slotted rotor for crankshaft sensor – removal and refitting

## Removal

1 The slotted rotor is located on the flywheel/driveplate end of the crankshaft. Remove the crankshaft as described in Chapter 2B.

2 Using a Torx key, unscrew the four screws securing the slotted rotor to the crankshaft, then remove the rotor over the end of the crankshaft.

## Refitting

3 Refitting is a reversal of removal. Note that the rotor can only be fitted in one position, since the bolt holes are unequally-spaced.

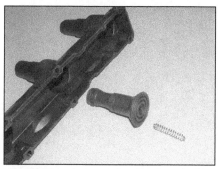

3.7 Rubber sleeve and spring from inside lower shroud

### 6 Ignition timing – general information

The ignition timing is preprogrammed into the system ECU, and cannot be adjusted or even checked with any accuracy. If the timing is thought to be incorrect, the car should be taken to a Saab dealer, who will have the necessary equipment to extract any fault codes stored in the ECU. For further information see Chapter 4A.

Notes

Notes

# Chapter 6
# Clutch

## Contents

## Degrees of difficulty

| | | | | |
|---|---|---|---|---|
| **Easy,** suitable for novice with little experience  | **Fairly easy,** suitable for beginner with some experience  | **Fairly difficult,** suitable for competent DIY mechanic  | **Difficult,** suitable for experienced DIY mechanic  | **Very difficult,** suitable for expert DIY or professional |

## Specifications

**System type** . . . . . . . . . . . . . . . . . . . . . . . . . . . . . . . . . . . . . . . Single dry-plate clutch with diaphragm spring, operated by master/slave cylinder hydraulic release system

**Friction plate**

Diameter . . . . . . . . . . . . . . . . . . . . . . . . . . . . . . . . . . . . . . . . . . . . 228 mm
Thickness:
   New . . . . . . . . . . . . . . . . . . . . . . . . . . . . . . . . . . . . . . . . . . . . 7.3 mm
   Minimum . . . . . . . . . . . . . . . . . . . . . . . . . . . . . . . . . . . . . . . . . 5.5 mm

**Hydraulic release mechanism**

Slave cylinder stroke . . . . . . . . . . . . . . . . . . . . . . . . . . . . . . . . . . . 8.0 mm
Master cylinder piston diameter . . . . . . . . . . . . . . . . . . . . . . . . . . . 15.87 mm

| **Torque wrench settings** | Nm | lbf ft |
|---|---|---|
| Clutch pedal/master cylinder mounting bracket to bulkhead . . . . . . . | 24 | 18 |
| Clutch pressure plate to flywheel . . . . . . . . . . . . . . . . . . . . . . . . . . | 22 | 16 |
| Master cylinder securing screws . . . . . . . . . . . . . . . . . . . . . . . . . . | 20 | 15 |
| Slave cylinder securing screws . . . . . . . . . . . . . . . . . . . . . . . . . . . | 10 | 7 |
| Supply pipe to slave cylinder . . . . . . . . . . . . . . . . . . . . . . . . . . . . | 22 | 16 |

## 1 General description

1 The hydraulic clutch system is of single dry-plate type, and consists of the following main components: the clutch pedal, master cylinder, release bearing/slave cylinder, friction plate, and pressure plate with its integral diaphragm spring and cover **(see illustration)**.
2 The friction plate is free to slide along the splines of the transmission input shaft. This is held in position between the flywheel and the pressure plate by the pressure exerted on the pressure plate by the diaphragm spring. Friction lining material is riveted to both sides of the friction plate. Spring cushioning between the friction linings and the hub absorbs transmission shocks, and helps to ensure a smooth take-up of power as the clutch is engaged.
3 The diaphragm spring is mounted on pins, and is held in place in the cover by annular fulcrum rings.
4 Effort is transmitted from the clutch pedal to the master cylinder, mounted on the rear of the engine compartment bulkhead, via a pushrod. The master cylinder piston forces hydraulic fluid through a supply pipe to the slave cylinder, which is located inside the transmission casing, mounted concentrically over the transmission input shaft. The fluid forces the piston out of the slave cylinder, thus actuating the release bearing.
5 When the clutch pedal is depressed, the release bearing is forced to slide along the input shaft sleeve, to bear against the centre of the diaphragm spring, thus pushing the centre of the diaphragm spring inwards. The diaphragm spring acts against a circular

fulcrum ring in the cover. When the centre of the spring is pushed in, the outside of the spring is pushed out, so allowing the pressure plate to move backwards away from the friction plate.
6 When the clutch pedal is released, the diaphragm spring forces the pressure plate into contact with the friction linings on the friction plate. This simultaneously pushes the friction plate forwards on its splines, forcing it against the flywheel. The friction plate is now firmly sandwiched between the pressure plate and the flywheel, and drive is taken up.
7 The fluid used in the hydraulic clutch system is the same as that used in the braking system, hence fluid is supplied to the master cylinder from a tapping on the brake fluid reservoir. The clutch hydraulic system must be sealed before work is carried out on any of its components and then, on completion, topped-up and bled to remove any air bubbles. Details of these procedures are given in Section 6 of this Chapter.

## 2 Clutch pedal – removal and refitting

**Note:** *The clutch pedal is part of the pedal bracket assembly and cannot be removed separately.*

### Removal

1 Remove the facia panel as described in Chapter 11.
2 On right-hand drive models, from inside the engine bay, remove the cover from the top of the engine and the intake manifold.
3 On left-hand drive models, remove the battery, then undo the retaining bolts/nuts

and remove the central electric unit and fuse holder from the left-hand side top strut mounting.
4 From inside the engine bay, undo the four retaining nuts from the pedal bracket assembly. **Note:** *two of the nuts are the clutch master cylinder retaining nuts.*
5 From inside the vehicle, undo the retaining bolts and remove the knee shield from across the lower part of the steering column and bulkhead.
6 Disconnect the wiring connector from the pedal switch, then undo the retaining bolts securing the pedal bracket to the facia mounting crossmember.
7 Unhook the spring from the clutch pedal, remove the securing clip and withdraw the pivot pin.
8 Undo the lower steering column shaft joint securing bolt, and detach it from the splines on the steering rack. **Note:** *Do not prise open the joint to remove (see Chapter 10 for further information).*

⚠️ **Warning: As the steering column is moved away from the bulkhead, take care that the upper and lower parts of the steering column do not separate, see Chapter 10.**

9 Undo the retaining bolts from the facia mounting crossmember, then withdraw the crossmember to allow enough room to withdraw the pedal bracket assembly from the footwell.

### Refitting

10 Refitting is a reversal of removal procedure. Ensure that the pedal return spring is correctly fitted and all retaining bolts are tightened to the specified torque.
11 On completion, bleed the clutch hydraulic system with reference to Section 6.

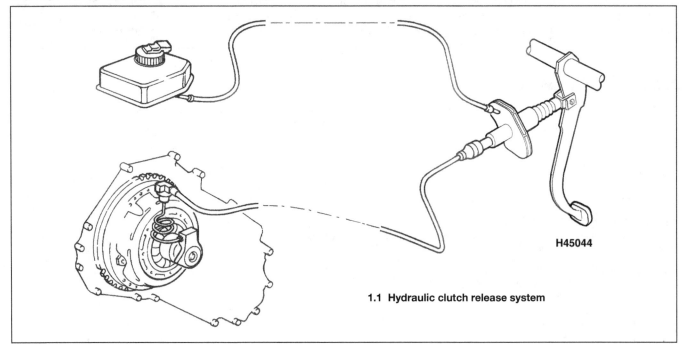

H45044

**1.1 Hydraulic clutch release system**

3.5 Lift off the pressure plate, then recover the friction plate, noting its orientation

## 3 Clutch assembly – removal, inspection and refitting

**Warning: Dust created by clutch wear and deposited on the clutch components may contain asbestos, which is a health hazard. DO NOT blow it out with compressed air, nor inhale any of it. DO NOT use petrol or petroleum-based solvents to clean off the dust. Brake system cleaner or methylated spirit should be used to flush the dust into a suitable receptacle. After the clutch components are wiped clean with clean rags, dispose of the contaminated rags and cleaner in a sealed, marked container.**
**Note:** *Although some friction materials may no longer contain asbestos, it is safest to assume that they DO, and to take precautions accordingly*

### Removal

**1** Unless the complete engine/transmission is to be removed from the car and separated for major overhaul (see Chapter 2B), the clutch can be accessed by removing the transmission, as described in Chapter 7A.
**2** Before disturbing any of the clutch components, mark the relationship between the pressure plate, friction plate and the flywheel.
**3** To aid the removal of the pressure plate, the flywheel should ideally be locked in position by bolting a locking tool to one of the transmission mounting holes, and engaging it with the flywheel ring gear. If a universal flywheel locking tool is not available, the crankshaft (and hence the flywheel) can be held stationary using a wrench and socket on the crankshaft sprocket bolt. The help of an assistant will be required to complete this task.
**4** Working diagonally across the pressure plate, progressively slacken the mounting bolts, half a turn at a time, until they can be removed by hand.
**5** With all the bolts removed, lift off the clutch assembly. Be prepared to catch the friction plate as the cover assembly is lifted from the flywheel, and note which way round the friction plate is fitted **(see illustration)**.

3.11 With the clutch removed, check the machined surface of the flywheel (arrowed)

### Inspection

**Note:** *Due to the amount of work necessary to remove and refit clutch components, it is usually considered good practice to renew the clutch friction plate, pressure plate assembly and release bearing as a matched set, even if only one of these is actually worn enough to require renewal.*
**6** When cleaning clutch components, observe the warning at the beginning of this Section regarding the hazards of handling the friction materials contained in clutch components; remove dust using a clean, dry cloth, and working in a well-ventilated atmosphere.
**7** Check the friction plate facings for signs of wear, damage or oil contamination. If the friction material is cracked, burnt, scored or damaged, or if it is contaminated with oil or grease (shown by shiny black patches), the friction plate must be renewed.
**8** If the friction material is still serviceable, check that the centre boss splines are unworn, that the torsion springs are in good condition and securely fastened, and that all the rivets are tightly fastened. If any wear or damage is found, the friction plate must be renewed.
**9** If the friction material is fouled with oil, this must be due to an oil leak from the crankshaft left-hand oil seal, from the sump-to-cylinder block joint, or from the transmission input shaft; renew the seal or repair the joint, as appropriate, as described in Chapter 2A or 7A before installing the new friction plate.
**10** Check the pressure plate assembly for obvious signs of wear or damage; shake it to check for loose rivets or worn or damaged fulcrum rings, and check that the drive straps securing the pressure plate to the cover do not show signs of overheating (such as a deep yellow or blue discoloration). If the diaphragm spring is worn or damaged, or if its pressure is in any way suspect, the pressure plate assembly should be renewed.
**11** Examine the machined bearing surfaces of the pressure plate and of the flywheel **(see illustration)**; they should be clean, completely flat and free from scratches or scoring. If either is discoloured from excessive heat or shows signs of cracks it should be renewed, although minor damage of this nature can sometimes be polished away using emery paper.

3.14 Place the friction plate against the flywheel; the stamped lettering FLYWHEEL SIDE should face towards the flywheel

**12** Check that the release bearing contact surface rotates smoothly and easily, with no sign of noise or roughness, and that the surface itself is smooth and unworn, with no signs of cracks, pitting or scoring. If there is any doubt about its condition, the bearing must be renewed; refer to Section 4 for guidance.

### Refitting

**13** On reassembly, ensure that the bearing surfaces of the flywheel and pressure plate are completely clean, smooth and free from oil or grease. Use solvent to remove any protective grease from new components.
**14** Offer up the friction plate so that its spring hub assembly faces away from the flywheel; observe any manufacturer's markings which show which way around the plate should be fitted **(see illustration)**.
**15** Refit the pressure plate assembly to the flywheel, engaging it with its locating dowels; align the marks made on dismantling if the original pressure plate is being re-used. Fit the pressure plate bolts, hand-tightening them only at this stage, so that the friction plate can be rotated to aid alignment, if necessary.
**16** The friction plate must now be centralised inside the pressure plate assembly, so that when the transmission is refitted, the input shaft will pass through the splines at the centre of the friction plate. This can be achieved by passing a large screwdriver or wrench extension bar through the friction plate and into the hole in the crankshaft; the friction plate can then be moved around until it is centred over the crankshaft hole. Alternatively, a universal clutch alignment tool can be used; these can be obtained from most car accessory shops. Ensure that the friction plate alignment is correct before proceeding any further.

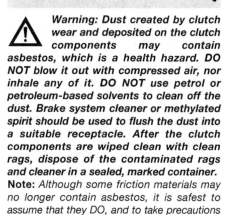

> **HAYNES HINT** *A clutch alignment device can be made up from a length of metal rod or wooden dowel which is either tapered at one end, or fits closely inside the crankshaft hole, and has insulating tape wound around it, to match the internal diameter of the friction plate splined hole.*

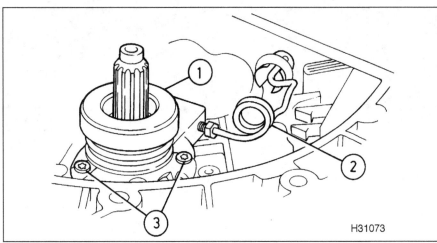

**4.3 Slave cylinder**

*1 Release bearing*    *2 Hydraulic fluid pipe*    *3 Securing screws*

**17** When the friction plate is centralised, progressively tighten the pressure plate bolts in a diagonal sequence and to the specified torque setting.

**18** Where applicable, remove the flywheel locking tool.

**19** Apply a thin smear of high-melting point grease to the splines of the friction plate and the transmission input shaft.

**20** Refit the transmission as described in Chapter 7A.

## 4 Clutch slave cylinder/ release bearing – removal and refitting

**Note:** *The clutch slave cylinder and thrust release bearing are integrated and can only be purchased as a complete assembly.*

### Removal

**1** Unless the complete engine/transmission unit is to be removed from the car and separated for major overhaul (see Chapter 2B), the clutch release cylinder can be reached by removing the transmission only, as described in Chapter 7A.

**2** Wipe clean the outside of the slave cylinder then slacken the union nut and disconnect the hydraulic pipe. Wipe up any spilt fluid with a clean cloth.

**3** Unscrew the three retaining bolts and slide the slave cylinder from the transmission input shaft **(see illustration)**. Where applicable, remove the sealing ring which is fitted between the cylinder and transmission housing and discard it; a new one must be used on refitting. Whilst the cylinder is removed, take care not to allow any debris to enter the transmission unit.

**4** The slave cylinder is a sealed unit and cannot be overhauled. If the cylinder seals have failed or the release bearing is noisy or rough in operation, then the complete unit must be renewed.

### Refitting

**5** Ensure the slave cylinder and transmission mating surfaces are clean and dry, then fit the new sealing ring to the transmission recess.

**6** Lubricate the slave cylinder seal with a smear of transmission oil then carefully ease the cylinder along the input shaft and into position. Ensure the sealing ring is still correctly seated in its groove then refit the slave cylinder retaining bolts and tighten them to the specified torque.

**7** Reconnect the hydraulic pipe to the slave cylinder, tightening its union nut to the specified torque.

**8** Prime and bleed the slave cylinder with hydraulic fluid, as described in Section 6.

**9** Refit the transmission unit as described in Chapter 7A.

## 5 Clutch master cylinder – removal and refitting

### Removal

**1** Remove the cover from the battery, then disconnect the battery negative cable and position it away from the terminal.

**2** Referring to Chapter 11 for guidance, remove the sound insulating trim panel from underneath the facia, on the driver's side.

**3** At the connection point between the master cylinder link rod and the clutch pedal, use a pair of long-nosed pliers to remove the clip from the spigot, then pull off the link rod. Also release the clutch pedal return spring.

**4** As a precaution, place a dust sheet under the clutch pedal in the footwell, to catch any hydraulic fluid spillage.

**5** On right-hand drive models, from inside the engine bay, remove the cover from the top of the intake manifold.

**6** On left-hand drive models, from inside the engine bay, undo the retaining bolts/nuts and remove the central electric unit and fuse holder from the left-hand side top strut mounting.

> ⚠ **Warning: Observe the warnings given in Section 6, regarding the hazards of handling hydraulic fluid.**

**7** From inside the engine bay, seal the flexible supply hose from the fluid reservoir, using a proprietary brake hose clamp between the fluid reservoir and the master cylinder.

**8** Release the hose clip, and pull the supply hose off the master cylinder port. Be prepared for a small amount of hydraulic fluid loss; position a container or a wad of rags underneath the joint to catch any spillage.

**9** Slide out the retaining clip and free the hydraulic delivery pipe from the front of the master cylinder **(see illustration)**. Plug the

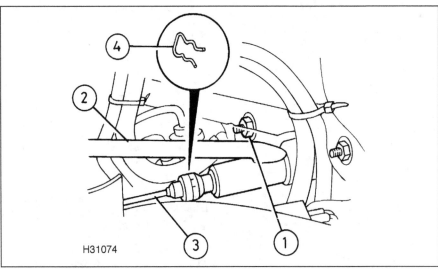

**5.9 Remove the nut securing the right-hand side of the clutch pedal/master cylinder bracket to the rear of the engine compartment bulkhead**

*1 Securing nut*    *2 Supply hose*    *3 Delivery pipe*    *4 Retaining clip*

pipe end and master cylinder port to minimise fluid loss and prevent the entry of dirt. Where applicable, recover the sealing ring from the union and discard it; a new one must be used on refitting. Refit the retaining clip to the master cylinder groove, to prevent loss of clip.

**10** Remove the two nuts from the retaining bolts, and lift the master cylinder away from the bulkhead, guiding the link rod through the aperture. Recover the gasket and inspect it for damage; renew it if necessary.

### Refitting

**11** Refit the master cylinder by following the removal procedure in reverse. Noting the following points:
   a) *Make sure the delivery pipe to the master cylinder is secured correctly in position with the retaining clip.*
   b) *Observe the specified torque wrench setting when tightening the master cylinder-to-pedal bracket nuts.*
   c) *On completion, refer to Section 6 and bleed the hydraulic system.*

## 6  Clutch hydraulic system – bleeding

### General information

⚠️ **Warning: Hydraulic fluid is poisonous; thoroughly wash off spills from bare skin without delay. Seek immediate medical advice if any fluid is swallowed or gets into the eyes. Certain types of hydraulic fluid are inflammable, and may ignite when brought into contact with hot components. When servicing any hydraulic system, it is safest to assume that the fluid IS inflammable, and to take precautions against the risk of fire as though it is petrol that is being handled. It is also hygroscopic (absorbs moisture from the air); excess moisture content lowers the fluid boiling point to an unacceptable level, resulting in a loss of hydraulic pressure. Old fluid may have suffered contamination, and should not be re-used. When topping-up or renewing the fluid, always use the recommended grade, and ensure that it comes from a freshly-opened sealed container.**

**HAYNES HiNT** *Hydraulic fluid is an effective paint stripper, and will also attack many plastics. If spillage occurs onto painted bodywork or fittings, it should be washed off immediately, using copious quantities of fresh water.*

**1** Whenever the clutch hydraulic lines are disconnected for service or repair, a certain amount of air will enter the system. The presence of air in any hydraulic system will cause a degree of elasticity; this will translate into poor pedal feel and reduced travel, leading to an inefficient clutch release action and difficult gear changes. For this reason, the hydraulic system must be bled after repair or servicing, to remove any air bubbles.

**2** The clutch hydraulic system is bled by pressurising it externally; the most effective way of achieving this is to use a pressure brake bleeding kit.

**3** These are readily available in motor accessory shops and are extremely effective; the following sub-section describes bleeding the clutch system using such a kit.

### Bleeding the clutch

**Note:** *If a new slave cylinder has been fitted, or if you suspect that the hydraulic fluid has been allowed to drain from the existing slave cylinder during servicing or repair, refer to the sub-section entitled 'Bleeding the slave cylinder' first.*

**4** Remove the dust cap from the bleed nipple **(see illustration).**

**5** Fit a ring spanner over the bleed nipple head, but do not slacken it at this point. Connect a length of clear plastic hose over the nipple, and insert the other end into a clean container. Pour hydraulic fluid into the container, such that the end of the hose is completely covered.

**6** Following the kit manufacturer's instructions, pour hydraulic fluid into the bleeding kit vessel.

**7** Unscrew the vehicle's fluid reservoir cap, then connect the bleeding kit fluid supply hose to the reservoir.

**8** Connect the pressure hose to a supply of compressed air – a spare tyre is a convenient source.

*Caution: Check that the pressure in the tyre does not exceed the maximum quoted by the kit manufacturer, let some air escape to reduce the pressure, if necessary. Gently open the air valve, and allow the air and fluid pressures to equalise. Check that there are no leaks before proceeding.*

**9** Using the spanner, slacken the bleed nipple

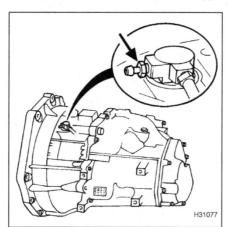

**6.4  Clutch hydraulic system bleed nipple (arrowed)**

until fluid and air bubbles can be seen to flow through the tube, into the container. Maintain a steady flow until the emerging fluid is free of air bubbles; keep a watchful eye on the level of fluid in the bleeding kit vessel and the vehicle's fluid reservoir – if it is allowed to drop too low, air may be forced into the system, defeating the object of the exercise. To refill the vessel, turn off the compressed air supply, remove the lid, and pour in an appropriate quantity of clean fluid from a new container – **do not** re-use the fluid collected in the receiving container. Repeat as necessary until the ejected fluid is bubble-free.

**10** On completion, pump the clutch pedal several times to assess its feel and travel. If firm, constant pedal resistance is not felt throughout the pedal stroke, it is probable that air is still present in the system – repeat the bleeding procedure until the pedal feel is restored.

**11** Depressurise the bleeding kit, and remove it from the vehicle.

**12** If a new slave cylinder has been fitted, or if you suspect that air has entered the existing slave cylinder, proceed as follows: with the receiving container still connected, open the bleed nipple, while an assistant fully depresses the clutch pedal and holds it there. Wait for the fluid to flow into the receiving container, then with the clutch pedal at the bottom of its stroke, tighten the bleed nipple, and allow the pedal to return to its rest position. Repeat this sequence until the fluid that flows from the bleed nipple into the receiving container is free from air bubbles. Keep a watchful eye on the level of fluid in the vehicle's fluid reservoir, topping-up if necessary.

**13** On completion of the bleeding process, tighten the bleed nipple securely, disconnect the receiving container and then refit the nipple dust cap.

**14** At this point, the fluid reservoir may well be 'over-full'; the excess should be removed using a *clean* pipette to reduce the level to the MAX mark.

**15** Finally, road test the vehicle and check the operation of the clutch.

### Bleeding the slave cylinder

**16** Providing that the slave cylinder has not been removed from the transmission during servicing or repair, the procedure described in the preceding sub-section should cause all air to be expelled from the clutch hydraulic system. If however, a large amount of fluid has drained from the slave cylinder, allowing air to enter, or if a new slave cylinder has been fitted, the procedure described above may not be sufficient to purge all the air from the slave cylinder. This is because the bleed nipple is positioned at the point where the hydraulic fluid enters the top of the slave cylinder – fluid is not forced through the slave cylinder during the bleeding process and the cylinder is not fully primed with hydraulic fluid. Consequently, some air may remain inside the slave cylinder housing.

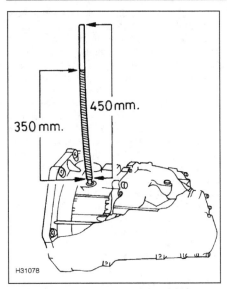

H31078

**6.20 Fill the hose to a height of 350 mm (measured from the bleed nipple ) with new brake fluid**

**17** To overcome this, the slave cylinder must be primed before the transmission is refitted to the transmission, as follows.

**18** Take a 450 mm length of 8 mm diameter clear plastic hose and fit it to the slave cylinder bleed nipple.

**19** Open the bleed nipple then press the release bearing along the input shaft sleeve towards the transmission, so that the piston is pushed fully into the slave cylinder. Catch any fluid ejected from the hose in a container.

**20** Hold the hose vertically, then fill it to a height of 350 mm (measured from the bleed nipple) with new brake fluid **(see illustration)**.

**21** Connect a foot pump or bicycle pump to the end of the hose, ensuring a good seal. Gradually apply pressure to the hose using the pump, until the brake fluid flows into the slave cylinder. Allow the piston to be pushed out of the slave cylinder to the end of its travel, *but no further* – the resistance felt at the pump should increase when the piston reaches the end of its travel.

**22** Press the release bearing back along the input shaft sleeve towards the transmission, so that the piston is pushed back fully into the slave cylinder. Allow the air bubbles now flowing through the brake fluid to escape from the end of the plastic hose.

**23** Repeat the steps described in paragraphs 21 and 22 until no more air escapes from the slave cylinder.

**24** Leave the piston fully retracted inside the slave cylinder, then disconnect and drain the plastic hose. Refit the transmission as described in Chapter 7A, without disturbing the slave cylinder. On completion, bleed the entire hydraulic system as described in the previous sub-section, paying particular attention to paragraph 12.

# Chapter 7 Part A:
# Manual transmission

## Contents

## Degrees of difficulty

| Easy, suitable for novice with little experience  | Fairly easy, suitable for beginner with some experience  | Fairly difficult, suitable for competent DIY mechanic  | Difficult, suitable for experienced DIY mechanic | Very difficult, suitable for expert DIY or professional |
|---|---|---|---|---|

## Specifications

### General

Type . . . . . . . . . . . . . . . . . . . . . . . . . . . . . . . . . . . . . . . . . . . . . . . . . . .  Transversely-mounted, front-wheel-drive layout, with integral transaxle differential/final drive. Five forward speeds, one reverse, all with synchromesh

### Gear ratios (typical)

Transmission code FM:

| | |
|---|---|
| 1st . . . . . . . . . . . . . . . . . . . . . . . . . . . . . . . . . . . . . . . . . . . . . . . . . . . | 3.38 : 1 |
| 2nd . . . . . . . . . . . . . . . . . . . . . . . . . . . . . . . . . . . . . . . . . . . . . . . . . . | 1.76 : 1 |
| 3rd . . . . . . . . . . . . . . . . . . . . . . . . . . . . . . . . . . . . . . . . . . . . . . . . . . | 1.12 : 1 |
| 4th . . . . . . . . . . . . . . . . . . . . . . . . . . . . . . . . . . . . . . . . . . . . . . . . . . | 0.89 : 1 |
| 5th . . . . . . . . . . . . . . . . . . . . . . . . . . . . . . . . . . . . . . . . . . . . . . . . . . | 0.70 : 1 |
| Reverse . . . . . . . . . . . . . . . . . . . . . . . . . . . . . . . . . . . . . . . . . . . . . . | 3.17 : 1 |
| Final drive . . . . . . . . . . . . . . . . . . . . . . . . . . . . . . . . . . . . . . . . . . . . | 3.61 : 1 |

### Torque wrench settings

| | Nm | lbf ft |
|---|---|---|
| Bellhousing-to-engine block bolts . . . . . . . . . . . . . . . . . . . . . . . . . . | 70 | 52 |
| Gear lever bracket-to-engine mounting bolts . . . . . . . . . . . . . . . . . | 8 | 6 |
| Gear lever housing-to-floorpan bolts . . . . . . . . . . . . . . . . . . . . . . . | 8 | 6 |
| Gear linkage-to-selector rod bolt . . . . . . . . . . . . . . . . . . . . . . . . . . | 22 | 16 |
| Left-hand oil seal retaining housing . . . . . . . . . . . . . . . . . . . . . . . . | 24 | 18 |
| Oil level, filler and drain plugs . . . . . . . . . . . . . . . . . . . . . . . . . . . . | 50 | 37 |
| Reversing light switch . . . . . . . . . . . . . . . . . . . . . . . . . . . . . . . . . . . | 24 | 18 |
| Selector rod pinch-bolt . . . . . . . . . . . . . . . . . . . . . . . . . . . . . . . . . . | 22 | 16 |

## 1  General information

The manual transmission is mounted transversely in the engine bay, bolted directly to the engine. This layout has the advantage of providing the shortest possible drive path to the front wheels, as well as locating the transmission in the airflow through the engine bay, optimising cooling.

The unit is cased in aluminium alloy, and has oil filler, drain and level plugs. The case has two mating faces; one to the bellhousing, which is sealed with 'liquid gasket' compound, and one to the gearbox end cover, which sealed with a solid gasket. A 'labyrinth' vent at the top of the gearcase allows for air expansion, and permits gases produced by the lubricant to escape. The vent also houses a filter to keep out ingress of water and dirt.

Drive from the crankshaft is transmitted via the clutch to the gearbox input shaft, which is splined to accept the clutch friction plate. All six driving gears (pinions) are mounted on the input shaft; reverse, first and second speed pinions are journalled on sliding contact bearings, and the third, fourth and fifth speed pinions are carried on needle bearings.

The driven gears for all five forward speeds are mounted on the output shaft, again with third, fourth and fifth speed gears carried on needle bearings. Reverse gear is integral with the first/second speed synchromesh sleeve.

The pinions are in constant mesh with their corresponding driven gears, and are free to rotate independently of the gearbox shafts until a speed is selected. The difference in diameter and number of teeth between the pinions and gears provides the necessary shaft speed reduction and torque multiplication. Drive is then transmitted to the final drive gears/differential through the output shaft.

All gears are fitted with syncromeshes, including reverse. When a speed is selected, the movement of the floor-mounted gear lever is communicated to the gearbox by a selector rod. This in turn actuates a series of selector forks inside the gearbox, which are slotted onto the synchromesh sleeves. The sleeves, which are locked to the gearbox shafts, but

**2.5a  Unscrew the drain plug from the transmission casing**

**2.5b  Note that the drain plug contains a removable magnetic insert**

can slide axially by means of splined hubs, press baulk rings into contact with the respective gear/pinion. The coned surfaces between the baulk rings and the pinion/gear act as a friction clutch, progressively matching the speed of the synchromesh sleeve (and hence the gearbox shaft) with that of the gear/pinion. The dog teeth on the outside of the baulk ring prevent the synchromesh sleeve ring from meshing with the gear/pinion until their speeds are exactly matched; this allows gearchanges to be carried out smoothly, and greatly reduces the noise and mechanical wear caused by rapid gearchanges.

When reverse gear is engaged, an idler gear is brought into mesh between the reverse pinion and the teeth on the outside of the first/second speed synchromesh sleeve. This arrangement introduces the necessary speed reduction, and also causes the output shaft to rotate in the opposite direction, allowing the vehicle to be driven in reverse.

## 2  Transmission – draining and refilling

### General information

1 The gearbox is filled with the correct quantity and grade of oil at manufacture. The level must be checked regularly, and if necessary topped-up in accordance with the maintenance schedule (see Chapter 1).

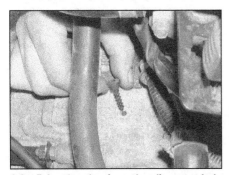

**3.3a  Prise the plug from the alignment hole at the top of the transmission casing . . .**

However, there is no requirement to drain and renew the oil during the normal lifetime of the gearbox, unless repair or overhaul is carried out.

### Draining

2 Take the car on a road test of sufficient length to warm the engine/transmission up to normal operating temperature; this will speed up the draining process, and any sludge and debris will be more likely to be drained out.

3 Park the car on level ground, switch off the ignition, and apply the handbrake firmly. For improved access, jack up the front of the car and support it securely on axle stands. **Note:** *The car must be lowered to the ground and parked on a level surface, to ensure accuracy when refilling and checking the oil level.*

4 Wipe clean the area around the filler plug, which is situated on the top surface of the transmission. Unscrew the plug from the casing, and recover the sealing washer.

5 Position a container with a capacity of at least 2.5 litres (ideally with a large funnel) under the drain plug **(see illustrations)**. The drain plug is located on the right-hand end of the transmission, under the driveshaft; use a wrench to unscrew the plug from the casing. Note that the drain plug contains an integral magnet, designed to catch the metal fragments produced as the transmission components wear. If the plug is clogged with a large amount of metal debris, this may be an early indication of component failure.

6 Allow all the oil to drain completely into the container. If the oil is still hot, take precautions

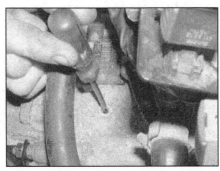

**3.3b  . . . then select fourth gear, and insert a screwdriver into the alignment hole; this will lock the transmission in fourth gear**

against scalding. Clean both the filler and drain plugs thoroughly, paying particular attention to the threads. Discard the original sealing washers; they should be always renewed whenever they are disturbed.

### Refilling

7 When the oil has drained out completely, clean the plug hole threads in the transmission casing. Fit a new sealing washer to the drain plug. Coat the thread with thread-locking compound, and tighten it into the transmission casing. If the car was raised for the draining operation, lower it to the ground.

8 When refilling the transmission, allow plenty of time for the oil level to settle completely before attempting to check it. Note that the car must be parked on a flat, level surface when checking the oil level. Use a funnel if necessary to maintain a gradual, constant flow and avoid spillage.

9 Refill the transmission with the specified grade and quantity of oil, then check the oil level as described in Chapter 1. If a large quantity flows out when the level checking plug is removed, refit both the filler and level plugs, then drive the car for a short distance so that the new oil is distributed fully around the transmission components. Recheck the level again upon your return.

10 On completion, fit the filler and level plugs with new sealing washers. Coat their threads with thread-locking compound and tighten them securely.

## 3  Gearchange linkage – adjustment

1 If the action of the gearchange linkage is stiff, slack or vague, the alignment between the gearchange linkage and the gearbox selector rod may be incorrect (also check the oil level and type is correct). The operations in the following paragraphs describe how to check and, if necessary, adjust the alignment.

2 Park the vehicle, apply the handbrake and switch off the ignition.

3 Locate the alignment hole at the top of the gearbox casing, adjacent to the part number plate **(see illustrations)**. Prise out the plug to expose the alignment hole. Select fourth gear, then take the locking tool (a screwdriver with a shaft diameter of approximately 4 mm), and insert it into the alignment hole; this will lock the gearbox in fourth gear. **Note:** *Use a screwdriver; the handle will prevent the screwdriver from falling into the gearbox.*

4 Inside the car, remove the gear lever gaiter and mounting frame to expose the gearchange lever housing. Using a locking pin (screwdriver or drill bit) with a diameter of approximately 4 mm, insert it into the alignment hole in the side of the lever housing **(see illustration)**.

5 If the locking pin can be inserted without difficulty, then the gearchange linkage

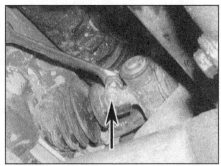

**3.4 Inside the vehicle, insert a locking tool (drill bit) into the alignment hole in the side of the lever housing**

**3.7 Slackening the selector rod pinch-bolt**

## 4 Gearchange linkage – removal, inspection and refitting

### Gear lever housing

#### Removal

**1** Park the vehicle, switch off the ignition, and apply the handbrake.
**2** Referring to Chapter 11, remove the gear lever gaiter, centre console and side carpet trim panels.
**3** Open the bonnet and undo the pinch-bolt clamp, to the gear selector rod universal joint.
**4** Slacken and remove the bolts that secure the gearchange lever housing to the floorpan.
**5** Disconnect the wiring plug from the ignition switch, then lift the gear lever housing up and withdraw it from the vehicle. Unbolt the gear lever from the selector shaft (see illustration). Recover all bushes, washers and spacers, and remove the housing.

#### Inspection

**6** It is possible to remove the gear lever from its housing, to allow the bearings to be inspected and renewed. It is most likely, however, that any slack found in the mechanism will be caused by worn bushes between the gear lever and the selector rod. Extract the bushes from the gear lever linkage (see illustration) and inspect them; if they appear worn or corroded, renew them.

alignment is correct, and hence cannot be blamed for the poor gearchange quality; the best course of action now is to remove the gearchange linkage and inspect it for wear or damage – refer to Section 4 for details.
**6** If the locking pin (screwdriver or drill bit) cannot be inserted into the alignment hole, then the gearchange linkage is incorrectly adjusted.
**7** From the engine bay, at the point where the selector rod passes through the bulkhead, slacken the pinch-bolt adjacent to the rubber coupling, to allow movement between the two halves of the selector rod (see illustration).
**8** Move the gearchange lever such that the locking pin (screwdriver shaft or drill bit) can be inserted into the alignment hole in the lever

housing; ensure that the lever is still in the 4th gear position.
**9** In the engine bay, tighten the pinch-bolt on the selector rod, observing the correct torque.
**10** Remove the screwdriver from the gearbox alignment hole, and fit the plastic plug.
**11** Remove the screwdriver from the gear lever housing alignment hole.
**12** Refit the gear lever gaiter and mounting frame.
**13** Before moving the vehicle, check that the gear lever can be moved from neutral to all six gear positions. **Note:** *Check the key can be removed while reverse is selected.*
**14** Finally, road test the vehicle, and check that all gears can be obtained smoothly and precisely.

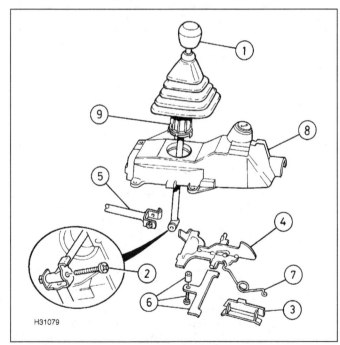

**4.5 Gearchange lever and housing assembly**

| 1 | Gearchange lever | 4 | Locking plate | 8 | Gearchange lever |
| 2 | Gearchange lever-to-selector rod screw | 5 | Selector rod | | housing |
| | | 6 | Screw and collar | 9 | Gear lever ball socket |
| 3 | Stop plate | 7 | Locking plate spring | | |

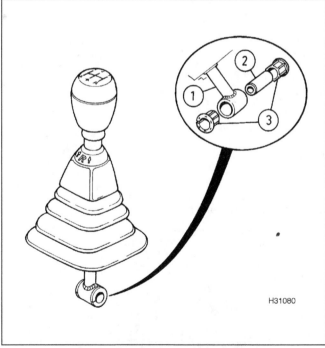

**4.6 Gearchange lever selector rod bushes (inset)**

| 1 | Gearchange lever | 2 | Sleeve |
| | | 3 | Bushes |

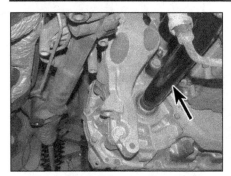

**5.4 Driveshaft intermediate shaft (arrowed)**

### Gear lever

**7** To remove the gear lever from the housing (see illustration 4.5), first withdraw the lock-plate holder then unclip the locking plate spring.
**8** Using a screwdriver, disengage the pawl which is controlled by the ignition switch. Lift up the locking plate together with its plastic bracket and remove the stop plate.
**9** Set the gear lever to reverse, then undo the screw securing the selector rod to the gear lever.
**10** Remove the gear lever and ball socket by carefully pressing the three locking tabs on the socket using a screwdriver.

#### Refitting

**11** Refit the gearchange lever and housing by reversing the removal sequence, noting the following:
  a) *Observe the correct torque for the gear lever-to-selector rod bolt and the gear lever housing-to-floorpan bolts.*
  b) *Refit the wiring plug connector to the ignition switch.*
  c) *On completion, check that the gear lever can be moved from neutral to all six gear positions.* **Note:** *check the key can be removed while reverse is selected.*
  d) *Finally, road test the vehicle, and check that all gears can be obtained smoothly and precisely.*

### Selector rod

#### Removal

**12** Refer to the previous sub-section, and remove the gear lever and housing. Ensure

**5.7 Using a large socket to refit the oil seal, making sure it seats squarely**

---

**5.5 Levering out the oil seal, using a block of wood to allow better leverage**

that 4th gear is selected before removal. Remove the plug from the alignment hole in the top of the gearbox casing, and lock the gearbox in 4th gear using a suitable screwdriver, as described in Section 3.
**13** From within the engine bay, at the point where the selector rod passes through the bulkhead, slacken the pinch-bolt collar to detach the selector rod from the gearbox.
**14** From inside the cabin, carefully withdraw the selector rod through the bulkhead, taking care to avoid damaging the rubber grommet in the bulkhead.

#### Refitting

**15** Lubricate the selector rod with silicone grease, and push it through the grommet in the bulkhead; do not tighten the pinch-bolt collar at the gearbox at this stage.
**16** Refit the gear lever and housing as described earlier in this Section. Fit the bushes, and bolt the gear lever to the selector rod.
**17** Lock the gear lever in 4th gear by inserting a screwdriver with a 4 mm shaft into the alignment hole on the gear lever housing, with reference to Section 3.
**18** Tighten the pinch-bolt collar on the selector rod at the gearbox, observing the specified torque.
**19** Remove the screwdriver from the housing, and refit the gear lever gaiter.
**20** Before moving the vehicle, check that the gear lever can be moved from neutral to all six gear positions. Finally, road test the vehicle, and check that all gears can be obtained smoothly and precisely.

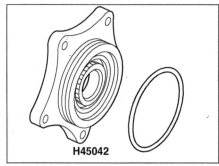

**5.16 O-ring seal fitted to the driveshaft seal retaining housing**

---

## 5 Oil seals – renewal

### Right-hand driveshaft oil seal

**1** Park the vehicle on a level surface, apply the handbrake, and chock the rear wheels. Remove the wheel centre caps, and slacken the wheel bolts.
**2** Apply the handbrake, then raise the front of the vehicle, rest it securely on axle stands and remove the roadwheels; refer to *Jacking and vehicle support* for guidance.
**3** Refer to Section 2 and drain the transmission oil. Clean and refit the drain plug as described in Section 2.
**4** Working from Chapter 8, remove the intermediate driveshaft and bearing assembly (see illustration).
**5** Using a suitable lever, prise the driveshaft oil seal out from the transmission housing (see illustration), taking care not to damage the sealing surface. Discard the old seal.
**6** Thoroughly clean the mating surfaces of the bearing housing and differential casing; take precautions to prevent debris entering the bearings of either assembly.
**7** Lubricate the new oil seal with clean oil, and carefully refit the it into the transmission housing, ensuring that it is seated squarely (see illustration).
**8** Refer to Chapter 8 and refit the intermediate driveshaft and bearing assembly.
**9** Refit the roadwheels, and lower the vehicle to the ground. Tighten the roadwheel bolts to the correct torque, and refit the wheel centre caps/trims.
**10** Refer to Section 2 and refill the transmission with oil of the correct grade.

### Left-hand driveshaft oil seal and O-ring

**11** Park the vehicle on a level surface, apply the handbrake, and chock the rear wheels. Remove the wheel centre caps, and slacken the wheel bolts.
**12** Apply the handbrake, then raise the front of the vehicle, rest it securely on axle stands and remove the roadwheels; refer to *Jacking and vehicle support* for guidance.
**13** Refer to Section 2 and drain the transmission oil. Clean and refit the drain plug as described in Section 2.
**14** Working from the relevant section of Chapter 8, disconnect the left-hand driveshaft from the transmission at the inboard universal joint.
**15** Place a container beneath the driveshaft housing mating face, then slacken and withdraw the five retaining screws.
**16** Withdraw the seal retaining housing from the transmission, then remove the O-ring seal from the housing (see illustration).
**17** Note the fitted depth of the oil seal in its housing and the correct fitted position. Using a suitable lever, carefully prise the oil seal out

from the housing, taking care not to damage the sealing surface.

18 Thoroughly clean the mating surfaces of the bearing housing and differential casing; take precautions to prevent debris entering the bearings of either assembly.

19 Lubricate the new oil seal with clean oil, and carefully refit the it into the oil seal retaining housing, ensuring that it is seated squarely (see illustration 5.7).

20 Refit the O-ring seal to the seal retaining housing, then refit the housing to the transmission. Tighten the five retaining screws to the specified torque setting.

21 Refer to Chapter 8, and reconnect the left-hand driveshaft at the universal joint.

22 Refit the roadwheels, and lower the vehicle to the ground. Tighten the roadwheel bolts to the correct torque, and refit the wheel centre caps/trims.

23 Refer to Section 2 and refill the transmission with oil of the correct grade.

### Input shaft oil seal

24 The oil seal is part of the clutch slave cylinder assembly and cannot be renewed separately, see Chapter 6, Section 4 (*Clutch slave cylinder/release bearing – removal and refitting*) for further information.

### Selector rod oil seal

25 Clean off the area around the selector rod seal in the transmission, to prevent dirt entering the transmission.

26 Ensure that 4th gear is selected, remove the plug from the alignment hole in the top of the gearbox casing, and lock the gearbox in 4th gear using a suitable 4 mm locking tool/screwdriver, as described in Section 3.

27 Slacken and remove the selector rod retaining bolt, then select 3rd gear to disengage the selector rod from the transmission.

28 Note the fitted position of the oil seal in its housing, then using a suitable lever carefully prise the oil seal out from the transmission, taking care not to damage the sealing surface.

29 Thoroughly clean the sealing surface and selector rod, check there are no burrs on the selector rod; take precautions to prevent debris entering the transmission.

30 Lubricate the new oil seal and selector rod with clean oil, and carefully refit the new seal into the transmission housing, ensuring that it is seated squarely.

31 Refit the selector rod and securely tighten the retaining bolt. Remove the locking tool/screwdriver from the housing, and check the gearchange linkage adjustment as described in Section 3.

32 Before moving the vehicle, check that the gear lever can be moved from neutral to all six gear positions. Check the transmission oil level. Finally, road test the vehicle, and check that all gears can be obtained smoothly and precisely.

## 6 Reversing light switch – testing, removal and refitting

### Testing

1 Disconnect the battery negative cable, and position it away from the terminal.

2 Unplug the wiring harness from the reversing light switch at the connector. The switch is located on the rear of the transmission casing (see illustration).

3 Connect the probes of a continuity tester, or a multi-meter set to the resistance function, across the terminals of the reversing light switch.

4 The switch contacts are normally open, so with any gear other than reverse selected, the tester/meter should indicate an open-circuit. When reverse gear is then selected, the switch contacts should close, causing the tester/meter to indicate a short-circuit.

5 If the switch appears to be constantly open- or short-circuit, or is intermittent in its operation, it should be renewed.

### Removal

6 If not already done, disconnect the battery negative cable, and position it away from the terminal.

7 Unplug the wiring harness from the reversing light switch at the connector.

8 Using a suitable spanner, unscrew the switch, recovering any washers that may be fitted; these must be refitted, to ensure that the correct clearance exists between the switch shaft and the reverse gear shaft.

### Refitting

9 Refit the switch by reversing the removal procedure, reconnect the battery negative cable.

## 7 Speedometer drive – removal and refitting

### General information

1 Vehicles are fitted with an electronic transducer in place of the drive gear. This device measures the rotational speed of the transmission final drive, and converts the information into an electronic signal, which is then sent to the speedometer module in the instrument panel. The signal is also used as an input by the engine management system ECU (and where fitted, by the cruise control ECU, the trip computer and the traction control system ECU).

### Removal

2 Locate the speed transducer, which is on the differential housing, at the rear of the transmission case.

3 Unplug the wiring harness from the transducer, at the connector.

**6.2 Reversing light switch location (arrowed)**

4 Remove the transducer retaining screw, and unscrew the unit from the transmission casing.

5 Where applicable, recover and discard the O-ring seal.

### Refitting

6 Refit the transducer by following the removal procedure in reverse. **Note:** *Where applicable, a new O-ring seal must be used on refitting.*

## 8 Transmission – removal and refitting

### Removal

**Note:** *Refer to Chapter 2B for details on removal of the engine and transmission as a complete assembly.*

1 Park the vehicle on a level surface, apply the handbrake and chock the rear wheels. Remove the wheel centre caps, and slacken the wheel bolts.

2 Apply the handbrake, then raise the front of the vehicle, rest it securely on axle stands and remove the roadwheels; refer to *Jacking and vehicle support* for guidance.

3 Refer to Section 2 of this Chapter and drain the oil from the transmission. Refit and tighten the drain plug as described in Section 2.

4 Refer to Section 3, and set the gearchange linkage in a reference position, to ensure correct alignment of the linkage on refitting. Undo the retaining bolt and disconnect the gear linkage from the transmission.

5 Referring to Chapter 5A, remove the battery cover, disconnect both battery cables and remove the battery.

6 Unbolt the battery tray from the side of the engine bay (see illustration).

7 Working from Chapter 6, seal off the clutch hydraulic system by fitting a clamp to the flexible section of the slave cylinder supply hose.

8 Release the securing clip and disconnect the connection for the fluid delivery at the top of the transmission. Refit the securing clip to the connector after it has been disconnected for safe-keeping. Plug both sides of the open

8.6 Undo the battery tray bolts (arrowed)

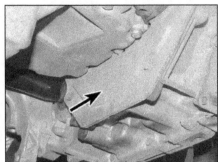

8.17 Remove the lower flywheel cover plate (arrowed)

8.20 Remove the retaining bolts and nut (arrowed)

fuel lines to minimise leakage and to prevent the ingress of foreign material.

**9** Unplug the wiring connector from the reversing light switch at the transmission; refer to Section 6 of this Chapter for further information.

**10** Slacken and remove the three upper transmission retaining bolts.

**11** Unplug the wiring connector(s) from the oxygen sensor; refer to Chapter 4B, Section 2, for further information.

**12** Slacken and remove the centre retaining nut from the rear engine mounting, then slacken the three outer mounting bolts.

**13** Position a lifting beam across the engine bay, locating the support legs securely in the sills at either side, in line with the strut top mountings. Hook the jib onto the engine lifting eyelet and raise it, so that the weight of the engine is taken off the transmission mounting. Most people won't have access to an engine lifting beam, but it may be possible to hire one. Alternatively, an engine hoist may be used to support the engine, but when using this method, bear in mind that if the vehicle is lowered on its axle stands to adjust the working height, for example, then the hoist will have to be lowered accordingly, to avoid straining the engine mountings.

**14** Remove the subframe from under the engine with reference to Chapter 10.

**15** Remove the three retaining bolts from the rear engine mounting bracket and withdraw it from the engine bay.

**16** With reference to Chapter 8, remove the both driveshafts from the transmission.

**17** Undo the retaining bolts and remove the lower cover plate from the flywheel **(see illustration). Note:** *On B235R models also remove the bolts between the transmission and the engine oil sump.*

**18** Undo the retaining bolt(s) and disconnect the earth cable(s) from the transmission housing.

**19** Position a jack underneath the transmission, and raise it to take the weight of the unit. Check that nothing remains

connected to the transmission before attempting to separate it from the engine.

**20** Unscrew the bolts securing the left-hand engine/transmission mounting bracket to the bodywork and the centre nut from the mounting **(see illustration)**. Make sure the transmission is supported, taking care to avoid straining the other engine mountings as you do this. Withdraw the mounting from the inner wing panel and transmission.

**21** Work around the circumference of the bellhousing, and remove the last retaining bolts from the bellhousing. Pull the transmission away from the engine, extracting the input shaft from the clutch friction plate – this task should only be attempted with the help of an assistant.

⚠ *Warning: Maintain firm support on the transmission, to ensure that it remains steady on the jack head.*

**22** When the input shaft is clear of the clutch friction plate, lower the transmission out of the engine bay using the jack.

**23** At this point with the transmission removed, it would be a good opportunity to check and if required renew the clutch assembly, see Chapter 6 for further information

### *Refitting*

#### All models

**24** Refit the transmission by reversing the removal procedure, noting the following points:
 a) *Apply a smear of high-melting point grease to the transmission input shaft. Do not apply an excessive amount, as there is a possibility of the clutch friction plate being contaminated.*
 b) *Refit the subframe with reference to Chapter 10.*
 c) *Refit the engine/transmission mountings with reference to Chapter 2A.*
 d) *Observe the specified torque wrench settings (where applicable) when tightening all nuts and bolts after refitting.*
 e) *Bleed the clutch hydraulic system, referring to Chapter 6 for reference.*

 f) *On completion, if the transmission was drained, refill with the specified type and quantity of oil as described in Section 2.*

### 9 Transmission overhaul – general information

The overhaul of a manual transmission is a complex (and often expensive) engineering task for the DIY home mechanic to undertake, which requires access to specialist equipment. It involves dismantling and reassembly of many small components, measuring clearances precisely, and if necessary adjusting them by the selection shims and spacers. Internal transmission components are also often difficult to obtain, and in many instances extremely expensive. Because of this, if the transmission develops a fault or becomes noisy, the best course of action is to have the unit overhauled by a specialist repairer, or to obtain an exchange reconditioned unit.

Nevertheless, it is not impossible for the more experienced mechanic to overhaul the transmission, if the special tools are available and the job is carried out in a deliberate step-by-step manner, to ensure that nothing is overlooked.

The tools necessary for an overhaul include internal and external circlip pliers, bearing pullers, a slide hammer, a set of pin punches, a dial test indicator (dial gauge), and possibly a hydraulic press. In addition, a large, sturdy workbench and a vice will be required.

During dismantling of the transmission, make careful notes of how each component is fitted, to make reassembly easier and accurate.

Before dismantling the transmission, it will help if you have some idea of where the problem lies. Certain problems can be closely related to specific areas in the transmission, which can make component examination and renewal easier. Refer to *Fault finding* at the end of this manual for more information.

# Chapter 7 Part B:
## Automatic transmission

# Contents

# Degrees of difficulty

| Easy, suitable for novice with little experience |  | Fairly easy, suitable for beginner with some experience |  | Fairly difficult, suitable for competent DIY mechanic | ⚒ | Difficult, suitable for experienced DIY mechanic | ⚒ | Very difficult, suitable for expert DIY or professional | ⚒ |

# Specifications

## General

| | |
|---|---|
| Designation ........................................... | AF30 (automatic transmission front-wheel-drive) |
| Type*: | |
|   FA47 ............................................... | Four speed electronically-controlled automatic with three (Normal, Sport and Winter) driving modes |
|   FA57 ............................................... | Electronically-controlled five stage automatic transmission, with facility to change gear manually |

*The type code is marked on a plate, attached to the top of the transmission casing*

| Torque wrench settings | Nm | lbf ft |
|---|---|---|
| Drain plug ............................................ | 40 | 30 |
| Driveplate/lower bellhousing cover plate ..................... | 7 | 5 |
| Engine-to-transmission unit bolts .......................... | See Chapter 2A | |
| Fluid filler pipe retaining nut ............................. | 22 | 16 |
| Fluid temperature sensor cover plate screw ................... | 25 | 18 |
| Fluid temperature sensor ................................ | 25 | 18 |
| Input shaft speed sensor bolt ............................. | 6 | 4 |
| Gear selector position sensor: | | |
|   Switch-to-transmission nut/screw ..................... | 8 | 6 |
|   Lever to position sensor ............................ | 25 | 18 |
| Left-hand engine mounting ............................... | See Chapter 2A | |
| Oil cooler unions ...................................... | 27 | 20 |
| Output shaft speed sensor bolt ............................ | 6 | 4 |
| Subframe mounting bolts ................................ | See Chapter 10 | |
| Torque converter-to-driveplate bolts ........................ | 30 | 22 |

## 1 General information

**1** The AF30 automatic transmission is an electronically-controlled four/five-speed unit (depending on model), incorporating a lock-up function. It consists mainly of a planetary gear unit, a torque converter with lock-up clutch, a hydraulic control system and an electronic control system. The unit is controlled by the electronic control unit (ECU) via four electrically-operated solenoid valves. The transmission unit has three driving modes: normal (economy), sport and winter modes.

**2** The normal (economy) mode is the standard mode for driving in which the transmission shifts up at relatively low engine speeds to combine reasonable performance with economy. If the transmission unit is switched into sport mode, using the button on the selector lever, the transmission shifts up only at high engine speeds, giving improved acceleration and overtaking performance. When the transmission is in sport mode, the indicator light in the instrument panel is illuminated. If the transmission is switched into winter mode, using the button on the selector lever indicator panel, the transmission will select third gear as the vehicle pulls away from a standing start; this helps to maintain traction on very slippery surfaces.

**3** The torque converter provides a fluid coupling between engine and transmission, which acts as an automatic clutch, and also provides a degree of torque multiplication when accelerating.

**4** The epicyclic geartrain provides one of the forward or reverse gear ratios, according to which of its component parts are held stationary or allowed to turn. The components of the geartrain are held or released by brakes and clutches which are activated by the control unit. A fluid pump within the transmission provides the necessary hydraulic pressure to operate the brakes and clutches.

**5** Driver control of the transmission is by a seven-position selector lever. The 'drive' D position, allows automatic changing throughout the range of all four/five gear ratios. An automatic kickdown facility shifts the transmission down a gear if the accelerator pedal is fully depressed. The transmission also has three 'hold' positions, 1 means only the first gear ratio can be selected, 2 allows both the first and second gear ratios position to be automatically selected and 3 allows automatic changing between the first three gear ratios. These 'hold' positions are useful for providing engine braking when travelling down steep gradients. Note, however, that the transmission should *never* be shifted down a position at high engine speeds.

**6** Due to the complexity of the automatic transmission, any repair or overhaul work must be left to a Saab dealer with the necessary special equipment for fault diagnosis and repair. The contents of the following Sections are therefore confined to supplying general information, and any service information and instructions that can be used by the owner.

## 2 Transmission fluid – draining and refilling

Refer to the information given in Chapter 1, Section 29.

## 3 Selector cable – adjustment

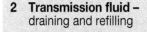

**1** Operate the selector lever throughout its entire range and check that the transmission engages the correct gear indicated on the selector lever position indicator.

**2** Check the play in the selector lever while it's in position N and position D. If it is not the same, then adjustment is necessary, continue as follows.

**3** Inside the vehicle, position the selector lever in the P (Park) position.

**4** Working in the engine compartment, lift the adjustment retaining clip on the transmission end of the selector cable **(see illustration)**.

**5** Locate the lever on the transmission range switch, to which the selector cable is

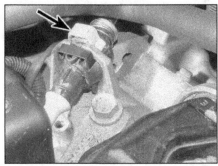

**3.4 Remove the locking clip (arrowed) from the selector cable**

connected. Position the lever so that the transmission is set in the Park position.

**6** With the handbrake in the off position, roll the car until the Park interlock engages.

**7** With the aid of an assistant, hold the selector lever rearward in the park position to take up the free-play.

**8** Working in the engine compartment, press down the adjustment clip at the transmission end to lock the cable.

**9** Check the selector lever as described in paragraphs 1 and 2, if necessary, repeat the adjustment procedure.

**10** On completion, road test the vehicle to check the correct operation of the gearchange.

## 4 Selector cable – removal and refitting

### Removal

**1** Working in the engine compartment, to gain access to the transmission end of the selector cable, remove the battery and battery tray (see Chapter 5A).

**2** With the gear selector in the Park position, locate the lever on the transmission range switch, to which the selector cable is connected. Remove the retaining nut and detach the lever from the range switch **(see illustration)**.

**3** Withdraw the locking clip and disengage the selector cable from the tra0nsmission casing **(see illustrations)**.

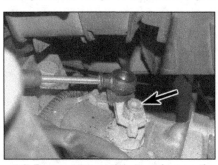

**4.2 Remove the retaining nut (arrowed) and detach the selector lever from the position sensor**

**4.3a Withdraw the locking clip . . .**

**4.3b . . . and release the selector cable from the bracket**

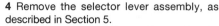

**5.2a Remove the locking clip . . .**

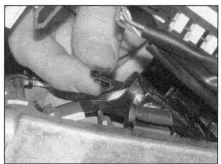

**5.2b . . . and the anti-rattle clip . . .**

**5.2c . . . then withdraw the pin from the selector**

**4** Remove the selector lever assembly, as described in Section 5.

**5** Work back along the cable, noting its correct routing, and free it from all the relevant retaining clips. Free the cable grommet from the bulkhead and remove it from the vehicle.

**6** Examine the cable, looking for worn end fittings or a damaged outer casing, and for signs of fraying of the inner cable. Check the cable's operation; the inner cable should move smoothly and easily through the outer casing. Remember that a cable that appears serviceable when tested off the car may well be much heavier in operation when curved into its working position. Renew the cable if it shows any signs of excessive wear or any damage.

### Refitting

**7** Refitting is a reversal of removal, noting the following points.

**8** Refit the selector lever assembly, as described in Section 5.

**9** Ensure the cable is correctly routed and passes through the selector lever housing then located securely in the bulkhead.

**10** Pass the transmission end of the cable through its mounting bracket and clip the outer cable securely in position. Connect the cable end to the transmission lever then secure it in position with the locking clip. Fit the lever to the transmission range switch, then fit the nut and tighten it securely.

---

**5  Selector lever assembly –**
removal and refitting

---

### Removal

**1** Remove the centre console, and rear compartment air ducts, as described in Chapter 11.

**2** Remove the locking clip and anti-rattle clip, the drive out the pin while removing the end of the cable from the ball **(see illustrations)**.

**3** Slacken and remove the retaining bolts then lift the gear selector lever housing away from the floorpan.

**4** Disconnect any wiring block connectors from the gear selector housing, release any

cable-ties from the wiring loom **(see illustrations)**.

**5** Using a screwdriver, withdraw the securing clip and release the selector cable from the housing **(see illustrations)**. Remove the gear selector housing from the vehicle.

**6** Inspect the selector lever mechanism for signs of wear or damage.

### Refitting

**7** Refitting is a reversal of removal, noting the following points.

**8** Refit the cable to the selector lever and housing, making sure all securing clips are correctly located.

**9** Adjust the selector cable as described in Section 3.

**10** On completion, refit the centre console, as described in Chapter 11, and refit all components removed to gain access to the transmission end of the cable.

**5.4a Disconnect the wiring connector from the gear selector . . .**

**5.5a Using a screwdriver lever out the securing clip . . .**

---

**6  Oil seals –**
renewal

---

### Driveshaft oil seals

**1** Refer to Chapter 7A.

### Torque converter oil seal

**2** Remove the transmission as described in Section 9.

**3** Carefully slide the torque converter off the transmission shaft whilst being prepared for fluid spillage.

**4** Note the correct fitted position of the seal in the oil pump housing then carefully lever the seal out of position taking care not to mark the housing or input shaft.

**5** Remove all traces of dirt from the area around the oil seal aperture then press the

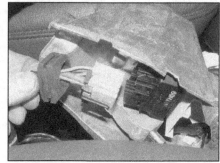

**5.4b . . . and the ignition switch**

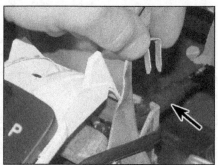

**5.5b . . . and release the selector cable (arrowed) from the housing**

new seal into position, ensuring its sealing lip is facing inwards.

**6** Lubricate the seal with clean transmission fluid then carefully ease the torque converter into position.

**7** Refit the transmission (see Section 9).

## 7 Fluid cooler –
general information

The transmission fluid cooler is an integral part of the radiator assembly. Refer to Chapter 3 for removal and refitting details. If the cooler is damaged the complete radiator assembly must be renewed.

## 8 Transmission control system electrical components –
removal and refitting

### Gear selector position sensor

#### General information

**1** As well as informing the transmission ECU which gear is currently selected, the gear selector position sensor also contains contacts which control the operation of the reversing lights relay, and the starter motor inhibitor relay.

#### Removal

**2** Remove the battery from its mounting tray as described in Chapter 5A, then undo the retaining bolts and remove the battery tray.

**3** Where necessary, release the power steering fluid hose from its mounting bracket and move it to one side.

**4** Undo the securing nut and release the transmission fluid dipstick tube from the side of the transmission position sensor **(see illustration)**.

**5** Select Park, then undo the retaining nut and disconnect the selector lever from the transmission position sensor **(see illustration)**.

**6** Slacken and remove the nuts/bolts that secure the gear selector position sensor to the transmission.

**7** Unplug the position sensor wiring connector, then withdraw the position sensor from the transmission selector shaft and remove it from the engine compartment.

#### Refitting

**8** Refitting is a reversal of removal. Tighten the switch securing nut/bolt to the specified torque and on completion, check the adjustment of the selector cable with reference to Section 3.

### Electronic control unit (ECU)

#### Removal

**9** The ECU is located in the front passenger footwell. Prior to removal, disconnect the battery negative terminal.

**10** Prise out the retaining clips and remove the undercover from the passenger side of the facia. Remove the glovebox from the facia (see Chapter 11) to gain access to the ECU.

**11** Release the retaining clip and disconnect the wiring connector from the ECU. Release the mounting bracket from the body and remove the ECU from the vehicle.

#### Refitting

**12** Refitting is the reverse of removal, ensuring that the wiring is securely reconnected.

### Input and output shaft speed sensors

#### Removal

**13** The speed sensors are fitted to the top of the transmission unit. The input shaft speed sensor is the front of the two sensors and is nearest to the left-hand end of the transmission. The output shaft sensor is the rear of the two **(see illustration)**.

**14** To gain access to the sensors, remove the battery from its mounting plate as described in Chapter 5A. Access can be further improved by unclipping the coolant expansion tank from its mountings and positioning it clear.

**15** Disconnect the wiring connector located on a mounting bracket at the left hand end of

**8.4 Remove the securing nut (arrowed) to release the fluid dipstick tube**

the cylinder head. Wipe clean the area around the relevant sensor.

**16** Undo the retaining bolt and remove the sensor from the transmission. Remove the sealing ring from the sensor and discard it, a new one should be used on refitting.

#### Refitting

**17** Fit the new sealing ring to the sensor groove and lubricate it with a smear of transmission fluid.

**18** Ease the sensor into position then refit the retaining bolt and tighten it to the specified torque setting. Reconnect the wiring connector.

**19** Refit the battery and clip the expansion tank (where necessary) back into position.

### Fluid temperature sensor

#### Removal

**20** The fluid temperature sensor is screwed into the base of the transmission unit, at the front. Before removing the sensor, disconnect the battery negative terminal.

**21** Firmly apply the handbrake then jack up the front of the vehicle and support it on axle stands (see *Jacking and vehicle support*).

**22** Trace the wiring back from the sensor, noting its correct routing. Disconnect the wiring connector and free the wiring from its retaining clips.

**23** Undo the retaining bolts and remove the cover plate from the sensor **(see illustration)**.

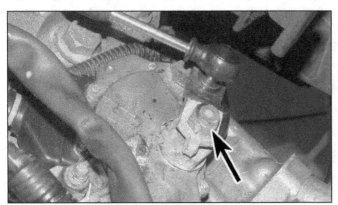

**8.5 Remove the retaining nut (arrowed) and detach the selector lever from the position sensor**

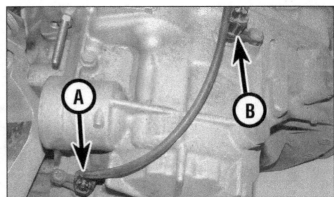

**8.13 Automatic transmission input shaft speed sensor (A) and output shaft speed sensor (B) locations**

**24** Wipe clean the area around the sensor and have a suitable plug ready to minimise fluid loss as the sensor is removed (see illustration).

**25** Unscrew the sensor and remove it from the transmission unit along with its sealing washer. Quickly plug the transmission aperture and wipe up any spilt fluid.

### Refitting

**26** Fit a new sealing washer to the sensor then remove the plug and quickly screw the sensor into the transmission unit. Tighten the sensor to the specified torque and wipe up any spilt fluid. Refit the cover plate and tighten its retaining bolts to the specified torque.

**27** Ensure the wiring is correctly routed and retained by all the necessary clips then securely reconnect the wiring connector.

**28** Lower the vehicle to the floor and reconnect the battery. Check the transmission fluid level as described in Chapter 1.

## 9 Transmission – removal and refitting

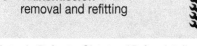

**Note 1:** *Refer to Chapter 2B for details on removal of the engine and transmission as a complete assembly.*

**Note 2:** *New torque converter-to-driveplate bolts and fluid cooler union sealing rings will be required on refitting.*

### Removal

**1** Chock the rear wheels, apply the handbrake, and place the selector lever in the N (Neutral) position. Jack up the front of the vehicle, and securely support it on axle stands (see *Jacking and vehicle support*). Remove both front roadwheels then remove the retaining screws and fasteners and (where necessary) remove the undercover panels from beneath the engine/transmission unit.

**2** Drain the transmission fluid as described in Chapter 1, then refit the drain plug and tighten it to the specified torque.

**3** Remove the battery from its mounting plate as described in Chapter 5A, then undo the retaining bolts and remove the battery tray.

**4** Disconnect the battery earthing cable(s) from the transmission casing (see illus-

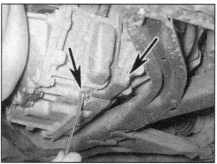

8.23 Undo the retaining bolts (arrowed) and remove the cover plate . . .

trations). Release the cabling from the transmission fluid dipstick tube.

**5** Withdraw the dipstick and its tube from the transmission casing and plug the open hole, to prevent contamination.

**6** Disconnect the breather hose (where fitted) from the top of the transmission unit.

**7** Disconnect the selector cable from the transmission as described in Sections 3 and 4.

**8** Unplug the transmission control system wiring at the two connectors, located at the front of the battery tray (see illustration).

**9** Trace the wiring back from the transmission switches and sensors and disconnect the various connectors by lifting their retaining clips. Release the main wiring harness from any clips or ties securing it to the transmission unit.

**10** Remove the air cleaner and intake ducting as described in Chapter 4A. Remove the cover panel from the top of the throttle body and remove the intercooler-to-throttle body ducting.

**11** Position a lifting beam across the engine bay, locating the support legs securely in the sills at either side, in line with the strut top mountings. Hook the jib onto the engine lifting eyelet and raise it, so that the weight of the engine is taken off the transmission mounting. Most people won't have access to an engine lifting beam, but it may be possible to hire one. Alternatively, an engine hoist may be used to support the engine, but when using this method, bear in mind that if the vehicle is lowered on its axle stands to adjust the working height, for example, then the hoist will have to be lowered accordingly, to avoid straining the engine mountings.

8.24 . . . to gain access to the fluid temperature sensor (arrowed)

**12** Unbolt and remove the exhaust system front pipe and catalytic converter (see Chapter 4A).

**13** Slacken the unions and disconnect the transmission fluid cooler pipes from the front of the transmission casing. Recover the sealing washers.

**14** Slacken and remove the three upper transmission retaining bolts.

**15** Slacken and remove the centre retaining nut from the rear engine mounting, then slacken the three outer mounting bolts.

**16** Remove the subframe from under the engine with reference to Chapter 10.

**17** Remove the three retaining bolts from the rear engine mounting bracket and withdraw it from the engine bay.

**18** With reference to Chapter 8, remove the both driveshafts from the transmission.

**19** Undo the retaining bolts and remove the lower cover plate from the flywheel. Using the crankshaft pulley to turn the engine, slacken and remove all the torque converter retaining bolts as they become accessible (see illustrations). Discard the retaining bolts, new ones must be used on refitting. **Note:** *As the transmission is removed, the torque converter must stay in the transmission bellhousing and not slide off the transmission shaft. A bracket can be made and bolted to the bellhousing to hold the torque converter in place.*

**20** Position a jack underneath the transmission, and raise it to take the weight of the unit. Check that nothing remains connected to the transmission before attempting to separate it from the engine.

**21** Unscrew the bolts securing the left-hand

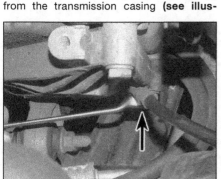

9.4a Disconnect the earth cable (arrowed) from the front of the transmission . . .

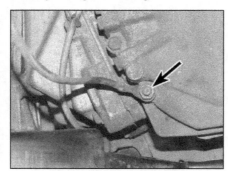

9.4b . . . and the earth cable (arrowed) from the end of the transmission

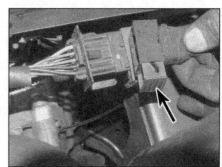

9.8 Release the securing clip (arrowed) and disconnect the wiring block connectors

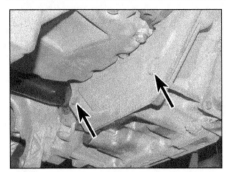

9.19a Undo the retaining bolts (arrowed) and remove the cover plate . . .

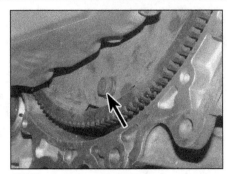

9.19b . . . then undo the torque converter bolts (one arrowed) – turn engine to access other bolts

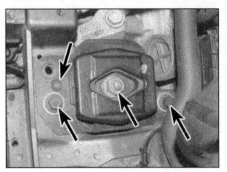

9.21 Undo the bolts and nut (arrowed) to remove mounting

engine/transmission mounting bracket to the bodywork and the centre nut from the mounting **(see illustration)**. Make sure the transmission is supported, taking care to avoid straining the other engine mountings as you do this. Withdraw the mounting from the inner wing panel and transmission.

**22** Work around the circumference of the bellhousing, and remove the last retaining bolts from the bellhousing.

 **Warning: Maintain firm support on the transmission, to ensure that it remains steady on the jack head.**

**23** Make a final check that any components which would prevent the removal of the transmission from the car have been removed or disconnected. Ensure that components such as the gear selector cable are secured so that they cannot be damaged on removal.

**24** Withdraw the transmission from the engine; keep the unit horizontal until the bell-housing is clear of the driveplate and its mounting dowels. Make sure the torque converter does not slide off the transmission shaft.

**25** Slowly lower the transmission assembly from the engine compartment, making sure that it clears the components on the surrounding panels. Lower the assembly to the ground and remove it from the underside of the engine compartment.

### Refitting

**26** The transmission is refitted by a reversal of the removal procedure, bearing in mind the following points.

a) *Prior to refitting, remove all traces of old locking compound from the torque converter threads by running a tap of the correct thread diameter and pitch down the holes. In the absence of a suitable tap, use one of the old bolts with slots cut in its threads.*

b) *Prior to refitting, ensure the engine/transmission locating dowels are correctly positioned and apply a smear of molybdenum disulphide grease to the torque converter locating pin and its centring bush in the crankshaft end.*

c) *Once the transmission and engine are correctly joined, refit the securing bolts, tightening them to the specified torque setting.*

d) *Fit the new torque converter-to-driveplate bolts and tighten them lightly only to start then go around and tighten them to the specified torque setting In a diagonal sequence.*

e) *Tighten all nuts and bolts to the specified torque (where given).*

f) *Renew the driveshaft oil seals (see Chapter 7A) and refit the driveshafts to the transmission as described in Chapter 8.*

g) *Fit new sealing rings to the fluid cooler*

hose unions and ensure both unions are securely retained by their clips.

h) *When refitting the subframe, ensure that the spacer washers are fitted to the two rearmost bolts and observe the alignment markings made during removal. Do not tighten the subframe bolt to their final torque until the full weight of the engine and transmission assembly is resting upon it.*

i) *Ensure that all earthing cables are securely refitted.*

j) *On completion, refill the transmission with the specified type and quantity of fluid as described in Chapter 1 and adjust the selector cable as described in Section 3.*

## 10 Transmission overhaul – general information

**1** In the event of a fault occurring with the transmission, it is first necessary to determine whether it is of a mechanical or hydraulic nature, and to do this, special test equipment is required. It is therefore essential to have the work carried out by a Saab dealer if a transmission fault is suspected.

**2** Do not remove the transmission from the car for possible repair before professional fault diagnosis has been carried out, since most tests require the transmission to be in the vehicle.

# Chapter 8
# Driveshafts

## Contents

## Degrees of difficulty

| Easy, suitable for novice with little experience  | Fairly easy, suitable for beginner with some experience  | Fairly difficult, suitable for competent DIY mechanic  | Difficult, suitable for experienced DIY mechanic  | Very difficult, suitable for expert DIY or professional |

## Specifications

### General

| | |
|---|---|
| Driveshaft type . . . . . . . . . . . . . . . . . . . . . . . . . . . . . . . . . . . . . . | Steel shafts with outer constant velocity joints and inner tripode joints. Intermediate shaft from right-hand side of transmission to driveshaft |
| Lubrication (overhaul or repair only) . . . . . . . . . . . . . . . . . . . . . . . | Use only special grease supplied in sachets with gaiter/overhaul kits; joints are otherwise prepacked with grease and sealed |

### Joint grease quantity

| | |
|---|---|
| Outer joint . . . . . . . . . . . . . . . . . . . . . . . . . . . . . . . . . . . . . . . . | 120 g |
| Inner joint: | |
| Standard . . . . . . . . . . . . . . . . . . . . . . . . . . . . . . . . . . . . . . . | 190 g |
| With tubular shaft and hexagonal housing (up to VIN 230011766) . . | 140 g |

### Torque wrench settings

| | Nm | lbf ft |
|---|---|---|
| Driveshaft/hub nut: | | |
| Nut without groove (1998/2001 models) . . . . . . . . . . . . . . . . . . . . . | 290 | 214 |
| Nut with groove: | | |
| 1998/2001 models: | | |
| Stage 1 . . . . . . . . . . . . . . . . . . . . . . . . . . . . . . . . . . . . . . | 170 | 125 |
| Stage 2 . . . . . . . . . . . . . . . . . . . . . . . . . . . . . . . . . . . . . . | Angle-tighten by 45° | |
| 2002-on models . . . . . . . . . . . . . . . . . . . . . . . . . . . . . . . . . | 230 | 170 |
| Front suspension lower balljoint clamp bolt: | | |
| 1998/1999 models . . . . . . . . . . . . . . . . . . . . . . . . . . . . . . . . | 100 | 74 |
| 2000/2001 models: | | |
| Stage 1 . . . . . . . . . . . . . . . . . . . . . . . . . . . . . . . . . . . . . . | 60 | 44 |
| Stage 2 . . . . . . . . . . . . . . . . . . . . . . . . . . . . . . . . . . . . . . | Angle-tighten by 90° | |
| 2002-on models . . . . . . . . . . . . . . . . . . . . . . . . . . . . . . . . . | 50 | 37 |
| Intermediate driveshaft bracket-to-engine bolts . . . . . . . . . . . . . . . | 30 | 22 |
| Wheel bolts . . . . . . . . . . . . . . . . . . . . . . . . . . . . . . . . . . . . . . . | 110 | 81 |

## 1  General information

Power is transmitted from the transmission final drive to the roadwheels by the driveshafts. The outer joints on all models are of 'constant velocity' (CV) type, consisting of six balls running in axial grooves. The driveshaft outer joints incorporate stub axles which are splined to the hubs located in the front suspension hub carriers. The inner 'universal' joints are designed to move in a smaller arc than the outer CV joints, and can also move axially to allow for movements of the front suspension. They are of tripod type consisting of a three-armed 'spider' with needle bearings and outer race splined to the driveshaft, and an outer housing with three corresponding cut-outs for the bearing races to slide in.

An intermediate shaft, with its own support bearing, is fitted between the transmission and right-hand driveshaft – a design which equalises driveshaft angles at all suspension positions, and reduces driveshaft flexing, improving directional stability under hard acceleration.

The universal and CV joints allow smooth transmission of drive to the wheels at all steering and suspension angles. The joints are protected by rubber gaiters which are packed with grease, to provide permanent lubrication. In the event of wear being detected, the joint can be renewed separately from the driveshaft. The joints do not require additional lubrication, unless they have been renovated or the rubber gaiters have been damaged, allowing the grease to become contaminated. Refer to Chapter 1 for guidance in checking the condition of the driveshaft gaiters.

2.2a  Use a small chisel to free the metal dust cover . . .

2.2b  . . . then remove the cover from the hub flange

## 2  Driveshafts – removal and refitting

### Removal

**1**  Jack up the front of the vehicle and support it on axle stands (see *Jacking and vehicle support*). Remove the relevant roadwheel and, where applicable, the engine undertray.

**2**  On 2002-on models, tap off the metal dust cover for access to the hub nut **(see illustrations)**. Note that the cover cannot be removed with the roadwheel in position, so it is not possible to loosen the hub nut before raising the front of the vehicle.

**3**  Temporarily refit two of the roadwheel bolts and tighten them to hold the brake disc onto the hub flange, then have an assistant depress the footbrake pedal, while the hub nut is being loosened. Unscrew and remove the hub nut **(see illustrations)**. Discard the nut as a new one must be used on refitting. Note if the nut has a groove in it, as there are two types of nut with different tightening torques.

**4**  If removing the driveshaft on 2002-on models, remove the inner splash cover from inside the wheel arch. If removing the right-hand driveshaft on 2002-on models fitted with a headlamp position sensor, unscrew the nut securing the sensor arm to the lower suspension arm, then unbolt the sensor from its mounting bracket and position it to one side.

**5**  Unscrew the clamp bolt securing the front suspension lower balljoint to the hub carrier, then lever down the lower arm and disconnect the balljoint. Secure the lower arm in this position using a block of wood positioned between the arm and anti-roll bar.

**6**  If removing the left-hand driveshaft, carefully lever the inner joint from the trans-

mission. Be prepared for some loss of oil, and take care not to force the inner joint apart.

**7**  If removing the right-hand driveshaft, use a soft-faced mallet to drive the driveshaft from the intermediate shaft. Note that the right-hand driveshaft inner joint splines incorporate a circlip which engages a groove inside the splined end of the intermediate shaft.

**8**  Release the brake hydraulic hose and ABS cable from the front suspension strut.

**9**  Pull out the front suspension strut, then use the soft-faced mallet to drive the driveshaft out from the hub. Withdraw it from under the vehicle **(see illustrations)**. Take care not to damage the hub nut threads on the driveshaft. If the driveshaft is tight, a suitable three-legged puller may be used to force it out of the hub.

### Refitting

**10**  Before refitting the left-hand driveshaft, check the oil seal in the transmission and if necessary renew it with reference to Chapter 7A or 7B. Lightly smear the oil seal with fresh transmission oil.

**11**  On both left- and right-hand driveshafts, check that the inner retaining circlip is in good condition and correctly located in the driveshaft groove **(see illustration)**.

**12**  Ensure that the splines at the outboard end of the driveshaft are clean, then pull out the strut and insert the driveshaft through the hub into engagement with the hub splines. Refit the new hub nut and hand-tighten it at this stage.

**13**  Lubricate the splines at the inner end of the driveshaft with transmission oil, then locate the inner end in the transmission sun gear (left-hand side) or intermediate shaft (right-hand side), pressing it fully in until the circlip is heard to snap into the groove.

**14**  Attach the brake hydraulic hose and ABS cable to the front suspension strut.

**15**  Relocate the front suspension lower balljoint to the hub carrier, make sure it is fully entered, then insert the clamp bolt and tighten to the specified torque.

*Caution: Make sure that the balljoint is fully entered in the hub carrier.*

**16**  On 2002-on models, refit the headlamp position sensor and inner splash cover as applicable.

2.3a  With an assistant depressing the footbrake pedal, loosen the hub nut . . .

2.3b  . . . then unscrew it completely

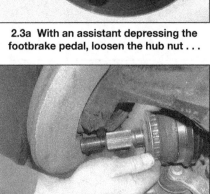

2.9a  Removing the driveshaft from the splines in the hub

2.9b  Withdrawing the driveshaft from the transmission

2.11  Checking the circlip on the inner end of the driveshaft

**17** With two of the roadwheel bolts holding the brake disc in position, have an assistant depress the footbrake pedal, then tighten the hub nut to the specified torque. Note that on early models there two types of nut with different tightening torques.

**18** On 2002-on models, tap the metal dust cover onto the hub flange.

**19** Check and if necessary top-up the transmission oil/fluid level with reference to Chapter 1.

**20** Refit the undertray where applicable, then refit the roadwheel and lower the vehicle to the ground. Tighten the wheel bolts to the specified torque.

**3.6 Remove the clip . . .**

**3.7 . . . release the rubber gaiter from the joint housing . . .**

## 3  Driveshafts –
inspection, joint renewal and cleaning

### *Inspection*

**1** If any of the checks described in Chapter 1 reveal apparent excessive wear or play, first remove the wheel cover and check that the hub nut (driveshaft outer nut) is tightened to the specified torque. Repeat this check on the hub nut on the other side.

**2** To check for driveshaft wear, road test the vehicle, driving it slowly in a circle on full steering lock (carry out the test on both left and right lock), while listening for a metallic clicking or knocking sound coming from the front wheels. An assistant in the passenger seat can listen for the sound from the nearside joint. If such a sound is heard, this indicates wear in the outer joint.

**3** If vibration proportional to road speed is felt through the car when accelerating or on over-run, there is a possibility of wear in the inner joints. For a more thorough check, remove and dismantle the driveshafts where possible as described in the following Sections. Refer to a Saab dealer for information on the availability of driveshaft components.

**4** Continual noise from the area of the right-hand driveshaft, increasing with road speed, may indicate wear in the support bearing.

### *Outer joint renewal*

**5** Remove the driveshaft as described in

**3.9a . . . then use circlip pliers to open the circlip . . .**

Section 2, then thoroughly clean it and mount it in a vice. It is important that foreign matter, such as dust and dirt, is prevented from entering the joint.

**6** Release the large clip securing the rubber gaiter to the outer joint housing **(see illustration)**, then similarly release the small clip securing the rubber gaiter to the driveshaft. Note the fitted position of the gaiter.

**7** Slide the rubber gaiter along the driveshaft, away from the joint **(see illustration)**. Scoop out as much of the grease as possible from the joint and gaiter.

**8** Using a dab of paint, mark the outer joint and driveshaft in relation to each other to ensure correct refitting.

**9** Using circlip pliers at the inner end of the joint, open the circlip then slide the joint from the end of the driveshaft **(see illustrations)**. If it is tight, use a hammer and soft drift to tap the joint hub from the splines. Note that on

**3.9b . . . and slide the outer joint from the end of the driveshaft**

later models, it may not be necessary to open the circlip, as it will release from the driveshaft as the joint is being tapped off.

**10** With the joint removed, slide the rubber gaiter and small clip from the driveshaft **(see illustration)**. Check the rubber gaiter for cracks or slits, and renew it if necessary.

**11** Thoroughly clean the splines of the driveshaft and outer joint, and also the rubber gaiter contact surfaces. If the joint has been contaminated with road grit or water, it must be dismantled and cleaned as described later in this Section. Check the condition of the circlip which is captive in the outer joint, and renew it if necessary **(see illustration)**.

**12** Locate the gaiter, together with small clip, on the outer end of the driveshaft. Smear a little grease onto the driveshaft to facilitate this.

**13** Pack the joint with the specified quantity of grease, working it well into the cavities of the housing **(see illustration)**.

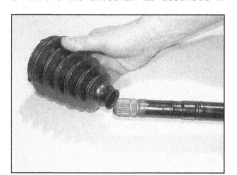

**3.10  Removing the outer rubber gaiter**

**3.11  The circlip is captive in the outer joint**

**3.13  Pack the CV joint with grease from the service kit**

**3.22a Remove the circlip...**

**14** Locate the outer joint onto the driveshaft splines in its previously-noted position, and press it on until the internal circlip engages with the groove.

**15** Reposition the rubber gaiter onto the joint outer housing in its previously-noted position, then refit the two clips. Tighten the clips securely.

**16** Refit the driveshaft with reference to Section 2.

### Inner joint renewal

**17** Remove the driveshaft as described in Section 2, then thoroughly clean it and mount it in a vice. It is important that foreign matter, such as dust and dirt, is prevented from entering the joint.

**18** Release the large clip securing the rubber gaiter to the inner joint housing, then similarly release the small clip securing the rubber gaiter to the driveshaft. Note the fitted position of the gaiter. Where the original factory gaiter is fitted, it will be necessary to bend up the metal plate to release it from the joint housing, however, it is not necessary to bend the plate down for the refitting procedure.

**19** Slide the rubber gaiter along the driveshaft, away from the joint.

**20** Scoop out as much of the grease as possible from the joint and gaiter.

**21** Mark the driveshaft and inner joint housing in relation to each other using a centre-punch or dab of paint, then withdraw the housing from the tripod.

**22** Mark the driveshaft and tripod in relation

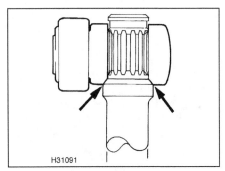

**3.26 On the inner joint, make sure that the chamfer is located against the inner shoulder on the driveshaft**

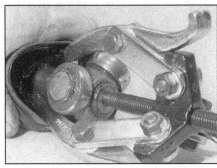

**3.22b ... then use a puller to remove the spider from the driveshaft splines**

to each other using a centre-punch or dab of paint. Using circlip pliers, expand and remove the circlip from the end of the driveshaft, then use a puller to remove the tripod together with needle roller bearings **(see illustrations)**. Note that the chamfered edge of the tripod faces the centre of the driveshaft.

**23** Slide the rubber gaiter and small clip from the driveshaft. Check the rubber gaiter for cracks or slits, and renew it if necessary.

**24** Thoroughly clean the splines of the driveshaft and inner joint, and also the rubber gaiter contact surfaces. If the joint has been exposed to road grit or water, it should be thoroughly cleaned as described later in this Section. Check the condition of the circlip and renew it if necessary. Check that the three tripod bearings are free to rotate without resistance, and that they are not excessively worn.

**25** Locate the gaiter, together with small clip, on the inner end of the driveshaft. Smear a little grease onto the driveshaft to facilitate this.

**26** Locate the tripod on the driveshaft splines, chamfered edge first, making sure that the previously-made marks are aligned **(see illustration)**. Using a socket or metal tube, drive the tripod fully onto the driveshaft, then refit the circlip, making sure that it is correctly located in its groove.

**27** Pack the tripod joint and inner joint housing with the specified quantity of grease, working it well into the bearings. Locate the inner joint housing onto the tripod in its previously-noted position.

**3.28 Using a crimping tool to tighten the gaiter clips**

**28** Reposition the rubber gaiter onto the inner joint housing in its previously-noted position, then refit the two clips. Tighten the clips securely. If crimp-type clips are being fitted, use a crimping tool to tighten them **(see illustration)**.

**29** Refit the driveshaft with reference to Section 2.

### Joint cleaning

**30** Where a joint has been contaminated with road grit or water through a damaged rubber gaiter, the joint should be completely dismantled and cleaned. Remove the joint as described previously in this Section.

**31** To dismantle the outer joint, mount it vertically in a soft-jawed vice, then turn the splined hub and ball cage so that the balls can be removed individually. Remove the hub followed by the ball cage.

**32** The inner joint is dismantled during removal, however, the tripod joint bearings should be washed in suitable solvent to remove all traces of grease.

**33** Thoroughly clean the inner and outer joint housings, together with the ball-bearings, cages and hubs, removing all traces of grease and foreign matter.

**34** To reassemble the outer joint, first insert the cage, followed by the splined hub. Manoeuvre the hub and carrier so that the balls can be inserted one at a time.

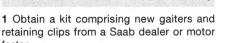

**4  Driveshaft gaiters –**
renewal

**1** Obtain a kit comprising new gaiters and retaining clips from a Saab dealer or motor factor.

**2** Removal and refitting of the gaiters is described in Section 3.

**5  Intermediate driveshaft and support bearing –**
removal, overhaul and refitting

### Removal

**1** Disconnect the battery negative lead (refer to *Disconnecting the battery* in the Reference Chapter).

**2** Apply the handbrake, then jack up the front of the vehicle and support it on axle stands (see *Jacking and vehicle support*). Remove the right-hand front roadwheel.

**3** Working under the right-hand wheel arch, undo the fasteners and remove the splash cover for access to the right-hand side of the engine.

**4** In the engine compartment, remove the engine top cover.

**5** Remove the clamp for the power steering servo pipe.

**6** Support the right-hand side of the engine with a trolley jack and block of wood beneath

**5.18 Intermediate driveshaft support bearing bracket bolts**

**5.19 Removing the intermediate driveshaft from the transmission**

**5.20 Intermediate driveshaft dust seal**

the sump. Alternatively, wedge a block of wood between the subframe and engine sump.

**7** Unbolt and remove the right-hand upper engine mounting bracket (refer to Chapter 2A if necessary).

**8** Note the fitted routing of the auxiliary drivebelt, and mark it with an arrow to indicate its normal running direction.

**9** Using a square-drive extension bar, turn the tensioner clockwise to release its tension, then slip the auxiliary drivebelt off of the crankshaft, alternator, air conditioning compressor and idler pulleys. Release the tensioner.

**10** Using an 8.0 mm Allen key, unbolt the tensioner from the engine. Also, unscrew and remove the alternator upper mounting bolt.

**11** Unclip the front brake hydraulic hose, and move the hose to one side. Also, disconnect the ABS wiring.

**12** On 2002-on models fitted with a headlamp position sensor, unscrew the nut securing the sensor arm to the lower suspension arm, then unbolt the sensor from its mounting bracket and position it to one side.

**13** Unscrew and remove the clamp bolt securing the front suspension lower balljoint to the hub carrier, noting which way round the bolt is fitted. Lever the lower arm downwards and disconnect the balljoint from the hub carrier, then hold the arm in this position with a block of wood between the arm and anti-roll bar.

**14** Using a soft-faced mallet, tap the driveshaft inner joint off of the intermediate shaft and lower the driveshaft onto the subframe and lower arm. If the retaining circlip is tight, hold the joint firmly against the circlip before tapping it with the mallet. If necessary, have an assistant pull out the strut while the driveshaft is being disconnected.

**15** On the rear of the alternator, unscrew the nuts and disconnect the battery positive cable together with the warning light cable.

**16** Unscrew the alternator lower mounting bolt and position the alternator to one side.

**17** Position a container beneath the transmission to catch spilled oil/fluid when the intermediate shaft is removed.

**18** Unscrew the bolts securing the support

bearing bracket to the rear of the cylinder block **(see illustration)**.

**19** Using a screwdriver, lever the bracket away from the dowels on the cylinder block, then withdraw the intermediate driveshaft from the splined sun gear in the transmission **(see illustration)**.

### Overhaul

**20** With the intermediate shaft and bracket on the bench, remove the dust seal from the end of the shaft. The seal may have come away with the right-hand driveshaft **(see illustration)**.

**21** Using circlip pliers, extract the outer small circlip from the end of the intermediate shaft **(see illustration)**.

**22** The intermediate shaft must now be pressed out of the bearing. To do this, support the bracket in a vice, then press or drive out the shaft. If the shaft is being renewed, extract the inner small circlip from the shaft **(see illustration)**.

**23** Using circlip pliers, extract the large circlip securing the bearing in the bracket. The bearing must now be pressed or driven out of the bracket. Support the bracket in a vice to do this.

**24** Support the bracket with its open end upwards, then locate the new bearing and press or drive it fully in using a metal tube on the outer race. Fit the large circlip to secure the bearing in the bracket.

**25** With the intermediate driveshaft mounted in the vice, refit the small circlip to the driveshaft, then refit the bearing with bracket

onto the driveshaft and press or drive on the bearing inner race until it contacts the circlip. Make sure that the bracket is fitted the correct way round, and press only on the inner race.

**26** Fit the small circlip in the groove, making sure that the concave side faces the bearing.

**27** Fit a new dust seal over the outer end of the intermediate shaft.

### Refitting

**28** Wipe clean the transmission oil seal then smear a little oil on the seal lips. It is recommended that the oil seal is always renewed, with reference to Chapter 7A or 7B, considering the amount of work necessary to renew it separately.

**29** Insert the intermediate driveshaft into the transmission side gear, and engage the splines with each other.

**30** Locate the bracket on the dowels, then refit the bolts and tighten to the specified torque.

**31** Refer to Chapter 5A and check that the alternator adjuster sleeves in the mounting bracket are tapped out approximately 1.0 mm, then refit the alternator mounting bolts and tighten securely.

**32** Reconnect the battery positive and warning light cables to the rear of the alternator and tighten securely.

**33** Pull out the strut, then locate the driveshaft inner joint splines in the splined intermediate shaft. Press on the joint until the internal circlip engages with its groove at the end of the splines.

**34** Remove the block of wood, and hold the

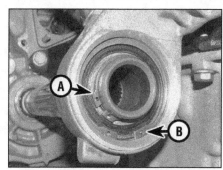

**5.21 Intermediate shaft bearing small circlip (A) and large circlip (B)**

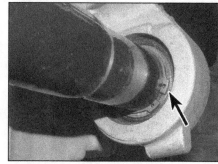

**5.22 Inner small circlip on the driveshaft**

suspension lower arm down while the balljoint is located in the hub carrier. Make sure the balljoint is fully entered in the hub carrier, then refit the clamp bolt with its head in the previously-noted position and tighten to the specified torque.

**35** On 2002-on models, refit the headlamp position sensor and tighten the mounting bolts/nut.

**36** Refit the brake hydraulic hose to the strut clips, and reconnect the ABS wiring.

**37** Refit the alternator upper mounting bolt and tighten securely.

**38** Refit the auxiliary drivebelt tensioner and tighten the bolts with the 8.0 mm Allen key.

**39** Using the square drive, turn the tensioner clockwise then refit the auxiliary drivebelt on the pulleys. Make sure that it is routed correctly, and engaged with all of the pulley grooves, then release the tensioner.

**40** Refit the right-hand upper engine mounting bracket and tighten the bolts to the specified torque (see Chapter 2A). Remove the support from the right-hand side of the engine.

**41** Refit the clamp for the power steering servo pipe.

**42** Top-up the transmission oil/fluid with reference to Chapter 1.

**43** Refit the engine top cover.

**44** Refit the splash cover under the right-hand wheel arch.

**45** Refit the roadwheel, then lower the vehicle to the ground.

**46** Reconnect the battery negative lead (refer to *Disconnecting the battery* in the Reference Chapter).

# Chapter 9
# Braking system

## Contents

## Degrees of difficulty

| Easy, suitable for novice with little experience |  | Fairly easy, suitable for beginner with some experience |  | Fairly difficult, suitable for competent DIY mechanic | 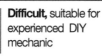 | Difficult, suitable for experienced DIY mechanic | 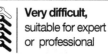 | Very difficult, suitable for expert DIY or professional |  |

## Specifications

### General

Brake system type and layout:

Footbrake . . . . . . . . . . . . . . . . . . . . . . . . . . . . . . . . . . . . . . . . . . . . . Diagonally-split dual hydraulic circuits; front left/rear right and front right/rear left. Discs fitted front and rear, ventilated at the front. Single-piston, sliding calipers on front, double-piston fixed calipers (early) or floating calipers (late) on rear. Anti-lock Braking System (ABS) fitted as standard on all models with vacuum servo assistance. Electronic Stability Program (ESP) option on some models

Handbrake . . . . . . . . . . . . . . . . . . . . . . . . . . . . . . . . . . . . . . . . . . . . . Lever and cable operation, acting on shoes in drums incorporated in rear discs

### Front brakes

Discs:
  Type . . . . . . . . . . . . . . . . . . . . . . . . . . . . . . . . . . . . . . . . . . . . . . . . Ventilated
  Outside diameter . . . . . . . . . . . . . . . . . . . . . . . . . . . . . . . . . . . . . . 288.0 mm
  Thickness (new disc) . . . . . . . . . . . . . . . . . . . . . . . . . . . . . . . . . . . 25.0 mm
  Minimum thickness after grinding . . . . . . . . . . . . . . . . . . . . . . . . 23.5 mm
  Minimum wear thickness . . . . . . . . . . . . . . . . . . . . . . . . . . . . . . . . 22.0 mm
  Maximum run-out . . . . . . . . . . . . . . . . . . . . . . . . . . . . . . . . . . . . . . 0.08 mm
  Maximum variation in disc thickness . . . . . . . . . . . . . . . . . . . . . . 0.015 mm
Calipers:
  Type . . . . . . . . . . . . . . . . . . . . . . . . . . . . . . . . . . . . . . . . . . . . . . . . Single-piston, floating
  Piston diameter . . . . . . . . . . . . . . . . . . . . . . . . . . . . . . . . . . . . . . . 57.0 mm
Pads:
  Minimum friction material thickness . . . . . . . . . . . . . . . . . . . . . . . . 5.0 mm
  Thickness for acoustic warning device . . . . . . . . . . . . . . . . . . . . . 3.0 mm

## Rear brakes

Discs:

| | |
|---|---|
| Type | Solid |
| Outside diameter | 286.0 mm |
| Thickness (new disc) | 10.0 mm |
| Minimum thickness after grinding | 8.5 mm |
| Minimum wear thickness | 8.0 mm |
| Maximum run-out | 0.08 mm |
| Maximum variation in disc thickness | 0.015 mm |
| Handbrake drum inner diameter | 160.0 mm |
| Handbrake drum maximum out-of-round | 0.08 mm |

Calipers:

Type:

| | |
|---|---|
| Early | Fixed, double-piston |
| Late | Floating, single-piston |
| Piston diameter | 38.0 mm |

Pads:

Minimum friction material thickness:

| | |
|---|---|
| Fixed caliper | 5.0 mm |
| Floating caliper | 4.0 mm |

Handbrake:

| | |
|---|---|
| Shoe minimum friction material thickness | 0.5 mm |

## ABS components

Wheel sensors:

| | |
|---|---|
| Resistance | 1600 ± 160 ohms at 20°C |
| Clearance between sensor and tooth (not adjustable) | 0.2 to 1.3 mm |

## Torque wrench settings

| | Nm | lbf ft |
|---|---|---|
| ABS hydraulic unit mounting nut | 20 | 15 |
| Brake caliper guide bolts | 28 | 21 |
| ESP hydraulic unit | 20 | 15 |
| Front brake caliper mounting bracket: | | |
| 1998 to 2001 | 117 | 86 |
| 2002-on: | | |
| Stage 1 | 140 | 103 |
| Stage 2 | Angle-tighten 45° | |
| Front brake hose to caliper: | | |
| 1998 to 2001 | 45 | 33 |
| 2002-on | 40 | 30 |
| Handbrake cable support bracket | 8 | 6 |
| Master cylinder | 25 | 18 |
| Master cylinder hydraulic lines: | | |
| 1998 to 2001: | | |
| RH | 12 | 9 |
| LH | 15 | 11 |
| 2002-on | 16 | 12 |
| Rear brake caliper to backplate (fixed caliper) | 80 | 59 |
| Rear brake caliper mounting bracket (floating caliper) | 80 | 59 |
| Rear brake hose to caliper (floating caliper) | 43 | 32 |
| Rear brake pipe union nut (fixed caliper) | 16 | 12 |
| Rear wheel hub to rear axle: | | |
| Stage 1 | 50 | 37 |
| Stage 2 | Angle-tighten by 30° | |
| Steering column-to-gear clamp bolt | 25 | 18 |
| Vacuum pump (mechanical) banjo bolt | 24 | 18 |
| Vacuum pump (mechanical) mounting bolt | 24 | 18 |
| Vacuum servo | 25 | 18 |
| Wheel bolts | 110 | 81 |

## 1 General information

Braking is achieved by a dual-circuit hydraulic system, assisted by a vacuum servo unit. All models have discs fitted at the front and rear. The front discs are ventilated, to improve cooling and reduce brake fade.

The dual hydraulic circuits are diagonally-split; on LHD models, the primary circuit operates the front left and rear right brakes, and the secondary circuit operates the front right and rear left brakes. On RHD models, the circuits are opposite. This design ensures that at least 50% of the vehicle's braking capacity will be available should pressure be lost in one of the hydraulic circuits. Under these circumstances, the diagonal layout should prevent the vehicle from becoming unstable if the brakes are applied when only one circuit is operational.

The front brake calipers are of floating single-piston type. Each caliper has two brake pads, one inboard and one outboard of the disc. During braking, hydraulic pressure forces the piston along its cylinder, and presses the inboard brake pad against the disc. The caliper body reacts to this effort by sliding along its guide pins, bringing the outboard pad into contact with the disc. In this manner, equal pressure is applied to each side of the disc by the brake pads. When the brake pedal is released, the hydraulic pressure drops and the piston seal retracts the piston from the brake pad.

The rear brake calipers on early models are of fixed double-piston type with two brake pads, one inboard and one outboard of the disc. Later models have a floating, single-piston caliper with two brake pads. The pistons in the early type operate independently of each other, although, the later type function as described earlier for the front calipers.

The rear discs incorporate drums with internal brake shoes for operation of the handbrake. A single primary cable, together with two secondary cables from the handbrake lever, operate the lever on each rear brake expander. The handbrake is not self-adjusting, and must be adjusted regularly.

The brake vacuum servo unit uses engine inlet manifold vacuum to boost the effort applied to the master cylinder by the brake pedal. In order to supply sufficient vacuum to the servo on automatic transmission models, the inlet manifold vacuum is supplemented by an additional vacuum pump driven from the exhaust camshaft. On models manufactured up to 2000, a voltage-variable-speed electric vacuum pump is located in front of the battery. The pump switches on when the inlet manifold vacuum is less than 0.35 bar, and switches off when the vacuum exceeds 0.4 bar. The pressure is monitored by a pressure sensor located on the inlet manifold. Non-return valves in the vacuum lines isolate the inlet manifold and electric vacuum pump to maintain the required vacuum in the lines. The system is only operational with the ignition on and D selected. From 2001-on, the supplementary vacuum is supplied by a mechanical vacuum pump mounted on the left-hand end of the cylinder head and driven by the camshaft. From 2001-on, manual transmission turbo models are fitted with an 'ejector' device to boost the vacuum to the vacuum servo. The device is fitted in the charge air pipe, and operates by speeding up the flow of air across a venturi, thus providing vacuum to the servo.

The anti-lock braking system (ABS) fitted as standard to all models, prevents wheel lock-up under heavy braking, and not only optimises stopping distances, but also improves steering control. By electronically monitoring the speed of each roadwheel in relation to the other wheels, the system can detect when a wheel is about to lock-up,

before control is actually lost. The brake fluid pressure applied to that wheel's brake caliper is then decreased and restored ('modulated') several times a second until control is regained. The system components comprise four wheel speed sensors, a hydraulic unit with integral Electronic Control Unit (ECU), brake lines and a dashboard-mounted warning light. The four wheel sensors are mounted on the wheel hub carriers. Each wheel has a rotating toothed hub mounted on the driveshaft (front) or on the hub (rear). The wheel speed sensors are mounted in close proximity to these hubs. The teeth produce a voltage waveform whose frequency varies with the speed of the hubs. These waveforms are transmitted to the ECU, and used to calculate the rotational speed of each wheel. The ECU has a self-diagnostic facility, to inhibit the operation of the ABS if a fault is detected, lighting the dashboard-mounted warning light. The braking system will then revert to conventional, non-ABS operation. If the nature of the fault is not immediately obvious upon inspection, the vehicle *must* be taken to a Saab dealer, who will have the diagnostic equipment required to interrogate the ABS ECU electronically and pin-point the problem.

The traction control system (TCS) is available as an option on some models, and uses the basic ABS system, with an additional pump and valves fitted to the hydraulic actuator. If wheelspin is detected at a speed below 30 mph, one of the valves opens, to allow the pump to pressurise the relevant brake, until the spinning wheel slows to a rotational speed corresponding to the speed of the vehicle. This has the effect of transferring torque to the wheel with most traction. At the same time, the throttle plate is closed slightly, to reduce the torque from the engine.

The electronic stability program (ESP) system adds another function to the ABS system. Sensors measure the position of the steering wheel, the pressure in the brake master cylinder, the yaw velocity/rate, and the lateral acceleration. With this information, the system can compare the driver's intention with the vehicle's movement, and apply the appropriate corrective action.

## 2  Hydraulic system – bleeding

**Warning: Hydraulic fluid is poisonous; wash off immediately and thoroughly in the case of skin contact, and seek immediate medical advice if any fluid is swallowed or gets into the eyes. Certain types of hydraulic fluid are inflammable, and may ignite when brought into contact with hot components; when servicing any hydraulic system, it is safest to assume that the fluid is inflammable, and to take precautions against the risk of fire as though it is petrol that is being handled. Hydraulic fluid is also an effective paint stripper, and will attack plastics; if any is spilt, it should be washed off immediately, using copious quantities of fresh water. Finally, it is hygroscopic (it absorbs moisture from the air) – old fluid may be contaminated and unfit for further use. When topping-up or renewing the fluid, always use the recommended type, and ensure that it comes from a freshly-opened sealed container.**

### General

1 The correct operation of any hydraulic system is only possible after removing all air from the components and circuit; this is achieved by bleeding the system.

2 During the bleeding procedure, add only clean, unused hydraulic fluid of the recommended type; never re-use fluid that has already been bled from the system. Ensure that sufficient fluid is available before starting work.

3 If there is any possibility of incorrect fluid being already in the system, the brake components and circuit must be flushed completely with uncontaminated, correct fluid, and new seals should be fitted to the various components.

4 If hydraulic fluid has been lost from the system, or air has entered because of a leak, ensure that the fault is cured before proceeding further.

5 Park the vehicle over an inspection pit or on car ramps. Alternatively, apply the handbrake then jack up the front and rear of the vehicle and support it on axle stands (see *Jacking and vehicle support*). For improved access with the vehicle jacked up, remove the roadwheels.

6 Check that all pipes and hoses are secure, unions tight and bleed screws closed. Clean any dirt from around the bleed screws.

7 Unscrew the master cylinder reservoir cap, and top the master cylinder reservoir up to the MAX level line; refit the cap loosely, and remember to maintain the fluid level at least above the MIN level line throughout the procedure, otherwise there is a risk of further air entering the system.

8 There is a number of one-man, do-it-yourself brake bleeding kits currently available from motor accessory shops. It is recommended that one of these kits is used whenever possible, as they greatly simplify the bleeding operation, and also reduce the risk of expelled air and fluid being drawn back into the system. If such a kit is not available, the basic (two-man) method must be used, which is described in detail below.

9 If a kit is to be used, prepare the vehicle as described previously, and follow the kit manufacturer's instructions, as the procedure may vary slightly according to the type being used; generally, they are as outlined below in the relevant sub-section.

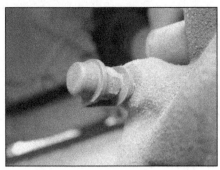

**2.14 Dust cap on the caliper bleed screw**

**2.22 Using a one-way valve kit to bleed the rear brake circuit**

**10** Whichever method is used, the same sequence must be followed (paragraphs 11 and 12) to ensure the removal of all air from the system.

### Bleeding sequence

**11** If the system has been only partially disconnected, and suitable precautions were taken to minimise fluid loss, it should only be necessary to bleed that part of the system (ie, the primary or secondary circuit).

**12** If the complete system is to be bled, then it should be done working in the following sequence:
a) Right-hand front brake.
b) Left-hand rear brake.
c) Left-hand front brake.
d) Right-hand rear brake.

### Bleeding

#### Basic (two-man) method

**13** Collect together a clean glass jar, a suitable length of plastic or rubber tubing which is a tight fit over the bleed screw, and a ring spanner to fit the screw. The help of an assistant will also be required.

**14** Remove the dust cap from the first bleed screw in the sequence **(see illustration)**. Fit the spanner and tube to the screw, place the other end of the tube in the jar, and pour in sufficient fluid to cover the end of the tube.

**15** Ensure that the master cylinder reservoir fluid level is maintained at least above the MIN level mark throughout the procedure.

**16** Have the assistant fully depress and release the brake pedal several times to build-up initial pressure in the system.

**17** Unscrew the bleed screw approximately half a turn then have the assistant slowly depress the brake pedal down to the floor and hold it there. Tighten the bleed screw and have the assistant slowly release the pedal to its rest position.

**18** Repeat the procedure given in paragraph 17 until the fluid emerging from the bleed screw is free from air bubbles. After every two or three depressions of the pedal, check the level of fluid in the reservoir and top up if necessary.

**19** When no more air bubbles appear, securely tighten the bleed screw, remove the tube and spanner, and refit the dust cap. Do not overtighten the bleed screw.

**20** Repeat the procedure on the remaining screws in the sequence, until all air is removed from the system and the brake pedal feels firm again.

#### Using a one-way valve kit

**21** As the name implies, these kits consist of a length of tubing with a one-way valve fitted, to prevent expelled air and fluid being drawn back into the system; some kits include a translucent container, which can be positioned so that the air bubbles can be more easily seen flowing from the end of the tube.

**22** The kit is connected to the bleed screw, which is then opened **(see illustration)**. The user returns to the driver's seat, depresses the brake pedal with a smooth, steady stroke, and slowly releases it; this is repeated until the expelled fluid is clear of air bubbles.

**23** Note that these kits simplify work so much that it is easy to forget the master cylinder reservoir fluid level; ensure that this is maintained at least above the MIN level at all times.

#### Using a pressure-bleeding kit

**24** These kits are usually operated by a reservoir of pressurised air contained in the spare tyre. However, note that it will probably be necessary to reduce the pressure to a lower level than normal; refer to the instructions supplied with the kit.

**25** By connecting a pressurised, fluid-filled container to the master cylinder reservoir, bleeding can be carried out simply by opening each screw in turn (in the specified sequence),

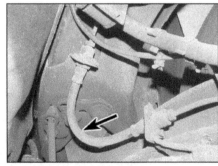

**3.2 Rear brake flexible hose located between the underbody and trailing arm**

and allowing the fluid to flow out until no more air bubbles can be seen in the expelled fluid.

**26** This method has the advantage that the large reservoir of fluid provides an additional safeguard against air being drawn into the system during bleeding.

**27** Pressure-bleeding is particularly effective when bleeding 'difficult' systems, or when bleeding the complete system at the time of routine fluid renewal.

#### All methods

**28** When bleeding is complete, and firm pedal feel is restored, wipe off any spilt fluid, securely tighten the bleed screws, and refit the dust caps.

**29** Check the hydraulic fluid level in the master cylinder reservoir, and top-up if necessary (see *Weekly checks*).

**30** Discard any hydraulic fluid that has been bled from the system; it will not be fit for re-use.

**31** Check the feel of the brake pedal. If it feels at all spongy, air must still be present in the system, and further bleeding is required. Failure to bleed satisfactorily after a reasonable repetition of the bleeding procedure may be due to worn master cylinder seals.

### 3  Hydraulic pipes and hoses – renewal

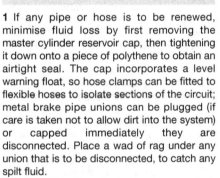

**1** If any pipe or hose is to be renewed, minimise fluid loss by first removing the master cylinder reservoir cap, then tightening it down onto a piece of polythene to obtain an airtight seal. The cap incorporates a level warning float, so hose clamps can be fitted to flexible hoses to isolate sections of the circuit; metal brake pipe unions can be plugged (if care is taken not to allow dirt into the system) or capped immediately they are disconnected. Place a wad of rag under any union that is to be disconnected, to catch any spilt fluid.

**2** If a flexible hose is to be disconnected, unscrew the brake pipe union nut before removing the spring clip which secures the hose to its mounting bracket **(see illustration)**. Where applicable, unscrew the banjo union bolt securing the hose to the caliper and recover the copper washers. When removing the front flexible hose, pull out the spring clip and disconnect it from the strut.

**3** To unscrew union nuts, it is preferable to obtain a 'split' brake pipe spanner of the correct size; these are available from most motor accessory shops. Failing this, a close-fitting open-ended spanner will be required, though if the nuts are tight or corroded, their flats may be rounded-off if the spanner slips. In such a case, a self-locking wrench is often the only way to unscrew a stubborn union, but it follows that the pipe and the damaged nuts

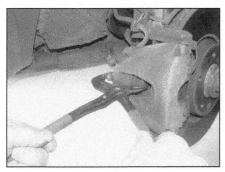

4.2  Using slip-joint pliers to press the piston into the caliper

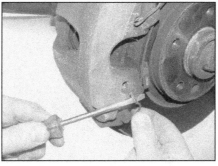

4.3a  Lever out the retaining spring . . .

4.3b  . . . and remove it from the caliper

must be renewed on reassembly. Always clean a union and surrounding area before disconnecting it. If disconnecting a component with more than one union, make a careful note of the connections before disturbing any of them.

4  If a brake pipe is to be renewed, it can be obtained, cut to length and with the union nuts and end flares in place, from a dealer's parts shop. All that is then necessary is to bend it to shape, following the line of the original, before fitting it to the car. Alternatively, most motor accessory shops can make up brake pipes from kits, but this requires very careful measurement of the original, to ensure that the new part is of the correct length. The safest answer is usually to take the original to the shop as a pattern.

5  On refitting, do not overtighten the union nuts.

6  When refitting hoses to the calipers, always use new copper washers and tighten the banjo union bolts to the specified torque. Make sure that the hoses are positioned so that they will not touch surrounding bodywork or the roadwheels.

7  Ensure that the pipes and hoses are correctly routed, with no kinks, and that they are secured in the clips or brackets provided. After fitting, remove the polythene from the reservoir, and bleed the hydraulic system as described in Section 2. Wash off any spilt fluid, and check carefully for fluid leaks.

## 4  Front brake pads – renewal

⚠ *Warning: Renew BOTH sets of front brake pads at the same time – NEVER renew the pads on only*

*one wheel, as uneven braking may result. Note that the dust created by wear of the pads may contain asbestos, which is a health hazard. Never blow it out with compressed air, and do not inhale any of it. Use brake cleaner or methylated spirit to clean brake components.*

1  Apply the handbrake, then jack up the front of the vehicle and support it on axle stands (see *Jacking and vehicle support*). Remove both front roadwheels.

2  Using slip-joint pliers, press the piston fully into the caliper **(see illustration)**. **Note:** *Provided that the master cylinder reservoir has not been overfilled with hydraulic fluid, there should be no spillage, but keep a careful watch on the fluid level while retracting the piston. If the fluid level rises above the MAX line at any time, the surplus should be syphoned off or ejected via a plastic tube connected to the bleed screw.*

3  Carefully lever off the retaining spring from the holes on the outer surface of the caliper, noting how the spring is located on the caliper mounting bracket **(see illustrations)**

4  Remove the dust caps from the inner ends of the guide bolts **(see illustration)**.

5  Unscrew the guide bolts from the caliper, and lift the caliper and pads away from the mounting bracket **(see illustrations)**. Tie the caliper to the suspension strut using a suitable piece of wire. Do not allow the caliper to hang unsupported on the flexible brake hose.

6  Remove the inner and outer pads from the caliper, noting that the inner one is retained in the piston by a spring clip attached to the pad backing plate **(see illustrations)**. **Note:** *An*

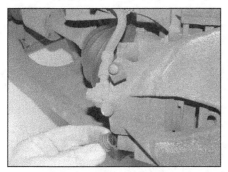

4.4  Remove the dust caps . . .

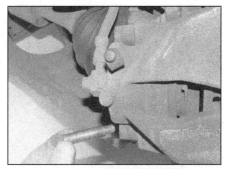

4.5a  . . . then unscrew the guide bolts . . .

4.5b  . . . and lift the caliper and pads away from the mounting bracket

4.6a  Remove the outer pad from the caliper . . .

4.6b  . . . then the inner pad, noting that it is retained in the piston by a spring clip

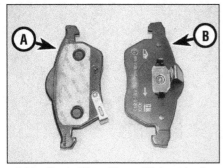

4.11a Outer (A) and inner (B) front brake pads

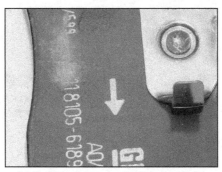

4.11b The pads must be fitted with the arrow pointing the normal, forward rotation of the brake disc

*acoustic wear warning device is fitted to the outer pad, consisting of a metal strip which contacts the brake disc when the thickness of the friction material is less than 3.0 mm. This device causes a scraping noise which warns the driver that the pads are worn excessively.*

**7** Brush the dirt and dust from the caliper, but take care not to inhale it. Carefully remove any rust from the edge of the brake disc.

**8** Measure the thickness of the friction material on each brake pad (excluding the backing plate). If either pad is worn at any point to the specified minimum thickness or less, all four pads must be renewed. The pads should also be renewed if any are contaminated with oil or grease; there is no satisfactory way of degreasing friction material. Trace and rectify the cause of contamination before reassembly.

**9** If the brake pads are still serviceable, clean them using a clean, fine wire brush or similar, paying particular attention to the sides and back of the metal backing. Carefully clean the pad locations in the caliper body/mounting bracket.

**10** Prior to fitting the pads, check that the guide bolts are a good fit in the caliper bushes. Brush the dust and dirt from the caliper and piston (see *Warning* at the beginning of this Section). Apply a little high melting-point copper brake grease to the areas on the pad backing plates which contact the caliper and piston. Inspect the dust seal around the piston for damage, and the piston for evidence of fluid leaks, corrosion or damage. If attention to any of these components is necessary, refer to Section 6.

**11** Fit the inner pad to the caliper, ensuring

that its clip is correctly located in the caliper piston. Make sure that the arrows on the pad point in the normal, forward direction of rotation of the brake disc **(see illustrations)**.

**12** Fit the outer pad to the caliper mounting bracket, ensuring that its friction material is facing the brake disc. The acoustic wear indicators must face downwards.

**13** Slide the caliper and inner pad into position over the outer pad, and locate it in the mounting bracket.

**14** Insert the caliper guide bolts, and tighten them to the specified torque setting.

**15** Refit the guide bolt dust caps.

**16** Refit the retaining spring to the caliper, ensuring that its ends are correctly located in the caliper holes.

**17** Depress the brake pedal repeatedly, until normal pedal pressure is restored.

**18** Repeat the above procedure on the remaining front brake caliper.

**19** Refit the roadwheels, then lower the vehicle to the ground and tighten the roadwheel bolts to the specified torque setting.

**20** Check the hydraulic fluid level as described in *Weekly checks*.

**5  Rear brake pads –**
renewal

⚠ *Warning: Renew BOTH sets of rear brake pads at the same time – NEVER renew the pads on only one wheel, as uneven braking may result. Note that the dust created by wear of the pads may contain asbestos, which is a health hazard. Never blow it out with compressed air, and do not inhale any of it. Use brake cleaner or methylated spirit to clean brake components.*

**1** Chock the front wheels, then jack up the rear of the vehicle and support on axle stands (see *Jacking and vehicle support*). Remove the rear roadwheels.

### Fixed caliper

**2** Note how the anti-squeal spring is located, then drive out the upper and lower pad retaining pins from the outside of the caliper using a punch **(see illustration)**.

**3** Remove the anti-squeal spring **(see illustration)**.

**4** Move the pads away from the disc slightly using a suitable lever or a pair of large adjustable pliers, then withdraw the outer pad from the caliper using pliers or a special removal tool.

**5** Withdraw the inner pad from the caliper **(see illustrations)**.

### Floating caliper

**6** Using slip-joint pliers, press the piston fully into the caliper **(see illustration)**. **Note:** *Provided that the master cylinder reservoir has*

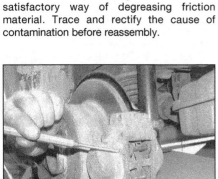

5.2 Using a punch to drive out the rear brake pad retaining pins

5.3 Removing the anti-squeal spring

5.5a Removing the inner rear brake pad

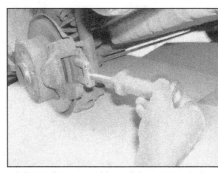

5.5b Using a removal tool to remove the inner rear brake pad

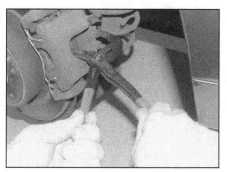

5.6 Using slip-joint pliers to press the piston fully into the caliper

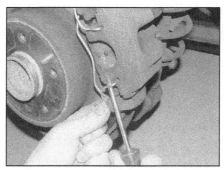

5.7 Use a screwdriver to lever off the retaining spring

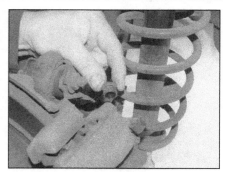

5.8a Remove the dust caps . . .

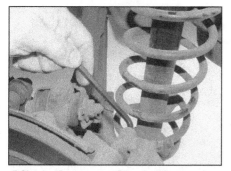

5.8b . . . then use an Allen key to unscrew the guide bolts . . .

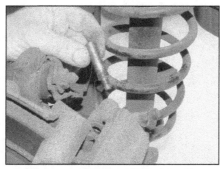

5.8c . . . and remove them from the caliper . . .

5.8d . . . then lift the caliper and pads from the mounting bracket . . .

*not been overfilled with hydraulic fluid, there should be no spillage, but keep a careful watch on the fluid level while retracting the piston. If the fluid level rises above the MAX level line at any time, the surplus should be syphoned off or ejected via a plastic tube connected to the bleed screw.*

**7** Carefully lever off the retaining spring from the holes on the outer surface of the caliper, noting how the spring is located on the caliper mounting bracket **(see illustration)**.

**8** Remove the dust caps, then use an Allen key to unscrew the guide bolts from the caliper, and lift the caliper and pads away from the mounting bracket. Tie the caliper to the suspension coil spring using a suitable piece of wire **(see illustrations)**. Do not allow the caliper to hang unsupported on the flexible brake hose.

**9** Remove the outer and inner pads from the caliper, noting that the inner one is retained in the piston by a spring clip attached to the pad backing plate **(see illustrations)**.

### All models

**10** Brush the dirt and dust from the caliper, but take care not to inhale it. Carefully remove any rust from the edge of the brake disc.

**11** Measure the thickness of the friction material on each brake pad (excluding the backing plate). If either pad is worn at any point to the specified minimum thickness or less, all four pads must be renewed. The pads should also be renewed if any are contaminated with oil or grease; there is no satisfactory way of degreasing friction material. Trace and rectify the cause of contamination before reassembly.

**12** If the brake pads are still serviceable,

clean them using a clean, fine wire brush or similar, paying particular attention to the sides and back of the metal backing. Carefully clean the pad locations in the caliper body/ mounting bracket.

**13** Prior to fitting the pads, clean and check the pad retaining pins on 1998 models, and check that the guide bolts are a good fit in the caliper bushes on later models. Brush the dust and dirt from the caliper and piston (see *Warning* at the beginning of this Section). Apply a little high melting-point copper brake grease to the areas on the pad backing plates which contact the caliper and piston **(see illustration)**. Inspect the dust seal around the piston(s) for damage, and the piston(s) for evidence of fluid leaks, corrosion or damage. If attention to any of these components is necessary, refer to Section 7.

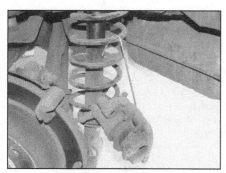

5.8e . . . and suspend the caliper from the suspension coil spring

5.9a Remove the outer pad . . .

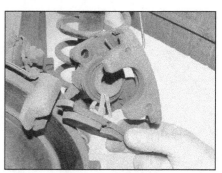

5.9b . . . and inner pad with location spring from the caliper

**5.13 Apply a little high-melting point brake grease to the backs of the brake pads**

14 If new brake pads are to be fitted, the caliper piston(s) must be pushed back into the cylinder(s) to make room for them. Either use a G-clamp or similar tool, or use suitable pieces of wood as levers. Provided that the master cylinder reservoir has not been overfilled with hydraulic fluid, there should be no spillage, but keep a careful watch on the fluid level while retracting the piston(s). If the fluid level rises above the MAX level line at any time, the surplus should be syphoned off or ejected via a plastic tube connected to the bleed screw.

 *Warning: Do not syphon the fluid by mouth, as it is poisonous; use a syringe or an old poultry baster.*

### Fixed caliper

15 Where applicable, use a steel rule to check that the cutaway recess in the pistons are positioned correctly (see illustration). The recesses must be at the bottom of the caliper. If necessary, carefully turn the pistons to their correct positions.
16 Locate the new pads in the caliper. Ensure that the friction material faces the disc, and check that the pads are free to move.
17 Locate the anti-squeal spring on the pads, then insert the pad retaining pins from the inside edge of the caliper, while depressing the spring. Tap the pins firmly into the caliper.

### Floating caliper

18 Locate the inner and outer pads in the caliper, making sure that the inner pad location spring is fully entered in the piston.

**6.5a Unscrew the bolts . . .**

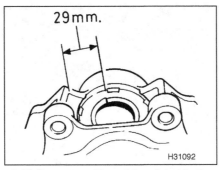

**5.15 Correct position of the piston in the rear brake caliper (early models)**

19 Slide the caliper and pads over the disc and onto the mounting bracket.
20 Insert the caliper guide bolts, and tighten them to the specified torque setting.
21 Refit the guide bolt dust caps.
22 Refit the retaining spring to the caliper, ensuring that its ends are correctly located in the caliper holes.

### All models

23 Depress the brake pedal repeatedly until normal pedal pressure is restored.
24 Repeat the above procedure on the remaining rear brake caliper.
25 Refit the roadwheels, then lower the vehicle to the ground and tighten the road-wheel bolts to the specified torque setting.
26 Check the hydraulic fluid level as described in *Weekly checks*.

### 6 Front brake caliper – removal, overhaul and refitting

### Removal

1 Apply the handbrake, then jack up the front of the vehicle and support it on axle stands (see *Jacking and vehicle support*). Remove the roadwheel.
2 Minimise fluid loss by first removing the master cylinder reservoir cap, then tightening it down onto a piece of polythene to obtain an airtight seal. Alternatively, use a brake hose clamp to clamp the flexible hose leading to the brake caliper.

**6.5b . . . and remove the caliper mounting bracket from the hub carrier**

3 Clean the area around the caliper brake hose union. Note the fitted angle of the hose (to ensure correct refitting), then unscrew and remove the union bolt and recover the copper sealing washer from each side of the hose union. Discard the washers; new ones must be used on refitting. Plug the hose end and caliper hole, to minimise fluid loss and prevent the ingress of dirt into the hydraulic system.
4 Remove the brake pads as described in Section 4, then remove the caliper from the vehicle.
5 If necessary, unbolt the caliper mounting bracket from the hub carrier (see illustrations).

### Overhaul

6 With the caliper on the bench, clean away all external dirt and debris.
7 Withdraw the piston from the caliper body, and remove the dust seal. The piston can be withdrawn by hand or, if necessary, pushed out by applying compressed air to the brake hose union hole. Only low pressure should be required, such as from a foot pump.
8 Using a small screwdriver, carefully remove the piston seal from the caliper, taking care not to mark the bore.
9 Remove the guide bushes from the caliper body.
10 Thoroughly clean all components, using only methylated spirit or clean hydraulic fluid. Never use mineral-based solvents such as petrol or paraffin. Dry the components using compressed air or a clean, lint-free cloth. If available, use compressed air to blow clear the fluid passages.
11 Check all components, and renew any that are worn or damaged. If the piston and/or cylinder bore are scratched excessively, renew the complete caliper body. Similarly check the condition of the guide bushes and bolts; both bushes and bolts should be undamaged and a reasonably tight sliding fit. If there is any doubt about the condition of any component, renew it. Renew the caliper seals and dust covers as a matter of course; these are available as a repair kit together with assembly grease.
12 On reassembly, ensure that all components are absolutely clean.
13 Lubricate the new seal with the grease supplied, or dip it in clean hydraulic fluid. Locate the seal in the cylinder bore groove, using only the fingers to manipulate it into position.
14 Fill the inner cavity of the dust seal with the grease supplied, or dip it in clean hydraulic fluid, then locate it on the piston.
15 Locate the piston on the caliper, then carefully press it fully into the bore, twisting it from side-to-side to ensure it enters the internal seal correctly. At the same time, make sure that the inner end of the dust seal enters the groove on the caliper body, and the outer end enters the groove in the piston.
16 Insert the guide bushes in the caliper body, using suitable grease to lubricate them.

## Refitting

**17** Locate the caliper mounting bracket on the hub carrier, then apply locking fluid to the threads of the mounting bolts, insert them, and tighten to the specified torque.

**18** Refit the brake pads as described in Section 4, together with the caliper which at this stage will not have the hose attached.

**19** Position a new copper sealing washer on each side of the hose union, and connect the brake hose to the caliper. Ensure that the hose is correctly positioned against the caliper body lug, then install the union bolt and tighten securely.

**20** Remove the brake hose clamp or the polythene, where fitted, and bleed the hydraulic system as described in Section 2. Note that, providing the precautions described were taken to minimise brake fluid loss, it should only be necessary to bleed the relevant front brake.

**21** Refit the roadwheel, then lower the vehicle to the ground and tighten the roadwheel bolts to the specified torque.

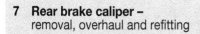

## 7  Rear brake caliper – removal, overhaul and refitting

### Removal

**1** Chock the front wheels, then jack up the rear of the vehicle and support on axle stands (see *Jacking and vehicle support*). Remove the roadwheel.

**2** Minimise fluid loss by first removing the master cylinder reservoir cap, then tightening it down onto a piece of polythene to obtain an airtight seal. Alternatively, use a brake hose clamp on the flexible hose leading to the brake line on the rear axle (early models with fixed caliper) **(see illustration)** or to the floating caliper (late models).

### Fixed caliper

**3** Clean the area around the hydraulic line union nut, then loosen the nut **(see illustration)**. Do not fully unscrew the nut at this stage.

**4** Remove the brake pads as described in Section 5.

**5** Unscrew and remove the mounting bolts securing the caliper to the backplate **(see illustration)**. Recover the cover plate from under the bolt heads.

**6** Fully unscrew the union nut and disconnect the hydraulic line from the caliper, then withdraw the caliper from the disc **(see illustration)**. Tape over or plug the hydraulic line to prevent entry of dust and dirt.

### Floating caliper

**7** Clean the area around the brake hose on the caliper, then loosen only the hose end fitting. The hose cannot be fully unscrewed from the caliper at this stage.

**7.2  Brake hose clamp fitted to the flexible hose leading from the body to the brake line on the rear axle (pre 2003)**

**8** At the other end of the brake hose, unscrew the union nut and disconnect the rigid brake line from the hose end fitting on the rear suspension trailing arm. Be prepared for some loss of brake fluid. Recover the clip, and withdraw the hose from the bracket. Tape over or plug the ends of the rigid line and hose to prevent entry of dust and dirt.

**9** Remove the brake pads as described in Section 5, then remove the caliper from the vehicle. Fully unscrew the hose from the caliper.

**10** If necessary, unbolt the caliper mounting bracket from the backplate.

### Overhaul

**11** With the caliper on the bench, clean away all external dirt and debris.

**12** Withdraw the piston(s) from the caliper body, and remove the dust seal(s). The piston(s) can be withdrawn by hand, or if necessary pushed out by applying compressed air to the brake hose union hole. Only low pressure should be required, such as from a foot pump.

*Caution: On the fixed caliper, keep each piston identified for position to ensure correct refitting.*

**13** Using a small screwdriver, carefully remove the piston seal(s) from the caliper, taking care not to mark the bore(s).

**14** On the floating caliper, remove the guide bushes from the caliper body.

**15** Thoroughly clean all components, using only methylated spirit or clean hydraulic fluid. Never use mineral-based solvents such as

**7.3  Unscrewing the hydraulic line union nut from the rear brake caliper**

petrol or paraffin. Dry the components using compressed air or a clean, lint-free cloth. If available, use compressed air to blow clear the fluid passages.

**16** Check all components, and renew any that are worn or damaged. If the piston(s) and/or cylinder bore(s) are scratched excessively, renew the complete caliper body. On the floating caliper, check the condition of the guide bushes and bolts; both bushes and bolts should be undamaged and a reasonably tight sliding fit. Renew the caliper seals and dust covers as a matter of course; these are available as a repair kit together with assembly grease.

**17** On reassembly, ensure that all components are absolutely clean.

**18** Lubricate the new seal(s) with the grease supplied, or dip them in clean hydraulic fluid, then locate them in the cylinder bore groove(s), using only the fingers to manipulate them into position.

**19** Fill the inner cavities of the dust seals with the grease supplied, or dip them in clean hydraulic fluid, then locate them on the piston(s).

**20** Locate the piston(s) on the caliper, then carefully press it fully into the caliper body, twisting it from side-to-side to ensure it enters the internal seal correctly. At the same time, make sure that the inner end of the dust seal(s) enters the groove on the caliper body, and the outer end enters the groove in the piston. On the fixed caliper, make sure that the piston cutaway recesses are positioned as described in Section 5.

**7.5  Removing the rear brake caliper mounting bolts**

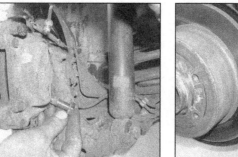

**7.6  Removing the rear brake caliper**

## Refitting

### Fixed caliper

**21** With both pistons refitted, locate the caliper over the disc and onto the backplate, then insert the hydraulic line and screw in the union nut. Do not fully tighten the nut at this stage.

**22** Apply a little locking fluid to the threads of the mounting bolts, then refit the cover plate and bolts, and tighten the bolts to the specified torque.

**23** Refit the brake pads (see Section 5).

**24** Fully tighten the hydraulic union nut.

### Floating caliper

**25** Locate the caliper mounting bracket on the backplate, then apply locking fluid to the threads of the mounting bolts, insert them, and tighten to the specified torque.

**26** Screw the brake hose into the caliper and tighten it to the specified torque.

**27** Refit the brake pads as described in Section 5, together with the caliper.

**28** Locate the brake hose in the bracket making sure that it is not twisted. Refit the clip, then insert and tighten the rigid brake line union nut.

### All models

**29** Remove the polythene, where fitted, and bleed the hydraulic system as described in Section 2. Note that, providing the precautions described were taken to minimise brake fluid loss, it should only be necessary to bleed the relevant rear brake.

**30** Refit the roadwheel, then lower the vehicle to the ground and tighten the road-wheel bolts to the specified torque.

## 8 Front brake disc – inspection, removal and refitting

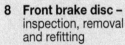

## Inspection

**1** Apply the handbrake, then jack up the front of the vehicle and support it on axle stands (see *Jacking and vehicle support*). Remove both front roadwheels.

**2** For an accurate check and for access to each side of the disc, the brake caliper should

**8.5 Checking the front brake disc with a dial gauge**

be unbolted and suspended to one side as described later in this Section. Alternatively, just the brake pads can be removed as described in Section 5.

**3** Check that the brake disc securing screw is tight, then fit spacers approximately 10.0 mm thick to each of the roadwheel bolts, and refit and tighten the bolts. This will hold the disc in its normal running position.

**4** Rotate the brake disc, and examine it for deep scoring or grooving. Light scoring is normal, but if excessive, the disc should be removed and either renewed or machined (within the specified limits) by an engineering works. The minimum thickness is given in the Specifications at the beginning of this Chapter.

**5** Using a dial gauge, or a flat metal block and feeler blades, check that the disc run-out does not exceed the figure given in the Specifications **(see illustration)**.

**6** If the disc run-out is excessive, remove the disc as described later, and check that the disc-to-hub surfaces are perfectly clean. Refit the disc and check the run-out again. If the run-out is still excessive, the disc should be renewed.

**7** Using a micrometer check that the disc thickness is not less than that given in the Specifications. Take readings at several points around the disc.

**8** Repeat the inspection on the other front brake disc.

## Removal

**9** Remove the roadwheel bolts and spacers used when checking the disc.

**10** Remove the disc pads as described in Section 4, and tie the caliper one side. Also remove the front brake caliper mounting bracket with reference to Section 6.

**11** Remove the securing screw and withdraw the disc from the hub. If the screw is tight, use an impact driver to loosen it **(see illustrations)**.

## Refitting

**12** Refitting is a reversal of removal, but make sure that the mating faces of the disc and hub are perfectly clean, and apply a little locking fluid to the threads of the securing screw before tightening it. If a new disc is being fitted, remove the protective coating from the surface, using an appropriate solvent. Refit the disc pads as described in Section 4, then refit the roadwheel and lower the vehicle to the ground.

## 9 Rear brake disc – inspection, removal and refitting

## Inspection

**1** Chock the front wheels, then jack up the rear of the vehicle and support on axle stands (see *Jacking and vehicle support*). Remove both rear roadwheels.

**2** For an accurate check and for access to each side of the disc, the brake caliper should be unbolted and suspended to one side as described later in this Section. Alternatively, just the brake pads can be removed as described in Section 5.

**3** Check that the brake disc securing screw is tight, then fit spacers approximately 10.0 mm thick to each of the roadwheel bolts, and refit and tighten the bolts. This will hold the disc in its normal running position.

**4** Rotate the brake disc, and examine it for deep scoring or grooving. Light scoring is normal, but if excessive, the disc should be removed and either renewed or machined (within the specified limits) by an engineering works. The minimum thickness is given in the Specifications at the beginning of this Chapter.

**8.11a Front brake disc securing screw**

**8.11b Using an impact driver to loosen the brake disc securing screw**

**8.11c Removing the front brake disc**

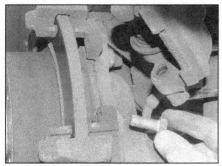

**9.13a Unscrew the bolts . . .**

**9.13b . . . and remove the caliper mounting bracket from the rear suspension trailing arm**

**9.14 Back off the handbrake shoe adjustment using a screwdriver through the access hole in the disc**

**5** Using a dial gauge, or a flat metal block and feeler blades, check that the disc run-out does not exceed the figure given in the Specifications.

**6** If the disc run-out is excessive, remove the disc as described later, and check that the disc-to-hub surfaces are perfectly clean. Refit the disc and check the run-out again. If the run-out is still excessive, the disc should be renewed.

**7** Using a micrometer check that the disc thickness is not less than that given in the Specifications. Take readings at several points around the disc.

**8** Repeat the inspection on the other rear brake disc.

### Removal

**9** Remove the roadwheel bolts and spacers used when checking the disc.

**10** Remove the disc pads as described in Section 5.

### Fixed caliper

**11** Carefully release the rear brake hydraulic line from the clip on the rear axle, taking care not to bend the line excessively.

**12** Unbolt and remove the rear brake caliper with reference to Section 7, and tie it to one side. A convenient place to secure the caliper on the left-hand side is to the exhaust system, using a long plastic cable tie.

### Floating caliper

**13** With the caliper already removed in order to remove the disc pads, unscrew the bolts and remove the mounting bracket from the rear suspension trailing arm **(see illustrations)**.

### All models

**14** Using a screwdriver through the access hole, back off the handbrake shoe adjustment with reference to Section 16 **(see illustration)**.

**15** Remove the securing screw and withdraw the disc from the hub **(see illustrations)**.

### Refitting

**16** Refitting is a reversal of removal, but make sure that the mating faces of the disc and hub are perfectly clean, and apply a little locking fluid to the threads of the securing screw before tightening it. If a new disc is being fitted, remove the protective coating

**9.15a Remove the screw . . .**

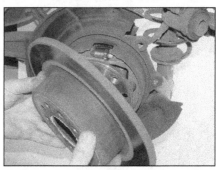

**9.15b . . . and remove the rear brake disc**

from the surface, using an appropriate solvent. Adjust the handbrake as described in Section 16 and the handbrake cables as described in Section 17. Refit the roadwheel and lower the vehicle to the ground.

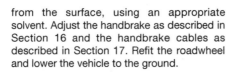

### 10 Handbrake shoes –
inspection, removal and refitting

> **Warning: Renew BOTH sets of rear brake shoes at the same time. Note that the dust created by wear of the pads may contain asbestos, which is a health hazard. Never blow it out with compressed air, and do not inhale any of it. Use brake cleaner or methylated spirit to clean brake components.**

### Inspection

**1** The handbrake operates independently of the footbrake, using brake shoes inside drums integral with the discs.

**2** A quick check of the handbrake shoe wear may be made without removing the rear brake disc. Chock the front wheels, then jack up the rear of the vehicle and support it on axle stands (see *Jacking and vehicle support*). Turn the brake disc so that the automatic adjuster is visible through the hole in the disc (see Chapter 9). If the adjuster has more than 10 threads visible, the shoes are worn excessively and should be renewed.

**3** For a thorough check, remove the rear brake disc as described in Section 9, then

check the minimum thickness of the friction material on each handbrake shoe. If any one of the shoes has worn below the specified limit, all four handbrake shoes must be renewed as a set.

### Removal

**4** With the rear brake disc removed, clean the dust and dirt from the brake shoes and backplate.

**5** It is possible to remove and refit the shoes without removing the rear hub, although we found it much easier with the hub removed and the backplate on the bench, particularly for the reassembly procedure. Refer to Chapter 10 and remove the rear hub, and the backplate complete with handbrake shoes.

**6** Unhook the cable return spring from the hole in the backplate and from the cable end fitting **(see illustration)**.

**10.6 Unhook and remove the cable return spring**

**10.7 Disconnecting the handbrake cable end fitting from the lever on the backplate**

**10.8a Handbrake shoes fitted to the rear brake backplate**

**10.8b Handbrake shoe adjuster (left-hand rear brake) . . .**

**10.8c . . . expander . . .**

**10.8d . . . and hold-down springs**

**10.9 Removing the handbrake shoe hold-down cups, springs and pins**

**7** Unhook the cable end fitting from the lever on the bottom of the backplate **(see illustration)**.

**8** Note the fitted position of all components, and if necessary make a sketch of them **(see illustrations)**.

**9** Remove the shoe hold-down cups, springs and pins by depressing the cups and turning them through 90° using a pair of pliers **(see illustration)**. If the hub is still fitted, insert a suitable tool through the hole in the hub flange.

**10** Carefully lift the shoes directly from the backplate anchors and guide the expander lever through the rubber grommet **(see illustration)**.

**11** Pull the shoes apart and remove the adjuster, followed by the upper return spring **(see illustrations)**.

**12** Swivel the upper ends of the shoes inwards, and remove the expander from the bottom ends **(see illustrations)**.

**13** Unhook the lower return spring from the shoes **(see illustration)**.

**14** Dismantle the adjuster and expander components for cleaning **(see illustration)**.

**15** If both handbrake assemblies are dismantled at the same time, take care not to mix them up.

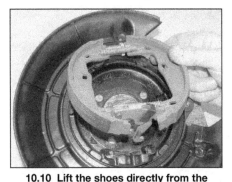

**10.10 Lift the shoes directly from the backplate**

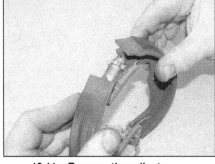

**10.11a Remove the adjuster . . .**

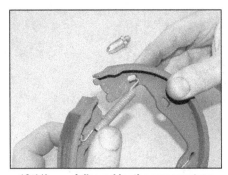

**10.11b . . . followed by the upper return spring**

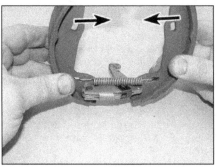

**10.12a Swivel the upper ends of the shoes inwards . . .**

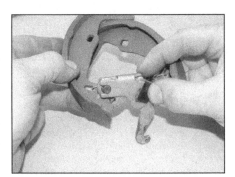

**10.12b . . . and remove the expander**

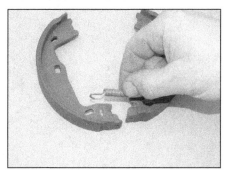

10.13 Unhook the lower return spring

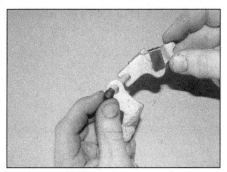

10.14 Dismantling the expander

10.17 Apply a little copper grease to the shoe contact points

16 Clean all components, then examine them for wear and damage. Renew worn or damaged components. Make sure that the expander and adjuster operate freely and not seized – apply a spot of oil to the expander pivots, and apply a little high melting-point grease to the threads of the adjuster before reassembling it. Set the adjuster to its minimum length.

### Refitting

17 Clean the backplate thoroughly, and apply a little copper grease to the shoe contact points **(see illustration)**.
18 Assemble the shoes onto the backplate using a reversal of the removal procedure.
19 Refit the backplate and rear hub with reference to Chapter 10.
20 Hook the cable end fitting on the expander lever and locate the cable holder in the bracket.
21 Hook the cable return spring in the backplate hole and on the end fitting.
22 Refit the rear brake disc and caliper as described in Section 9.
23 Adjust the handbrake shoes as described in Section 16, then refit the roadwheels and lower the vehicle to the ground.

### 11 Master cylinder –
removal, overhaul and refitting

### Removal

1 Exhaust the vacuum present in the brake servo unit by repeatedly depressing the brake pedal.
2 On left-hand drive models, remove the main fusebox and holder, then disconnect the wiring from the anti-theft alarm switch. To provide more working room, unbolt and remove the bracket.
3 Disconnect the wiring from the brake fluid warning switch in the reservoir filler cap.
4 Syphon out the fluid from the reservoir. Alternatively, open any convenient bleed screw in the system, and gently pump the brake pedal to expel the fluid through a plastic tube connected to the bleed screw (see Section 2).

> **Warning: Do not syphon the fluid by mouth, as it is poisonous; use a syringe or an old poultry baster.**

5 Place cloth rags beneath the master cylinder to catch spilt fluid.
6 On manual transmission models, disconnect the clutch hydraulic hose from the brake fluid reservoir.
7 Refit the filler cap on the reservoir, then carefully lever the reservoir from the rubber grommets in the top of the master cylinder using a wide-bladed screwdriver.
8 Note the position of the brake lines, then unscrew the union nuts and move the lines to one side so that they are just clear of the master cylinder. Do not bend the brake lines excessively. If available use a split spanner to unscrew the nuts, as they can be very tight.

Tape over or plug the outlets of the brake lines and master cylinder.
9 Unscrew the mounting nuts and withdraw the master cylinder from the front of the vacuum servo. Recover the seal. Wrap the master cylinder in cloth rags and remove it from the engine compartment. Take care not to spill fluid on the vehicle paintwork.

### Overhaul

10 Before dismantling the master cylinder check on the availability and cost of parts, as it may be more economical to renew the complete unit.
11 Clean all dirt and debris from the exterior of the master cylinder.
12 Prise out the reservoir rubber seals from the top of the master cylinder **(see illustration)**.

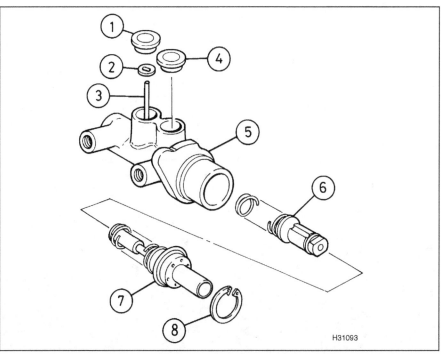

**11.12 Exploded view of the brake master cylinder**

1 Fluid reservoir rubber seal
2 Cover
3 Lockpin
4 Fluid reservoir rubber seal
5 Master cylinder body
6 Secondary piston assembly
7 Primary piston assembly
8 Circlip

**13** Remove the cover and the lockpin from the fluid aperture to the secondary piston.

**14** Using circlip pliers, extract the circlip from the mouth of the master cylinder while slightly depressing the piston against the spring tension.

**15** Remove the primary and secondary pistons, together with their springs, from the master cylinder bore, noting their order of removal. If the pistons are tight, tap the cylinder on the work bench or on a block of wood to release them.

**16** Thoroughly clean the master cylinder components with methylated spirit or clean brake fluid, and examine them for wear and damage. In particular, check the bore surfaces and rubber seals. The bore surface must not be pitted or scored, and the rubber seals must not be perished or worn. Clean the fluid entry ports of any rust or sediment.

**17** If the cylinder bore is in good condition but the rubber seals are worn excessively, obtain new seals or complete new pistons and seals.

**18** Lubricate the seals and bore surface with clean brake fluid. Insert the secondary piston assembly with the slot in line with the top of the cylinder, and then insert the lockpin and cover to hold the piston in place. Make sure that the seal lip is not damaged as it enters the cylinder.

**19** Insert the primary piston assembly, again making sure that the seal lip is not damaged as it enters the cylinder.

**20** Depress the primary piston, then fit the circlip in the groove in the cylinder mouth. Release the piston.

**21** Dip the rubber seals in clean fluid and locate them in the apertures on the top of the master cylinder.

### Refitting

**22** Ensure the mating surfaces are clean and dry then fit the new seal to the rear of the master cylinder.

**23** Fit the master cylinder to the studs on the vacuum servo unit, ensuring that the servo unit pushrod enters the master cylinder piston centrally. Fit the retaining nuts and tighten them securely.

**24** Remove the tape or plugs, and reconnect the brake lines to the master cylinder. Tighten

the union nuts initially with the fingers to prevent cross-threading, then fully tighten them with a spanner.

**25** Locate the fluid reservoir stubs in the rubber seals, and press firmly until it is fully entered.

**26** On manual transmission models, reconnect the clutch hydraulic hose to the brake fluid reservoir.

**27** Fill the fluid reservoir with fresh brake fluid up to the MAX level mark.

**28** Reconnect the wiring to the brake fluid warning switch in the reservoir filler cap.

**29** On left-hand drive models, reconnect the wiring to the anti-theft alarm switch. Refit the bracket, main fusebox and holder.

**30** Bleed the hydraulic system as described in Section 2. Thoroughly check the operation of the braking system before using the vehicle on the road.

---

## 12 Vacuum servo unit non-return valve – removal, testing and refitting

### Removal

**1** The non-return valve is located in the hose leading from the vacuum servo unit to the inlet manifold. It cannot be obtained separately from the hose.

**2** Carefully ease the hose adapter from the rubber grommet on the front of the servo unit.

**3** Unscrew the union nut and disconnect the hose from the inlet manifold.

**4** Release the hose from the support and remove from the engine compartment.

### Testing

**5** Examine the check valve and hose for signs of damage, and renew if necessary. The valve may be tested by blowing through the hose in both directions. Air should flow through the valve in one direction only – when blown through from the servo unit end. Renew the valve and hose complete if necessary.

**6** Examine the sealing grommet in the vacuum servo unit for signs of damage or deterioration, and renew as necessary.

### Refitting

**7** Refitting is a reversal of removal, but

tighten the union nut securely. On completion, start the engine and check the function of the brakes; also check that there are no air leaks.

---

## 13 Vacuum servo unit – testing, removal and refitting

### Testing

**1** To test the operation of the servo unit, with the engine off, depress the footbrake several times to dissipate the vacuum. Now start the engine, keeping the pedal firmly depressed. As the engine starts, there should be a noticeable 'give' in the brake pedal as the vacuum builds-up. Allow the engine to run for at least two minutes, then switch it off. The brake pedal should now feel normal, but further applications should result in the pedal feeling firmer, the pedal stroke decreasing with each application.

**2** If the servo does not operate as described, first inspect the servo unit check valve as described in Section 12.

**3** If the servo unit still fails to operate satisfactorily, the fault lies within the unit itself. Repairs to the unit are not possible; if faulty, the servo unit must be renewed.

### Right-hand drive models

#### Removal

**4** Remove the master cylinder as described in Section 11.

**5** Remove both windscreen wiper arms as described in Chapter 12. Remove the plastic cover from the engine compartment rear bulkhead area for access to the wiper linkage.

**6** Ease the vacuum hose adapter from the rubber grommet in the front of the vacuum servo unit.

**7** To provide more working room, remove the crankcase breather valve and hoses.

**8** Working inside the vehicle, remove the facia lower trim panel from beneath the steering column.

**9** Unhook the brake pedal return spring, then extract the spring clip and pull out the pivot pin securing the pushrod clevis to the brake pedal **(see illustrations)**.

**13.9a Unhook the brake pedal return spring . . .**

**13.9b . . . extract the spring clip . . .**

**13.9c . . . and remove the pushrod pivot pin**

**10** On the bulkhead next to the wiper linkage, unscrew the servo bracket mounting bolt and nuts. Withdraw the servo unit and upper mounting bracket from the bulkhead, and remove from the engine compartment.

**11** Undo the nuts and remove the bracket from the rear of the servo unit.

### Refitting

**12** Fit the bracket to the rear of the servo unit, and tighten the nuts.

**13** Locate the servo unit and mounting bracket on the bulkhead making sure that the upper bracket locates correctly on the lower bracket. Refit the mounting bolt and nuts, and tighten securely.

**14** Inside the vehicle, connect the pushrod clevis on the pedal, then insert the pivot pin and secure with the spring clip. Reconnect the brake pedal return spring **(see illustration)**.

**15** Refit the facia lower trim panel beneath the steering column.

**16** Refit the crankcase breather valve and hoses.

**17** Press the vacuum hose adapter in the rubber grommet in the front of the vacuum servo unit.

**18** Refit the plastic cover to the rear bulkhead area, then refit the windscreen wiper arms with reference to Chapter 12.

**19** Refit the master cylinder with reference to Section 11, and bleed the brake hydraulic system as described in Section 2.

### *Left-hand drive models*

#### Removal

**20** Remove the master cylinder as described in Section 11.

**21** Clean the area around the master cylinder-to-ABS unit rear brake line, note its position, then unscrew the union nut and remove the line from the ABS unit. Tape over or plug the aperture and line ends to prevent entry of dust and dirt.

**22** Ease the vacuum hose adapter from the rubber grommet in the front of the vacuum servo unit.

**23** Unscrew the mounting nuts securing the servo unit to the bracket, then remove the clip from the pushrod and withdraw the servo unit from the vehicle.

#### Refitting

**24** Locate the servo unit on the bracket and engage the brake pedal pushrod with the servo pushrod. Refit and tighten the mounting nuts.

**25** Refit the clip to the pushrod, then depress the brake pedal to lock the clip.

**26** Press the vacuum hose adapter into the rubber grommet on the front of the servo unit.

**27** Refit the rear brake line to the ABS unit in its previously-noted position, then tighten the union nut.

**28** Refit the brake master cylinder with reference to Section 11, and bleed the brake hydraulic system as described in Section 2.

**13.14  Fitted position of the brake pedal return spring**

### 14  Vacuum pump (electric) – removal and refitting

#### *Removal*

**1** Apply the handbrake, then jack up the front of the vehicle and support it on axle stands (see *Jacking and vehicle support*). Remove the left-hand front wheel.

**2** Remove the wheel arch liner, and where applicable, the engine undershield.

**3** Disconnect the vacuum hose from the pump.

**4** Disconnect the wiring.

**5** Unscrew the mounting nuts and bolts and withdraw the vacuum pump.

#### *Refitting*

**6** Refitting is a reversal of removal.

### 15  Vacuum pump (mechanical) – removal and refitting

#### *Removal*

**1** Unclip and remove the engine top cover.

**2** Disconnect the vacuum hose from the pressure sensor located on the side of the turbocharger.

**3** Undo the screw, and detach the bypass pipe from the turbocharger inlet pipe.

**4** Disconnect the bypass valve from the charge air pipe.

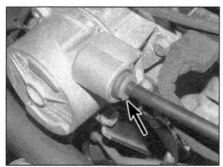

**15.7  Depress the red locking ring to release the vacuum hose**

**5** Disconnect the wiring from the temperature sensor on the charge air pipe.

**6** Loosen the clips securing the charge air pipe to the throttle body and turbocharger, then unscrew the mounting bolt from the bracket on the cylinder head, and withdraw the pipe from the engine compartment. Temporarily tape over or cover the turbocharger and throttle body apertures.

**7** Disconnect the vacuum hose from the vacuum pump on the left-hand end of the cylinder head. To do this, press in the red locking ring while pulling the hose out **(see illustration)**.

**8** Disconnect the wiring from the ignition discharge module on the cylinder head.

**9** Place some cloth rags below the vacuum pump lubrication banjo, then unscrew and remove the banjo bolt. Recover the outer seal.

**10** Unscrew the pump mounting bolts, including the bracket bolt, then withdraw it from the cylinder head **(see illustration)**. Recover the inner lubrication seal and the main pump seal. Discard all seals as new ones must be used for refitting.

#### *Refitting*

**11** Clean the contact surfaces of the pump and cylinder head. Position the new inner and main seals on the pump and retain with a little grease.

**12** Position the pump drive dog so that it will engage with the slot in the end of the camshaft when refitted. Locate the pump on the cylinder head, and refit the mounting bolts, hand-tight at this stage. Wipe away any spilt oil from the cylinder head.

**13** Refit the banjo bolt together with a new O-ring seal, and tighten it to the specified torque.

**14** Insert the mounting bolts, and first tighten the two in the cylinder head to the specified torque, then tighten the remaining bolt in the bracket to the specified torque.

**15** Reconnect the wiring to the ignition discharge module, then reconnect the vacuum hose to the pump.

**16** Refit the charge air pipe to the throttle body and turbocharger, and tighten the mounting bolt. If necessary, apply a little petroleum jelly to the throttle body O-ring to facilitate refitting it. Tighten the pipe securing clips.

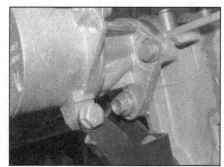

**15.10  Mechanical brake vacuum pump mounting bolts**

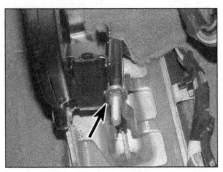

**16.7  Handbrake cable adjustment nut on the handbrake lever**

17  Reconnect the wiring to the temperature sensor on the charge air pipe.
18  Reconnect the bypass valve to the charge air pipe, then reconnect the bypass pipe to the turbocharger inlet pipe and tighten the screw.
19  Reconnect the vacuum hose to the pressure sensor.
20  Refit the engine top cover.

## 16  Handbrake – adjustment

1  First chock the front wheels, then jack up the rear of the vehicle and support on axle stands (see *Jacking and vehicle support*). Remove both rear wheels. Fully release the handbrake lever.
2  Check that the cables are not pulling the expander levers on the rear backplates. If they are, loosen the cable adjusting nut as necessary with reference to paragraph 6.
3  Working on each side at a time, adjust the shoe positions as follows. Turn the rear disc/drum until the access hole is positioned over the upper adjuster serrations. Using a screwdriver through the hole, turn the adjuster serrations until the disc/drum is locked. Now back off the serrations until the disc/drum is just free to turn. Repeat the adjustment on the remaining disc/drum.
4  Refit the rear wheels and tighten the bolts.
5  Set the handbrake lever on the 1st notch.
6  Open the lid of the centre console, and remove the mat for access to the handbrake cable adjusting nut.
7  Tighten the cable adjusting nut until slight resistance is felt when turning the rear wheels **(see illustration)**. Fully release the handbrake lever and check that the rear wheels turn freely, then set the lever on the 2nd or 3rd notch and check that the rear wheels are locked firmly. If necessary, make a final adjustment of the adjusting nut.
8  If only one rear wheel locks, one of the brake cables may be seized, and this must be attended to before finally adjusting the handbrake.
9  On completion, lower the vehicle to the ground.

## 17  Handbrake cables – removal and refitting

### Removal

1  One primary and a double secondary cable are fitted. An equalizer is permanently attached to the front of the secondary inner cables, and the primary cable is attached to the centre of the equalizer. The secondary cables are supplied as one assembly. First, chock the front wheels then jack up the rear of the vehicle and support on axle stands (see *Jacking and vehicle support*).
2  Refer to Chapter 4A and separate the exhaust front and rear sections, then disconnect the rubber mounting from the left-hand side of the exhaust and lower the exhaust.
3  Unscrew the rear nuts from the heatshield on the underbody, then bend down the heatshield for access to the handbrake equalizer.
4  At the rear brake backplates, disconnect the handbrake cable return springs from the expander levers.
5  Unhook each cable end fitting from the expander levers.
6  Turn the primary cable end fitting through 90° and disconnect it from the equalizer.
7  Release the front ends of each cable from the supports.
8  Support the fuel tank with a trolley jack and large block of wood, then unscrew the fuel tank front support strap bolts. Pull down the straps to release the handbrake secondary cables.
9  Release the cables from the supports and withdraw from under the vehicle.

### Refitting

10  Refitting is a reversal of removal, but adjust the handbrake as described in Section 16.

## 18  Handbrake lever – removal and refitting

### Removal

1  Chock the front wheels, then jack up the rear of the vehicle and support on axle stands (see *Jacking and vehicle support*). Remove both rear wheels.
2  Working at each rear wheel brake, disconnect the left- and right-hand return springs from the holes in the backplates then unhook the cable fittings from the handbrake shoe operating levers.
3  Remove the centre console as described in Chapter 11, and lift up the gaiter.
4  Disconnect the wiring from the handbrake warning light switch, and release the wiring from the cable ties.

5  Unscrew the nuts securing the handbrake assembly to the floor.
6  Raise the handbrake assembly directly from the floor, and carefully ease the equalizer up through the floor aperture. Tie a length of string to the equalizer so that it can be recovered for refitting.
7  Turn the primary cable end fitting through 90° and disconnect it from the equalizer. Withdraw the handbrake lever assembly from inside the vehicle.

### Refitting

8  Refitting is a reversal of removal, but finally adjust the handbrake as described in Section 16. Tighten the handbrake lever mounting bolts securely.

## 19  Handbrake ON warning light switch – removal, testing and refitting

### Removal

1  The handbrake ON warning light switch is mounted on the front of the handbrake lever mounting bracket **(see illustration)**. Refer to Chapter 11 and remove the centre console.
2  Disconnect the wiring from the switch.
3  Undo the mounting screw and remove the switch.

### Testing

4  Connect a multimeter or battery test probe to the wiring contact and switch body.
5  With the switch plunger at rest, there should be continuity and the multimeter should read no resistance, or the test light should light. With the plunger depressed, there should be infinity resistance or the test light should be extinguished.
6  Failure to operate correctly may indicate corroded contacts or ultimately a faulty switch. Check that there is a 12 volt supply to the wiring with the ignition switched on. Renew the switch if necessary.

### Refitting

7  Refitting is a reversal of removal.

**19.1  Handbrake ON warning light switch**

## 20 Brake pedal –
removal and refitting

### Removal

**1** Move the driver's seat fully rearwards.

#### Right-hand drive models

**2** Remove the brake vacuum servo unit as described in Section 13.

**3** With the vacuum servo removed, unscrew the four nuts securing the brake pedal bracket to the bulkhead.

**4** Working inside the vehicle, remove the facia panel complete as described in Chapter 11.

**5** Refer to Chapter 10 and detach the steering column from the steering gear pinion, taking care not to separate the splined/telescopic section. The front wheels must be pointing straight-ahead and the steering wheel should be taped to the facia panel as a precaution.

**6** Disconnect the wiring from the pedal switches.

**7** Unbolt the steering column assembly from the bulkhead and pedal bracket, and move it rearwards as far as possible without straining the wiring.

**8** Lift the pedal bracket assembly from the bulkhead and remove from the vehicle. Recover the foam packing.

#### Left-hand drive models

**9** Remove the battery from the front left-hand corner of the engine compartment (Chapter 5A).

**10** Remove the ABS/TCS/ESP hydraulic unit as described in Section 23.

**11** Unbolt and remove the main fusebox from the rear left-hand corner of the engine compartment after disconnecting the wiring.

**12** Disconnect the engine wiring harness and remove the retaining box from the bulkhead partition behind the engine.

**13** Unscrew the four nuts securing the brake pedal bracket to the bulkhead.

**14** Refer to Chapter 11 and remove the lower facia trim from the driver's side.

**15** Remove the stepping motor located beneath the brake pedal.

**16** Refer to Chapter 10 and detach the steering column from the steering gear pinion, taking care not to separate the splined/telescopic section. The front wheels must be pointing straight-ahead and the steering wheel should be taped to the facia panel as a precaution.

**17** Unscrew the two bolts securing the pedal assembly to the steering column assembly.

**18** Disconnect the wiring from the pedal switches.

**19** Unhook the return spring from the pedal, then remove the circlip and pull out the clevis pin connecting the pedal to the pushrod.

**20** Lift the pedal bracket assembly from the bulkhead and remove from the vehicle. Recover the foam packing.

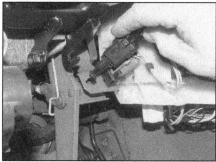

**21.3  Remove the stop-light switch from the bracket . . .**

### Refitting

**21** Refitting is a reversal of removal, but tighten all nuts and bolts to their correct specified torque where given.

## 21 Stop-light switch –
removal, testing and refitting

### Removal

**1** The stop-light switch is mounted on top of the pedal bracket. An internal spring tensions the switch plunger so that the contacts are normally closed, however, when the brake pedal is released, the pedal return spring tension is greater than the switch spring, so the contacts are separated when the pedal is in its released position. When the brake pedal is depressed, the switch supplies a current of 12 volts to the central electronic control unit, which then supplies the stop-lights with power. The control unit checks the three stop-light bulbs and if necessary displays a warning on the instrument panel. Where a trailer is being towed, current to the trailer stop-lights is supplied direct from the stop-light switch.

**2** To remove the switch, first remove the lower trim panel from the facia with reference to Chapter 11.

**3** Twist the switch anti-clockwise 90° and withdraw it from the mounting bracket **(see illustration)**.

**4** Disconnect the wiring from the switch **(see illustration)**.

### Testing

**5** The switch is a single-pole device, and has normally-closed contacts. The operation of the switch can be tested using either a multimeter (switched to the ohmmeter function), or a continuity tester made up of a flashlight bulb, dry cell battery and two pieces of wire. Connect the meter/tester to the switch connector terminals with the switch in its rest position, and check that the meter reads zero resistance or the tester lights up.

**6** Press the switch plunger down, and check that the meter reads infinity resistance (open-circuit) or the tester is extinguished.

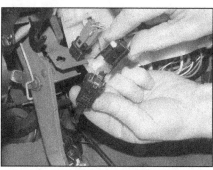

**21.4  . . . and disconnect the wiring**

**7** If the switch does not behave as described, or is intermittent in its operation, then a new switch must be fitted; the unit is not serviceable.

### Refitting

**8** Refit the brake stop-light switch by reversing the removal procedure.

## 22 Anti-lock Braking System (ABS) – general information and fault finding

### General information

**1** The Anti-lock Braking System (ABS) is managed by an Electronic Control Unit (ECU), which has the capacity to monitor the status and condition of all the components in the system, including itself. If the ECU detects a fault it responds by shutting down the ABS and illuminating the dashboard-mounted ABS warning light. Under these circumstances, conventional non-ABS braking is maintained. Note also that the warning light will be illuminated if the power supply to the ABS ECU is disconnected (eg, if the supply fuse blows). On models manufactured from late 1998, when the ABS warning light is illuminated the standard brake warning light and central warning light are also illuminated.

**2** If the ABS warning lights indicate a fault, it is very difficult to diagnose problems without the equipment and expertise to electronically 'interrogate' the ECU for fault codes. Therefore, this Section is limited firstly to a list of the basic checks that should be carried out, to establish the integrity of the system.

**3** If the cause of the fault cannot be immediately identified using the check list described, the only course of action open is to take the vehicle to a Saab dealer for examination. Dedicated test equipment is needed to interrogate the ABS ECU, to determine the nature of the fault.

### Basic fault finding checks

#### Brake fluid level

**4** Check the brake fluid level (see *Weekly checks*). If the level is low, check the complete braking system for signs of leaks. Refer to Chapter 1 and carry out a check of the brake hoses and pipes throughout the vehicle. If no leaks are apparent, remove each roadwheel in turn, and check for leaks at the brake caliper pistons.

### Fuses and relays

**5** The fuse for the ABS is located beneath a cover on the end of the instrument panel. Remove the cover and pull out the fuse. Visually check the fuse filament; if it is difficult to see whether or not it has blown, use a multimeter to check the continuity of the fuse. If any of the fuses are blown, determine the cause before fitting a new one – if necessary, have the vehicle inspected by a Saab dealer.

**6** The ABS system relay is located beneath a cover on the left-hand side of the engine compartment. In general, relays are difficult to test conclusively without any electrical specification. However, the metal contacts inside a relay can usually be felt (and often heard) to open or close as it operates – if the relay in question does not behave in this way when the ignition switch is turned on, it may be faulty. It should be noted that this is not a conclusive test, and substitution with a known good relay *of the same type* is the only way to verify the component operation. If any of the relays is suspected of being faulty, it can be renewed by pulling it out of its socket – noting its orientation – and pushing in a new unit.

### Electrical connections and earthing points

**7** The engine bay is a hostile environment for electrical connections, and even the best seals can sometimes be penetrated. Water, chemicals and air will induce corrosion on the connector's contacts and prevent good continuity, sometimes intermittently. Disconnect the battery negative cable, then check the security and condition of all connectors at the ABS hydraulic unit, situated on the left-hand side of the engine bay.

**8** Unplug each connector, and examine the contacts inside. Clean any contacts that are found to be dirty or corroded. Avoid scraping the contacts clean with a blade, as this will accelerate corrosion later. Use a piece of lint-free cloth in conjunction with a proprietary cleaning solvent to produce a clean, shiny contact surface.

**9** In addition, check the security and condition of the system electrical earthing point on the side of the hydraulic unit.

### 23 Anti-lock Braking System (ABS) components – removal and refitting

**Note:** *If the ABS system is faulty, have it checked by a Saab dealer before removing any component.*

### Front wheel sensor

#### Removal

**1** Apply the handbrake, then jack up the front of the vehicle and support it on axle stands (see *Jacking and vehicle support*). Remove the relevant roadwheel.

**2** Disconnect the wiring plug in the engine compartment. For the front left-hand sensor, it is located next to the battery, and it is recommended that the battery and battery tray are removed (see Chapter 5A); on 2002-on models, also unclip the coolant expansion tank and position it to one side. For the right-hand sensor it is located behind the power steering fluid reservoir, and it will be necessary to release the locking tab on the wiring connector; on 2002-on models, remove the power steering fluid reservoir and position it to one side.

**3** Clean the area around the wheel sensor on the front hub carrier, then unscrew the mounting bolt and remove the sensor.

**4** Prise the rubber grommet from the inner wing panel, and pull out the wiring.

**5** Release the wiring from the retaining clips on the inner wing panel and brake hose.

#### Refitting

**6** Refitting is a reversal of removal, but tighten the mounting bolt securely.

### Rear wheel sensor

#### Removal

**7** The rear wheel sensors are integral with the rear wheel hubs, so this section essentially describes the removal of the hub. First, chock the front wheels then jack up the rear of the vehicle and support on axle stands (see *Jacking and vehicle support*). Remove the relevant roadwheel.

**8** Remove the rear brake disc as described in Section 9.

**9** On 1999-on models (VIN X3025752-on), remove the protective cover from the bottom of the rear suspension trailing arm, and unbolt the handbrake cable support bracket.

**10** Disconnect the wiring from the wheel sensor on the rear of the hub.

**11** Unscrew the mounting nuts and withdraw the hub assembly from the rear axle. Leave the backplate, handbrake shoes and the spacer(s) hanging on the cable. **Note:** *Discard the hub nuts as new ones must be used on refitting.* Recover the shims where fitted.

#### Refitting

**12** Clean the mounting faces of the rear axle, backplate, spacer(s) and hub then mount the components in the correct order. Fit and progressively tighten the new nuts to the torque wrench setting and angle given in the Specifications.

**13** Reconnect the wiring to the wheel sensor.

**14** On 1999-on models (VIN X3025752-on), refit the handbrake cable support bracket and the protective cover to the bottom of the rear suspension trailing arm.

**15** Refit the rear brake disc (see Section 9) and adjust the handbrake shoes (see Section 16).

**16** Refit the roadwheel, then lower the vehicle to the ground.

**17** Depress the footbrake pedal firmly to set the rear brake pads in their normal position.

### ABS/ESP/TCS hydraulic unit

**Note:** *The ABS electronic control unit (ECU) is supplied as an integral part of the hydraulic unit and cannot be removed separately. After fitting a new unit, the ECU must be calibrated by a Saab dealer using the Saab Tech2 hand-held diagnostic instrument. It is recommended that the ESP system is switched off until the calibration has been carried out.*

#### Removal

**18** Disconnect the battery negative lead (refer to *Disconnecting the battery* in the Reference Chapter). On 2002-on models, remove the battery and battery tray as described in Chapter 5A.

**19** Working in the left-hand rear corner of the engine compartment, release the fusebox holder.

**20** On pre-2002 models, disconnect the wiring from the anti-theft alarm.

**21** Cut the plastic cable ties holding the battery positive cable to the main fusebox, then unscrew the nuts and position the fusebox to one side without disconnecting the wiring. If necessary, suspend the fusebox using a piece of string.

**22** Minimise fluid loss by first removing the master cylinder reservoir cap, then tightening it down onto a piece of polythene to obtain an airtight seal. As the cap includes a fluid level warning switch, it may be preferable to fit a plain used cap if available. Also, place cloth rags beneath the unit to catch spilt fluid. On 2002-on LHD models with manual transmission, syphon the brake fluid from the master cylinder reservoir, and disconnect the clutch hydraulic fluid hose from it.

**23** Disconnect the wiring plug from the electronic control unit and position the plug to one side. On 2002-on models, disconnect the wiring from the fuel pressure sensor on the rear of the unit.

**24** Identify each hydraulic brake pipe for its location on the hydraulic unit, then unscrew the union nuts and disconnect the pipes. Tape over or plug the apertures and pipe ends to prevent entry of dust and dirt.

**25** Unscrew the mounting nuts and remove the ABS hydraulic unit from the engine compartment. On 2002-on models, the outer mounting nut is difficult to reach, and it may be necessary to prise the bracket away from the inner wheel housing with a screwdriver. Take care not to spill hydraulic fluid on the vehicle paintwork.

#### Refitting

**26** Refitting is a reversal of removal, but tighten the unit mounting nuts and the hydraulic brake pipe union nuts to the specified torque, and finally bleed the hydraulic system as described in Section 2.

## 24 Electronic Stability Program (ESP) components –
removal and refitting

### *Yaw Rate (gyro) Sensor*

#### Removal

**1** Remove the centre console as described in Chapter 11.

**2** On manual transmission models, remove the gear lever housing with reference to Chapter 7A; on automatic transmission models, remove the selector lever housing with reference to Chapter 7B.

**3** Note the fitted position of the sensor, and the forward direction of the arrow on the upper face, then undo the mounting screws. Prise away the air duct for access to the left-hand screw.

**4** Release the locking tab, then disconnect the wiring and remove the sensor.

#### Refitting

**5** Refitting is a reversal of removal, but make sure that the arrow points to the front of the vehicle.

### *Steering wheel angle sensor*

**Note:** *After fitting a new steering wheel angle sensor, the sensor must be calibrated by a Saab dealer using the Saab Tech2 hand-held diagnostic instrument. It is recommended that the ESP system is switched off until the calibration has been carried out.*

⚠️ **Warning: Never fit a damaged steering wheel angle sensor, as the vehicle may react dangerously in the event of an emergency. Do not use excessive force when removing or refitting the sensor.**

#### Removal

**6** Remove the steering column assembly as described in Chapter 10.

**7** The inner steering column consists of two splined sections, which are collapsible and will only fit together in one position. First, mark both inner column sections and the outer column housing in relation to each other.

**8** Carefully pull the lower inner column together with the bearing bracket and angle sensor from the outer column.

**9** Undo the locking screw securing the

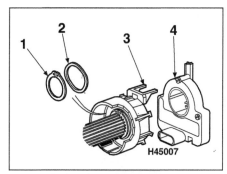

**24.10 Steering wheel angle sensor components**

1  Circlip
2  Spring washer
3  Bearing carrier
4  Steering wheel angle sensor

bearing bracket to the bearing carrier, then use a screwdriver to depress the plastic retaining catch on the opposite side, and withdraw the bracket over the lower inner column.

**10** Using circlip pliers, expand the circlip and remove it from the lower inner column/intermediate shaft, followed by the spring washer **(see illustration)**.

**11** Remove the bearing carrier and the steering wheel angle sensor from the lower inner column/intermediate shaft.

#### Refitting

**12** Locate the sensor on the lower inner column/intermediate shaft, and engage its groove with the raised tab **(see illustration)**. If a new sensor is being fitted, complete the label and attach it to the sensor.

**13** Locate the bearing carrier onto the shaft, engaging the arms with the sensor leg.

**14** Refit the spring washer and the circlip, making sure that the circlip fully enters the groove.

**15** Locate the bracket onto the bearing carrier, making sure that the plastic retaining catch engages correctly, then insert and tighten the locking screw.

**16** Align the marks made on both inner column sections with the marks made on the outer column housing, then engage the upper and lower inner columns with each other. Do not force the columns if they are not correctly aligned.

**17** Refit the steering column assembly with reference to Chapter 10.

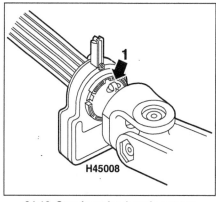

**24.12 Steering wheel angle sensor location raised tab (1) on the intermediate shaft**

**18** Have the steering wheel angle sensor calibrated by a Saab dealer at the earliest opportunity.

### *Brake pressure sensor*

#### Removal

**19** The brake pressure sensor is located on the rear of the hydraulic unit, at the left-hand rear corner of the engine compartment. Have ready a means of plugging the sensor hole to prevent loss of brake fluid.

**20** Disconnect the wiring from the sensor.

**21** Using a 24.0 mm spanner, unscrew the sensor from the hydraulic unit. Plug the opening immediately, taking care not to allow dust and dirt to enter the circuit.

#### Refitting

**22** Refitting is a reversal of removal, but tighten the sensor securely. Finally, bleed the hydraulic circuit with reference to Section 2; if minimal fluid was lost, it is only necessary to bleed the front left- and rear right-hand brakes.

### *ESP/TCS switch*

#### Removal

**23** The ESP/TCS on/off switch is located on the instrument panel. To remove it, carefully ease it out using two screwdrivers.

**24** Disconnect the wiring.

#### Refitting

**25** Refitting is a reversal of removal.

# Chapter 10
# Suspension and steering

## Contents

## Degrees of difficulty

| Easy, suitable for novice with little experience |  | Fairly easy, suitable for beginner with some experience | | Fairly difficult, suitable for competent DIY mechanic | 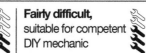 | Difficult, suitable for experienced DIY mechanic | | Very difficult, suitable for expert DIY or professional | 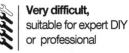 |
|---|---|---|---|---|---|---|---|---|---|

## Specifications

### General

| | |
|---|---|
| Front suspension type . . . . . . . . . . . . . . . . . . . . . . . . . . . . . . . . . . . . . . | Independent with MacPherson struts, hub carriers and anti-roll bar. Struts incorporate gas-filled shock absorbers and coil springs. Subframe with lower arms and balljoints |
| Rear suspension type . . . . . . . . . . . . . . . . . . . . . . . . . . . . . . . . . . . . . . | Independent with struts and anti-roll bar. The struts incorporate gas-filled shock absorbers and coil springs. Subframe with upper and lower transverse links to trailing arms |
| Steering type . . . . . . . . . . . . . . . . . . . . . . . . . . . . . . . . . . . . . . . . . . . . . | Rack-and-pinion, hydraulic power assistance on all models |

### Wheel alignment

Front:
  Toe-in:

| | |
|---|---|
|     15 in wheels . . . . . . . . . . . . . . . . . . . . . . . . . . . . . . . . . . . . . . . . . . . . | 2.0 ± 0.6 mm |
|     16 in wheels . . . . . . . . . . . . . . . . . . . . . . . . . . . . . . . . . . . . . . . . . . . . | 2.2 ± 0.6 mm |
|     17 in wheels . . . . . . . . . . . . . . . . . . . . . . . . . . . . . . . . . . . . . . . . . . . . | 2.2 ± 0.6 mm |

  Camber:

| | |
|---|---|
|     15 in wheels . . . . . . . . . . . . . . . . . . . . . . . . . . . . . . . . . . . . . . . . . . . . | -0.8° (at body height of 600 mm) |
|     16 in wheels . . . . . . . . . . . . . . . . . . . . . . . . . . . . . . . . . . . . . . . . . . . . | -0.9° (at body height of 610 mm) |
|     17 in wheels . . . . . . . . . . . . . . . . . . . . . . . . . . . . . . . . . . . . . . . . . . . . | -0.8° (at body height of 630 mm) |
|   Castor . . . . . . . . . . . . . . . . . . . . . . . . . . . . . . . . . . . . . . . . . . . . . . . . . . | 2.9° ± 0.5° |
|   Swivel pin inclination . . . . . . . . . . . . . . . . . . . . . . . . . . . . . . . . . . . . . . . | 12.6° ± 0.5° |

Rear:
  Toe-in:

| | |
|---|---|
|     15 in wheels . . . . . . . . . . . . . . . . . . . . . . . . . . . . . . . . . . . . . . . . . . . . | 3.0 ± 1.4 mm |
|     16 in wheels . . . . . . . . . . . . . . . . . . . . . . . . . . . . . . . . . . . . . . . . . . . . | 3.2 ± 1.4 mm |
|     17 in wheels . . . . . . . . . . . . . . . . . . . . . . . . . . . . . . . . . . . . . . . . . . . . | 3.4 ± 1.4 mm |

  Camber:

| | |
|---|---|
|     15 in wheels . . . . . . . . . . . . . . . . . . . . . . . . . . . . . . . . . . . . . . . . . . . . | -0.9° (at body height of 590 mm) |
|     16 in wheels . . . . . . . . . . . . . . . . . . . . . . . . . . . . . . . . . . . . . . . . . . . . | -0.8° (at body height of 605 mm) |
|     17 in wheels . . . . . . . . . . . . . . . . . . . . . . . . . . . . . . . . . . . . . . . . . . . . | -0.8° (at body height of 620 mm) |

Steering angle toe-out on turns:

| | |
|---|---|
|   Outer wheel . . . . . . . . . . . . . . . . . . . . . . . . . . . . . . . . . . . . . . . . . . . . . | 20.0° |
|   Inner wheel . . . . . . . . . . . . . . . . . . . . . . . . . . . . . . . . . . . . . . . . . . . . . . | 21.25° ± 0.5° |

## Roadwheels
Size:
    Standard . . . . . . . . . . . . . . . . . . . . . . . . . . . . . . . . . . . . . . . .   6 x 15, 6.5 x 16 or 7 x 17
    Compact spare . . . . . . . . . . . . . . . . . . . . . . . . . . . . . . . . . . . .   4 x 16

## Tyres
Size:
    Winter . . . . . . . . . . . . . . . . . . . . . . . . . . . . . . . . . . . . . . . . . . .   195/65R15, 205/55R16 or 215/55R16
    Summer . . . . . . . . . . . . . . . . . . . . . . . . . . . . . . . . . . . . . . . . .   205/65R15, 215/55R16 or 225/45R17
Tyre pressures . . . . . . . . . . . . . . . . . . . . . . . . . . . . . . . . . . . . . . .   See end of *Weekly checks* on page 0•17

## Power steering
Steering wheel turns, lock to lock . . . . . . . . . . . . . . . . . . . . . . . . .   2.9 turns

## Torque wrench settings

| | Nm | lbf ft |
|---|---|---|
| **Front suspension** | | |
| Anti-roll bar link . . . . . . . . . . . . . . . . . . . . . . . . . . . . . . . . . . . . . . . . . . . . | 90 | 66 |
| Anti-roll bar to subframe . . . . . . . . . . . . . . . . . . . . . . . . . . . . . . . . . . . . . | 25 | 18 |
| Engine rear mounting to engine bracket . . . . . . . . . . . . . . . . . . . . . . . | 50 | 37 |
| Engine rear mounting to subframe . . . . . . . . . . . . . . . . . . . . . . . . . . . . | 25 | 18 |
| Hub bearing and backplate to carrier (2002-on): | | |
|     Stage 1 . . . . . . . . . . . . . . . . . . . . . . . . . . . . . . . . . . . . . . . . . . . . . | 90 | 66 |
|     Stage 2 . . . . . . . . . . . . . . . . . . . . . . . . . . . . . . . . . . . . . . . . . . . . . | Angle-tighten 45° | |
| Hub centre (driveshaft) nut (new): | | |
|     Nut without groove (1998/2001 models) . . . . . . . . . . . . . . . . . . . . | 290 | 214 |
|     Nut with groove: | | |
|         1998/2001 models: | | |
|             Stage 1 . . . . . . . . . . . . . . . . . . . . . . . . . . . . . . . . . . . . . . | 170 | 125 |
|             Stage 2 . . . . . . . . . . . . . . . . . . . . . . . . . . . . . . . . . . . . . . | Angle-tighten by 45° | |
|         2002-on models . . . . . . . . . . . . . . . . . . . . . . . . . . . . . . . . . . | 230 | 170 |
| Shock absorber piston rod upper retaining nut . . . . . . . . . . . . . . . . . . | 75 | 55 |
| Strut to hub carrier: | | |
|     1998 to 2001: | | |
|         Stage 1 . . . . . . . . . . . . . . . . . . . . . . . . . . . . . . . . . . . . . . . . . | 110 | 81 |
|         Stage 2 . . . . . . . . . . . . . . . . . . . . . . . . . . . . . . . . . . . . . . . . . | Angle-tighten 45° | |
|     2002-on: | | |
|         Stage 1 . . . . . . . . . . . . . . . . . . . . . . . . . . . . . . . . . . . . . . . . . | 100 | 74 |
|         Stage 2 . . . . . . . . . . . . . . . . . . . . . . . . . . . . . . . . . . . . . . . . . | Angle-tighten 90° | |
| Strut top mounting bolts: | | |
|     1998 to 2001 . . . . . . . . . . . . . . . . . . . . . . . . . . . . . . . . . . . . . . . . . | 18 | 13 |
|     2002-on . . . . . . . . . . . . . . . . . . . . . . . . . . . . . . . . . . . . . . . . . . . . . | 30 | 22 |
| Subframe mounting to underbody: | | |
|     Stage 1 . . . . . . . . . . . . . . . . . . . . . . . . . . . . . . . . . . . . . . . . . . . . . | 100 | 74 |
|     Stage 2 . . . . . . . . . . . . . . . . . . . . . . . . . . . . . . . . . . . . . . . . . . . . . | Angle-tighten 45° | |
| Subframe rear crossmember support bracket . . . . . . . . . . . . . . . . . . . | 65 | 48 |
| Suspension lower balljoint to hub carrier: | | |
|     1998 to 2001 . . . . . . . . . . . . . . . . . . . . . . . . . . . . . . . . . . . . . . . . . | 95 | 70 |
|     2002-on . . . . . . . . . . . . . . . . . . . . . . . . . . . . . . . . . . . . . . . . . . . . . | 49 | 36 |
| Suspension lower balljoint to lower arm: | | |
|     1998 to 2001 . . . . . . . . . . . . . . . . . . . . . . . . . . . . . . . . . . . . . . . . . | 20 | 15 |
|     2002-on: | | |
|         Stage 1 . . . . . . . . . . . . . . . . . . . . . . . . . . . . . . . . . . . . . . . . . | 20 | 15 |
|         Stage 2 . . . . . . . . . . . . . . . . . . . . . . . . . . . . . . . . . . . . . . . . . | Angle-tighten 90° | |
| Suspension lower arm mounting to subframe: | | |
|     1998 to 2001 . . . . . . . . . . . . . . . . . . . . . . . . . . . . . . . . . . . . . . . . . | 95 | 70 |
|     2002-on: | | |
|         Stage 1 . . . . . . . . . . . . . . . . . . . . . . . . . . . . . . . . . . . . . . . . . | 120 | 89 |
|         Stage 2 . . . . . . . . . . . . . . . . . . . . . . . . . . . . . . . . . . . . . . . . . | Angle-tighten 90° | |
| Suspension lower arm rear mounting to lower arm . . . . . . . . . . . . . . | 75 | 55 |
| **Rear suspension** | | |
| Anti-roll bar to crossmember . . . . . . . . . . . . . . . . . . . . . . . . . . . . . . | 50 | 37 |
| Hub assembly to trailing arm: | | |
|     Stage 1 . . . . . . . . . . . . . . . . . . . . . . . . . . . . . . . . . . . . . . . . . . . . . | 50 | 37 |
|     Stage 2 . . . . . . . . . . . . . . . . . . . . . . . . . . . . . . . . . . . . . . . . . . . . . | Angle-tighten 30° | |
| Shock absorber/strut lower mounting bolt . . . . . . . . . . . . . . . . . . . . | 190 | 140 |
| Shock absorber/strut piston rod top mounting . . . . . . . . . . . . . . . . | 20 | 15 |
| Shock absorber/strut to body . . . . . . . . . . . . . . . . . . . . . . . . . . . . . | 55 | 41 |

## Torque wrench settings (continued)

| | Nm | lbf ft |
|---|---|---|
| **Rear suspension (continued)** | | |
| Suspension subframe: | | |
| Stage 1 .......................................... | 90 | 66 |
| Stage 2 .......................................... | Angle-tighten 60° | |
| Suspension trailing arm bracket to underbody: | | |
| Stage 1 .......................................... | 90 | 66 |
| Stage 2 .......................................... | Angle-tighten 30° | |
| Suspension trailing arm to mounting bracket: | | |
| Stage 1 .......................................... | 90 | 66 |
| Stage 2 .......................................... | Angle-tighten 60° | |
| Suspension upper and lower transverse links to trailing arm: | | |
| Stage 1 .......................................... | 90 | 66 |
| Stage 2 .......................................... | Angle-tighten 60° | |
| **Steering** | | |
| Power steering pump ..................................... | 25 | 18 |
| Power steering pump delivery pipe support ...................... | 30 | 22 |
| Power steering pump delivery pipe union nut ................... | 30 | 22 |
| Steering column ........................................ | 25 | 18 |
| Steering column-to-pinion gear clamp bolt .................... | 30 | 22 |
| Steering gear mounting bolts ............................... | 95 | 70 |
| Steering gear supply and return pipe union bolts ................ | 30 | 22 |
| Steering wheel ......................................... | 38 | 28 |
| Track rod end locknut ..................................... | 70 | 52 |
| Track rod end to steering arm: | | |
| 1998 to 2001 ........................................ | 60 | 44 |
| 2002-on ............................................ | 35 | 26 |
| **Wheels** | | |
| Roadwheel bolts ........................................ | 110 | 81 |

## 1  General information

The front suspension is fully independent, with MacPherson struts and an anti-roll bar. The struts incorporate shock absorbers and gas-filled coil springs, and the hub carriers are bolted to the bottom of the struts. The hub carriers are located on the outer ends of the lower arms by renewable balljoints bolted onto the arms. The hub bearings can be renewed separately, however, on later models the hub and bearings are integral, and are bolted to the carriers separately. The lower arms and anti-roll bar are mounted on the front suspension subframe located beneath the engine compartment.

The rear suspension is fully independent, with trailing arms, struts, upper and lower transverse links and an anti-roll bar. The struts incorporate shock absorbers and coil springs, and the hubs are bolted to the trailing arms. The transverse links and anti-roll bar are mounted on the rear suspension subframe. The rear hubs have double-row bearings and are supplied as integral units which cannot be dismantled; they are attached to the trailing arms by studs and nuts. Each rear hub incorporates an internal ABS sensor to monitor the wheel speed.

Power-assisted steering is fitted to all

models. The steering rack is essentially a hydraulic ram, which is actuated mechanically by a pinion gear, and hydraulically by pressurised hydraulic fluid, supplied by the power steering pump. The steering column transmits effort applied at the steering wheel to the pinion, and a control valve supplies hydraulic fluid to the steering rack ram. When the steering wheel is turned, the valve directs fluid to the appropriate side of the ram, assisting the movement of the rack. The power steering pump is mounted externally on the engine, and is driven by the auxiliary drivebelt.

The design and mounting position of the steering column are such that, in the event of a head-on collision, it will absorb impact by crumpling longitudinally, and will also be deflected away from the driver.

2.2a  Unscrew the nut . . .

## 2  Front suspension strut – removal, overhaul and refitting

### Removal

1 Apply the handbrake, then jack up the front of the vehicle and support it on axle stands (see *Jacking and vehicle support*). Remove the roadwheel.
2 Unscrew the nut and remove the anti-roll bar link from the suspension strut. Hold the link spindle with one spanner while the nut is being loosened **(see illustrations)**.
3 Note that the bolts securing the strut to the hub carrier are fitted with their heads facing forwards. Unscrew and remove the bolts, and move the holder for the ABS wheel sensor

2.2b  . . . and remove the anti-roll bar link from the suspension strut

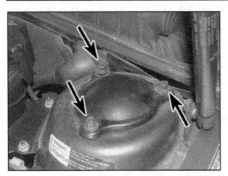

2.5 Front suspension strut upper mounting bolts

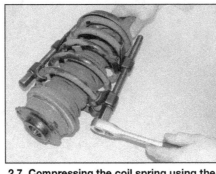

2.7 Compressing the coil spring using the spring compressor tools

2.8a Hold the piston rod with an Allen key while loosening the top bearing retaining nut . . .

2.8b . . . then unscrew and remove the nut

and brake hydraulic hose to one side. The bolts have small location splines on their shanks, and must not be turned within the hub carrier; hold the bolt head stationary and unscrew the nut from it.

4 Hold the strut inwards while the hub carrier is tilted outwards from it. Do not strain the brake flexible hydraulic hose.
5 Support the strut, then unscrew the upper mounting bolts on the suspension tower in the

rear corner of the engine compartment. Note that the mounting bolts also secure an upper cover. Withdraw the strut from under the front wing (see illustration).

### Overhaul

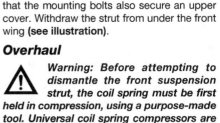

**Warning: Before attempting to dismantle the front suspension strut, the coil spring must be first held in compression, using a purpose-made tool. Universal coil spring compressors are available from motor factors or car accessory shops, and are essential for this operation. DO NOT attempt to dismantle the strut without such a tool, as damage and/or personal injury is likely.**

**Note:** *A new top mounting nut must be used on reassembly.*

6 Support the strut by clamping it in a soft-jawed vice.
7 Using the spring compressor, compress the coils of the spring just enough to relieve **all** pressure from the upper spring seat **(see illustration)**.
8 The shock absorber piston rod must be held stationary while the top bearing retaining nut is unscrewed. To do this, use a ring spanner and Allen key **(see illustrations)**. Discard the nut as a new one must be fitted on reassembly.
9 Remove the top mounting, race, upper spring seat and rubber gaiter, followed by the bump stop and coil spring **(see illustrations)**.
10 Further dismantling of the strut is not possible, therefore if the shock absorber is faulty, the strut itself must be renewed **(see illustration)**.

2.9a Remove the top mounting . . .

2.9b . . . race . . .

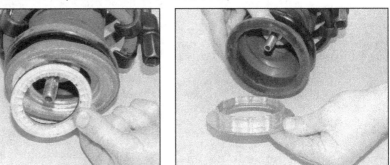

2.9c . . . upper spring seat and rubber gaiter . . .

2.9d . . . followed by the bump stop . . .

2.9e . . . and coil spring

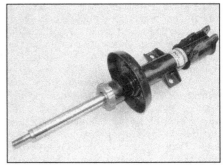

2.10 Front suspension strut with coil spring removed

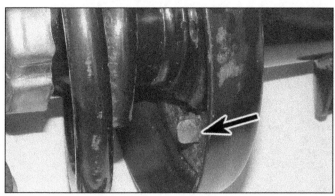

2.12 Location stop on the lower spring seat

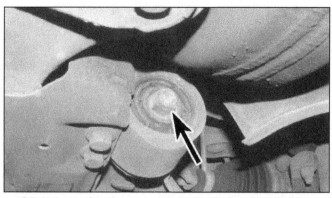

3.5 Nut securing the rear mounting to the front suspension lower arm

**11** Clean all the components and examine them for wear and damage. Check the upper mounting bearing for smooth operation by turning it by hand. Renew the components as necessary.

**12** Locate the bottom end (small diameter) of the coil spring onto the strut, making sure its end abuts the location stop on the lower spring seat **(see illustration)**. **Note:** *If a new spring is being fitted, first compress the coils using the spring compressor.*

**13** Fit the bump stop over the piston rod, followed by the rubber gaiter.

**14** Fit the upper spring seat on top of the spring, followed by the bearing race, top mounting and a new retaining nut.

**15** Tighten the nut to the specified torque while holding the piston rod stationary with the Allen key.

**16** Carefully loosen the spring compressor while at the same time making sure that the bottom of the spring remains located correctly in the lower spring seat. Remove the compressor.

### *Refitting*

**17** Locate the strut under the front wing and lift it into position. Note that the small hole is used for locating the upper bearing in the strut tower. Insert the upper mounting bolts and tighten them to the specified torque.

**18** Tilt the hub carrier inwards and engage it with the bottom of the strut. Insert the bolts from the front and refit the ABS wheel sensor/brake hose holder. Apply locking fluid to the threads of the bolts, then screw on the

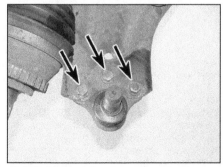

3.6 Bolts retaining the suspension lower balljoint to the lower arm

nuts and tighten them to the specified torque. Hold the bolt heads stationary while the nuts are tightened.

**19** Refit the anti-roll bar link to the strut and tighten the nut to the specified torque.

**20** Refit the roadwheel and lower the vehicle to the ground.

---

### 3 Front suspension lower arm – removal, overhaul and refitting

### *Removal*

**1** Apply the handbrake, then jack up the front of the vehicle and support it on axle stands (see *Jacking and vehicle support*). Remove the roadwheel.

**2** Unscrew and remove the bolts securing the lower arm rear mounting to the subframe.

**3** Unscrew and remove the lower arm front mounting bolt, and pull the lower arm down from the subframe.

**4** Unscrew and remove the clamp bolt securing the lower arm balljoint to the bottom of the hub carrier. If necessary, prise the clamp apart slightly using a screwdriver or lever. Withdraw the lower arm from the hub carrier.

**5** Note the fitted position of the rear mounting on the lower arm, then unscrew the nut and remove the mounting **(see illustration)**.

**6** Unscrew the bolts and remove the front suspension lower balljoint from the lower arm **(see illustration)**.

### *Overhaul*

**7** Clean the components and examine them for wear and damage.

**8** If the front mounting bush is worn excessively, press out the old bush and similarly press in the new bush. If a standard press is not available, use a long bolt together with tubing and washers to complete the task. Saab technicians use a tapered tool for the fitting procedure; the outer rubber is compressed to a diameter less than that of the bore in the lower arm.

**9** Check the rear mounting for wear, and renew it if necessary.

**10** Check the lower arm for damage and if necessary renew it.

**11** Check the lower balljoint stub for good articulation. If it is dry or seized, renew it. Also, check that the balljoint rubber boot is not damaged.

### *Refitting*

**12** Fit the lower balljoint to the arm and tighten the bolts to the specified torque.

**13** Locate the rear mounting on the lower arm so that its axis is in line with the arm **(see illustration)**. Refit the nut and tighten to the specified torque.

**14** Lift the lower arm into position and insert the lower balljoint stub into the bottom of the hub carrier. Make sure that the stub is fully entered so that the annular groove is opposite the clamp bolt hole. Insert the clamp bolt and tighten to the specified torque and angle.

**15** Locate the inner end of the lower arm on the subframe and insert the front mounting bolt hand-tight at this stage.

**16** Insert the rear mounting bolt hand-tight, then raise the outer end of the lower arm with a trolley jack until the weight of the front of the vehicle is on the front suspension, and fully tighten the arm mounting bolts to their specified torque. If preferred, the bolts can be fully tightened after lowering the vehicle to the ground.

**17** Refit the roadwheel and lower the vehicle to the ground.

**18** Have the front wheel alignment checked and if necessary adjusted at the earliest opportunity.

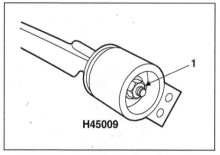

3.13 Align the front suspension rear mounting bush before tightening the retaining nut (1)

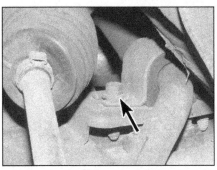

**4.9 Front anti-roll bar mounting clamp bolt**

## 4 Front anti-roll bar – removal, overhaul and refitting

### Removal

**1** Apply the handbrake, then jack up the front of the vehicle and support it on axle stands (see *Jacking and vehicle support*). Remove both front roadwheels.

**2** The engine assembly must be supported while the rear of the subframe is lowered. To do this, use a suitable hoist or engine support bar which straddles the engine compartment. Slightly lift the engine assembly so that its weight is supported.

**3** At the rear of the engine, unscrew the nut securing the rear engine mounting to the engine bracket, then unbolt the mounting from the subframe and remove it.

**5.5 Removing the front brake disc**

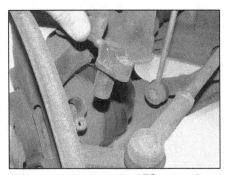

**5.6b ... and remove the ABS sensor from the hub carrier**

**4** Working under the vehicle, unbolt the crossmember from the rear of the subframe.

**5** The exhaust front section must be lowered before lowering the subframe. To do this, refer to Chapter 4A and either remove the exhaust or separate it at the joint and release it from the rubber mountings.

**6** Unscrew and remove the two bolts securing the steering gear to the subframe.

**7** Support the subframe with a trolley jack, then unscrew and remove the centre mounting bolts and lower the rear of the subframe as far as possible for access to the front anti-roll bar mountings.

**8** Note the fitted position of the side links on the anti-roll bar, then unscrew the nuts and detach them. If preferred, the side links may be detached from the strut.

**9** Note the position of the two anti-roll bar mounting clamps, then unscrew the bolts and remove the clamps **(see illustration)**.

**10** Withdraw the anti-roll bar from one side of the vehicle, taking care not to damage the brake hoses and wiring.

**11** Note the fitted position of the split clamp mounting rubbers, then prise them from the anti-roll bar.

### Overhaul

**12** Check the anti-roll bar and mountings for signs of wear and damage. Also check the side links.

**13** Check the split clamp mounting rubbers and renew them if necessary.

### Refitting

**14** Clean the anti-roll bar, then dip the split

**5.6a Unscrew the bolt ...**

**5.8a Undo the screws ...**

clamp mounting rubbers in soapy water and fit them with their splits facing rearwards.

**15** Locate the anti-roll bar onto the subframe and refit the mounting clamps. Insert the mounting bolts and tighten them to the specified torque.

**16** Refit the side links to the anti-roll bar (or strut if applicable) and tighten the nuts to the specified torque.

**17** Raise the subframe and refit the centre mounting bolts. Tighten the bolts to the specified torque and angle. Remove the trolley jack.

**18** Insert the steering gear mounting bolts and tighten them to the specified torque.

**19** Refit the exhaust front section with reference to Chapter 4A.

**20** Refit the crossmember to the rear of the subframe and tighten the mounting bolts to the specified torque.

**21** Refit the rear engine mounting and tighten the bolts to the specified torques.

**22** Remove the hoist or support bar.

**23** Refit the roadwheels and lower the vehicle to the ground.

## 5 Front suspension hub carrier – removal and refitting

### Removal

**1** Jack up the front of the vehicle and support it on axle stands (see *Jacking and vehicle support*). Remove the relevant roadwheel and, where applicable, the engine undertray.

**2** On 2002-on models, tap off the metal dust cover for access to the hub nut. Note that the cover cannot be removed with the roadwheel in position, so it is not possible to loosen the hub nut before raising the front of the vehicle.

**3** Temporarily refit two of the roadwheel bolts and tighten them to hold the brake disc onto the hub flange, then have an assistant depress the footbrake pedal, while the hub nut is being loosened. Unscrew and remove the hub nut. Discard the nut as a new one must be used on refitting.

**4** On 2002-on models fitted with a headlamp position sensor, unscrew the nut securing the sensor arm to the lower suspension arm, then unbolt the sensor from its mounting bracket and position it to one side.

**5** Refer to Chapter 9 and remove the front brake disc **(see illustration)**. Suspend the caliper from the front coil spring with a piece of wire or cable tie, without disconnecting the flexible hydraulic fluid hose.

**6** Unscrew the bolt and remove the ABS sensor from the hub carrier **(see illustrations)**. Position it to one side.

**7** Detach the steering track rod end from the hub carrier with reference to Section 21.

**8** Undo the screws and remove the brake backplate from the hub carrier – access to the screws is gained through the holes in the hub flange **(see illustrations)**.

5.8b . . . and remove the brake backplate

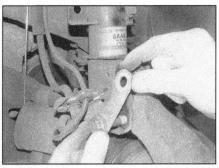
5.9 Removing the strut-to-hub carrier bolts together with the wiring/hose holding plate

5.10 Removing the lower arm balljoint clamp bolt

5.11a Slide the driveshaft from the hub . . .

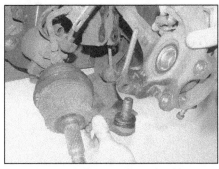
5.11b . . . and lift the hub carrier from the lower balljoint

5.17 The location cut-out (arrowed) must align with the bolt hole

9 Note that the bolts securing the strut to the hub carrier are fitted with their heads facing forwards. Unscrew and remove the bolts, and move the holding plate for the ABS wheel sensor wiring and brake hydraulic hose to one side (see illustration). The bolts have fine location splines on their shanks, and must not be turned within the hub carrier; hold the bolt head stationary and unscrew the nut from it. Lower the assembly so that the driveshaft is resting on the front subframe.
10 Unscrew and remove the clamp bolt securing the lower arm balljoint to the bottom of the hub carrier (see illustration).
11 Push the splined section of the driveshaft out of the hub. If it is tight, temporarily refit the hub nut onto the threads and tap the end of the driveshaft using a soft-faced mallet to free it. Lift the hub carrier from the lower balljoint and withdraw from the vehicle (see illustrations). If necessary, prise the clamp apart slightly using a screwdriver or lever.
12 If required, remove the hub bearing from the carrier as described in Section 6.

### Refitting

13 Refit the hub bearing to the carrier with reference to Section 6.
14 Locate the hub onto the end of the driveshaft and engage the hub splines with the driveshaft splines. Draw the hub onto the driveshaft using the new hub centre nut, but do not fully tighten the nut at this stage.
15 Locate the top of the hub carrier in the bottom of the strut, and insert the bolts with their heads facing forwards, together with the

holder for the ABS wheel sensor and brake hydraulic hose. Apply locking fluid to the threads of the bolts, then screw on the nuts and tighten them to the specified torque. Hold the bolt heads stationary while the nuts are tightened.
16 Refit the brake backplate and tighten the retaining screws securely.
17 Lift the lower arm into position and insert the lower balljoint stub into the bottom of the hub carrier. Make sure that the stub is fully entered and the location cut-out is opposite the clamp bolt hole (see illustration). Insert the clamp bolt and tighten to the specified torque and angle.
18 Refit the steering track rod end to the hub carrier and tighten the nut to the specified torque.
19 Refit the ABS sensor to the hub carrier and tighten the bolt securely.

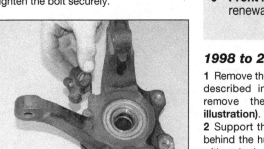
6.1 Removing the ABS sensor holder from the hub carrier

20 Refit the front brake caliper and disc with reference to Chapter 9.
21 On 2002-on models, refit the headlamp position sensor and inner splash cover as applicable.
22 With two of the roadwheel bolts holding the brake disc in position, have an assistant depress the footbrake pedal, then tighten the hub nut to the specified torque. Note that there two types of nut with different tightening torques.
23 On 2002-on models, tap the metal dust cover onto the hub flange.
24 Refit the undertray where applicable, then refit the roadwheel and lower the vehicle to the ground. Tighten the wheel bolts to the specified torque.

### 6 Front hub bearing – renewal

#### 1998 to 2001 models

1 Remove the front suspension hub carrier as described in Section 5, then unbolt and remove the ABS sensor holder (see illustration).
2 Support the hub carrier on its outer face behind the hub flange. This is best achieved with an hydraulic press. Press or drive the hub from the bearings using a metal tube or large socket in contact with the inner end of the hub. An alternative method is to screw two bolts through the hub flange, bearing on nuts

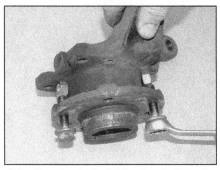

**6.2a Progressively tighten two bolts onto nuts, to press the hub from the bearing . . .**

**6.2b . . . then remove the hub**

**6.3 Removing the circlip from the outer side of the hub bearing**

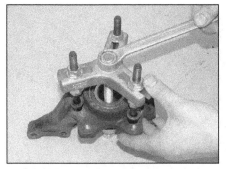

**6.4 Using a puller to remove the hub bearing**

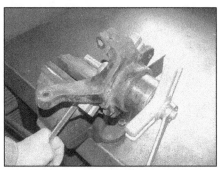

**6.7 Using a puller to fit the new bearing**

**6.9 Using a long bolt and metal tubing to fit the hub**

positioned on the hub carrier **(see illustrations)**. **Note:** *The action of pressing out the hub will damage the bearing, therefore the bearing **must not** be re-used.*

**3** Using circlip pliers, extract the circlip from the outer side of the hub bearing **(see illustration)**.

**4** Support the hub carrier on its outer face

and press or drive out the bearing using a metal tube or large socket in contact with the bearing outer race. Alternatively, use a puller together with a long bolt, washers and tubing **(see illustration)**.

**5** Clean the hub and the inside of the hub carrier.

**6** Smear some multi-purpose grease on the

outer periphery of the new bearing and in the hub carrier.

**7** Support the inner face of the hub carrier and press or drive in the bearing until it contacts the shoulder, using a metal tube or large socket on the bearing outer race. Alternatively, use the puller to draw the bearing into the carrier, but make sure that pressure is only applied to the outer race **(see illustration)**.

**8** Fit the circlip to its groove in the hub carrier, positioning the circlip opening at the bottom. Where fitted, refit the spacer.

**9** Support the inner end of the bearing with a metal tube or large socket on the inner race, then press or drive in the hub from the outside. Alternatively, support the hub flange and press the inner race of the bearing onto the hub. The hub can also be pressed into the bearing using a long bolt and metal tube in contact with the inner race **(see illustration)**.

**10** Refit the front suspension hub carrier as described in Section 5.

### 2002-on models

**11** On 2002-on models, the hub and bearing assembly is bolted to the carrier separately **(see illustration)**. With the vehicle parked on a level surface, remove the wheel trim (and hub dust cap where applicable). Loosen the hub centre nut half a turn.

**12** Apply the handbrake, then jack up the front of the vehicle and support it on axle stands (see *Jacking and vehicle support*). Remove the roadwheel.

**13** Fully unscrew and remove the hub centre nut. Discard the nut as a new one must be used on refitting.

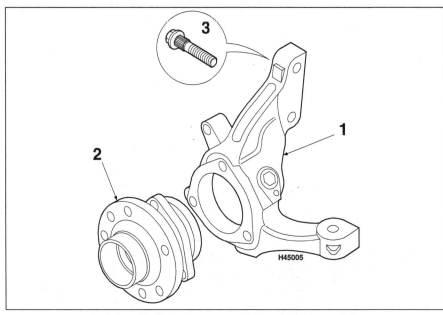

**6.11 Front hub carrier components on 2002-on models**

1 Hub carrier
2 Hub and bearing assembly

3 Splined bolt securing the hub carrier to the front suspension strut

**14** Refer to Chapter 9 and remove the front brake disc. Suspend the caliper from the front coil spring with a piece of wire or cable tie, without disconnecting the flexible hydraulic fluid hose.

**15** Unscrew the bolt and remove the ABS sensor from the hub carrier. Position it to one side.

**16** Detach the steering track rod end from the hub carrier with reference to Section 21.

**17** Unscrew and remove the clamp bolt securing the lower arm balljoint to the bottom of the hub carrier. If necessary, prise the clamp apart slightly using a screwdriver or lever. Pull down the lower arm from the hub carrier.

**18** Push the splined section of the driveshaft out of the hub. If it is tight, temporarily refit the hub nut onto the threads and tap the end of the driveshaft using a soft-faced mallet to free it, while supporting the hub carrier.

**19** Unscrew the bolts and withdraw the hub bearing and backplate assembly from the carrier **(see illustration)**.

**20** Clean the carrier, then locate the new hub bearing and backplate assembly on the carrier and tighten the mounting bolts to the specified torque.

**21** Locate the hub and carrier onto the end of the driveshaft and engage the hub splines with those of the driveshaft. Draw the hub onto the driveshaft using the new hub centre nut, but do not fully tighten the nut at this stage.

**22** Lift the lower arm into position and insert the lower balljoint stub into the bottom of the hub carrier. Make sure that the stub is fully entered so that the annular groove is opposite the clamp bolt hole. Insert the clamp bolt and tighten to the specified torque and angle.

**23** Refit the steering track rod end to the hub carrier and tighten the nut to the specified torque.

**24** Refit the ABS sensor to the hub carrier and tighten the bolt securely.

**25** Refit the front brake caliper and disc with reference to Chapter 9.

**6.19 One of the bolts securing the hub bearing to the carrier**

**26** Refit the roadwheel and lower the vehicle to the ground.

**27** Tighten the hub centre nut to the specified torque and angle.

**7 Front suspension subframe –** removal, overhaul and refitting

### Removal

**1** Apply the handbrake, then jack up the front of the vehicle and support it on axle stands (see *Jacking and vehicle support*). Remove both front wheels, then remove the underbody splash covers.

**2** Unbolt the engine rear mounting from the subframe with reference to Chapter 2A.

**3** Support the weight of the engine and transmission with a hoist attached to the rear engine lifting eye.

**4** Support the radiator and air conditioning condenser on the engine compartment front crossmember using cable ties.

**5** Disconnect the wiring connector for the oxygen sensors.

**6** Where applicable, unbolt the oil cooler and allow it to hang from its hoses.

**7** Unscrew the power steering fluid cooler mounting bolts and support the cooler with cable ties.

**8** Mark the position of the subframe on the underbody to ensure correct refitting. One way to do this is to spray paint around the subframe mountings using an aerosol; the outline of the mountings will be marked clearly on the underbody.

**9** Unbolt the reinforcement crossmember from the rear of the subframe. Note that the outer bolts are also the subframe rear mounting bolts **(see illustration)**. **Note:** *On early models, the reinforcement crossmember is in one piece, however, on late models the two outer triangles are separate from the centre section.*

**10** Unscrew the steering gear mounting bolts from the subframe **(see illustration)**. To support the steering gear while the subframe is lowered, use cable ties between the track rods and underbody.

**11** Remove the exhaust front pipe section with reference to Chapter 4A.

**12** Unbolt the front engine mounting/transmission torque arm from the subframe.

**13** Unscrew and remove the clamp bolts securing the lower arm balljoints to the bottom of the hub carriers. If necessary, prise the clamps apart slightly using a screwdriver or lever. Pull down the lower arms from the hub carriers.

**14** Unscrew the nuts and disconnect the anti-roll bar links from the front suspension struts. Hold the link stubs with one spanner while loosening the retaining nuts.

**15** Where applicable, disconnect the wiring from the load angle sensor.

**16** Unscrew the nuts retaining the air cleaner to the subframe.

**17** Remove the air conditioning pipes from their mounting brackets. Also, detach the power steering pipe from the support clips.

**18** Support the weight of the front suspension subframe on trolley jacks.

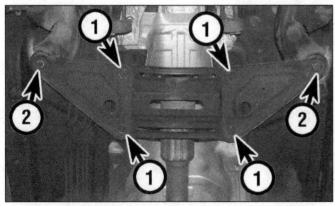

**7.9 Reinforcement crossmember on the rear of the subframe (late models)**

1 Bolts retaining the centre section and inner ends of the triangular plates

2 Bolts retaining the outer ends of the triangular plates and the rear of the subframe

**7.10 Steering gear mounting bolts on the subframe**

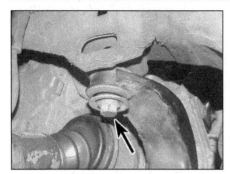

7.19a Subframe side mounting bolt

7.19b Subframe front mounting bolt

7.19c Radiator and air conditioning mounting stubs and rubber grommets

**19** Unscrew the side and front mounting bolts and lower the subframe to the ground. Make sure that the radiator upper mountings remain located in the crossmember; the lower mounting stubs will be released from the rubber grommets in the subframe **(see illustrations)**. Note that the reinforcement crossmember mounting bolts have smaller washers and 20 mm heads when compared to the main subframe mounting bolts.

### Overhaul

**20** Check the subframe and mounting bushes for wear and damage, and renew as necessary.
**21** The mounting bushes can be renewed if necessary using a press or, alternatively, metal tubing, washers and a long bolt. Press in the new bushes using the same method.

### Refitting

**22** Refitting is a reversal of removal, but

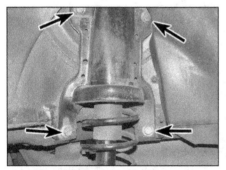

8.2 Rear shock absorber/strut mounting bolts

position the subframe as noted before removal, and tighten the mounting bolts to the specified torque.

---

**8 Rear strut/shock absorber –** removal, overhaul and refitting

**Note:** *Optional self-levelling rear suspension may be fitted for certain markets, however, at the time of writing, no information was available.*

### Removal

**1** Chock the front wheels then jack up the rear of the vehicle and support on axle stands (see *Jacking and vehicle support*). Remove the roadwheel.
**2** The shock absorber/strut is mounted on the body with 4 bolts; unscrew and remove the two lower bolts and loosen the upper bolts

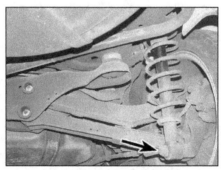

8.3 Rear shock absorber/strut lower mounting bolt

two or three turns **(see illustration)**. The upper bolt holes are open-ended, however, with the lower bolts removed, the rear anti-roll bar will still exert some upward pressure.
**3** Support the strut, then unscrew and remove the mounting bolt securing the rear shock absorber/strut to the trailing arm, and recover the washer **(see illustration)**. Discard both the bolt and washer as new ones must be used on refitting.
**4** Withdraw the rear shock absorber/strut from the vehicle **(see illustration)**.

### Overhaul

⚠️ *Warning: Before attempting to dismantle the rear shock absorber/ strut, the coil spring must be first held in compression, using a purpose-made tool. Universal coil spring compressors are available from motor factors or car accessory shops, and are essential for this operation. DO NOT attempt to dismantle the strut without such a tool, as damage and/or personal injury is likely.*
**Note:** *A new top mounting nut must be used on reassembly.*
**5** Use a dab of paint to mark the rear coil spring for position. Note that the small diameter coils are at the bottom of the spring.
**6** Support the strut by clamping it in a soft-jawed vice.
**7** Using the spring compressor, compress the coils of the spring just enough to relieve **all** pressure from the upper spring seat **(see illustration)**.
**8** The shock absorber piston rod must be held stationary while the top bearing retaining

8.4 Removing the rear shock absorber/strut from the vehicle

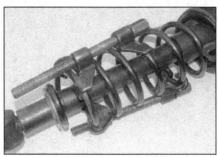

8.7 Using a spring compressor tool, compress the coil sufficiently to relieve all pressure from the upper spring seat

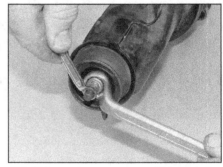

8.8 Using a ring spanner and Allen key to loosen the top bearing retaining nut

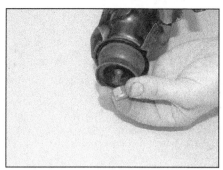

8.9a  Unscrew and remove the nut . . .

8.9b  . . . recover the upper domed washer . . .

8.9c  . . . and remove the upper rubber bush

8.10a  Lift off the upper bracket . . .

8.10b  . . . and remove the upper spring seat . . .

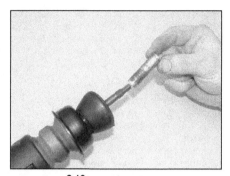

8.10c  . . . spacer . . .

nut is unscrewed. To do this, use a ring spanner and Allen key (see illustration). Discard the nut as a new one must be fitted on reassembly.

**9** Fully unscrew the nut and recover the

upper domed washer and upper rubber bush (see illustrations).

**10** Lift off the upper bracket, then remove the upper spring seat, followed by the spacer, lower rubber bush, lower domed washer,

buffer stop and coil spring, noting their fitted locations (see illustrations).

**11** Clean all the components and examine them for wear and damage. With the shock absorber mounted in the vice, operate the piston rod over its full stroke several times and check for tight spots or seizing. The rod should move smoothly with constant resistance. Renew the components as necessary.

**12** Refit the coil spring with its small diameter coils downwards, making sure that its lower end locates correctly on the lower spring seat.

**13** Refit the buffer stop, followed by the washer, lower rubber bush and spacer.

**14** Refit the upper spring seat to the upper bracket, then locate the assembly on the coil spring, making sure that the end of the coil locates in the special recess in the spring seat.

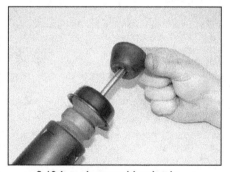

8.10d  . . . lower rubber bush . . .

8.10e  . . . lower domed washer . . .

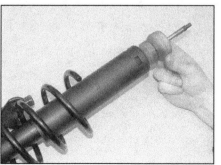

8.10f  . . . buffer stop . . .

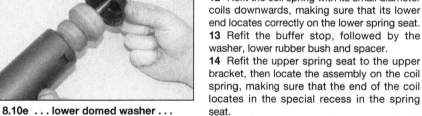

8.10g  . . . and coil spring . . .

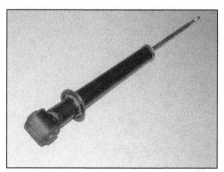

8.10h  . . . rear shock absorber/strut with coil spring components removed

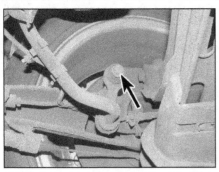

**9.2 Bolt securing the rear anti-roll bar link to the trailing arm**

**15** Screw on the new top mounting nut by hand as far as possible.
**16** Hold the piston rod stationary (as for dismantling) and tighten the mounting nut to the specified torque.

### Refitting

**17** Locate the shock absorber/strut on the loose upper mounting bolts, then insert the lower mounting bolts loosely. Push the strut upwards, then tighten the bolts to the specified torque.
**18** Fit the new lower mounting bolt and washer on the trailing arm, and tighten to the specified torque.
**19** Refit the roadwheel and lower the vehicle to the ground.

## 9  Rear anti-roll bar – removal, overhaul and refitting

### Removal

**1** Chock the front wheels then jack up the rear of the vehicle and support on axle stands (see *Jacking and vehicle support*). Remove both rear roadwheels.
**2** Unscrew the bolts securing the anti-roll bar links to the trailing arms **(see illustration)**.
**3** As applicable, release the ABS wiring from the clips on the rear anti-roll bar.
**4** Unscrew the nuts and bolts from the clamps, and remove the anti-roll bar from the rear crossmember **(see illustration)**. The bolts will probably remain in the clamps.

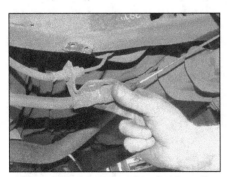

**10.2 Unbolt the support bracket from the trailing arm**

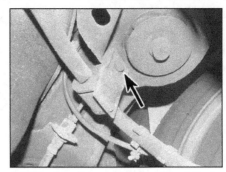

**9.4 Clamp bolt securing the anti-roll bar to the rear crossmember**

### Overhaul

**5** Check the split mounting rubbers and side links mountings for wear and damage, and renew them as necessary.
**6** To renew the split mounting rubbers, first note their fitted position on the anti-roll bar. To remove them, mount the clamps in a vice and tap out the bolts, then unhook the clamp retaining plates from the slot in the intermediate plates. Prise the rubbers from the anti-roll bar. Clean the bar, then dip the split clamp mounting rubbers in soapy water and fit them in the previously-noted positions. Assemble the intermediate plates and hook on the retaining plates. Make sure that the split sides of the rubbers contact the intermediate plates.
**7** To renew the side links, mount the anti-roll bar in a vice then press off the links. It may be possible to renew the link mountings, but check with your Saab dealer first. To remove the mountings, press them out using metal tubing and a vice. Press in the new mountings using the same method.

### Refitting

**8** Locate the anti-roll bar on the rear crossmember, insert the nuts and bolts and tighten to the specified torque.
**9** Insert the bolts securing the anti-roll bar links to the trailing arms and tighten securely.
**10** Clip the ABS wiring to the anti-roll bar as applicable.
**11** Refit the roadwheels and lower the vehicle to the ground.

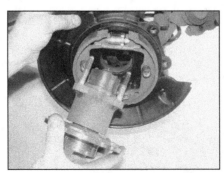

**10.4 Removing the rear hub assembly from the trailing arm and brake backplate**

## 10  Rear hub assembly – removal and refitting

**Note:** *The rear hub bearings cannot be renewed separately; if they are worn excessively, the hub assembly must be renewed.*

### Removal

**1** Remove the rear brake disc as described in Chapter 9.
**2** On 1999-on models (VIN X3025752-on), remove the protective cover from the bottom of the rear suspension trailing arm, and unbolt the handbrake cable, wiring and brake pipe support brackets **(see illustration)**.
**3** Disconnect the wiring from the ABS sensor located on the rear of the hub assembly.
**4** Unscrew the nuts securing the rear hub assembly to the trailing arm, noting the location of the bracket on one of the hub studs, then withdraw the hub assembly, leaving the brake backplate suspended by the handbrake cable **(see illustration)**. Recover the two shims located between the backplate and trailing arm. Discard the nuts as new ones must be used on refitting.

### Refitting

**5** Clean the contact surfaces of the hub, backplate and trailing arm.
**6** Locate the backplate on the hub studs, followed by the shims, then locate the assembly on the trailing arm and tighten the new nuts to the specified torque. Make sure the shims are positioned correctly between the backplate and trailing arm.
**7** Reconnect the wiring to the ABS sensor.
**8** On 1999-on models (VIN X3025752-on), refit the support brackets for the handbrake cable, wiring and brake pipe, then refit the protective cover to the bottom of the rear suspension lower arm.
**9** Refit the rear brake disc with reference to Chapter 9.

## 11  Rear suspension trailing arm – removal, overhaul and refitting

### Removal

**1** Remove the hub assembly as described in Section 9.
**2** Unscrew and remove the lower mounting bolt securing the rear shock absorber/strut to the trailing arm, and recover the washer. Discard both the bolt and washer as new ones must be used on refitting.
**3** Unscrew the bolt and remove the lower transverse link from the trailing arm. Note that the bolt head faces forward.
**4** Unbolt the handbrake cable support bracket from the trailing arm.
**5** Unhook the handbrake cable return spring and remove the cable.

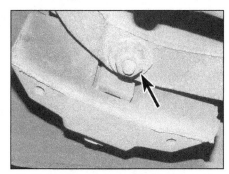

**11.10 Nut securing the rubber damper to the front of the trailing arm**

6 Unscrew the bolt and remove the anti-roll bar link from the trailing arm.

7 Unscrew the bolt and remove the upper transverse link from the trailing arm. Note that the bolt head faces forward.

8 Mark the trailing arm front mounting bracket in relation to the underbody, then unscrew and remove the bolts and withdraw from the vehicle.

9 At this stage, Saab technicians fit a small jig tool to hold the trailing arm in its normal position in relation to the mounting bracket. If this tool is not available, mark the two parts in relation to each other to ensure correct refitting. Unscrew the nut and bolt and remove the mounting bracket from the trailing arm. Note that the bolt head faces the outside of the arm.

10 Where fitted, unscrew the nut and remove the rubber damper from the front of the trailing arm **(see illustration)**.

### Overhaul

11 Check the trailing arm for wear and damage, and renew if necessary.

12 The front mounting bush can be renewed if necessary using metal tubing and a vice to press it out. First, cut off the edges of the rubber bush with a hacksaw for ease of removal. The transverse link bushes can also be renewed in the same way.

13 Press in the new bush using the same method, but position it correctly **(see illustration)**. Note that the rubber bush outer sides will swell, and this is quite normal.

### Refitting

14 Where fitted, refit the rubber damper to the front of the trailing arm and tighten the nut securely.

15 Locate the bracket on the front of the trailing arm and insert the bolt. Position the bracket and arm in their previously-noted position, and tighten the bolt to the specified torque and angle.

16 Lift the trailing arm and bracket onto the underbody and insert the mounting bolts. Position the bracket to align the previously-made marks, then insert the bolts and tighten them to the specified torque and angle.

17 Refit the upper transverse link and tighten the bolt to the specified torque.

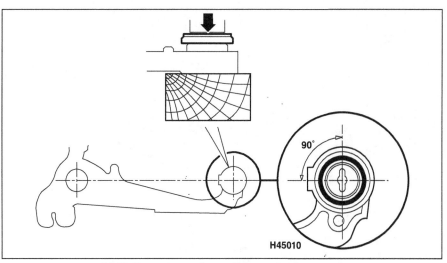

**11.13 Rear suspension trailing arm bush renewal**

18 Refit the anti-roll bar link and tighten the bolt securely.

19 Refit the handbrake cable and reconnect the return spring.

20 Refit the handbrake cable support bracket, and tighten the bolt securely.

21 Refit the lower transverse link and tighten the bolt to the specified torque.

22 Refit the rear shock absorber/strut to the trailing arm, and secure with a new lower mounting bolt and washer. Tighten the bolt to the specified torque.

23 Refit the hub assembly with reference to Section 9.

24 Have the rear wheel alignment checked and adjusted at the earliest opportunity.

---

**12 Rear suspension upper transverse link – removal and refitting**

### Removal

1 Chock the front wheels then jack up the rear of the vehicle and support on axle stands (see *Jacking and vehicle support*). Remove the roadwheel.

2 If removing the left-hand transverse link, unhook the exhaust system central and rear

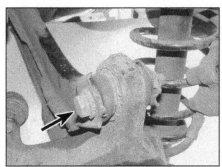

**12.4 The bolt head for the upper transverse link must face forward**

mounting rubbers and lower the exhaust onto axle stands. Make sure that the front flexible section is not unduly strained.

3 Unscrew the nut and bolt, and remove the lower transverse link from the trailing arm. Note that the bolt head faces forward. Discard the nut as a new one must be used on refitting.

4 Unscrew the bolt and remove the upper transverse link from the trailing arm **(see illustration)**. Note that the bolt head faces forward. Discard the nut as a new one must be used on refitting.

5 Unscrew the bolt and remove the anti-roll bar link from the trailing arm.

6 Support the rear suspension crossmember on a trolley jack, then unscrew and remove the crossmember-to-underbody bolts on the side being worked on. Loosen the crossmember mounting bolts on the opposite side. Lower the crossmember slightly.

7 Unscrew the bolt and remove the lower transverse link from the suspension crossmember. Note that the bolt head faces forward. Discard the nut as a new one must be used on refitting.

8 Unscrew the bolt and remove the upper transverse link from the suspension crossmember. Note that the bolt head faces forward. Discard the nut as a new one must be used on refitting.

### Refitting

9 Refitting is a reversal of removal, but tighten all nuts and bolts to the specified torque where given. Note that the transverse link-to-crossmember mounting bolts and (new) nuts should initially be tightened by hand only, and finally fully tightened with the full weight of the vehicle on the rear suspension. Note that the bolts incorporate special sleeves to protect the fuel tank and fuel filler pipe in the event of a collision; **do not** use different types of bolt.

10 Have the rear wheel alignment checked and adjusted at the earliest opportunity.

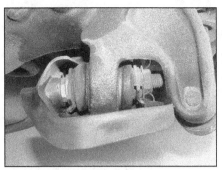

**13.3 Lower transverse link mounting on the trailing arm**

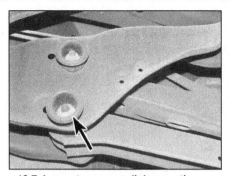

**13.7 Lower transverse link mounting on the crossmember**

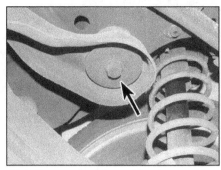

**14.4 Rear suspension subframe mounting bolt**

## 13 Rear suspension lower transverse link – removal and refitting

### Removal

**1** Chock the front wheels then jack up the rear of the vehicle and support on axle stands (see *Jacking and vehicle support*). Remove the roadwheel.

**2** If removing the left-hand transverse link, unhook the exhaust system central and rear mounting rubbers and lower the exhaust onto axle stands. Make sure that the front flexible section is not unduly strained.

**3** Unscrew the nut and bolt, and remove the lower transverse link from the trailing arm **(see illustration)**. Note that the bolt head faces forward. Discard the nut as a new one must be used on refitting.

**4** Unscrew the bolt and remove the upper transverse link from the trailing arm. Note that the bolt head faces forward. Discard the nut as a new one must be used on refitting.

**5** Unscrew the bolt and remove the anti-roll bar link from the trailing arm.

**6** Support the rear suspension crossmember on a trolley jack, then unscrew and remove the crossmember-to-underbody bolts on the side being worked on. Loosen the crossmember mounting bolts on the opposite side. Lower the crossmember slightly.

**7** Unscrew the bolt and remove the lower transverse link from the suspension crossmember **(see illustration)**. Note that the

bolt head faces forward. Discard the nut as a new one must be used on refitting.

### Refitting

**8** Refitting is a reversal of removal, but tighten all nuts and bolts to the specified torque where given. Note that the transverse link-to-crossmember mounting bolts and (new) nuts should initially be tightened by hand only, and finally fully tightened with the full weight of the vehicle on the rear suspension. Note that the bolts incorporate special sleeves to protect the fuel tank and fuel filler pipe in the event of a collision; **do not** use a different type of bolt.

**9** Have the rear wheel alignment checked and adjusted at the earliest opportunity.

## 14 Rear suspension subframe – removal, overhaul and refitting

### Removal

**1** Remove the rear suspension anti-roll bar as described in Section 9.

**2** Remove the right-hand and left-hand rear suspension upper and lower transverse links as described in Sections 12 and 13, however, do not remove the subframe mounting bolts.

**3** Support the subframe with a trolley jack and length of wood.

**4** Unscrew and remove the subframe mounting bolts and washers **(see illustration)**.

**5** Lower the subframe from the underbody and withdraw from beneath the vehicle.

### Overhaul

**6** Check the subframe and mounting bushes for wear and damage, and renew as necessary.

**7** The mounting bushes can be renewed if necessary using a press or alternatively, metal tubing, washers and a long bolt. Press in the new bushes using the same method.

### Refitting

**8** Raise the subframe onto the underbody, and insert the mounting bolts hand-tight at this stage.

**9** Refit the right-hand and left-hand rear suspension upper and lower transverse links with reference to Sections 12 and 13.

**10** Refit the rear suspension anti-roll bar with reference to Section 9.

**11** Fully tighten the subframe mounting bolts to the specified torque, and lower the vehicle to the ground.

## 15 Steering wheel – removal and refitting

### Removal

**1** Turn the front wheels to the 'straight-ahead' position, then turn the ignition to the OFF position, leaving the key in the switch so that the steering lock is released.

**2** Using a screwdriver, prise the plugs from over the airbag module retaining screw positions. Undo the screws and withdraw the airbag module from the steering wheel, then disconnect the airbag, horn and where applicable the audio wiring. On later models, the wiring is secured with Velcro. Store the airbag in a safe place with its metal bracket facing downwards.

*Caution: Observe the safety instructions given in Chapter 11.*

**3** Mark the relationship between the steering wheel and steering column with a dab of paint, then unscrew the steering wheel retaining nut, and remove the vibration damper plate and washer where fitted **(see illustrations)**.

*Caution: Do not use the steering lock to brace the column whilst the nut is being removed, as this may cause damage.*

**15.3a Unscrew the steering wheel retaining nut . . .**

**15.3b . . . and remove the vibration damper plate**

**4** Carefully ease the steering wheel from the column splines while feeding the horn and airbag wiring through the hole. If it is tight, temporarily leave the retaining nut and washer on the last few threads, to prevent damage when it releases from the column.

*Caution: Do not drive the steering wheel from the splines, as this may damage the collapsible inner column. Also take care not to damage the airbag contact spring unit located over the top of the column.*

**5** Using adhesive tape, secure the contact spring unit in its central position **(see illustration)**.

### Refitting

**6** Remove the adhesive tape from the contact spring unit. If its central position has been lost, first check that the front wheels are pointing straight-ahead, then turn the unit fully clockwise. Now turn the unit back 2.0 turns exactly.

**7** Locate the steering wheel on the column splines, while feeding the airbag and horn wiring through the hole. Make sure the previously-made marks are correctly aligned.

**8** Refit the washer and retaining nut and tighten the nut to the specified torque.

**9** Reconnect the airbag, horn and audio wiring, and on later models, secure it with the Velcro.

**10** Locate the driver's airbag module on the steering wheel, and tighten the retaining screws (refer to Chapter 11).

**11** Have the vehicle electronic control system checked for fault codes by a Saab dealer.

**15.5 Secure the contact spring unit in its central position with adhesive tape**

### 16 Steering column –
removed and refitting

> *Warning: Do not separate the steering intermediate shaft from the inner column during removal of the steering column.*

### Removal

**1** Remove the steering wheel as described in Section 15.

**2** Release the steering wheel height adjustment lever.

**3** Remove the steering column upper and lower shrouds. There are two screws facing upwards in the upper shroud, and one screw located beneath the lower shroud **(see illustrations)**.

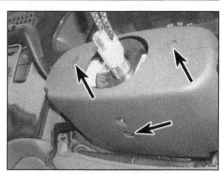

**16.3a Undo the screws . . .**

**4** Remove the lighting and wiper combination switches from the column and disconnect the wiring with reference to Chapter 12. On 2002-on models, unclip the wiring conduit from the steering column.

**5** Disconnect the wiring then remove the airbag contact spring unit (see Chapter 11).

**6** Mark the position of the holder for the contact spring unit and combination switches on the steering column, then loosen the clamp screw. Using a screwdriver, release the airbag wiring socket from the holder, then withdraw the holder from the steering column. Also release the airbag wiring socket from the support **(see illustrations)**.

**7** Remove the facia lower trim panel and air duct on the driver's side with reference to Chapter 11. On 2002-on models, remove the knee protector from the steering column **(see illustration)**.

**16.3b . . . then remove the upper shroud . . .**

**16.3c . . . and lower shroud**

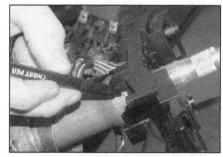

**16.6a Use a felt-tip pen to mark the position of the holder on the steering column . . .**

**16.6b . . . then loosen the clamp screw . . .**

**16.6c . . . and use a screwdriver to release the airbag socket . . .**

**16.6d . . . withdraw the contact spring holder . . .**

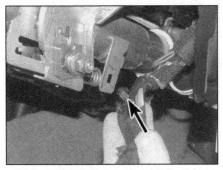

16.6e ... and release the airbag wiring socket from the support

16.7 Removing the knee protector

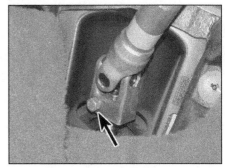

16.8a Unscrew the clamp bolt ...

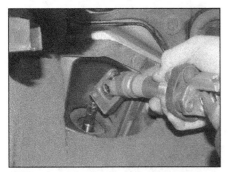

16.8b ... and slide the universal joint from the steering gear pinion shaft

16.9 Unscrew the steering column lower mounting bolt (note it cannot be removed completely at this stage)

16.12 Steering column upper mounting bolts

8 At the bottom of the steering column, unscrew and remove the clamp bolt and slide the universal joint from the steering gear pinion shaft **(see illustrations)**. Mark the shaft and column if necessary to ensure correct refitting. Make sure that the column intermediate shaft remains together with the upper column for the period when the steering column is removed.

9 Unscrew the steering column lower mounting bolt. The bolt cannot be removed completely at this stage **(see illustration)**.

10 Release the relevant wiring from the plastic cable ties, and move to one side.

11 Manoeuvre the rubber dust excluder gaiter over the steering wheel height adjustment lever, to allow the lever to be removed together with the steering column.

12 Unscrew and remove the upper mounting bolts **(see illustration)** and withdraw the steering column from inside the vehicle. The lower mounting bolt can now be removed from the column.

### Refitting

13 Locate the lower mounting bolt in the steering column, then position the steering column onto the bulkhead and hand-tighten the bolt to hold the assembly. Insert the upper mounting bolts, then fully tighten all the bolts to the specified torque.

14 Engage the universal joint on the bottom of the column with the splines on the steering gear pinion shaft, making sure that the bolt hole is aligned with the cut-out in the shaft and the alignment marks are adjacent as

previously noted. Tighten the clamp bolt to the specified torque.

15 Reposition the rubber dust excluder gaiter over the steering wheel height adjustment lever, so that the lever protrudes through its hole in the gaiter.

16 Secure the relevant wiring with new plastic cable ties. On 2002-on models, secure the wiring conduit to the steering column.

17 Refit the facia lower trim panel and air duct on the driver's side with reference to Chapter 11. On 2002-on models refit the knee protector to the steering column.

18 Refit the holder for the contact spring unit and combination switches with the groove uppermost, and tighten the bolts. Make sure that it is still held in its central position with the adhesive tape.

19 Reconnect the wiring for the airbag contact spring unit at the connector.

20 Refit the lighting and wiper combination switches and reconnect the wiring with reference to Chapter 12.

21 Refit the steering column upper and lower shrouds and tighten the screws.

22 Refit the steering wheel with reference to Section 14.

### 17 Steering gear assembly – removal and refitting

### Removal

1 Apply the handbrake, then jack up the front

of the vehicle and support it on axle stands (see *Jacking and vehicle support*). Remove both front roadwheels.

2 Drain the hydraulic fluid from the power steering system as described in Section 18, then return the steering to the straight-ahead position. The steering wheel must remain in its central position during the following procedure; use adhesive tape to secure it to the facia.

*Caution: Damage will occur to the airbag contact spring unit if the steering wheel is not secured in its central position.*

3 Disconnect the battery negative lead (refer to *Disconnecting the battery* in the Reference Chapter).

4 At the bottom of the steering column, unscrew and remove the clamp bolt and slide the universal joint from the steering gear pinion shaft. Mark the shaft and column if necessary to ensure correct refitting. Make sure that the column intermediate shaft remains together with the upper column for the period when the steering gear is removed.

5 The engine assembly must be supported while the rear of the subframe is lowered. To do this, use a suitable hoist or engine support bar which straddles the engine compartment. Slightly lift the engine assembly so that its weight is supported. If a support bar is being used, it may be necessary to remove the cover from over the inlet manifold.

6 At the rear of the engine, unscrew the nut securing the rear engine mounting to the engine bracket, then unbolt the mounting from the subframe and remove it.

**7** If the track rod ends are to be removed from the steering gear, loosen the adjusting nuts securing the ends to the track rods a quarter of a turn at this stage.

**8** Using a balljoint separator tool, disconnect the steering track rod ends from the steering arms on the hub carriers with reference to Section 21. If required, unscrew the track rod ends from the track rods, counting the exact number of turns necessary to remove them, to ensure correct refitting.

**9** Working under the vehicle, unbolt the crossmember and support bracket from the rear of the subframe.

**10** The exhaust front section must be lowered before lowering the subframe. To do this, refer to Chapter 4A and either remove the exhaust or separate it at the joint and release it from the rubber mountings.

**11** Support the subframe with a trolley jack, then unscrew and remove the centre mounting bolts and lower the rear of the subframe as far as possible.

**12** Position a container beneath the steering gear to catch spilt fluid. Identify the supply and return hydraulic pipes for location, then unscrew the union nuts and carefully position the pipes to one side. Recover the O-ring seals and valve body dust cover. Tape over or plug the ends of the pipes and the steering gear apertures to prevent entry of dust and dirt. Where applicable, cut the plastic cable ties securing the wiring to the pipes.

**13** Unscrew and remove the two nuts and bolts securing the steering gear to the subframe. Note the position of the nut retaining the support bracket for the delivery pipe.

**14** Withdraw the steering gear from one side of the vehicle, taking care not to damage the rubber gaiters.

**15** Examine the mounting rubbers for wear and damage and renew them if necessary. If a new steering gear is to be fitted, transfer the internal pipes from the old unit and fit new O-ring seals. Tighten the union nuts securely. Check the bulkhead rubber gaiter and renew if necessary.

### Refitting

**16** Before refitting the steering gear make sure that its rack is in its central position, and that the front wheels are still pointing straight-ahead.

**17** Locate the steering gear onto the subframe and connect the supply and return hydraulic pipes together with new O-ring seals. Do not fully tighten the union bolts at this stage.

**18** Insert the steering gear mounting bolts from under the subframe and screw on the nuts, but do not fully tighten them at this stage. But make sure the delivery pipe support bracket is fitted as previously-noted.

**19** Fully tighten the supply and return hydraulic pipe union bolts to their specified torque. Hold the pipes against rotation while the bolts are tightened.

**20** Fully tighten the steering gear mounting bolts to the specified torque.

**21** Secure the wiring to the hydraulic pipes with new plastic cable ties.

**22** Raise the subframe and refit the centre mounting bolts. Tighten the bolts to the specified torque and angle. Remove the trolley jack.

**23** Refit the exhaust front section with reference to Chapter 4A.

**24** Refit the crossmember and support bracket to the rear of the subframe and tighten the mounting bolts to the specified torque.

**25** If removed, screw on the track rod ends to the track rods the exact number of turns previously-noted.

**26** Refit the track rod ends to the steering arms on the hub carriers, then refit the nuts and tighten to the specified torque. With the track rod ends held in their central positions, tighten the locknuts securely.

**27** Refit the rear engine mounting and tighten the bolts to the specified torques.

**28** Remove the hoist or support bar, and where necessary refit the cover over the inlet manifold.

**29** Make sure that the steering wheel is still in its central position, then engage the universal joint on the bottom of the column with the splines on the steering gear pinion shaft, making sure that the bolt hole is aligned with the cut-out in the shaft and the alignment marks are adjacent as previously noted. Tighten the clamp bolt to the specified torque. Remove the adhesive tape from the steering wheel.

**30** Reconnect the battery negative lead (refer to *Disconnecting the battery* in the Reference Chapter).

**31** Fill the power steering system with the specified hydraulic fluid and bleed the system with reference to Section 18.

**32** Refit the front roadwheels and lower the vehicle to the ground.

**33** Have the front wheel alignment checked at the earliest opportunity.

### 18 Power steering hydraulic system – draining, refilling and bleeding

**Note:** *The power steering hydraulic system must be bled if any part of the system has been disconnected.*

### Draining

**1** To drain the complete hydraulic system of fluid, position a container (having a capacity of at least one litre) beneath the power steering pump on the right-hand front of the engine. Unclip the reservoir from its mounting, then loosen the clip and disconnect the return hose from the pump. Allow the fluid to drain into the container from the return hose.

**2** Secure the container in the engine bay, away from any moving components and direct sources of heat. Start the engine, and allow the hydraulic fluid to be pumped into the container. Turn the steering wheel lock-to-lock several times, to purge the fluid from the steering rack. When the flow of fluid ceases, turn off the engine immediately; **do not** allow the power steering pump to run dry for any length of time.

**3** Reconnect the return hose and tighten the clip, then reposition the reservoir on its mounting.

### Refilling

**4** Remove the fluid reservoir filler cap, and top-up to the maximum level mark with fluid of the specified type and grade; refer to *Weekly checks* for guidance.

### Bleeding

**5** Park the vehicle on a level surface and apply the handbrake.

**6** With the engine stopped, slowly move the steering from lock-to-lock several times to purge any trapped air, then top-up the level in the fluid reservoir. Repeat this procedure until the fluid level in the reservoir does not drop any further.

**7** Start the engine, then slowly move the steering from lock-to-lock several times to purge out any remaining air in the system. Repeat this procedure until bubbles cease to appear in the fluid reservoir.

**8** If an abnormal noise is heard from the pump or fluid pipes when the steering is operated, this is an indication that there is still air in the system. Confirm this by turning the wheels to the straight-ahead position and switching off the engine. If the fluid level in the reservoir rises, then air is present in the system, and further bleeding will be necessary. Repeat the above procedure as necessary.

**9** Once all traces of air have been purged from the power steering hydraulic system, stop the engine and allow the system to cool. Finally, check that the fluid level is up to the maximum mark on the reservoir, and top-up if necessary.

### 19 Power steering pump – removal and refitting

### Removal

**1** Drain the hydraulic fluid from the power steering system as described in Section 18, then return the steering to the straight-ahead position and refit the fluid reservoir.

**2** At the right-hand front corner of the engine compartment, loosen the clips and disconnect the air inlet hose and mass airflow meter. Place the hose and meter to one side.

**3** Remove the auxiliary drivebelt as described in Chapter 1.

**4** Place a container beneath the power steering pump, then loosen the clip and disconnect the fluid reservoir-to-pump hose.

**5** Unscrew the bolt securing the delivery pipe support to the pump, then unscrew the union nut and disconnect it from the pump. Access to the support bolt is gained through the hole in the pulley. Recover the O-ring seal.

**6** Unscrew the bolts securing the power steering pump to the mounting bracket, and withdraw it from the engine. Note that the pump and mounting bracket were changed for 2002-on models. On earlier models, access to the bolt at the pulley end is gained through the hole in the pulley. Wrap the pump in cloth rag to prevent fluid dropping onto the vehicle paintwork.

### Refitting

**7** Locate the pump on the engine, then insert the mounting bolts and tighten them to the specified torque.

**8** Fit a new O-ring seal to the delivery pipe end fitting, then locate it on the pump. Tighten the union nut and support bolt to the specified torque.

**9** Reconnect the reservoir-to-pump hose and tighten the clip.

**10** Refit the auxiliary drivebelt as described in Chapter 1.

**11** Refit the air inlet hose and mass airflow meter.

**12** Refill and bleed the power steering hydraulic system with reference to Section 18.

## 20 Steering rack rubber gaiter – renewal

**1** Apply the handbrake, then jack up the front of the vehicle and support it on axle stands (see *Jacking and vehicle support*). Remove the relevant roadwheel.

**2** Loosen the track rod end locknut on the track rod a quarter of a turn.

**3** Using a balljoint separator tool, disconnect the steering track rod end from the steering arm on the hub carrier **(see illustration)**.

**4** Unscrew the track rod end from the track rod, counting the exact number of turns necessary to remove it, to ensure correct refitting.

**5** Note the position of the track rod end locknut, then unscrew it from the track rod.

**20.3 Using a balljoint separator tool to release the track rod end balljoint**

**6** Wipe clean the track rod, then loosen the rubber gaiter retaining clips on the rod and steering gear housing.

**7** Release the gaiter from the housing groove and slide it from the track rod.

**8** Wipe clean the steering gear housing and track rod, and lubricate the track rod inner balljoint with lithium grease. Smear a little grease on the track rod to assist sliding on the new gaiter.

**9** Slide on the new gaiter and locate in the grooves. Fit and tighten the retaining clips. If new Saab clips are fitted, they must be tightened by crimping with a pair of pliers or pincers.

**10** Screw on the track rod end locknut to its previously-noted position.

**11** Screw on the track rod end by the number of turns previously noted.

**12** Locate the track rod end on the steering arm, and tighten the nut to the specified torque.

**13** Tighten the track rod end locknut to the specified torque.

**14** Refit the roadwheel and lower the vehicle to the ground.

**15** Have the front wheel alignment checked at the earliest opportunity.

## 21 Track rod end – removal and refitting

### Removal

**1** Apply the handbrake, then jack up the front of the vehicle and support it on axle stands (see *Jacking and vehicle support*). Remove the relevant roadwheel.

**2** On 2002-on models, note that the track rod ends are 'handed', and curve slightly rearwards in relation to the track rods. They are marked LH and RH on top of the balljoint for identification.

**3** Loosen the track rod end locknut on the track rod a quarter of a turn.

**4** Using a balljoint separator tool, disconnect the steering track rod end from the steering arm on the hub carrier.

**5** Unscrew the track rod end from the track rod, counting the exact number of turns necessary to remove it, to ensure correct refitting.

### Refitting

**6** Screw on the track rod end the exact number of turns noted on removal.

**7** Locate the track rod end stub on the steering arm, then tighten the nut to the specified torque.

**8** Tighten the track rod end locknut to the specified torque.

**9** Refit the roadwheel and lower the vehicle to the ground.

**10** Have the front wheel alignment checked at the earliest opportunity.

## 22 Wheel alignment and steering angles – general information

**1** Accurate front wheel alignment is essential to provide positive steering, and to prevent excessive tyre wear. Before considering the steering/suspension geometry, check that the tyres are correctly inflated, that the wheels are not buckled, and that the steering linkage and suspension joints are in good order, without slackness or wear. Alignment of the front subframe is also critical to the front suspension geometry.

**2** Wheel alignment consists of four factors **(see illustration)**:

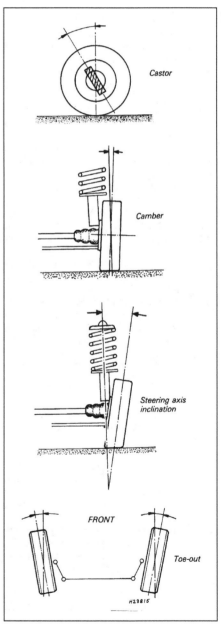

**21.2 Wheel alignment and steering angles**

**Camber** is the angle at which the front wheels are set from the vertical, when viewed from the front of the vehicle. 'Positive camber' is the amount (in degrees) that the wheels are tilted outward at the top of the vertical.

**Castor** is the angle between the steering axis and a vertical line, when viewed from each side of the car. 'Positive castor' is when the steering axis is inclined rearward at the top.

**Steering axis inclination** is the angle (when viewed from the front of the vehicle) between the vertical and an imaginary line drawn through the suspension strut upper mounting and the lower suspension arm balljoint.

**Toe setting** is the amount by which the distance between the front inside edges of the roadwheel rims (measured at hub height) differs from the diametrically-opposite distance measured between the rear inside edges of the roadwheel rims.

**3** Owing to the need for precision gauges to measure the small angles of the steering and suspension settings, the checking of camber, castor and steering axis inclination must be carried out by a service station having the necessary equipment. The camber readings vary according to body height as given in the Specifications; the heights are measured on the underbody, just inside of the roadwheels. Any deviation from the specified angle will be due to accident damage or gross wear in the suspension mountings.

**4** Two methods are available to the home mechanic for checking the front wheel toe setting. One method is to use a gauge to measure the distance between the front and rear inside edges of the roadwheels. The other method is to use a scuff plate, in which each front wheel is rolled across a movable plate which records any deviation, or scuff, of the tyre from the straight-ahead position as it moves across the plate. Relatively-inexpensive equipment of both types is available from accessory outlets.

**5** If, after checking the toe setting using whichever method is preferable, it is found that adjustment is necessary, proceed as follows.

**6** Turn the steering wheel onto full-left lock, and record the number of exposed threads on the right-hand track rod. Now turn the steering onto full-right lock, and record the number of threads on the left-hand track rod. If there are the same number of threads visible on both sides, then subsequent adjustment can be made equally on both sides. If there are more threads visible on one side than the other, it will be necessary to compensate for this during adjustment. After adjustment, there must be the same number of threads visible on each track rod. This is most important.

**7** To alter the toe setting, slacken the locknuts on the track rods, and turn the track rods using self-locking pliers to achieve the desired setting. Only turn the track rods by a quarter of a turn each time, and then recheck the setting.

**8** After adjustment, tighten the locknuts and check that the exposed threads on each track rod is the same. Reposition the steering gear rubber gaiters, to remove any twist caused by turning the track rods.

### Rear wheel alignment

**9** The rear wheel toe setting may also be checked and adjusted, but as this additionally requires alignment with the front wheels, it should be left to a service station having the necessary equipment.

# Chapter 11
# Bodywork and fittings

## Contents

## Degrees of difficulty

| Easy, suitable for novice with little experience  | Fairly easy, suitable for beginner with some experience  | Fairly difficult, suitable for competent DIY mechanic | Difficult, suitable for experienced DIY mechanic | Very difficult, suitable for expert DIY or professional  |
|---|---|---|---|---|

## Specifications

| Torque wrench settings | Nm | lbf ft |
|---|---|---|
| Front seats | 24 | 18 |
| Front seat belt: | | |
|    Reel | 45 | 33 |
|    Stalk | 33 | 24 |
| Rear bumper | 40 | 30 |
| Rear seat belt | 45 | 33 |
| Rear seat belt guide (Estate models) | 22 | 16 |
| Rear seat hinge pin (Estate models) | 24 | 18 |
| Side airbag | 7 | 5 |
| Side impact sensor | 5 | 4 |

## 1 General information

The vehicle's body is constructed from pressed-steel sections that are either spot-welded or seam-welded together. The overall rigidity of the body is increased by the use of stiffening beams built into the body panels, steel flanges in the window and door openings, and the application of adhesive in fixed glass joints.

The front subframe assembly provides mounting points for the engine/transmission unit, front suspension and steering gear. The front wings are bolted on, rather than welded on, allowing accident damage to be repaired easily.

The vehicle's underside is coated with underseal and an anti-corrosion compound. This treatment provides protection against the elements, and also serves as an effective sound insulation layer. The cabin, luggage area and engine compartment are also lined with bituminous felt and other sound-insulating materials, to provide further noise damping.

All models are fitted with electric windows at the front and rear. The window glass is raised and lowered by an electric motor, directly operating a window regulator.

Electrically-operated front seats are available as an option, with a control module located on the underside of the driver's seat. The module contains the memory for position and movement control, and a communication function for diagnosis. The system also

memorises the position of the electrically-operated rear view mirrors. With reverse gear engaged, it is possible to tilt down the passenger door mirror towards the rear wheel; when reverse gear is disengaged, the system automatically repositions the mirrors.

Remote control central locking is fitted to all models, and operates the locks on all four doors, the boot lid/tailgate, and the fuel filler cap. The lock mechanisms are actuated by servo motor units, and the system is controlled by an Electronic Control Unit (ECU).

All models are fitted with a driver's airbag located in the centre of the steering wheel, side airbags and seat belt tensioners on driver's and passenger's sides. The passenger airbag is an optional extra. A knee shield made of foam plastic, sheet metal and aluminium is attached to the steering column.

On the passenger side, the glovebox lid is reinforced with sheet metal to protect the passenger's knees.

The front seat belts incorporate automatic tensioners which operate in the event of a front-end collision. The airbags form part of the Supplementary Restraint System (SRS) which is controlled by an Electronic Control Unit (ECU). Sensors, built into the ECU casing and the front of the engine bay, are triggered in the event of a front-end collision, and prompt the ECU to activate the airbag(s) and the seat belt tensioners.

## 2 Maintenance – bodywork and underframe

The general condition of a vehicle's bodywork is the one thing that significantly affects its value. Maintenance is easy, but needs to be regular. Neglect, particularly after minor damage, can lead quickly to further deterioration and costly repair bills. It is important also to keep watch on those parts of the vehicle not immediately visible, for instance the underside, inside all the wheel arches, and the lower part of the engine compartment.

The basic maintenance routine for the bodywork is washing – preferably with a lot of water, from a hose. This will remove all the loose solids which may have stuck to the vehicle. It is important to flush these off in such a way as to prevent grit from scratching the finish. The wheel arches and underframe need washing in the same way, to remove any accumulated mud which will retain moisture and tend to encourage rust. Paradoxically enough, the best time to clean the underframe and wheel arches is in wet weather, when the mud is thoroughly wet and soft. In very wet weather, the underframe is usually cleaned of large accumulations automatically, and this is a good time for inspection.

Periodically, except on vehicles with a wax-based underbody protective coating, it is a good idea to have the whole of the underframe of the vehicle steam-cleaned, engine compartment included, so that a thorough inspection can be carried out to see what minor repairs and renovations are necessary. Steam-cleaning is available at many garages, and is necessary for the removal of the accumulation of oily grime, which sometimes is allowed to become thick in certain areas. If steam-cleaning facilities are not available, there are one or two excellent grease solvents available, which can be brush-applied; the dirt can then be simply hosed off. Note that these methods should not be used on vehicles with wax-based underbody protective coating, or the coating will be removed. Such vehicles should be inspected annually, preferably just prior to Winter, when the underbody should be washed down, and any damage to the wax

coating repaired. Ideally, a completely fresh coat should be applied. It would also be worth considering the use of such wax-based protection for injection into door panels, sills, box sections, etc, as an additional safeguard against rust damage, where such protection is not provided by the vehicle manufacturer.

After washing paintwork, wipe off with a chamois leather to give an unspotted clear finish. A coat of clear protective wax polish will give added protection against chemical pollutants in the air. If the paintwork sheen has dulled or oxidised, use a cleaner/polisher combination to restore the brilliance of the shine. This requires a little effort, but such dulling is usually caused because regular washing has been neglected. Care needs to be taken with metallic paintwork, as special non-abrasive cleaner/polisher is required to avoid damage to the finish. Always check that the door and ventilator opening drain holes and pipes are completely clear, so that water can be drained out. Brightwork should be treated in the same way as paintwork. Windscreens and windows can be kept clear of the smeary film which often appears, by the use of proprietary glass cleaner. Never use any form of wax or other body or chromium polish on glass.

## 3 Maintenance – upholstery and carpets

Mats and carpets should be brushed or vacuum-cleaned regularly, to keep them free of grit. If they are badly stained, remove them from the vehicle for scrubbing or sponging, and make quite sure they are dry before refitting. Seats and interior trim panels can be kept clean by wiping with a damp cloth. If they do become stained (which can be more apparent on light-coloured upholstery), use a little liquid detergent and a soft nail brush to scour the grime out of the grain of the material. Do not forget to keep the headlining clean in the same way as the upholstery. When using liquid cleaners inside the vehicle, do not over-wet the surfaces being cleaned. Excessive damp could get into the seams and padded interior, causing stains, offensive odours or even rot. If the inside of the vehicle gets wet accidentally, it is worthwhile taking some trouble to dry it out properly, particularly where carpets are involved. *Do not leave oil or electric heaters inside the vehicle for this purpose.*

## 4 Minor body damage – repair

### Minor scratches

If the scratch is very superficial, and does not penetrate to the metal of the bodywork,

repair is very simple. Lightly rub the area of the scratch with a paintwork renovator, or a very fine cutting paste, to remove loose paint from the scratch, and to clear the surrounding bodywork of wax polish. Rinse the area with clean water.

Apply touch-up paint to the scratch using a fine paint brush; continue to apply fine layers of paint until the surface of the paint in the scratch is level with the surrounding paintwork. Allow the new paint at least two weeks to harden, then blend it into the surrounding paintwork by rubbing the scratch area with a paintwork renovator or a very fine cutting paste. Finally, apply wax polish.

Where the scratch has penetrated right through to the metal of the bodywork, causing the metal to rust, a different repair technique is required. Remove any loose rust from the bottom of the scratch with a penknife, then apply rust-inhibiting paint, to prevent the formation of rust in the future. Using a rubber or nylon applicator, fill the scratch with bodystopper paste. If required, this paste can be mixed with cellulose thinners, to provide a very thin paste which is ideal for filling narrow scratches. Before the stopper-paste in the scratch hardens, wrap a piece of smooth cotton rag around the top of a finger. Dip the finger in cellulose thinners, and quickly sweep it across the surface of the stopper-paste in the scratch; this will ensure that the surface of the stopper-paste is slightly hollowed. The scratch can now be painted over as described earlier in this Section.

### Dents

When deep denting of the vehicle's bodywork has taken place, the first task is to pull the dent out, until the affected bodywork almost attains its original shape. There is little point in trying to restore the original shape completely, as the metal in the damaged area will have stretched on impact, and cannot be reshaped fully to its original contour. It is better to bring the level of the dent up to a point which is about 3 mm below the level of the surrounding bodywork. In cases where the dent is very shallow anyway, it is not worth trying to pull it out at all. If the underside of the dent is accessible, it can be hammered out gently from behind, using a mallet with a wooden or plastic head. Whilst doing this, hold a suitable block of wood firmly against the outside of the panel, to absorb the impact from the hammer blows and thus prevent a large area of the bodywork from being 'belled-out'.

Should the dent be in a section of the bodywork which has a double skin, or some other factor making it inaccessible from behind, a different technique is called for. Drill several small holes through the metal inside the area – particularly in the deeper section. Then screw long self-tapping screws into the holes, just sufficiently for them to gain a good purchase in the metal. Now the dent can be pulled out by pulling on the protruding heads of the screws with a pair of pliers.

The next stage of the repair is the removal of the paint from the damaged area, and from an inch or so of the surrounding 'sound' bodywork. This is accomplished most easily by using a wire brush or abrasive pad on a power drill, although it can be done just as effectively by hand, using sheets of abrasive paper. To complete the preparation for filling, score the surface of the bare metal with a screwdriver or the tang of a file, or alternatively, drill small holes in the affected area. This will provide a really good 'key' for the filler paste.

To complete the repair, see the Section on filling and respraying.

### Rust holes or gashes

Remove all paint from the affected area, and from an inch or so of the surrounding 'sound' bodywork, using an abrasive pad or a wire brush on a power drill. If these are not available, a few sheets of abrasive paper will do the job most effectively. With the paint removed, you will be able to judge the severity of the corrosion, and therefore decide whether to renew the whole panel (if this is possible) or to repair the affected area. New body panels are not as expensive as most people think, and it is often quicker and more satisfactory to fit a new panel than to attempt to repair large areas of corrosion.

Remove all fittings from the affected area, except those which will act as a guide to the original shape of the damaged bodywork (eg headlamp shells etc). Then, using tin snips or a hacksaw blade, remove all loose metal and any other metal badly affected by corrosion. Hammer the edges of the hole inwards, in order to create a slight depression for the filler paste.

Wire-brush the affected area to remove the powdery rust from the surface of the remaining metal. Paint the affected area with rust-inhibiting paint; if the back of the rusted area is accessible, treat this also.

Before filling can take place, it will be necessary to block the hole in some way. This can be achieved by the use of aluminium or plastic mesh, or aluminium tape.

Aluminium or plastic mesh, or glass-fibre matting is probably the best material to use for a large hole. Cut a piece to the approximate size and shape of the hole to be filled, then position it in the hole so that its edges are below the level of the surrounding bodywork. It can be retained in position by several blobs of filler paste around its periphery.

Aluminium tape should be used for small or very narrow holes. Pull a piece off the roll, trim it to the approximate size and shape required, then pull off the backing paper (if used) and stick the tape over the hole; it can be overlapped if the thickness of one piece is insufficient. Burnish down the edges of the tape with the handle of a screwdriver or similar, to ensure that the tape is securely attached to the metal underneath.

### Filling and respraying

Before using this Section, see the Sections on dent, deep scratch, rust holes and gash repairs.

Many types of bodyfiller are available, but generally speaking, those proprietary kits which contain a tin of filler paste and a tube of resin hardener are best for this type of repair. A wide, flexible plastic or nylon applicator will be found invaluable for imparting a smooth and well-contoured finish to the surface of the filler.

Mix up a little filler on a clean piece of card or board – measure the hardener carefully (follow the maker's instructions on the pack), otherwise the filler will set too rapidly or too slowly. Using the applicator, apply the filler paste to the prepared area; draw the applicator across the surface of the filler to achieve the correct contour and to level the surface. As soon as a contour that approximates to the correct one is achieved, stop working the paste – if you carry on too long, the paste will become sticky and begin to 'pick-up' on the applicator. Continue to add thin layers of filler paste at 20-minute intervals, until the level of the filler is just proud of the surrounding bodywork.

Once the filler has hardened, the excess can be removed using a metal plane or file. From then on, progressively-finer grades of abrasive paper should be used, starting with a 40-grade production paper, and finishing with a 400-grade wet-and-dry paper. Always wrap the abrasive paper around a flat rubber, cork, or wooden block – otherwise the surface of the filler will not be completely flat. During the smoothing of the filler surface, the wet-and-dry paper should be periodically rinsed in water. This will ensure that a very smooth finish is imparted to the filler at the final stage.

At this stage, the 'dent' should be surrounded by a ring of bare metal, which in turn should be encircled by the finely 'feathered' edge of the good paintwork. Rinse the repair area with clean water, until all of the dust produced by the rubbing-down operation has gone.

Spray the whole area with a light coat of primer – this will show up any imperfections in the surface of the filler. Repair these imperfections with fresh filler paste or bodystopper, and once more smooth the surface with abrasive paper. If bodystopper is used, it can be mixed with cellulose thinners, to form a really thin paste which is ideal for filling small holes. Repeat this spray-and-repair procedure until you are satisfied that the surface of the filler, and the feathered edge of the paintwork, are perfect. Clean the repair area with clean water, and allow to dry fully.

The repair area is now ready for final spraying. Paint spraying must be carried out in a warm, dry, windless and dust-free atmosphere. This condition can be created artificially if you have access to a large indoor working area, but if you are forced to work in the open, you will have to pick your day very carefully. If you are working indoors, dousing the floor in the work area with water will help to settle the dust which would otherwise be in the atmosphere. If the repair area is confined to one body panel, mask off the surrounding panels; this will help to minimise the effects of a slight mis-match in paint colours. Bodywork fittings (eg chrome strips, door handles etc) will also need to be masked off. Use genuine masking tape, and several thicknesses of newspaper, for the masking operations.

Before commencing to spray, agitate the aerosol can thoroughly, then spray a test area (an old tin, or similar) until the technique is mastered. Cover the repair area with a thick coat of primer; the thickness should be built up using several thin layers of paint, rather than one thick one. Using 400 grade wet-and-dry paper, rub down the surface of the primer until it is really smooth. While doing this, the work area should be thoroughly doused with water, and the wet-and-dry paper periodically rinsed in water. Allow to dry before spraying on more paint.

Spray on the top coat, again building up the thickness by using several thin layers of paint. Start spraying at the top of the repair area, and then, using a side-to-side motion, work downwards until the whole repair area and about 2 inches of the surrounding original paintwork is covered. Remove all masking material 10 to 15 minutes after spraying on the final coat of paint.

Allow the new paint at least two weeks to harden, then, using a paintwork renovator or a very fine cutting paste, blend the edges of the paint into the existing paintwork. Finally, apply wax polish.

### Plastic components

With the use of more and more plastic body components by the vehicle manufacturers (eg bumpers. spoilers, and in some cases major body panels), rectification of more serious damage to such items has become a matter of either entrusting repair work to a specialist in this field, or renewing complete components. Repair of such damage by the DIY owner is not really feasible, owing to the cost of the equipment and materials required for effecting such repairs. The basic technique involves making a groove along the line of the crack in the plastic, using a rotary burr in a power drill. The damaged part is then welded back together, using a hot air gun to heat up and fuse a plastic filler rod into the groove. Any excess plastic is then removed, and the area rubbed down to a smooth finish. It is important that a filler rod of the correct plastic is used, as body components can be made of a variety of different types (eg polycarbonate, ABS, polypropylene).

Damage of a less serious nature (abrasions, minor cracks etc) can be repaired by the DIY owner using a two-part epoxy filler repair. Once mixed in equal, this is used in similar

6.1 Removing the splash guards

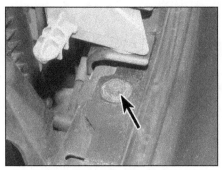

6.6 Front bumper mounting bolt located near the horns

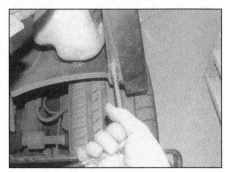

6.8 Unscrewing the nuts securing the front bumper to the front wings

fashion to the bodywork filler used on metal panels. The filler is usually cured in twenty to thirty minutes, ready for sanding and painting.

If the owner is renewing a complete component himself, or if he has repaired it with epoxy filler, he will be left with the problem of finding a suitable paint for finishing which is compatible with the type of plastic used. At one time, the use of a universal paint was not possible, owing to the complex range of plastics encountered in body component applications. Standard paints, generally speaking, will not bond to plastic or rubber satisfactorily, but suitable paints to match any plastic or rubber finish, can be obtained from dealers. However, it is now possible to obtain a plastic body parts finishing kit which consists of a pre-primer treatment, a primer and coloured top coat. Full instructions are normally supplied with a kit, but basically, the method of use is to first apply the pre-primer to the component concerned, and allow it to dry for up to 30 minutes. Then the primer is applied, and left to dry for about an hour before finally applying the special-coloured top coat. The result is a correctly-coloured component, where the paint will flex with the plastic or rubber, a property that standard paint does not normally posses.

## 5 Major body damage – repair

Where serious damage has occurred, or large areas need renewal due to neglect, it

means that complete new panels will need welding-in, and this is best left to professionals. If the damage is due to impact, it will also be necessary to check completely the alignment of the bodyshell, and this can only be carried out accurately by a dealer using special jigs. If the body is left misaligned, it is primarily dangerous, as the car will not handle properly, and secondly, uneven stresses will be imposed on the steering, suspension and possibly transmission, causing abnormal wear, or complete failure, particularly to such items as the tyres.

## 6 Front bumper – removal and refitting

### Removal

1 Apply the handbrake, then jack up the front of the vehicle and support it on axle stands (see *Jacking and vehicle support*). Undo the screws and remove the splash guards from under the radiator (see illustration).
2 With the bonnet open, remove the radiator grille as described in Section 8.
3 Remove the front direction indicator light units as described in Chapter 12.
4 Where fitted, remove both headlamp wiper arms as described in Chapter 12.
5 On 2002-on models, remove the battery cover, and also remove the headlight units as described in Chapter 12.
6 Working through the light unit apertures,

undo the two screws securing the front bumper to the bumper crossmember noting the locating pins. Also undo the two screws located near the horns (see illustration).
7 On 2002-on models, where applicable, remove the washer nozzles, using two small screwdrivers to release the clips. After disconnecting them, refit the clips.
8 Working through the access holes, undo the nuts securing the front bumper to the front wings (see illustration).
9 Working beneath the wheel arches on each side, undo the screws securing the wheel arch liners to the front bumper (see illustration).
10 Under the front of the vehicle, undo the screws and remove the splash shield from the front bumper and subframe.
11 Disconnect the wiring from the front foglights and from the exterior temperature sensor on the front bumper. If preferred, the sensor may be removed completely (see illustration).
12 With the aid of an assistant, release the outer corners of the front bumper from the wings and wheel arch liners, then withdraw the bumper from the crossmember on the front of the vehicle.
13 If the bumper is being renewed, remove the spoiler, number plate, foglights, and lower grille as applicable, and transfer them to the new bumper.

### Refitting

14 Make sure that the retaining tabs on the crossmember are undamaged and not bent.
15 With the aid of an assistant, locate the bumper onto the crossmember, making sure that the headlight wiper blade spindles and washer tubes are correctly engaged, and the bumper location pins engage with the holes in the bracket (see illustrations).
16 Press the bumper into position, then attach the outer corners, making sure that the metal reinforcements are located between the wings and liners.
17 Locate the bumper shell over the liners, then refit and tighten the screws securing the wheel arch liners.
18 Reconnect the wiring to the front foglights and exterior temperature sensor.
19 Refit the splash shield to the bumper lower edge and subframe.

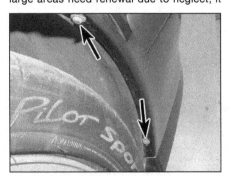

6.9 Screws securing the wheel arch liners to the front bumper

6.11 Removing the exterior temperature sensor from the front bumper

**20** Refit and tighten the nuts securing the front bumper to the front wings.
**21** On 2002-on models, refit the washer nozzles.
**22** Refit and tighten the screws securing the bumper to the crossmember.
**23** On 2002-on models, refit the headlight unit with reference to Chapter 12. Also, refit the battery cover.
**24** Refit the headlamp wiper arms and front direction indicator light units with reference to Chapter 12. Make sure that the indicator light units engage with the headlamps correctly.
**25** Refit the radiator grille (see Section 8), then lower the vehicle to the ground.

### 7  Rear bumper – removal and refitting

#### Removal

**1** With the boot lid/tailgate open, release the rubber weatherstrips and pull back the carpet at the rear of the luggage area, for access to the bumper mounting nuts.

#### Saloon models

**2** On models fitted with a towbar, unbolt the corner panels from under the rear light units.
**3** On 2002-on models, undo the screws and remove the rear valance cover plate.

#### Estate models

**4** Remove the storage compartments and insulating pads (see illustrations).

**7.4a  On Estate models, remove the storage compartments . . .**

**7.7 . . . then unscrew the mounting nuts on the rear valance**

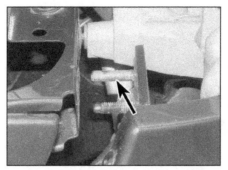

**6.15a  Front bumper locating pin**

**5** On models fitted with a towbar, remove the bumper upper shell, rear light units, disconnect the towbar wiring, and unscrew the bolts securing the towbar to the underbody.

#### All models

**6** At the front ends of the bumper on each side of the vehicle, undo the two screws securing the bumper to the wheel arches (see illustration).
**7** Unscrew and remove the rear bumper mounting nuts on the rear valance (see illustration).
**8** With the help of an assistant, pull the bumper rearwards while releasing it from the side brackets. Take care not to damage the vehicle paintwork. Where applicable, disconnect the wiring from the Saab Parking Assistance (SPA) system (see illustrations).

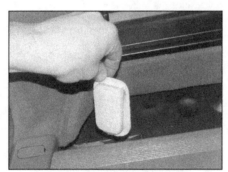

**7.4b . . . and insulating pads**

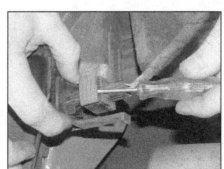

**7.8a  Prise up the lock . . .**

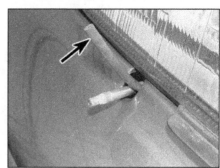

**6.15b  Make sure the washer tubes are located correctly**

#### Refitting

**9** Refitting is a reversal of removal, but tighten all nuts and bolts to the specified torque, where given. Make sure the bumper engages correctly with the side brackets.

### 8  Radiator grille – removal and refitting

#### Pre-2002 models

#### Removal

**1** With the bonnet open, unscrew the centre pins/screws and carefully prise out the upper retaining fasteners (see illustrations).
**2** Lift the grille from the lower holes (see illustration).

**7.6  Undo the front securing screws . . .**

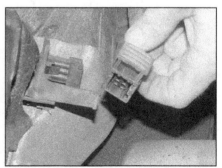

**7.8b . . . and disconnect the wiring for the Saab Parking Assistance (SPA) system**

**8.1a Unscrew the centre pins . . .**

**8.1b . . . and prise out the fasteners . . .**

**8.2 . . . then lift the radiator grille from the lower holes**

### Refitting

**3** Locate the grille in the lower holes.
**4** Insert the upper retaining fasteners, then press in the centre pins or refit the screws to secure.

### 2002-on models

#### Removal

**5** To remove the centre grille, with the bonnet open, lift the centre of the centre grille to release the bottom edge, then pull the grille forward and downward to release the upper spring clips **(see illustration)**.
**6** To remove the side grilles, reach in through the centre grille aperture and bend up the lower clips. The grilles can then be withdrawn **(see illustration)**.
**7** To remove the lower grille, apply the handbrake, then jack up the front of the vehicle and support it on axle stands (see *Jacking and vehicle support*). Remove the splash guard from under the radiator, detach the exterior temperature sensor, then use a screwdriver to depress the clips, and carefully withdraw the grille.

#### Refitting

**8** Refitting is a reversal of removal.

---

### 9 Bonnet, struts and hinges – removal and refitting

### Bonnet

#### Removal

**1** Support the bonnet in its open position, then place some cloth rags or card between the rear edge of the bonnet and the windscreen valance.
**2** Release the sound insulation, and disconnect the washer tube at the connection. Unclip and remove the tubing from the bonnet hinge.
**3** Using a pencil, mark the position of the hinges on the bonnet.
**4** With the help of an assistant, support both sides of the bonnet, then disconnect the gas-filled struts by prising out the special springs. Lower the struts onto the inner wings.

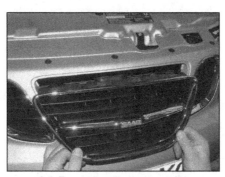

**8.5 Removing the centre grille (2002-on models)**

**5** Unscrew the mounting nuts and carefully remove the bonnet from the hinges. Place it away from the vehicle in a safe position, taking care not to damage the paintwork. Note that it is only necessary to loosen the upper hinge bolts, since the bolt hole is open-ended.
**6** If necessary, remove the weatherseal, sound insulation and washer jets from the old bonnet, and transfer them to the new unit.

#### Refitting

**7** Refitting is a reversal of removal. When first closing the bonnet, lower it slowly and check that the striker is aligned with the lock. Also check that the bonnet is positioned centrally between the front wings. If necessary, loosen the bolts and reposition the bonnet on the hinges before fully closing the bonnet. Tighten the bolts on completion. Check that the front of the bonnet is level with the front wings, and if necessary screw in or out the rubber stops located in the front corners of the engine compartment – it may also be necessary to adjust the two strikers located on the underside of the bonnet. The rear height is adjusted by loosening the bolts securing the hinges to the body.

### Struts

#### Removal

**8** Open the bonnet. If removing just one strut, the remaining strut will hold the bonnet up, however if removing both struts an assistant will be required to hold the bonnet open. Alternatively, use a length of wood to prop the bonnet open.

**8.6 Removing a side grille (2002-on models)**

**9** Using a screwdriver, prise the spring clip from the top of the strut and disconnect the strut from the ball-pin.
**10** Disconnect the bottom of the strut from the lower ball-pin by prising out the spring clip.

#### Refitting

**11** Refitting is a reversal of removal.

### Hinges

#### Removal

**12** Remove the bonnet as described earlier in this Section.
**13** Using a pencil, mark the position of the hinge on the body, then unscrew the bolts and remove the hinge.

#### Refitting

**14** Refitting is a reversal of removal, but tighten the bolts securely and adjust the bonnet as described earlier.

---

### 10 Bonnet release cable and lever – removal and refitting

### Removal

**1** With the bonnet open, remove the radiator grille as described in Section 8.
**2** Loosen the clamp screws on the crossmember, and release the main outer cable and intermediate outer cable.
**3** Loosen the inner cable end stop screws on both locks, and pull out the cable from the

**10.6 Bonnet release lever and cable**

lock spring eyes. If necessary, the removed items may be refitted to the cable and the end stop screws retightened.

**4** Remove the windscreen wiper arms (see Chapter 12), and remove the rubber seals from the spindles.

**5** Pull off the weatherstrip located at the rear of the engine compartment, then undo the screws and remove the scuttle cover by lifting its front edge and pulling it from the rear retaining clips.

**6** Inside the vehicle, remove the lower facia trim panel on the driver's side for access to the lever **(see illustration)**.

**7** Remove the kick-plate from the inner sill panel on the driver's side footwell, and fold back the carpet.

**8** Depress the top and bottom of the bonnet lever holder, and release the bonnet lever by sliding it rearwards.

**9** Pull the lever and cable into the passenger compartment and withdraw from the vehicle. As an aid to refitting, tie a length of string to the front end of the cable and leave it in position until the refitting procedure. To prevent the cable catching, wrap adhesive tape around its sharp edges.

### Refitting

**10** Refitting is a reversal of removal, but adjust the position of the end stops to provide approximately 1.0 mm clearance between the stop and return spring.

**11** Close the bonnet and check that the cable operates the release springs correctly.

## 11 Bonnet lock – removal and refitting

### Removal

**1** With the bonnet open, remove the radiator grille as described in Section 8.

**2** Loosen the inner cable end stop screws on both locks, and pull out the cable until it is released from the lock spring eyes.

**3** Unscrew the mounting bolts and remove the bonnet lock(s) from the crossmember.

### Refitting

**4** Refitting is a reversal of removal, but adjust the position of the end stops to provide

approximately 1.0 mm clearance between the stop and return spring. Lubricate the spring contacts with a little grease.

## 12 Doors – removal, refitting and adjustment

### *Front*

#### Removal

**1** Before removing the door, check the gap between the door and surrounding bodywork with the door shut. Any adjustment to the hinges on the A-pillar can then be made with the door removed, as the adjustment may not be possible with the door fitted. Similarly, adjustment of the front edge of the door in relation to the front wing is best achieved with the door removed.

**2** Open the door, then prise out the rubber grommet and disconnect the wiring located between the door and A-pillar.

**3** Unbolt the check strap from the A-pillar **(see illustration)**.

**4** Mark the position of the door hinge plates on the A-pillar hinge brackets.

**5** With the help of an assistant, unscrew first the lower mounting bolt then the upper bolt, and withdraw the door from the A-pillar hinge brackets **(see illustration)**. Take care not to damage the paintwork.

#### Refitting and adjustment

**6** Refitting is a reversal of removal. Check

that the gap between the door and surrounding bodywork is equal when the door is shut, and where necessary remove the door to make the adjustment. Note, however, that adjustment of the door front edge in relation to the front wing is possible with the door fitted, but with the front wing removed. To adjust the vertical or horizontal position of the door, loosen the hinge bracket bolts on the A-pillar (there are 3 bolts per hinge); to adjust the position of the door front edge, loosen the nuts securing the door hinge plates to the hinge brackets. Tighten all nuts and bolts to their specified torque, where given.

**7** If only minor adjustment is necessary, it is possible to remove the sleeves from the nuts securing the door hinge plates to the hinge brackets. With the door open, unscrew the nuts and remove the sleeves, then refit the nuts, adjust the door position as necessary and retighten the nuts.

**8** Check that the door lock aligns correctly with the striker on the B-pillar as the door is closed, and if necessary adjust the striker by loosening the two screws **(see illustration)**. Do not fully unscrew the screws, as the spacer plate will drop down inside the B-pillar.

### *Rear*

#### Removal

**9** Open the front door on the relevant side in order to access the rear door wiring harness rubber grommet in the B-pillar. Remove the rubber grommet and disconnect the wiring **(see illustration)**.

**12.3 Front door check strap retaining bolt**

**12.5 Door hinge bolt**

**12.8 Front door striker on the B-pillar**

**12.9 Disconnecting the rear door wiring at the B-pillar**

**12.10 Rear door check strap mounting bolt on the B-pillar**

**12.12 Rear door upper hinge plate bolt**

**12.14 Rear door striker on the C-pillar**

10 Open the rear door and unbolt the check strap from the B-pillar **(see illustration)**.
11 Mark the position of the door hinge plates on the B-pillar hinge brackets
12 With the help of an assistant, unscrew first the lower mounting bolt then the upper bolt, and withdraw the door from the B-pillar hinge brackets **(see illustration)**. Take care not to damage the paintwork.

**Refitting and adjustment**

13 Refitting is a reversal of removal. Check that the gap between the door and surrounding bodywork is equal when the door is shut. To adjust the vertical or horizontal position of the door, loosen the hinge bracket bolts on the B-pillar (there are 2 upper and 3 lower bolts); to adjust the position of the door front edge, loosen the nuts securing the door hinge plates to the hinge brackets. Tighten all nuts and bolts to their specified torque, where given.

14 Check that the door lock aligns correctly with the striker on the C-pillar as the door is closed **(see illustration)**, and if necessary adjust the striker by loosening the two screws. Do not fully unscrew the screws, as the spacer plate will drop down inside the C-pillar.

## 13 Door inner trim panel – removal and refitting

### *Front door*

#### Removal

1 Carefully prise the curved trim panel from the upper half of the door (around the window glass opening) using a wide-bladed screwdriver. The clips may pull out of the metal frame, in which case they should be

removed from the trim and pressed back into position.
2 Disconnect the wiring plug for the exterior door mirror and remove the curved trim panel.
3 Prise out the plastic cover, undo the screw, then remove the interior door handle and unclip it from the operating rod **(see illustrations)**.
4 Prise out the plastic covers, then undo the screws and remove the door grip **(see illustrations)**.
5 Using a wide-bladed screwdriver, carefully prise out the clips and release the trim panel from the door **(see illustration)**. Take care not to damage the trim panel or break the clips by prising as near to the clip positions as possible.
6 With the clips released, lift the trim panel upwards over the locking button.
7 Disconnect the wiring, and release the door courtesy light from the bottom of the trim panel **(see illustration)**. Also disconnect the wiring from the electric window switch.

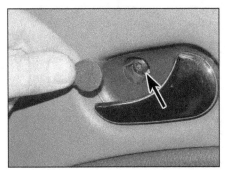

**13.3a Prise out the cover and undo the screw . . .**

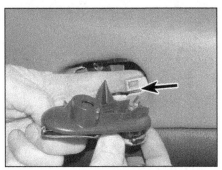

**13.3b . . . then unclip the interior door handle**

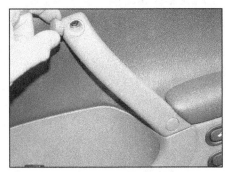

**13.4a Prise out the plastic covers . . .**

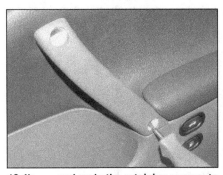

**13.4b . . . and undo the retaining screws to remove the door grip**

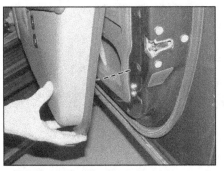

**13.5 Removing the front door trim panel**

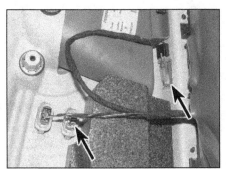

**13.7 Disconnect the wiring from the trim panel**

**13.10  Removing the curved trim panel**

**13.11a  Prise out the plastic cover . . .**

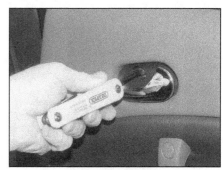

**13.11b  . . . undo the screw . . .**

**8** If necessary carefully pull the waterproof membrane from the door inner panel.

### Refitting

**9** Refitting is a reversal of removal.

### *Rear door*

#### Removal

**10** Carefully prise the curved trim panel from the upper half of the door (around the window glass opening) using a wide-bladed screwdriver **(see illustration)**. The clips may pull out of the metal frame, in which case they should be removed from the trim and pressed back into position.

**11** Prise out the plastic cover, undo the screw, then remove the interior door handle and unclip it from the operating rod **(see illustrations)**.

**12** Prise out the plastic covers, then undo the screws and remove the door grip **(see illustrations)**.

**13** Using a wide-bladed screwdriver, carefully

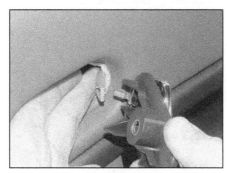

**13.11c  . . . then unhook the interior door handle**

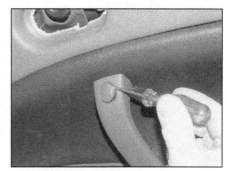

**13.12a  Prise out the plastic covers . . .**

prise out the clips securing the trim panel to the door **(see illustration)**. Take care not to damage the trim panel or break the clips by prising as near to the clip positions as possible.

**14** With the clips released, lift the trim panel upwards over the locking button **(see illustration)**.

**15** Disconnect the wiring from the electrically-operated window switch and courtesy light; if necessary, remove the switch and courtesy light from the trim panel **(see illustrations)**.

**16** If necessary carefully cut the waterproof membrane from the door inner panel **(see illustration)**.

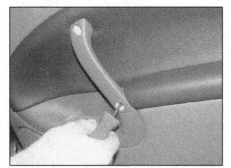

**13.12b  . . . and unscrew the door grip retaining screws**

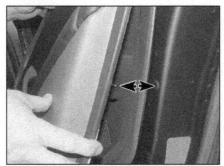

**13.13  Releasing the trim panel from the rear door**

**13.14  Removing the rear door trim panel**

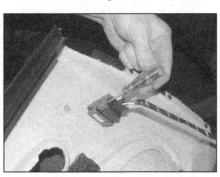

**13.15a  Disconnect the wiring from the electrically-operated window switch . . .**

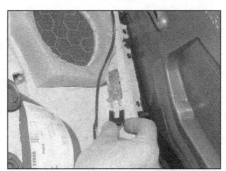

**13.15b  . . . and courtesy light**

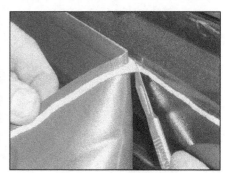

**13.16  Cutting the waterproof membrane from the door inner panel**

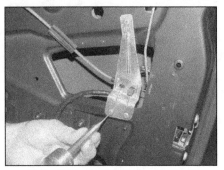

**14.8a Drive out the rivet centre pin remains . . .**

**14.8b . . . then drill out the rivets . . .**

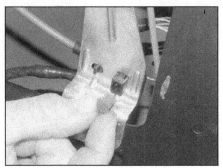

**14.8c . . . detach the cable . . .**

### Refitting

**17** Refitting is a reversal of removal.

## 14 Door handle and lock components – removal and refitting

### Interior door handle

**1** Prise the plastic cover from the inner door handle, then undo the screw and unclip the handle from the operating rod.
**2** Refitting is a reversal of removal.

### Front door lock

**3** Open the window, then remove the door trim and waterproof membrane as described in Section 13.

**4** Slightly loosen the door exterior mirror retaining screws to release the front of the exterior glass weatherstrip, then undo the screw from its rear end and withdraw the weatherstrip from the door.
**5** Lower the window so that the lower glass channel is visible in the large inner door panel aperture. Using tape, support the glass in this position while the winder arms are disconnected from the lower channel.
**6** Disconnect the window winder arms from the rollers in the glass lower channel by pulling out the clips, then using a wide-bladed screwdriver to prise out the arms. Insert the screwdriver near the ball, between the arm and channel, to prevent deforming the arm.
**7** Carefully lift and tilt the rear of the glass, and withdraw it from the outside of the door frame. Position it in a safe place.

**8** The window regulator cable support bracket must now be removed. To do this, drive out the rivet centre pin remains, then drill out the rivets, remove the bracket and release the cable, and unhook it from the lock **(see illustrations)**.
**9** Undo the nut and bolt from the security guard plate, then undo the screws securing the bottom of the rear glass channel to the door, pull the channel forwards, and withdraw the guard plate **(see illustrations)**.
**11** Undo the lock mounting screws from the rear edge of the door, then tilt the lock and disconnect the pullrods. At the same time, disconnect the exterior handle pushrod **(see illustrations)**.
**12** Disconnect the wiring and withdraw the front door lock from the door **(see illustrations)**. Recover the lock seal.

**14.8d . . . remove the bracket . . .**

**14.8e . . . and unhook the cable from the lock**

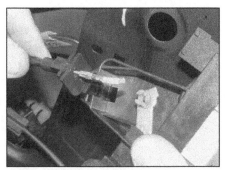

**14.9a Unscrew the nut and bolt securing the security guard plate . . .**

**14.9b . . . and unscrew the window rear glass channel mounting bolts . . .**

**14.9c . . . then remove the guard plate**

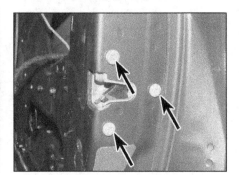

**14.11a Undo the lock mounting screws . . .**

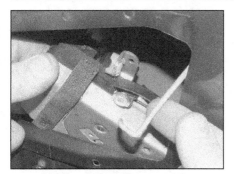

14.11b . . . then disconnect the pullrods . . .

14.11c . . . and exterior door handle pushrod

14.12a Disconnect the wiring . . .

13 Refitting is a reversal of removal, however, lightly grease the winder rollers and channel, then refit the clips to the rollers. With the clips refitted, press the arm balls fully into the rollers until they are heard to engage. Before refitting the door trim, make sure that the lock operates correctly. Use new rivets to secure the metal support bracket.

### Rear door lock

14 Remove the door trim and waterproof membrane as described in Section 13.
15 Undo the lock mounting screws from the rear edge of the door (see illustration).
16 Release the locking knob and inner handle cables from their support clips (see illustrations).
17 Unhook the exterior handle locking rod from the lock, then withdraw the rear door lock through the aperture in the inner door panel (see illustration).

14.12b . . . and remove the front door lock

18 Disconnect the wiring from the lock (see illustration).
19 Unhook the locking knob operating cable. Unhook the interior door handle operating cable from the lock (see illustrations).

14.15 Removing the rear door lock mounting screws

20 Refitting is a reversal of removal.

### Exterior door handle

21 Remove the door lock as described earlier in this Section.

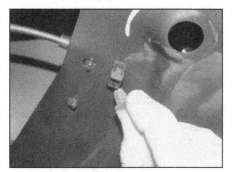

14.16a Release the clips . . .

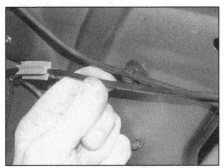

14.16b . . . and unclip the cables

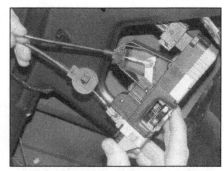

14.17 Withdraw the rear door lock . . .

14.18 . . . and disconnect the wiring

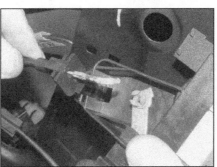

14.19a Unhook the locking knob operating cable . . .

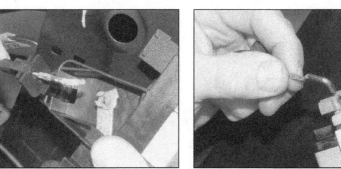

14.19b . . . and interior door handle operating cable

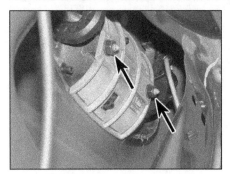

14.22a Unscrew the nuts . . .

14.22b . . . and remove the security plate

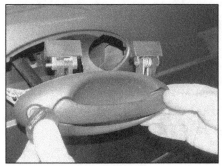

14.24 Removing the exterior handle from the front door

14.25 Removing the exterior door handle from the rear door

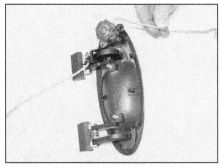

14.28a Unhook the operating rod . . .

**22** Reach through the aperture in the door inner panel, unscrew the nut(s) and remove the security plate from the exterior door handle **(see illustrations)**.

### Front doors

**23** Insert the ignition key in the door lock and turn it anti-clockwise. Tilt the rear of the handle, so that the end of the operating pullrod locates in the lever groove, then pull up the handle and withdraw it as far as possible from the door. Take care not to damage the paintwork; if necessary tape some card to the door as a precaution.
**24** Hold the handle away from the door, then undo the lock cylinder holder retaining screw. Ideally, use an angled screwdriver to do this. Rotate the lock cylinder holder clockwise (viewed from the rear of the handle) while pressing it through the handle. Unhook the lock cylinder lever from the operating rod, and

withdraw the exterior door handle **(see illustration)**. Recover the gasket.

### Rear doors

**25** Withdraw the door handle from the door panel **(see illustration)**. Recover the gasket.

### All doors

**26** Refitting is a reversal of removal.

### *Front door lock cylinder*

**27** Remove the front door exterior door handle and lock cylinder holder as described earlier.
**28** On some models, the cylinder is separate from the holder and is retained by screws, however on other models, the holder and cylinder are supplied as one unit. Where applicable, unhook the operating rod, undo the screws and remove the lock cylinder **(see illustrations)**.
**29** Refitting is a reversal of removal.

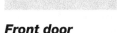

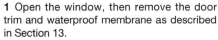

## 15 Door window glass – removal and refitting

### *Front door*

#### Removal

**1** Open the window, then remove the door trim and waterproof membrane as described in Section 13.
**2** Loosen slightly the door exterior mirror retaining screws to release the front of the exterior glass weatherstrip, then undo the screw from its rear end and withdraw the weatherstrip from the door.
**3** Lower the window so that the lower glass channel is visible in the large inner door panel aperture. To do this, temporarily reconnect the switch to the winder motor, however, keep hands and clothing clear of the winder while repositioning it, and disconnect the switch before continuing. Using tape, support the glass in this position while the winder arms are disconnected from the lower channel.
**4** Disconnect the window winder arms from the rollers in the glass lower channel by pulling out the clips, then using a wide-bladed screwdriver to prise out the arms. Insert the screwdriver near the ball, between the arm and channel, to prevent deforming the arm.
**5** Carefully lift and tilt the rear of the glass, and withdraw it from the outside of the door frame **(see illustration)**.
**6** Remove the rollers from the channel.

14.28b . . . undo the screws . . .

14.28c . . . and remove the lock cylinder

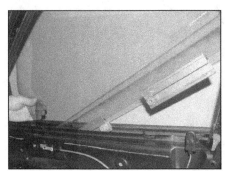

15.5 Removing the front door window glass

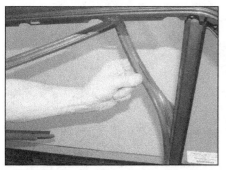

**15.9  Pull the weatherstrip from the outer edge of the window aperture**

**15.13a  Undo the screw . . .**

**15.13b  . . . then carefully prise out the weatherstrip. Note the tape to protect the paintwork**

**15.14  Removing the window rear guide channel screws**

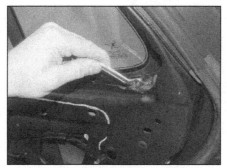

**15.15a  Unscrew the mounting nuts . . .**

**15.15b  . . . and remove the fixed window from the rear door**

## Refitting

**7** Refitting is a reversal of removal, however, lightly grease the winder rollers and channel, then refit the clips to the rollers. With the clips refitted, press the arm balls fully into the rollers until they are heard to engage.

## *Rear door*

### Removal

**8** Open the window, then remove the door trim and waterproof membrane as described in Section 13.
**9** Carefully pull the weatherstrip from the outer edge of the window aperture **(see illustration)**.
**10** Lower the window so that the lower glass channel is visible in the inner door panel aperture. To do this, temporarily reconnect the switch to the winder motor, however, keep

**15.16  Removing the window glass from the rear door**

hands and clothing clear of the winder while repositioning it, and disconnect the switch before continuing. Using tape, support the glass in this position while the winder arm is disconnected from the lower channel.
**11** Disconnect the window winder arm from the glass lower channel by removing the clip from the roller, then using a wide-bladed screwdriver to prise out the arm. Insert the screwdriver near the ball, between the arm and channel, to prevent the arm deforming.
**12** Lower the glass to the bottom of the door.
**13** Undo the screw securing the front of the glass weatherstrip to the door frame, then carefully prise out the weatherstrip. Use tape to protect the paintwork **(see illustrations)**.
**14** Unscrew and remove the window rear guide channel upper and lower screws **(see illustration)**.
**15** Unscrew the mounting nuts from the fixed window, then press the window forward and withdraw it upwards from the door **(see illustrations)**. Take care not to damage the paintwork.
**16** Lift up the door window glass and withdraw it from the outside of the door **(see illustration)**.

### Refitting

**17** Refitting is a reversal of removal, however, lightly grease the winder roller and channel before inserting the window glass in the door. With the spring clip in position, press the ball of the winder arm into the clip until a 'double click' is heard to engage. On completion, check the operation of the window.

## 16  Door window regulator – removal and refitting

## *Front door*

### Removal

**1** Open the window, then remove the door trim and waterproof membrane as described in Section 13.
**2** Lower the window so that the lower glass channel is visible in the large aperture at the bottom of the inner door panel **(see illustration)**. To do this, temporarily reconnect the switch to the winder motor, however, keep the hands clear of the winder while repositioning it, and disconnect the switch before continuing. Using tape, support the

**16.2  Lower the glass channel into the aperture . . .**

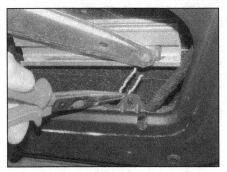

16.3a . . . then pull out the retaining clips . . .

16.3b . . . and prise the arms from the rollers

16.4a Drive out the remains of the rivet centre pins . . .

glass in this position while the winder arms are disconnected from the lower channel.

**3** Disconnect the window winder arms from the rollers in the glass lower channel by pulling out the clips, then using a wide-bladed screwdriver to prise the arms from the rollers. Insert the screwdriver near the ball, between the arm and channel, to prevent deforming the arm (**see illustrations**).

**4** Drive out the remains of the rivet centre pins securing the window regulator to the door, then drill out the rivets (**see illustrations**).

**5** Disconnect the window regulator wiring at the plug (**see illustration**).

**6** Mark the regulator guide rail nut positions on the inner door panel, then unscrew and remove them together with the regulator mounting nuts (**see illustration**).

**7** Withdraw the regulator through the large hole in the door inner panel (**see illustration**).

### Refitting and adjustment

**8** Refitting is a reversal of removal, but use new rivets to secure the regulator. Lightly grease the winder rollers and channel before inserting the glass in the door. With the clips refitted, press the arm balls fully into the rollers until they are heard to engage.

**9** Check that the window glass is aligned with the door frame when closed, and if necessary adjust it as follows. Position the glass half open, then loosen the guide rail screws and push the glass firmly to the rear so that its rear edge is fully engaged with the rear channel. With the glass held in this position, fully tighten the screws.

### *Rear door*

#### Removal

**10** Open the window, then remove the door

trim and waterproof membrane as described in Section 13.

**11** Lower the window so that the lower glass channel is visible in the inner door panel aperture. To do this, temporarily reconnect the switch to the winder motor, however, keep the hands clear of the winder while repositioning it, and disconnect the switch before continuing. Using tape, support the glass in this position while the winder arm is disconnected from the lower channel (**see illustrations**).

**12** Disconnect the window winder arm from the glass lower channel by removing the clip from the roller, then using a wide-bladed screwdriver to prise out the arm. Insert the screwdriver near the ball, between the arm and channel, to prevent the arm deforming (**see illustrations**).

**13** Lower the glass to the bottom of the door.

16.4b . . . then drill out the rivets

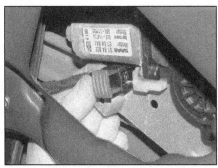

16.5 Disconnecting the window regulator wiring

16.6 Undo the mounting nuts . . .

16.7 . . . and withdraw the regulator through the door inner panel aperture

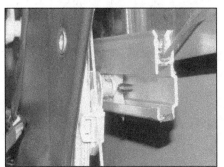

16.11a Lower the window glass channel into the door aperture . . .

16.11b . . . then use tape to support the glass

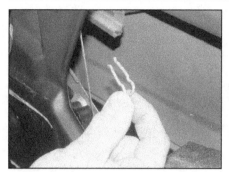

**16.12a  Remove the clip from the roller . . .**

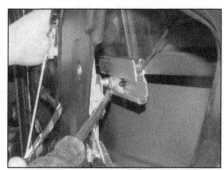

**16.12b  . . . then prise out the arm using a screwdriver**

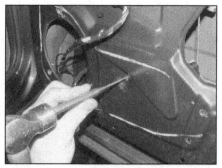

**16.15a  Drive out the rivet centre pins . . .**

**16.15b  . . . then drill out the rivets**

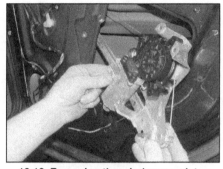

**16.16  Removing the window regulator through the door aperture**

**16.17  Secure the window regulator with new rivets**

14 Disconnect the window regulator wiring at the plug.

15 Drive out the remains of the rivet centre pins securing the window regulator to the door, then drill out the rivets **(see illustrations)**.

16 Lower the regulator and withdraw the upper part through the hole in the inner door panel **(see illustration)**. **Note:** *The motor and regulator cannot be separated.*

### Refitting

17 Refitting is a reversal of removal, but use new rivets to secure the regulator **(see illustration)**. Lightly grease the winder roller and channel before inserting the window glass in the door. With the spring clip in position, press the ball of the winder arm into the roller until a 'double click' is heard to engage. On completion, check the operation of the window. No adjustment is possible for the rear window glass.

**17  Boot lid, support struts and hinges –**
removal and refitting

## Boot lid

### Removal

1 Open the boot lid, then reach into the rear left-hand corner of the luggage compartment and open the hatch for access to the boot lid wiring harness connector. Disconnect the plug from the connector.

2 Prise out the wiring grommet from the body

and release it from the hinge. Pull the wiring up from the luggage compartment.

3 With the help of an assistant, support the boot lid open, then prise out the clips and disconnect the support strut upper ends from the hinges.

4 Using a pencil, mark the outline of the hinges on the boot lid **(see illustration)**.

5 Unscrew and remove the lower nuts securing the hinges to the boot lid, then loosen the upper bolts and carefully lift the boot lid from the hinges. The upper bolt holes in the hinges are open-ended.

### Refitting and adjustment

6 With the upper bolts loosely fitted, lower the boot lid onto them and refit the lower bolts. Tighten the bolts securely.

7 When first closing the boot lid, lower it slowly and check that the striker is aligned with the lock – if not, loosen the bolt(s),

reposition the striker, then tighten the bolt(s) **(see illustration)**. Check that the boot lid is positioned central in its body aperture. Forward and backward adjustment is made by loosening the nuts and repositioning the boot lid on the hinges. Height adjustment of the front of the boot lid is made by repositioning the front end of the hinges on the body. Height adjustment of the rear of the boot lid (when it is closed) is made by turning the two rubber buffers in or out. Height adjustment of the **entire** boot lid is made by loosening the bolts securing the hinges to the body. Tighten all nuts and bolts.

8 Reconnect the support strut upper ends to the hinges and refit the clips.

9 Insert the wiring into the luggage compartment, and refit the wiring grommet. Attach the grommet to the hinge.

10 Reconnect the wiring plug and close the hatch.

**17.4  Boot lid hinge and mounting nuts**

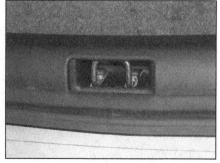

**17.7  Boot lid striker**

**17.11a Boot lid support strut lower mounting . . .**

### Support struts

#### Removal

**11** Support the boot lid in its open position, and note the fitted positions of the support struts. The piston end of the strut faces downwards **(see illustrations)**.
**12** Prise out the clips and disconnect the support strut upper and lower ends from the hinges. Withdraw the strut from the vehicle.

#### Refitting

**13** Refitting is a reversal of removal.

### Hinges

#### Removal

**14** Remove the boot lid as described earlier in this Section.
**15** Prise out the clip and disconnect the support strut lower end from the hinge. Place the strut to one side.

**18.2 Removing the tailgate hinge covers/seals**

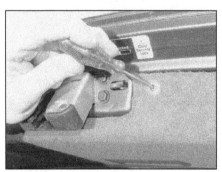

**18.5a Depress the centre pins . . .**

**17.11b . . . and upper mounting**

**16** Using a pencil, mark the outline of the hinge on the body, then unscrew the bolts and remove the hinge.

#### Refitting

**17** Refitting is a reversal of removal, but tighten the bolts securely and adjust the boot lid as described earlier.

---

### 18 Tailgate, support struts and hinges – removal and refitting

### Tailgate

#### Removal

**1** With the tailgate open, place some cloth rags or card between the tailgate and the bodywork to prevent any damage.
**2** Remove the covers/seals from the tailgate

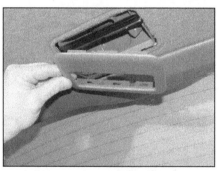

**18.4 Removing the surround from the inner door handle**

**18.5b . . . and remove the fasteners . . .**

hinges **(see illustration)**, then prise apart and remove the wiring duct.
**3** Carefully prise out the covers then undo the screws and remove the upper trim mouldings from around the rear window aperture inside the tailgate.
**4** Remove the tailgate leading lights (see Chapter 12, Section 5), then undo the screws and remove the inner hand grip. Also carefully prise off the surround from the inner door handle **(see illustration)**.
**5** Release the fasteners from the lower edge of the trim panel be depressing their centre pins, then pull down the top of the panel to release it from the upper clips, and pull it to the rear to release the guide pin at the hand grip **(see illustrations)**.
**6** Note the fitted location of the wiring harness, then disconnect it and release it from the support clips. Also, disconnect the rear washer tube. Carefully extract the wiring from the tailgate at the hinges. **Note:** *If it is required to remove the tailgate complete with all the wiring, the D-pillar trim must be removed and the rear headlining lowered for access to the wiring connectors and earth cables.*
**7** Using a pencil, mark the outline of the hinges on the tailgate.
**8** With the help of an assistant, support the weight of the tailgate, then unscrew the bolts and withdraw the tailgate from the hinges.

#### Refitting

**9** Locate the tailgate on the hinges and insert the bolts. With the tailgate aligned with the previously-made marks, tighten the mounting bolts securely. When first closing the tailgate, lower it slowly and check that the striker is aligned with the lock – if not, loosen the bolt, reposition the striker, then tighten the bolt. Check that the tailgate is positioned central in its body aperture. Forward, backward and sideway adjustment is made by loosening the bolts and repositioning the boot lid on the hinges. Upward and downward adjustment is made by loosening the bolts securing the hinges to the body, however, it will be necessary to remove the D-pillar trim and lower the rear headlining. Check that the two rubber support pads located above the rear tail light positions, are adjusted so that the tailgate is supported adequately when closed.

**18.5c . . . then release the trim panel from the upper retaining clips**

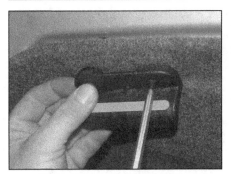

19.1a Remove the handgrip . . .

19.1b . . . then depress their centres . . .

19.1c . . . and remove the fastenings . . .

## Support struts

### Removal

**10** Remove the D-pillar trim, the rear headlining trim, and the two mouldings between the C- and D-pillars. Extract the clips from the headlining, and also remove the cargo safety net holders. Carefully bend down the rear of the headlining for access to the strut mountings.
**11** Support the tailgate in its open position, and note the fitted position of the support struts. Unbolt the metal yokes from over the front mountings of the struts on the roof panel crossmember.
**12** Prise out the clips and disconnect the support strut upper and lower ends from the hinge and body. Withdraw the strut from the vehicle.

### Refitting

**13** Refitting is a reversal of removal, but lubricate the strut ball sockets with grease before refitting them.

## Hinges

### Removal

**14** Remove the tailgate complete with wiring as described earlier in this Section.
**15** Prise out the clips and disconnect the rear ends of the support struts from the hinges.
**16** Working through the hole in the roof rear crossmember, unscrew and remove the hinge inner mounting bolts.
**17** Mark the positions of the tailgate rubber buffers, then unbolt and remove them.

**18** Pull down the rubber weatherstrip from the upper half of the tailgate body aperture, and remove the side and upper cover plates.
**19** Unscrew the mounting bolts and withdraw the hinges from the roof rear crossmember.

### Refitting

**20** Refitting is a reversal of removal, but lubricate the strut ball sockets with grease before refitting them. Adjust the tailgate as described earlier in this Section.

---

### 19 Boot lid/tailgate lock components – removal and refitting

## Boot lid lock

### Removal

**1** With the boot lid open, undo the screws and remove the handgrip, then release the fastenings and carefully prise away the trim panel, using a wide-bladed screwdriver positioned next to each retaining clip (**see illustrations**).
**2** Unscrew and remove the lock mounting bolts located on the boot lid lower edge (**see illustration**).
**3** Working through the hole on the boot lid inner panel, disconnect the lock operating rod from the lock motor. To do this, press the plastic retainer to one side.
**4** Remove the boot lid lock together with the operating rod (**see illustration**).

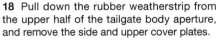

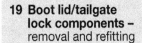

19.1d . . . and prise the trim from the boot lid

### Refitting

**5** Refitting is a reversal of removal but tighten the mounting bolts securely.

## Tailgate lock

### Removal

**6** With the tailgate open, carefully prise off the surround from the inner door handle.
**7** Undo the screws from the lower edge of the trim panel, then pull down the top of the panel to release it from the upper clips, and pull it to the rear to release the guide pin at the hand grip. **Do not** pull down the rear of the panel before releasing the top, as the guide pin will be broken.
**8** Inside the tailgate, note the location of the operating rods on the lock, then press the plastic retainers to one side and disconnect them (**see illustration**).

19.2 Boot lid lock mounting bolts

19.4 Removing the boot lid lock

19.8 Disconnecting the operating rods

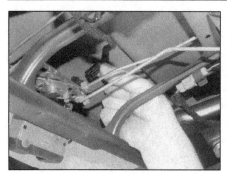

19.9a Disconnect the wiring . . .

19.9b . . . then unscrew the mounting bolts . . .

19.9c . . . and withdraw the tailgate lock

9 Disconnect the wiring plug, then unscrew the mounting bolts and withdraw the lock (see illustrations).

### Refitting

10 Refitting is a reversal of removal.

## Boot lid lock motor

### Removal

11 With the boot lid open, undo the screws and remove the handgrip, then release the fasteners and carefully prise away the trim panel, using a wide-bladed screwdriver positioned next to each retaining clip.
12 Remove the lock motor cover, then, working through the hole on the boot lid inner panel, disconnect the lock operating rod from the lock motor (see illustrations). To do this, press the plastic retainer to one side.
13 Disconnect the private lock operating rod driver from the motor by pressing out the

centre pin, using a hooked instrument. Allow the driver to hang loose on the private lock operating rod.
14 Unscrew the mounting bolts, withdraw the motor, and disconnect the wiring plug.

### Refitting

15 Refitting is a reversal of removal.

## Tailgate lock motor

### Removal

16 With the tailgate open, carefully prise off the surround from the inner door handle.
17 Undo the screws from the lower edge of the trim panel, then pull down the top of the panel to release it from the upper clips, and pull it to the rear to release the guide pin at the hand grip. Do not pull down the rear of the panel before releasing the top, as the guide pin will be broken.
18 Working through the hole on the tailgate

inner panel, disconnect the wiring plug from the lock motor (see illustration).
19 Unscrew the mounting bolts, then disconnect the private lock operating rod driver from the motor by pressing out the centre pin, using a hooked instrument. Allow the driver to hang loose on the private lock operating rod. Carefully lower and tilt the motor, and withdraw it from the tailgate. Take care not to damage the pin on the driver (see illustrations).

### Refitting

20 Refitting is a reversal of removal.

## Tailgate lock cylinder

### Removal

21 With the tailgate open, carefully prise off the surround from the inner door handle.
22 Undo the screws from the lower edge of the trim panel, then pull down the top of the

19.12a Remove the cover . . .

19.12b . . . for access to the boot lid lock motor

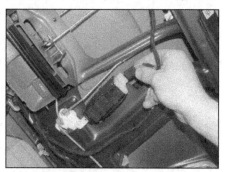

19.18 Disconnect the wiring . . .

19.19a . . . unscrew the mounting bolts . . .

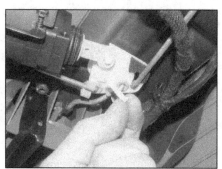

19.19b . . . remove the centre pin . . .

19.19c . . . and withdraw the tailgate lock motor

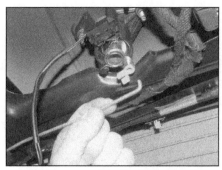

19.23  Disconnecting the lock operating rod from the lever on the lock cylinder

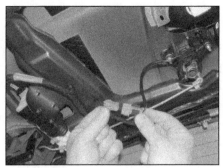

19.24a  Disconnect the wiring . . .

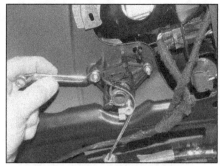

19.24b  . . . unscrew the mounting nuts . . .

19.24c  . . . and withdraw the lock cylinder from the tailgate

19.34a  Disconnect the manual operating rod . . .

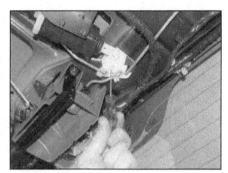

19.34b  . . . and central locking operating rod

panel to release it from the upper clips, and pull it to the rear to release the guide pin at the hand grip. **Do not** pull down the rear of the panel before releasing the top, as the guide pin will be broken.

**23**  Disconnect the lock operating rod from the lever on the lock cylinder. To do this, press the plastic clip to one side **(see illustration)**.

**24**  Disconnect the wiring, unscrew the mounting nuts, and withdraw the lock cylinder from the tailgate **(see illustrations)**. Check the seal and if necessary obtain a new one.

### Refitting

**25**  Refitting is a reversal of removal, but tighten all nuts and bolts securely.

## *Boot lid handle*

### Removal

**26**  Remove the number plate.

**27**  With the boot lid open, undo the screws and remove the handgrip, then carefully prise away the trim panel, using a wide-bladed screwdriver positioned next to each retaining clip.

**28**  Undo the four nuts and remove the decor panel.

**29**  Remove the left-hand rear light unit by unscrewing the nuts and depressing the clips (refer to Chapter 12, Section 7).

**30**  Unscrew the mounting bolts, withdraw the handle, and disconnect the wiring.

### Refitting

**31**  Refitting is a reversal of removal.

## *Tailgate inner handle*

### Removal

**32**  With the tailgate open, undo the screws and remove the inner hand grip. Also carefully prise off the surround from the inner door handle.

**33**  Undo the screws from the lower edge of the trim panel, then pull down the top of the panel to release it from the upper clips, and pull it to the rear to release the guide pin at the hand grip.

**34**  Disconnect the two operating rods **(see illustrations)**.

**35**  Undo the mounting screws and withdraw the inner handle from the tailgate **(see illustration)**.

### Refitting

**36**  Refitting is a reversal of removal.

19.35  Removing the inner door handle from the tailgate

## *Tailgate outer handle*

### Removal

**37**  With the tailgate open, undo the screws and remove the inner hand grip. Also carefully prise off the surround from the inner door handle.

**38**  Undo the screws from the lower edge of the trim panel, then pull down the top of the panel to release it from the upper clips, and pull it to the rear to release the guide pin at the hand grip.

**39**  Remove the left-hand rear tailgate light cluster as described in Chapter 12, Section 7.

**40**  Undo the retaining nuts and bolts, release the clips, and withdraw the outer handle from the tailgate, then disconnect the wiring **(see illustrations)**.

### Refitting

**41**  Refitting is a reversal of removal.

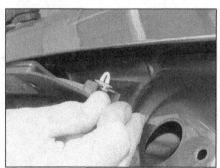

19.40a  Undo the nuts and bolts, and release the clips . . .

**19.40b ... then withdraw the outer handle ...**

**19.40c ... and disconnect the wiring**

**20.1a Prise off the window surround ...**

## 20 Exterior door mirror and glass –
removal and refitting

### Mirror

#### Removal

**1** Carefully prise off the window surround from the inside the door, then disconnect the switch wiring **(see illustrations)**.
**2** Remove the foam seal and disconnect the wiring from the exterior door mirror **(see illustrations)**.
**3** Support the exterior door mirror, then unscrew the mounting bolts. Note that the front bolt is located on the front edge of the door **(see illustration)**.
**4** Unhook the mirror and remove it from the outside of the door **(see illustration)**. Check the sealing gasket and renew it if necessary.

#### Refitting

**5** Refitting is a reversal of removal, but tighten the mounting bolts progressively.

### Glass

#### Removal

**6** Swivel the exterior door mirror fully forwards, then angle-out the inner edge of the mirror glass. Hold a piece of cloth over the glass to prevent it falling out.
**7** Carefully insert a small screwdriver behind the glass, and release the retaining spring **(see illustration)**.
**8** Withdraw the glass and disconnect the heater wiring **(see illustration)**.

#### Refitting

**9** Make sure the spring clips are correctly located on the rear of the mirror.
**10** Reconnect the heater wiring.

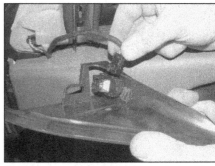

**20.1b ... and disconnect the switch wiring**

**11** Locate the glass on the motor, and use a wad of cloth to press it on until it is fully engaged.
**12** Swivel the mirror rearwards, and check that it operates correctly.

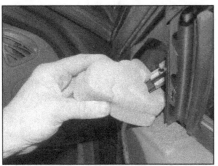

**20.2a Remove the foam seal ...**

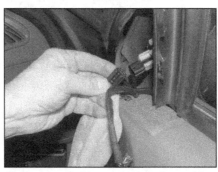

**20.2b ... and disconnect the mirror wiring**

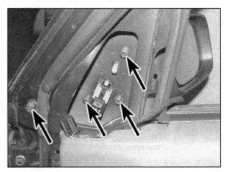

**20.3 Unscrew the mounting bolts ...**

**20.4 ... and remove the exterior door mirror**

**20.7 Release the retaining spring with a screwdriver ...**

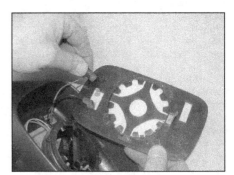

**20.8 ... withdraw the mirror and disconnect the wiring**

## 21 Windscreen, rear window and fixed windows –
general information

### Windscreen and rear window

1 The windscreen and rear window glass are bonded in position with a special adhesive. Renewal of such fixed glass is a complex, messy and time-consuming task, which is beyond the scope of the home mechanic; without the benefit of extensive practice, it is difficult to attain a secure, waterproof fit. Furthermore, the task carries a high risk of accidental breakage – this applies especially to the laminated glass windscreen. In view of this, owners are strongly advised to entrust work of this nature to a Saab dealer, or one of the many specialist windscreen fitters.

### Fixed rear side window

2 On Estate models, the fixed rear side window is bonded in position the same as the windscreen and rear window. Refer to paragraph 1.

## 22 Sunroof assembly –
removal and refitting

1 Due to the complexity of the tilt/slide sunroof mechanism, considerable expertise is required to repair, renew or adjust the sunroof components successfully. Removal of the sunroof first requires that the headlining be removed, which is a tedious, time-consuming operation. Therefore, this Section is limited to removal of the glass hatch and drive motor, and it is recommended that any other work related to the sunroof is referred to a Saab dealer.

### Glass hatch

#### Removal

2 Open the sunroof then undo the screws from the front cover strip.
3 Close the sunroof and tilt the rear edge. Pull the rear edge of the cover strip rearwards to release the clips, then pull out the strip taking care not to damage the paintwork.
4 Carefully pull the side cover strips from the retaining clips.
5 Raise the rear of the hatch, undo the two retaining bolts and lift out the glass hatch.

#### Refitting

6 Refitting is a reversal of removal, but adjust the glass hatch so that it is level with the surrounding roof panel. The front edge of the hatch can be slightly lower than the roof panel.

### Drive motor assembly

**Note:** *If the drive motor is faulty, it is possible to operate the sunroof using a screwdriver. Slide off the cover from the overhead switch panel, and turn the motor shaft with the screwdriver. Turn the shaft anti-clockwise to close the sunroof.*

#### Removal

7 Open the sunroof then undo the screws from the front cover strip.
8 Close the sunroof and tilt the rear edge. Pull the rear edge of the cover strip rearwards to release the clips, then pull out the strip taking care not to damage the paintwork.
9 Carefully pull the side cover strips from the retaining clips.
10 Close the sunroof and check that the wires' slide mountings are centred between the two marks on the slide rail. **Note:** *The sunroof must be closed when fitting a new motor, as it is supplied in the closed position.*
11 Undo the screws and remove the sun visors; disconnect the wiring for the mirror light.
12 Prise out the lens from the interior light with a screwdriver, then undo the screws and remove the roof console.
13 Undo the screws and remove the rear view mirror.
14 Carefully bend down the front of the headlining and unscrew the drive motor mounting bolts. Take care not do damage the headlining. Withdraw the motor and disconnect the wiring.

#### Refitting

15 Refitting is a reversal of removal. Move the motor backwards and forwards as required to ensure the gears engage correctly before inserting the mounting bolts.

## 23 Body exterior fittings –
removal and refitting

### Door protective mouldings

#### Removal

1 Use a screwdriver to prise away the rear edge of the moulding – protect the paintwork with adhesive tape.
2 Pull the moulding and retaining clips from the sockets in the door panel, and slide it rearwards from the front mounting hole. If the clips come away from the moulding, or the sockets come out of the door panel, refit them in their correct positions.

#### Refitting

3 Refitting is a reversal of removal. Where fitted, leave the protective tape on the front of the moulding as this will allow it to slide forwards in the front mounting hole.

### Sill scuff plate

#### Removal

4 Undo the screw securing the front of the scuff plate to the front wheel arch liner.
5 Unscrew the nut securing the front of the scuff plate to the front wing.

6 Prise out the rubber strip from the top of the scuff plate.
7 Unscrew the nut securing the scuff plate to the rear wheel arch liner.
8 Undo the screws and nuts securing the scuff plate to the sill.
9 Pull out the rear wheel arch liner, and withdraw the scuff plate.

#### Refitting

10 Refitting is a reversal of removal.

### Wheel arch liners

#### Removal

11 Raise the front or rear of the vehicle (as applicable) and support it on axle stands (see *Jacking and vehicle support*). Remove the roadwheel.
12 Undo the plastic retaining nuts/bolts securing the liner to the body or wing.
13 Press the liner away from the outer edge of the wing, and withdraw it from the wheel housing.

#### Refitting

14 Refitting is a reversal of removal.

## 24 Seats –
removal and refitting

### Front seat

#### Removal

1 Adjust the seat fully forwards. On models with an electrically-operated front seat, if the seat motor is seized or inoperative, raise the seat as high as possible using the spring-loaded lever, and remove the upper seat cowl, then remove the front bolt. Undo the Torx screws, grasp the shaft and pull out the bevel gear. The gear can now be dismantled and a suitable tool attached to it with Jubilee clips to manually move the front seat.
2 Unscrew and remove the seat rear mounting bolts **(see illustration)**.
3 Adjust the seat fully rearwards.
4 Unscrew and remove the seat front mounting bolts **(see illustration)**.

**24.2 Removing the front seat rear mounting bolts**

**24.4 Removing the front seat front mounting bolts**

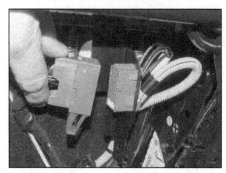

**24.5a Disconnect the multi-pin wiring plug . . .**

**24.5b . . . and release the cable tie and clip**

**5** Lift the front of the seat and disconnect the multi-pin wiring plug – also release the cable tie and clip **(see illustrations)**.
**6** Lift the seat from inside the vehicle, and, if necessary, release the seat belt from it (refer to Section 26).

### Refitting

**7** Refitting is a reversal of removal, but tighten the mounting bolts to the specified torque. The inner bolt should be tightened first both at the front and rear.

### *Rear seat cushion*

#### Removal

**8** Fold the rear seat cushion forwards.
**9** Release the plastic clip from the hinge **(see illustration)**.
**10** Where applicable, disconnect the multi-pin plug from the underside of the seat cushion.

**11** Withdraw the cushion from the vehicle **(see illustration)**.

#### Refitting

**12** Refitting is a reversal of removal.

### *Rear seat backrest (40% section)*

#### Removal

**13** On Saloon and Estate models, fold the rear seat cushion forwards and the backrest downwards, then fasten the seat belts in their holders on the C-pillars.
**14** Fold the backrest slightly forwards and unhook the upholstery hooks at the seatbelt mounting.
**15** Release the outer pivot pin using a screwdriver to prise out the catch retainer plate, then lift the backrest and withdraw it from the inner pivot pin **(see illustration)**. Note that the backrest will only release in one

position, when it is folded approximately 20° from vertical. Lift the backrest from inside the vehicle.

#### Refitting

**16** Refitting is a reversal of removal. Press down on the backrest until the catch locks. Make sure that the centre seat belt is located in front of the backrest.

### *Rear seat backrest (60% section)*

#### Removal

**17** Remove the 40% section rear seat backrest as described earlier.
**18** On Saloon models, release the lock by pressing with a finger, then pull the backrest from the anchor pins. Lift the backrest from inside the vehicle.
**19** On Estate models, unscrew the bolt from the centre seat belt lower mounting, and

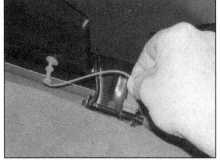

**24.9 Removing the plastic clip from the hinge . . .**

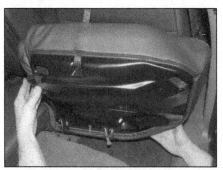

**24.11 . . . and remove the rear seat cushion**

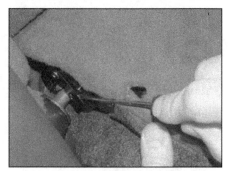

**24.15 Use a screwdriver to release the catch retainer plate**

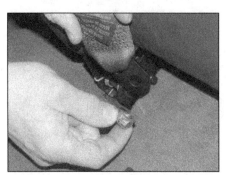

**24.19a Unscrew the bolt from the centre seat belt lower mounting . . .**

**24.19b . . . unscrew the hinge pin from the centre support . . .**

**24.19c . . . unhook the upholstery clip . . .**

unscrew the hinge pin from the centre support. Unhook the upholstery clip, then lift the backrest from the left-hand side mounting. Slide the backrest towards the door to release the centre pin lug from the support, and withdraw the backrest from inside the vehicle **(see illustrations)**.

### Refitting

**20** Refitting is a reversal of removal. Press down on the backrest until the catch locks. On Saloon models, make sure that the centre seat belt is located in front of the backrest.

## 25 Driver's seat control module – removal and refitting

**Note:** *The control module is only fitted to models with an electrically-operated seat.*

### Removal

**1** The front seat control module is located on the underside of the driver's seat. It contains the memory for position and movement control, and a communication function for diagnosis. The system also memorises the position of the electrically-operated rear view mirrors.
**2** Remove the front seat as described in Section 24.
**3** Disconnect the wiring from the module.
**4** Undo the retaining screws and withdraw the module from the seat. Note that one of the module body bolt holes is open-ended and it is only necessary to loosen the bolt in this position, and slide the module from it.

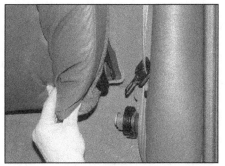
24.19d ... release the outer left-hand side mounting ...

### Refitting

**5** Refitting is a reversal of removal.

## 26 Seat belts – removal and refitting

⚠️ *Warning: If the vehicle has been involved in an accident which causes the seat belt pretensioner to be activated, the complete seat belt, together with pretensioner, must be renewed.*

### Front belt and tensioner

#### Removal

**1** Adjust the seat as far forward as possible. Make sure that the ignition is switched off.
**2** Release the seat belt from the front seat by pressing in the catch with a 90° angled

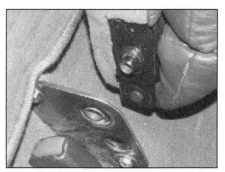
24.19e ... and release the centre pin lug from the support

screwdriver. The end of the screwdriver blade must have a tip 3.0 mm wide. If necessary for improved access, remove the plastic side cover and use a screwdriver to depress the catch **(see illustrations)**.
**3** Pull back the weatherstrip locally then, using a wide-bladed screwdriver, carefully lever the trim from the B-pillar and lift it from the air duct. Pull the seat belt through the trim **(see illustrations)**.
**4** Disconnect the wiring for the belt pretensioner **(see illustration)**.
**5** Unscrew the two nuts/bolts and single screw, and withdraw the front seat inertia reel and belt tensioner **(see illustration)**.
**6** To remove the stalk from the inner side of the front seat, first remove the seat (see Section 24), then disconnect the reminder warning light wiring on the underside of the seat and cut the plastic cable tie. Unscrew the bolt and remove the stalk.

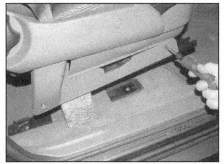
26.2a  Undo the screws ...

26.2b  ... and remove the plastic side cover ...

26.2c  ... then depress the catch with a screwdriver ...

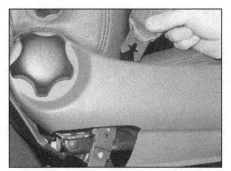
26.2d  ... and release the seat belt

26.3a  Remove the trim from the B-pillar ...

26.3b  ... and pull through the seat belt

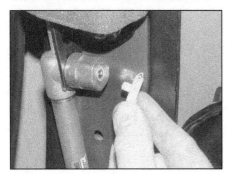

**26.4 Disconnecting the belt pretensioner wiring**

### Refitting

**7** Refitting is a reversal of removal, but tighten the mounting bolts to the specified torque. Check that the belt is fitted correctly to the front seat by pulling it directly upwards; the catch must be visible on the outside of the mounting. Saab recommend that the airbag system is checked for fault codes after fitting the front seat belt inertia reel and belt tensioner.

### *Rear outer belt (Saloon models)*

#### Removal

**8** Fold the seat cushion forwards, then unscrew the nut securing the lower end of the seat belt to the floor.
**9** Pull back the weatherstrip locally, then remove the trim panel from the C-pillar by carefully prising it away with a wide-bladed screwdriver to release the retaining clips.

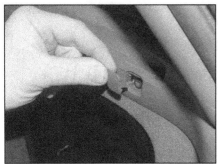

**26.22a Prise out the covers . . .**

**26.22c . . . and remove the parcel shelf support**

**26.5 Front seat belt inertia reel and belt tensioner mounting bolts**

Draw the seat belt through the hole in the panel.
**10** Unscrew the mounting nuts and remove the seat belt reel from the C-pillar.
**11** To remove the stalk, unscrew the mounting nut and remove it from the floor. On later models it will be necessary to remove both backrests, then unclip the carpet from the floor for access to the nut.

#### Refitting

**12** Refitting is a reversal of removal, but tighten the mounting nuts and bolts to the specified torque.

### *Rear centre belt (Saloon models)*

#### Removal

**13** Fold down the rear seat backrest and remove the head restraint from the seat.
**14** Remove both speaker grilles, then remove

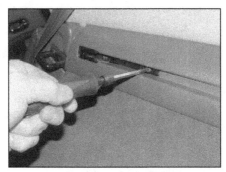

**26.22b . . . undo the screws . . .**

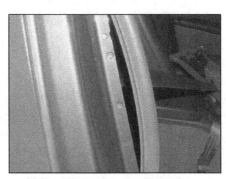

**26.24a Lift the door weatherstrip . . .**

**26.19 Rear luggage compartment storage box removal**

the clips from the front of the parcel shelf, lift out the shelf trim and pull out the centre belt.
**15** Unscrew the mounting nut and remove the centre belt from the floor.
**16** Unscrew the mounting nut and remove the seat belt reel from the rear parcel shelf crossmember.
**17** To remove the stalk, unscrew the mounting nut and remove it from the floor. On later models it will be necessary to remove both backrests, then unclip the carpet from the floor for access to the nut.

#### Refitting

**18** Refitting is a reversal of removal but tighten the mounting nuts to the specified torque. Make sure the belt is located over the front of the backrest.

### *Rear outer belt (Estate models)*

#### Removal

**19** Remove the rear parcel shelf (where fitted), and also remove the storage box from the luggage compartment **(see illustration)**.
**20** Remove the scuff plate from the tailgate opening.
**21** Remove the headlining rear trim, then prise away the D-pillar trim using a wide-bladed screwdriver.
**22** Prise out the covers, then undo the screws and prise away the parcel shelf support **(see illustrations)**.
**23** Fold up the rear seat cushion, and fold down the backrest.
**24** Lift the door weatherstrip and pull out the top of the side bolster, then unhook the bottom and withdraw **(see illustrations)**.

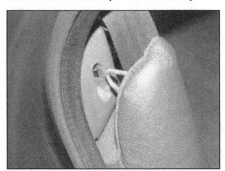

**26.24b . . . then unhook the side bolster**

**25** Undo the screws and pull the trim from the backrest, then disconnect the wiring for the CD player, where fitted.
**26** Starting at the top, pull away the trim from the C-pillar, noting the locating pin at the bottom rear **(see illustration)**.
**27** Unscrew the nut and remove the lower end of the belt from the floor.
**28** Remove the guide from the C-pillar trim, then feed the belt tongue and belt through the guide.
**29** Remove the insulating pad and guide, then unbolt and remove the seat belt reel **(see illustrations)**.
**30** To remove the stalk, unscrew the retaining nut/bolt and withdraw it from the rear floor panel **(see illustration)**.

## Refitting

**31** Refitting is a reversal of removal, but tighten the mounting nuts/bolts to the specified torque. Make sure that the rubber weatherstrip is located correctly over the D-pillar trim, headlining and scuff plate.

### Rear centre belt (Estate models)

#### Removal

**32** Fold the rear seat cushions forwards, and secure the rear seat belts in their holders.
**33** Fold the 40% backrest slightly forwards and remove the trim retaining clip.
**34** Using a screwdriver, release the lower catch and lift out the backrest.
**35** Unscrew the centre belt lower mounting, remove the centre pivot hinge pin, however, do not remove the retaining bolts.
**36** Unclip the trim from the 60% backrest. With the backrest upright, release it from the left-hand side bracket. Now move it towards the door and release the centre pivot pin. Withdraw the backrest.
**37** Undo the screw and unclip the cover from the catch.
**38** Unclip the plate from the backrest, remove the trim from the groove and withdraw the plate. Take care not the break the corner.
**39** Undo the screws and remove the belt plate from the rear of the backrest.
**40** Remove the guide from the backrest and belt.
**41** Cut the foam as necessary, undo the screws and remove the guide. Release the guide from the belt.
**42** Unbolt and remove the inertia reel together with the seat belt.
**43** To remove the stalk, unscrew the retaining nut/bolt and withdraw it from the rear floor panel.

#### Refitting

**44** Refitting is a reversal of removal, but tighten the mounting nuts/bolts to the specified torque.

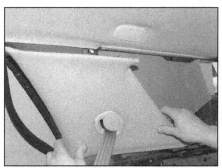

**26.26  Removing the trim from the C-pillar**

**26.29b  Rear seat belt reel and anchor mounting bolts**

### 27 Interior trim panels – removal and refitting

#### A-pillar trim panels

**Note:** *As from 2002 models, special absorbent material is fitted between the headlining and roof panel to protect the driver's and passenger's heads in the event of a collision. The A-pillar trim panel clips are attached to these pads and must not be detached.*
**1** Open the relevant front door, and pull the rubber weatherstrip from the door aperture at the A-pillar.
**2** Working from the headlining down, grasp the trim panel firmly and progressively ease it away from the pillar, allowing the press-studs beneath to disengage one at a time.
**3** On 2002-on models, release the upper clips from the trim panel, however, **do not** remove the clip and strap from the pillar as this forms part of the energy absorption system fitted to the headlining.
**4** Refitting is a reversal of removal.

#### B-pillar trim panels

**Note:** *On 2002-on models, take care not to disturb the special absorbent material fitted between the headlining and roof panel.*
**5** Move the front seat fully forwards, then carefully pull off the B-pillar trim panel and lift it out of the air duct.
**6** Using an angled screwdriver, press in the

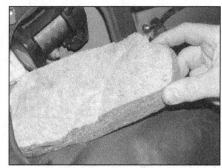

**26.29a  Removing the insulation pad**

**26.30  Rear seat belt stalks**

catch and release the seat belt mounting from the front seat.
**7** Remove the belt guide and pull the belt through the B-pillar trim panel. Withdraw the trim panel.
**8** Refitting is a reversal of removal.

#### C-pillar trim panels

**Note:** *On 2002-on models, take care not to disturb the special absorbent material fitted between the headlining and roof panel.*

##### Saloon models

**9** Fold down the rear seat backrest, then undo the screw and remove the head restraint.
**10** Undo the screw and unclip the radio speaker grille from the parcel shelf.
**11** Carefully pull the trim panel from the C-pillar, then unbolt the seat belt and feed it through the panel.
**12** Refitting is a reversal of removal.

##### Estate models

**13** Remove the rear roof cross panel from the rear of the headlining. This is necessary to provide sufficient clearance for the D-pillar trim.
**14** Carefully pull the D-pillar trim panel forwards and release it from the retaining clips.
**15** Undo the screws and remove the parcel shelf support from under the rear side window.
**16** Starting at the top, pull away the C-pillar trim panel, noting the location pin at the rear lower edge.

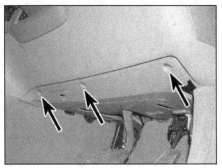

**27.34a Undo the screws . . .**

**17** Fold the rear seat cushion forwards, then unscrew the lower seat belt mounting nut.
**18** Remove the guide from the C-pillar and pull the belt through the trim.
**19** Refitting is a reversal of removal.

### Luggage area side trim panel

#### Saloon models

**20** Where applicable, remove the CD changer on the left-hand side of the luggage compartment and the protective net from the right-hand side.
**21** Lift up the floor panel and unclip the scuff plate from the rear valance.
**22** Fold down the rear seat backrest, then undo the screws and unclip the floor panel at the front.
**23** Undo the screw and unclip the radio speaker grille from the parcel shelf.
**24** Unscrew the plastic nuts and withdraw the side trim panel.

**27.35a Undo the screws . . .**

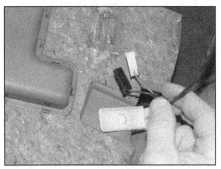

**27.36 Disconnecting the wiring from the footwell light**

**27.34b . . . and remove the lower facia trim panel with air duct**

**25** Refitting is a reversal of removal.

#### Estate models

**26** Remove the storage compartment from the luggage compartment.
**27** Prise off the covers and undo the screws, then unclip the scuff plate from the rear valance.
**28** Remove the rear roof cross panel from the rear of the headlining. This is necessary to provide sufficient clearance for the D-pillar trim.
**29** Carefully pull the D-pillar trim panel forwards and release it from the retaining clips.
**30** Undo the screws and remove the parcel shelf support from under the rear side window.
**31** Pull out the top of the side bolster, then unhook the bottom and withdraw.
**32** Undo the screws from the top of the side trim panel, then, where necessary, carefully

**27.35b . . . and remove the diagnostic socket and data link wiring**

**27.41 Rear view mirror retaining screws**

pull out the panel and disconnect the wiring from the CD player. Withdraw the panel.
**33** Refitting is a reversal of removal. When refitting the side trim panel, insert the rearmost retaining screw first.

### Lower facia panel (driver's side)

**34** Undo the screws and remove the lower facia trim panel together with the air duct on the driver's side **(see illustrations)**.
**35** Undo the screws and remove the diagnostic socket and data link wiring **(see illustrations**.
**36** Remove the footwell light from the lower facia trim panel, or disconnect the wiring **(see illustration)**.
**37** Refitting is a reversal of removal.

### Headlining

**Note:** *On 2002-on models, the headlining is fitted with special energy-absorbent pads which must not be damaged.*
**38** Undo the screws and remove the sun visors. Where applicable, disconnect the wiring from the mirror light.
**39** Carefully prise out the interior light lens from the roof console.
**40** Undo the screws and remove the roof console. Where fitted, it will be necessary to disconnect the wiring from the interior temperature sensor and microphone.
**41** Undo the screws and remove the rear view mirror **(see illustration)**.
**42** Remove the A-pillar trim panels as described earlier in this Section.
**43** Undo the screws and remove the handgrips located over the door apertures.
**44** On models with a sunroof, remove the three clips from the rear of the sunroof aperture.
**45** Remove the B-pillar trim panel on the passenger's side as described earlier in this Section.

#### Saloon models

**46** Unclip the top of each C-pillar trim.
**47** Unclip the high-level brake light cover and disconnect the wiring. Pull the wiring clear of the console.
**48** Release the rear of the headlining by twisting the two clips through 90°.
**49** Adjust the front seats as low and as far rearwards as possible, and fold down the backrests to provide as much working room as possible.
**50** Carefully pull out the headlining from the driver's and passenger's door sealing mouldings.
**51** On models with a sunroof, release the headlining from the hooks near the sunroof.
**52** Note that some wiring is taped to the top of the headlining. Disconnect the wiring in the roof console aperture, and where applicable disconnect the alarm wiring.
**53** Adjust the steering wheel fully forwards. On manual transmission models, select reverse. On automatic transmission models, select first.

**54** With the help of an assistant, carefully lift the headlining through the passenger door aperture. Take care not to crack the headlining.
*Caution: On 2002-on models, check that the energy-absorbent pads on the top of the headlining are still intact. If any are damaged, the complete headlining must be renewed.*

### Estate models

**55** Release the clips securing the headlining rear crossmember to the roof.
**56** Disconnect the wiring from the glass breakage sensor and luggage compartment light.
**57** Carefully pull away the trim panels from the D-pillars, then remove the trim panels from between the C- and D-pillars.
**58** Release the clips securing the top of the C-pillar trim panels.
**59** Remove the cargo safety net mountings, prise off the covers and undo the clips.
**60** Release the rear of the headlining by twisting the two clips through 90°.
**61** Carefully pull out the headlining from the driver's and passenger's door sealing mouldings.
**62** On models with a sunroof, release the headlining from the hooks near the sunroof.
**63** Note that some wiring is taped to the top of the headlining. Disconnect the wiring in the roof console aperture, and where applicable disconnect the alarm wiring.
**64** With the help of an assistant, carefully lift the headlining through the tailgate aperture. Take care not to crack the headlining.
*Caution: On 2002-on models, check that the energy-absorbent pads on the top of the headlining are still intact. If any are damaged, the complete headlining must be renewed.*

### All models

**65** If a new headlining is being fitted, transfer the wiring from the old one and secure with new tape.
**66** Refitting is a reversal of removal.

## 28 Centre console – removal and refitting

### Removal

**1** On manual transmission models, prise the gear lever gaiter from the centre console. On automatic transmission models, use a screwdriver to prise up the selector lever surround **(see illustration)**.
**2** Where an ashtray is fitted, open it and detach the outer (veneered) panel with the ashtray **(see illustration)**.
**3** Using a screwdriver, prise back the retaining tabs and prise the ashtray/oddments box from the centre console **(see illustrations)**. Use tape to protect the walnut veneer.
**4** Undo the screws and remove the gear

**28.1 Removing the selector lever surround (automatic transmission models)**

**28.2 Removing the outer (veneered) panel from the ashtray**

**28.3a Prise back the retaining tabs . . .**

**28.3b . . . and remove the ashtray box from the centre console**

lever/selector cover. Identify the wiring locations then disconnect the plugs – there are plugs for the seat heating, seat ventilation and cigarette lighter. Also disconnect the

wiring from the central locking switch **(see illustrations)**.
**5** Remove the rear end part of the console by lifting it, and disconnect the wiring from the

**28.4a Undo the screws . . .**

**28.4b . . . remove the gear/selector cover . . .**

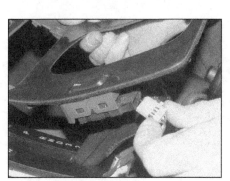
**28.4c . . . then disconnect the wiring from the central locking switch . . .**

**28.4d . . . and remaining switches**

28.5a Lift the rear end part of the console . . .

28.5b . . . and disconnect the wiring from the rear seat cushion heating switches

28.7a Remove the theft protection antenna unit . . .

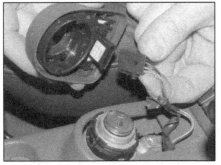

28.7b . . . and disconnect the wiring

28.8a Prise out the small panel . . .

28.8b . . . then push out the electric window switch panel . . .

rear seat cushion heating switches **(see illustrations)**.

6 Select reverse (manual transmission) or P (automatic transmission). Remove the ignition key.

7 Twist the theft protection antenna unit bayonet fitting from the ignition switch and disconnect the wiring **(see illustrations)**. Insert the ignition key and select Neutral.

8 Prise out the electric window switch panel

and disconnect the wiring. If necessary, access may be gained by first prising out the small panel behind the switch **(see illustrations)**.

9 Undo the screws and remove the upper surround panel from the centre console, at the

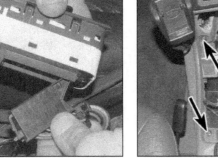

28.8c . . . and disconnect the wiring

28.9a Undo the front screws . . .

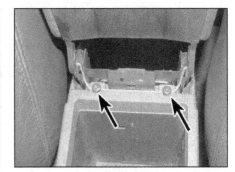

28.9b . . . and rear screws . . .

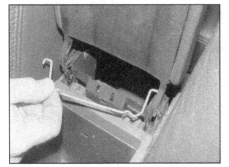

28.9c . . . noting the location of the spring for the storage compartment lid . . .

28.9d . . . then remove the upper surround panel from the centre console

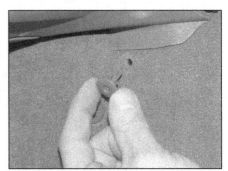

28.10a Remove the fasteners . . .

28.10b . . . undo the side screws . . .

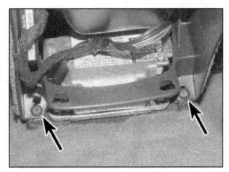

28.10c . . . and rear screws . . .

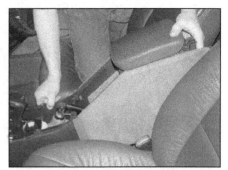

28.11 . . . then remove the centre console

same time pulling off the handbrake lever gaiter. Note that the rear screws secure the spring for the storage compartment lid **(see illustrations)**.

**10** Remove the fasteners and fold back the carpet, then undo the console front and rear mounting screws **(see illustrations)**.

**11** Withdraw the centre console from inside the vehicle **(see illustration)**.

### Refitting

**12** Refitting is a reversal of removal.

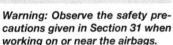

### 29 Facia assembly –
removal and refitting

⚠ *Warning: Observe the safety precautions given in Section 31 when working on or near the airbags.*

### Removal

**1** Disconnect the battery negative lead (refer to *Disconnecting the battery* in the Reference Chapter).

**2** Carefully prise out the speaker grilles from each side of the facia **(see illustration)**. They are secured with clips.

**3** Undo the screws and lift out the speakers. Disconnect the wiring **(see illustrations)**.

**4** Carefully remove the cover from the centre top of the facia by initially pushing it forwards, then lifting it. Remove the anti-theft warning LED, then disconnect the wiring from the solar sensor and push it down through the hole in the facia, noting its routing **(see illustrations)**.

**5** Remove the glovebox as described in Section 30 and lift out the air duct.

**6** Remove the steering wheel as described in Chapter 10.

**7** Undo the screws and remove the lower

facia trim panel together with the air duct on the driver's side.

**8** Undo the screws from the diagnostic socket, and also disconnect the wiring.

**9** Remove the footwell light from the lower facia trim panel, or disconnect the wiring.

**10** On manual transmission models, prise the gear lever gaiter from the centre console. On automatic transmission models, use a screwdriver to prise up the selector lever surround.

**11** Using a screwdriver, prise out the ashtray and holder, or oddments tray as applicable. Undo the screws located behind the aperture.

**12** Disconnect the wiring from the central locking switch.

**13** Raise the gear lever cover and disconnect the wiring for the seat heater and cigarette lighter.

**14** Remove the instrument panel and surround as described in Chapter 12.

**15** Unbolt the fusebox from the bulkhead.

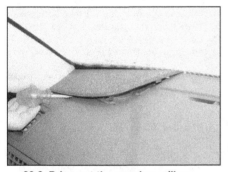

29.2 Prise out the speaker grilles . . .

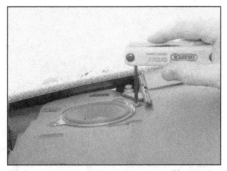

29.3a . . . then undo the screws, lift out the speaker . . .

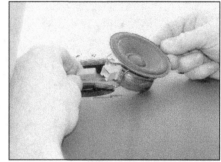

29.3b . . . and disconnect the wiring

29.4a Remove the centre cover from the facia . . .

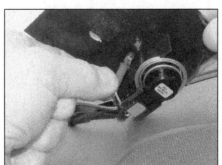

29.4b . . . remove the anti-theft warning LED . . .

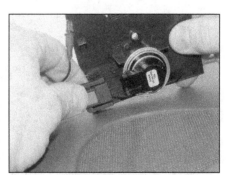

29.4c . . . and disconnect the solar sensor wiring

29.16a Undo the screws . . .

29.16b . . . and remove the steering column gaiter

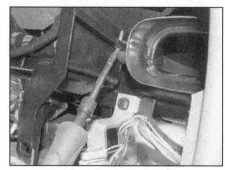

29.17a Undo the screws . . .

29.17b . . . and remove the air ducts on both sides

29.18 Velcro retaining the wiring near the passenger airbag

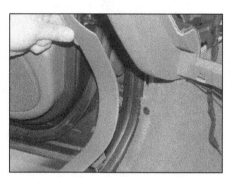
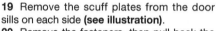
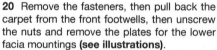
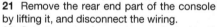

29.19 Removing the door sill scuff plates

**16** Undo the screws and remove the steering column gaiter **(see illustrations)**.
**17** Undo the screws and remove the air ducts on the driver's and passenger's sides **(see illustrations)**.

**18** On models with a passenger airbag, disconnect the airbag wiring, then undo the screw and remove the airbag retaining strap. Also release the wiring loom from the Velcro near the airbag **(see illustration)**.

**19** Remove the scuff plates from the door sills on each side **(see illustration)**.
**20** Remove the fasteners, then pull back the carpet from the front footwells, then unscrew the nuts and remove the plates for the lower facia mountings **(see illustrations)**.
**21** Remove the rear end part of the console by lifting it, and disconnect the wiring.
**22** Select reverse (manual transmission) or P (automatic transmission). Remove the ignition key.
**23** Twist the theft protection antenna unit bayonet fitting from the ignition switch and disconnect the wiring. Insert the ignition key and select Neutral.
**24** Prise out the electric window switch and disconnect the wiring.
**25** Undo the screws and remove the upper surround panel from the centre console.
**26** Mark its fitted position, then unbolt and remove the metal bracket and locating pin

29.20a Remove the fasteners . . .

29.20b . . . pull back the carpet . . .

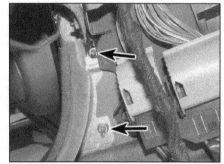

29.20c . . . undo the nuts . . .

29.20d . . . and remove the plates for the lower facia mountings

29.26a Unscrew the bolts . . .

**29.26b** . . . and remove the locating pin bracket from the front of the centre console

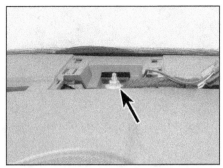

**29.27 Facia upper central mounting nut – it is only necessary to loosen this nut**

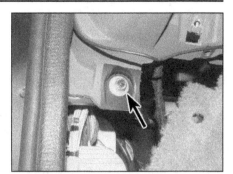

**29.28a Unscrew the facia lower outer nuts . . .**

**29.28b** . . . and the central nuts securing the facia to the heater

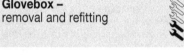

**29.29 Removing the facia assembly from inside the car**

nuts, and the central nuts securing the facia to the heater **(see illustrations)**.

**29** With the help of an assistant, carefully lift the facia assembly from the bulkhead and withdraw it through one of the front door apertures **(see illustration)**.

**30** Where fitted, unscrew the nuts and remove the passenger airbag from the facia panel.

### Refitting

**31** Refitting is a reversal of removal, but refer to Section 31 for details of refitting the airbags.

from the front of the centre console **(see illustrations)**.

**27** Unscrew the centre nut and outer bolts from the front edge of the facia panel **(see**

illustration). Note that it is only necessary to loosen the centre nut as its hole is slotted, however, the outer bolts must be removed.

**28** Unscrew the facia lower outer mounting

## 30 Glovebox – removal and refitting

### Removal

**1** Remove the carpet cover from the heater/ ventilation unit beneath the glovebox **(see illustration)**.

**2** Undo the screws and remove the lower facia trim panel, then remove the footwell light or disconnect the wiring from it **(see illustrations)**.

**3** Unscrew the three mounting screws underneath and three screws inside the glovebox, then withdraw the glovebox sufficiently to disconnect the wiring from the illumination light **(see illustrations)**.

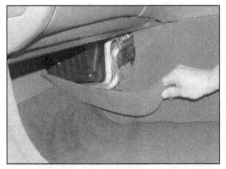

**30.1 Removing the carpet cover from the heater/ventilation unit beneath the glovebox**

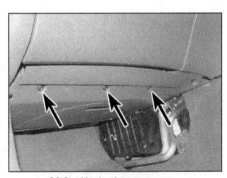

**30.2a Undo the screws . . .**

**30.2b** . . . remove the lower facia trim panel, and disconnect the footwell light wiring

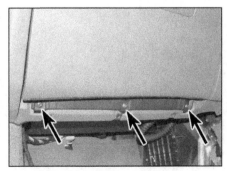

**30.3a Undo the lower screws . . .**

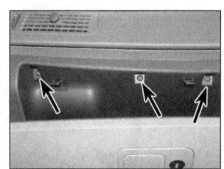

**30.3b** . . . and upper screws . . .

30.3c . . . then withdraw the glovebox . . .

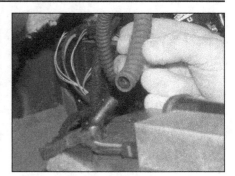

30.3d . . . disconnect the wiring from the illumination light . . .

30.4 . . . and release the air conditioning cold air hose from the glovebox

**4** On models with air conditioning, release the cold air hose from the glovebox **(see illustration)**.

**5** Withdraw the glovebox from the facia.

### Refitting

**6** Refitting is a reversal of removal.

## 31 Supplementary Restraint System (SRS) components – removal and refitting

### General information

The operation of the SRS is managed by an Electronic Control Unit (ECU). When the vehicle's ignition switch is turned on, the ECU performs self-test checks of the system's components; if a fault is detected, the ECU records it in memory as a fault. Following this, the ECU illuminates the instrument panel-mounted SRS warning light. If this should occur, the vehicle should be taken to a Saab dealer for examination. Dedicated test equipment is needed to interrogate the SRS ECU, firstly to determine the nature and incidence of the fault, and secondly to clear the stored fault, thus preventing the fault from being displayed by the warning light once the fault has been rectified.

The SRS ECU incorporates an electro-mechanical safety sensor of magnetic reed type, a microprocessor, three back-up power sources, a voltage converter and an accelerometer. After deployment of either the driver's or passenger's airbag, a permanent

fault code is generated in the ECU which cannot be cleared, requiring the renewal of the ECU.

*Caution: The SRS ECU must be renewed after deployment of either the driver's or passenger's airbag. However, it may be re-used a total of three times after deployment of the side airbags and/or seat belt tensioners.*

The ECU's wiring connector incorporates short-circuiting jumpers which are activated when the connector is unplugged. The circuits concerned are the electric detonators for the front airbags and side airbags, and also the circuit for the airbag warning lamp. This ensures the airbags cannot be deployed with the ECU connector unplugged.

For safety reasons, owners are strongly advised against attempting to diagnose problems with the SRS using standard workshop equipment. The information in this Section is therefore limited to those components in the SRS which must occasionally be removed to gain access to other components on the vehicle.

⚠ **Warning: A number of additional precautions must be observed when working on vehicles with airbags/SRS:**

a) *Always switch the ignition off and remove the ignition key before working on the SRS system components. Although not a manufacturer's requirement, the battery may also be disconnected as a further precaution.*

b) ***Do not*** *attempt to splice into any of the electric cables in the SRS wiring harness.*

c) *Avoid hammering or causing any harsh vibration at the front of the vehicle, particularly in the engine bay, as this may trigger the crash sensors and activate the SRS.*

d) *Do not use ohmmeters or any other device capable of supplying current on any of the SRS components, as this may cause accidental detonation.*

e) *Airbags (and seat belt tensioners) are classed as pyrotechnical (explosive) devices, and must be stored and handled according to the relevant laws in the country concerned. In general, do not leave these components disconnected from their electrical wiring any longer than is absolutely necessary; in this state they are unstable, and the risk of accidental detonation is introduced. Rest a disconnected airbag with the metal bracket facing downwards, away from flammable materials – never leave it unattended.*

f) *The seat belt tensioners must not be exposed to temperatures in excess of 100°C.*

### Driver's airbag

#### Removal

**1** Ensure the ignition is switched off and turn the steering wheel to the straight-ahead position.

**2** Prise out the plugs then undo the screws securing the airbag to the steering wheel. The screws are located on each side of the steering wheel **(see illustrations)**.

**3** Carefully lift the airbag from the steering wheel sufficiently to disconnect the wiring. Where necessary on later models, release the wiring from the Velcro tape **(see illustrations)**.

**4** Rest the airbag in a safe place with the metal bracket facing downwards.

#### Refitting

**5** Locate the airbag over the steering wheel and reconnect the wiring, making sure that it is firmly pressed onto the terminal.

**6** Lower the airbag into the steering wheel, then insert and tighten the retaining screws. Refit the rubber plugs.

31.2a Prise out the plugs . . .

31.2b . . . and undo the screws securing the airbag to the steering wheel

**7** Switch on the ignition and check that the SRS warning light goes out. If the warning light does not go out, the control unit probably has a fault code stored in it and it will be necessary to have a Saab dealer check the system.

### Passenger's airbag

#### Removal

**8** Ensure the ignition is switched off, then remove the facia as described in Section 29.
**9** Disconnect the wiring from the passenger airbag module **(see illustration)**.
**10** Undo the retaining nuts and remove the passenger's airbag from the facia **(see illustration)**.
**11** Rest the airbag in a safe place with the metal bracket facing downwards (ie, airbag facing upwards).

#### Refitting

**12** Position the airbag in the facia and tighten the nuts securely.
**13** Refit the facia with reference to Section 29.
**14** Switch on the ignition and check that the SRS warning light goes out. If the warning light does not go out, the control unit probably has a fault code stored in it and it will be necessary to have a Saab dealer check the system.

### Side airbag

**Note:** *This work involves removing the rear fabric from the seat, and may be considered a job for an upholsterer rather than the home mechanic.*

#### Removal

**15** Ensure the ignition is switched off.
**16** Remove the front seat as described in Section 24.
**17** Release the seat backrest upholstery from the bottom of the seat and remove the retaining strip.
**18** Release the staples and remove the cardboard.
**19** Remove the retaining strips and fold out the upholstery.
**20** Disconnect the wiring from the side airbag, then unscrew the retaining nuts and withdraw the unit.

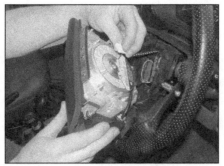

**31.3a Disconnect the wiring . . .**

**31.9 Disconnect the passenger airbag wiring . . .**

#### Refitting

**21** Locate the side airbag on the front seat and tighten the nuts to the specified torque.
**22** Refit the upholstery and cardboard and secure with new staples.
**23** Refit the front seat with reference to Section 24.

### Airbag contact spring unit

#### Removal

**24** Ensure the ignition is switched off.
**25** Turn the steering wheel to the straight-ahead position.
**26** Remove the steering wheel as described in Chapter 10.
**27** Remove the steering column upper and lower shrouds. There are two screws facing upwards in the upper shroud, and one screw located beneath the lower shroud.

**31.3b . . . and on later models, release the wiring from the Velcro tape**

**31.10 . . . then undo the retaining nuts**

**28** Retain the contact spring unit in its central position using tape. **Note:** *New contact spring units are supplied preset to the central position, and retained with a transport safety catch.*
**29** Cut the cable tie, then disconnect the wiring for the contact spring unit at the connector, and release the wiring from the hook **(see illustrations)**.
**30** Note its fitted position, then undo the screws and remove the airbag contact spring unit from the steering column holder **(see illustrations)**.

#### Refitting

**31** If a new unit is being fitted, release the transport safety catch, but retain the unit in its central position with tape.
**32** Locate the unit onto the steering column then insert and tighten the retaining bolts.

**31.29a Cut the cable tie . . .**

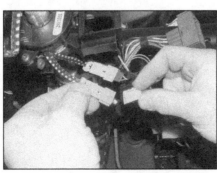

**31.29b . . . and disconnect the wiring**

**31.30a Undo the screws . . .**

**31.30b . . . and remove the airbag contact spring unit from the steering column**

Make sure it is still in its central position, however, it this has been lost, reset it as follows. With the wheels in their straight-ahead position, rotate the contact spring unit fully clockwise to its end position, then turn it back two complete turns.

**33** Plug in the wiring connector and locate the loom in the hook. Make sure the wiring is not twisted.

**34** Refit the steering column shrouds, then refit the steering wheel with reference to Chapter 10.

**35** Switch on the ignition and check that the SRS warning light goes out. If the warning light does not go out, the control unit probably

**31.40 SRS airbag electronic control unit**

has a fault code stored in it and it will be necessary to have a Saab dealer check the system.

### Side impact sensor

#### Removal

**36** The side impact sensor is located inside the door, behind the loudspeaker. First, remove the door inner trim panel and water-proof membrane as described in Section 13.

**37** Undo the retaining screws, withdraw the sensor from inside the door, and disconnect the wiring.

#### Refitting

**38** Refitting is a reversal of removal, but tighten the retaining screws to the specified torque. The sensor wiring connector must face downwards.

### Electronic control unit (ECU)

**Note:** *If a new ECU if fitted, it must be programmed by a Saab dealer using a special diagnostic tool.*

#### Removal

**39** Ensure the ignition is switched off.

**40** Remove the centre console as described in Section 28. The electronic control unit is located centrally on the floor panel beneath the centre console **(see illustration)**.

**41** Disconnect the wiring from the control unit.

**42** Note its fitted position, then undo the mounting bolts and withdraw the control unit from inside the vehicle.

#### Refitting

**43** Refitting is a reversal of removal, but tighten the mounting bolts securely. **Do not** connect the wiring before tightening the mounting bolts. Make sure that the arrow on the ECU points to the **rear** of the vehicle; this is important, as otherwise the airbag system will not function.

# Chapter 12
# Body electrical system

## Contents

## Degrees of difficulty

| Easy, suitable for novice with little experience |  | Fairly easy, suitable for beginner with some experience | | Fairly difficult, suitable for competent DIY mechanic |  | Difficult, suitable for experienced DIY mechanic | | Very difficult, suitable for expert DIY or professional | |

## Specifications

**System type** . . . . . . . . . . . . . . . . . . . . . . . . . . . . . . . . . . . . . . . . . . . . . . 12 volt negative earth

### Bulb ratings
| | Watts |
|---|---|
| Front and rear direction indicators | 21 |
| Front foglights | 55 |
| Headlights – main and dipped: | |
|     Standard | 55 |
|     Xenon lights | 37 |
| High-level stop-light: | |
|     Estate (LED) | 4 |
|     Saloon | 5 |
| Illumination for switches and front ashtray | 1.2 or 2.0 |
| Interior dome light, courtesy light, luggage compartment light, glove compartment light | 10 |
| Number plate lights | 5 |
| Reading light (rear) | 4 |
| Rear foglight, reversing light | 21 |
| Seat belt warning, reading light (front), overhead console | 5 |
| Sidelights | 5 |
| Side repeater light | 5 (or 2.2 for certain markets) |
| Stop/tail lights | 21/5 |

### Torque wrench setting
| | Nm | lbf ft |
|---|---|---|
| Windscreen wiper motor and linkage | 8 | 6 |

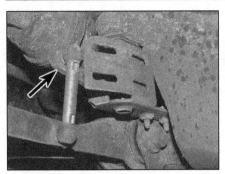

**1.3a Xenon load sensor fitted to the front suspension lower arm . . .**

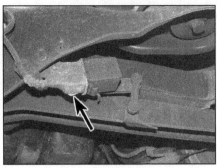

**1.3b . . . and rear suspension lower arm**

**1.4 Diagnostic socket located beneath the driver's side of the facia**

## 1 General information and precautions

⚠ *Warning: Before carrying out any work on the electrical system, read through the precautions given in 'Safety First!' at the beginning of this manual and Chapter 5A.*

⚠ *Warning: When working on Xenon headlights, always switch off the ignition and turn the key to its LOCK position. Never connect voltage to the Xenon headlight without its protective cover being fitted. Never attempt to repair the wiring of Xenon headlights; faulty wiring must be renewed in its entirety. It is recommended that protective gloves and glasses are worn.*

The electrical system is of 12 volt negative earth type and comprises a 12 volt battery, an alternator with integral voltage regulator, a starter motor and related electrical accessories, components and wiring.

All models are fitted with an anti-theft alarm and immobiliser system including door sensors, a boot lid/tailgate sensor, a bonnet sensor and a glass breakage sensor. The system is controlled by a central electronic control module which operates the warning horn on getting a signal from one of the sensors. A tilt angle sensor (fluid filled) is also fitted to some models to monitor any attempt to jack up the vehicle while the alarm is enabled. Both the glass and tilt sensors can be disabled individually if required, leaving just the main alarm functional. The system antenna is incorporated in the ignition switch, and the transponder for the immobiliser is located in the ignition key fob.

Some models are equipped with Xenon dipped headlights which are designed to last the life of the vehicle. To ensure these headlights do not dazzle oncoming traffic, an automatic levelling system is fitted incorporating load sensors on the front and rear suspension arms **(see illustrations)**.

This Chapter covers repair and service procedures for the various electrical components not associated with the engine.

Information on the battery, alternator and starter motor can be found in Chapter 5A. Many of the electrical circuits are linked to control units, which can be tested for faults using a purpose-made diagnostic instrument connected to the socket located beneath the driver's side of the facia **(see illustration)**.

It should be noted that prior to disconnecting wiring from any components in the electrical system, the battery negative terminal should first be disconnected, to prevent the possibility of electrical short circuits and/or fires. Note also that the alarm must be disabled before disconnecting the battery.

## 2 Electrical fault finding – general information

**Note:** *Refer to the precautions given in 'Safety first!' and in Section 1 of this Chapter before starting work. The following tests relate to testing of the main electrical circuits, and should not be used to test delicate electronic circuits (such as engine management systems, anti-lock braking systems, etc), particularly where an electronic control unit (ECU) is used.*

### General

A typical electrical circuit consists of an electrical component, any switches, relays, motors, fuses, fusible links or circuit breakers related to that component, and the wiring and connectors which link the component to both the battery and the body. To help pinpoint a problem in an electrical circuit, wiring diagrams are included at the end of this Chapter.

Before attempting to diagnose an electrical fault, first study the appropriate wiring diagram, to obtain a complete understanding of the components included in the particular circuit concerned. The possible sources of a fault can be narrowed down by noting if other components related to the circuit are operating properly. If several components or circuits fail at one time, the problem is likely to be related to a shared fuse or earth connection.

Electrical problems usually stem from simple causes, such as loose or corroded connections, a faulty earth connection, a blown fuse, a melted fusible link, or a faulty relay (refer to Section 3 for details of testing relays). Visually inspect the condition of all fuses, wires and connections in a problem circuit before testing the components. Use the wiring diagrams to determine which terminal connections will need to be checked in order to pinpoint the trouble spot.

The basic tools required for electrical fault finding include a circuit tester or voltmeter (a 12 volt bulb with a set of test leads can also be used for certain tests), an ohmmeter (to measure resistance and check for continuity), a battery and set of test leads, and a jumper wire (preferably with a circuit breaker or fuse incorporated), which can be used to bypass suspect wires or electrical components. Before attempting to locate a problem with test instruments, use the wiring diagram to determine where to make the connections.

To find the source of an intermittent wiring fault (usually due to a poor or dirty connection, or damaged wiring insulation), a 'wiggle' test can be performed on the wiring. This involves wiggling the wiring by hand to see if the fault occurs as the wiring is moved. It should be possible to narrow down the source of the fault to a particular section of wiring. This method of testing can be used in conjunction with any of the tests described in the following sub-Sections.

Apart from problems due to poor connections, two basic types of fault can occur in an electrical circuit – open-circuit or short-circuit.

Open circuit faults are caused by a break somewhere in the circuit, which prevents current from flowing. An open circuit fault will prevent a component from working, but will not cause the relevant circuit fuse to blow.

Short circuit faults are caused by a 'short' somewhere in the circuit, which allows the current flowing in the circuit to 'escape' along an alternative route, usually to earth. Short circuit faults are normally caused by a breakdown in wiring insulation, which allows a feed wire to touch either another wire, or an earthed component such as the bodyshell. A short circuit fault will normally cause the relevant circuit fuse to blow.

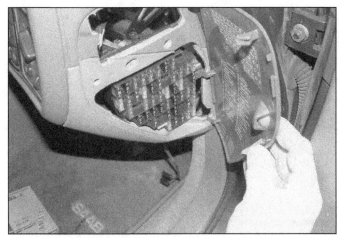

3.2a  Fusebox located on the right-hand end of the facia

3.2b  Removing a fuse from the fusebox located in the engine compartment

## Finding an open-circuit

To check for an open circuit, connect one lead of a circuit tester or the negative lead of a voltmeter either to the battery negative terminal or to a known good earth.

Connect the other lead to a connector in the circuit being tested, preferably nearest to the battery or fuse.

Switch on the circuit, bearing in mind that some circuits are live only when the ignition switch is moved to a particular position.

If voltage is present (indicated either by the tester bulb lighting or a voltmeter reading, as applicable), this means that the section of the circuit between the relevant connector and the switch is problem-free.

Continue to check the remainder of the circuit in the same fashion.

When a point is reached at which no voltage is present, the problem must lie between that point and the previous test point with voltage. Most problems can be traced to a broken, corroded or loose connection.

## Finding a short-circuit

To check for a short circuit, first disconnect the load(s) from the circuit (loads are the components which draw current from a circuit, such as bulbs, motors, heating elements, etc).

Remove the relevant fuse from the circuit, and connect a circuit tester or voltmeter to the fuse connections.

Switch on the circuit, bearing in mind that some circuits are live only when the ignition switch is moved to a particular position.

If voltage is present (indicated either by the tester bulb lighting or a voltmeter reading, as applicable), this means that there is a short circuit.

If no voltage is present during this test, but the fuse still blows with the load(s) reconnected, this indicates an internal fault in the load(s).

## Finding an earth fault

The battery negative terminal is connected to 'earth' – the metal of the engine/transmission unit and the vehicle body – and many systems are wired so that they only receive a positive feed, the current returning via the metal of the car body. This means that the component mounting and the body form part of that circuit. Loose or corroded mountings can therefore cause a range of electrical faults, ranging from total failure of a circuit, to a puzzling partial failure. In particular, lights may shine dimly (especially when another circuit sharing the same earth point is in operation), motors (eg, wiper motors or the radiator cooling fan motor) may run slowly, and the operation of one circuit may have an apparently unrelated effect on another. Note that on many vehicles, earth straps are used between certain components, such as the engine/transmission and the body, usually where there is no metal-to-metal contact between components, due to flexible rubber mountings, etc.

To check whether a component is properly earthed, disconnect the battery and connect one lead of an ohmmeter to a known good earth point. Connect the other lead to the wire or earth connection being tested. The resistance reading should be zero; if not, check the connection as follows.

If an earth connection is thought to be faulty, dismantle the connection, and clean

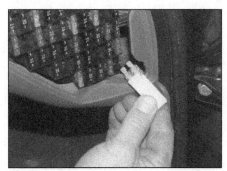

3.4  Using the plastic tool to remove a fuse

back to bare metal both the bodyshell and the wire terminal or the component earth connection mating surface. Be careful to remove all traces of dirt and corrosion, then use a knife to trim away any paint, so that a clean metal-to-metal joint is made. On reassembly, tighten the joint fasteners securely; if a wire terminal is being refitted, use serrated washers between the terminal and the bodyshell, to ensure a clean and secure connection. When the connection is remade, prevent the onset of corrosion in the future by applying a coat of petroleum jelly or silicone-based grease, or by spraying on (at regular intervals) a proprietary ignition sealer or a water dispersant lubricant.

## 3  Fuses and relays – general information

### Fuses

**1**  Fuses are designed to break an electrical circuit when a predetermined current limit is reached, in order to protect the components and wiring which could be damaged by excessive current flow. Any excessive current flow will be due to a fault in the circuit, usually a short-circuit (see Section 2).

**2**  The fuses are located either in the fusebox located on the right-hand end of the facia, or in the fusebox located in the left-hand rear of the engine compartment **(see illustrations)**. High amp fusible links are also located behind the fusebox on early models, or next to the battery on the left-hand front corner of the engine compartment on later models.

**3**  Access to the facia fusebox is gained by opening the driver's door and releasing the plastic cover. The engine compartment fusebox is opened by opening the bonnet and lifting the plastic cover.

**4**  To remove a fuse, use the plastic tool provided in the fusebox to pull the fuse from its socket **(see illustration)**.

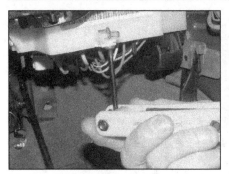

**3.8a Undo the screw ...**

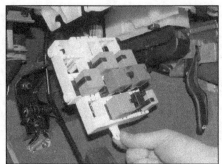

**3.8b ... and lower the relay holder from its housing**

## 4 Switches and controls – removal and refitting

5 Inspect the fuse from the side, through the transparent plastic body – a blown fuse can be recognised by its melted or broken wire.

6 Spare fuses are provided in the blank terminal positions in the fusebox.

7 Before renewing a blown fuse, trace and rectify the cause, and always use a fuse of the correct rating (see wiring diagrams at the end of this Chapter).

*Caution: Never substitute a fuse of a higher rating, or make temporary repairs using wire or metal foil; more serious damage, or even a fire, could result.*

### Relays

8 Relays are remote electrically-operated switches used in certain circuits. The relays are located under the right-hand side of the facia, or on the left-hand side of the engine compartment. Access to the facia-mounted

relays is gained by undoing the screw and lowering the relay holder **(see illustrations)**.

9 If a component controlled by a relay becomes inoperative and the relay is suspect, listen to the relay as the circuit is operated. If the relay is functioning, it should be possible to hear it click as it is energised. If the relay proves satisfactory, the fault lies with the components or wiring of the system. If the relay is not being energised, then either the relay is not receiving a switching voltage, or the relay itself is faulty. Do not overlook the relay socket terminals when tracing faults. Testing is by the substitution of a known good unit, but be careful; some relays are identical in appearance and in operation, but perform different functions.

10 To renew a relay first ensure that the ignition switch is off. The relay can then simply be pulled out from the socket and the new relay pressed in.

### Ignition switch cylinder

#### Removal

1 Remove the ignition key antenna unit from around the switch cylinder by turning it slightly clockwise and lifting it up.

2 Turn the ignition key to the OFF position, but leave it inserted.

3 Bend a length of welding rod at right-angles and insert it through the rear hole in the switch housing so that the locking catch is released. The lock cylinder can now be withdrawn directly from the housing. Refer to the cylinder removal included in *Ignition switch and lock removal* below for the location to insert the rod.

#### Refitting

4 Refitting is a reversal of removal.

### Ignition switch and lock

#### Removal

5 The ignition switch and lock is incorporated in the gearchange assembly between the front seats. Remove the centre console as described in Chapter 11; the ignition switch is incorporated in the gearchange housing.

6 To remove the manual transmission gearchange housing, select 4th gear then loosen the clamp at the universal joint. Unscrew the bolts securing the housing to the

**4.7a Remove the air duct ...**

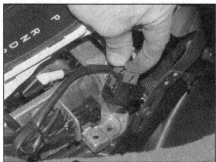

**4.7b ... disconnect the upper wiring ...**

**4.7c ... then extract the circlip ...**

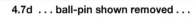

**4.7d ... ball-pin shown removed ...**

**4.7e ... and remove the cable ball-pin ...**

**4.7f ... lift the housing ...**

4.7g . . . disconnect the lower wiring . . .

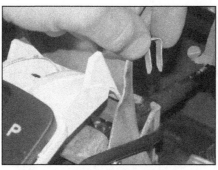

4.7h . . . and detach the selector cable from the housing

4.8a Depress the catch . . .

4.8b . . . remove the ignition switch cylinder . . .

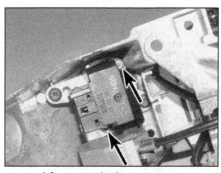

4.8c . . . undo the screws . . .

4.8d . . . and remove the ignition switch . . .

floor, then lift the housing and disconnect the wiring. Also remove the heater air duct.

**7** To remove the automatic transmission selector housing, remove the air duct, disconnect the upper wiring, then extract the circlip and drive out the cable ball-pin while

disconnecting the cable end fitting. Unscrew the bolts securing the housing to the floor, then lift the housing and disconnect the wiring and release the cable ties. Pull out the clip and lift the selector cable from the housing **(see illustrations)**.

**8** Remove the ignition switch cylinder as described earlier in this Section, then undo the screws and remove the switch, from the housing. Note the location of the spacer **(see illustrations)**.

**Refitting**

**9** Refitting is a reversal of removal.

### *Steering column switch*

**Removal**

**10** Adjust the steering wheel to its lowest and most rearward position, then lock it.

**11** Remove the steering column upper and lower shrouds. There are two screws facing upwards in the upper shroud, and one screw located beneath the lower shroud.

**12** Release the retaining clips and slide out the combination switch, then disconnect the wiring **(see illustrations)**.

4.8e . . . and spacer

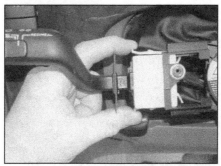

4.12a Remove the indicator/lighting combination switch . . .

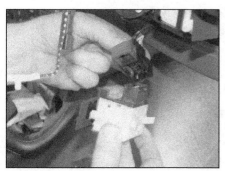

4.12b . . . and disconnect the wiring

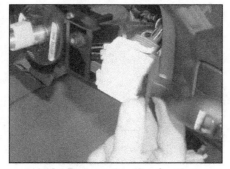

4.12c Remove the wiper/washer combination switch . . .

4.12d . . . and disconnect the wiring

4.15 Disconnecting the wiring from the electric window control switch

4.20 Removing the map reading light switch

4.23 Press out the lighting switch from behind . . .

### Refitting

13 Refitting is a reversal of removal.

## Electric window control switch

### Removal

14 Using a screwdriver, carefully prise up the front of the switch from the centre console.
15 Disconnect the wiring (see illustration).

### Refitting

16 Refitting is a reversal of removal.

## Headlight height switch

### Removal

17 Using a screwdriver, carefully prise the switch from the facia panel. If it is tight, remove the lighting switch and press the switch out from behind.
18 Disconnect the wiring.

### Refitting

19 Refitting is a reversal of removal.

## Interior lighting control switch

### Removal

20 Using a screwdriver, carefully prise the switch from the centre console rear section. Access to the lighting switches on the headlining console is gained after removing the lens and cover (see illustration).
21 Disconnect the wiring.

### Refitting

22 Refitting is a reversal of removal.

## Lighting and rear foglight switch/instrument illumination rheostat

### Removal

23 Remove the lid from the main fusebox on the end of the facia. Insert a finger through the fusebox opening and press out the lighting switch from behind (see illustration).
24 Disconnect the wiring (see illustration).

### Refitting

25 Refitting is a reversal of removal.

## Stop-light switch

### Removal

26 To remove the switch, first remove the lower trim panel from the facia with reference to Chapter 11.
27 Twist the switch anti-clockwise 90° and withdraw it from the mounting bracket.
28 Disconnect the wiring from the switch.

### Refitting

29 Refitting is a reversal of removal.

## Hazard warning light switch

### Removal

30 The switch is held in position by two tensioned plastic tabs which have both fitting and removal ramps. Carefully prise the switch from the facia using a screwdriver, or alternatively press out the switch from behind after removing the SID module (see illustration).
31 Disconnect the wiring.

### Refitting

32 Refitting is a reversal of removal.

## Electric door mirror switch

### Removal

33 Carefully prise the switch from the triangular cover on the front door or the inner trim panel on the rear door.
34 Disconnect the wiring.

### Refitting

35 Refitting is a reversal of removal.

## Courtesy light switch

### Removal

36 Open the door then undo the screw securing the courtesy light switch to the B- or C-pillar (see illustration).
37 Remove the switch and disconnect the wiring. Tape the wire to the pillar to prevent it dropping inside.

### Refitting

38 Refitting is a reversal of removal.

## TCS switch

### Removal

39 Carefully prise out the switch from the facia, or alternatively remove the radio/cassette unit and press out the switch from behind (see illustration).
40 Disconnect the wiring.

### Refitting

41 Refitting is a reversal of removal.

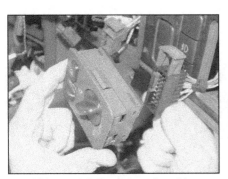

4.24 . . . and disconnect the wiring

4.30 Removing the hazard warning light switch

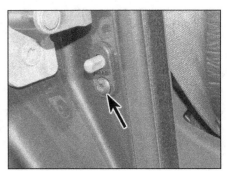

4.36 Courtesy light switch retaining screw

## Front foglight switch

### Removal

42 Carefully prise out the switch from the facia, or alternatively remove the lighting switch and press out the switch from behind (see illustration).
43 Disconnect the wiring.

### Refitting

44 Refitting is a reversal of removal.

## 5   Interior light bulbs – renewal

**4.39  Removing the TCS switch**

**4.42  Removing the front foglight switch**

## Instrument panel

1 Remove the instrument panel as described in Section 9.

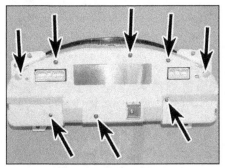

**5.2  Undo the screws . . .**

2 Undo and remove the 8 screws securing the back panel to the module (see illustration). Note that 4 screws are short and 4 are long, so record their positions.
3 Release the 2 side clips and withdraw the

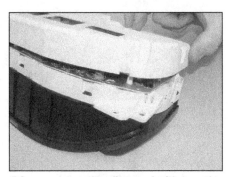

**5.3  . . . release the clips, and withdraw the back panel**

back panel (see illustration).
4 Disconnect the wiring plugs and remove the printed circuit boards (see illustrations).
5 Twist the relevant bulbholder and remove it from the instrument panel; the bulbholder positions are marked on the printed circuit board (see illustrations).
6 Fit the new bulb using a reversal of the removal procedure.

### Rear interior lights

#### Passenger compartment

7 Using a screwdriver carefully prise down the interior light lens (see illustration). Note that the glass breakage sensor is located in the light cover.
8 To remove the side bulbs, depress and twist them; to remove the centre festoon type bulb, release it from the terminals (see illustration).

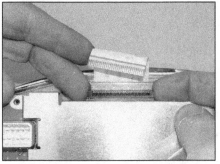

**5.4a  Disconnect the wiring plugs . . .**

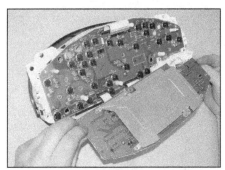

**5.4b  . . . and remove the printed circuit boards**

**5.5a  Removing a bulb/bulbholder from the printed circuit board**

**5.5b  The bulb positions are marked on the printed circuit**

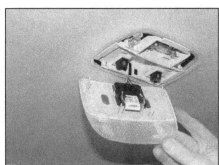

**5.7  Prise down the interior light lens . . .**

**5.8  . . . then depress and twist the side bulbs, or release the central festoon type bulb from its terminals**

5.10 Removing the luggage compartment interior light lens . . .

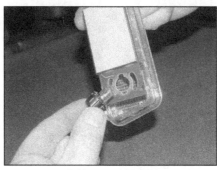

5.11 . . . and bulb

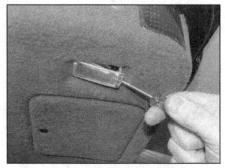

5.16 Prise out the interior light lens . . .

5.17 . . . and remove the festoon type bulb from the terminals

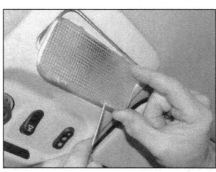

5.22a Prise off the lens . . .

5.22b . . . and remove the festoon type bulb

9 Fit the new bulb using a reversal of the removal procedure.

### Estate luggage compartment

10 Using a screwdriver carefully prise out the interior light lens (see illustration).
11 Remove the festoon type bulb from the terminals (see illustration).
12 Fit the new bulb using a reversal of the removal procedure.

### Saloon luggage compartment

13 Using a screwdriver carefully prise the interior light lens from the trim panel.
14 Remove the festoon type bulb from the terminals.
15 Fit the new bulb using a reversal of the removal procedure.

### Tailgate loading light

16 Using a screwdriver carefully prise the interior light/lens from the trim panel (see illustration).
17 Remove the festoon type bulb from the terminals (see illustration).
18 Fit the new bulb using a reversal of the removal procedure.

### Glovebox illumination

19 With the glovebox open, use a screwdriver to prise out the lens/light unit.
20 Remove the festoon type bulb from the terminals.
21 Fit the new bulb using a reversal of the removal procedure.

### Front interior/map reading lights

22 Prise off the lens using a small screwdriver, and remove the festoon type bulb from the terminals (see illustrations).
23 Undo the cover retaining screw. Where applicable, remove the microphone and temperature sensor from the cover (see illustrations).
24 To remove the spotlight bulb, turn the spotlight reflector anti-clockwise and pull out the wedge-type bulb. To remove the illumination bulbs, use a length of washer tubing to grip the wedge-type bulbs (see illustrations).
25 Fit the new bulb using a reversal of the removal procedure.

5.23a Undo the retaining screw . . .

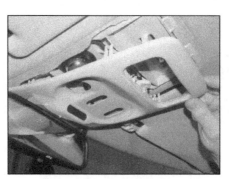

5.23b . . . lower the cover . . .

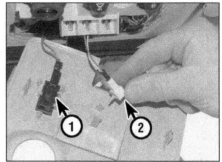

5.23c . . . and remove the microphone (1) and temperature sensor (2)

**5.24a  Turn the spotlight reflector anti-clockwise from the housing . . .**

**5.24b  . . . and pull out the wedge-type bulb**

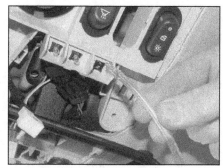

**5.24c  Use washer tubing to remove. . .**

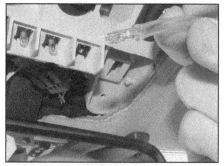

**5.24d  . . . the wedge-type illumination bulbs**

**5.26  Removing the selector lever surround (automatic transmission models)**

**5.27  Removing the outer (veneered) panel from the ashtray**

## Cigarette lighter

**26** On manual transmission models, prise the gear lever gaiter from the centre console. On automatic transmission models, use a screwdriver to prise up the selector lever surround **(see illustration)**.

**27** Open the ashtray and remove the outer (veneered) panel together with the ashtray **(see illustration)**.

**28** Using a screwdriver, prise back the retaining tabs and prise the ashtray/oddments box from the centre console **(see illustrations)**. Use tape to protect the walnut veneer.

**29** Undo the screws and remove the gear lever/selector cover. Identify the wiring locations then disconnect the plugs – there are plugs for the seat heating, seat ventilation and cigarette lighter. Also disconnect the wiring from the central locking switch **(see illustrations)**.

**30** With the cover removed, disconnect the bulb wiring from the rear of the cigarette lighter, then remove the bulbholder and extract the bulb.

**31** Fit the new bulb using a reversal of the removal procedure.

## Window switch illumination

**32** Remove the electric window control switch as described in Section 4.

**33** Using a screwdriver, twist the bulbholder anti-clockwise to remove it.

**34** Fit the new bulb using a reversal of the removal procedure.

## Automatic transmission selector illumination

**35** Remove the position indicator panel, followed by the green strip and slider **(see illustrations)**.

**5.28a  Prise back the retaining tabs . . .**

**5.29  Removing the gear lever/selector cover**

**36** Remove the graded strip, then use a suitable rubber tube to extract the illumination bulb **(see illustrations)**.

**37** Fit the new bulb using a reversal of the removal procedure.

**5.28b  . . . and remove the ashtray box from the centre console**

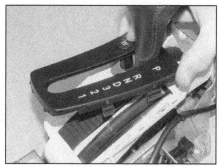

**5.35a  Remove the position indicator panel . . .**

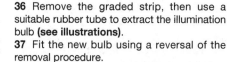

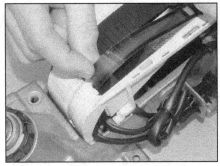

5.35b . . . followed by the green strip . . .

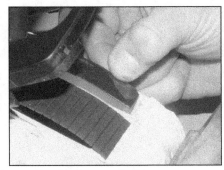

5.35c . . . and slider . . .

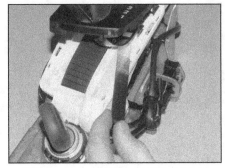

5.36a . . . remove the graded strip . . .

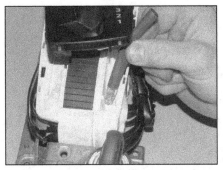

5.36b . . . and use a suitable rubber tube to extract the bulb

5.39 Removing the bulbholder from the Saab Information Display (SID) module

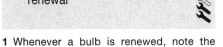

5.42 Removing the bulbholder from the rear of the lighting switch

### Saab Information Display module illumination

**38** Remove the SID module (see Section 10).
**39** Using a screwdriver, twist the bulbholder anti-clockwise and remove it from the module

5.45 Removing the bulbholder from the side of the hazard switch

5.48 Removing the bulbholder from the rear of the climate control module

**(see illustration)**. There are 6 bulbholders in all, and Saab recommend that all are renewed at the same time as they all have an identical life expectancy.
**40** Fit the new bulb using a reversal of the removal procedure.

### Lighting switch illumination

**41** Remove the lighting switch (see Section 4).
**42** Twist the bulbholder from the rear of the switch **(see illustration)**.
**43** Fit the new bulb using a reversal of the removal procedure.

### Hazard switch illumination

**44** Remove the hazard switch as described in Section 4.
**45** Twist the bulbholder from the side of the switch **(see illustration)**.
**46** Fit the new bulb using a reversal of the removal procedure.

6.2 Unscrew the plastic cover . . .

### Climate control module illumination

**47** Remove the climate control module as described in Chapter 3, Section 9.
**48** Using a screwdriver, twist the bulbholder from the rear of the module **(see illustration)**.
**49** Fit the new bulb using a reversal of the removal procedure.

---

### 6 Exterior light bulbs – renewal

**1** Whenever a bulb is renewed, note the following points:
  a) *Switch off all exterior lights and the ignition.*
  b) *Remember that if the light has just been in use, the bulb may be extremely hot.*
  c) *Always check the bulb contacts and holder, ensuring that there is clean metal-to-metal contact.*
  d) *Always ensure that the new bulb is of the correct rating and that it is completely clean before fitting it.*
  e) *Do not touch the glass of halogen-type bulbs (headlights, front foglights) with the fingers, as this may lead to premature failure of the new bulb; if the glass is accidentally touched, clean it with methylated spirit.*

### Headlight (halogen)

**2** With the bonnet open, unscrew the plastic cover anti-clockwise from the rear of the headlight **(see illustration)**. Access to the left-hand headlight can be improved by unclipping

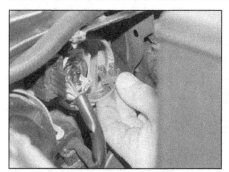

6.3 ... disconnect the wiring ...

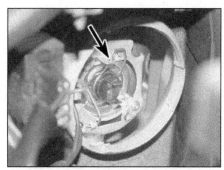

6.4a ... release the spring clip ...

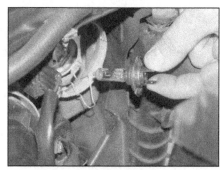

6.4b ... and remove the bulb

6.7 Remove the cover ...

6.8a ... release the clip ...

6.8b ... and withdraw the Xenon light bulb ...

the cover from the battery. Access to the right-hand headlight can be improved by moving the air inlet hose to one side.

**3** Disconnect the wiring from the bulb **(see illustration)**.

**4** Release the spring clip and remove the bulb **(see illustrations)**. Use a tissue or clean cloth to prevent touching the bulb.

**5** Fit the new bulb using a reversal of the removal procedure, but make sure that the bulb location lugs engage correctly in the rear of the headlight. The plastic cover must be refitted with the UP arrow facing upwards.

### Headlight (Xenon)

 *Warning: It is recommended that protective gloves and safety glasses are worn when renewing Xenon headlamp bulbs. The*

*bulbs contain mercury and are highly pressurised. Do not switch on the headlamps with the bulb removed – high voltages (23 000 volts minimum) are present which could cause personal injury!*

### Dipped beam

**6** Remove the headlight as described in Section 7.

**7** Remove the cover from the rear of the headlight **(see illustration)**.

**8** Release the spring clip and withdraw the Xenon light bulb unit from the headlight **(see illustrations)**.

**9** Disconnect the wiring and remove the bulb unit **(see illustrations)**.

**10** Fit the new bulb unit using a reversal of the removal procedure.

### Main beam

**11** With the bonnet open, unscrew the plastic cover anti-clockwise from the rear of the headlight **(see illustration)**. On later models, access to the left-hand headlight can be improved by unclipping the cover from the battery. Access to the right-hand headlight can be improved by moving the air inlet hose to one side.

**12** Disconnect the wiring from the main beam bulb **(see illustration)**.

**13** Release the spring clip and remove the bulb **(see illustrations)**.

**14** Fit the new bulb using a reversal of the removal procedure, but make sure that the bulb location lugs engage correctly in the rear of the headlight. On later models, the plastic cover must be refitted with the tab facing upwards.

6.9 ... then disconnect the wiring

6.11 Unscrew the plastic cover ...

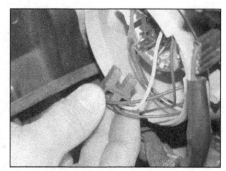

6.12 ... disconnect the wiring ...

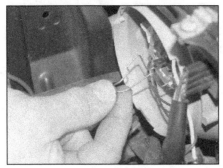

6.13a . . . release the spring clip . . .

6.13b . . . and remove the bulb

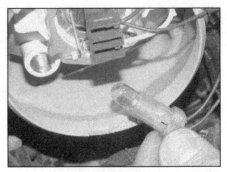

6.16a Pull the front sidelight bulbholder from the headlight . . .

6.16b . . . and pull out the wedge-type bulb

6.19a Pull out the bulbholder with the reinforced wires . . .

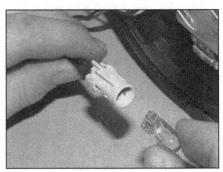

6.19b . . . then pull out the wedge-type sidelight bulb

### Front sidelight

#### Models with halogen dipped beam

15 With the bonnet open, unscrew the plastic cover anti-clockwise from the rear of the main headlight. Access to the left-hand headlight can be improved by unclipping the cover from the battery. Access to the right-hand headlight can be improved by moving the air inlet hose to one side.

16 Pull the bulbholder from the headlight, then pull the wedge-type bulb from the bulbholder (see illustrations).

17 Fit the new bulb using a reversal of the removal procedure.

#### Models with Xenon dipped beam

18 With the bonnet open, unscrew the plastic cover anti-clockwise from the rear of the main headlight. Access to the left-hand headlight

can be improved by unclipping the cover from the battery. Access to the right-hand headlight can be improved by moving the air inlet hose to one side.

19 Pull the bulbholder wires and remove the bulbholder from the headlight, then pull the wedge-type bulb from the bulbholder. Note that the wires are reinforced to withstand pulling out the bulbholder (see illustrations).

20 Fit the new bulb using a reversal of the removal procedure. If necessary, look through the front of the headlight lens to help locate the bulbholder.

### Front direction indicator

21 Open the bonnet. On pre-2002 models, use a socket to loosen the direction indicator retaining screw located on the engine compartment front crossmember. On 2002-on models, reach into the front corner of the

engine compartment and depress the front direction indicator retaining catch. Access to the left-hand side can be improved by unclipping the cover from the battery. Access to the right-hand side can be improved by moving the air inlet hose to one side.

22 Withdraw the front direction indicator forwards, then twist the bulbholder anti-clockwise to remove it (see illustration).

23 Depress and twist the bulb to remove it (see illustration).

24 Fit the new bulb using a reversal of the removal procedure.

### Side repeater lights

25 Carefully press the light forwards against the tension of the plastic clip, then release the rear of the light from the front wing (see illustration).

6.22 Twist the front direction bulbholder anti-clockwise to remove it . . .

6.23 . . . then depress and twist the bulb

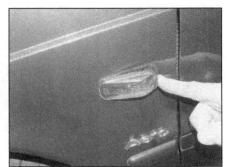

6.25 Press the side repeater light forwards . . .

6.26a ... remove the bulbholder ...

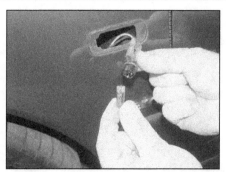

6.26b ... then pull out the wedge-type bulb

6.30a  Squeeze together the locking tabs and remove the body bulbholder ...

6.30b ... or boot lid bulbholder ...

6.31 ... then depress and twist the bulb to remove it

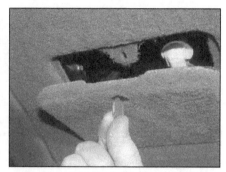

6.34  To access the tailgate cluster bulb, open the access flap ...

26  Twist the bulbholder and remove the lens unit, then pull out the wedge-type bulb **(see illustrations)**. Do not allow the wiring to drop into the space behind the wing.

27  Fit the new bulb using a reversal of the removal procedure.

### Rear light cluster

#### Saloon models

28  The rear light cluster consists of light units in the rear body and also in the boot lid.

29  To access the body cluster, open the boot lid and pull back the carpet flap in the luggage compartment. To access the boot lid cluster, release the trim by removing the grab handle and relevant fasteners (depress the fastener centres).

30  Squeeze together the locking tabs and remove the bulbholder from the cluster **(see illustrations)**.

31  Depress and twist the relevant bulb and remove it from the bulbholder **(see illustration)**.

32  Fit the new bulb using a reversal of the removal procedure. Before refitting the fasteners, pull out their centres.

#### Estate models

33  The rear light cluster consists of light units in the rear body and also in the tailgate.

34  To access the body cluster bulb, open the tailgate then turn the fasteners a quarter turn anti-clockwise and remove the cover from the side of the rear light cluster. Undo the retaining screws and pull the cluster from the body while tilting it outwards. Remove the fastener from the body and refit it to the cluster. To access the tailgate cluster bulb, open the tailgate then turn the fastener a quarter turn anti-clockwise and remove the cover **(see illustration)**.

35  Twist the relevant bulbholder and remove it from the cluster.

36  Depress and twist the bulb and remove it from the bulbholder **(see illustrations)**.

37  Fit the new bulb using a reversal of the removal procedure.

### Front foglight

38  Apply the handbrake, then jack up the front of the vehicle and support it on axle stands (see *Jacking and vehicle support*).

39  Reach up behind the foglight and twist the bulbholder anti-clockwise to remove it **(see illustration)**. If necessary, the bulbholder can be disconnected from the wiring.

40  Pull the bulb from the bulbholder **(see illustration)**.

41  Fit the new bulb using a reversal of the removal procedure.

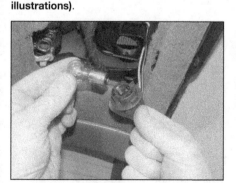

6.36a ... remove the bulbholder, then depress and twist the bulb to remove it

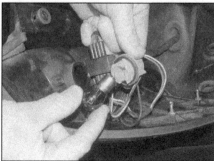

6.36b  Removing a body rear light cluster bulb

6.39  Remove the bulbholder from the front foglight ...

6.40 ... then pull out the bulb

6.42a Undo the screws ...

6.42b ... withdraw the lens ...

6.43 ... and pull out the wedge-type bulb

6.48a Remove the rear window side trim covers ...

## Number plate light

42 Undo the screws and withdraw the lens from the number plate light (see illustrations). Recover the seal, and check it for damage.

43 Pull out the wedge-type bulb from the bulbholder (see illustration).
44 Fit the new bulb using a reversal of the removal procedure.

## High-level stop-light

### Saloon models

45 Remove the cover panel from the rear of the headlining by carefully pressing in the two clips on each side.
46 Unclip the bulbholder from the cover panel, then pull out the relevant wedge-type bulb.
47 Fit the new bulb using a reversal of the removal procedure. Make sure the cover panel is fully entered in the clips.

### Estate models

48 With the tailgate open, prise off the covers, then undo the screws and remove the rear window side and upper trim covers (see illustrations).
49 Disconnect the wiring from the high-level stop-light, then unscrew the nuts and withdraw the light unit from the tailgate (see illustrations).

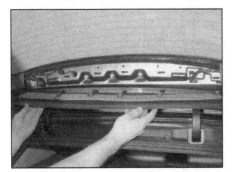

6.48b ... and upper trim cover

6.49a Disconnect the wiring ...

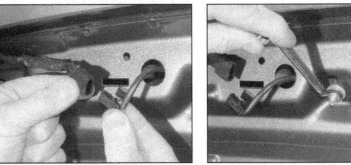

6.49b ... then unscrew the nuts ...

6.49c ... and withdraw the light unit from the tailgate

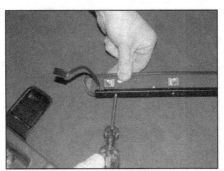

6.50a Undo the screws ...

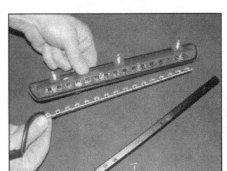

6.50b ... and separate the printed circuit board and LEDs

7.3a Unscrew the headlight upper . . .

7.3b . . . and lower mounting screws

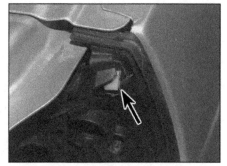

7.3c Headlight side protective cover clip

**50** Undo the screws and separate the printed circuit board together with the LEDs **(see illustrations)**. Take care not to damage the guide pins.
**51** Fit the new printed circuit board using a reversal of the removal procedure.

## 7 Exterior light units –
removal and refitting

### Headlight

⚠️ **Warning: On models with Xenon headlights, the ignition switch must be OFF and in its LOCK position.**

**1** With the bonnet open, remove the radiator grille as described in Chapter 11. On 2002-on models it is only necessary to remove the

centre and side grilles. On pre-2002 models, remove the front bumper as described in Chapter 11.
**2** Remove the relevant direction indicator light as described later in this Section.
**3** Undo the upper and lower headlight mounting screws. On later models, also unclip the headlight side protective cover from the front wing **(see illustrations)**.
**4** If fitted, lift the wiper arms from the headlamps, then withdraw the headlight unit forwards, at the same time releasing it from the height adjustment arm.
**5** Disconnect the wiring plug and withdraw the headlight from the vehicle. Note the location peg on the valance **(see illustrations)**.
**6** Refitting is a reversal of removal, but on 2002-on models, make sure that the headlight drain hose is located free of any obstruction

and pointing downwards. Have the headlight beam alignment checked and adjusted as soon as possible.

### Front direction indicator light

**7** Open the bonnet. On pre-2002 models, use a socket to loosen the direction indicator retaining screw located on the engine compartment front crossmember. On 2002-on models, reach into the front corner of the engine compartment and depress the front direction indicator retaining catch. Access to the left-hand side can be improved by unclipping the cover from the battery **(see illustrations)**. Access to the right-hand side can be improved by moving the air inlet hose to one side.
**8** Withdraw the front direction indicator forwards, then twist the bulbholder anti-clockwise to remove it **(see illustrations)**.
**9** Refitting is a reversal of removal, but make

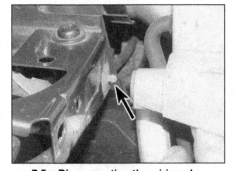

7.5a Disconnecting the wiring plug

7.5b Headlight location peg on the valance

7.5c Removing the headlight on 2002-on models

7.7a Loosen the screw . . .

7.7b . . . remove the battery cover on 2002-on models . . .

7.8a . . . then withdraw the front direction indicator forwards . . .

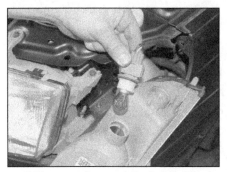

7.8b . . . and remove the bulbholder

7.9 Front direction indicator light location peg

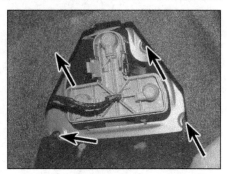

7.16 Rear light cluster mounting nut locations (Saloon models)

sure the rear location peg is located in the front wing, and the front location tangs engage with the slots in the headlight unit (see illustration).

### Side repeater light

**10** Carefully press the light forwards against the tension of the plastic clip, then release the rear of the light from the front wing.
**11** Twist the bulbholder and remove the lens unit. Do not allow the wiring to drop into the space behind the wing.
**12** Refitting is a reversal of removal.

### Rear light cluster

#### Saloon models

**13** The rear light cluster consists of light units in the rear body and also in the boot lid.
**14** To remove the body cluster, open the boot lid and pull back the carpet flap in the luggage compartment. To remove the boot lid cluster, release the trim by removing the grab handle and relevant fasteners (depress the fastener centres). Remove the number plate and decor panel as necessary.
**15** Squeeze together the locking tabs and remove the bulbholder from the cluster.
**16** Unscrew the nuts and withdraw the cluster (see illustration). On the boot lid cluster, depress the catches to release it.
**17** Refitting is a reversal of removal, but firmly tighten the nuts.

#### Estate models

**18** The rear light cluster consists of light units in the rear body and also in the tailgate.
**19** To remove the body cluster, open the tailgate then, on pre-2002 models, prise out the covers concealing the retaining screws. On later models, turn the fasteners a quarter turn anti-clockwise and remove the cover from the

side of the rear light cluster. Undo the retaining screws and pull the cluster from the body while tilting it outwards. Disconnect the wiring by prising up the lock (see illustrations).
**20** To remove the tailgate cluster, open the tailgate and carefully prise away the upper trim mouldings from around the rear window aperture inside the tailgate. Undo the screws and remove the inner hand grip. Undo the screws from the lower edge of the trim panel, then pull down the top of the panel to release it from the upper clips, and pull it to the rear to release the guide pin at the hand grip. Where necessary, remove the number plate and decor panel. On RHD models, remove the private lock and leave it suspended; on LHD models without a lock cylinder, remove the clip and cable. Undo the retaining nuts and remove the clamp plate, then withdraw the cluster and disconnect the wiring (see illustrations).

7.19a On pre-2002 models, prise out the plastic covers

7.19b Undo the retaining screws . . .

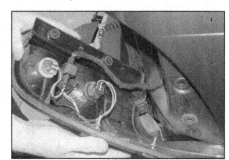

7.19c . . . and withdraw the rear light cluster from the body while releasing the location pins from the grommets . . .

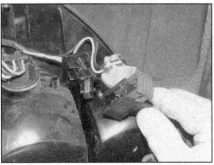

7.19d . . . and disconnect the wiring

7.20a Remove the private lock . . .

7.20b . . . disconnect the cluster wiring . . .

**21** Refitting is a reversal of removal. Before refitting the body cluster, remove the fastener from the body and refit it to the cluster. Check the tailgate cluster seal before refitting it.

### Front foglight

**22** Apply the handbrake, then jack up the front of the vehicle and support it on axle stands (see *Jacking and vehicle support*).
**23** Reach up behind the foglight and twist the bulbholder anti-clockwise to remove it. If necessary, the bulbholder can be disconnected from the wiring.
**24** Undo the retaining nut and bolts as applicable, then withdraw the foglight from the bumper.
**25** Refitting is a reversal of removal. To adjust the foglight, park the vehicle 10 metres from a wall and mark the wall with a cross at the same height as the centre of the lens. Make a further mark 10 to 20 cm below the cross, then adjust the foglight beam onto this mark by turning the knob on the rear of the light unit.

### Number plate light

**26** Undo the screws and lower the number plate light from the tailgate.
**27** Disconnect the wiring.
**28** Refitting is a reversal of removal.

### High-level stop-light

#### Saloon models

**29** Remove the cover panel from the rear of the headlining by carefully pressing in the two clips on each side.

**30** Undo the console retaining screws then unplug the wiring and withdraw the light unit.
**31** Refitting is a reversal of removal.

#### Estate models

**32** With the tailgate open, prise off the covers, then undo the screws and remove the rear window trim covers.
**33** Unscrew the nuts, withdraw the high-level stop-light and disconnect the wiring.
**34** Undo the screws and separate the printed circuit board together with the LEDs. Take care not to damage the guide pins.
**35** Refitting is a reversal of removal.

### Headlight manual adjustment unit

**36** The manual adjustment unit can be removed without removing the headlight unit. Reach in behind the headlight and disconnect the wiring **(see illustration)**.
**37** Twist the unit anti-clockwise and unhook the arm from the headlight reflector **(see illustration)**. Withdraw the unit.
**38** Refitting is a reversal of removal, however, to facilitate connecting the arm to the reflector, remove the cover from the outer headlight and pull the reflector towards the beam adjustment unit.

### Xenon headlight control module

 *Warning: Observe the safety precautions for models with Xenon headlights, given earlier in this Chapter. Also, note that the module is sensitive to static electricity; earth yourself regularly during the module removal and refitting procedure.*

**Note:** *If the module is renewed, it must be programmed by a Saab dealer using specialist equipment.*
**39** Remove the headlight as described earlier in this Section.
**40** Undo the six screws and withdraw the module from the headlight **(see illustrations)**.
**41** Disconnect the wiring and remove the module.
**42** Check the condition of the module seal and renew it if necessary.
**43** Refitting is a reversal of removal.

### 8  Headlight beam adjustment – general information

**1** Accurate adjustment of the headlight beam is only possible using optical beam-setting equipment, and this work should therefore be carried out by a Saab dealer or suitably-equipped workshop. In an emergency, it is possible to adjust the headlights by turning the knobs located on the rear of the headlight.
**2** Some models have a headlight beam adjustment control, which allows the aim of the headlights to be adjusted to compensate for variation in the vehicle's payload. The aim is altered by means of facia-mounted switch, which controls electric adjuster motors located in the rear of the headlight assemblies. The switch should be positioned as follows, according to the load being carried in the vehicle:

7.20c ... unscrew the nuts and remove the clamp plate ...

7.20d ... and withdraw the rear light cluster from the tailgate

7.36 Disconnect the wiring ...

7.37 ... then twist the headlight beam adjustment unit and disconnect the arm

7.40a Undo the screws ...

7.40b ... and withdraw the Xenon headlight control module

| Switch position | Vehicle load |
|---|---|
| 0 | Up to 3 occupants (no more than one in the rear seat), no luggage. |
| 1 | Up to 3 occupants in rear seats, up to 30 kg in luggage. |
| 2 | Up to 3 occupants in rear seats, up to 80 kg in luggage. |
| 3 | Up to 5 occupants, luggage area full – or up to 5 occupants, luggage area full, towing caravan/trailer. |

**3** Models with Xenon headlights have an automatic levelling system. If a fault occurs in this system, a warning light will show up on the instrument panel, and the headlights will be angled down to avoid dazzling oncoming traffic. If this happens, the driving speed must be adjusted accordingly to allow for decreased visibility.

**4** To make a temporary adjustment of the headlights, position the vehicle on a level surface 10 metres from a wall. The tyres must all be at the correct pressure, the fuel tank half full, and a person must be sitting in the driver's seat. Turn on the ignition, and where applicable check that the manual headlight setting is at 0. Measure the distance from the ground to the cross in the centre of the headlight, then deduct 5.0 cm for models with halogen lights and 7.5 cm for models with Xenon lights. Draw a mark on the wall at this height, then adjust the headlight beam centre point onto this mark by turning the adjustment knobs on the rear of the headlight unit **(see illustration)**.

**8.4 The headlight height adjustment is made on the manual adjustment unit**

## 9 Instrument panel and electronic unit – removal and refitting

### Instrument panel

#### Removal

**1** Adjust the steering wheel to its lowest and most rearward position, then lock it.

**2** Remove the steering column upper and lower shrouds. There are two screws facing upwards in the upper shroud, and one screw located beneath the lower shroud.

**3** Depress the retaining clips and withdraw the direction indicator and windscreen wiper combination switches, then disconnect the wiring.

**4** Remove the radio/cassette player and mounting box as described in Section 17.

**5** Remove the Saab Information Display (SID) unit as described in Section 10.

**6** Remove the air conditioning/heating ventilation unit as described in Chapter 3. Do not remove the seat heating unit.

**7** Remove the facia switches located on the inner side of the steering column.

**8** Remove the lid from the main fusebox on the end of the facia. Insert a finger through the fusebox opening and press out the lighting switches from behind. Disconnect the black, green and orange wiring connectors, noting their location.

**9** Carefully prise out the button blanks from the facia.

**10** Undo the screws and remove the instrument surround panel – there are 6 screws and 4 clips located inside the various apertures. With the surround removed, if necessary the cup holder may be removed after undoing the retaining screws **(see illustrations)**.

**11** Undo the instrument panel mounting screws, then withdraw the unit and unplug the wiring connectors. Withdraw the unit from the bulkhead **(see illustrations)**.

#### Refitting

**12** Refitting is a reversal of removal.

### Electronic unit

#### Removal

**13** Remove the instrument panel as described.

**14** Undo and remove the 8 screws securing the back panel to the module. Note that 4 screws are short and 4 are long, so record their positions.

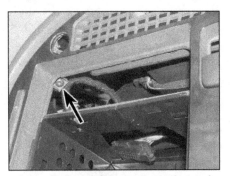

**9.10a The retaining screws are located inside the apertures**

**9.10b Removing the instrument surround panel**

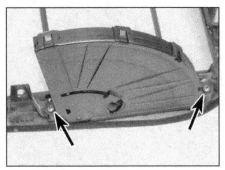

**9.10c Screws retaining the cup holder to the instrument surround panel**

**9.11a Undo the mounting screws on each side . . .**

**9.11b . . . withdraw the instrument panel from the facia . . .**

**9.11c . . . and disconnect the wiring**

**15** Release the 2 side clips and withdraw the back panel.

**16** Disconnect the wiring plugs and remove the printed circuit boards, then undo the screws and withdraw the electronic unit **(see illustrations)**.

**Refitting**

**17** Refitting is a reversal of removal.

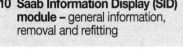

**10 Saab Information Display (SID) module** – general information, removal and refitting

**Note:** *If a new SID module is fitted, it must be programmed by a Saab dealer using the special Saab Tech2 diagnostic tool.*

**General information**

**1** The Saab Information Display (SID) module provides the driver with information, and also controls the display lighting and trip computer. The module also displays service reminders. It uses the following components:
a) *Outside temperature sensor.*
b) *Steering wheel horn and audio controls.*
c) *Coolant level sensor.*
d) *Washer fluid level sensor.*
e) *Headlight filament sensor.*
f) *Display lighting rheostat.*
g) *Interior light sensor for automatic control of the display illumination.*

**Removal**

**2** The Saab Information Display (SID) module is located in the centre of the facia above the

**9.16a  Undo the screws . . .**

radio. First remove the radio/cassette player as described in Section 17.

**3** Reach in behind the SID module and push it out of the facia panel **(see illustrations)**.

**4** Disconnect the wiring and remove the module **(see illustration)**.

**Refitting**

**5** Refitting is a reversal of removal.

**11 Cigarette lighter –** removal and refitting

**Removal**

**1** There are two cigarette lighters, one above the ashtray and the other on the rear of the centre console.

**10.3b  Remove the SID unit . . .**

**9.16b  . . . and remove the electronic unit**

**Front cigarette lighter**

**2** To remove the front cigarette lighter, on manual transmission models, prise the gear lever gaiter from the centre console. On automatic transmission models, use a screwdriver to prise up the selector lever surround.

**3** Using a screwdriver, prise out the ashtray and holder, or oddments tray as applicable.

**4** Undo the screws and remove the gear lever cover. Identify the wiring locations then disconnect the plugs – there are plugs for the seat heating, seat ventilation and cigarette lighter.

**5** Remove the lighter element, then release the cigarette lighter socket and illumination ring from the cover.

**Rear cigarette lighter**

**6** Remove the rear end part of the centre console by lifting it straight up, then disconnect the wiring.

**7** Remove the lighter element, then release the cigarette lighter socket and illumination ring.

**Refitting**

**8** Refitting is a reversal of removal.

**12 Horn –** removal and refitting

**Removal**

**1** Remove the radiator grille as described in Chapter 11.

**2** Disconnect the wiring from the horn **(see illustration)**.

**10.3a  Reach through the radio/cassette aperture and push out the SID unit**

**10.4  . . . and disconnect the wiring**

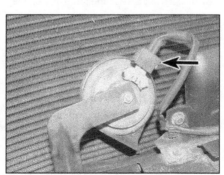
**12.2  Horn wiring plug**

**12.4  The two horn positions**

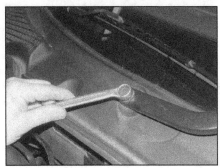

**13.3 Unscrew the nut . . .**

**13.4 . . . then use a small puller to remove the wiper arm from the spindle**

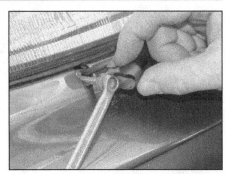

**13.12 Removing the headlight wiper arm**

**3** Note that the horns are each marked to indicate their tone – the high tone horn is marked with an H, and the low tone horn with an L.
**4** Unscrew the bracket mounting nut and withdraw the horn assembly **(see illustration)**.

### Refitting

**5** Refitting is a reversal of removal. When fitted, the horn must be angled downwards and outwards by 45° for 1998 to 2001 models, and 15° to 20° for later models.

## 13 Windscreen, tailgate and headlight wiper arms – removal and refitting

### Windscreen wiper arm

**1** Make sure that the windscreen wipers are at their rest positions. Use a piece of tape to mark the position on the windscreen.
**2** Prise up the cover from the windscreen wiper arm.
**3** Unscrew the nut securing the wiper arm to the spindle **(see illustration)**.
**4** Ease the arm from the spindle by carefully rocking it side-to-side. If it is tight, use a small puller to remove it **(see illustration)**.
**5** Refitting is a reversal of removal.

### Tailgate wiper arm

**6** Make sure that the tailgate wipers are at their rest positions. Use a piece of tape to mark the position on the windscreen.

**15.5 Removing the rubber seals from the spindles**

**7** Lift up the cover at the base of the tailgate wiper arm.
**8** Unscrew the nut securing the wiper arm to the shaft.
**9** Ease the arm from the shaft by carefully rocking it side-to-side. If it is tight, use a small puller to remove it.
**10** Refitting is a reversal of removal.

### Headlight wiper arm

**Note:** *On later models, high pressure headlight washers are fitted in the front bumper, without the need for wiper blades.*
**11** Note the rest position of the headlight wiper arms. Use a piece of tape to mark the position on the headlight.
**12** Unscrew the nut securing the wiper arm to the shaft **(see illustration)**.
**13** Ease the arm from the shaft by rocking it side-to-side, then disconnect the washer tubing. Remove the arm.
**14** Refitting is a reversal of removal.

## 14 Rain sensor – removal and refitting

### Removal

**1** The rain sensor is located centrally, at the top of the windscreen, just in front of the rear view mirror.
**2** Saab technicians use a special removal tool to remove the cover from the rain sensor, however, a suitable plastic or wooden lever may be used. To spread the force and prevent

**15.6 Pulling off the rubber weatherstrip**

the windscreen from cracking, place a thin piece of wood on the windscreen to lever against. Carefully lever off the cover, by pressing the sides individually towards the headlining.
**3** Carefully press the sensor towards the windscreen, then bend out the retaining clamps and withdraw the sensor from the bracket. Take care not to scratch or damage the windscreen.
**4** Disconnect the wiring and withdraw the sensor.

### Refitting

**5** Thoroughly clean the windscreen surface before refitting the sensor. Check that the sensor retaining clamps are in good condition; if not, renew them.
**6** Refitting is a reversal of removal.

## 15 Windscreen, tailgate and headlight wiper motor and linkage – removal and refitting

### Windscreen wiper motor

#### Removal

**1** Make sure that the windscreen wipers are at their rest positions. Use a piece of tape to mark the position on the windscreen.
**2** Where applicable, use a screwdriver to prise up the covers from each windscreen wiper arm.
**3** Unscrew the nuts securing the wiper arms to the shafts.
**4** Ease the arms from the spindles by carefully rocking them side-to-side. If they are tight, use a small puller to remove them.
**5** Remove the rubber seals from the spindles **(see illustration)**.
**6** Pull off the rubber weatherstrip from the front of the scuttle area **(see illustration)**.
**7** Remove the fasteners, then withdraw the windscreen scuttle cover from the spindles, noting the location of the catches beneath the windscreen **(see illustrations)**.
**8** Remove the plastic cover, then disconnect the wiring from the wiper motor **(see illustrations)**.
**9** Unscrew the mounting bolts and lift the

15.7a  Unscrew the centre pins . . .

15.7b  . . . remove the fasteners . . .

15.7c  . . . and withdraw the scuttle cover

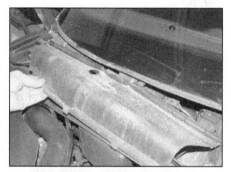

15.8a  Remove the plastic cover . . .

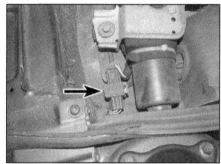

15.8b  . . . and disconnect the wiring from the wiper motor

15.9  Removing the wiper motor and linkage

wiper motor and linkage from the bulkhead **(see illustration)**.

**10** If necessary, the wiper motor may be unbolted from the frame after disconnecting the link arm and removing it from the driveshaft **(see illustration)**. Note that it may be necessary to turn the crank arm slightly in order to access one of the mounting bolts.

### Refitting

**11** Refitting is a reversal of removal, but tighten the mounting bolts to the specified torque.

## Tailgate wiper motor

### Removal

**12** Make sure that the tailgate wiper is at its rest position. Use a piece of tape to mark the position on the windscreen.
**13** Lift up the cover at the base of the tailgate wiper arm.
**14** Unscrew the nut securing the wiper arm to the shaft **(see illustration)**.
**15** Ease the arm from the shaft by carefully rocking it side-to-side **(see illustration)**. If it is tight, use a small puller to remove it.
**16** With the tailgate open, prise off the covers, then undo the screws and remove the rear window trim covers.
**17** Undo the screws and remove the inner hand grip from the tailgate trim panel.
**18** Undo the screws from the lower edge of the trim panel, then pull down the top of the panel to release it from the upper clips, and pull it to the rear to release the guide pin at the hand grip.

**19** Disconnect the washer hose and wiring from the tailgate wiper motor **(see illustrations)**.
**20** Undo the mounting bracket screws, and withdraw the wiper motor assembly from the

15.10  Wiper motor-to-frame mounting bolts

15.15  . . . and ease the arm from the shaft

tailgate, while guiding the spindle housing through the rubber grommet **(see illustrations)**.
**21** Unbolt the mounting bracket from the wiper motor.

15.14  Unscrew the nut . . .

15.19a  Disconnect the washer hose . . .

15.19b . . . and wiring from the tailgate wiper motor

15.20a Undo the mounting bracket screws . . .

15.20b . . . and withdraw the wiper motor assembly from the tailgate

15.27 The headlight wiper motor assembly

### Refitting

22 Refitting is a reversal of removal.

## Headlight wiper motor

### Removal

23 Remove the headlight and front direction indicator light units as described in Section 7.
24 Disconnect the headlight wiper motor wiring at the plug.
25 Disconnect the washer hose from the wiper arm.
26 Remove the wiper arm and blade as described in Section 13.
27 Unscrew the mounting bolts and withdraw the headlight wiper motor assembly from the front valance (see illustration).

### Refitting

28 Refitting is a reversal of removal.

## 16 Windscreen, tailgate and headlight washer system – removal and refitting

### Removal

1 The washer fluid reservoir and pump are located beneath the front left-hand wing (see illustration). For access to them, remove the wheel arch liner. For additional working room, remove the front bumper.
2 To remove the pump, position a container beneath the reservoir, then disconnect the pump wiring and washer tubes and allow the fluid to drain (see illustration). Pull the pump out of the reservoir then remove the bush.
3 To remove the reservoir, first remove the pump. Unscrew the nut and disconnect the

upper filler neck from the reservoir, then unscrew the mounting bolts and remove the reservoir (see illustration). If necessary, remove the level sensor from the reservoir.
4 To remove the windscreen washer jets, release the insulation from the bonnet, disconnect the tubes then depress the locking tabs and withdraw the jets from the bonnet. To remove the headlight washer jets, first remove the headlight and front direction indicator lights, then release the jet from the front bumper by depressing the retaining tabs with two screwdrivers, and disconnect the tube and cover.

### Refitting

5 Refitting is a reversal of removal.

## 17 Radio/cassette player – removal and refitting

Caution: All models are fitted with a radio/cassette player programmed for the specific vehicle it is fitted to, and no radio code is supplied or required. If a unit is removed from one vehicle and fitted to another vehicle, it must be reprogrammed by a Saab dealer using the special Tech2 equipment. Note also that the equipment must be used to 'divorce' the unit from the original vehicle before it is removed.

### Removal

1 The standard radio/cassette is retained by DIN fixings, and two DIN removal tools will be required to release the retaining clips. The tools are available from car accessory shops, and are inserted into the holes on each side of the unit until they are felt to engage with the retaining strips (see illustration). Non-standard radios may be retained by other means, but the method of removal is similar.
2 With the clips released, carefully withdraw the unit from the facia. Note the wiring and aerial sockets which engage with the plugs attached to the mounting box (see illustration).
3 Where applicable, the radio mounting box

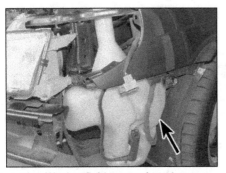

16.1 Washer fluid reservoir and pump (front bumper removed)

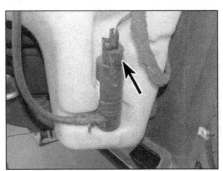

16.2 Washer pump wiring plug

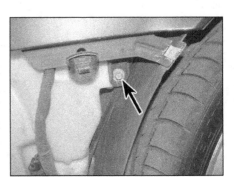

16.3 Washer fluid reservoir mounting bolt

**17.1 Using two DIN removal tools to release the radio/cassette retaining clips**

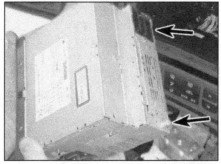

**17.2 Wiring and aerial cable connection sockets on the rear of the radio/cassette**

**17.3 Disconnecting the aerial and radio wiring from the rear of the mounting box**

can be removed from the facia by bending up the retaining tabs, withdrawing it, then disconnecting the wiring and aerial plugs **(see illustration)**.

### Refitting

**4** Refitting is a reversal of removal. Press the radio/cassette unit firmly into the mounting box until the retaining strips engage.

## 18 Loudspeakers – removal and refitting

### Facia-mounted speakers

#### Removal

**1** Using a screwdriver carefully prise out the grille from the relevant speaker **(see illustration)**.
**2** Using a Torx key, undo the screws securing the speaker in the facia, and carefully lift it out.
**3** Disconnect the wiring and tape it to the facia to prevent it dropping down inside **(see illustration)**.

#### Refitting

**4** Refitting is a reversal of removal.

### Door-mounted speaker

#### Removal

**5** Remove the door inner trim panel as described in Chapter 11.
**6** Undo the mounting screws, then withdraw the speaker and disconnect the wiring **(see illustrations)**.

#### Refitting

**7** Refitting is a reversal of removal.

### Parcel shelf speaker

#### Removal

**8** Lower the rear seat backrest then unclip the speaker grille.
**9** Undo the screws and lift out the speaker, then disconnect the wiring.

#### Refitting

**10** Refitting is a reversal of removal.

### Luggage compartment speaker

#### Removal

**11** Lower the rear seat backrest, then remove the right-hand side bolster from between the right-hand door and backrest by pulling out the top and lifting it from the lower mounting. Also remove the trim panel.
**12** Remove the right-hand storage compartment from the floor.
**13** Remove the tailgate opening scuff plate by prising out the covers and undoing the screws. The plate is retained with clips as well.
**14** Remove the headlining rear trim panel and disconnect the lighting wiring.
**15** Remove the trim from the right-hand D-pillar, then undo the screws and remove the right-hand shelf support.
**16** Undo the screws and remove the luggage compartment right-hand trim panel.

**18.1 Prise out the grille . . .**

**18.6a Undo the mounting screws . . .**

**17** Unscrew the mounting bolts and withdraw the bass speaker, then disconnect the wiring.

#### Refitting

**18** Refitting is a reversal of removal.

## 19 Audio amplifier – removal and refitting

**Note:** *Although similar in appearance, the amplifiers for Saloon and Estate models are different due to the different cabin areas inside each vehicle.*

### Removal

**1** With the passenger's door open, remove the inner sill trim panel.

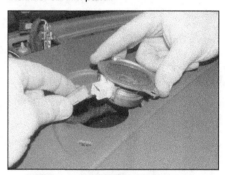

**18.3 . . . unbolt the speaker, and disconnect the wiring**

**18.6b . . . remove the door-mounted speaker, and disconnect the wiring**

**2** Remove the facia lower trim panel from under the glovebox.

**3** Fold back the carpet and unscrew the audio amplifier lower mounting nuts. Loosen only the upper mounting nut.

**4** Lift out the amplifier and disconnect the wiring plug.

### Refitting

**5** Refitting is a reversal of removal.

## 20 CD changer – removal and refitting

**Caution: As with the radio/cassette player, the CD changer is programmed for the specific vehicle it is fitted to, and no radio code is supplied or required. If a unit is removed from one vehicle and fitted to another vehicle, it must be reprogrammed by a Saab dealer using the special Tech2 equipment. Note also that the equipment must be used to 'divorce' the unit from the original vehicle before it is removed.**

### Removal

**1** The CD changer is located in the luggage compartment. Undo the mounting screws – there are two at the front and two at the rear.

**2** Move the CD changer to one side and disconnect the wiring. Withdraw the unit from the luggage compartment.

**3** If the CD changer is to be stored in a horizontal position, change the end setting so that the pointer points to the H mark. Note that four red transport screws are fitted to new units.

### Refitting

**4** Refitting is a reversal of removal.

## 21 Aerial amplifier and filter – removal and refitting

**1** On Saloon models, the separate AM aerial loop is integrated into the top of the rear window, and the FM aerial is integral with the rear or side window heater element. The aerial signal is amplified by an amplifier located on the right-hand C-pillar, and an aerial filter located on the left-hand C-pillar.

**2** One of two systems is fitted to Estate models. The first system uses an AM/FM aerial integrated into the rear right-hand side window and an adjacent amplifier and filter located on the D-pillar. In addition, the second system uses an FM aerial integrated into the rear left-hand side window and an adjacent amplifier and filter located on the D-pillar. The second system has a diversity function whereby the aerial with the best signal reception is used by the radio receiver.

### Aerial amplifier (Saloon models)

#### Removal

**3** Remove the trim panel from the right-hand C-pillar as described in Chapter 11.

**4** Note the location of the wiring to the amplifier, then disconnect it.

**5** Disconnect the aerial from the amplifier, however, take care not to damage the internal contacts.

**6** Unscrew the retaining nuts and withdraw the amplifier from inside the car.

#### Refitting

**7** Refitting is a reversal of removal.

### Aerial filter (Saloon models)

#### Removal

**8** Remove the trim panel from the left-hand C-pillar as described in Chapter 11.

**9** Disconnect the single wire leading to the filter at the connector.

**10** Undo the nut securing the filter lead to the body, and withdraw the filter from inside the car.

#### Refitting

**11** Refitting is a reversal of removal.

### Aerial amplifier and filter (Estate models)

#### Removal

**12** Refer to Chapter 11 and remove the D-pillar trim, the rear headlining trim, and the two mouldings between the C- and D-pillars. Extract the clips from the headlining, and also remove the cargo safety net holders. Carefully bend down the rear of the headlining for access to the amplifier.

**13** Note the location of the wiring to the amplifier and filter, then disconnect it.

**14** Disconnect the aerial from the amplifier, however, take care not to damage the internal contacts.

**15** Unscrew the retaining nuts and withdraw the amplifier and filter from inside the car.

#### Refitting

**16** Refitting is a reversal of removal.

## 22 Heated and ventilated seat components – general information, removal and refitting

### General information

**1** Certain models are fitted with thermostatically-regulated heated front and rear seats. Individual control switches are provided for each seat, which allow the heating element temperature to be set to one of three levels, or switched off completely. Two heating element pads are fitted to each seat – one in the backrest, and one in the seat cushion. Access to the heating elements can only be gained by removing the upholstery

from the seat – this is an operation which should be entrusted to a Saab dealer.

**2** Seat cooling is also available for the front seats on certain models, with individual control switches for each seat providing three fan speeds together with an off position. The fans extract the warm air from the seat fabric in contact with the body.

### Removal and refitting

**3** To remove the cooling fan, first remove the front seat as described in Chapter 11. Where a programmable control module is fitted to the driver's seat, remove this as described in Chapter 11 for access to the cooling fan. Unscrew the fan motor retaining nuts, disconnect the wiring and release the wiring from the cable ties. Refitting is a reversal of removal.

## 23 DICE control module – general information, removal and refitting

### General information

**1** The Dash Integrated Central Electronics (DICE) system is a central control system for the vehicle main electrical circuits. The control module communicates with the various systems via the vehicle wiring harness and the instrument bus (I-bus). DICE is able to diagnose faults within the circuits and generate trouble codes, which can then be read to determine the faulty component or circuit. The main functions controlled by DICE is as follows:

a) Exterior lighting.
b) Interior lighting.
c) Rheostat control.
d) Acoustic warning for ignition and parking lights.
e) Intermittent wiper operation between 2 and 15 seconds.
f) Headlight washer system operation.
g) Electrically-heated rear window and door mirrors.
h) Radiator cooling fan.
i) Air conditioning.

**2** The DICE control module is programmable according to the country of origin. With the lighting system, this affects how main and dipped beam lighting functions, and whether daylight driving lights are necessary. The module is located next to the fusebox on the driver's side of the facia.

### Removal

**3** Disconnect the battery negative lead (refer to *Disconnecting the battery* in the Reference Chapter).

**4** Remove the lower facia panel from the driver's side.

**5** Undo the screw and lower the relay holder from the housing for improved access to the DICE control module.

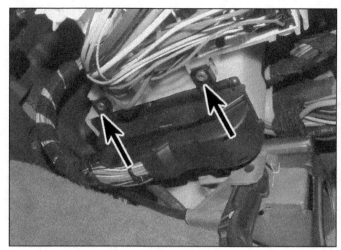

23.6a  Undo the screws . . .

23.6b  . . . and withdraw the module from the housing

6  Undo the screws and withdraw the module from the housing (see illustrations).
7  Disconnect the wiring from the control module.

### Refitting

8  Refitting is a reversal of removal. If a new module is being fitted, it must be programmed specifically for the car by a Saab dealer.

## 24  Parking aid components –
general information, removal and refitting

### General information

1  The Saab Parking Assistance (SPA) system is available as an option for models manufactured from 2000-onwards. Four ultrasound sensors located in the rear bumper measure the distance to the closest object behind the car, and inform the driver using acoustic signals on the facia SID display unit. The nearer the object, the more frequent the acoustic signals. The text PARK ASSIST appears on the display unit when reverse gear is selected, and the signal tone

changes to continuous when an object is closer than 12 inches (30 cm).
2  On Saloon models, the SPA control module is located behind the rear backrest, beneath the side trim on the left-hand side. On Estate models, it is located beneath the floor in the luggage compartment.

### Control module

#### Saloon models

3  With the left-hand rear door open, fold the 60% rear seat cushion and backrest forwards.
4  Pull back the door weatherseal for access to the rear side trim. Release the upper clip and carefully bend out the side trim.
5  Remove the sound insulation cushion.
6  Loosen the control module retaining screws, then lift the module and withdraw the screws through the slotted holes.
7  Disconnect the wiring and remove the module from inside the vehicle.
8  Refitting is a reversal of removal. Make sure that the grey plug is fitted to the grey socket, and the black plug to the black socket. Where fitted, the washers must be located in front of the mounting plate.

#### Estate models

9  Lift the rear seat cushions and fold the backrest forwards.
10  Unclip the front floor of the luggage compartment for access to the front of the lower trim. Remove the lower trim from the clips and lift it up.
11  Disconnect the wiring.
12  Unscrew the mounting nuts and withdraw the module from inside the vehicle.
13  Refitting is a reversal of removal. Make sure that the grey plug is fitted to the grey socket, and the black plug to the black socket. Where fitted, the washers must be located in front of the mounting plate.

### Range/distance sensor

#### 1998 to 2001 models

14  With the thumb, press the centre of the distance sensor into the retainer for access to the retaining clips.
15  Using a small screwdriver, release the clips, then withdraw the sensor from the rear bumper (see illustration).
16  Slide the retainer from the sensor and disconnect the wiring (see illustrations).

24.15a  Remove the range/distance sensor from the rear bumper . . .

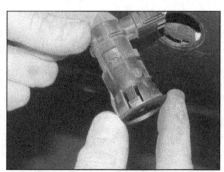

24.15b  . . . then slide out the retainer . . .

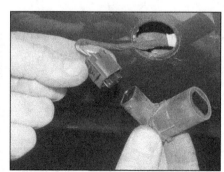

24.16  . . . and disconnect the wiring

**17** Slide the retainer onto the sensor, making sure that the raised tab locates in the special slot.

**18** Reconnect the wiring, then insert the sensor into the rear bumper, making sure that the location rib engages with the slot in the left-hand side of the hole in the bumper. Press the sensor firmly into position until the retaining clips engage.

### 2002-on Saloon models

**19** Working on each side, carefully prise out the rear bumper corner protection strips where they abut the centre strip. Saab technicians use a special tool to do this, however, careful use of a screwdriver is possible.

**20** Prise out the centre strip from the bumper for access to the four distance sensors.

**21** Release the plastic clips and remove the sensors from the retainers, then disconnect the wiring.

**22** Depress the large and small fasteners and remove the retainers from the centre strip.

**23** Refitting is a reversal of removal. Press the retainers firmly into the centre strip so that the fasteners engage.

### 2002-on Estate models

**24** The distance sensors are fitted to the rear bumper upper centre panel which can be removed separately to the main part of the rear bumper.

**25** Working on each side, carefully prise off the rear bumper corner protection strips.

**26** With the tailgate open, undo the rear bumper upper centre panel mounting screws.

**27** Release the bottom of the centre panel from the retaining clips, then lift the panel to free the tabs from the screws. Press in the corners of the panel and withdraw it directly rearwards.

**28** Release the plastic clips and remove the sensors from the retainers, then disconnect the wiring.

**29** Depress the large and small fasteners and remove the retainers from the centre strip.

**30** Refitting is a reversal of removal. Press the retainers firmly into the centre strip so that the fasteners engage.

**25.8 Glass breakage sensor located in the rear passenger interior light**

### 25 Anti-theft alarm system components – general information, removal and refitting

### General information

**1** The Saab anti-theft alarm system is referred to as TWICE (Theft Warning Integrated Central Electronics). The TWICE electronic control module operates the following systems:

a) *Lamp check including parking and brake lights.*

b) *Seat belt warning including passenger seat occupation sensor.*

c) *Electrically-heated rear seat.*

d) *Electrically-powered passenger seat.*

e) *Central locking.*

f) *Electric opening of the boot lid.*

g) *Theft protection immobilisation.*

h) *Anti-theft alarm including glass breakage and angle sensors.*

### Electronic control module

**Caution: If a new electronic control module is to be fitted, it must be reprogrammed by a Saab dealer using the special Tech2 equipment. All transponders and remote controls must be renewed, and all new ignition keys must be programmed at the same time.**

### Removal

**2** Remove the left-hand front seat as described in Chapter 11.

**3** Fold back the carpet and if necessary remove the moulding for access to the control module on the floor panel.

**4** Disconnect the wiring multiplug from the control module.

**5** Unscrew the plastic nuts and remove the module from inside the car.

### Refitting

**6** Refitting is a reversal of removal. If a new module is being fitted, it must be programmed specifically for the car by a Saab dealer.

### Glass breakage sensor

**Note:** *On Estate models there are two glass breakage sensors, a central one over the rear passenger area, and a rear one in the luggage compartment interior light. The rear sensor is integral with the light unit and cannot be renewed separately.*

### Removal

**7** Carefully prise off the lens from the rear interior light, then use a screwdriver to release the light retainers and withdraw the unit from the headlining.

**8** Disconnect the wiring and remove the glass breakage sensor from the lens cover **(see illustration)**.

### Refitting

**9** Refitting is a reversal of removal, however, note that there are two types of sensor, one for models with fabric seat covers and the other for models with leather seats.

### Warning LED on top of facia

### Removal

**10** The LED is fitted to a plate; slide the plate forwards and remove it.

**11** Press the LED from the plate, then disconnect the wiring and remove the diode. The LED terminal legs are fragile, so take care not to break them.

### Refitting

**12** Refitting is a reversal of removal.

### Bonnet switch

### Removal

**13** With the bonnet open, slide the bonnet switch up from its location on the fusebox in the left-hand rear of the engine compartment.

**14** Disconnect the wiring.

### Refitting

**15** Refitting is a reversal of removal.

### Luggage compartment switch

**Note:** *On Estate models, the switch is integral with the tailgate lock and cannot be renewed separately.*

### Removal

**16** Remove the boot lid lock as described in Chapter 11.

**17** With the lock on the bench, prise off the grip washers and remove the switch from the lock.

### Refitting

**18** Refitting is a reversal of removal.

### Alarm horn/siren

### Removal

**19** Apply the handbrake, then jack up the front of the vehicle and support it on axle stands (see *Jacking and vehicle support*). Remove the left-hand front roadwheel.

**20** Working beneath the front left-hand wheel arch, remove the front section of the wheel arch liner for access to the alarm horn.

**21** Disconnect the wiring from the horn.

**22** Undo the retaining nut and bolt and withdraw the alarm horn from under the front wing.

### Refitting

**23** Refitting is a reversal of removal.

### Tilt angle sensor

### Removal

**24** Refer to Chapter 11 and remove the inner sill trim from the front and rear of the B-pillar.

**25** Remove the right-hand front seat (Chapter 11) then release the lower B-pillar clips and unclip the carpet. Fold the carpet to one side for access to the tilt sensor.

**26** Disconnect the wiring then unscrew the retaining nuts and withdraw the tilt sensor from inside the car.

### Refitting

**27** Refitting is a reversal of removal. After fitting the tilt sensor, check the system by activating the alarm and checking that the diode glows for about 10 seconds, then flashes. Wait for 15 seconds then deactivate the alarm. Ideally, the system should be checked for trouble codes by a Saab dealer.

## Remote control receiver

### Removal

**28** Raise the armrest on the centre console, then use a screwdriver to release the front edge of the console rear panel until the clip is released. Lift the rear panel up and tilt it outwards, then disconnect the switch wiring.
**29** Where fitted, remove the clip from the console side wall. Remove the control receiver and disconnect the wiring **(see illustrations)**.

### Refitting

**30** Refitting is a reversal of removal. Where necessary, use additional tape to secure the wiring to the console, and also use an extra clip.

25.29a  Remote control receiver location

25.29b  Removing the remote control receiver

## Saab 9-5 wiring diagrams

**Diagram 1**

## Key to symbols

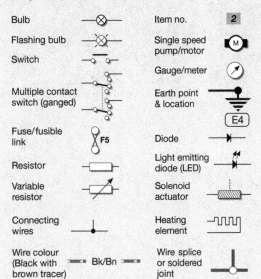

| | |
|---|---|
| Bulb | ⊗ |
| Flashing bulb | ⊗ |
| Switch | |
| Multiple contact switch (ganged) | |
| Fuse/fusible link | F5 |
| Resistor | |
| Variable resistor | |
| Connecting wires | |
| Wire colour (Black with brown tracer) | Bk/Bn |

| | |
|---|---|
| Item no. | 2 |
| Single speed pump/motor | M |
| Gauge/meter | |
| Earth point & location | E4 |
| Diode | |
| Light emitting diode (LED) | |
| Solenoid actuator | |
| Heating element | |
| Wire splice or soldered joint | |

Dashed outline denotes part of a larger item, containing in this case an electronic or solid state device. e.g. 30 - standard DIN terminal designation (battery positive), pin no. 2.

## Key to circuits

| | |
|---|---|
| Diagram 1 | Information for wiring diagrams. |
| Diagram 2 | Starting, charging, engine cooling fan & horn. |
| Diagram 3 | Side, tail, number plate, stop & reversing lights. |
| Diagram 4 | Halogen & xenon headlights. |
| Diagram 5 | Foglights, direction indicators & hazard warning lights. |
| Diagram 6 | Instrument cluster, cigarette lighter & electric sunroof. |
| Diagram 7 | Heated seats, heated rear window, electric mirrors & fuel filler cap release. |
| Diagram 8 | Central locking & electric windows. |
| Diagram 9 | Interior lighting & audio system. |
| Diagram 10 | Headlight levelling, front & rear wash/wipe, headlight washer. |

## Earth locations

| | |
|---|---|
| E1 | On slam panel behind LH headlight |
| E2 | In luggage compartment under LH tail light |
| E3 | On centre console between front seats |
| E4 | On engine |
| E5 | On cross member under LH front seat |
| E6 | On cross member under RH front seat |
| E7 | On gearbox |
| E8 | LH inner wing behind battery |
| E9 | On slam panel behind RH headlight |
| E10 | Behind LH kick panel at bottom LH end of dashboard |
| E11 | On LH 'A' pillar at LH end of dashboard |
| E12 | Behind centre of dashboard |
| E13 | Behind centre of dashboard |
| E14 | On RH 'A' pillar at RH end of dashboard |
| E15 | Behind centre of dashboard |
| E16 | On parcel shelf by RH rear speaker |
| E17 | In roof above LH 'D' pillar |
| E18 | On RH inner wing by filler cap opening |

## Typical engine compartment fuses

| Fuse | Rating | Circuit protected |
|---|---|---|
| F1 | 40A | LH & RH engine cooling fan |
| F2 | 60A | ABS/TCS/ESP |
| F3 | - | - |
| F4 | 7.5A | Load angle sensor |
| F5 | 15A | Auxiliary heater |
| F6 | 10A | Alarm, A/C compressor |
| F7 | 15A | Headlight flasher, main beam relay |
| F8 | - | - |
| F9 | - | - |
| F10 | 15A | LH main beam |
| F11 | 15A | LH dipped beam |
| F12 | 15A | RH main beam |
| F13 | 15A | RH dipped beam |
| F14 | 30A | RH radiator fan, high speed |
| F15 | 15A | Fog lights |
| F16 | 30A | Rear window wiper, headlight, headlight washer motor |
| F17 | 15A | Horn |

## Typical passenger compartment fuses

| Fuse | Rating | Circuit protected |
|---|---|---|
| FA | 30A | Trailer lighting |
| FB | 10A | Traction control |
| FC | 7.5A | Electric door mirrors, DICE, manual headlight adjustment |
| F1 | 15A | Stop light switch |
| F2 | 15A | Reversing lights |
| F3 | 10A | LH sidelight |
| F4 | 10A | RH sidelight |
| F5 | 7.5A | DICE/TWICE |
| F6 | 30A | Electric windows RH |
| F6B | 10A | Stop lights - pre-installed trailer wiring |
| F7 | 10A | Fuel injection |
| F8 | 15A | Luggage compartment lighting, luggage compartment lock, door lighting, circulation pump, parking assistance, SID |
| F9 | 15A | Audio system, CD changer |
| F10 | 15A | Heated rear seat, sunroof |
| F11 | 30A | Electrically adjusted passenger's seat |
| F12 | 7.5A | Traction control |
| F13 | 20A | Amplifier |
| F14 | 30A | Engine management |
| F15 | 20A | Fuel pump |
| F16 | 20A | DICE, direction indicators |
| F16B | 7.5A | Road toll provision |
| F17 | 20A | Engine management, instrument cluster, DICE/TWICE |
| F18 | 40A | Heated rear window and mirrors |
| F19 | 10A | Provision for mobile phone |
| F20 | 15A | Automatic climate control, interior lighting, rear foglights |
| F21 | 10A | Radio, automatic dimming mirror, navigation, automatic headlight levelling, cruise control |
| F22 | 40A | Blower motor |
| F23 | 15A | Sunroof |
| F24 | 40A | Secondary air injection |
| F25 | 30A | Electrically adjusted driver's seat, fuel filler flap |
| F26 | 7.5A | Parking assistance, memory seats, sunroof, door mirrors |
| F27 | 10A | Engine management, instrument cluster, SID |
| F28 | 7.5A | Airbag |
| F29 | 7.5A | ABS, TCS, ESP |
| F30 | 7.5A | Starter motor |
| F31 | 7.5A | Cruise control, water valve, front fog lights, rain sensor |
| F32 | 15A | Seat ventilation |
| F33 | 7.5A | Direction indicator switch |
| F34 | 30A | Cigarette lighter |
| F35 | 15A | Daytime driving lights |
| F36 | 30A | Electric window LH |
| F37 | 30A | Windscreen wipers |
| F38 | 30A | Heated seats |
| F39 | 20A | Limp home solenoid (auto. trans.), provision for mobile phone |

H32883

## Wire colours

| | | | |
|---|---|---|---|
| **Bu** | Blue | **Rd** | Red |
| **Vt** | Violet | **Ye** | Yellow |
| **Og** | Orange | **Bn** | Brown |
| **Pk** | Pink | **Wh** | White |
| **Gy** | Grey | **Bk** | Black |
| **Gn** | Green | | |

## Key to items

| | | | | | |
|---|---|---|---|---|---|
| 1 | Battery | 10 | Low speed relay | 19 | Horn relay |
| 2 | Starter motor | 11 | LH fan high speed relay | 20 | Horn switch |
| 3 | Alternator | 12 | DICE control unit | 21 | Steering wheel clock spring |
| 4 | Ignition switch | 13 | 2 speed fan resistor | 22 | Remote audio controls |
| 5 | Maxi-fusebox | 14 | LH engine cooling fan | | |
| 6 | Engine fusebox | 15 | RH engine cooling fan | | |
| 7 | Passenger fusebox | 16 | RH fan high speed relay | | |
| 8 | Transmission range switch | 17 | SID control unit | | |
| 9 | Starter relay | 18 | Horn | | |

**Diagram 2**

H32884

### Typical starting & charging system

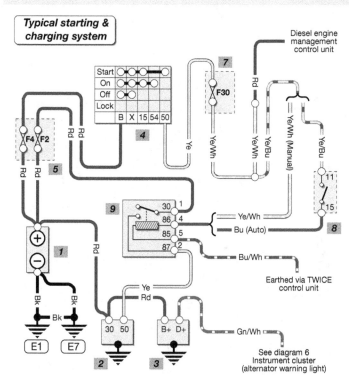

### Typical engine cooling fan - twin speed

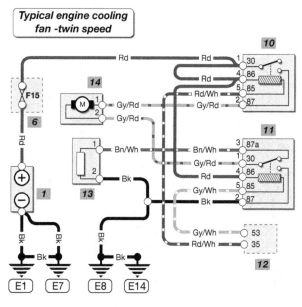

### Typical horn

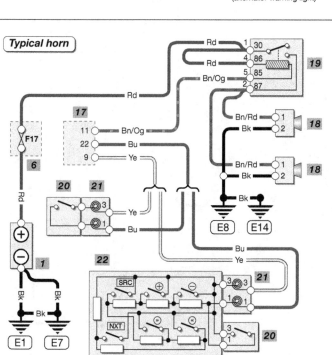

### Typical engine cooling fans - dual fans

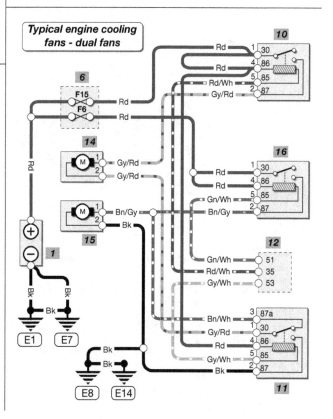

## Wire colours

| | | | |
|---|---|---|---|
| **Bu** | Blue | **Rd** | Red |
| **Vt** | Violet | **Ye** | Yellow |
| **Og** | Orange | **Bn** | Brown |
| **Pk** | Pink | **Wh** | White |
| **Gy** | Grey | **Bk** | Black |
| **Gn** | Green | | |

## Key to items

1 Battery
4 Ignition switch
5 Maxi-fusebox
7 Passenger fusebox
8 Transmission range switch
12 DICE control unit
25 Stop light switch
26 TWICE control unit
27 LH rear light unit
  a = stop light
  b = tail light
28 RH rear light unit
  a = stop light
  b = tail light
29 High level brake light
30 Reversing light switch
31 LH Boot/tailgate lid light unit
  a = reversing light
  b = tail light
32 RH Boot/tailgate lid light unit
  a = reversing light
  b = tail light
33 Number plate light
34 LH headlight unit
  a = sidelight
35 RH headlight unit
  a = sidelight
36 Combined lighting switch
  a = light switch
  c = switch illumination

**Diagram 3**

H32885

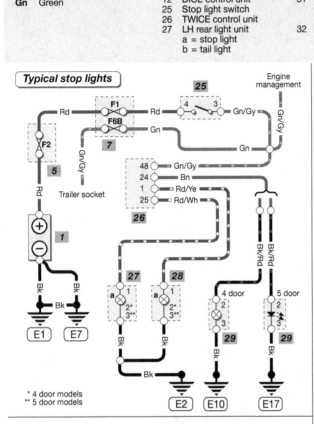

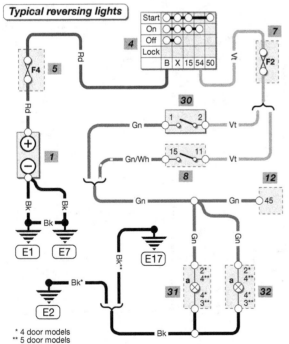

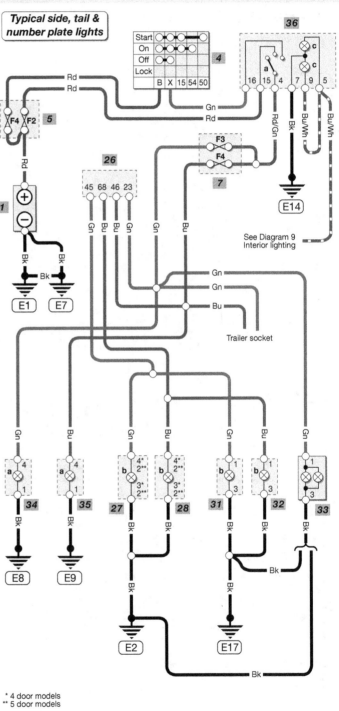

## Wire colours

| | | | |
|---|---|---|---|
| **Bu** | Blue | **Rd** | Red |
| **Vt** | Violet | **Ye** | Yellow |
| **Og** | Orange | **Bn** | Brown |
| **Pk** | Pink | **Wh** | White |
| **Gy** | Grey | **Bk** | Black |
| **Gn** | Green | | |

## Key to items

1 Battery
4 Ignition switch
5 Maxi-fusebox
6 Engine fusebox
7 Passenger fusebox
12 DICE control unit
34 LH headlight unit
   a = side light
   b = main beam
   c = dipped beam
   d = xenon light unit
   e = levelling motor

f = Auto. headlight levelling
    control unit
g = xenon light screen solenoid
35 RH headlight unit
   a = side light
   b = main beam
   c = dipped beam
   d = xenon light unit
   e = levelling motor
36 Combined lighting switch
   a = light switch
39 Dip switch

40 Filament monitor
41 Dipped beam relay
42 Main beam relay

**Diagram 4**

H32886

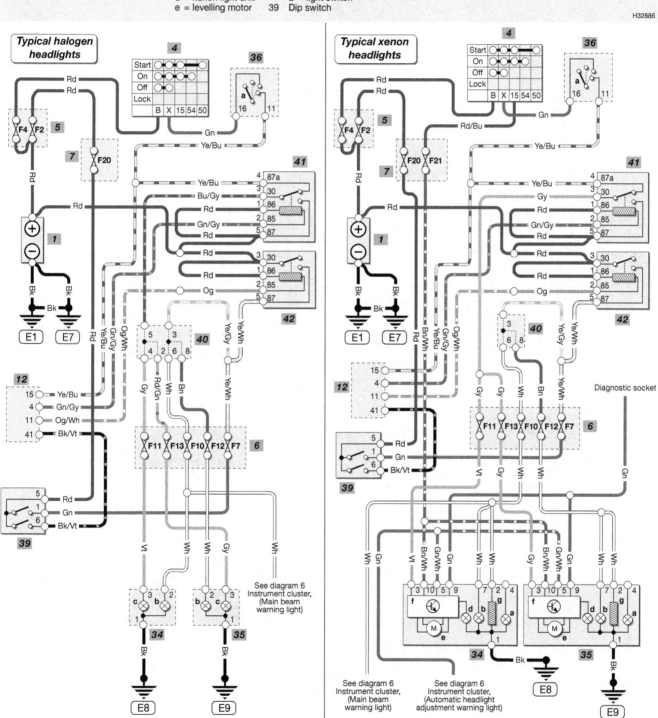

Typical halogen headlights

Typical xenon headlights

See diagram 6
Instrument cluster,
(Main beam
warning light)

See diagram 6
Instrument cluster,
(Main beam
warning light)

See diagram 6
Instrument cluster,
(Automatic headlight
adjustment warning light)

Diagnostic socket

## Wire colours

**Bu** Blue    **Rd** Red
**Vt** Violet    **Ye** Yellow
**Og** Orange    **Bn** Brown
**Pk** Pink    **Wh** White
**Gy** Grey    **Bk** Black
**Gn** Green

## Key to items

1  Battery
4  Ignition switch
5  Maxi-fusebox
6  Engine fusebox
7  Passenger fusebox
12  DICE control unit
27  LH rear light unit
   c = direction indicator
28  RH rear light unit
   c = direction indicator
31  LH Boot/tailgate lid light unit
   c = rear foglight

32  RH Boot/tailgate lid light unit
   c = rear foglight
34  LH headlight unit
   h = direction indicator
35  RH headlight unit
   h = direction indicator
36  Combined lighting switch
   a = light switch
   b = rear foglight switch
45  Front foglight relay
46  Front foglight switch
47  LH front foglight

48  RH front foglight
50  Ignition relay
51  Direction indicator switch
52  Hazard warning switch
53  LH indicator side repeater
54  RH indicator side repeater

**Diagram 5**

H32887

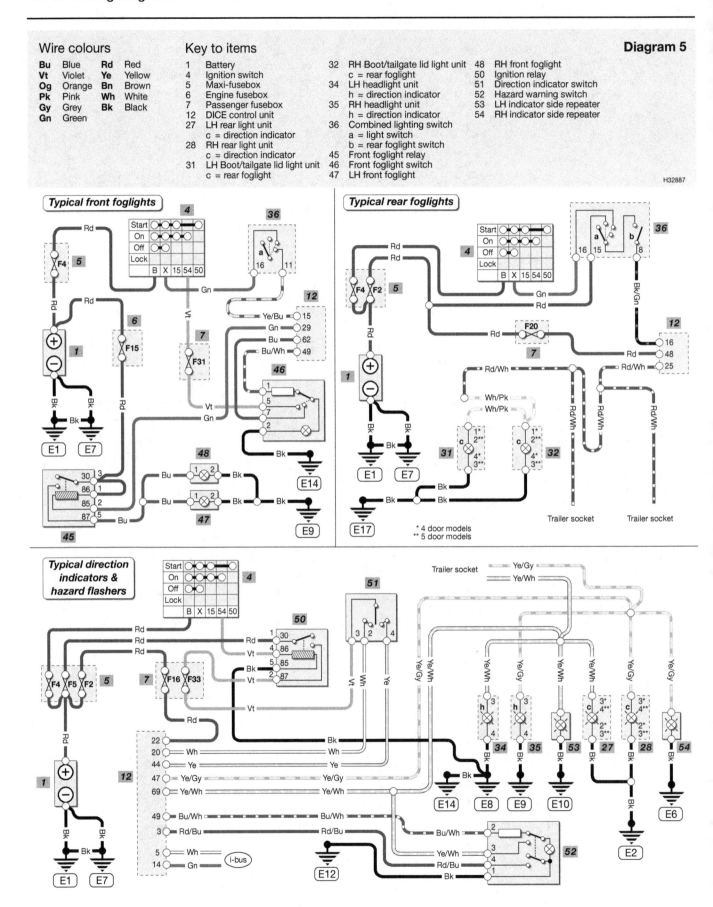

* 4 door models
** 5 door models

## Wire colours

| | | | |
|---|---|---|---|
| **Bu** | Blue | **Rd** | Red |
| **Vt** | Violet | **Ye** | Yellow |
| **Og** | Orange | **Bn** | Brown |
| **Pk** | Pink | **Wh** | White |
| **Gy** | Grey | **Bk** | Black |
| **Gn** | Green | | |

## Key to items

1   Battery
4   Ignition switch
5   Maxi-fusebox
7   Passenger fusebox
36   Combined lighting switch
    a = light switch
50   Ignition relay
56   Low brake fluid switch
57   Handbrake switch
58   Fuel gauge sender unit
59   Oil pressure switch

60   Instrument cluster
    a = instrument control unit
    b = tachometer
    c = speedometer
    d = fuel gauge
    e = temperature gauge
    f = turbo pressure gauge
    g = odometer
    h = door ajar graphic
    i = auto. trans. graphic
    j = all other warning indicators

k = AHL indicator
61   Front cigarette lighter
62   Rear cigarette lighter
63   Electric sunroof motor
64   Electric sunroof switch

**Diagram 6**

H32888

**Typical instrument cluster**

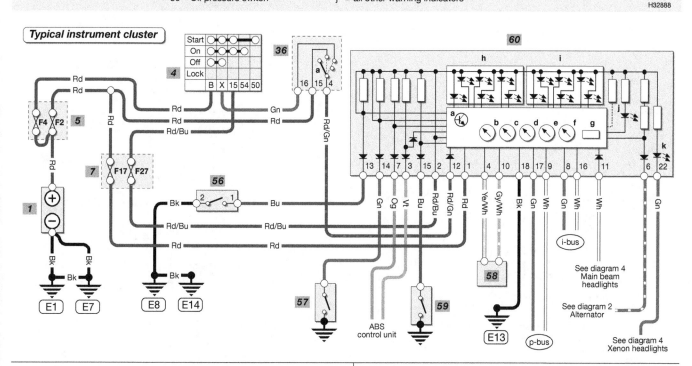

**Typical cigarette lighter**

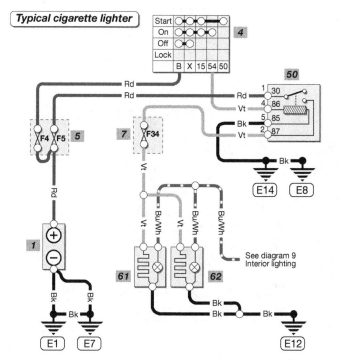

**Typical electric sunroof**

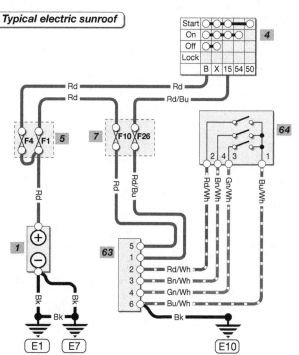

Diagram 7

## Wire colours

| | | | |
|---|---|---|---|
| Bu | Blue | Rd | Red |
| Vt | Violet | Ye | Yellow |
| Og | Orange | Bn | Brown |
| Pk | Pink | Wh | White |
| Gy | Grey | Bk | Black |
| Gn | Green | | |

## Key to items

1 Battery
4 Ignition switch
5 Maxi-fusebox
7 Passenger fusebox
12 DICE control unit
50 Ignition relay
67 LH front heated seat switch
68 RH front heated seat switch
69 LH heated seat pad
70 RH heated seat pad
71 Heated rear window
72 Heated rear window relay
73 Antenna module
74 Noise suppressing filter
75 Fuel filler cap release switch
76 Fuel filler cap release solenoid
77 Fuel filler cap release relay
78 Electric mirror switch
79 Driver's door mirror assembly
80 Passenger's door mirror assembly

H32889

**Typical heated seats**

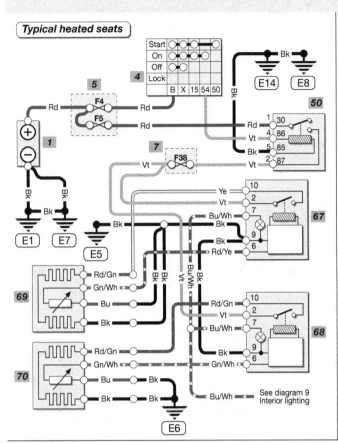

**Typical heated rear window**

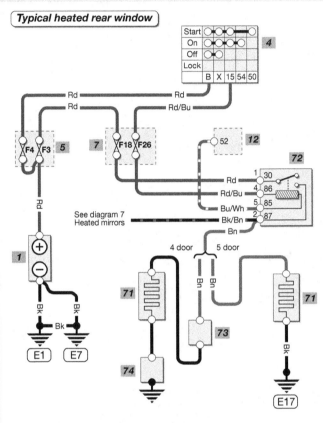

**Electric mirrors**

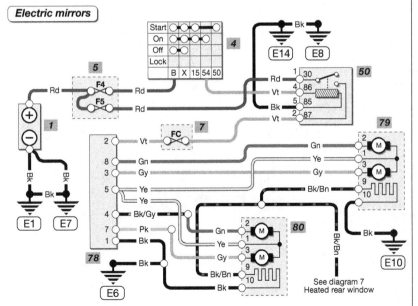

**Fuel filler cap release**

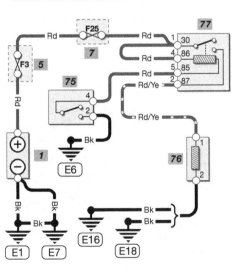

## Wire colours

| | | | |
|---|---|---|---|
| **Bu** | Blue | **Rd** | Red |
| **Vt** | Violet | **Ye** | Yellow |
| **Og** | Orange | **Bn** | Brown |
| **Pk** | Pink | **Wh** | White |
| **Gy** | Grey | **Bk** | Black |
| **Gn** | Green | | |

## Key to items

1  Battery
4  Ignition switch
5  Maxi-fusebox
7  Passenger fusebox
26  TWICE control unit
50  Ignition relay
83  Electric window switch control unit
84  Driver's window motor
85  Passenger's window motor
86  LH rear window motor
87  RH rear window motor
88  LH rear window switch
89  RH rear window switch
90  Central locking remote control receiver
91  Boot lock motor (4 door)
92  Tailgate lock motor (5 door)
93  Luggage compatment light switch
94  Tailgate lock microswitch (5 door)
95  Tailgate lock relay (5 door)
96  Boot/tailgate release switch
97  Central locking master switch
98  Driver's lock assembly
99  Passenger's lock assembly
100  LH rear lock motor
101  RH rear lock motor

## Diagram 8

H32890

**Typical electric windows**

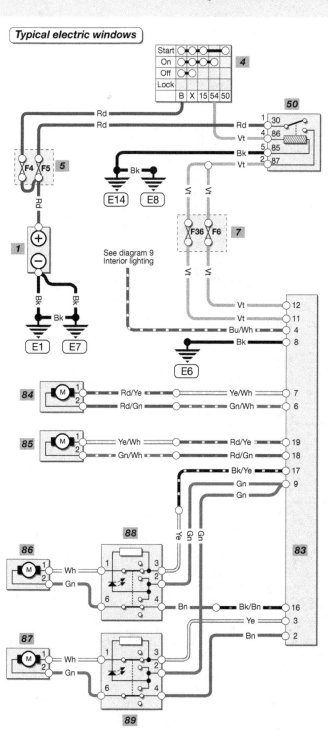

**Typical central locking**

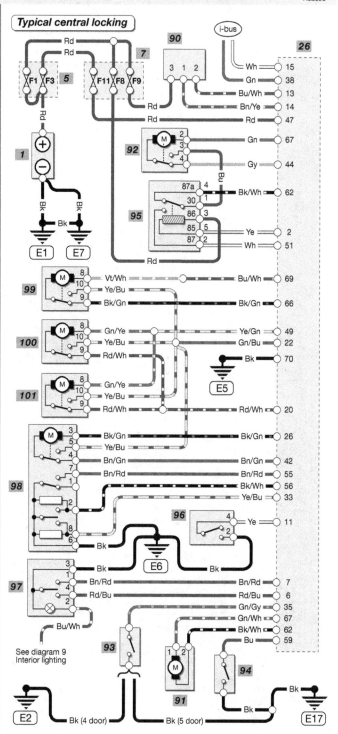

## Wire colours

| | | | |
|---|---|---|---|
| Bu | Blue | Rd | Red |
| Vt | Violet | Ye | Yellow |
| Og | Orange | Bn | Brown |
| Pk | Pink | Wh | White |
| Gy | Grey | Bk | Black |
| Gn | Green | | |

## Key to items

1 Battery
4 Ignition switch
5 Maxi-fusebox
7 Passenger fusebox
12 DICE control unit
17 SID control unit
26 TWICE control unit
93 Luggage compartment light switch
103 Interior lighting rheostat
104 Glove box light & switch
105 LH footwell illumination
106 RH footwell illumination
107 Front roof light
   a = map reading
   b = interior light switch

108 LH vanity mirror
109 RH vanity mirror
110 Centre roof light
   a = reading light
   b = interior light switch
111 Driver's door courtesy light
112 Passenger's door courtesy light
113 LH rear door courtesy light
114 RH rear door courtesy light
115 Tailgate courtesy light LH
116 Tailgate courtesy light RH
117 Luggage compartment light
118 Audio unit
119 Amplifier (if fitted)
120 CD player

121 Connection to mobile phone
122 LH dash speaker
123 RH dash speaker
124 LH rear door speaker
125 RH rear door speaker
126 Driver's door speaker
127 Passenger's door speaker

**Diagram 9**

H32891

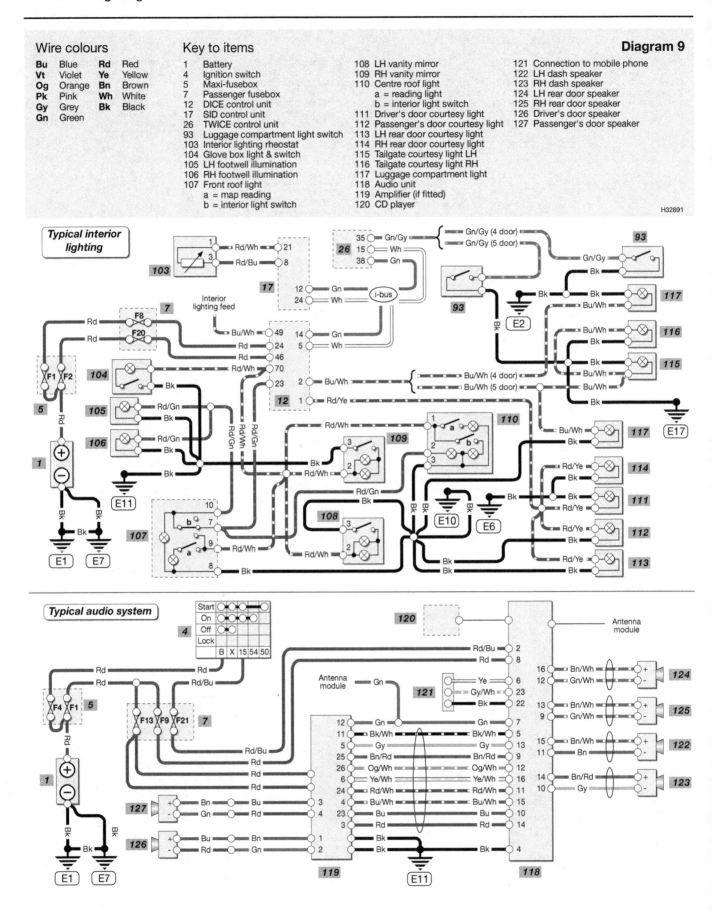

## Wire colours

| | | | |
|---|---|---|---|
| **Bu** | Blue | **Rd** | Red |
| **Vt** | Violet | **Ye** | Yellow |
| **Og** | Orange | **Bn** | Brown |
| **Pk** | Pink | **Wh** | White |
| **Gy** | Grey | **Bk** | Black |
| **Gn** | Green | | |

## Key to items

| | |
|---|---|
| 1 | Battery |
| 4 | Ignition switch |
| 5 | Maxi-fusebox |
| 6 | Engine fusebox |
| 7 | Passenger fusebox |
| 12 | DICE control unit |
| 50 | Ignition relay |
| 34 | LH headlight unit |
| | e = levelling motor |

| | |
|---|---|
| 35 | RH headlight unit |
| | e = levelling motor |
| 130 | Headlight adjustment switch |
| 131 | Front wiper motor |
| 132 | Front washer pump |
| 133 | Front wash/wipe switch |
| | a = washer switch |
| | b = wiper switch |
| | c = wiper delay |

| | |
|---|---|
| 134 | Front wiper relay |
| 135 | Headlight washer relay |
| 136 | Headlight washer pump |
| 137 | Rear wiper relay |
| 138 | Rear wiper motor |
| 139 | Rear washer pump |
| 140 | Rear wash/wipe switch |
| | a = washer switch |
| | b = wiper switch |

**Diagram 10**

H32892

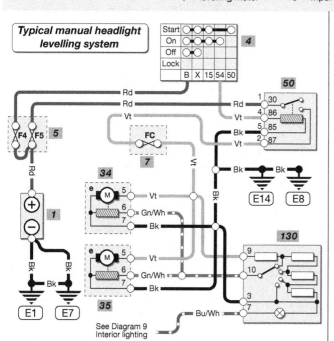

**Typical manual headlight levelling system**

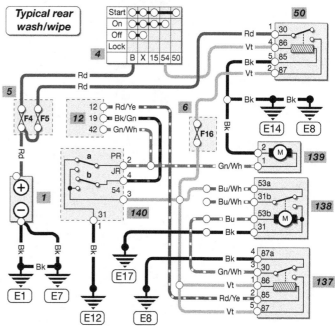

**Typical rear wash/wipe**

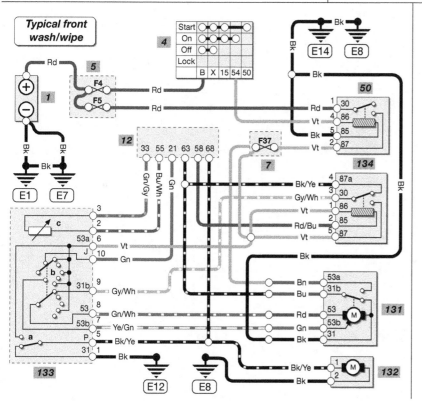

**Typical front wash/wipe**

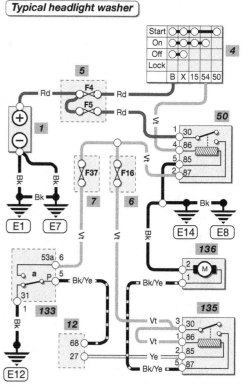

**Typical headlight washer**

**Notes**

# Dimensions and weights

**Note:** *All figures are approximate, and vary according to model. Refer to manufacturer's data for exact figures.*

## Dimensions

Overall length (including bumpers):
| | |
|---|---|
| Saloon | 4827 mm |
| Estate | 4828 mm |

Overall width (including wing mirrors) ........................ 2042 mm

Overall height:
| | |
|---|---|
| Saloon | 1475 mm |
| Estate | 1501 mm |

Wheelbase ............................ 2703 mm

Track width:
| | |
|---|---|
| Front | 1522 mm |
| Rear | 1522 mm |

Ground clearance (typical) .............................. 116 mm

Turning circle diameter:
| | |
|---|---|
| Wall to wall | 11.9 m |
| Kerb to kerb | 11.3 m |

Luggage compartment length:
Saloon:
| | |
|---|---|
| Rear seat upright | 1092 mm |
| Rear seat folded down | 1714 mm |

Estate:
| | |
|---|---|
| Rear seat upright | 1087 mm |
| Rear seat folded down | 1732 mm |

## Weights

Kerb weight:
| | |
|---|---|
| Saloon | 1525 to 1700 kg |
| Estate | 1590 to 1775 kg |

Maximum axle load:
Saloon:
| | |
|---|---|
| Front axle | 1175 kg |
| Rear axle | 1050 kg |

Estate:
| | |
|---|---|
| Front axle | 1175 kg |
| Rear axle | 1125 kg |

Maximum roof rack load ............................... 100 kg

Maximum towing weight:
| | |
|---|---|
| Un-braked trailer | 750 kg |
| Braked trailer | 1800 kg |

Maximum load on ball hitch ............................... 50 to 75 kg

# Conversion factors

## Length (distance)

| | | | | | |
|---|---|---|---|---|---|
| Inches (in) | x 25.4 | = Millimetres (mm) | x 0.0394 | = Inches (in) |
| Feet (ft) | x 0.305 | = Metres (m) | x 3.281 | = Feet (ft) |
| Miles | x 1.609 | = Kilometres (km) | x 0.621 | = Miles |

## Volume (capacity)

| | | | | |
|---|---|---|---|---|
| Cubic inches (cu in; in³) | x 16.387 | = Cubic centimetres (cc; cm³) | x 0.061 | = Cubic inches (cu in; in³) |
| Imperial pints (Imp pt) | x 0.568 | = Litres (l) | x 1.76 | = Imperial pints (Imp pt) |
| Imperial quarts (Imp qt) | x 1.137 | = Litres (l) | x 0.88 | = Imperial quarts (Imp qt) |
| Imperial quarts (Imp qt) | x 1.201 | = US quarts (US qt) | x 0.833 | = Imperial quarts (Imp qt) |
| US quarts (US qt) | x 0.946 | = Litres (l) | x 1.057 | = US quarts (US qt) |
| Imperial gallons (Imp gal) | x 4.546 | = Litres (l) | x 0.22 | = Imperial gallons (Imp gal) |
| Imperial gallons (Imp gal) | x 1.201 | = US gallons (US gal) | x 0.833 | = Imperial gallons (Imp gal) |
| US gallons (US gal) | x 3.785 | = Litres (l) | x 0.264 | = US gallons (US gal) |

## Mass (weight)

| | | | | |
|---|---|---|---|---|
| Ounces (oz) | x 28.35 | = Grams (g) | x 0.035 | = Ounces (oz) |
| Pounds (lb) | x 0.454 | = Kilograms (kg) | x 2.205 | = Pounds (lb) |

## Force

| | | | | |
|---|---|---|---|---|
| Ounces-force (ozf; oz) | x 0.278 | = Newtons (N) | x 3.6 | = Ounces-force (ozf; oz) |
| Pounds-force (lbf; lb) | x 4.448 | = Newtons (N) | x 0.225 | = Pounds-force (lbf; lb) |
| Newtons (N) | x 0.1 | = Kilograms-force (kgf; kg) | x 9.81 | = Newtons (N) |

## Pressure

| | | | | |
|---|---|---|---|---|
| Pounds-force per square inch (psi; lbf/in²; lb/in²) | x 0.070 | = Kilograms-force per square centimetre (kgf/cm²; kg/cm²) | x 14.223 | = Pounds-force per square inch (psi; lbf/in²; lb/in²) |
| Pounds-force per square inch (psi; lbf/in²; lb/in²) | x 0.068 | = Atmospheres (atm) | x 14.696 | = Pounds-force per square inch (psi; lbf/in²; lb/in²) |
| Pounds-force per square inch (psi; lbf/in²; lb/in²) | x 0.069 | = Bars | x 14.5 | = Pounds-force per square inch (psi; lbf/in²; lb/in²) |
| Pounds-force per square inch (psi; lbf/in²; lb/in²) | x 6.895 | = Kilopascals (kPa) | x 0.145 | = Pounds-force per square inch (psi; lbf/in²; lb/in²) |
| Kilopascals (kPa) | x 0.01 | = Kilograms-force per square centimetre (kgf/cm²; kg/cm²) | x 98.1 | = Kilopascals (kPa) |
| Millibar (mbar) | x 100 | = Pascals (Pa) | x 0.01 | = Millibar (mbar) |
| Millibar (mbar) | x 0.0145 | = Pounds-force per square inch (psi; lbf/in²; lb/in²) | x 68.947 | = Millibar (mbar) |
| Millibar (mbar) | x 0.75 | = Millimetres of mercury (mmHg) | x 1.333 | = Millibar (mbar) |
| Millibar (mbar) | x 0.401 | = Inches of water (inH₂O) | x 2.491 | = Millibar (mbar) |
| Millimetres of mercury (mmHg) | x 0.535 | = Inches of water (inH₂O) | x 1.868 | = Millimetres of mercury (mmHg) |
| Inches of water (inH₂O) | x 0.036 | = Pounds-force per square inch (psi; lbf/in²; lb/in²) | x 27.68 | = Inches of water (inH₂O) |

Note: subscript/superscript — $\text{in}^3$, $\text{cm}^3$, $\text{lbf/in}^2$, $\text{lb/in}^2$, $\text{kgf/cm}^2$, $\text{kg/cm}^2$, $\text{inH}_2\text{O}$

## Torque (moment of force)

| | | | | |
|---|---|---|---|---|
| Pounds-force inches (lbf in; lb in) | x 1.152 | = Kilograms-force centimetre (kgf cm; kg cm) | x 0.868 | = Pounds-force inches (lbf in; lb in) |
| Pounds-force inches (lbf in; lb in) | x 0.113 | = Newton metres (Nm) | x 8.85 | = Pounds-force inches (lbf in; lb in) |
| Pounds-force inches (lbf in; lb in) | x 0.083 | = Pounds-force feet (lbf ft; lb ft) | x 12 | = Pounds-force inches (lbf in; lb in) |
| Pounds-force feet (lbf ft; lb ft) | x 0.138 | = Kilograms-force metres (kgf m; kg m) | x 7.233 | = Pounds-force feet (lbf ft; lb ft) |
| Pounds-force feet (lbf ft; lb ft) | x 1.356 | = Newton metres (Nm) | x 0.738 | = Pounds-force feet (lbf ft; lb ft) |
| Newton metres (Nm) | x 0.102 | = Kilograms-force metres (kgf m; kg m) | x 9.804 | = Newton metres (Nm) |

## Power

| | | | | |
|---|---|---|---|---|
| Horsepower (hp) | x 745.7 | = Watts (W) | x 0.0013 | = Horsepower (hp) |

## Velocity (speed)

| | | | | |
|---|---|---|---|---|
| Miles per hour (miles/hr; mph) | x 1.609 | = Kilometres per hour (km/hr; kph) | x 0.621 | = Miles per hour (miles/hr; mph) |

## Fuel consumption*

| | | | | |
|---|---|---|---|---|
| Miles per gallon, Imperial (mpg) | x 0.354 | = Kilometres per litre (km/l) | x 2.825 | = Miles per gallon, Imperial (mpg) |
| Miles per gallon, US (mpg) | x 0.425 | = Kilometres per litre (km/l) | x 2.352 | = Miles per gallon, US (mpg) |

## Temperature

Degrees Fahrenheit = (°C x 1.8) + 32          Degrees Celsius (Degrees Centigrade; °C) = (°F - 32) x 0.56

*It is common practice to convert from miles per gallon (mpg) to litres/100 kilometres (l/100km), where mpg x l/100 km = 282*

Spare parts are available from many sources, including maker's appointed garages, accessory shops, and motor factors. To be sure of obtaining the correct parts, it will sometimes be necessary to quote the vehicle identification number. If possible, it can also be useful to take the old parts along for positive identification. Items such as starter motors and alternators may be available under a service exchange scheme – any parts returned should be clean.

Our advice regarding spare parts is as follows.

## Officially appointed garages

This is the best source of parts which are peculiar to your car, and which are not otherwise generally available (eg, badges, interior trim, certain body panels, etc). It is also the only place at which you should buy parts if the vehicle is still under warranty.

## Accessory shops

These are very good places to buy materials and components needed for the maintenance of your car (oil, air and fuel filters, light bulbs, drivebelts, greases, brake pads, touch-up paint, etc). Components of this nature sold by a reputable shop are of the same standard as those used by the car manufacturer.

Besides components, these shops also sell tools and general accessories, usually have convenient opening hours, charge lower prices, and can often be found close to home. Some accessory shops have parts counters where components needed for almost any repair job can be purchased or ordered.

## Motor factors

Good factors will stock all the more important components which wear out comparatively quickly, and can sometimes supply individual components needed for the overhaul of a larger assembly (eg, brake seals and hydraulic parts, bearing shells, pistons, valves). They may also handle work such as cylinder block reboring, crankshaft regrinding, etc.

## Tyre and exhaust specialists

These outlets may be independent, or members of a local or national chain. They frequently offer competitive prices when compared with a main dealer or local garage, but it will pay to obtain several quotes before making a decision. When researching prices, also ask what 'extras' may be added – for instance fitting a new valve and balancing the wheel are both commonly charged on top of the price of a new tyre.

## Other sources

Beware of parts or materials obtained from market stalls, car boot sales or similar outlets. Such items are not invariably sub-standard, but there is little chance of compensation if they do prove unsatisfactory. In the case of safety-critical components such as brake pads, there is the risk not only of financial loss, but also of an accident causing injury or death.

Second-hand components or assemblies obtained from a car breaker can be a good buy in some circumstances, but his sort of purchase is best made by the experienced DIY mechanic.

Modifications are a continuing and unpublicised process in vehicle manufacture, quite apart from major model changes. Spare parts manuals and lists are compiled upon a numerical basis, the individual vehicle identification numbers being essential to correct identification of the component required.

When ordering spare parts, always give as much information as possible. Quote the car model, year of manufacture, body and engine numbers as appropriate.

The *Vehicle Identification Number (VIN)* or *chassis number* appears in several places on the vehicle:

a) *On a metal plate riveted to the left-hand inner wing panel* **(see illustration).**
b) *Stamped on the bulkhead at the rear of the engine compartment* **(see illustration).**
c) *On the left-hand side of the facia, so that it can be seen through the bottom left-hand corner of the windscreen*

On early models, the *E approval plate* is attached to the right-hand inner wing panel **(see illustration).**

The *Engine number* is stamped on the front left-hand side of the cylinder block.

The *Transmission number* is printed on a plate, attached to the front/top of the transmission casing.

The *Body number* is stamped on a metal plate riveted to the crossmember at the front left hand side of the engine compartment.

The *Tyre pressures and colour code label* is attached to the front facing edge on the passenger door B-pillar **(see illustration).**

Vehicle Identification Number (VIN) stamped on a plate riveted to the left-hand inner wing panel

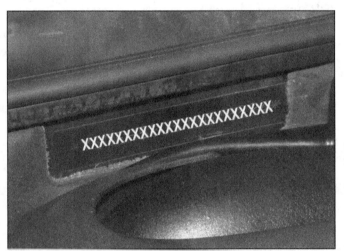

Chassis number stamped on the bulkhead at the rear of the engine compartment

E approval plate attached to the right-hand inner wing panel

Tyre pressures and colour code label attached to the passenger door B-pillar

Whenever servicing, repair or overhaul work is carried out on the car or its components, observe the following procedures and instructions. This will assist in carrying out the operation efficiently and to a professional standard of workmanship.

## Joint mating faces and gaskets

When separating components at their mating faces, never insert screwdrivers or similar implements into the joint between the faces in order to prise them apart. This can cause severe damage which results in oil leaks, coolant leaks, etc upon reassembly. Separation is usually achieved by tapping along the joint with a soft-faced hammer in order to break the seal. However, note that this method may not be suitable where dowels are used for component location.

Where a gasket is used between the mating faces of two components, a new one must be fitted on reassembly; fit it dry unless otherwise stated in the repair procedure. Make sure that the mating faces are clean and dry, with all traces of old gasket removed. When cleaning a joint face, use a tool which is unlikely to score or damage the face, and remove any burrs or nicks with an oilstone or fine file.

Make sure that tapped holes are cleaned with a pipe cleaner, and keep them free of jointing compound, if this is being used, unless specifically instructed otherwise.

Ensure that all orifices, channels or pipes are clear, and blow through them, preferably using compressed air.

## Oil seals

Oil seals can be removed by levering them out with a wide flat-bladed screwdriver or similar implement. Alternatively, a number of self-tapping screws may be screwed into the seal, and these used as a purchase for pliers or some similar device in order to pull the seal free.

Whenever an oil seal is removed from its working location, either individually or as part of an assembly, it should be renewed.

The very fine sealing lip of the seal is easily damaged, and will not seal if the surface it contacts is not completely clean and free from scratches, nicks or grooves. If the original sealing surface of the component cannot be restored, and the manufacturer has not made provision for slight relocation of the seal relative to the sealing surface, the component should be renewed.

Protect the lips of the seal from any surface which may damage them in the course of fitting. Use tape or a conical sleeve where possible. Lubricate the seal lips with oil before fitting and, on dual-lipped seals, fill the space between the lips with grease.

Unless otherwise stated, oil seals must be fitted with their sealing lips toward the lubricant to be sealed.

Use a tubular drift or block of wood of the appropriate size to install the seal and, if the seal housing is shouldered, drive the seal down to the shoulder. If the seal housing is unshouldered, the seal should be fitted with its face flush with the housing top face (unless otherwise instructed).

## Screw threads and fastenings

Seized nuts, bolts and screws are quite a common occurrence where corrosion has set in, and the use of penetrating oil or releasing fluid will often overcome this problem if the offending item is soaked for a while before attempting to release it. The use of an impact driver may also provide a means of releasing such stubborn fastening devices, when used in conjunction with the appropriate screwdriver bit or socket. If none of these methods works, it may be necessary to resort to the careful application of heat, or the use of a hacksaw or nut splitter device.

Studs are usually removed by locking two nuts together on the threaded part, and then using a spanner on the lower nut to unscrew the stud. Studs or bolts which have broken off below the surface of the component in which they are mounted can sometimes be removed using a stud extractor. Always ensure that a blind tapped hole is completely free from oil, grease, water or other fluid before installing the bolt or stud. Failure to do this could cause the housing to crack due to the hydraulic action of the bolt or stud as it is screwed in.

When tightening a castellated nut to accept a split pin, tighten the nut to the specified torque, where applicable, and then tighten further to the next split pin hole. Never slacken the nut to align the split pin hole, unless stated in the repair procedure.

When checking or retightening a nut or bolt to a specified torque setting, slacken the nut or bolt by a quarter of a turn, and then retighten to the specified setting. However, this should not be attempted where angular tightening has been used.

For some screw fastenings, notably cylinder head bolts or nuts, torque wrench settings are no longer specified for the latter stages of tightening, "angle-tightening" being called up instead. Typically, a fairly low torque wrench setting will be applied to the bolts/nuts in the correct sequence, followed by one or more stages of tightening through specified angles.

## Locknuts, locktabs and washers

Any fastening which will rotate against a component or housing during tightening should always have a washer between it and the relevant component or housing.

Spring or split washers should always be renewed when they are used to lock a critical component such as a big-end bearing retaining bolt or nut. Locktabs which are folded over to retain a nut or bolt should always be renewed.

Self-locking nuts can be re-used in non-critical areas, providing resistance can be felt when the locking portion passes over the bolt or stud thread. However, it should be noted that self-locking stiffnuts tend to lose their effectiveness after long periods of use, and should then be renewed as a matter of course.

Split pins must always be replaced with new ones of the correct size for the hole.

When thread-locking compound is found on the threads of a fastener which is to be re-used, it should be cleaned off with a wire brush and solvent, and fresh compound applied on reassembly.

## Special tools

Some repair procedures in this manual entail the use of special tools such as a press, two or three-legged pullers, spring compressors, etc. Wherever possible, suitable readily-available alternatives to the manufacturer's special tools are described, and are shown in use. In some instances, where no alternative is possible, it has been necessary to resort to the use of a manufacturer's tool, and this has been done for reasons of safety as well as the efficient completion of the repair operation. Unless you are highly-skilled and have a thorough understanding of the procedures described, never attempt to bypass the use of any special tool when the procedure described specifies its use. Not only is there a very great risk of personal injury, but expensive damage could be caused to the components involved.

## Environmental considerations

When disposing of used engine oil, brake fluid, antifreeze, etc, give due consideration to any detrimental environmental effects. Do not, for instance, pour any of the above liquids down drains into the general sewage system, or onto the ground to soak away. Many local council refuse tips provide a facility for waste oil disposal, as do some garages. If none of these facilities are available, consult your local Environmental Health Department, or the National Rivers Authority, for further advice.

With the universal tightening-up of legislation regarding the emission of environmentally-harmful substances from motor vehicles, most vehicles have tamperproof devices fitted to the main adjustment points of the fuel system. These devices are primarily designed to prevent unqualified persons from adjusting the fuel/air mixture, with the chance of a consequent increase in toxic emissions. If such devices are found during servicing or overhaul, they should, wherever possible, be renewed or refitted in accordance with the manufacturer's requirements or current legislation.

OIL CARE

FOLLOW THE CODE

OIL BANK LINE

**0800 66 33 66**

www.oilbankline.org.uk

**Note: It is antisocial and illegal to dump oil down the drain. To find the location of your local oil recycling bank, call this number free.**

The jack supplied with the vehicle tool kit should only be used for changing the roadwheels – see *Wheel changing* at the front of this manual. When carrying out any other kind of work, raise the vehicle using a hydraulic trolley jack, and always supplement the jack with axle stands positioned under the vehicle jacking points.

When using a trolley jack or axle stands, always position the jack head or axle stand head under, or adjacent to one of the relevant jacking points **(see illustration)**. Both front wheels can be raised by positioning the jack head beneath the front of the suspension subframe. Both rear wheels can be raised with the jack head adjacent to the rear towing eye, or beneath the towbar where fitted.

Do **not** attempt to jack the vehicle under the rear axle, floorpan, engine sump, transmission sump, or any of the suspension components.

The jack supplied with the vehicle locates in the jacking points on the underside of the sills – see *Wheel changing* at the front of this manual. Ensure that the jack head is correctly engaged before attempting to raise the vehicle.

**Never** work under, around, or near a raised vehicle, unless it is adequately supported in at least two places.

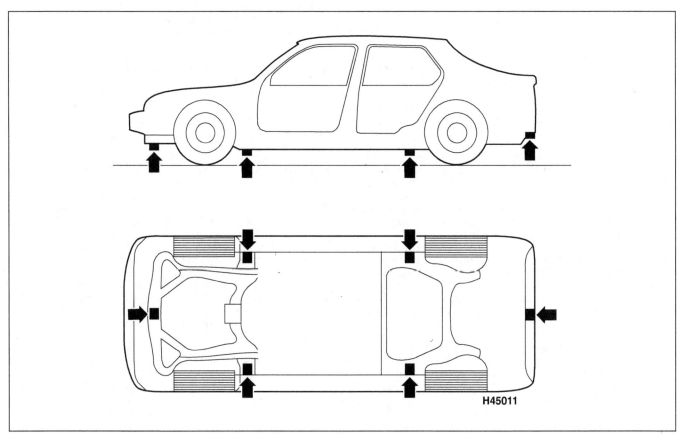

H45011

**Jacking points for a trolley jack**

**The battery is located on the front left-hand side of the engine compartment**

**Always disconnect the negative terminal first**

**Note:** *If a non-standard radio/cassette unit is installed, note the security code before disconnecting the battery.*

 **Warning: Never disconnect the battery while the engine is running.**

The battery is located on the front left-hand side of the engine compartment.

Lift off the battery heat protection cover/box, then slacken the battery negative (-) terminal and lift it from the battery post. Always disconnect the negative terminal first.

Similarly slacken the battery positive (+) terminal and lift it from the battery post.

When reconnecting the battery terminals, always connect the negative terminal last.

# Radio/cassette unit anti-theft system – precautions

The radio/cassette unit fitted as standard equipment to the Saab 9-5, has an electronic security lock which is unique to the car in which the unit is fitted. When the audio system is switched on, a check is made to ensure that the vehicle and audio unit codes match each other. If they do, the unit is fully switched on, however, if they do not, the display will indicate that the unit is locked and it will be impossible to switch it on.

If a non-standard radio/cassette unit is fitted, it may be equipped with a built-in security code, to deter thieves. If the power source to the unit is cut, the anti-theft system will activate. Even if the power source is immediately reconnected, the radio/cassette unit will not function until the correct security code has been entered. Therefore if you do not know the correct security code for the unit, **do not** disconnect the battery negative lead, or remove the radio/cassette unit from the vehicle.

If the security code is lost or forgotten, seek the advice of your Saab dealer. On presentation of proof of ownership, a Saab dealer will be able to provide you with a new security code.

## Introduction

A selection of good tools is a fundamental requirement for anyone contemplating the maintenance and repair of a motor vehicle. For the owner who does not possess any, their purchase will prove a considerable expense, offsetting some of the savings made by doing-it-yourself. However, provided that the tools purchased meet the relevant national safety standards and are of good quality, they will last for many years and prove an extremely worthwhile investment.

To help the average owner to decide which tools are needed to carry out the various tasks detailed in this manual, we have compiled three lists of tools under the following headings: *Maintenance and minor repair, Repair and overhaul*, and *Special*. Newcomers to practical mechanics should start off with the *Maintenance and minor repair* tool kit, and confine themselves to the simpler jobs around the vehicle. Then, as confidence and experience grow, more difficult tasks can be undertaken, with extra tools being purchased as, and when, they are needed. In this way, a *Maintenance and minor repair* tool kit can be built up into a *Repair and overhaul* tool kit over a considerable period of time, without any major cash outlays. The experienced do-it-yourselfer will have a tool kit good enough for most repair and overhaul procedures, and will add tools from the *Special* category when it is felt that the expense is justified by the amount of use to which these tools will be put.

## Maintenance and minor repair tool kit

The tools given in this list should be considered as a minimum requirement if routine maintenance, servicing and minor repair operations are to be undertaken. We recommend the purchase of combination spanners (ring one end, open-ended the other); although more expensive than open-ended ones, they do give the advantages of both types of spanner.

☐ *Combination spanners:*
*Metric - 8 to 19 mm inclusive*
☐ *Adjustable spanner - 35 mm jaw (approx.)*
☐ *Spark plug spanner (with rubber insert) - petrol models*
☐ *Spark plug gap adjustment tool - petrol models*
☐ *Set of feeler gauges*
☐ *Brake bleed nipple spanner*
☐ *Screwdrivers:*
*Flat blade - 100 mm long x 6 mm dia*
*Cross blade - 100 mm long x 6 mm dia*
*Torx - various sizes (not all vehicles)*
☐ *Combination pliers*
☐ *Hacksaw (junior)*
☐ *Tyre pump*
☐ *Tyre pressure gauge*
☐ *Oil can*
☐ *Oil filter removal tool*
☐ *Fine emery cloth*
☐ *Wire brush (small)*
☐ *Funnel (medium size)*
☐ *Sump drain plug key (not all vehicles)*

## Repair and overhaul tool kit

These tools are virtually essential for anyone undertaking any major repairs to a motor vehicle, and are additional to those given in the *Maintenance and minor repair* list. Included in this list is a comprehensive set of sockets. Although these are expensive, they will be found invaluable as they are so versatile - particularly if various drives are included in the set. We recommend the half-inch square-drive type, as this can be used with most proprietary torque wrenches.

The tools in this list will sometimes need to be supplemented by tools from the *Special* list:

☐ *Sockets (or box spanners) to cover range in previous list (including Torx sockets)*
☐ *Reversible ratchet drive (for use with sockets)*
☐ *Extension piece, 250 mm (for use with sockets)*
☐ *Universal joint (for use with sockets)*
☐ *Flexible handle or sliding T "breaker bar" (for use with sockets)*
☐ *Torque wrench (for use with sockets)*
☐ *Self-locking grips*
☐ *Ball pein hammer*
☐ *Soft-faced mallet (plastic or rubber)*
☐ *Screwdrivers:*
*Flat blade - long & sturdy, short (chubby), and narrow (electrician's) types*
*Cross blade – long & sturdy, and short (chubby) types*
☐ *Pliers:*
*Long-nosed*
*Side cutters (electrician's)*
*Circlip (internal and external)*
☐ *Cold chisel - 25 mm*
☐ *Scriber*
☐ *Scraper*
☐ *Centre-punch*
☐ *Pin punch*
☐ *Hacksaw*
☐ *Brake hose clamp*
☐ *Brake/clutch bleeding kit*
☐ *Selection of twist drills*
☐ *Steel rule/straight-edge*
☐ *Allen keys (inc. splined/Torx type)*
☐ *Selection of files*
☐ *Wire brush*
☐ *Axle stands*
☐ *Jack (strong trolley or hydraulic type)*
☐ *Light with extension lead*
☐ *Universal electrical multi-meter*

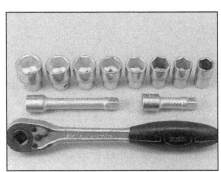

**Sockets and reversible ratchet drive**

**Brake bleeding kit**

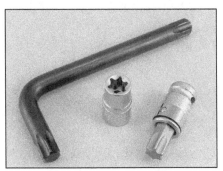

**Torx key, socket and bit**

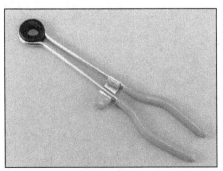

**Hose clamp**

**Angular-tightening gauge**

## Special tools

The tools in this list are those which are not used regularly, are expensive to buy, or which need to be used in accordance with their manufacturers' instructions. Unless relatively difficult mechanical jobs are undertaken frequently, it will not be economic to buy many of these tools. Where this is the case, you could consider clubbing together with friends (or joining a motorists' club) to make a joint purchase, or borrowing the tools against a deposit from a local garage or tool hire specialist. It is worth noting that many of the larger DIY superstores now carry a large range of special tools for hire at modest rates.

The following list contains only those tools and instruments freely available to the public, and not those special tools produced by the vehicle manufacturer specifically for its dealer network. You will find occasional references to these manufacturers' special tools in the text of this manual. Generally, an alternative method of doing the job without the vehicle manufacturers' special tool is given. However, sometimes there is no alternative to using them. Where this is the case and the relevant tool cannot be bought or borrowed, you will have to entrust the work to a dealer.

- ☐ Angular-tightening gauge
- ☐ Valve spring compressor
- ☐ Valve grinding tool
- ☐ Piston ring compressor
- ☐ Piston ring removal/installation tool
- ☐ Cylinder bore hone
- ☐ Balljoint separator
- ☐ Coil spring compressors (where applicable)
- ☐ Two/three-legged hub and bearing puller
- ☐ Impact screwdriver
- ☐ Micrometer and/or vernier calipers
- ☐ Dial gauge
- ☐ Stroboscopic timing light
- ☐ Dwell angle meter/tachometer
- ☐ Fault code reader
- ☐ Cylinder compression gauge
- ☐ Hand-operated vacuum pump and gauge
- ☐ Clutch plate alignment set
- ☐ Brake shoe steady spring cup removal tool
- ☐ Bush and bearing removal/installation set
- ☐ Stud extractors
- ☐ Tap and die set
- ☐ Lifting tackle
- ☐ Trolley jack

## Buying tools

Reputable motor accessory shops and superstores often offer excellent quality tools at discount prices, so it pays to shop around.

Remember, you don't have to buy the most expensive items on the shelf, but it is always advisable to steer clear of the very cheap tools. Beware of 'bargains' offered on market stalls or at car boot sales. There are plenty of good tools around at reasonable prices, but always aim to purchase items which meet the relevant national safety standards. If in doubt, ask the proprietor or manager of the shop for advice before making a purchase.

## Care and maintenance of tools

Having purchased a reasonable tool kit, it is necessary to keep the tools in a clean and serviceable condition. After use, always wipe off any dirt, grease and metal particles using a clean, dry cloth, before putting the tools away. Never leave them lying around after they have been used. A simple tool rack on the garage or workshop wall for items such as screwdrivers and pliers is a good idea. Store all normal spanners and sockets in a metal box. Any measuring instruments, gauges, meters, etc, must be carefully stored where they cannot be damaged or become rusty.

Take a little care when tools are used. Hammer heads inevitably become marked, and screwdrivers lose the keen edge on their blades from time to time. A little timely attention with emery cloth or a file will soon restore items like this to a good finish.

## Working facilities

Not to be forgotten when discussing tools is the workshop itself. If anything more than routine maintenance is to be carried out, a suitable working area becomes essential.

It is appreciated that many an owner-mechanic is forced by circumstances to remove an engine or similar item without the benefit of a garage or workshop. Having done this, any repairs should always be done under the cover of a roof.

Wherever possible, any dismantling should be done on a clean, flat workbench or table at a suitable working height.

Any workbench needs a vice; one with a jaw opening of 100 mm is suitable for most jobs. As mentioned previously, some clean dry storage space is also required for tools, as well as for any lubricants, cleaning fluids, touch-up paints etc, which become necessary.

Another item which may be required, and which has a much more general usage, is an electric drill with a chuck capacity of at least 8 mm. This, together with a good range of twist drills, is virtually essential for fitting accessories.

Last, but not least, always keep a supply of old newspapers and clean, lint-free rags available, and try to keep any working area as clean as possible.

**Micrometers**

**Dial test indicator ("dial gauge")**

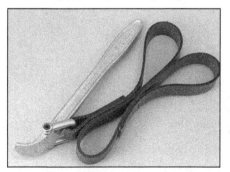

**Strap wrench**

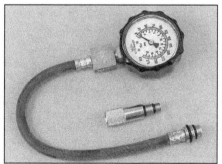

**Compression tester**

**Fault code reader**

This is a guide to getting your vehicle through the MOT test. Obviously it will not be possible to examine the vehicle to the same standard as the professional MOT tester. However, working through the following checks will enable you to identify any problem areas before submitting the vehicle for the test.

It has only been possible to summarise the test requirements here, based on the regulations in force at the time of printing. Test standards are becoming increasingly stringent, although there are some exemptions for older vehicles.

An assistant will be needed to help carry out some of these checks.

*The checks have been sub-divided into four categories, as follows:*

**1** Checks carried out **FROM THE DRIVER'S SEAT**

**2** Checks carried out **WITH THE VEHICLE ON THE GROUND**

**3** Checks carried out **WITH THE VEHICLE RAISED AND THE WHEELS FREE TO TURN**

**4** Checks carried out on **YOUR VEHICLE'S EXHAUST EMISSION SYSTEM**

---

**1** Checks carried out **FROM THE DRIVER'S SEAT**

### Handbrake

☐ Test the operation of the handbrake. Excessive travel (too many clicks) indicates incorrect brake or cable adjustment.
☐ Check that the handbrake cannot be released by tapping the lever sideways. Check the security of the lever mountings.

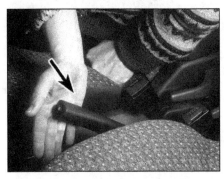

### Footbrake

☐ Depress the brake pedal and check that it does not creep down to the floor, indicating a master cylinder fault. Release the pedal, wait a few seconds, then depress it again. If the pedal travels nearly to the floor before firm resistance is felt, brake adjustment or repair is necessary. If the pedal feels spongy, there is air in the hydraulic system which must be removed by bleeding.

☐ Check that the brake pedal is secure and in good condition. Check also for signs of fluid leaks on the pedal, floor or carpets, which would indicate failed seals in the brake master cylinder.
☐ Check the servo unit (when applicable) by operating the brake pedal several times, then keeping the pedal depressed and starting the engine. As the engine starts, the pedal will move down slightly. If not, the vacuum hose or the servo itself may be faulty.

### Steering wheel and column

☐ Examine the steering wheel for fractures or looseness of the hub, spokes or rim.
☐ Move the steering wheel from side to side and then up and down. Check that the steering wheel is not loose on the column, indicating wear or a loose retaining nut. Continue moving the steering wheel as before, but also turn it slightly from left to right.
☐ Check that the steering wheel is not loose on the column, and that there is no abnormal

movement of the steering wheel, indicating wear in the column support bearings or couplings.

### Windscreen, mirrors and sunvisor

☐ The windscreen must be free of cracks or other significant damage within the driver's field of view. (Small stone chips are acceptable.) Rear view mirrors must be secure, intact, and capable of being adjusted.

☐ The driver's sunvisor must be capable of being stored in the "up" position.

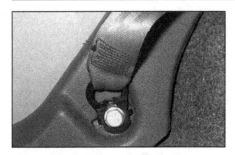

## Seat belts and seats

**Note:** *The following checks are applicable to all seat belts, front and rear.*

☐ Examine the webbing of all the belts (including rear belts if fitted) for cuts, serious fraying or deterioration. Fasten and unfasten each belt to check the buckles. If applicable, check the retracting mechanism. Check the security of all seat belt mountings accessible from inside the vehicle.

☐ Seat belts with pre-tensioners, once activated, have a "flag" or similar showing on the seat belt stalk. This, in itself, is not a reason for test failure.

☐ The front seats themselves must be securely attached and the backrests must lock in the upright position.

## Doors

☐ Both front doors must be able to be opened and closed from outside and inside, and must latch securely when closed.

## 2 Checks carried out WITH THE VEHICLE ON THE GROUND

## Vehicle identification

☐ Number plates must be in good condition, secure and legible, with letters and numbers correctly spaced – spacing at (A) should be at least twice that at (B).

☐ The VIN plate and/or homologation plate must be legible.

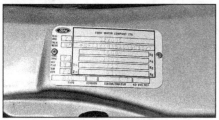

## Electrical equipment

☐ Switch on the ignition and check the operation of the horn.

☐ Check the windscreen washers and wipers, examining the wiper blades; renew damaged or perished blades. Also check the operation of the stop-lights.

☐ Check the operation of the sidelights and number plate lights. The lenses and reflectors must be secure, clean and undamaged.

☐ Check the operation and alignment of the headlights. The headlight reflectors must not be tarnished and the lenses must be undamaged.

☐ Switch on the ignition and check the operation of the direction indicators (including the instrument panel tell-tale) and the hazard warning lights. Operation of the sidelights and stop-lights must not affect the indicators - if it does, the cause is usually a bad earth at the rear light cluster.

☐ Check the operation of the rear foglight(s), including the warning light on the instrument panel or in the switch.

☐ The ABS warning light must illuminate in accordance with the manufacturers' design. For most vehicles, the ABS warning light should illuminate when the ignition is switched on, and (if the system is operating properly) extinguish after a few seconds. Refer to the owner's handbook.

## Footbrake

☐ Examine the master cylinder, brake pipes and servo unit for leaks, loose mountings, corrosion or other damage.

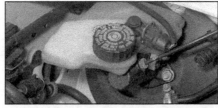

☐ The fluid reservoir must be secure and the fluid level must be between the upper (A) and lower (B) markings.

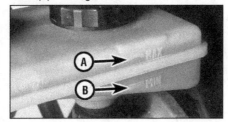

☐ Inspect both front brake flexible hoses for cracks or deterioration of the rubber. Turn the steering from lock to lock, and ensure that the hoses do not contact the wheel, tyre, or any part of the steering or suspension mechanism. With the brake pedal firmly depressed, check the hoses for bulges or leaks under pressure.

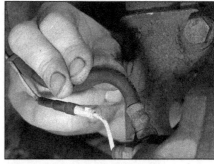

## Steering and suspension

☐ Have your assistant turn the steering wheel from side to side slightly, up to the point where the steering gear just begins to transmit this movement to the roadwheels. Check for excessive free play between the steering wheel and the steering gear, indicating wear or insecurity of the steering column joints, the column-to-steering gear coupling, or the steering gear itself.

☐ Have your assistant turn the steering wheel more vigorously in each direction, so that the roadwheels just begin to turn. As this is done, examine all the steering joints, linkages, fittings and attachments. Renew any component that shows signs of wear or damage. On vehicles with power steering, check the security and condition of the steering pump, drivebelt and hoses.

☐ Check that the vehicle is standing level, and at approximately the correct ride height.

## Shock absorbers

☐ Depress each corner of the vehicle in turn, then release it. The vehicle should rise and then settle in its normal position. If the vehicle continues to rise and fall, the shock absorber is defective. A shock absorber which has seized will also cause the vehicle to fail.

## Exhaust system

☐ Start the engine. With your assistant holding a rag over the tailpipe, check the entire system for leaks. Repair or renew leaking sections.

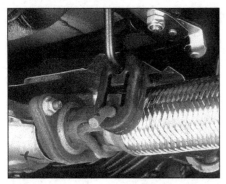

**3** Checks carried out
**WITH THE VEHICLE RAISED AND THE WHEELS FREE TO TURN**

*Jack up the front and rear of the vehicle, and securely support it on axle stands. Position the stands clear of the suspension assemblies. Ensure that the wheels are clear of the ground and that the steering can be turned from lock to lock.*

## Steering mechanism

☐ Have your assistant turn the steering from lock to lock. Check that the steering turns smoothly, and that no part of the steering mechanism, including a wheel or tyre, fouls any brake hose or pipe or any part of the body structure.

☐ Examine the steering rack rubber gaiters for damage or insecurity of the retaining clips. If power steering is fitted, check for signs of damage or leakage of the fluid hoses, pipes or connections. Also check for excessive stiffness or binding of the steering, a missing split pin or locking device, or severe corrosion of the body structure within 30 cm of any steering component attachment point.

## Front and rear suspension and wheel bearings

☐ Starting at the front right-hand side, grasp the roadwheel at the 3 o'clock and 9 o'clock positions and rock gently but firmly. Check for free play or insecurity at the wheel bearings, suspension balljoints, or suspension mountings, pivots and attachments.

☐ Now grasp the wheel at the 12 o'clock and 6 o'clock positions and repeat the previous inspection. Spin the wheel, and check for roughness or tightness of the front wheel bearing.

☐ If excess free play is suspected at a component pivot point, this can be confirmed by using a large screwdriver or similar tool and levering between the mounting and the component attachment. This will confirm whether the wear is in the pivot bush, its retaining bolt, or in the mounting itself (the bolt holes can often become elongated).

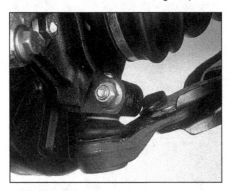

☐ Carry out all the above checks at the other front wheel, and then at both rear wheels.

## Springs and shock absorbers

☐ Examine the suspension struts (when applicable) for serious fluid leakage, corrosion, or damage to the casing. Also check the security of the mounting points.

☐ If coil springs are fitted, check that the spring ends locate in their seats, and that the spring is not corroded, cracked or broken.

☐ If leaf springs are fitted, check that all leaves are intact, that the axle is securely attached to each spring, and that there is no deterioration of the spring eye mountings, bushes, and shackles.

☐ The same general checks apply to vehicles fitted with other suspension types, such as torsion bars, hydraulic displacer units, etc. Ensure that all mountings and attachments are secure, that there are no signs of excessive wear, corrosion or damage, and (on hydraulic types) that there are no fluid leaks or damaged pipes.

☐ Inspect the shock absorbers for signs of serious fluid leakage. Check for wear of the mounting bushes or attachments, or damage to the body of the unit.

## Driveshafts
## (fwd vehicles only)

☐ Rotate each front wheel in turn and inspect the constant velocity joint gaiters for splits or damage. Also check that each driveshaft is straight and undamaged.

## Braking system

☐ If possible without dismantling, check brake pad wear and disc condition. Ensure that the friction lining material has not worn excessively, (A) and that the discs are not fractured, pitted, scored or badly worn (B).

☐ Examine all the rigid brake pipes underneath the vehicle, and the flexible hose(s) at the rear. Look for corrosion, chafing or insecurity of the pipes, and for signs of bulging under pressure, chafing, splits or deterioration of the flexible hoses.

☐ Look for signs of fluid leaks at the brake calipers or on the brake backplates. Repair or renew leaking components.

☐ Slowly spin each wheel, while your assistant depresses and releases the footbrake. Ensure that each brake is operating and does not bind when the pedal is released.

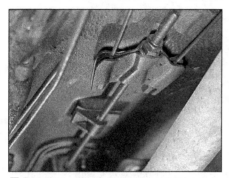

☐ Examine the handbrake mechanism, checking for frayed or broken cables, excessive corrosion, or wear or insecurity of the linkage. Check that the mechanism works on each relevant wheel, and releases fully, without binding.

☐ It is not possible to test brake efficiency without special equipment, but a road test can be carried out later to check that the vehicle pulls up in a straight line.

## Fuel and exhaust systems

☐ Inspect the fuel tank (including the filler cap), fuel pipes, hoses and unions. All components must be secure and free from leaks.

☐ Examine the exhaust system over its entire length, checking for any damaged, broken or missing mountings, security of the retaining clamps and rust or corrosion.

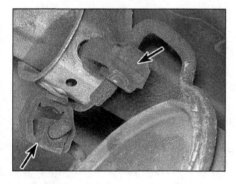

## Wheels and tyres

☐ Examine the sidewalls and tread area of each tyre in turn. Check for cuts, tears, lumps, bulges, separation of the tread, and exposure of the ply or cord due to wear or damage. Check that the tyre bead is correctly seated on the wheel rim, that the valve is sound and properly seated, and that the wheel is not distorted or damaged.

☐ Check that the tyres are of the correct size for the vehicle, that they are of the same size

and type on each axle, and that the pressures are correct.

☐ Check the tyre tread depth. The legal minimum at the time of writing is 1.6 mm over at least three-quarters of the tread width. Abnormal tread wear may indicate incorrect front wheel alignment.

## Body corrosion

☐ Check the condition of the entire vehicle structure for signs of corrosion in load-bearing areas. (These include chassis box sections, side sills, cross-members, pillars, and all suspension, steering, braking system and seat belt mountings and anchorages.) Any corrosion which has seriously reduced the thickness of a load-bearing area is likely to cause the vehicle to fail. In this case professional repairs are likely to be needed.

☐ Damage or corrosion which causes sharp or otherwise dangerous edges to be exposed will also cause the vehicle to fail.

# 4 Checks carried out on YOUR VEHICLE'S EXHAUST EMISSION SYSTEM

## Petrol models

☐ The engine should be warmed up, and running well (ignition system in good order, air filter element clean, etc).

☐ Before testing, run the engine at around 2500 rpm for 20 seconds. Let the engine drop to idle, and watch for smoke from the exhaust. If the idle speed is too high, or if dense blue or black smoke emerges for more than 5 seconds, the vehicle will fail. Typically, blue smoke signifies oil burning (engine wear); black smoke means unburnt fuel (dirty air cleaner element, or other fuel system fault).

☐ An exhaust gas analyser for measuring carbon monoxide (CO) and hydrocarbons (HC) is now needed. If one cannot be hired or borrowed, have a local garage perform the check.

## CO emissions (mixture)

☐ The MOT tester has access to the CO limits for all vehicles. The CO level is measured at idle speed, and at 'fast idle' (2500 to 3000 rpm). The following limits are given as a general guide:

At idle speed – Less than 0.5% CO
At 'fast idle' – Less than 0.3% CO
Lambda reading – 0.97 to 1.03

☐ If the CO level is too high, this may point to poor maintenance, a fuel injection system problem, faulty lambda (oxygen) sensor or catalytic converter. Try an injector cleaning treatment, and check the vehicle's ECU for fault codes.

## HC emissions

☐ The MOT tester has access to HC limits for all vehicles. The HC level is measured at 'fast idle' (2500 to 3000 rpm). The following limits are given as a general guide:

At 'fast idle' – Less then 200 ppm

☐ Excessive HC emissions are typically caused by oil being burnt (worn engine), or by a blocked crankcase ventilation system ('breather'). If the engine oil is old and thin, an oil change may help. If the engine is running badly, check the vehicle's ECU for fault codes.

## Diesel models

☐ The only emission test for diesel engines is measuring exhaust smoke density, using a calibrated smoke meter. The test involves accelerating the engine at least 3 times to its maximum unloaded speed.

**Note:** *On engines with a timing belt, it is VITAL that the belt is in good condition before the test is carried out.*

☐ With the engine warmed up, it is first purged by running at around 2500 rpm for 20 seconds. A governor check is then carried out, by slowly accelerating the engine to its maximum speed. After this, the smoke meter is connected, and the engine is accelerated quickly to maximum speed three times. If the smoke density is less than the limits given below, the vehicle will pass:

Non-turbo vehicles: 2.5m-1
Turbocharged vehicles: 3.0m-1

☐ If excess smoke is produced, try fitting a new air cleaner element, or using an injector cleaning treatment. If the engine is running badly, where applicable, check the vehicle's ECU for fault codes. Also check the vehicle's EGR system, where applicable. At high mileages, the injectors may require professional attention.

## Engine

- ☐ Engine fails to rotate when attempting to start
- ☐ Starter motor turns engine slowly
- ☐ Engine rotates, but will not start
- ☐ Engine difficult to start when cold
- ☐ Engine difficult to start when hot
- ☐ Starter motor noisy or excessively-rough in engagement
- ☐ Engine starts, but stops immediately
- ☐ Engine idles erratically
- ☐ Engine misfires at idle speed
- ☐ Engine misfires throughout the driving speed range
- ☐ Engine stalls
- ☐ Engine hesitates on acceleration
- ☐ Engine lacks power
- ☐ Engine backfires
- ☐ Oil pressure warning light illuminated with engine running
- ☐ Engine runs-on after switching off
- ☐ Engine noises

## Cooling system

- ☐ Overheating
- ☐ Overcooling
- ☐ External coolant leakage
- ☐ Internal coolant leakage
- ☐ Corrosion

## Fuel and exhaust systems

- ☐ Excessive fuel consumption
- ☐ Fuel leakage and/or fuel odour
- ☐ Excessive noise or fumes from exhaust system

## Clutch

- ☐ Pedal travels to floor – no pressure or very little resistance
- ☐ Clutch fails to disengage (unable to select gears)
- ☐ Clutch slips (engine speed increases, with no increase in vehicle speed)
- ☐ Judder as clutch is engaged
- ☐ Noise when depressing or releasing clutch pedal

## Manual transmission

- ☐ Gear lever rattles
- ☐ Difficulty engaging gears
- ☐ Jumps out of gear
- ☐ Vibration
- ☐ Noisy in neutral with engine running
- ☐ Noisy in one particular gear
- ☐ Lubricant leaks

## Automatic transmission

- ☐ Fluid leakage
- ☐ Transmission fluid brown, or has burned smell
- ☐ General gear selection problems
- ☐ Transmission will not downshift (kickdown) with accelerator pedal fully depressed
- ☐ Engine will not start in any gear, or starts in gears other than Park or Neutral
- ☐ Transmission slips, shifts roughly, is noisy, or has no drive in forward or reverse gears

## Driveshafts

- ☐ Clicking or knocking noise on turns (at slow speed on full-lock)
- ☐ Vibration when accelerating or decelerating

## Braking system

- ☐ Vehicle pulls to one side under braking
- ☐ Noise (grinding or high-pitched squeal) when brakes applied
- ☐ Brake pedal feels spongy when depressed
- ☐ Excessive brake pedal travel
- ☐ Excessive brake pedal effort required to stop vehicle
- ☐ Judder felt through brake pedal or steering wheel when braking
- ☐ Brakes binding
- ☐ Rear wheels locking under normal braking

## Suspension and steering systems

- ☐ Vehicle pulls to one side
- ☐ Wheel wobble and vibration
- ☐ Excessive pitching and/or rolling around corners, or during braking
- ☐ Wandering or general instability
- ☐ Excessively-stiff steering
- ☐ Excessive play in steering
- ☐ Lack of power assistance
- ☐ Tyre wear excessive

## Electrical system

- ☐ Battery will not hold a charge for more than a few days
- ☐ Ignition/no-charge warning light remains illuminated with engine running
- ☐ Ignition/no-charge warning light fails to come on
- ☐ Lights inoperative
- ☐ Instrument readings inaccurate or erratic
- ☐ Horn inoperative, or unsatisfactory in operation
- ☐ Windscreen/tailgate wipers inoperative, or unsatisfactory in operation
- ☐ Windscreen/tailgate washers inoperative, or unsatisfactory in operation
- ☐ Electric windows inoperative, or unsatisfactory in operation
- ☐ Central locking system inoperative, or unsatisfactory in operation

# Introduction

The vehicle owner who does his or her own maintenance according to the recommended service schedules should not have to use this section of the manual very often. Modern component reliability is such that, provided those items subject to wear or deterioration are inspected or renewed at the specified intervals, sudden failure is comparatively rare. Faults do not usually just happen as a result of sudden failure, but develop over a period of time. Major mechanical failures in particular are usually preceded by characteristic symptoms over hundreds or even thousands of miles. Those components which do occasionally fail without warning are often small and easily carried in the vehicle.

With any fault-finding, the first step is to decide where to begin investigations. Sometimes this is obvious, but on other occasions, a little detective work will be necessary. The owner who makes half a dozen haphazard adjustments or replacements may be successful in curing a fault (or its symptoms), but will be none the wiser if the fault recurs, and ultimately may have spent more time and money than was necessary. A calm and logical approach will be found to be more satisfactory in the long run. Always take into account any warning signs or abnormalities that may have been noticed in the period preceding the fault – power loss, high or low gauge readings, unusual smells, etc – and remember that failure of components such as fuses or spark plugs may only be pointers to some underlying fault.

The pages which follow provide an easy-reference guide to the more common problems which may occur during the operation of the vehicle. These problems and their possible causes are grouped under headings denoting various components or systems, such as Engine, Cooling system, etc. The general Chapter which deals with the problem is also shown in brackets; refer to the relevant part of that Chapter for system-specific information. Whatever the fault, certain basic principles apply. These are as follows:

*Verify the fault.* This is simply a matter of being sure that you know what the symptoms are before starting work. This is particularly important if you are investigating a fault for someone else, who may not have described it very accurately.

*Don't overlook the obvious.* For example, if the vehicle won't start, is there fuel in the tank? (Don't take anyone else's word on this particular point, and don't trust the fuel gauge either!) If an electrical fault is indicated, look for loose or broken wires before digging out the test gear.

*Cure the disease, not the symptom.* Substituting a flat battery with a fully-charged one will get you off the hard shoulder, but if the underlying cause is not attended to, the new battery will go the same way. Similarly, changing oil-fouled spark plugs for a new set will get you moving again, but remember that the reason for the fouling (if it wasn't simply an incorrect grade of plug) will have to be established and corrected.

*Don't take anything for granted.* Particularly, don't forget that a 'new' component may itself be defective (especially if it's been rattling around in the boot for months), and don't leave components out of a fault diagnosis sequence just because they are new or recently-fitted. When you do finally diagnose a difficult fault, you'll probably realise that all the evidence was there from the start.

# Engine

## Engine fails to rotate when attempting to start
- [ ] Battery terminal connections loose or corroded (*Weekly checks*).
- [ ] Battery discharged or faulty (Chapter 5A).
- [ ] Broken, loose or disconnected wiring in the starting circuit (Chapter 5A).
- [ ] Defective starter solenoid or switch (Chapter 5A).
- [ ] Defective starter motor (Chapter 5A).
- [ ] Starter pinion or flywheel/driveplate ring gear teeth loose or broken (Chapters 2A or 5A).
- [ ] Engine earth cable broken or disconnected (Chapter 2A).

## Starter motor turns engine slowly
- [ ] Partially-discharged battery (recharge, use jump leads, or push start) (Chapter 5A).
- [ ] Battery terminals loose or corroded (*Weekly checks*).
- [ ] Battery earth to body defective (Chapter 5A).
- [ ] Engine earth strap loose (Chapter 2A).
- [ ] Starter motor (or solenoid) wiring loose (Chapter 5A).
- [ ] Starter motor internal fault (Chapter 5A).

## Engine rotates, but will not start
- [ ] Fuel tank empty.
- [ ] Battery discharged (engine rotates slowly) (Chapter 5A).
- [ ] Battery terminal connections loose or corroded (*Weekly checks*).
- [ ] Ignition components damp or damaged (Chapters 1 and 5B).
- [ ] Broken, loose or disconnected wiring in the ignition circuit (Chapters 1 and 5B).
- [ ] Worn, faulty or incorrectly-gapped spark plugs (Chapter 1).
- [ ] Fuel injection system fault (Chapter 4A).
- [ ] Major mechanical failure (eg broken timing chain) (Chapter 2A).

## Engine difficult to start when cold
- [ ] Battery discharged (Chapter 5A).
- [ ] Battery terminal connections loose or corroded (*Weekly checks*).
- [ ] Worn, faulty or incorrectly-gapped spark plugs (Chapter 1).
- [ ] Fuel injection system fault (Chapter 4A).
- [ ] Other ignition system fault (Chapters 1 and 5B).
- [ ] Low cylinder compressions (Chapter 2A).

## Engine difficult to start when hot
- [ ] Air filter element dirty or clogged (Chapter 1).
- [ ] Fuel injection system fault (Chapter 4A).
- [ ] Low cylinder compressions (Chapter 2A).

## Starter motor noisy or excessively-rough in engagement
- [ ] Starter pinion or flywheel/driveplate ring gear teeth loose or broken (Chapters 2A or 5A).
- [ ] Starter motor mounting bolts loose or missing (Chapter 5A).
- [ ] Starter motor internal components worn or damaged (Chapter 5A).

## Engine starts, but stops immediately
- [ ] Loose or faulty electrical connections in the ignition circuit (Chapters 1 and 5B).
- [ ] Vacuum leak at the throttle body or inlet manifold (Chapter 4A).
- [ ] Fuel injection system fault (Chapter 4A).

## Engine idles erratically
- [ ] Air filter element clogged (Chapter 1).
- [ ] Vacuum leak at the throttle body, inlet manifold or associated hoses (Chapter 4A or 4B).
- [ ] Worn, faulty or incorrectly-gapped spark plugs (Chapter 1).
- [ ] Uneven or low cylinder compressions (Chapter 2A).
- [ ] Camshaft lobes worn (Chapter 2A).
- [ ] Fuel injection system fault (Chapter 4A).

## Engine misfires at idle speed
- [ ] Worn, faulty or incorrectly-gapped spark plugs (Chapter 1).
- [ ] Faulty DI cartridge (Chapter 5B).
- [ ] Vacuum leak at the throttle body, inlet manifold or associated hoses (Chapter 4A or 4B).
- [ ] Fuel injection system fault (Chapter 4A).
- [ ] Uneven or low cylinder compressions (Chapter 2A).
- [ ] Disconnected, leaking, or perished crankcase ventilation hoses (Chapter 4B).

## Engine misfires throughout the driving speed range
- [ ] Fuel filter choked (Chapter 1).
- [ ] Fuel pump faulty, or delivery pressure low (Chapter 4A).
- [ ] Fuel tank vent blocked, or fuel pipes restricted (Chapter 4A).
- [ ] Vacuum leak at the throttle body, inlet manifold or associated hoses (Chapter 4A).
- [ ] Worn, faulty or incorrectly-gapped spark plugs (Chapter 1).
- [ ] Faulty DI cartridge (Chapter 5B).
- [ ] Uneven or low cylinder compressions (Chapter 2A).
- [ ] Fuel injection system fault (Chapter 4A).

## Engine stalls
- [ ] Vacuum leak at the throttle body, inlet manifold or associated hoses (Chapter 4A or 4B).
- [ ] Fuel filter choked (Chapter 1).
- [ ] Fuel pump faulty, or delivery pressure low (Chapter 4A).
- [ ] Fuel tank vent blocked, or fuel pipes restricted (Chapter 4A).
- [ ] Fuel injection system fault (Chapter 4A).

## Engine hesitates on acceleration
- [ ] Worn, faulty or incorrectly-gapped spark plugs (Chapter 1).
- [ ] Vacuum leak at the throttle body, inlet manifold or associated hoses (Chapter 4A or 4B).
- [ ] Fuel injection system fault (Chapter 4A).

# Engine (continued)

## Engine lacks power

- ☐ Fuel filter choked (Chapter 1).
- ☐ Fuel pump faulty, or delivery pressure low (Chapter 4A).
- ☐ Uneven or low cylinder compressions (Chapter 2A).
- ☐ Worn, faulty or incorrectly-gapped spark plugs (Chapter 1).
- ☐ Vacuum leak at the throttle body, inlet manifold or associated hoses (Chapter 4A or 4B).
- ☐ Fuel injection system fault (Chapter 4A).
- ☐ Faulty turbocharger (Chapter 4A).
- ☐ Brakes binding (Chapters 1 and 9).
- ☐ Clutch slipping (Chapter 6).

## Engine backfires

- ☐ Vacuum leak at the throttle body, inlet manifold or associated hoses (Chapter 4A or 4B).
- ☐ Fuel injection system fault (Chapter 4A).

## Oil pressure warning light illuminated with engine running

- ☐ Low oil level, or incorrect oil grade (*Weekly checks*).
- ☐ Faulty oil pressure sensor (Chapter 2A).
- ☐ Worn engine bearings and/or oil pump (Chapter 2A or 2B).
- ☐ Excessively high engine operating temperature (Chapter 3).
- ☐ Oil pressure relief valve defective (Chapter 2A).
- ☐ Oil pick-up strainer clogged (Chapter 2A).

**Note:** *Low oil pressure in a high-mileage engine at tick-over is not necessarily a cause for concern. Sudden pressure loss at speed is far more significant. In any event, check the gauge or warning light sender before condemning the engine.*

## Engine runs-on after switching off

- ☐ Excessive carbon build-up in engine (Chapter 2A or 2B).
- ☐ Excessively high engine operating temperature (Chapter 3).

## Engine noises

### Pre-ignition (pinking) or knocking during acceleration or under load

- ☐ Ignition system fault (Chapters 1 and 5B).
- ☐ Incorrect grade of spark plug (Chapter 1).
- ☐ Incorrect grade of fuel (Chapter 4A).
- ☐ Vacuum leak at throttle body, inlet manifold or associated hoses (Chapter 4A or 4B).
- ☐ Excessive carbon build-up in engine (Chapter 2A or 2B).
- ☐ Fuel injection system fault (Chapter 4A).

### Whistling or wheezing noises

- ☐ Leaking inlet manifold or throttle body gasket (Chapter 4A).
- ☐ Leaking exhaust manifold gasket (Chapter 4A).
- ☐ Leaking vacuum hose (Chapters 4A, 4B and 9).
- ☐ Blowing cylinder head gasket (Chapter 2A).

### Tapping or rattling noises

- ☐ Worn valve gear, timing chain, camshaft or hydraulic tappets (Chapter 2A).
- ☐ Ancillary component fault (water pump, alternator, etc) (Chapters 3, 5A, etc).

### Knocking or thumping noises

- ☐ Worn big-end bearings (regular heavy knocking, perhaps less under load) (Chapter 2B).
- ☐ Worn main bearings (rumbling and knocking, perhaps worsening under load) (Chapter 2B).
- ☐ Piston slap (most noticeable when cold) (Chapter 2B).
- ☐ Ancillary component fault (water pump, alternator, etc) (Chapters 3, 5A, etc).

# Cooling system

### Overheating

☐ Auxiliary drivebelt broken – or, where applicable, incorrectly adjusted (Chapter 1).
☐ Insufficient coolant in system (*Weekly checks*).
☐ Thermostat faulty (Chapter 3).
☐ Radiator core blocked, or grille restricted (Chapter 3).
☐ Electric cooling fan or thermostatic switch faulty (Chapter 3).
☐ Pressure cap faulty (Chapter 3).
☐ Ignition timing incorrect, or ignition system fault (Chapters 1 and 5B).
☐ Inaccurate temperature gauge sender unit (Chapter 3).
☐ Airlock in cooling system (Chapter 1).

### Overcooling

☐ Thermostat faulty (Chapter 3).
☐ Inaccurate temperature gauge sender unit (Chapter 3).

### External coolant leakage

☐ Deteriorated or damaged hoses or hose clips (Chapter 1).
☐ Radiator core or heater matrix leaking (Chapter 3).
☐ Pressure cap faulty (Chapter 3).
☐ Water pump internal seal leaking (Chapter 3).
☐ Water pump-to-block O-ring or housing gasket leaking (Chapter 3).
☐ Boiling due to overheating (Chapter 3).
☐ Core plug leaking (Chapter 2B).

### Internal coolant leakage

☐ Leaking cylinder head gasket (Chapter 2A).
☐ Cracked cylinder head or cylinder block (Chapter 2A or 2B).

### Corrosion

☐ Infrequent draining and flushing (Chapter 1).
☐ Incorrect coolant mixture or inappropriate coolant type (*Weekly checks*).

# Fuel and exhaust systems

### Excessive fuel consumption

☐ Air filter element dirty or clogged (Chapter 1).
☐ Fuel injection system fault (Chapter 4A).
☐ Ignition system fault (Chapters 1 and 5B).
☐ Brakes binding (Chapter 9).
☐ Tyres under-inflated (*Weekly checks*).

### Fuel leakage and/or fuel odour

☐ Damaged fuel tank, pipes or connections (Chapters 1 and 4A).

### Excessive noise or fumes from exhaust system

☐ Leaking exhaust system or manifold joints (Chapters 1 and 4A).
☐ Leaking, corroded or damaged silencers or pipe (Chapters 1 and 4A).
☐ Broken mountings causing body or suspension contact (Chapter 4A).

# Clutch

### Pedal travels to floor – no pressure or very little resistance
☐ Broken clutch release bearing (Chapter 6).
☐ Broken diaphragm spring in clutch pressure plate (Chapter 6).

### Clutch fails to disengage (unable to select gears)
☐ Clutch disc sticking on gearbox input shaft splines (Chapter 6).
☐ Clutch disc sticking to flywheel or pressure plate (Chapter 6).
☐ Faulty pressure plate assembly (Chapter 6).
☐ Clutch release mechanism worn or incorrectly assembled (Chapter 6).

### Clutch slips (engine speed increases, with no increase in vehicle speed)
☐ Clutch disc linings excessively worn (Chapter 6).
☐ Clutch disc linings contaminated with oil or grease (Chapter 6).
☐ Faulty pressure plate or weak diaphragm spring (Chapter 6).

### Judder as clutch is engaged
☐ Clutch disc linings contaminated with oil or grease (Chapter 6).
☐ Clutch disc linings excessively worn (Chapter 6).
☐ Faulty or distorted pressure plate or diaphragm spring (Chapter 6).
☐ Worn or loose engine or gearbox mountings (Chapter 2A or 2B).
☐ Clutch disc hub or gearbox input shaft splines worn (Chapter 6).

### Noise when depressing or releasing clutch pedal
☐ Worn clutch release bearing (Chapter 6).
☐ Worn or dry clutch pedal bushes (Chapter 6).
☐ Faulty pressure plate assembly (Chapter 6).
☐ Pressure plate diaphragm spring broken (Chapter 6).
☐ Broken clutch disc cushioning springs (Chapter 6).

# Manual transmission

### Gear lever rattles
☐ Fit a modified O-ring around the base of the gear lever ball socket (Chapter 7A, Section 4).

### Difficulty engaging gears
☐ Clutch fault (Chapter 6).
☐ Worn or damaged gear linkage (Chapter 7A).
☐ Incorrectly-adjusted gear linkage (Chapter 7A).
☐ Worn synchroniser units (Chapter 7A).*

### Jumps out of gear
☐ Worn or damaged gear linkage (Chapter 7A).
☐ Incorrectly-adjusted gear linkage (Chapter 7A).
☐ Worn synchroniser units (Chapter 7A).*
☐ Worn selector forks (Chapter 7A).*

### Vibration
☐ Lack of oil (Chapter 1).
☐ Worn bearings (Chapter 7A).*

### Noisy in neutral with engine running
☐ Input shaft bearings worn (noise apparent with clutch pedal released, but not when depressed) (Chapter 7A).*
☐ Clutch release bearing worn (noise apparent with clutch pedal depressed, possibly less when released) (Chapter 6).

### Noisy in one particular gear
☐ Worn, damaged or chipped gear teeth (Chapter 7A).*

### Lubricant leaks
☐ Leaking oil seal (Chapter 7A).
☐ Leaking housing joint (Chapter 7A).*

*Although the corrective action necessary to remedy the symptoms described is beyond the scope of this manual, the above information should be helpful in isolating the cause of the condition, so that the owner can communicate clearly with a professional mechanic.*

# Automatic transmission

**Note:** *Due to the complexity of the automatic transmission, it is difficult for the home mechanic to properly diagnose and service this unit. For problems other than the following, the vehicle should be taken to a dealer service department or automatic transmission specialist.*

### Fluid leakage

☐ Automatic transmission fluid is usually deep red in colour. Fluid leaks should not be confused with engine oil, which can easily be blown onto the transmission by air flow.

☐ To determine the source of a leak, first remove all built-up dirt and grime from the transmission housing and surrounding areas, using a degreasing agent or by steam-cleaning. Drive the vehicle at low speed, so that air flow will not blow the leak far from its source. Raise and support the vehicle, and determine where the leak is coming from. The following are common areas of leakage.

a) *Fluid pan (transmission 'sump').*
b) *Dipstick tube (Chapter 1).*
c) *Transmission-to-fluid cooler fluid pipes/unions (Chapter 7B).*

### Transmission fluid brown, or has burned smell

☐ Transmission fluid level low, or fluid in need of renewal (Chapter 1).

### General gear selection problems

☐ The most likely cause of gear selection problems is a faulty or poorly-adjusted gear selector mechanism. The following are common problems associated with a faulty selector mechanism.

a) *Engine starting in gears other than Park or Neutral.*

b) *Indicator on gear selector lever pointing to a gear other than the one actually being used.*
c) *Vehicle moves when in Park or Neutral.*
d) *Poor gear shift quality, or erratic gear changes.*
   Refer any problems to a Saab dealer, or an automatic transmission specialist.

### Transmission will not downshift (kickdown) with accelerator pedal fully depressed

☐ Low transmission fluid level (Chapter 1).
☐ Incorrect selector cable adjustment (Chapter 7B).

### Engine will not start in any gear, or starts in gears other than Park or Neutral

☐ Incorrect starter inhibitor switch adjustment – where applicable (Chapter 7B).
☐ Incorrect selector cable adjustment (Chapter 7B).

### Transmission slips, shifts roughly, is noisy, or has no drive in forward or reverse gears

☐ There are many probable causes for the above problems, but the home mechanic should be concerned with only one possibility – incorrect transmission fluid level. Before taking the vehicle to a dealer or transmission specialist, check the fluid level and condition of the fluid as described in Chapter 1. Correct the fluid level as necessary, or change the fluid and filter if needed. If the problem persists, professional help will be necessary.

# Driveshafts

### Clicking or knocking noise on turns (at slow speed on full-lock)

☐ Lack of constant velocity joint lubricant, possibly due to damaged gaiter (Chapter 8).
☐ Worn outer constant velocity joint (Chapter 8).

### Vibration when accelerating or decelerating

☐ Worn inner constant velocity joint (Chapter 8).
☐ Damaged or distorted driveshaft (Chapter 8).

# Braking system

**Note:** *Before assuming that a brake problem exists, make sure that the tyres are in good condition and correctly inflated, that the front wheel alignment is correct, and that the vehicle is not loaded with weight in an unequal manner. Apart from checking the condition of all pipe and hose connections, any faults occurring on the anti-lock braking system should be referred to a Saab dealer for diagnosis.*

## Vehicle pulls to one side under braking

☐ Worn, defective, damaged or contaminated front or rear brake pads on one side (Chapters 1 and 9).
☐ Seized or partially-seized front or rear brake caliper piston (Chapter 9).
☐ A mixture of brake pad lining materials fitted between sides (Chapter 9).
☐ Brake caliper mounting bolts loose (Chapter 9).
☐ Worn or damaged steering or suspension components (Chapters 1 and 10).

## Noise (grinding or high-pitched squeal) when brakes applied

☐ Brake pad friction lining material worn down to metal backing (Chapters 1 and 9).
☐ Excessive corrosion of brake disc – may be apparent after the vehicle has been standing for some time (Chapters 1 and 9).

## Brake pedal feels spongy when depressed

☐ Air in hydraulic system (Chapter 9).
☐ Deteriorated flexible rubber brake hoses (Chapters 1 and 9).
☐ Master cylinder mountings loose (Chapter 9).
☐ Faulty master cylinder (Chapter 9).

## Excessive brake pedal travel

☐ Faulty master cylinder (Chapter 9).
☐ Air in hydraulic system (Chapter 9).
☐ Faulty vacuum servo unit (Chapter 9).

## Excessive brake pedal effort required to stop vehicle

☐ Air in hydraulic system (Chapter 9).
☐ Brake fluid requires renewal (Chapter 1).
☐ Faulty vacuum servo unit (Chapter 9).
☐ Disconnected, damaged or insecure brake servo vacuum hose (Chapters 1 and 9).
☐ Primary or secondary hydraulic circuit failure (Chapter 9).
☐ Seized brake caliper piston(s) (Chapter 9).
☐ Brake pads incorrectly fitted (Chapter 9).
☐ Incorrect grade of brake pads fitted (Chapter 9).
☐ Brake pads contaminated (Chapter 9).

## Judder felt through brake pedal or steering wheel when braking

☐ Excessive run-out or distortion of brake disc(s) (Chapter 9).
☐ Brake pad linings worn (Chapters 1 and 9).
☐ Brake caliper mounting bolts loose (Chapter 9).
☐ Wear in suspension or steering components or mountings (Chapters 1 and 10).

## Brakes binding

☐ Seized brake caliper piston(s) (Chapter 9).
☐ Incorrectly-adjusted handbrake mechanism (Chapter 9).
☐ Faulty master cylinder (Chapter 9).

## Rear wheels locking under normal braking

☐ Seized brake caliper piston(s) (Chapter 9).
☐ Faulty brake pressure regulator (Chapter 9).

# Suspension and steering

**Note:** *Before diagnosing suspension or steering faults, be sure that the trouble is not due to incorrect tyre pressures, mixtures of tyre types, or binding brakes.*

## Vehicle pulls to one side
☐ Defective tyre (*Weekly checks*).
☐ Excessive wear in suspension or steering components (Chapters 1 and 10).
☐ Incorrect front wheel alignment (Chapter 10).
☐ Accident damage to steering or suspension components (Chapters 1 and 10).

## Wheel wobble and vibration
☐ Front roadwheels out of balance (vibration felt mainly through the steering wheel) (*Weekly checks*).
☐ Rear roadwheels out of balance (vibration felt throughout the vehicle) (*Weekly checks*).
☐ Roadwheels damaged or distorted (*Weekly checks*).
☐ Faulty or damaged tyre (*Weekly checks*).
☐ Worn steering or suspension joints, bushes or components (Chapters 1 and 10).
☐ Wheel bolts loose.

## Excessive pitching and/or rolling around corners, or during braking
☐ Defective shock absorbers (Chapters 1 and 10).
☐ Broken or weak coil spring and/or suspension component (Chapters 1 and 10).
☐ Worn or damaged anti-roll bar or mountings (Chapter 10).

## Wandering or general instability
☐ Incorrect front wheel alignment (Chapter 10).
☐ Worn steering or suspension joints, bushes or components (Chapters 1 and 10).
☐ Roadwheels out of balance (*Weekly checks*).
☐ Faulty or damaged tyre (*Weekly checks*).
☐ Wheel bolts loose.
☐ Defective shock absorbers (Chapters 1 and 10).

## Excessively-stiff steering
☐ Lack of steering gear lubricant (Chapter 10).
☐ Seized track rod end balljoint or suspension balljoint (Chapters 1 and 10).
☐ Broken or incorrectly adjusted auxiliary drivebelt (Chapter 1).
☐ Incorrect front wheel alignment (Chapter 10).
☐ Steering rack or column bent or damaged (Chapter 10).

## Excessive play in steering
☐ Worn steering column universal joint(s) (Chapter 10).
☐ Worn steering track rod end balljoints (Chapters 1 and 10).
☐ Worn rack-and-pinion steering gear (Chapter 10).
☐ Worn steering or suspension joints, bushes or components (Chapters 1 and 10).

## Lack of power assistance
☐ Broken or incorrectly-adjusted auxiliary drivebelt (Chapter 1).
☐ Incorrect power steering fluid level (*Weekly checks*).
☐ Restriction in power steering fluid hoses (Chapter 1).
☐ Faulty power steering pump (Chapter 10).
☐ Faulty rack-and-pinion steering gear (Chapter 10).

## Tyre wear excessive

### Tyres worn on inside or outside edges
☐ Tyres under-inflated (wear on both edges) (*Weekly checks*).
☐ Incorrect camber or castor angles (wear on one edge only) (Chapter 10).
☐ Worn steering or suspension joints, bushes or components (Chapters 1 and 10).
☐ Excessively-hard cornering.
☐ Accident damage.

### Tyre treads exhibit feathered edges
☐ Incorrect toe setting (Chapter 10).

### Tyres worn in centre of tread
☐ Tyres over-inflated (*Weekly checks*).

### Tyres worn on inside and outside edges
☐ Tyres under-inflated (*Weekly checks*).
☐ Worn shock absorbers (Chapters 1 and 10).

### Tyres worn unevenly
☐ Tyres out of balance (*Weekly checks*).
☐ Excessive wheel or tyre run-out (*Weekly checks*).
☐ Worn shock absorbers (Chapters 1 and 10).
☐ Faulty tyre (*Weekly checks*).

# Electrical system

**Note:** *For problems associated with the starting system, refer to the faults listed under 'Engine' earlier in this Section.*

### Battery will not hold a charge for more than a few days

- [ ] Battery defective internally (Chapter 5A).
- [ ] Battery electrolyte level low – where applicable (Chapter 5A).
- [ ] Battery terminal connections loose or corroded (*Weekly checks*).
- [ ] Auxiliary drivebelt worn (Chapter 1).
- [ ] Alternator not charging at correct output (Chapter 5A).
- [ ] Alternator or voltage regulator faulty (Chapter 5A).
- [ ] Short-circuit causing continual battery drain (Chapters 5A and 12).

### Ignition/no-charge warning light remains illuminated with engine running

- [ ] Auxiliary drivebelt broken or worn (Chapter 1).
- [ ] Alternator brushes worn, sticking, or dirty (Chapter 5A).
- [ ] Alternator brush springs weak or broken (Chapter 5A).
- [ ] Internal fault in alternator or voltage regulator (Chapter 5A).
- [ ] Broken, disconnected, or loose wiring in charging circuit (Chapter 5A).

### Ignition/no-charge warning light fails to come on

- [ ] Warning light bulb blown (Chapter 12).
- [ ] Broken, disconnected, or loose wiring in warning light circuit (Chapter 12).
- [ ] Alternator faulty (Chapter 5A).

### Lights inoperative

- [ ] Bulb blown (Chapter 12).
- [ ] Corrosion of bulb or bulbholder contacts (Chapter 12).
- [ ] Blown fuse (Chapter 12).
- [ ] Faulty relay (Chapter 12).
- [ ] Broken, loose, or disconnected wiring (Chapter 12).
- [ ] Faulty switch (Chapter 12).

### Instrument readings inaccurate or erratic

#### Instrument readings increase with engine speed

- [ ] Faulty voltage regulator (Chapter 12).

#### Fuel or temperature gauges give no reading

- [ ] Faulty gauge sender unit (Chapters 3 and 4).
- [ ] Wiring open-circuit (Chapter 12).
- [ ] Faulty gauge (Chapter 12).

#### Fuel or temperature gauges give continuous maximum reading

- [ ] Faulty gauge sender unit (Chapters 3 and 4).
- [ ] Wiring short-circuit (Chapter 12).
- [ ] Faulty gauge (Chapter 12).

### Horn inoperative, or unsatisfactory in operation

#### Horn operates all the time

- [ ] Horn contacts permanently bridged or horn push stuck down (Chapter 12).

#### Horn fails to operate

- [ ] Blown fuse (Chapter 12).
- [ ] Cable or cable connections loose, broken or disconnected (Chapter 12).
- [ ] Faulty horn (Chapter 12).

#### Horn emits intermittent or unsatisfactory sound

- [ ] Cable connections loose (Chapter 12).
- [ ] Horn mountings loose (Chapter 12).
- [ ] Faulty horn (Chapter 12).

### Windscreen/tailgate wipers inoperative, or unsatisfactory in operation

#### Wipers fail to operate, or operate very slowly

- [ ] Wiper blades stuck to screen, or linkage seized or binding (*Weekly checks* and Chapter 12).
- [ ] Blown fuse (Chapter 12).
- [ ] Cable or cable connections loose, broken or disconnected (Chapter 12).
- [ ] Faulty relay (Chapter 12).
- [ ] Faulty wiper motor (Chapter 12).

#### Wiper blades sweep over too large or too small an area of the glass

- [ ] Wiper arms incorrectly positioned on spindles (Chapter 12).
- [ ] Excessive wear of wiper linkage (Chapter 12).
- [ ] Wiper motor or linkage mountings loose or insecure (Chapter 12).

#### Wiper blades fail to clean the glass effectively

- [ ] Wiper blade rubbers worn or perished (*Weekly checks*).
- [ ] Wiper arm tension springs broken, or arm pivots seized (Chapter 12).
- [ ] Insufficient windscreen washer additive to adequately remove road film (*Weekly checks*).

### Windscreen/tailgate washers inoperative, or unsatisfactory in operation

#### One or more washer jets inoperative

- [ ] Blocked washer jet.
- [ ] Disconnected, kinked or restricted fluid hose (Chapter 12).
- [ ] Insufficient fluid in washer reservoir (*Weekly checks*).

#### Washer pump fails to operate

- [ ] Broken or disconnected wiring or connections (Chapter 12).
- [ ] Blown fuse (Chapter 12).
- [ ] Faulty washer switch (Chapter 12).
- [ ] Faulty washer pump (Chapter 12).

#### Washer pump runs for some time before fluid is emitted from jets

- [ ] Faulty one-way valve in fluid supply hose (Chapter 12).

### Electric windows inoperative, or unsatisfactory in operation

#### Window glass will only move in one direction

- [ ] Faulty switch (Chapter 12).

#### Window glass slow to move

- [ ] Regulator seized or damaged, or in need of lubrication (Chapter 11).
- [ ] Door internal components or trim fouling regulator (Chapter 11).
- [ ] Faulty motor (Chapter 11).

#### Window glass fails to move

- [ ] Blown fuse (Chapter 12).
- [ ] Regulator seized or jammed (Chapter 12)
- [ ] Faulty relay (Chapter 12).
- [ ] Broken or disconnected wiring or connections (Chapter 12).
- [ ] Faulty motor (Chapter 11).

### Central locking system inoperative, or unsatisfactory in operation

#### Complete system failure

- [ ] Blown fuse (Chapter 12).
- [ ] Faulty relay (Chapter 12).
- [ ] Broken or disconnected wiring or connections (Chapter 12).

# A

**ABS (Anti-lock brake system)** A system, usually electronically controlled, that senses incipient wheel lockup during braking and relieves hydraulic pressure at wheels that are about to skid.

**Air bag** An inflatable bag hidden in the steering wheel (driver's side) or the dash or glovebox (passenger side). In a head-on collision, the bags inflate, preventing the driver and front passenger from being thrown forward into the steering wheel or windscreen.

**Air cleaner** A metal or plastic housing, containing a filter element, which removes dust and dirt from the air being drawn into the engine.

**Air filter element** The actual filter in an air cleaner system, usually manufactured from pleated paper and requiring renewal at regular intervals.

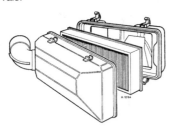

*Air filter*

**Allen key** A hexagonal wrench which fits into a recessed hexagonal hole.

**Alligator clip** A long-nosed spring-loaded metal clip with meshing teeth. Used to make temporary electrical connections.

**Alternator** A component in the electrical system which converts mechanical energy from a drivebelt into electrical energy to charge the battery and to operate the starting system, ignition system and electrical accessories.

*Alternator (exploded view)*

**Ampere (amp)** A unit of measurement for the flow of electric current. One amp is the amount of current produced by one volt acting through a resistance of one ohm.

**Anaerobic sealer** A substance used to prevent bolts and screws from loosening. Anaerobic means that it does not require oxygen for activation. The Loctite brand is widely used.

**Antifreeze** A substance (usually ethylene glycol) mixed with water, and added to a vehicle's cooling system, to prevent freezing of the coolant in winter. Antifreeze also contains chemicals to inhibit corrosion and the formation of rust and other deposits that

would tend to clog the radiator and coolant passages and reduce cooling efficiency.

**Anti-seize compound** A coating that reduces the risk of seizing on fasteners that are subjected to high temperatures, such as exhaust manifold bolts and nuts.

*Anti-seize compound*

**Asbestos** A natural fibrous mineral with great heat resistance, commonly used in the composition of brake friction materials. Asbestos is a health hazard and the dust created by brake systems should never be inhaled or ingested.

**Axle** A shaft on which a wheel revolves, or which revolves with a wheel. Also, a solid beam that connects the two wheels at one end of the vehicle. An axle which also transmits power to the wheels is known as a live axle.

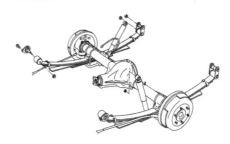

*Axle assembly*

**Axleshaft** A single rotating shaft, on either side of the differential, which delivers power from the final drive assembly to the drive wheels. Also called a driveshaft or a halfshaft.

# B

**Ball bearing** An anti-friction bearing consisting of a hardened inner and outer race with hardened steel balls between two races.

*Bearing*

**Bearing** The curved surface on a shaft or in a bore, or the part assembled into either, that permits relative motion between them with minimum wear and friction.

**Big-end bearing** The bearing in the end of the connecting rod that's attached to the crankshaft.

**Bleed nipple** A valve on a brake wheel cylinder, caliper or other hydraulic component that is opened to purge the hydraulic system of air. Also called a bleed screw.

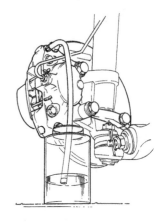

*Brake bleeding*

**Brake bleeding** Procedure for removing air from lines of a hydraulic brake system.

**Brake disc** The component of a disc brake that rotates with the wheels.

**Brake drum** The component of a drum brake that rotates with the wheels.

**Brake linings** The friction material which contacts the brake disc or drum to retard the vehicle's speed. The linings are bonded or riveted to the brake pads or shoes.

**Brake pads** The replaceable friction pads that pinch the brake disc when the brakes are applied. Brake pads consist of a friction material bonded or riveted to a rigid backing plate.

**Brake shoe** The crescent-shaped carrier to which the brake linings are mounted and which forces the lining against the rotating drum during braking.

**Braking systems** For more information on braking systems, consult the *Haynes Automotive Brake Manual*.

**Breaker bar** A long socket wrench handle providing greater leverage.

**Bulkhead** The insulated partition between the engine and the passenger compartment.

# C

**Caliper** The non-rotating part of a disc-brake assembly that straddles the disc and carries the brake pads. The caliper also contains the hydraulic components that cause the pads to pinch the disc when the brakes are applied. A caliper is also a measuring tool that can be set to measure inside or outside dimensions of an object.

**Camshaft** A rotating shaft on which a series of cam lobes operate the valve mechanisms. The camshaft may be driven by gears, by sprockets and chain or by sprockets and a belt.

**Canister** A container in an evaporative emission control system; contains activated charcoal granules to trap vapours from the fuel system.

*Canister*

**Carburettor** A device which mixes fuel with air in the proper proportions to provide a desired power output from a spark ignition internal combustion engine.

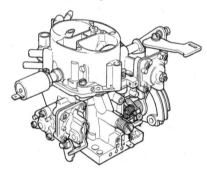

*Carburettor*

**Castellated** Resembling the parapets along the top of a castle wall. For example, a castellated balljoint stud nut.

*Castellated nut*

**Castor** In wheel alignment, the backward or forward tilt of the steering axis. Castor is positive when the steering axis is inclined rearward at the top.

**Catalytic converter** A silencer-like device in the exhaust system which converts certain pollutants in the exhaust gases into less harmful substances.

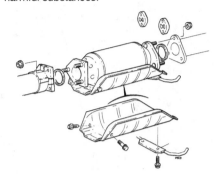

*Catalytic converter*

**Circlip** A ring-shaped clip used to prevent endwise movement of cylindrical parts and shafts. An internal circlip is installed in a groove in a housing; an external circlip fits into a groove on the outside of a cylindrical piece such as a shaft.

**Clearance** The amount of space between two parts. For example, between a piston and a cylinder, between a bearing and a journal, etc.

**Coil spring** A spiral of elastic steel found in various sizes throughout a vehicle, for example as a springing medium in the suspension and in the valve train.

**Compression** Reduction in volume, and increase in pressure and temperature, of a gas, caused by squeezing it into a smaller space.

**Compression ratio** The relationship between cylinder volume when the piston is at top dead centre and cylinder volume when the piston is at bottom dead centre.

**Constant velocity (CV) joint** A type of universal joint that cancels out vibrations caused by driving power being transmitted through an angle.

**Core plug** A disc or cup-shaped metal device inserted in a hole in a casting through which core was removed when the casting was formed. Also known as a freeze plug or expansion plug.

**Crankcase** The lower part of the engine block in which the crankshaft rotates.

**Crankshaft** The main rotating member, or shaft, running the length of the crankcase, with offset "throws" to which the connecting rods are attached.

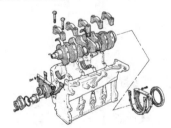

*Crankshaft assembly*

**Crocodile clip** See Alligator clip

# D

**Diagnostic code** Code numbers obtained by accessing the diagnostic mode of an engine management computer. This code can be used to determine the area in the system where a malfunction may be located.

**Disc brake** A brake design incorporating a rotating disc onto which brake pads are squeezed. The resulting friction converts the energy of a moving vehicle into heat.

**Double-overhead cam (DOHC)** An engine that uses two overhead camshafts, usually one for the intake valves and one for the exhaust valves.

**Drivebelt(s)** The belt(s) used to drive accessories such as the alternator, water pump, power steering pump, air conditioning compressor, etc. off the crankshaft pulley.

*Accessory drivebelts*

**Driveshaft** Any shaft used to transmit motion. Commonly used when referring to the axleshafts on a front wheel drive vehicle.

*Driveshaft*

**Drum brake** A type of brake using a drum-shaped metal cylinder attached to the inner surface of the wheel. When the brake pedal is pressed, curved brake shoes with friction linings press against the inside of the drum to slow or stop the vehicle.

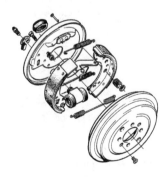

*Drum brake assembly*

## E

**EGR valve** A valve used to introduce exhaust gases into the intake air stream.

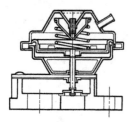

*EGR valve*

**Electronic control unit (ECU)** A computer which controls (for instance) ignition and fuel injection systems, or an anti-lock braking system. For more information refer to the *Haynes Automotive Electrical and Electronic Systems Manual.*

**Electronic Fuel Injection (EFI)** A computer controlled fuel system that distributes fuel through an injector located in each intake port of the engine.

**Emergency brake** A braking system, independent of the main hydraulic system, that can be used to slow or stop the vehicle if the primary brakes fail, or to hold the vehicle stationary even though the brake pedal isn't depressed. It usually consists of a hand lever that actuates either front or rear brakes mechanically through a series of cables and linkages. Also known as a handbrake or parking brake.

**Endfloat** The amount of lengthwise movement between two parts. As applied to a crankshaft, the distance that the crankshaft can move forward and back in the cylinder block.

**Engine management system (EMS)** A computer controlled system which manages the fuel injection and the ignition systems in an integrated fashion.

**Exhaust manifold** A part with several passages through which exhaust gases leave the engine combustion chambers and enter the exhaust pipe.

*Exhaust manifold*

## F

**Fan clutch** A viscous (fluid) drive coupling device which permits variable engine fan speeds in relation to engine speeds.

**Feeler blade** A thin strip or blade of hardened steel, ground to an exact thickness, used to check or measure clearances between parts.

*Feeler blade*

**Firing order** The order in which the engine cylinders fire, or deliver their power strokes, beginning with the number one cylinder.

**Flywheel** A heavy spinning wheel in which energy is absorbed and stored by means of momentum. On cars, the flywheel is attached to the crankshaft to smooth out firing impulses.

**Free play** The amount of travel before any action takes place. The "looseness" in a linkage, or an assembly of parts, between the initial application of force and actual movement. For example, the distance the brake pedal moves before the pistons in the master cylinder are actuated.

**Fuse** An electrical device which protects a circuit against accidental overload. The typical fuse contains a soft piece of metal which is calibrated to melt at a predetermined current flow (expressed as amps) and break the circuit.

**Fusible link** A circuit protection device consisting of a conductor surrounded by heat-resistant insulation. The conductor is smaller than the wire it protects, so it acts as the weakest link in the circuit. Unlike a blown fuse, a failed fusible link must frequently be cut from the wire for replacement.

## G

**Gap** The distance the spark must travel in jumping from the centre electrode to the side

*Adjusting spark plug gap*

electrode in a spark plug. Also refers to the spacing between the points in a contact breaker assembly in a conventional points-type ignition, or to the distance between the reluctor or rotor and the pickup coil in an electronic ignition.

**Gasket** Any thin, soft material - usually cork, cardboard, asbestos or soft metal - installed between two metal surfaces to ensure a good seal. For instance, the cylinder head gasket seals the joint between the block and the cylinder head.

*Gasket*

**Gauge** An instrument panel display used to monitor engine conditions. A gauge with a movable pointer on a dial or a fixed scale is an analogue gauge. A gauge with a numerical readout is called a digital gauge.

## H

**Halfshaft** A rotating shaft that transmits power from the final drive unit to a drive wheel, usually when referring to a live rear axle.

**Harmonic balancer** A device designed to reduce torsion or twisting vibration in the crankshaft. May be incorporated in the crankshaft pulley. Also known as a vibration damper.

**Hone** An abrasive tool for correcting small irregularities or differences in diameter in an engine cylinder, brake cylinder, etc.

**Hydraulic tappet** A tappet that utilises hydraulic pressure from the engine's lubrication system to maintain zero clearance (constant contact with both camshaft and valve stem). Automatically adjusts to variation in valve stem length. Hydraulic tappets also reduce valve noise.

## I

**Ignition timing** The moment at which the spark plug fires, usually expressed in the number of crankshaft degrees before the piston reaches the top of its stroke.

**Inlet manifold** A tube or housing with passages through which flows the air-fuel mixture (carburettor vehicles and vehicles with throttle body injection) or air only (port fuel-injected vehicles) to the port openings in the cylinder head.

## J

**Jump start** Starting the engine of a vehicle with a discharged or weak battery by attaching jump leads from the weak battery to a charged or helper battery.

## L

**Load Sensing Proportioning Valve (LSPV)** A brake hydraulic system control valve that works like a proportioning valve, but also takes into consideration the amount of weight carried by the rear axle.

**Locknut** A nut used to lock an adjustment nut, or other threaded component, in place. For example, a locknut is employed to keep the adjusting nut on the rocker arm in position.

**Lockwasher** A form of washer designed to prevent an attaching nut from working loose.

## M

**MacPherson strut** A type of front suspension system devised by Earle MacPherson at Ford of England. In its original form, a simple lateral link with the anti-roll bar creates the lower control arm. A long strut - an integral coil spring and shock absorber - is mounted between the body and the steering knuckle. Many modern so-called MacPherson strut systems use a conventional lower A-arm and don't rely on the anti-roll bar for location.

**Multimeter** An electrical test instrument with the capability to measure voltage, current and resistance.

## N

**NOx** Oxides of Nitrogen. A common toxic pollutant emitted by petrol and diesel engines at higher temperatures.

## O

**Ohm** The unit of electrical resistance. One volt applied to a resistance of one ohm will produce a current of one amp.

**Ohmmeter** An instrument for measuring electrical resistance.

**O-ring** A type of sealing ring made of a special rubber-like material; in use, the O-ring is compressed into a groove to provide the sealing action.

*O-ring*

**Overhead cam (ohc) engine** An engine with the camshaft(s) located on top of the cylinder head(s).

**Overhead valve (ohv) engine** An engine with the valves located in the cylinder head, but with the camshaft located in the engine block.

**Oxygen sensor** A device installed in the engine exhaust manifold, which senses the oxygen content in the exhaust and converts this information into an electric current. Also called a Lambda sensor.

## P

**Phillips screw** A type of screw head having a cross instead of a slot for a corresponding type of screwdriver.

**Plastigage** A thin strip of plastic thread, available in different sizes, used for measuring clearances. For example, a strip of Plastigage is laid across a bearing journal. The parts are assembled and dismantled; the width of the crushed strip indicates the clearance between journal and bearing.

*Plastigage*

**Propeller shaft** The long hollow tube with universal joints at both ends that carries power from the transmission to the differential on front-engined rear wheel drive vehicles.

**Proportioning valve** A hydraulic control valve which limits the amount of pressure to the rear brakes during panic stops to prevent wheel lock-up.

## R

**Rack-and-pinion steering** A steering system with a pinion gear on the end of the steering shaft that mates with a rack (think of a geared wheel opened up and laid flat). When the steering wheel is turned, the pinion turns, moving the rack to the left or right. This movement is transmitted through the track rods to the steering arms at the wheels.

**Radiator** A liquid-to-air heat transfer device designed to reduce the temperature of the coolant in an internal combustion engine cooling system.

**Refrigerant** Any substance used as a heat transfer agent in an air-conditioning system. R-12 has been the principle refrigerant for many years; recently, however, manufacturers have begun using R-134a, a non-CFC substance that is considered less harmful to the ozone in the upper atmosphere.

**Rocker arm** A lever arm that rocks on a shaft or pivots on a stud. In an overhead valve engine, the rocker arm converts the upward movement of the pushrod into a downward movement to open a valve.

**Rotor** In a distributor, the rotating device inside the cap that connects the centre electrode and the outer terminals as it turns, distributing the high voltage from the coil secondary winding to the proper spark plug. Also, that part of an alternator which rotates inside the stator. Also, the rotating assembly of a turbocharger, including the compressor wheel, shaft and turbine wheel.

**Runout** The amount of wobble (in-and-out movement) of a gear or wheel as it's rotated. The amount a shaft rotates "out-of-true." The out-of-round condition of a rotating part.

## S

**Sealant** A liquid or paste used to prevent leakage at a joint. Sometimes used in conjunction with a gasket.

**Sealed beam lamp** An older headlight design which integrates the reflector, lens and filaments into a hermetically-sealed one-piece unit. When a filament burns out or the lens cracks, the entire unit is simply replaced.

**Serpentine drivebelt** A single, long, wide accessory drivebelt that's used on some newer vehicles to drive all the accessories, instead of a series of smaller, shorter belts. Serpentine drivebelts are usually tensioned by an automatic tensioner.

*Serpentine drivebelt*

**Shim** Thin spacer, commonly used to adjust the clearance or relative positions between two parts. For example, shims inserted into or under bucket tappets control valve clearances. Clearance is adjusted by changing the thickness of the shim.

**Slide hammer** A special puller that screws into or hooks onto a component such as a shaft or bearing; a heavy sliding handle on the shaft bottoms against the end of the shaft to knock the component free.

**Sprocket** A tooth or projection on the periphery of a wheel, shaped to engage with a chain or drivebelt. Commonly used to refer to the sprocket wheel itself.

**Starter inhibitor switch** On vehicles with an automatic transmission, a switch that prevents starting if the vehicle is not in Neutral or Park.

**Strut** See MacPherson strut.

# T

**Tappet** A cylindrical component which transmits motion from the cam to the valve stem, either directly or via a pushrod and rocker arm. Also called a cam follower.

**Thermostat** A heat-controlled valve that regulates the flow of coolant between the cylinder block and the radiator, so maintaining optimum engine operating temperature. A thermostat is also used in some air cleaners in which the temperature is regulated.

**Thrust bearing** The bearing in the clutch assembly that is moved in to the release levers by clutch pedal action to disengage the clutch. Also referred to as a release bearing.

**Timing belt** A toothed belt which drives the camshaft. Serious engine damage may result if it breaks in service.

**Timing chain** A chain which drives the camshaft.

**Toe-in** The amount the front wheels are closer together at the front than at the rear. On rear wheel drive vehicles, a slight amount of toe-in is usually specified to keep the front wheels running parallel on the road by offsetting other forces that tend to spread the wheels apart.

**Toe-out** The amount the front wheels are closer together at the rear than at the front. On front wheel drive vehicles, a slight amount of toe-out is usually specified.

**Tools** For full information on choosing and using tools, refer to the *Haynes Automotive Tools Manual*.

**Tracer** A stripe of a second colour applied to a wire insulator to distinguish that wire from another one with the same colour insulator.

**Tune-up** A process of accurate and careful adjustments and parts replacement to obtain the best possible engine performance.

**Turbocharger** A centrifugal device, driven by exhaust gases, that pressurises the intake air. Normally used to increase the power output from a given engine displacement, but can also be used primarily to reduce exhaust emissions (as on VW's "Umwelt" Diesel engine).

# U

**Universal joint or U-joint** A double-pivoted connection for transmitting power from a driving to a driven shaft through an angle. A U-joint consists of two Y-shaped yokes and a cross-shaped member called the spider.

# V

**Valve** A device through which the flow of liquid, gas, vacuum, or loose material in bulk may be started, stopped, or regulated by a movable part that opens, shuts, or partially obstructs one or more ports or passageways. A valve is also the movable part of such a device.

**Valve clearance** The clearance between the valve tip (the end of the valve stem) and the rocker arm or tappet. The valve clearance is measured when the valve is closed.

**Vernier caliper** A precision measuring instrument that measures inside and outside dimensions. Not quite as accurate as a micrometer, but more convenient.

**Viscosity** The thickness of a liquid or its resistance to flow.

**Volt** A unit for expressing electrical "pressure" in a circuit. One volt that will produce a current of one ampere through a resistance of one ohm.

# W

**Welding** Various processes used to join metal items by heating the areas to be joined to a molten state and fusing them together. For more information refer to the *Haynes Automotive Welding Manual*.

**Wiring diagram** A drawing portraying the components and wires in a vehicle's electrical system, using standardised symbols. For more information refer to the *Haynes Automotive Electrical and Electronic Systems Manual*.

**Note:** *References throughout this index are in the form "Chapter Number" • "Page Number"*